Computation and Intelligence

Collected Readings

Computation and Intelligence

Collected Readings

EDITED BY

George F. Luger

Menlo Park / Cambridge / London
AAAI Press / The MIT Press

Copublished and distributed by The MIT Press, Massachusetts Institute of Technology, Cambridge, Massachusetts and London, England.

ISBN 0-262-62101-0

Library of Congress Cataloging-in-Publication Data

Computation and intelligence / collected readings / edited by George F. Luger.
     p.   cm.
  Includes bibliographical references and index.
  ISBN 0-262-62101-0 (pbk.)
  1. Artificial intelligence. 2. Machine learning. 3. Computer science. I. Luger,
George F.
Q335.C55 1995   95-21293
006.3--dc20   CIP

PRINTED IN THE UNITED STATES OF AMERICA

Contents

Acknowledgments

Chapter 1: "The Prehistory of Android Epistemology," by C. Glymour, K. Ford, & P. Hayes is reprinted with permission from *Android Epistemology,* edited by Clark Glymour, Kenneth Ford, and Patrick Hayes. Menlo Park, Calif.: AAAI Press, 1995.

Chapter 2: "Computing Machinery and Intelligence," by A. Turing is reprinted with permission from *Mind,* October, 1950, 59: 433-460.

Chapter 3: "Steps Towards Artificial Intelligence," by M. Minsky is reprinted with permission from *Proceedings of the Institute of Radio Engineers* (now IEEE), January, 1961.

Chapter 4: "Computer Science as Empirical Enquiry: Symbols and Search," by A. Newell & H. A. Simon is reprinted with permission from *Communications of the Association of Computing Machinery,* 1976.

Chapter 5: "The Knowledge Level," by A. Newell is reprinted with permission from *Artificial Intelligence* 18: 87-127, 1982.

Chapter 6: "A Framework for Representing Knowledge" by M. Minsky is reprinted with permission from *Mind Design,* edited by John Haugeland. Cambridge, Massachusetts: The MIT Press, 1981.

Chapter 7: "Retrieval Time from Semantic Memory," by A. M. Collins, & M. R. Quillian is reprinted with permission from *The Journal of Verbal Learning and Verbal Behavior* 8: 240-247, 1969.

Chapter 8: "A Procedural Model of Language Understanding," by T. Winograd is reprinted with permission from *Computer Models of Thought and Language* by T. Winograd. San Francisco: W. H. Freeman, 1973.

Chapter 9: "The Structure of Episodes in Memory," by R. Schank is reprinted with permission from *Representation and Understanding: Studies in Cognitive Science,* edited by D. G. Bobrow and A. Collins. New York: Academic Press, 1975.

Chapter 10: "In Defense of Logic," by P. Hayes is reprinted with permission from *Proceedings from the International Jointo Conference on Artificial Intelligence,* 1975. San Francisco: Morgan Kaufmann, Inc., 1977.

Chapter 11: "Escaping Brittleness: The Possibility of General Purpose Learning: Algorithms Applied to Parallel Rule-Based Systems," by J. Holland is reprinted with permission from *Machine Learning: An AI Approach,* edited by R. Michaelski. San Francisco: Morgan Kaufmann, 1986.

Chapter 12: "The Appeal of Parallel Distributed Processing," by J. L. McClelland, D. E. Rumelhart, and G. E. Hinton is reprinted with permission from *Parallel Distributed Processing* edited by D. E. Rumelhart and J. McClelland. Cambridge, Massachusetts: The MIT Press, 1986.

Chapter 13: "Intelligence Without Representation," by R. A. Brooks is reprinted with permission from *Artificial Intelligence* 47: 139-59, 1991.

Chapter 14: "Empirical Explorations with the Logic Theory Machine," by A. Newell, J. C. Shaw, and H. A. Simon is reprinted with permission from *Proceedings of the Western Joint Computer Conference.* New York: IEEE, 1957.

Chapter 15: "Some Studies in Machine Learning Using the Game of Checkers," by A. L. Samuel, is reprinted with permission from *IBM Journal of Research and Development,* 3: 211-229, July, 1959.

Chapter 16: "GPS, A Program that Simulates Human Thought," by A. Newell and H. A. Simon is reprinted with permission from *Lernende Automaten.* Munich: R. Oldenbourg KG, 1961.

Chapter 17: "STRIPS: A New Approach in the Application of Theorem Proving to Problem Solving," by R. E. Fikes and N. J. Nilsson is reprinted with permission from *Artificial Intelligence* 2: 189–208, 1971.

Chapter 18: "Blackboard Systems: The Blackboard Model of Problem Solving and the Evolution of Blackboard Architectures," by H. P. Nii is reprinted with permission from *AI Magazine* (Summer 1986).

Chapter 19: "Programs with Common Sense," by J. McCarthy is reprinted with permission from *Semantic Information Processing,* edited by Marvin Minsky. Cambridge, Massachusetts: The MIT Press, 1968.

Chapter 20: "Dendral and Meta-Dendral: Their Application Dimension," by B. G. Buchanan and E. A. Feigenbaum is reprinted with permission from *Artificial Intelligence* 11: 5-24, 1978.

Chapter 21: "Consultation Systems for Physicians," by E. Shortliffe, is reprinted with permission from the *Proceedings of the Canadian Society for Computational Studies of Intelligence,* 1980.

Chapter 22: "A Truth Maintenance System," by J. Doyle is reprinted with permission from *Artificial Intelligence* 12 (3): 231-272, 1979.

Chapter 23: "Circumscription—A Form of Non-Monotonic Reasoning," by J. McCarthy is reprinted from *Artificial Intelligence* 13(1,2), 1980.

Chapter 24: "The Second Naive Physics Manifesto," by P. Hayes is reprinted with permission from *Formal Theories of the Common Sense World* edited by Jobbs and Moore. Norwood, New Jersey: Ablex Publishers, 1985.

Chapter 25: "Paradigms for Machine Learning," by J. G. Carbonell is reprinted with permission from *Artificial Intelligence* 40: 1-9, 1989.

Chapter 26: "Improving Human Decision Making Through Case Based Decision Aiding," by J. Kolodner is reprinted with permission from *AI Magazine* 12 (2): 52-69 (Summer 1991).

Chapter 27: "Diagnosis Based on Description of Structure and Function," by Randall Davis, Howard Shrobe, Walter Hamscher, Kären Wieckert, Mark Shirley, and Steve Polit is reprinted with permission from *Proceedings of the National Conference on Artificial Intelligence*. Menlo Park, California: AAAI Press, 1982.

Chapter 28: "Pengi: An Implementation of a Theory of Activity" by Philip E. Agre and David Chapman is reprinted with permission from *Proceedings of the National Conference on Artificial Intelligence*. Menlo Park, California: AAAI Press, 1987.

Chapter 29: "Logical Versus Analogical or Symbolic Versus Connectionist or Neat Versus Scruffy," by M. Minsky is reprinted with permission from *AI Magazine* 12(2): 52-69, Summer, 1991.

Chapter 30: "Machine as Mind," by H. A. Simon is reprinted with permission from *Android Epistemology*, edited by Clark Glymour, Kenneth Ford, and Patrick Hayes Menlo Park, Calif.: AAAI Press, 1995.

Preface

The idea for this book grew from introducing new research students and applications programmers to the discipline of artificial intelligence. Early in this introduction, the words used to describe AI concepts often fail to have meaning and the ideas that support the study of AI are vague and difficult. At this time it is important to begin the process of integrating the newcomer into the background issues and contexts that make up the study of AI, and define the concerns of the evolving AI community.

The goal of this collection of papers is to assist in this task. There were two criteria used in the selection of papers: First, that the papers reflect the historical foundations and research questions of the artificial intelligence community. Second, that the papers also be important for understanding the current practice of AI. If a paper was once considered important but has little influence in the current focus of the discipline, it is not included; and a number of more recent papers whose concerns are reflected in the present practice of AI are included.

This book is divided into five sections. Part I, Foundations, reflects the linkage between computation and intelligence, between mechanism and the formalization and use of knowledge. These papers address elements of the Western philosophical tradition and show how they are integrated into the foundational questions supporting AI research. It is important to realize that the AI community is bringing new tools and techniques to reformulate ancient questions.

Part II, Knowledge Representation, presents ideas and issues central to the AI enterprise. In fact, a not inappropriate definition of AI is the study of the representation of information and the search for useful solutions. Over the first forty years of growth of AI, a number of representational schemes have emerged, each with its own strengths, weaknesses, and controversies. Part II is intended to reflect both the wealth and diversity of these schemes.

Part III, Weak Method Problem Solving, reflects the research and design of general problem solving methods using syntax-based symbol manipulation. The most famous of these include the Logic Theorist and GPS. Their extensions include planning systems and blackboards.

Part IV reflects the AI community's work in Knowledge Intensive Problem Solving. Much of this effort was inspired by Edward Feigenbaum's research at Stanford University, especially his guidance of the MYCIN, DENDRAL, and Prospector projects. Other research in this area includes the design of reasoning systems exhibiting "common sense" and the ability to support belief revision.

Part V, Foundations Revisited, collects together more recent thoughts of two of the pioneers of the AI community, Marvin Minsky and Herbert Simon. Their papers touch on many of the concepts and controversies developed during the evolution of the tools and techniques that make up the present practice of AI. Their reflections add an important focus on current work in AI.

My editorial objective in presenting these papers has been to preserve the author's intent but in a form that does not create irrelevant distractions for the reader. Consequently, spelling has been normalized (in accordance with the *American Heritage Dictionary),* and section numbering has been applied consistently; added when entirely absent, and normalized when the original style deviated from the style chosen for this book. I have also applied a consistent citation style throughout the book, and collected all the references at the end of the volume.

In three cases, chapters were edited for length. Chapters 22 and 24 were shortened with the help of the authors. The appendix was eliminated from Chapter 15, although a reference to the missing material was added. The result of this modest editorial intrusion is, I hope, a unified modern presentation of the material

I would like to thank my fellow members on the AAAI Press editorial board for their acceptance of my original proposal for this book, as well as their continuing support and suggestions as it developed. Ken Ford and Pat Hayes were particularly helpful in this regard. Finally, I would especially like to thank Mike Hamilton of AAAI Press for his dedicated and careful work in scanning in and re-formatting these papers, often from difficult earlier manuscripts.

George Luger
Albuquerque
August, 1995

Dedicated to the
artificial intelligence community

ᴤ PART ONE ᴤ

Foundations

The artificial intelligence tradition, contrary to some modern commentators, is not an isolated or disassociated phenomenon. Rather it is the effort of a society of researchers, revisiting through their work and with the aid of modern tools, many ancient questions. We begin the presentation with a set of four papers that place artificial intelligence research firmly within the evolution of our philosophical and scientific traditions.

Although the AI community has existed as an identifiable entity only since the mid-1950s, the questions it asks and investigates are much older. Research in AI extends the ongoing Western epistemological tradition questioning the nature of knowledge and intelligence and the use of various formalisms for describing intelligent activity. This tradition in philosophy and science extends from the Presocratic period, through the Enlightenment philosophers Descartes, Locke, Hobbes, and Hume, and into the twentieth century work of Hilbert, Russell and Whitehead, Frege, Tarski, and Turing.

One of the most significant early authors in this tradition is Aristotle. In his Logic, Aristotle presented his epistemology, or science of knowing. He viewed logic as the instrument of (organon) and basis for all knowledge. Aristotle investigated whether certain propositions can be said to be true because they are related to other things that are known to be true. Thus, if we know that "all athletes are strong" and that "Socrates is an athlete," then we can conclude that "Socrates is strong." This argument is an example of what Aristotle referred to as a syllogism that uses the reasoning form modus ponens. Aristotle went on to describe another form of inference, now called abduction, by which one can conclude with some lesser degree of confidence that "Socrates is an athlete" from the observation that "Socretes is strong." Finally, in his Rhetoric, Aristotle discusses the interpretation of information or "signs" in the world and the nature of perception in that it leads to the act of interpretation. Although the formal axiomatization of reasoning required another two thousand years and the work of Boole, Frege, Russell and Whitehead, and Tarski, its roots may be traced to Aristotle.

We are not claiming that AI is or should be focused on the use of logic alone, although several of the papers of Part II might want to make this claim! Rather, the questions asked by both Aristotle and modern researchers in AI concern the nature of intelligence, modes for the perception and interpretation of an external world, and the constitution of meaning.

Mathematicians and philosophers over the centuries have also claimed some of the same goals that inspire modern AI research. For example, George Boole (1854) the creator of the algebraic system that supports digital computation, entitled his major work, An Investigation of the Laws of Thought, on which are Founded the Mathematical Theories of Logic and Probabilities. In it he described his goals:

> ... to investigate the fundamental laws of those operations of the mind by which reasoning is performed: to give expression to them in the symbolic language of a calculus, and upon this foundation to establish the science of logic and instruct its method; ... and finally, to collect ...in the course of these inquiries some probable intimations concerning the nature and constitution of the human mind...

Many modern AI workers (see especially Part V) would be quite comfortable with such goals!

In the first chapter of Part I, Glymour, Ford, and Hayes fill out more details of the historical evolution of Western philosophical thought, continuing the task of placing AI squarely within its scope. In the second chapter, Alan Turing, the renowned mathematician and complexity theorist, with his 1950 paper "Computing Machinery and Intelligence," makes one of the first explicit linkages between computational mechanism and the specification of intelligence.

In this same tradition, Minsky in "Steps Towards Artificial Intelligence" draws important lessons for AI from the insights of operations research and control theory. Minsky also points forward to the growing issues of pattern recognition, planning, and machine learning. To finish Part I, Newell and Simon, in their Turing Award lecture, "Computer Science as Empirical Inquiry", propose the physical symbol system hypothesis, and offer a methodology that raises the evaluation of computational descriptions of intelligence to the level of an empirical science.

Other papers important in defining the nexus of mathematics, computation, and intelligence include those of Frege (1884) with his codification of the predicate calculus, Tarski (1944) who creates a foundation for semantics and a mathematics of meaning, that is, a mathematics by which sets of expressions can have interpretations in possible worlds, and Church (1941) with his creation of the lambda calculus. McCulloch & Pitts (1943) in their paper, "A Logical Calculus of the Ideas Immanent in Nervous Activity," are the precursors of modern connectionist approaches to the description of intelligence.

1

The Prehistory of Android Epistemology

Clark Glymour, Kenneth Ford, and Patrick Hayes

1. Introduction

Contemporary artificial intelligence (AI) can be viewed as essays in the epistemology of androids, an exploration of the principles underlying the cognitive behavior of any possible kind of mechanical agents. Occasional hyperbole and flimflam aside, artificial intelligence is a wonderful subject, full of new ideas and possibilities, unfettered by tradition or concern (other than inspirational) for the accidents of human constitution, but disciplined by the limits of mechanical computation. More than other new sciences, AI and philosophy have things to say to one another: any attempt to create and understand minds must be of philosophical interest. In fact, AI *is* philosophy, conducted by novel means. That AI emerges from ideas of computer science is, of course, a familiar observation. The central insights of

Babbage, Turing, von Neumann and other pioneers on how a machine might actually be built that could manipulate and be influenced by symbols are widely recognized. But for all the novelty, many of the central ideas that animate artificial intelligence, and even particular techniques and themes prominent in contemporary practice, have a long philosophical ancestry. In fact, the sources of key assumptions and insights underlying much of AI—such as that the mind is computational, that computational devices can be a simulacrum of the mind, the fundamental idea that machines can "calculate" with symbols for things other than numbers, and that there is a plethora of possible artificial minds yet to be invented—are deeply embedded in the history of philosophy. This background includes the history of logic, the emergence of combinatorics, the merging and separating of theories of deduction and computation from psychological theories, the formation of the first program for a possible cognitive agent, characteristic designs of programs for machine learning, characterizations of conditions for causal inference, and no doubt a good deal more. In addition to any list of ideas, there is what might best be characterized as an attitude towards machinery. AI has an engineer's respect for things that work and a pragmatic willingness to try anything that will produce the results needed. In the spirit of medieval astronomy, it wants only to save the phenomena, not to hypothesize psychological truth. While important parts of modern science have emerged from trying to understand machines—thermodynamics and steam engines, for example—the direct intellectual merging of philosophy and engineering seems strange, even rather outrageous, in our modern academic culture. But many earlier philosophers seem to have had a similar kind of affection and respect for machinery. This essay attempts briefly to survey some of the philosophical sources of contemporary ideas about artificial intelligence. More extended treatments can be found in Glymour (1992) and in Haugeland (1985).

2. Back to the Greeks: Plato and Aristotle

According to both Plato and Aristotle, the objects of knowledge have a special *formal structure*. The sort of thing a person may know is that one thing or kind of property is a *finite combination* of other things or kinds of properties. *Man* is a combination of *rational* and *animal. Triangle* is a combination of *closed, rectilinear, figure,* and *three-sided.* Plato and Aristotle differed about the metaphysics, of course. For Plato these combinations are ideal objects or forms; for Aristotle they are essential attributes of concrete objects. For both philosophers, however, all knowledge consists of knowing such combinations of forms or essential attributes of a thing or kind. For example, according to Plato, knowledge of virtue is knowledge of which simple forms are combined into the form of virtue. Any AI knowledge engineer will recognize the idea and be attracted by its computational virtues. The anticipations are, however, more detailed. In the *Meno*, Socrates and Meno search for an answer to the question "What is virtue?" Socratic method is to collect positive and negative examples and to search for hypotheses that cover the positive and exclude the negative. In the course of the dialogue, Meno points out through a question the first theorem of computational learning theory: how will they know when they have found the correct answer? Meno's point, of course, is that they cannot, solely on the basis of a finite sample, decide the truth of a contingent, universal claim by any rule that will yield the truth in all logically possible circumstances consistent with the sample. Socrates' response to Meno is that the process of discovery is what is now called in artificial intelligence *explanation-based reasoning*. Everyone, according to Plato, already knows implicitly at birth all of the laws of forms. The process we think of as empirical discovery is simply a matter of realizing which formal truth, or consequence of laws of forms, applies to a particular set of cases and adding that truth to one's explicit knowledge.

The conjunctive view of the objects of knowledge suggests questions about combinations of properties. Ultimately, on either the Platonic or Aristotelian view, any kind of property that can be the object of scientific knowledge can be analyzed into a combination of simple properties that cannot be further analyzed. The number of distinct kinds that can be the objects of knowledge then consists of the number of distinct combinations of these simple properties, whatever they are. What is the number of pairs of distinct properties if there are n properties altogether? What is the number of triples of distinct properties if there are n properties altogether? What is the number of distinct combinations of any particular number m of properties drawn from n properties? How can these distinct combinations be enumerated and surveyed? If one has the Platonic-Aristotelian conception of the form of knowledge, these are fundamental questions.

In Europe, it was just such questions that gave rise to the mathematical subject of combinatorics, the study of the numbers of possible combinations satisfying given conditions. The first mathematical results of this kind in the West seem to occur in a commentary on Aristotle by Porphyry, written in the 3rd century A.D. Porphyry wished to comment on all of the similarities and differences among five Aristotelian "voices," and so he posed the problem of enumerating all the distinct pairs of things that can be obtained from a collection of five things. He observed that one might think that this number is 20, because one can choose the first thing of a pair in any of five ways, and the remaining member of the pair in four distinct ways. But Porphyry correctly argued that the number of pairings is not 20:

> Such is not the case; for though the first of the five can be paired with the remaining four, when we come to the second, one of the pairs will already have been

counted; with the third, two; with the fourth, three and with the fifth, four; thus there are in all only ten differences: 4+3+2+1. (cited in Edwards, 1987, p. 20)

Roughly 250 years later, Boethius wrote commentaries on Porphyry's commentary on Aristotle, and in them he provided a more general, alternative proof. But Porphyry's combinatoric result seems not to have been significantly extended until the Renaissance. Even without technical advances, however, combinatoric ideas remained important.

In the Middle Ages, the conception of the objects of knowledge as combinations of simple attributes that make up a kind or a complex property led to a conception of the method for acquiring knowledge. The method, insofar as it deserves the name, consisted of trying to "analyze" a thing into its simple properties (analysis) and then trying to put it back together by combining those properties (synthesis). Sometimes—in Renaissance chemistry, for example—"analysis" meant physically decomposing a substance into "simpler" substances, and "synthesis" meant physically reconstituting a substance of that kind, but for the most part the analysis and synthesis were purely mental.

3. Ramón Lull and the Infidels

After the reintroduction of classical learning into Christian Europe, one would expect that Christian intellectuals would have applied the methods they had learned from Aristotle and Plato to the study of God, and they did. God, too, had fundamental properties, and one could consider the combinations of His attributes. In the 13th century, the questions of how to enumerate, organize, and display God's attributes led to a fundamental insight, one that we nowadays take for granted. It concerns the odd life of the great Spanish philosopher, Ramón Lull, a 13th century Franciscan monk.

The notion of mechanical aids in carrying out an algorithm and the notion of an algorithm itself are ancient, perhaps prehistoric. But one of the central insights of modern computational thinking, the idea that machines can aid nonnumerical and nongeometrical reasoning through manipulating discrete symbols, first appeared in the West, as far as we know, in the writings of Ramón Lull. The source of Lull's idea lay in a traditional metaphysical view and in the slowly emerging mathematics of combinatorics. Lull's motives, however, were entirely religious.

Lull's life illustrates that a philosopher can also be a man (or woman) of action, if only bizzare action. Lull grew up in a wealthy family and passed his early adulthood in the court of James II of Spain. He spent his time with games and pleasantries and is reputed to have made great efforts to seduce the wives of other courtiers. Accounts have it that after considerable effort to seduce a particular lady, she finally let him into her chambers and revealed a withered breast. Taking this sight as a sign from God, Lull gave up the life of a courtier and joined the Franciscan order, determined that he would dedicate his life to converting Moslem civilization to Christianity, and in a curious way, philosophy gained from that dedication.

Lull moved to Majorca and spent several years mastering the Arabic language, studying and writing tracts (of which he eventually authored hundreds) against Islam and for Christianity. About 1274, Lull had a vision of the means by which Moslems could be converted to Christianity. Stimulated by the idea, he wrote another book, his *Ars Magna*. While Lull's fundamental style of thought is mystical and obscure, it contains one logical gem.

In effect, Lull's idea was that Moslems (and others) may fail to convert to Christianity because of a cognitive defect. They simply were unable to appreciate the vast array of the combinations of God's or Christ's virtues. But thanks to this vision, Lull believed that infidels could be converted if they could be brought to see the *combinations* of God's attributes. Further, he thought that a *representation* of those combinations could be effectively presented by means of appropriate machines, and that supposition was the key to his new method. Lull designed and built a series of machines to be used to present the combinations of God's virtues.

A typical Lullian machine consisted of two or more disks having a common spindle. Each disk could be rotated independently of the others. The rim of each disk was divided into sections or *camerae,* and each section bore a letter. According to the application for which the machine was intended, the letters would each have a special significance. They might denote, for example, an attribute of God. One Lullian machine, for example, has the letters "B" through "R" around the rims of an inner disk, and around the outer disk Latin words signifying attributes of God: Bonitas (B), Magnitudo (C), Eternitas (D) and so on. A Lullian machine was operated by rotating the two disks independently, much as we would a star finder or (some years ago) a circular slide rule. At any setting of the disks, *pairs* of God's attributes would be juxtaposed on the rims of the inner and outer disks. Rotating the disks would create different pairings. One would thus discover that God is Good *and* Great, Good *and* Eternal, Great *and* Eternal, and so forth. The heretic and the infidel were supposed to be brought to the True Faith by these revelations.

Lull lectured on several occasions at the University of Paris. He traveled throughout Europe attempting to raise money for missions to North Africa to convert Moslems to Christianity. He himself is reported to have made three such trips to Africa. Tradition has it that on his third trip, at the age of 83, he was stoned to death, but some biographers are so lacking in romantic sentiment that they dispute this account.

This story may seem a bizarre and slightly amusing tale of no particular philosophical significance. But buried within Lull's mysticism and his machines is the seed of a collection of powerful ideas that only began to bear fruit

350 years later, in the 17th century. One of the great ideas implicit in Lull's work is that nonmathematical reasoning can be done, or at least assisted, by a mechanical process; the other is that reasoning does not proceed by syllogism, but by combinatorics. Reasoning is the decomposition and recombination of representations. The decomposition and recombination of attributes can be represented by the decomposition and recombination of *symbols,* and that, as Lull's devices illustrate, is a process that can be made mechanical.

4. Computation and Discovery in the 17th Century: Pascal, Leibniz and Bacon

Lull's work was known even in the 17th century, when a version of his ideas was taken up by Leibniz. Interestingly, the 17th century has a hidden history that strived, but failed, to articulate a theory of reasoning that combines logic, algebra, and combinatorics.

In 1642, Blaise Pascal, the French philosopher, mathematician, and inventor, perfected what until recently had been generally thought of as the first automatic calculating machine.[1] Like Lullian machines, Pascal's machine used rotating wheels, but unlike Lull's, it actually did something—addition and subtraction—including carries or borrows. This machine, called Pascaline, seems very simple now but was a contemporary public sensation raising both excitement and fear—not unlike today's AI research program; and, skeptics might add, Pascal's machine had a defect that AI may share: it cost more to produce than people were willing to pay for it. Although the Pascaline's functionality was limited, it showed that tasks that previously might have been expected to require human attention or thought could be made fully, automatically mechanical. The process of building the calculating device seems to have had a substantial impact on Pascal's philosophical thinking. With a prescience for enduring controversy, in his *Pensées,* Pascal (1670/1932) remarked that "The arithmetical machine produces effects which approach nearer to thought than all the actions of animals." What animals have that the calculator lacked, Pascal wrote, is will.

Pascal's *Treatise of the Arithmetical Triangle*, in which the Binomial Theorem is first established, helped to make it evident that the analysis of combinations arising from the Aristotelian and Platonic traditions was an aspect of algebraic relations among numbers. Descartes' mathematical work had shown that geometry, the traditional mathematical language of the sciences, also had an algebraic side and that important geometrical properties could be characterized algebraically. By the middle and latter parts of the 17th century, algebraic relations, usually presented as geometrical statements of ratios, had become the form in which natural science expressed the laws of nature. Kepler's third law was essentially such a relation, and so was the Boyle-Mariotte law of gases, and the inverse square law of gravitation. It was only natural to suppose that the actions of the mind—thought—must also have laws that can be described by such relations, and that the combinatorics of analysis and synthesis are a hint of them. Gottfried Leibniz came to that very conclusion.

Pascal's *Treatise* was published in 1654. The next year Leibniz, then 19 years of age, published his first work, a Latin treatise on logic and combinatorics, *De Arte Combinatoria*. He did not yet know of Pascal's work, but he learned of it subsequently, and in later years when he journeyed to Paris, he tried unsuccessfully to meet with Pascal, who had retreated to religious quarters at Port Royal. Pascal had shown that the same combinatorial numbers or binomial coefficients also arise in relations between the terms of certain infinite series, and reflection on the properties of series eventually helped lead Leibniz to the discovery of the differential and integral calculus.

Leibniz's first work was really a combinatorial study of logic in the Aristotelian tradition. It is the only work on logic that Leibniz ever published. Over the course of the rest of his life, Leibniz wrote a long series of unpublished and incomplete papers on logic. They show the formation of some of the key modern ideas about deductive inference and proof, and they also show how very difficult the issues were for one of the greatest philosophers and mathematicians of the century. Leibniz's logical theory is not consistent and thorough (Leibniz had a difficult time completing anything), but it contains many ideas that were successfully elaborated in later centuries, and it also shows clearly the limitations of the Aristotelian framework.

Following tradition, Leibniz assumed that every proposition consists of a predicate applied to a subject and that in this regard the structure of language reflects the structure of the world. In the world, substances *have* attributes. But Leibniz gave this notion a twist. Substances don't, in his view, *have* attributes in the sense that one and the same substance could have an attribute or not have it. A substance *just is* a combination of attributes. You, for example, are nothing but the combination of all of the properties that you have. So there is no property that you in fact have that *you* could not have—an entity that didn't have some property you have wouldn't be you. So, finally, every property you have, you have *necessarily*. The same holds for any other substance in the world. Whatever properties a substance has, it has necessarily.

In Leibniz's theory, every concept *just is* a list or combination of primitive concepts. All true propositions are true because the list of primitive concepts of the subject term is appropriately related to the list of primitive concepts of the predicate term. Leibniz says that every true proposition is true because it is an instance of the identity $A = A$. He meant that if a proposition is true, the subject and predicate lists will be such that by eliminating irrelevant parts of one or the other, the same combination of concepts or attributes is found in the subject as is found in the predicate. So every true proposition can be given a proof. The proof of a proposition consists of the following:

1. Producing the combinations of simple concepts that are, respectively, the concept denoted by the predicate of the proposition and the concept denoted by the subject of the proposition.

2. Showing that the concept of the predicate is included in the concept of the subject, or vice-versa, according to what the proposition asserts.

Leibniz wrote extensively about these two steps. He never succeeded in making clear just how the analysis of concepts was to be obtained—of course, neither had Aristotle or the Scholastic tradition of analysis and synthesis. Leibniz envisioned the creation of an enormous dictionary or encyclopedia; his vision was ridiculed by Swift in the latter's account of Laputan scholarship and has not had a good reputation since the 18th century. In the 1950s, Bar-Hillel noted that a successful mechanical translator, in order to properly distinguish ambiguities such as "pen" in "the ink is in the pen" and "the sheep are in the pen," would have to have access to a huge database of all of human knowledge. Bar-Hillel's observation was considered a *reductio ad absurdum* argument for the impossibility of machine translation. But something like Leibnizian "dictionaries" are indeed being constructed in AI and used in machine translation, albeit with a rather more complex theory of the structure of knowledge, but still based on the idea—now with the backing of 20th century logical theory—that in a computational sense a concept simply is a combination of all that is known about it, so that a suitably rich enumeration and organization of all this knowledge is sufficient to capture the concept.

If a universal dictionary could be assembled that expressed each concept in terms of the simplest concepts, Leibniz was convinced that the production of scientific knowledge would become *automatic*. He thought an *algorithm* or mechanical procedure could be found to carry out the second part of the procedure for giving proofs. The way to formulate such a procedure is to treat the problem as though it is part of *algebra*. Each simple term and each complex term should be given a letter or other symbol (Leibniz sometimes suggested using numbers as symbols for concepts), and then one would use algebraic methods to search for algebraic identities. On other occasions, he suggested representing concepts by geometrical figures, such as lines, and trying to carry out the second step of the aforementioned two-step process by geometrical procedures. The essential thing is that there is a *mathematics of reason* (in fact, that is the title of one of the logical papers Leibniz completed), and this mathematics can be carried out automatically.

Again, much current AI research, given more adequate flesh by developments in logic, is based on a modification of Leibniz's vision. One entire subfield of AI is concerned with "computational logic," a phrase that Leibniz would have understood immediately. Pascal and Leibniz would perhaps also have understood one aspect of the computational difficulties of this field. The reasoning process is indeed governed by combinatorics, quite aside from problems of undecidability. Combinatorial analysis shows that the search spaces of reasoning expand too rapidly to submit to straightforward enumeration, so the mathematics of reasoning seems to require "dictionaries" of heuristics, which are the subject of active research.

Pascal's success with calculating machines inspired Leibniz to devise his own machine, which he called the *Stepped Reckoner.* Although conceptually much more sophisticated than either the Calculating Clock or the Pascaline, Leibniz's Stepped Reckoner appears never to have operated properly; its manufacture was beyond machining techniques of the day. Leibniz's efforts to build a better machine led him to realize that a binary notation would permit a much simpler mechanism than required for his and Pascal's decimal-based devices. He envisioned a binary calculator that would use moving balls to represent binary digits (Leibniz 1679).[2] As noted by Augarten (1985), the notion of binary representation had more than practical import for Leibniz. He regarded the remarkable expressiveness of binary enumeration as a sort of natural proof of the existence of God, asserting that it demonstrated that God, the omniscient *one* (1), had created everything out of *nothing* (0). Thus as did Lull and Pascal before him, Leibniz attached deep religious significance to his efforts at mechanization.

Pascaline's wheels carried numerals, and it performed arithmetic, but Leibniz saw that these machines were manipulating symbols in ways that were best understood in combinatoric terms and that there was nothing about the idea which restricted it solely to arithmetic. During the first half of this, the 20th century, when the idea of mechanical arithmetic had become commonplace, this insight was still rare. An early British government report on the significance of computing machines declared that they were not worth the investment of much research effort, on the grounds that there was not a great need for more gun-aiming tables.

In 1620, Francis Bacon's *Novum Organum* sought to provide the inductive method for the new science. Bacon describes a nearly algorithmic procedure, often ridiculed by 20th century philosophers of science for whom the very idea of discovery by algorithm was anathema. Bacon's discovery procedure assumes the investigator is in search of the "form" of a phenomenon, which for Bacon, as for Aristotle and Plato, meant at least a conjunction of features essential, necessary, and sufficient for the phenomenon. The investigator should then collect positive instances of the phenomenon, forming them in a table. Again, negative instances, otherwise as like positive instances as possible, should be collected in a table. Third, a table should be formed of instances exhibiting the phenomenon in varying degrees, if the phenomenon admits of such variation. Now the investigator should find—Bacon doesn't say how—whatever combination of features is common to all positive instances, absent from all negative instances, and concomitant in degree with the degree of the phenomenon in the table of degrees.

Bacon's problem setting, and his method, were revived around the middle of this century in the study in cognitive psychology of "concept learning." Procedures proposed by Bruner, and later by Hunt, and still later by statistical concept learners, have their logical and historical roots in Bacon's new method.

5. The Cartesian Way

René Descartes' mathematical innovations created linkages that proved essential to the very idea of a mechanics of mind. Descartes' algebraic geometry transformed aspects of the traditional geometrical formalism for the mathematical description of nature into systems of algebraic equations. With that transformation, an algebraic expression became possible for Kepler's laws, Boyle's law, and so on. The binomial theorem in turn established connections between algebra and combinatorics, the mathematics of mind.

Yet, philosophically, Descartes was unconnected with the invisible thread that bound Hobbes, Leibniz and Pascal. The Cartesian conception of mind was not, like Hobbes', of a material device that represents by physical symbols and reasons by computation. Descartes' mind, it is almost too banal to note, was of an entirely different substance than matter; Descartes' mind could exist were nothing material to exist; Descartes' mind could be influenced by material conditions, but it was not bound by and characterized by the principles that constrain matter.

This idea is tantalizingly close to the modern conception of software. Software is also immaterial and remarkably unconstrained by physical principles, yet when provided with a suitable material substrate (not a pineal gland), it can have startling material effects. The Cartesian error was only to think of it as a *substance* rather than something like a pattern or a specification. But perhaps Descartes can be forgiven—philosophers and lawyers are still not quite clear about exactly how to describe software. Fortunately, however, programmers are able to create and use it with some confidence.

For the purposes of our topic, Descartes' principal contemporary influence is on the opponents of artificial intelligence, through two ideas. First, Descartes thought of procedures, algorithms, methods, and rules as inextricable from meaning and intention. Descartes' rules for inquiry are not even approximately mechanical as are Bacon's; instead, Descartes formulated his rules in terms for which there are only inner criteria: examine whether ideas are *clear*; examine whether ideas are *distinct* from others. It was this very subjective twist on method that irritated Descartes' materialist critics, such as Pierre Gassendi. In our century, the Cartesian view of method seems to have prompted (no doubt through more proximate sources, such as phenomenalism) Wittgenstein's argument that a purely subjective language is impossible, because extra-linguistic criteria are required to constitute correct or incorrect usage, and a language without standards of use is not a language at all. Wittgenstein's private language argument has been recast by Saul Kripke as an argument about the irreducibility of rules or algorithms to material or physical relations. Briefly, Kripke argues that rules—for example, the rule for addition—require *meanings* that somehow determine how the rules apply to a potential infinity of as yet unexamined cases. But meanings are *normative*; meanings have to do with how language ought to be used. And, to conclude the argument, norms are not part of the physical world.

The second Cartesian influence on contemporary discussions occurs through a strategy of argument that is ubiquitous in contemporary philosophical opposition to artificial intelligence. Descartes' criterion for possibility is imagination: If p is (or can be) imagined, then p is possible. Hence, if the denial of p can be imagined, then p is not necessary. In combination with some other ideas about possibility and necessity—for example, the idea that fundamental scientific identifications of properties ("water is H_2O") entail that the identity claims are necessary—the Cartesian fallacy sows considerable confusion. A well-known recent example of this confusion is Searle's Chinese room argument. Searle wants to refute the thesis that *any* physically possible system that implements an appropriate program for understanding Chinese with sufficient speed therefore understands Chinese. Searle imagines that he is placed in a room containing baskets full of Chinese symbols and a rule book (in English) for matching Chinese symbols with other Chinese symbols. People outside the room (who understand Chinese) slide questions written in Chinese under the door. In response he manipulates the symbols according to the rules in the book and answers by sliding strings of Chinese symbols back out under the door. The rule book is supposed to be analogous to the computer program, and Searle to the computer. These answers are indistinguishable from those of a native Chinese speaker, although, according to Searle, neither he nor the room nor the two of them together understand Chinese. Even if one were to (mistakenly) grant his second conclusion (that the whole system didn't understand Chinese), Searle's thought experiment is only a counter-example to anything of interest to artificial intelligence if one supposes that because Searle can imagine himself running the program with sufficient speed, that this *is* actually possible. But before he could generate a single output Searle-in-the-box would become bored and his Chinese friends would have long since found better things to do.

6. Minds and Procedures: Hobbes to Kant

Thomas Hobbes, the 17th century autodidact and mathematical eccentric best known for his writings on political philosophy, also formulated a rather clear anticipation of Newell and Simon's notion of intelligence as a physical system that manipulates symbols:

> By ratiocination, I mean computation. Now to compute is either to collect the sum of many things that are added together, or to know what remains when one thing is taken out of another. Ratiocination, therefore, is the same with addition and subtraction; and if any man add multiplication and division, I will not be against it, seeing multiplication is nothing but addition of equals one to another, and division nothing but a subtraction of equals one from another, as often as is possible. So that all ratiocination is comprehended in these two operations of the mind, addition and subtraction.
>
> But how by the *ratiocination* of our mind, we add and subtract in our silent thoughts, without the use of words, it will be necessary for me to make intelligible by an example or two. If therefore a man sees something afar off and obscurely, although no appellation had yet been given to anything, he will, notwithstanding, have the same idea of that thing for which now, by imposing a name on it, we call it *body*. Again, when by coming nearer, he sees the same thing thus and thus, now in one place and now in another, he will have a new idea thereof, namely, that for which we now call such a thing *animated*. Thirdly, when standing nearer, he perceives the figure, hears the voice, and sees other things which are signs of a rational mind, he has a third idea, though it have yet no appellation, namely, that for which we now call anything *rational*. Lastly, when, by looking fully and distinctly upon it, he conceives all that he has seen as one thing, the idea he has now is compounded of his former ideas, which are put together in the mind in the same order in which these three single names, *body, animated, rational*, are in speech compounded into this one name, *body-animated-rational*, or *man*. In like manner, of the several conceptions of *four sides, equality of sides, and right angles,* is compounded the conception of a *square*. For the mind may conceive a figure of four sides without any conception of their equality, and of that equality without conceiving a right angle; and may join together all these single conceptions into one conception or one idea of a square. And thus we see how the conceptions of the mind are compounded. Again, whosoever sees a man standing near him, conceives the whole idea of that man; and if, as he goes away, he follows him with his eyes only, he will lose the idea of those things which were signs of his being rational, whilst, nevertheless, the idea of a body-animated remains still before his eyes, so that the idea of rational is subtracted from the whole idea of man, that is to say, of body-animated-rational, and there remains that of body-animated; and a while after, at a greater distance, the idea of animated will be lost, and that of body only will remain; so that at last, when nothing at all can be seen, the whole idea will vanish out of sight. By which examples, I think, it is manifest enough what is the internal ratiocination of mind without words.
>
> We must not therefore, think that computation, that is, ratiocination, has place only in numbers, as if man were distinguished from other living creatures (which is said to have been the opinion of *Pythagoras*) by nothing but the faculty of numbering; for *magnitude, body, motion, time, degrees of quality, action, conception proportion, speech and names* (in which all the kinds of philosophy consist) are capable of addition and subtraction. (Hobbes 1962, pp. 25-26)

There are several important thoughts in this passage. One is that reasoning is a psychological process, so that a theory of logical inference should be a theory of the operations of the mind. Another is that representations can have an encoding by, or be analogous to, numbers. A third is that the theory of reasoning is a theory of appropriate combinations; just what the objects are that are combined is obscure in this passage, but other passages suggest that Hobbes thought of the mind as composed of particles, and some of these particles, or collections of them, serve as symbols (or, as Hobbes would say, names) for things, and it is these physical symbols that are combined or decomposed in reasoning.

Later English writers of philosophical psychology, Locke, Hume, Mill, and Maudsley, for example, thought of the content of a theory of mind as, at least in part, a theory of mental procedures, specifically procedures in which mental objects—"ideas"—are linked or "associated." Associationist psychology typically avoided Hobbes' mechanical formulations, and his connection of procedures with algorithms and numerical encodings had no influence. Instead, mental procedures were explained in terms of "similarity" and "vivacity" and temporal proximity of occurrence of ideas.

The procedural viewpoint was given a very different turn in the closing decades of the 18th century in Kant's *Critique of Pure Reason* and his related works. As with the associationist writers who influenced him, Kant gives few hints that mental processes are computational, but he offers an original view of those processes themselves, quite unlike anything before. Kant is the modern father of the notion of top-down processing.

Kant recognized that the logical theory which he had inherited from Aristotle, and which he assumed to be sound and complete, could not account for mathematical inference. Euclid's geometrical proofs, which prove by construction the existence of objects with specified properties, cannot be turned into valid syllogistic arguments, nor can Euclid's proofs of theorems in number theory be obtained by syllogism. Yet Kant was convinced that classical mathematics and much else (including that all events are governed by causal regularities and features of Newtonian physics) is known *a priori* and not derived from inductions founded on experience. Kant's solution to the conundrum is that the content of experience is literally a *function* (in the mathematical sense) of the procedures of mind and of unknowable features of things in themselves. The difference between what is needed to obtain Euclid's proofs and what Aristotle's logic can do is built into the mind itself, not as axioms but as procedures that automatically construct the content of experience from the deliverances of sense. Things in themselves deliver, in unknowable ways, sensation, or what Kant sometimes calls the matter of experience; the "faculty of intuition" then contributes spatial and temporal features; and the "schematism of the understanding" contributes object identity, causal regularity, and the synthesis of the individual pieces into a unified experience.

The faculty of intuition automatically constructs images, for example, that satisfy the requirements of Euclidean axioms, and the schematism ensures that nothing random happens in experience. Kant repeatedly remarks that the process of synthesis and the operation of the schematism are unconscious, and he observes that how the schematism works will likely remain unknown (immediately thereafter he plunges into lengthy remarks about how the schematism works).

7. The 19th Century: Boole, Frege and Freud

George Boole's work can be seen as a continuation of Leibniz's vision. Boole provided an algebra of logic and considered the algebra important because it provided a method for correct reasoning. Boole, too, viewed the mathematical theory of reasoning as a description of psychological laws of nature, but he also realized the contradiction between this analysis and the obvious fact that humans make errors of reasoning.

The truth that the ultimate laws of thought are mathematical in their form, viewed in connection with the fact of the possibility of error, establishes a ground for some remarkable conclusions. If we directed our attention to the scientific truth alone, we might be led to infer an almost exact parallelism between the intellectual operations and the movements of external nature. Suppose any one conversant with physical science, but unaccustomed to reflect upon the nature of his own faculties, to have been informed, that it had been proved, that the laws of those faculties were mathematical; it is probable that after the first feelings of incredulity had subsided, the impression would arise, that the order of thought must, *therefore*, be as necessary as that of the material universe. We know that in the realm of natural science, the absolute connection between the initial and final elements of a problem, exhibited in the mathematical form, fitly symbolizes that physical necessity which binds together effect and cause. The necessary sequence of states and conditions in the inorganic world, and the necessary connection of premises and conclusion in the processes of exact demonstration thereto applied, seem to be coordinate.

Were, then, the laws of valid reasoning uniformly obeyed, a very close parallelism would exist between the operations of the intellect and those of external Nature. Subjection to laws mathematical in their form and expression, even the subjection of an absolute obedience, would stamp upon the two series one common character. The reign of necessity over the intellectual and the physical world would be alike complete and universal.

But while the observation of external Nature testifies with ever-strengthening evidence to the fact, that uniformity of operation and unvarying obedience to appointed laws prevail throughout her entire domain, the slightest attention to the processes of the intellectual world reveals to us another state of things. The mathematical laws of reasoning are, properly speaking, the laws of *right* reasoning only, and their actual transgression is a perpetually recurring phenomenon.

Error, which has no place in the material system, occupies a large one here. We must accept this as one of those ultimate facts, the origin of which it lies beyond the province of science to determine. We must admit that there exist laws which even the rigor of their mathematical forms does not preserve from violation. We must ascribe to them an authority the essence of which does not consist in power, a supremacy which the analogy of the inviolable order of the natural world in no way assists us to comprehend. (Boole 1951, pp. 407-408)

Caught by the image of logic as the laws of reasoning akin to the law of gravitation, Boole did not try to resolve this difficulty by supposing that his was the theory of some ideal agent; he did not think that he was describing other minds than ours, imaginary minds still somehow recognizably similar to our own.

About thirty years later, Frege gave the first adequate formulation of the logic of propositions—Boole had in effect described something closer to mod 2 arithmetic—and formalized a system of logic that included both first-order logic and the quantification over properties, although the latter part of his system was, as Russell showed, not consistent. Frege insisted on separating logic from psychology, and so he did not suffer Boole's embarrassment over human error. Frege's achievement, and the logical developments of the next fifty years that extended it, at last put in place one of the principal tools for the study, among many other things, of android epistemology. Another conceptual tool arose at nearly the same time from physiology.

While the 18th and early 19th centuries witnessed thinkers such as Pascal, Leibniz, and Boole struggling to find a mechanical basis for reasoning, the end of the 19th and the beginning of the 20th century saw two remarkably different ways of reconciling psychology with the notion that reasoning is computation. Each of these lines of work leads to a branch of contemporary AI research. The "symbolic" approach to AI emphasizes structures of reasoning, while "connectionist" artificial intelligence focuses on brain-like architectures.

Prefaces to modern connectionist works usually trace the ideas back as far as Hebb's (1949) *The Organization of Behavior;* occasionally writers will note passages of William James near the turn of the century that have a connectionist flavor. But the basics of connectionist models of computation and of mind were fully developed by the late 19th century in the private views, and some of the public views, of neuropsychologists. We know of no better statement from this time than Sigmund Freud's private writings, where a great many details, including what is now called "Hebbian learning" and the "Hebbian synapse" are described. Freud was trained as a neuroanatomist by Ernst Brucke, one of Europe's leading physiologists and an uncompromising materialist. Early in the 1890s physiologists learned of synaptic junctions, and in Vienna that revelation immediately led to connectionist speculations by the senior research assistants in Brucke's laboratory, including Freud. While others published similar views, Freud developed his ideas in his unpublished *Project for a Scientific Psychology,* written in 1895. Freud's theory of dreams began in that essay, and the last chapter of Freud's first book on dreams is clearly derived from it. (For a more detailed account of Freud's connection with connectionism, see Glymour, 1991.)

We return now to the symbolic tradition. Kant held that the objects of experience are constructed or "synthesized," but he was not at all clear about what they are constructed from or how the details of such a construction could work. After Frege's work, a few philosophers began to have novel ideas about what a "construction" or "synthesis" might be. The three most important philosophers first influenced by Frege were Bertrand Russell, Ludwig Wittgenstein, and Rudolf Carnap. Russell had an important correspondence with Frege, and Carnap went to Jena to study with him. Frege's antipsychologism may have had a curious and healthy effect, for Carnap especially had no hesitation in developing a mathematics of cognition that, while motivated by psychological ideas, did not pretend to describe how people actually reason. This attitude was crucial to the pragmatic approach of early work in AI.

Russell and Carnap each proposed (at about the same time) that extensions of Frege's logical theory, or Frege's logic in combination with set theory, could be used to describe the construction of physical objects from the data of sensation. Russell and Whitehead had developed techniques to carry on Frege's logicist program to reduce mathematics to logic; Russell and Carnap, independently, thought that the same techniques could be used to give an account of the possibility of knowledge of the external world.

Russell's idea was that starting with variables ranging over basic entities (the sense data) and with predicates denoting properties of sense data (such as red), one could then define terms that would denote sets of sense data. Physical objects would literally be sets of sense data, or sets of sets of sense data or sets of sets of sets of sense data, and so on. Similarly, higher order properties of physical objects (such as the property of being a tree) would also be appropriate sets of sense data (or sets of sets of sense data, etc.). Russell sketched these ideas in a popular book, *Our Knowledge of the External World,* but he made no attempt to describe any logical details. Meanwhile, Carnap actually produced an outline of such a system.

Carnap's book, *The Logical Structure of the World,* was published in 1928. Carnap assumed that the fundamental entities over which the variables of his system range are what he called *elementary experiences*—an elementary experience is all that appears to someone at a particular moment. In addition, he assumed one relation between elementary experiences is given in experience, namely, the relation that obtains when one recollects that two experiences are similar in some respect or other. (For example, they might both be experiences that contain a red patch somewhere.) The construction of the world begins with a finite list of pairs of elementary experiences; for each pair in the list, the person whose experiences they are recollects that the first element in the pair is in some respect similar to the second element in the pair. Qualities such as color and tone are then defined as certain sets (or sets of sets or sets of sets of sets, etc.) formed from this list. Objects are to be constructed in the same way.

One of the most remarkable things about Carnap's logical construction of the world is that it is not presented only as a collection of logical formulas that are to be applied to terms denoting elementary experiences and the relation of recollection. Carnap also described the construction as a *computational procedure*. That is, along with each logical construction he gave what he called a "fictitious procedure" that shows how to calculate a representation of the object constructed from any list of pairs of elementary experiences. The procedures are perfectly explicit, and they could be represented in any modern computer language. Carnap was the first philosopher (indeed the first person) to present a theory of the mind as a computational program. The use of logical representations immediately suggested (to Carnap anyway) that computation can be done not just on numbers, but on symbols that represent nonnumerical objects. This was really Ramón Lull's idea, and Hobbes' idea after that, but in Carnap's work it begins to look as though it might really work.

William Aspray (1981) has given a persuasive account of the origins of the theory of computation, as it emerged in this century, from philosophical issues in the foundations of mathematics rooted in the 19th century. We think it is fair to say, however, that while the development of the essentials of recursion computation theory was motivated by philosophical issues, the profession of philosophy contributed nothing to them. Gödel gave an account of his incompleteness results to the Vienna Circle, but the audience seems to have missed their import. Alonzo Church was at the center of things, but in the 30s and 40s he was in the mathematics department at Princeton, and there is no evidence that anyone in the philosophy department at the time had an inkling of the revolution going on around them.

Late in the 1920s or thereabouts, Frank Ramsey developed the idea of subjective utility theory and the theory of measurement of subjective utilities. Belatedly, Carnap approached Ramsey's conception of probability, and by the middle of the century, Carnap proposed that we think of inductive norms as the design principles for an android that would begin life with some probability distribution and carry on by conditioning on the evidence it acquired throughout life. When, early in the 1960s, electronic digital computers began to be available for research, the first expert systems for medical diagnosis used Bayesian methods much as Carnap had imagined. Whether there was any direct influence from the philosophical tradition, we do not know. Russell, too, came late in life to think of epistemology as principles of android design. His last serious work, *Human Knowledge, Its Scope and Limits*, abandons the idea of building up the world from sense data and considers especially the general knowledge of kinds and causes that systems must innately have in order to convert sensation into knowledge of the world.

Carnap had two students, Walter Pitts and Herbert Simon, who contributed directly to the formation of the subject of artificial intelligence in the middle of this century, and Simon, of course, contributed many of the leading ideas in the subject. And Carnap had another student, Carl Hempel, who contributed indirectly to the first commercial computer programs for automated scientific discovery. For all of their influence, neither Carnap nor Hempel seems to have had a glimmer of the possibilities in android epistemology, and both flatly denied—Hempel repeatedly and vehemently—the possibility of machine discovery.

Hempel's influence came through his students. One of his doctoral students at Princeton, Gerald Massey, had a doctoral student at Michigan State, Bruce Buchanan, who went to work at Stanford in what was then a very odd job: helping to design and implement programs for chemical identification with mass spectroscopy. Joshua Lederberg and others had developed algorithms for identifying the hydrocarbon compounds consistent with chemical law and a given formula, and the task was to use these algorithms as part of an inference engine. In the Dendral and Meta-Dendral programs, Hempel's theory of explanation and his instance-based approach to hypothesis confirmation were adapted and applied.

8. Conclusion

The history of modern computing has as a central theme the development of methods for representing information in a physical form which is both stable enough to be reliable as a memory and plastic enough to be changed mechanically. The algorithms of Pascal's and Leibniz's calculating machines were physically represented in their mechanical structure. It was not until Babbage's (1792-1871) Analytical Engine that a machine was designed that did not directly physically embody the algorithms that it could execute. Significantly, it used a punched-card technique for encoding information and algorithms which was originally developed for use in mechanical looms of the late 19th century. The engineers were beginning, quite serendipitously, to provide the ideas which could give flesh to Leibniz's vision.

AI is re-establishing the cooperation between philosophy and engineering which so motivated and enlightened Pascal and Leibniz, but now android epistemology is working with richer tools. In the centuries of philosophical discussion since Pascal and Leibniz first saw how arithmetic could be mechanized, the concept of "machine" has not been much extended beyond Pascaline. But AI is working with new kinds of machines—not just physical computing machines but also "virtual" machines which consist of software (run on other, "actual" machines) but perform real feats in the world. Through the work of Turing's student, Robin Gandy, and others, theorists are developing new and more general formal conceptions of machines that compute.

Some of the early work in artificial intelligence seems to have taken philosophical theories more or less off the shelf, specialized them to particular tasks, and automated them, so that some of the early work in the subject has the flavor of automated philosophy of science, and even some of the more recent work in machine learning—for example, work on discovering laws and work on causal inference—bears the mark of philosophical sources. But the period is past in which android epistemology could rely substantially on independent work in philosophical logic and philosophy of science. What future development requires is not separation of labor by disciplines, but rigor and imagination, clarity of broad motive and clarity of detail, and a willingness to take off the blinkers of disciplines. Philosophy should not be just one more set of blinkers.

Notes

1. It is now clear that Pascal was preceded by the German polymath Wilhelm Schickard and his Calculating Clock. Schickard was a protege of Kepler.

2. Leibniz is often erroneously credited with inventing binary arithmetic, but its roots are much older, reaching at least back to the ancient Chinese. Binary counting systems have been found in many of the world's ethnologically oldest tribes (Phillips 1936). It seems that ancient man was much taken with the pairwise nature of his body—two legs, arms, eyes and ears. Binary multiplication is first described in the wonderfully named manuscript "Directions for Obtaining Knowledge of All Dark Things," believed to have been written by a scribe named Ahmes in about 1650 B.C.

2

Computing Machinery and Intelligence

A. M. Turing

1. The Imitation Game

I propose to consider the question, "Can machines think?" This should begin with definitions of the meaning of the terms "machine" and "think." The definitions might be framed so as to reflect so far as possible the normal use of the words, but this attitude is dangerous. If the meaning of the words "machine" and "think" are to be found by examining how they are commonly used it is difficult to escape the conclusion that the meaning and the answer to the question, "Can machines think?" is to be sought in a statistical survey such as a Gallup poll. But this is absurd. Instead of attempting such a definition I shall replace the question by another, which is closely related to it and is expressed in relatively unambiguous words.

The new form of the problem can be described in terms of a game which we call the "imitation game." It is played with three people, a man (A), a woman (B), and an interrogator (C) who may be of either sex. The interrogator stays in a room apart from the other two. The object of the game for the interrogator is to determine which of the other two is the man and which is the woman. He knows them by labels X and Y, and at the end of the game he says either "X is A and Y is B" or "X is B and Y is A." The interrogator is allowed to put questions to A and B thus:

C: Will X please tell me the length of his or her hair?

Now suppose X is actually A, then A must answer. It is A's object in the game to try and cause C to make the wrong identification. His answer might therefore be:

"My hair is shingled, and the longest strands are about nine inches long." In order that tones of voice may not help the interrogator the answers should be written, or better still, typewritten. The ideal arrangement is to have a teleprinter communicating between the two rooms. Alternatively the question and answers can be repeated by an intermediary. The object of the game for the third player (B) is to help the interrogator. The best strategy for her is probably to give truthful answers. She can add such things as "I am the woman, don't listen to him!" to her answers, but it will avail nothing as the man can make similar remarks.

We now ask the question, "What will happen when a machine takes the part of A in this game?" Will the interrogator decide wrongly as often when the game is played like this as he does when the game is played between a man and a woman? These questions replace our original, "Can machines think?"

2. Critique of the New Problem

As well as asking, "What is the answer to this new form of the question," one may ask, "Is this new question a worthy one to investigate?" This latter question we investigate without further ado, thereby cutting short an infinite regress.

The new problem has the advantage of drawing a fairly sharp line between the physical and the intellectual capacities of a man. No engineer or chemist claims to be able to produce a material which is indistinguishable from the human skin. It is possible that at some time this might be done, but even supposing this invention available we should feel there was little point in trying to make a "thinking machine" more human by dressing it up in such artificial flesh. The form in which we have set the problem reflects this fact in the condition which prevents the interrogator from seeing or touching the other competitors, or hearing their voices. Some other advantages of the proposed criterion may be shown up by specimen questions and answers. Thus:

Q: Please write me a sonnet on the subject of the Forth Bridge.

A: Count me out on this one. I never could write poetry.

Q: Add 34957 to 70764.

A: (Pause about 30 seconds and then give as answer) 105621.

Q: Do you play chess?

A: Yes.

Q: I have K at my K1, and no other pieces. You have only K at K6 and R at R1. It is your move. What do you play?

A: (After a pause of 15 seconds) R-R8 mate.

The question and answer method seems to be suitable for introducing almost any one of the fields of human endeavor that we wish to include. We do not wish to penalize the machine for its inability to shine in beauty competitions, nor to penalize a man for losing in a race against an airplane. The conditions of our game make these disabilities irrelevant. The "witnesses" can brag, if they consider it advisable, as much as they please about their charms, strength or heroism, but the interrogator cannot demand practical demonstrations.

The game may perhaps be criticized on the ground that the odds are weighted too heavily against the machine. If the man were to try and pretend to be the machine he would clearly make a very poor showing. He would be given away at once by slowness and inaccuracy in arithmetic. May not machines carry out something which ought to be described as thinking but which is very different from what a man does? This objection is a very strong one, but at least we can say that if, nevertheless, a machine can be constructed to play the imitation game satisfactorily, we need not be troubled by this objection.

It might be urged that when playing the "imitation game" the best strategy for the machine may possibly be something other than imitation of the behavior of a man. This may be, but I think it is unlikely that there is any great effect of this kind. In any case there is no intention to investigate here the theory of the game, and it will be assumed that the best strategy is to try to provide answers that would naturally be given by a man.

3. The Machines Concerned in the Game

The question which we put in Section 1 will not be quite definite until we have specified what we mean by the word "machine." It is natural that we should wish to permit every kind of engineering technique to be used in our machines. We also wish to allow the possibility that an engineer or team of engineers may construct a machine which works, but whose manner of operation cannot be satisfactorily described by its constructors because they have applied a method which is largely experimental. Finally, we wish to exclude from the machines men born in the usual manner. It is difficult to frame the definitions so as to satisfy these three conditions. One might for instance insist that the team of engineers should be all of one sex, but this would not really be satisfactory, for it is probably possible to rear a complete individual from a single cell of the skin (say) of a man. To do so would be a feat of biological technique deserving of the very highest praise, but we would not be inclined to regard it as a case of "constructing a thinking machine." This prompts us to abandon the requirement that every kind of technique should be permitted. We are the more ready to do so in view of the fact that the present interest in "thinking machines" has been aroused by a particular kind of machine, usually called an "electronic computer" or "digital computer." Following this suggestion we only permit digital computers to take part in our game. This restriction appears at first sight to be a very drastic one. I shall attempt to show that it is not so in reality. To do this necessitates a short account of the nature and properties of these computers.

It may also be said that this identification of machines with digital computers, like our criterion for "thinking," will only be unsatisfactory if (contrary to my belief), it turns out that digital computers are unable to give a good showing in the game.

There are already a number of digital computers in working order, and it may be asked, "Why not try the experiment straight away? It would be easy to satisfy the conditions of the game. A number of interrogators could be used, and statistics compiled to show how often the right identification was given." The short answer is that we are not asking whether all digital computers would do well in the game nor whether the computers at present available would do well, but whether there are imaginable computers which would do well. But this is only the short answer. We shall see this question in a different light later.

4. Digital Computers

The idea behind digital computers may be explained by saying that these machines are intended to carry out any operations which could be done by a human computer. The human computer is supposed to be following fixed rules; he has no authority to deviate from them in any detail. We may suppose that these rules are supplied in a book, which is altered whenever he is put on to a new job. He has also an unlimited supply of paper on which he does his calculations. He may also do his multiplications and additions on a "desk machine," but this is not important.

If we use the above explanation as a definition we shall be in danger of circularity of argument. We avoid this by giving an outline of the means by which the desired effect is achieved. A digital computer can usually be regarded as consisting of three parts:
• Store.
• Executive unit.
• Control.
The store is a store of information, and corresponds to the human computer's

paper, whether this is the paper on which he does his calculations or that on which his book of rules is printed. In so far as the human computer does calculations in his head a part of the store will correspond to his memory.

The executive unit is the part which carries out the various individual operations involved in a calculation. What these individual operations are will vary from machine to machine. Usually fairly lengthy operations can be done such as "Multiply 3540675445 by 7076345687" but in some machines only very simple ones such as "Write down 0" are possible.

We have mentioned that the "book of rules" supplied to the computer is replaced in the machine by a part of the store. It is then called the "table of instructions." It is the duty of the control to see that these instructions are obeyed correctly and in the right order. The control is so constructed that this necessarily happens.

The information in the store is usually broken up into packets of moderately small size. In one machine, for instance, a packet might consist of ten decimal digits. Numbers are assigned to the parts of the store in which the various packets of information are stored, in some systematic manner. A typical instruction might say: "Add the number stored in position 6809 to that in 4302 and put the result back into the latter storage position."

Needless to say it would not occur in the machine expressed in English. It would more likely be coded in a form such as 6809430217. Here 17 says which of various possible operations is to be performed on the two numbers. In this case the operation is that described above, viz., "Add the number...." It will be noticed that the instruction takes up 10 digits and so forms one packet of information, very conveniently. The control will normally take the instructions to be obeyed in the order of the positions in which they are stored, but occasionally an instruction such as "Now obey the instruction stored in position 5606, and continue from there" may be encountered, or again "If position 4505 contains 0 obey next the instruction stored in 6707, otherwise continue straight on."

Instructions of these latter types are very important because they make it possible for a sequence of operations to be replaced over and over again until some condition is fulfilled, but in doing so to obey, not fresh instructions on each repetition, but the same ones over and over again. To take a domestic analogy. Suppose Mother wants Tommy to call at the cobbler's every morning on his way to school to see if her shoes are done, she can ask him afresh every morning. Alternatively she can stick up a notice once and for all in the hall which he will see when he leaves for school and which tells him to call for the shoes, and also to destroy the notice when he comes back if he has the shoes with him.

The reader must accept it as a fact that digital computers can be constructed, and indeed have been constructed, according to the principles we have described, and that they can in fact mimic the actions of a human computer very closely.

The book of rules which we have described our human computer as using is of course a convenient fiction. Actual human computers really remember what they have got to do. If one wants to make a machine mimic the behavior of the human computer in some complex operation one has to ask him how it is done, and then translate the answer into the form of an instruction table. Constructing instruction tables is usually described as "programming." To "program a machine to carry out the operation A" means to put the appropriate instruction table into the machine so that it will do A.

An interesting variant on the idea of a digital computer is a "digital computer with a random element." These have instructions involving the throwing of a die or some equivalent electronic process; one such instruction might for instance be, "Throw the die and put the resulting number into store 1000." Sometimes such a machine is described as having free will (though I would not use this phrase myself). It is not normally possible to determine from observing a machine whether it has a random element, for a similar effect can be produced by such devices as making the choices depend on the digits of the decimal for π.

Most actual digital computers have only a finite store. There is no theoretical difficulty in the idea of a computer with an unlimited store. Of course only a finite part can have been used at any one time. Likewise only a finite amount can have been constructed, but we can imagine more and more being added as required. Such computers have special theoretical interest and will be called infinitive capacity computers.

The idea of a digital computer is an old one. Charles Babbage, Lucasian Professor of Mathematics at Cambridge from 1828 to 1839, planned such a machine, called the Analytical Engine, but it was never completed. Although Babbage had all the essential ideas, his machine was not at that time such a very attractive prospect. The speed which would have been available would be definitely faster than a human computer but something like 100 times slower than the Manchester machine, itself one of the slower of the modern machines. The storage was to be purely mechanical, using wheels and cards.

The fact that Babbage's Analytical Engine was to be entirely mechanical will help us to rid ourselves of a superstition. Importance is often attached to the fact that modern digital computers are electrical, and that the nervous system also is electrical. Since Babbage's machine was not electrical, and since all digital computers are in a sense equivalent, we see that this use of electricity cannot be of theoretical importance. Of course electricity usually comes in where fast signalling is concerned, so that it is not surprising that we find it in both these connections. In the nervous system chemical phenomena are at least as important as electrical. In certain computers the storage system is mainly acoustic. The feature of using electricity is thus seen to be only a very superficial similarity. If we wish to find such similarities we should look rather for mathematical analogies of function.

5. Universality of Digital Computers

The digital computers considered in the last section may be classified amongst the "discrete-state machines." These are the machines which move by sudden jumps or clicks from one quite definite state to another. These states are sufficiently different for the possibility of confusion between them to be ignored. Strictly speaking there are no such machines. Everything really moves continuously. But there are many kinds of machine which can profitably be *thought of* as being discrete-state machines. For instance in considering the switches for a lighting system it is a convenient fiction that each switch must be definitely on or definitely off. There must be intermediate positions, but for most purposes we can forget about them. As an example of a discrete state machine we might consider a wheel which clicks round through 120° once a second, but may be stopped by a lever which can be operated from outside; in addition a lamp is to light in one of the positions of the wheel. This machine could be described abstractly as follows. The internal state of the machine (which is described by the position of the wheel) may be q_1, q_2 or q_3. There is an input signal i_0 or i_1 (position of lever). The internal state at any moment is determined by the last state and input signal according to the table

		Last State		
		q_1	q_2	q_3
Input	i_0	q_2	q_3	q_1
	i_1	q_1	q_2	q_3

The output signals, the only externally visible indication of the internal state (the light) are described by the table

State	q_1	q_2	q_3
Output	0_0	0_0	0_1

This example is typical of discrete-state machines. They can be described by such tables provided they have only a finite number of possible states.

It will seem that given the initial state of the machine and the input signals it is always possible to predict all future states. This is reminiscent of Laplace's view that from the complete state of the universe at one moment of time, as described by the positions and velocities of all particles, it should be possible to predict all future states. The prediction which we are considering is, however, rather nearer to practicability than that considered by Laplace. The system of the "universe as a whole" is such that quite small errors in the initial conditions can have an overwhelming effect at a later time. The displacement of a single electron by a billionth of a centimeter at one moment might make the difference between a man being killed by an avalanche a year later, or escaping. It is an essential property of the mechanical systems which we have called "discrete-state machines" that this phenomenon does not occur. Even when we consider the actual physical machines instead of the idealized machines, reasonably accurate knowledge of the state at one moment yields reasonably accurate knowledge any number of steps later.

As we have mentioned, digital computers fall within the class of discrete state machines. But the number of states of which such a machine is capable is usually enormously large. For instance, the number for the machine now working at Manchester is about $2^{165,000}$, i.e., about $10^{50,000}$. Compare this with our example of the clicking wheel described above, which had three states. It is not difficult to see why the number of states should be so immense. The computer includes a store corresponding to the paper used by a human computer. It must be possible to write into the store any one of the combinations of symbols which might have been written on the paper. For simplicity suppose that only digits from 0 to 9 are used as symbols. Variations in handwriting are ignored. Suppose the computer is allowed 100 sheets of paper each containing 50 lines each with room for 30 digits. Then the number of states is $10^{100 \times 50 \times 30}$, i.e., $10^{150,000}$. This is about the number of states of three Manchester machines put together. The logarithm to the base two of the number of states is usually called the "storage capacity" of the machine. Thus the Manchester machine has a storage capacity of about 165,000 and the wheel machine of our example about 1.6. If two machines are put together their capacities must be added to obtain the capacity of the resultant machine. This leads to the possibility of statements such as "The Manchester machine contains 64 magnetic tracks each with a capacity of 2560, eight electronic tubes with a capacity of 1280. Miscellaneous storage amounts to about 300 making a total of 174,380."

Given the table corresponding to a discrete-state machine it is possible to predict what it will do. There is no reason why this calculation should not be carried out by means of a digital computer. Provided it could be carried out sufficiently quickly the digital computer could mimic the behavior of any discrete-state machine. The imitation game could then be played with the machine in question (as B) and the mimicking digital computer (as A) and the interrogator would be unable to distinguish them. Of course the digital computer must have an adequate storage capacity as well as working sufficiently fast. Moreover, it must be programmed afresh for each new machine which it is desired to mimic.

This special property of digital computers, that they can mimic any discrete-state machine, is described by saying that they are *universal* machines. The existence of machines with this property has the important consequence that, considerations of speed apart, it is unnecessary to design various new machines to do various computing processes. They can all be done with one digital computer, suitably programmed for each case. It will be seen that as a consequence of this all digital computers are in a sense equivalent.

We may now consider again the point raised at the end of Section 3. It was suggested tentatively that the question, "Can machines think?" should be replaced by "Are there imaginable digital computers which would do well in the imitation game?" If we wish, we can make this superficially more general and ask "Are there discrete-state machines which would do well?" But in view of the universality property we see that either of these questions is equivalent to this, "Let us fix our attention on one particular digital computer C. Is it true that by modifying this computer to have an adequate storage, suitably increasing its speed of action, and providing it with an appropriate program, C can be made to play satisfactorily the part of A in the imitation game, the part of B being taken by a man?"

6. Contrary Views on the Main Question

We may now consider the ground to have been cleared and we are ready to proceed to the debate on our question, "Can machines think?" and the variant of it quoted at the end of the last section. We cannot altogether abandon the original form of the problem, for opinions will differ as to the appropriateness of the substitution and we must at least listen to what has to be said in this connection.

It will simplify matters for the reader if I explain first my own beliefs in the matter. Consider first the more accurate form of the question. I believe that in about fifty years time it will be possible to program computers, with a storage capacity of about 10^9, to make them play the imitation game so well that an average interrogator will not have more than 70 per cent chance of making the right identification after five minutes of questioning. The original question, "Can machines think?" I believe to be too meaningless to deserve discussion. Nevertheless I believe that at the end of the century the use of words and general educated opinion will have altered so much that one will be able to speak of machines thinking without expecting to be contradicted. I believe further that no useful purpose is served by concealing these beliefs. The popular view that scientists proceed inexorably from well-established fact to well-established fact, never being influenced by any improved conjecture, is quite mistaken. Provided it is made clear which are proved facts and which are conjectures, no harm can result. Conjectures are of great importance since they suggest useful lines of research. I now proceed to consider opinions opposed to my own.

6.1 The Theological Objection

Thinking is a function of man's immortal soul. God has given an immortal soul to every man and woman, but not to any other animal or to machines.

Hence no animal or machine can think.[1]

I am unable to accept any part of this, but will attempt to reply in theological terms. I should find the argument more convincing if animals were classed with men, for there is a greater difference, to my mind, between the typical animate and the inanimate than there is between man and the other animals. The arbitrary character of the orthodox view becomes clearer if we consider how it might appear to a member of some other religious community. How do Christians regard the Moslem view that women have no souls? But let us leave this point aside and return to the main argument. It appears to me that the argument quoted above implies a serious restriction of the omnipotence of the Almighty. It is admitted that there are certain things that He cannot do such as making one equal to two, but should we not believe that He has freedom to confer a soul on an elephant if He sees fit? We might expect that He would only exercise this power in conjunction with a mutation which provided the elephant with an appropriately improved brain to minister to the needs of this soul. An argument of exactly similar form may be made for the case of machines. It may seem different because it is more difficult to "swallow." But this really only means that we think it would be less likely that He would consider the circumstances suitable for conferring a soul. The circumstances in question are discussed in the rest of this paper. In attempting to construct such machines we should not be irreverently usurping His power of creating souls, any more than we are in the procreation of children: rather we are, in either case, instruments of His will providing mansions for the souls that He creates.

However, this is mere speculation. I am not very impressed with theological arguments whatever they may be used to support. Such arguments have often been found unsatisfactory in the past. In the time of Galileo it was argued that the texts, "And the sun stood still... and hasted not to go down about a whole day" (Joshua x. 13) and "He laid the foundations of the earth, that it should not move at any time" (Psalm cv. 5) were an adequate refutation of the Copernican theory. With our present knowledge, such an argument appears futile. When that knowledge was not available it made a quite different impression.

6.2 The "Heads in the Sand" Objection

"The consequences of machines thinking would be too dreadful. Let us hope and believe that they cannot do so."

This argument is seldom expressed quite so openly as in the form above. But it affects most of us who think about it at all. We like to believe that Man is in some subtle way superior to the rest of creation. It is best if he can be shown to be *necessarily* superior, for then there is no danger of him losing his commanding position. The popularity of the theological argument is clearly connected with this feeling. It is likely to be quite strong in intellectual people, since they value the power of thinking more highly than others, and are more inclined to base their belief in the superiority of Man on this power.

I do not think that this argument is sufficiently substantial to require refutation. Consolation would be more appropriate: perhaps this should be sought in the transmigration of souls.

6.3 The Mathematical Objection

There are a number of results of mathematical logic which can be used to show that there are limitations to the powers of discrete state machines. The best known of these results is known as Godel's theorem (1931) and shows that in any sufficiently powerful logical system statements can be formulated which can neither be proved nor disproved within the system, unless possibly the system itself is inconsistent. There are other, in some respects similar, results due to Church (1936), Kleene (1935). The latter result is the most convenient to consider, since it refers directly to machines, whereas the others can only be used in a comparatively indirect argument: for instance if Godel's theorem is to be used we need in addition to have some means of describing logical systems in terms of machines, and machines in terms of logical systems. The result in question refers to a type of machine which is essentially a digital computer with an infinite capacity. It states that there are certain things that such a machine cannot do. If it is rigged up to give answers to questions as in the imitation game, there will be some questions to which it will either give a wrong answer, or fail to give an answer at all, however much time is allowed for a reply. There may, of course, be many such questions, and questions which cannot be answered by one machine may be satisfactorily answered by another. We are of course supposing for the present that the questions are of the kind to which an answer "Yes" or "No" is appropriate, rather than questions such as "What do you think of Picasso?" The questions that we know the machines must fail on are of this type, "Consider the machine specified as follows.... Will this machine ever answer 'Yes' to any question?" The dots are to be replaced by a description of some machine in a standard form, which could be something like that used in Section 5. When the machine described bears a certain comparatively simple relation to the machine which is under interrogation, it can be shown that the answer is either wrong or not forthcoming. This is the mathematical result: it is argued that it proves a disability of machines to which the human intellect is not subject.

The short answer to this argument is that although it is established that there are limitations to the powers of any particular machine, it has only been stated, without any sort of proof, that no such limitations apply to the human intellect. But I do not think this view can be dismissed quite so lightly.

Whenever one of these machines is asked the appropriate critical question, and gives a definite answer, we know that this answer must be wrong, and this gives us a certain feeling of superiority. Is this feeling illusory? It is no doubt quite genuine, but I do not think too much importance should be attached to it. We too often give wrong answers to questions ourselves to be justified in being very pleased at such evidence of fallibility on the part of the machines. Further, our superiority can only be felt on such an occasion in relation to the one machine over which we have scored our petty triumph. There would be no question of triumphing simultaneously over *all* machines. In short, then, there might be men cleverer than any given machine, but then again there might be other machines cleverer again, and so on.

Those who hold to the mathematical argument would, I think, mostly he willing to accept the imitation game as a basis for discussion. Those who believe in the two previous objections would probably not be interested in any criteria.

6.4 The Argument from Consciousness

This argument is very well expressed in Professor Jefferson's Lister Oration for 1949, from which I quote. "Not until a machine can write a sonnet or compose a concerto because of thoughts and emotions felt, and not by the chance fall of symbols, could we agree that machine equals brain—that is, not only write it but know that it had written it. No mechanism could feel (and not merely artificially signal, an easy contrivance) pleasure at its successes, grief when its valves fuse, be warmed by flattery, be made miserable by its mistakes, be charmed by sex, be angry or depressed when it cannot get what it wants."

This argument appears to be a denial of the validity of our test. According to the most extreme form of this view the only way by which one could be sure that a machine thinks is to *be* the machine and to feel oneself thinking. One could then describe these feelings to the world, but of course no one would be justified in taking any notice. Likewise according to this view the only way to know that a *man* thinks is to be that particular man. It is in fact the solipsist point of view. It may be the most logical view to hold but it makes communication of ideas difficult. A is liable to believe "A thinks but B does not" whilst B believes "B thinks but A does not." Instead of arguing continually over this point it is usual to have the polite convention that everyone thinks.

I am sure that Professor Jefferson does not wish to adopt the extreme and solipsist point of view. Probably he would be quite willing to accept the imitation game as a test. The game (with the player B omitted) is frequently used in practice under the name of viva voce to discover whether some one really understands something or has "learned it parrot fashion." Let us listen in to a part of such a viva voce:

Interrogator: In the first line of your sonnet which reads "Shall I compare thee to a summer's day," would not "a spring day" do as well or better?

Witness: It wouldn't scan.

Interrogator: How about "a winter's day." That would scan all right.

Witness: Yes, but nobody wants to be compared to a winter's day.

Interrogator: Would you say Mr. Pickwick reminded you of Christmas?

Witness: In a way.

Interrogator: Yet Christmas is a winter's day, and I do not think Mr. Pickwick would mind the comparison.

Witness: I don't think you're serious. By a winter's day one means a typical winter's day, rather than a special one like Christmas.

And so on. What would Professor Jefferson say if the sonnet-writing machine was able to answer like this in the viva voce? I do not know whether he would regard the machine as "merely artificially signalling" these answers, but if the answers were as satisfactory and sustained as in the above passage I do not think he would describe it as "an easy contrivance." This phrase is, I think, intended to cover such devices as the inclusion in the machine of a record of someone reading a sonnet, with appropriate switching to turn it on from time to time.

In short then, I think that most of those who support the argument from consciousness could be persuaded to abandon it rather than be forced into the solipsist position. They will then probably be willing to accept our test.

I do not wish to give the impression that I think there is no mystery about consciousness. There is, for instance, something of a paradox connected with any attempt to localize it. But I do not think these mysteries necessarily need to be solved before we can answer the question with which we are concerned in this chapter.

6.5 Arguments from Various Disabilities

These arguments take the form, "I grant you that you can make machines do all the things you have mentioned but you will never be able to make one to do X." Numerous features X are suggested in this connection. I offer a selection:

Be kind, resourceful, beautiful, friendly, have initiative, have a sense of humor, tell right from wrong, make mistakes, fall in love, enjoy strawberries and cream, make some one fall in love with it, learn from experience, use words properly, be the subject of its own thought, have as much diversity of behavior as a man, do something really new.

No support is usually offered for these statements. I believe they are mostly founded on the principle of scientific induction. A man has seen thousands of machines in his lifetime. From what he sees of them he draws a number of general conclusions. They are ugly, each is designed for a very limited purpose, when required for a minutely different purpose they are useless, the variety of behavior of any one of them is very small, etc., etc. Naturally he concludes that these are necessary properties of machines in general. Many of these limitations are associated with the very small storage capacity of most machines. (I am assuming that the idea of storage capacity is extended in some way to cover machines other than discrete state machines. The exact definition does not matter as no mathematical accuracy is claimed in the present discussion.) A few years ago, when very little had been heard of digital computers, it was possible to elicit much incredulity concerning them, if one mentioned their properties without describing their construction. That was presumably due to a similar application of the principle of scientific induction. These applications of the principle are of course largely unconscious. When a burnt child fears the fire and shows that he fears it by avoiding it, I should say that he was applying scientific induction. (I could of course also describe his behavior in many other ways.) The works and customs of mankind do not seem to be very suitable material to which to apply scientific induction. A very large part of space-time must be investigated, if reliable results are to be obtained. Otherwise we may (as most English children do) decide that everybody speaks English, and that it is silly to learn French.

There are, however, special remarks to be made about many of the disabilities that have been mentioned. The inability to enjoy strawberries and cream may have struck the reader as frivolous. Possibly a machine might be made to enjoy this delicious dish but any attempt to make one do so would be idiotic. What is important about this disability is that it contributes to some of the other disabilities, e.g., to the difficulty of the same kind of friendliness occurring between man and machine as between white man and white man, or between black man and black man.

The claim that "machines cannot make mistakes" seems a curious one. One is tempted to retort, "Are they any the worse for that?" But let us adopt a more sympathetic attitude, and try to see what is really meant. I think this criticism can be explained in terms of the imitation game. It is claimed that the interrogator could distinguish the machine from the man simply by setting them a number of problems in arithmetic. The machine would be unmasked because of its deadly accuracy. The reply to this is simple. The machine (programmed for playing the game) would not attempt to give the *right* answers to the arithmetic problems. It would deliberately introduce mistakes in a manner calculated to confuse the interrogator. A mechanical fault would probably show itself through an unsuitable decision as to what sort of a mistake to make in the arithmetic. Even this interpretation of the criticism is not sufficiently sympathetic. But we cannot afford the space to go into it much further. It seems to me that this criticism depends on a confusion between two kinds of mistake. We may call them "errors of functioning" and "errors of conclusion." Errors of functioning are due to some mechanical or electrical fault which causes the machine to behave otherwise than it was designed to do. In philosophical discussions, one likes to ignore the possibility of such errors; one is therefore discussing "abstract machines." These abstract machines are mathematical fictions rather than physical objects. By definition they are incapable of errors of functioning. In this sense we can truly say that "machines can never make mistakes." Errors of conclusion can only arise when some meaning is attached to the output signals from the machine. The machine might, for instance, type out mathematical equations, or sentences in English. When a false proposition is typed we say that the machine has committed an error of conclusion. There is clearly no reason at all for saying that a machine cannot make this kind of mistake. It might do nothing but type out repeatedly "0 = 1." To take a less perverse example, it might have some method for drawing conclusions by scientific induction. We must expect such a method to lead occasionally to erroneous results.

The claim that a machine cannot be the subject of its own thought can of course only be answered if it can be shown that the machine has some thought with some subject matter. Nevertheless, "the subject matter of a machine's operations" does seem to mean something, at least to the people who deal with it. If, for instance, the machine was trying to find a solution of the equation $x^2 - 40x - 11 = 0$ one would be tempted to describe this equation as part of the machine's subject matter at that moment. In this sort of sense a machine undoubtedly can be its own subject matter. It may be used to help in making up its own programs or to predict the effect of alterations in its own structure. By observing the results of its own behavior it can modify its own programs so as to achieve some purpose more effectively. These are possibilities of the near future, rather than Utopian dreams.

The criticism that a machine cannot have much diversity of behavior is just a way of saying that it cannot have much storage capacity. Until fairly recently a storage capacity of even a thousand digits was very rare. The criticisms that we are considering here are often disguised forms of the argument from consciousness. Usually if one maintains that a machine *can* do one of these things, and describes the kind of method that the machine could use, one will not make much of an impression. It is thought that the method (whatever it may be, for it must be mechanical) is really rather base. Compare the parentheses in Jefferson's statement quoted earlier.

6.6 Lady Lovelace's Objection

Our most detailed information of Babbage's Analytical Engine comes from a memoir by Lady Lovelace (1842). In it she states, "The Analytical Engine has no pretensions to originate anything. It can do *whatever we know how to order it* to perform" (her italics). This statement is quoted by Hartree (1949) who adds: "This does not imply that it may not be possible to construct electronic equipment which will 'think for itself,' or in which, in biological terms, one could set up a conditioned reflex, which would serve as a basis for 'learning.' Whether this is possible in principle or not is a stimulating and exciting question, suggested by some of these recent developments. But it did not seem that the machines constructed or projected at the time had this property."

I am in thorough agreement with Hartree over this. It will be noticed that he does not assert that the machines in question had not got the property, but rather that the evidence available to Lady Lovelace did not encourage her to believe that they had it. It is quite possible that the machines in question had, in a sense, got this property. For suppose that some discrete-state machine has the property. The Analytical Engine was a universal digital computer, so that, if its storage capacity and speed were adequate, it could by suitable programming be made to mimic the machine in question. Probably this argument did not occur to the Countess or to Babbage. In any case there was no obligation on them to claim all that could be claimed.

This whole question will be considered again under the heading of learning machines.

A variant of Lady Lovelace's objection states that a machine can "never do anything really new." This may be parried for a moment with the saw, "There is nothing new under the sun." Who can be certain that "original work" that he has done was not simply the growth of the seed planted in him by teaching, or the effect of following well-known general principles. A better variant of the objection says that a machine can never "take us by surprise." This statement is a more direct challenge and can be met directly. Machines take me by surprise with great frequency. This is largely because I do not do sufficient calculation to decide what to expect them to do, or rather because, although I do a calculation, I do it in a hurried, slipshod fashion, taking risks. Perhaps I say to myself, "I suppose the voltage here ought to be the same as there: anyway let's assume it is." Naturally I am often wrong, and the result is a surprise for me for by the time the experiment is done these assumptions have been forgotten. These admissions lay me open to lectures on the subject of my vicious ways, but do not throw any doubt on my credibility when I testify to the surprises I experience.

I do not expect this reply to silence my critic. He will probably say that such surprises are due to some creative mental act on my part, and reflect no credit on the machine. This leads us back to the argument from consciousness, and far from the idea of surprise. It is a line of argument we must consider closed, but it is perhaps worth remarking that the appreciation of something as surprising requires as much of a "creative mental act" whether the surprising event originates from a man, a book, a machine or anything else.

The view that machines cannot give rise to surprises is due, I believe, to a fallacy to which philosophers and mathematicians are particularly subject. This is the assumption that as soon as a fact is presented to a mind all consequences of that fact spring into the mind simultaneously with it. It is a very useful assumption under many circumstances, but one too easily forgets that it is false. A natural consequence of doing so is that one then assumes that there is no virtue in the mere working out of consequences from data and general principles.

6.7 Argument from Continuity in the Nervous System

The nervous system is certainly not a discrete-state machine. A small error in the information about the size of a nervous impulse impinging on a neuron, may make a large difference to the size of the outgoing impulse. It may be argued that, this being so, one cannot expect to be able to mimic the behavior of the nervous system with a discrete-state system.

It is true that a discrete-state machine must be different from a continuous machine. But if we adhere to the conditions of the imitation game, the interrogator will not be able to take any advantage of this difference. The situation can be made clearer if we consider some other simpler continuous machine. A differential analyzer will do very well. (A differential analyzer is a certain kind of machine not of the discrete-state type used for some kinds of calculation.) Some of these provide their answers in a typed form, and so are suitable for taking part in the game. It would not be possible for a digital computer to predict exactly what answers the differential analyzer would give to a problem, but it would be quite capable of giving the right sort of answer. For instance, if asked to give the value of π (actually about 3.1416) it would be reasonable to choose at random between the values 3.12, 3.13, 3.14, 3.15, 3.16 with the probabilities of 0.05, 0.15, 0.55, 0.19, 0.06 (say). Under these circumstances it would be very difficult for the interrogator to distinguish the differential analyzer from the digital computer.

6.8 The Argument from Informality of Behavior

It is not possible to produce a set of rules purporting to describe what a man should do in every conceivable set of circumstances. One might for instance have a rule that one is to stop when one sees a red traffic light, and to go if one sees a green one, but what if by some fault both appear together? One may perhaps decide that it is safest to stop. But some further difficulty may well arise from this decision later. To attempt to provide rules of conduct to cover every eventuality, even those arising from traffic lights, appears to be impossible. With all this I agree.

From this it is argued that we cannot be machines. I shall try to reproduce the argument, but I fear I shall hardly do it justice. It seems to run something like this. "If each man had a definite set of rules of conduct by which he regulated his life he would be no better than a machine. But there are no such rules, so men cannot be machines." The undistributed middle is glaring. I do not think the argument is ever put quite like this, but I believe this is the argument used nevertheless. There may however be a certain confusion between "rules of conduct" and "laws of behavior" to cloud the issue. By "rules of conduct" I mean precepts such as "Stop if you see red lights," on which one can act, and of which one can be conscious. By "laws of behavior" I mean laws of nature as applied to a man's body such as "if you pinch him he will squeak." If we substitute "laws of behavior which regulate his life" for "laws of conduct by which he regulates his life" in the argument quoted the undistributed middle is no longer insuperable. For we believe that it is not only true that being regulated by laws of behavior implies being some sort of machine (though not necessarily a discrete-state machine), but that conversely being such a machine implies being regulated by such laws. However, we cannot so easily convince ourselves of the absence of complete laws of behavior as of complete rules of conduct. The only way we know of for finding such laws is scientific observation, and we certainly know of no circumstances under which we could say, "We have searched enough. There are no such laws."

We can demonstrate more forcibly that any such statement would be unjustified. For suppose we could be sure of finding such laws if they existed. Then given a discrete-state machine it should certainly be possible to discover by observation sufficient about it to predict its future behavior, and this within a reasonable time, say a thousand years. But this does not seem to be the case. I have set up on the Manchester computer a small program using only 1,000 units of storage, whereby the machine supplied with one sixteen-figure number replies with another within two seconds. I would defy anyone to learn from these replies sufficient about the program to be able to predict any replies to untried values.

6.9 The Argument from Extrasensory Perception

I assume that the reader is familiar with the idea of extrasensory perception, and the meaning of the four items of it, viz., telepathy, clairvoyance, precognition and psychokinesis. These disturbing phenomena seem to deny all our usual scientific ideas. How we should like to discredit them! Unfortunately the statistical evidence, at least for telepathy, is overwhelming. It is very difficult to rearrange one's ideas so as to fit these new facts in. Once one has accepted them it does not seem a very big step to believe in ghosts and bogies. The idea that our bodies move simply according to the known laws of physics, together with some others not yet discovered but somewhat similar, would be one of the first to go.

This argument is to my mind quite a strong one. One can say in reply that many scientific theories seem to remain workable in practice, in spite of clashing with ESP; that in fact one can get along very nicely if one forgets about it. This is rather cold comfort, and one fears that thinking is just the kind of phenomenon where ESP may be especially relevant.

A more specific argument based on ESP might run as follows: "Let us play the imitation game, using as witnesses a man who is good as a telepathic receiver, and a digital computer. The interrogator can ask such questions as 'What suit does the card in my right hand belong to?' The man by telepathy or clairvoyance gives the right answer 130 times out of 400 cards. The machine can only guess at random, and perhaps gets 104 right, so the interrogator makes the right identification." There is an interesting possibility which opens here. Suppose the digital computer contains a random number generator. Then it will be natural to use this to decide what answer to give. But then the random number generator will be subject to the psychokinetic powers of the interrogator. Perhaps this psychokinesis might cause the machine to guess right more often than would be expected on a probability calculation, so that the interrogator might still be unable to make the right identification. On the other hand, he might be able to guess right without any questioning, by clairvoyance. With ESP anything may happen.

If telepathy is admitted it will be necessary to tighten our test up. The situation could be regarded as analogous to that which would occur if the interrogator were talking to himself and one of the competitors was listening with his ear to the wall. To put the competitors into a "telepathy-proof room" would satisfy all requirements

7. Learning Machines

The reader will have anticipated that I have no very convincing arguments of a positive nature to support my views. If I had I should not have taken such pains to point out the fallacies in contrary views. Such evidence as I have I shall now give.

Let us return for a moment to Lady Lovelace's objection, which stated that the machine can only do what we tell it to do. One could say that a man can "inject" an idea into the machine, and that it will respond to a certain extent and then drop into quiescence, like a piano string struck by a hammer. Another simile would be an atomic pile of less than critical size: an injected idea is to correspond to a neutron entering the pile from without. Each such neutron will cause a certain disturbance which eventually dies away. If, however, the size of the pile is sufficiently increased, the disturbance caused by such an incoming neutron will very likely go on and on increasing until the whole pile is destroyed. Is there a corresponding phenomenon for minds, and is there one for machines? There does seem to be one for the human mind. The majority of them seem to be "subcritical," i.e., to correspond in this analogy to piles of subcritical size. An idea presented to such a mind will on average give rise to less than one idea in reply. A smallish proportion are supercritical. An idea presented to such a mind may give rise to a whole "theory" consisting of secondary, tertiary and more remote ideas. Animals' minds seem to be very definitely subcritical. Adhering to this analogy we ask, "Can a machine be made to be supercritical?"

The "skin-of-an-onion" analogy is also helpful. In considering the functions of the mind or the brain we find certain operations which we can explain in purely mechanical terms. This we say does not correspond to the real mind: it is a sort of skin which we must strip off if we are to find the real mind. But then in what remains we find a further skin to be stripped off, and so on. Proceeding in this way do we ever come to the "real" mind, or do we eventually come to the skin which has nothing in it? In the latter case the whole mind is mechanical. (It would not be a discrete-state machine however. We have discussed this.)

These last two paragraphs do not claim to be convincing arguments. They should rather be described as "recitations tending to produce belief."

The only really satisfactory support that can be given for the view expressed at the beginning of Section 6, will be that provided by waiting for the end of the century and then doing the experiment described. But what can we say in the meantime? What steps should be taken now if the experiment is to be successful?

As I have explained, the problem is mainly one of programming. Advances in engineering will have to be made too, but it seems unlikely that these will not be adequate for the requirements. Estimates of the storage capacity of the brain vary from 10^{10} to 10^{15} binary digits. I incline to the lower values and believe that only a very small fraction is used for the higher types of thinking. Most of it is probably used for the retention of visual impressions. I should be surprised if more than 10^9 was required for satisfactory playing of the imitation game, at any rate against a blind man. (Note: The capacity of the *Encyclopedia Britannica,* eleventh edition, is 2×10^9.) A storage capacity of 10^7 would be a very practicable possibility even by present techniques. It is probably not necessary to increase the speed of operations of the machines at all. Parts of modern machines which can be regarded as analogs of nerve cells work about a thousand times faster than the latter. This should provide a "margin of safety" which could cover losses of speed arising in many ways. Our problem then is to find out how to program these machines to play the game. At my present rate of working I produce about a thousand digits of program a day, so that about sixty workers, working steadily through the fifty years might accomplish the job, if nothing went into the wastepaper basket. Some more expeditious method seems desirable.

In the process of trying to imitate an adult human mind we are bound to think a good deal about the process which has brought it to the state that it is in. We may notice three components.

- The initial state of the mind, say at birth,

- The education to which it has been subjected,

- Other experience, not to be described as education, to which it has been subjected.

Instead of trying to produce a program to simulate the adult mind, why not rather try to produce one which simulates the child's? If this were then subjected to an appropriate course of education one would obtain the adult brain. Presumably the child brain is something like a notebook as one buys it from the stationers. Rather little mechanism, and lots of blank sheets. (Mechanism and writing are, from our point of view, almost synonymous.) Our hope is that there is so little mechanism in the child brain that something like it can be easily programmed. The amount of work in the education we can assume, as a first approximation, to be much the same as for the human child.

We have thus divided our problem into two parts. The child program and the education process. These two remain very closely connected. We cannot expect to find a good child machine at the first attempt. One must experiment with teaching one such machine and see how well it learns. One can then try another and see if it is better or worse. There is an obvious connection between this process and evolution, by the identifications

Structure of the child machine   =   hereditary material

Changes of the child machine   =   mutations

Natural selection   =   judgment of the experimenter

One may hope, however, that this process will be more expeditious than evolution. The survival of the fittest is a slow method for measuring advantages. The experimenter, by the exercise of intelligence, should be able to speed it up. Equally important is the fact that he is not restricted to random mutations. If he can trace a cause for some weakness he can probably think of the kind of mutation which will improve it.

It will not be possible to apply exactly the same teaching process to the machine as to a normal child. It will not, for instance, be provided with legs, so that it could not be asked to go out and fill the coal scuttle. Possibly it might not have eyes. But however well these deficiencies might be overcome by clever engineering, one could not send the creature to school without the other children making excessive fun of it. It must be given some tuition. We need not be too concerned about the legs, eyes, etc. The example of Miss Helen Keller shows that education can take place provided that communication in both directions between teacher and pupil can take place by some means or other.

We normally associate punishments and rewards with the teaching process. Some simple child machines can be constructed or programmed on this sort of principle. The machine has to be so constructed that events which shortly preceded the occurrence of a punishment signal are unlikely to be repeated, whereas a reward signal increased the probability of repetition of the events which led up to it. These definitions do not presuppose any feelings on the part of the machine. I have done some experiments with one such child machine, and succeeded in teaching it a few things, but the teaching method was too unorthodox for the experiment to be considered really successful.

The use of punishments and rewards can at best be a part of the teaching process. Roughly speaking, if the teacher has no other means of communicating to the pupil, the amount of information which can reach him does not exceed the total number of rewards and punishments applied. By the time a child has learned to repeat "Casabianca" he would probably feel very sore indeed, if the text could only be discovered by a "Twenty Questions" technique, every "NO" taking the form of a blow. It is necessary therefore to have some other "unemotional" channels of communication. If these are available it is possible to teach a machine by punishments and rewards to obey orders given in some language, e.g., a symbolic language. These orders are to be transmitted through the "unemotional" channels. The use of this language will diminish greatly the number of punishments and rewards required.

Opinions may vary as to the complexity which is suitable in the child machine. One might try to make it as simple as possible consistently with the general principles. Alternatively one might have a complete system of logical inference "built in."[2] In the latter case the store would be largely occupied with definitions and propositions. The propositions would have various kinds of status, e.g., well-established facts, conjectures, mathematically proved theorems, statements given by an authority, expressions having the logical form of proposition but not belief-value. Certain propositions may be described as "imperatives." The machine should be so constructed that as soon as an imperative is classed as "well established" the appropriate action automatically takes place. To illustrate this, suppose the teacher says to the machine, "Do your homework now." This may cause "Teacher says 'Do your homework now'" to be included amongst the well-established facts. Another such fact might be, "Everything that teacher says is true." Combining these may eventually lead to the imperative, "Do your homework now," being included amongst the well-established facts, and this, by the construction of the machine, will mean that the homework actually gets started, but the effect is very satisfactory. The processes of inference used by the machine need not be such as would satisfy the most exacting logicians. There might for instance be no hierarchy of types. But this need not mean that type fallacies will occur, any more than we are bound to fall over unfenced cliffs. Suitable imperatives (expressed *within* the systems, not forming part of the rules of the system) such as "Do not use a class unless it is a subclass of one which has been mentioned by teacher" can have a similar effect to "Do not go too near the edge."

The imperatives that can be obeyed by a machine that has no limbs are bound to be of a rather intellectual character, as in the example (doing homework) given above. Important amongst such imperatives will be ones which regulate the order in which the rules of the logical system concerned are to be applied. For at each stage when one is using a logical system, there is a very large number of alternative steps, any of which one is permitted to apply, so far as obedience to the rules of the logical system is concerned. These choices make the difference between a brilliant and a footling reasoner, not the difference between a sound and a fallacious one. Propositions leading to imperatives of this kind might be "When Socrates is mentioned, use the syllogism in Barbara" or "If one method has been proved to be quicker than another, do not use the slower method." Some of these may be "given by authority," but others may be produced by the machine itself, e.g., by scientific induction.

The idea of a learning machine may appear paradoxical to some readers. How can the rules of operation of the machine change? They should describe completely how the machine will react whatever its history might be, whatever changes it might undergo. The rules are thus quite time invariant. This is quite true. The explanation of the paradox is that the rules which get changed in the learning process are of a rather less pretentious kind, claiming only an ephemeral validity. The reader may draw a parallel with the Constitution of the United States.

An important feature of a learning machine is that its teacher will often be very largely ignorant of quite what is going on inside, although he may still be able to some extent to predict his pupil's behavior. This should apply most strongly to the later education of a machine arising from a child machine of well-tried design (or program). This is in clear contrast with normal procedure when using a machine to do computations: one's object is then to have a clear mental picture of the state of the machine at each moment in the computation. This object can only be achieved with a struggle. The view that "the machine can only do what we know how to order it to do,"[3] appears strange in face of this. Most of the programs which we can put into the machine will result in its doing something that we cannot make sense of at all, or which we regard as completely random behavior. Intelligent behavior presumably consists in a departure from the completely disciplined behavior involved in computation, but a rather slight one, which does not give rise to random behavior, or to pointless repetitive loops. Another important result of preparing our machine for its part in the imitation game by a process of teaching and learning is that "human fallibility" is likely to be omitted in a rather natural way, i.e., without special "coaching." (The reader should reconcile this with the point of view expressed in Section 6.5.) Processes that are learned do not produce a hundred per cent certainty of result; if they did they could not be unlearned.

It is probably wise to include a random element in a learning machine. A random element is rather useful when we are searching for a solution of some problem. Suppose for instance we wanted to find a number between 50 and 200 which was equal to the square of the sum of its digits, we might start at 51 then try 52 and go on until we got a number that worked. Alternatively we might choose numbers at random until we got a good one. This method has the advantage that it is unnecessary to keep track of the values that have been tried, but the disadvantage that one may try the same one twice, but this is not very important if there are several solutions. The systematic method has the disadvantage that there may be an enormous block without any solutions in the region which has to be investigated first. Now the learning process may be regarded as a search for a form of behavior which will satisfy the teacher (or some other criterion). Since there is probably a very large number of satisfactory solutions the random method seems to be better than the systematic. It should be noticed that it is used in the analogous process of evolution. But there the systematic method is not possible. How could one keep track of the different genetical combinations that had been tried, so as to avoid trying them again?

We may hope that machines will eventually compete with men in all purely intellectual fields. But which are the best ones to start with? Even this is a difficult decision. Many people think that a very abstract activity, like the playing of chess, would be best. It can also be maintained that it is best to provide the machine with the best sense organs that money can buy, and then teach it to understand and speak English. This process could follow the normal teaching of a child. Things would be pointed out and named, etc. Again I do not know what the right answer is, but I think both approaches should be tried.

We can only see a short distance ahead, but we can see plenty there that needs to be done.

Notes

1. Possibly this view is heretical. St. Thomas Aquinas *(Summa Theologica,* quoted by Bertrand Russell [1945, p. 458]) states that God cannot make a man to have no soul. But this may not be a real restriction on His powers, but only a result of the fact that men's souls are immortal, and therefore indestructible.

2. Or rather "programmed in" for our child machine will be programmed in a digital computer. But the logical system will not have to be learned.

3. Compare Lady Lovelace's statement which does not contain the word "only."

3

Steps Toward Artificial Intelligence

Marvin Minsky

1. Introduction

A visitor to our planet might be puzzled about the role of computers in our technology. On the one hand, he would read and hear all about wonderful "mechanical brains" baffling their creators with prodigious intellectual performance. And he (or it) would be warned that these machines must be restrained, lest they overwhelm us by might, persuasion, or even by the revelation of truths too terrible to be borne. On the other hand, our visitor would find the machines being denounced, on all sides, for their slavish obedience, unimaginative literal interpretations, and incapacity for innovation or initiative; in short, for their inhuman dullness.

Our visitor might remain puzzled if he set out to find, and judge for himself, these monsters. For he would find only a few machines (mostly "general-purpose" computers, programmed for the moment to behave according to some specification) doing things that might claim any real intellectual status. Some would be proving mathematical theorems of rather undistinguished character. A few machines might be playing certain games, occasionally defeating their designers. Some might be distinguishing between hand-printed letters. Is this enough to justify so much interest, let alone deep concern? I believe that it is; that we are on the threshold of an era that will be strongly influenced, and quite possibly dominated, by intelligent problem-solving machines. But our purpose is not to guess about what the future may bring; it is only to try to describe and explain what seem now to be our first steps toward the construction of "artificial intelligence."

Along with the development of general-purpose computers, the past few years have seen an increase in effort toward the discovery and mechanization of problem-solving processes. Quite a number of papers have appeared describing theories or actual computer programs concerned with game playing, theorem proving, pattern recognition, and other domains which would seem to require some intelligence. The literature does not include any general discussion of the outstanding problems of this field.

In this chapter, an attempt will be made to separate out, analyze, and find the relations between some of these problems. Analysis will be supported with enough examples from the literature to serve the introductory function of a review article, but there remains much relevant work not described here. This chapter is highly compressed, and therefore, cannot begin to discuss all these matters in the available space.

There is, of course, no generally accepted theory of "intelligence;" the analysis is our own and may be controversial. We regret that we cannot give full personal acknowledgments here—suffice it to say that we have discussed these matters with almost every one of the cited authors.

It is convenient to divide the problems into five main areas: search, pattern recognition, learning, planning, and induction; these comprise the main divisions of the chapter. Let us summarize, the entire argument very briefly:

A computer can do, in a sense, only what it is told to do. But even when we do not know exactly how to solve a certain problem, we may program a machine to *search* through some large space of solution attempts. Unfortunately, when we write a straightforward program for such a search, we usually find the resulting process to be enormously inefficient. With *pattern recognition techniques,* efficiency can be greatly improved by restricting the machine to use its methods only on the kind of attempts for which they are appropriate. And with *learning,* efficiency is further improved by directing search in accord with earlier experiences. By actually analyzing the situation, using what we call *planning* methods, the machine may obtain a really fundamental improvement by replacing the originally given search by a much smaller, more appropriate exploration. Finally, in the section on *induction,* we consider some rather more global concepts of how one might obtain intelligent machine behavior.

2. The Problem of Search[1]

If, for a given problem, we have a means for checking a proposed solution, then we can solve the problem by testing all possible answers. But this always takes much too long to be of practical interest. Any device that can reduce this search may be of value. If we can detect relative improvement, then "hill-climbing" (Section 2.2) may be feasible, but its use requires some structural knowledge of the search space. And unless this structure meets certain conditions, hill-climbing may do more harm than good.

When we talk of problem-solving in what follows we will usually suppose that all the problems to be solved are initially *well defined* (McCarthy 1956). By this we mean that with each problem we are given some systematic way to decide when a proposed solution is acceptable. Most of the experimental work discussed here is concerned with such well-defined problems as are met in theorem proving, or in games with precise rules for play and scoring.

In one sense all such problems are trivial. For if there exists a solution to such a problem, that solution can be found eventually by any blind exhaustive process which searches through all possibilities. And it is usually not difficult to mechanize or program such a search.

But for any problem worthy of the name, the search through all possibilities will be too inefficient for practical use. And on the other hand, systems like chess, or nontrivial parts of mathematics, are too complicated for complete analysis. Without complete analysis, there must always remain some core of search, or "trial and error." So we need to find techniques through which the results of *incomplete analysis* can be used to make the search more efficient. The necessity for this is simply overwhelming: a search of all the paths through the game of checkers involves some 10^{40} move choices (Samuel 1959a), in chess, some 10^{120} (Shannon, in Newman 1956). If we organized all the particles in our galaxy into some kind of parallel computer operating at the frequency of hard cosmic rays, the latter computation would still take impossibly long; we cannot expect improvements in "hardware" alone to solve all our problems! Certainly we must use whatever we know in advance to guide the trial generator. And we must also be able to make use of results obtained along the way [2, 3]

2.1 Relative Improvement, Hill-Climbing, and Heuristic Connections

A problem can hardly come to interest us if we have no background of information about it. We usually have some basis, however flimsy, for detecting improvement; some trials will be judged more successful than others. Suppose, for example, that we have a comparator which selects as the better, one from any pair of trial outcomes. Now the comparator cannot, alone, serve to make a problem well defined. No goal is defined. But if the comparator defined relation between trials is "transitive" (i.e., if *A dominates B* and *B dominates C* implies that *A dominates C),* then we can at least define "progress," and ask our machine, given a time limit, to do the best it can.

But it is essential to observe that a comparator by itself, however shrewd, cannot alone give any improvement over exhaustive search. The comparator gives us information about partial success, to be sure. But we need also some way of using this information to direct the pattern of search in promising directions; to select new trial points which are in some sense "like," or "similar to," or "in the same direction as" those which have given the best previous results. To do this we need some additional structure on the search space. This structure need not bear much resemblance to the ordinary spatial notion of direction, or that of distance, but it must somehow tie together points which are heuristically related.

We will call such a structure a *heuristic connection.* We introduce this term for informal use only—that is why our definition is itself so informal. But we need it. Many publications have been marred by the misuse, for this purpose, of precise mathematical terms, *e.g., metric* and *topological.* The term "connection," with its variety of dictionary meanings, seems just the word to designate a relation without commitment as to the exact nature of the relation.

An important and simple kind of heuristic connection is that defined when a space has coordinates (or parameters) and there is also defined a numerical "success function" *E* which is a reasonably smooth function of the coordinates. Here we can use local optimization or *hill-climbing* methods.

2.2 Hill-Climbing

Suppose that we are given a black-box machine with inputs $\lambda_1,\ldots, \lambda_n$ and an output $E(\lambda_1,\ldots, \lambda_n)$. We wish to maximize E by adjusting the input values. But we are not given any mathematical description of the function E; hence we cannot use differentiation or related methods. The obvious approach is to explore locally about a point, finding the direction of steepest ascent. One moves a certain distance in that direction and repeats the process until improvement ceases. If the hill is smooth this may be done, approximately, by estimating the gradient component $\delta E/\delta\lambda_i$ separately for each coordinate λ_i. There are more sophisticated approaches (one may use noise added to each variable, and correlate the output with each input, see Figure 1), but this is the general idea. It is a fundamental technique, and we see it always in the background of far more complex systems. Heuristically, its great virtue is this: the sampling effort (for determining the direction of the gradient) grows, in a sense, only linearly with the number of parameters. So if we can solve, by such a method, a certain kind of problem involving many parameters, then the addition of more parameters of the same kind ought not cause an inordi-

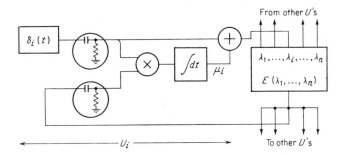

Figure 1. "Multiple simultaneous optimizers" search for a (local) maximum value of some function $E(\lambda_1, ..., \lambda_n)$ of several parameters. Each unit U_i independently "jitters" its parameter λ_i, perhaps randomly, by adding a variation $\sigma_i(t)$ to a current mean value, μ_i. The changes in the quantities σ_i and E_i are correlated, and the result is used to (slowly) change μ_i. The filters are to move d-c components. This simultaneous technique, really a form of coherent detection, usually has an advantage over methods dealing separately and sequentially with each parameter. [Cf. the discussion of "informative feedback" in Wiener (1948, pp. 133ff.).]

nate increase in difficulty. We are particularly interested in problem solving methods which can be so extended to more difficult problems. Alas, most interesting systems which involve combinational operations usually grow exponentially more difficult as we add variables.

A great variety of hill-climbing systems have been studied under the names of "adaptive" or "self-optimizing" servomechanisms.

2.3 Troubles with Hill-Climbing

Obviously, the gradient-following hill-climber would be trapped if it should reach a *local peak* which is not a true or satisfactory optimum. It must then be forced to try larger steps or changes.

It is often supposed that this false-peak problem is the chief obstacle to machine learning by this method. This certainly can be troublesome. But for really difficult problems, it seems to us that usually the more fundamental problem lies in finding any significant peak at all. Unfortunately the known E functions for difficult problems often exhibit what we have called (Minsky and Selfridge, 1960) the "mesa phenomenon" in which a small change in a parameter usually leads to either no change in performance or to a large change in performance. The space is thus composed primarily of flat regions or "mesas." Any tendency of the trial generator to make small steps then results in much aimless wandering without compensating information gains. A profitable search in such a space requires steps so large that hill-climbing is essentially ruled out. The problem solver must find other methods; hill-climbing might still be feasible with a different heuristic connection.

Certainly, in our own intellectual behavior we rarely solve a tricky problem by a steady climb toward success. I doubt that in any one simple mechanism, e.g., hill-climbing, will we find the means to build an efficient and general problem-solving machine. Probably, an intelligent machine will require a variety of different mechanisms. These will be arranged in hierarchies, and in even more complex, perhaps recursive, structures. And perhaps what amounts to straightforward hill-climbing on one level may sometimes appear (on a lower level) as the sudden jumps of "insight."

3. The Problem of Pattern Recognition

In order not to try all possibilities, a resourceful machine must classify problem situations into categories associated with the domains of effectiveness of the machine's different methods. These pattern-recognition methods must extract the heuristically significant features of the objects in question. The simplest methods simply match the objects against standards or prototypes. More powerful "property-list" methods subject each object to a sequence of tests, each detecting some *property* of heuristic importance. These properties have to be invariant under commonly encountered forms of distortion. Two important problems arise here—inventing new useful properties, and combining many properties to form a recognition system. For complex problems, such methods will have to be augmented by facilities for subdividing complex objects and describing the complex relations between their parts. Any powerful heuristic program is bound to contain a variety of different methods and techniques. At each step of the problem solving process the machine will have to decide what aspect of the problem to work on, and then which method to use. A choice must be made, for we usually cannot afford to try all the possibilities. In order to deal with a goal or a problem, that is, to choose an appropriate method, we have to recognize what kind of thing it is. Thus the need to choose among actions compels us to provide the machine with classification techniques, or means of evolving them. It is of overwhelming importance that the machine have classification techniques which are realistic. But "realistic" can be defined only with respect to the environments to be encountered by the machine, and with respect to the methods available to it. Distinctions which cannot be exploited are not worth recognizing. And methods are usually worthless without classification schemes which can help decide when they are applicable.

3.1 Teleological Requirements of Classification

The useful classifications are those which match the goals and methods of the machine. The objects grouped together in the classifications should have something of heuristic value in common; they should be "similar" in a useful sense; they should depend on relevant or essential features. We should not be surprised, then, to find ourselves using inverse or teleological expressions to define the classes. We really do want to have a grip on "the class of objects which can be transformed into a result of form Y," that is, the class of objects which will satisfy some goal. One should be wary of the familiar injunction against using teleological language in science. While it is true that talking of goals in some contexts may dispose us towards certain kinds of animistic explanations, this need not be a bad thing in the field of problem-solving; it is hard to see how one can solve problems without thoughts of purposes. The real difficulty with teleological definitions is technical, not philosophical, and arises when they have to be used and not just mentioned. One obviously cannot afford to use for classification a method which actually requires waiting for some remote outcome, if one needs the classification precisely for deciding whether to try out that method. So, in practice, the ideal teleological definitions often have to be replaced by practical approximations, usually with some risk of error; that is, the definitions have to be made *heuristically effective,* or economically usable. This is of great importance. (We can think of "heuristic effectiveness" as contrasted to the ordinary mathematical notion of "effectiveness" which distinguishes those definitions which can be realized at all by machine, regardless of efficiency.)

3.2 Patterns and Descriptions

It is usually necessary to have ways of assigning names—symbolic expressions—to the defined classes. The structure of the names will have a crucial influence on the mental world of the machine, for it determines what kinds of things can be conveniently thought about. There are a variety of ways to assign names. The simplest schemes use what we will call *conventional* (or *proper)* names; here, arbitrary symbols are assigned to classes. But we will also want to use complex *descriptions* or *computed names;* these are constructed for classes by processes which *depend on the class definitions.* To be useful, these should reflect some of the structure of the things they designate, abstracted in a manner relevant to the problem area. The notion of description merges smoothly into the more complex notion of *model;* as we think of it, a model is a sort of active description. It is a thing whose form reflects some of the structure of the thing represented, but which also has some of the character of a working machine.

In Section 4 we will consider "learning" systems. The behavior of those systems can be made to change in reasonable ways depending on what happened to them in the past. But by themselves, the simple learning systems are useful only in recurrent situations; they cannot cope with any significant novelty. Nontrivial performance is obtained only when learning systems are supplemented with classification or pattern-recognition methods of some inductive ability. For the variety of objects encountered in a nontrivial search is so enormous that we cannot depend on recurrence, and the mere accumulation of records of past experience can have only limited value. Pattern recognition, by providing a heuristic connection which links the old to the new, can make learning broadly useful.

What is a "pattern?" We often use the term teleologically to mean a set of objects which can in some (useful) way be treated alike. For each problem area we must ask, "What patterns would be useful for a machine working on such problems?"

The problems of *visual* pattern recognition have received much attention in recent years and most of our examples are from this area.

3.3 Prototype-Derived Patterns

The problem of reading printed characters is a clearcut instance of a situation in which the classification is based ultimately on a fixed set of "prototypes"—e.g., the dies from which the type font was made. The individual marks on the printed page may show the results of many distortions. Some distortions are rather systematic: change in size, position, orientation. Some are of the nature of noise: blurring, grain, low contrast, etc.

If the noise is not too severe, we may be able to manage the identification by what we call a *normalization* and *template matching* process. We first remove the differences related to size and position—that is, we *normalize* the input figure. One may do this, for example, by constructing a similar figure inscribed in a certain fixed triangle (see Figure 2); or one may transform the figure to obtain a certain fixed center of gravity and a unit second central moment. [There is an additional problem with rotational equivalence where it is not easy to avoid all ambiguities. One does not want to equate "6" and "9." For that matter, one does not want to equate $(0,o)$, or (X,x) or the o's in x_0 and x^0, so that there may be context dependency involved.] Once normalized, the unknown figure can be compared with *templates* for the prototypes and, by means of some measure of *matching,* choose the best fitting template. Each "matching criterion" will be sensitive to particular forms of noise and distortion, and so will each normalization procedure. The inscribing or boxing method may be sensitive to small specks, while the moment method will be especially sensitive to smearing, at least for thin-line figures, etc. The choice of a matching criterion must depend on the kinds of noise and transformations commonly encountered. Still, for many problems we may get acceptable results by using straightforward correlation methods.

When the class of equivalence transformations is very large, e.g., when local stretching and distortion are present, there will be difficulty in finding a uniform normalization method. Instead, one may have to consider a process of adjusting locally for best fit to the template. (While measuring the match-

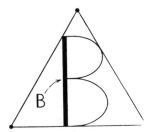

Figure 2. A simple normalization technique. If an object is expanded uniformly, without rotation, until it touches all three sides of a triangle, the resulting figure will be unique, and pattern recognition can proceed without concern about relative size and position.

ing, one could "jitter" the figure locally; if an improvement were found the process could be repeated using a slightly different change, etc.) There is usually no practical possibility of applying to the figure all of the admissible transformations. And to recognize the *topological* equivalence of pairs such as those in Figure 3 is likely beyond any practical kind of iterative local-improvement or hill-climbing matching procedure. (Such recognitions can be mechanized, though, by methods which follow lines, detect vertices, and build up a *description* in the form, say, of a vertex-connection table.)

The template-matching scheme, with its normalization and direct comparison and matching criterion, is just too limited in conception to be of much use in more difficult problems. If the transformation set is large, normalization, or "fitting," may be impractical, especially if there is no adequate heuristic connection on the space of transformations. Furthermore, for each defined pattern, the system has to be presented with a prototype. But if one has in mind a fairly abstract class, one may simply be unable to represent its essential features with one or a very few concrete examples. How could one represent with a single prototype the class of figures which have an even number of disconnected parts? Clearly, the template system has negligible descriptive power. The property-list system frees us from some of these limitations.

3.4 Property Lists and "Characters"

We define a *property* to be a two-valued function which divides figures into two classes; a figure is said to have or not have the property according to whether the function's value is 1 or 0. Given a number N of distinction properties, we could define as many as 2^n subclasses by their set intersections and, hence, as many as 2^{2n} *patterns* by combining the properties with AND's and OR's. Thus, if we have three properties, *rectilinear, connected,* and *cyclic,* there are eight subclasses (and 256 patterns) defined by their intersections (see Figure 4).

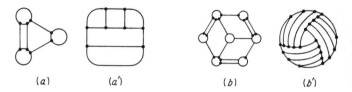

Figure 3. The figures a, a' and b, b' are topologically equivalent pairs. Lengths have been distorted in an arbitrary manner, but the connectivity relations between corresponding points have been preserved. In Sherman (1959) and Haller (1959) we find computer programs which can deal with such equivalences.

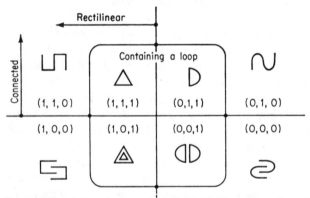

Figure 4. The eight regions represent all the possible configurations of values of the three properties "rectilinear," "connected," "containing a loop." Each region contains a representative figure, and its associated binary "character" sequence.

If the given properties are placed in a fixed order then we can represent any of these elementary regions by a vector, or string of digits. The vector so assigned to each figure will be called the *character* of that figure (with respect to the sequence of properties in question). (In "Some Aspects of Heuristic Programming and Artificial Intelligence" (1959), we use the term *characteristic* for a property without restriction to 2 values.) Thus a square has the character $(1,1,1)$ and a circle the character $(0,1,1)$ for the given sequence of properties.

For many problems one can use such characters as names for categories and as primitive elements with which to define an adequate set of patterns. Characters are more than conventional names. They are instead very rudimentary forms of description (having the form of the simplest symbolic expression—the list) whose structure provides some information about the designated classes. This is a step, albeit a small one, beyond the template method; the characters are not simple instances of the patterns, and the properties may themselves be very abstract. Finding a good set of properties is the major concern of many heuristic programs.

3.5 Invariant Properties

One of the prime requirements of a good property is that it be invariant under the commonly encountered equivalence transformations. Thus for visual pattern recognition we would usually want the object identification to be independent of uniform changes in size and position. In their pioneering paper Pitts and McCulloch (1947) describe a general technique for forming invariant properties from noninvariant ones, assuming that the transformation space has a certain (group) structure. The idea behind their mathematical argument is this: suppose that we have a function P of figures, and suppose that for a given figure F we define $[F] = \{F_1, F_2, \ldots\}$ to be the set of all figures equivalent to F under the given set of transformations; further, define $P[F]$ to be the set $\{P(F_1), P(F_1), \ldots\}$ of values of P on those figures. Finally, define $P^*[F]$ to be AVERAGE $(P[F])$. Then we have a new property P^* whose values are independent of the selection of F from an equivalence class defined by the transformations. We have to be sure that when different representatives are chosen from a class the collection $[F]$ will always be the same in each case. In the case of continuous transformation spaces, there will have to be a measure or the equivalent associated with the set $[F]$ with respect to which the operation AVERAGE is defined, say, as an integration.[4]

This method is proposed (Pitts and McCulloch 1947) as a neurophysiological model for pitch-invariant hearing and size invariant visual recognition (supplemented with visual centering mechanisms). This model is discussed also by Wiener.[5] Practical application is probably limited to one-dimensional groups and analog scanning devices.

In much recent work this problem is avoided by using properties already invariant under these transformations. Thus a property might count the number of connected components in a picture—this is invariant under size and position. Or a property may count the number of vertical lines in a picture—this is invariant under size and position (but not rotation).

3.6 Generating Properties

The problem of generating useful properties has been discussed by Selfridge (1955); we shall summarize his approach. The machine is given, at the start, a few basic transformations $A_1, \ldots, A_n$, each of which transforms, in some significant way, each figure into another figure. A_1 might, for example, remove all points not on a boundary of a solid region; A_2 might leave only *vertex* points; A_3 might fill up hollow regions, etc. (see Figure 5). Each sequence $A_{i1}A_{i2} \ldots A_{ik}$ of these forms a new transformation, so that there is available an infinite variety. We provide the machine-also with one or more

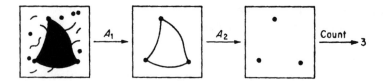

Figure 5. An arbitrary sequence of picture transformations, followed by a numerical-valued function, can be used as a *property* function for pictures. A_1 removes all points which are not at the edge of a solid region. A_2 leaves only vertex points—at which an arc suddenly changes direction. The function C simply counts the number of points remaining in the picture. All remarks in the text could be generalized to apply to properties like A_1A_2C, which can have more than two values.

"terminal" operations which convert a picture into a number, so that any sequence of the elementary transformations, followed by a terminal operation, defines a property. [Dineen (1955) describes how these processes were programmed in a digital computer.] We can start with a few short sequences, perhaps chosen randomly. Selfridge describes how the machine might learn new useful properties.

> We now feed the machine A's and O's telling the machine each time which letter it is. Beside each sequence under the two letters, the machine builds up distribution functions from the results of applying the sequences to the image. Now, since the sequences were chosen completely randomly, it may well be that most of the sequences have very flat distribution functions; that is, they [provide] no information, and the sequences are therefore [by definition] not significant. Let it discard these and pick some others. Sooner or later, however, some sequences will prove significant; that is, their distribution functions will peak up somewhere. What the machine does now is to build up new sequences like the significant ones. This is the important point. If it merely chose sequences at random it might take a very long while indeed to find the best sequences. But with some successful sequences, or partly successful ones, to guide it, we hope that the process will be much quicker. The crucial question remains: how do we build up sequences "like" other sequences, but not identical? As of now we think we shall merely build sequences from the transition frequencies of the significant sequences. We shall build up a matrix of transition frequencies from the significant ones, and use those as transition probabilities with which to choose new sequences.
>
> We do not claim that this method is necessarily a very good way of choosing sequences—only that it should do better than not using at all the knowledge of what kind of sequences has worked. It has seemed to us that this is the crucial point of learning.[6]

It would indeed be remarkable if this failed to yield properties more useful than would be obtained from completely random sequence selection. The generating problem is discussed further in Minsky (1956a). Newell, Shaw, and Simon (1960b) describe more deliberate, less statistical, techniques that might be used to discover sets of properties appropriate to a given problem area. One may think of the Selfridge proposal as a system which uses a finite-state language to describe its properties. Solomonoff (1957, 1960) proposes some techniques for discovering common features of a set of expressions, e.g., of the descriptions of those properties of already established utility; the methods can then be applied to generate new properties with the same common features. I consider the lines of attack in Selfridge (1955), Newell, Shaw and Simon (1960a), and Solomonoff (1960, 1958), although still incomplete, to be of the greatest importance.

3.7 Combining Properties

One cannot expect easily to find a *small* set of properties which will be just right for a problem area. It is usually much easier to find a large set of properties each of which provides a little useful information. Then one is faced with the problem of finding a way to combine them to make the desired distinctions. The simplest method is to choose, for each class, a typical character (a particular sequence of property values) and then to use some matching procedure, e.g., counting the numbers of agreements and disagreements, to compare an unknown with these chosen "character prototypes." The linear weighting scheme described just below is a slight generalization on this. Such methods treat the properties as more or less independent evidence for and against propositions; more general procedures (about which we have yet little practical information) must account also for nonlinear relations between properties, i.e., must contain weighting terms for joint subsets of property values.

3.6.1 "Bayes Nets" for Combining Independent Properties

We consider a single experiment in which an object is placed in front of a property-list machine. Each property E_i will have a value, 0 or 1. Suppose that there has been defined some set of "object classes" F_j, and that we want to use the outcome of this experiment to decide in which of these classes the object belongs.

Assume that the situation is basically probabilistic, and that we know the probability P_{ij} that, if the object is in class F_j then the ith property E_i will have value 1. Assume further that these properties are independent; that is, even given F_j, knowledge of the value of E_i tells us nothing more about the value of a different E_k in the same experiment. (This is a strong condition—see below.) Let ϕ_j be the absolute probability that an object is in class F_j. Finally, for this experiment define V to be the particular set of i's for which the E_i's are 1. Then this V represents the character of the object. From the definition of conditional probability, we have

$$\Pr(F_j, V) = \Pr(V) \cdot \Pr(F_j \mid V) = \Pr(F_j) \cdot \Pr(V \mid F_j)$$

Given the character V, we want to guess which F_j has occurred (with the least

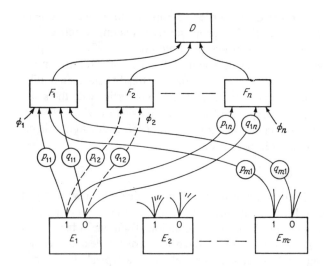

Figure 6. "Net" model for maximum-likelihood decisions based on linear weightings of property values. The input data are examined by each "property filter" E_i. Each E_i has "0" and "1" output channels, one of which is excited by each input. These outputs are weighted by the corresponding p_{ij}'s, as shown in the text. The resulting signals are multiplied in the F_j units, each of which "collects evidence" for a particular figure class. [We could have used here log (p_{ij}), and added at the F_j units.] The final decision is made by the *topmost* unit D, who merely chooses that F_j with the largest score. Note that the logarithm of the coefficient p_{ij}/q_{ij} in the second expression of (1) can be construed as the "weight of the evidence" of E_i, in favor of F_j. [See also Papert (1961) and Rosenblatt (1958).]

chance of being wrong—the so-called *maximum likelihood* estimate); that is, for which j is $\Pr(F_j \mid V)$ the largest? Since in the above $\Pr(V)$ does not depend on j, we have only to calculate for which j is

$$\Pr(F_j) \cdot \Pr(V \mid F_j) = \phi_j \Pr(V \mid F_j)$$

the largest. Hence, by our independence hypothesis, we have to maximize

$$\phi_j \cdot \prod_{i \in V} p_{ij} \cdot \prod_{i \in \overline{V}} q_{ij} = \phi_j \prod_{i \in V} \frac{p_{ij}}{q_{ij}} \cdot \prod_{\text{all } i} q_{ij} \tag{1}$$

These "maximum-likelihood" decisions can be made (Figure 6) by a simple network device.[7]

These nets resemble the general schematic diagrams proposed in the "Pandemonium" model of Selfridge (1959) (see his Figure 3). It is proposed there that some intellectual processes might be carried out by a hierarchy of simultaneously functioning submachines suggestively called "demons." Each unit is set to detect certain patterns in the activity of others and the output of each unit announces the degree of confidence of that unit that it sees what it is looking for. Our E_i units are Selfridge's "data demons." Our units F_j are his "cognitive demons;" each collects from the abstracted data evidence for a specific proposition. The topmost "decision demon" D responds to that one in the multitude below it whose shriek is the loudest.[8]

It is quite easy to add to this "Bayes network model" a mechanism which will enable it to learn the optimal connection weightings. Imagine that, after each event, the machine is told which F_j has occurred; we could implement this by sending back a signal along the connections leading to that F_j unit. Suppose that the connection for p_{ij} (or q_{ij}) contains a two-terminal device (or "synapse") which stores a number w_{ij}. Whenever the joint event $(F_j, E_j = 1)$ occurs, we modify w_{ij} by replacing it by $(w_{ij} + 1)\theta$, where θ is a factor slightly less than unity. And when the joint event $(F_j, E_i = 0)$ occurs, we decrement w_{ij} by replacing it with $(w_{ij})\theta$. It is not difficult to show that the expected values of the w_{ij}'s will become proportional to the p_{ij}'s [and, in fact, approach $p_{ij}[\theta/(1-\theta)]$. Hence, the machine tends to learn the optimal weighting on the basis of experience. (One must put in a similar mechanism for estimating the F_j's.) The variance of the normalized weight $w_{ij}[(1-\theta)/\theta]$ approaches $[(1-\theta)/(1+\theta]p_{ij}q_{ij}$. Thus a small value for θ means rapid learning but is associated with a large variance, hence, with low reliability. Choosing θ close to unity means slow, but reliable, learning. θ is really a sort of memory decay constant, and its choice must be determined by the noise and stability of the environment—much noise requires long averaging times, while a changing environment requires fast adaptation. The two requirements are, of course, incompatible and the decision has to be based on an economic compromise.[9]

3.6.2 Possibilities of Using Random Nets for Bayes Decisions

The nets of Figure 6 are very orderly in structure. Is all this structure necessary? Certainly if there were a great many properties, *each of which provided very little marginal information,* some of them would not be missed. Then one might expect good results with a mere sampling of all the possible connection paths w_{ij}. And one might thus, *in this special situation,* use a random connection net.

The two-layer nets here resemble those of the "Perceptron" proposal of Rosenblatt (1958). In the latter, there is an additional level of connections coming directly from randomly selected points of a "retina." Here the properties, the devices which abstract the visual input data, are simple functions which add some inputs, subtract others, and detect whether the result exceeds a threshold. Equation (1), we think, illustrates what is of value in this scheme. It does seem clear that a maximum-likelihood type of analysis of the output of the property functions can be handled by such nets. But these nets, with their simple, randomly generated, connections can probably never achieve recognition of such patterns as "the class of figures having two separated parts," and they cannot even achieve the effect of template recognition without size and position normalization (unless sample figures have been presented previously in essentially all sizes and positions). For the chances are extremely small of finding, by random methods, enough properties usefully correlated with patterns appreciably more abstract than those of the prototype-derived kind. And these networks can really only separate out (by weighting) information in the individual input properties; they cannot extract further information present in nonadditive form. The "Perceptron" class of machines have facilities neither for obtaining better-than-chance properties nor for assembling better-than-additive combinations of those it gets from random construction.[10]

For recognizing *normalized* printed or hand-printed characters, single point properties do surprisingly well (Highleyman and Kamentsky 1960); this amounts to just "averaging" many samples. Bledsoe and Browning (1959) claim good results with point-pair properties. Roberts (1960) describes a series of experiments in this general area. Doyle (1959) without normalization but with quite sophisticated properties obtains excellent results; his properties are already substantially size- and position-invariant. A general review of Doyle's work and other pattern-recognition experiments will be found in Selfridge and Neisser (1960).

For the complex discrimination, e.g., between one and two connected objects, the property problem is very serious, especially for long wiggly objects such as are handled by Kirsch (1957). Here some kind of recursive processing is required and combinations of simple properties would almost certainly fail even with large nets and long training.

We should not leave the discussion of some decision net models without noting their important limitations. The hypothesis that, for given j, the p_{ij} represent independent events, is a very strong condition indeed. Without this hypothesis we could still construct maximum-likelihood nets, but we would need an additional layer of cells to represent all of the joint events V; that is, we would need to know all the $\Pr(F_j \mid V)$. This gives a general (but trivial) solution, but requires 2^n cells for n properties, which is completely impractical for large systems. What is required is a system which computes some sampling of all the joint conditional probabilities, and uses these to estimate others when needed. The work of Uttley (1956, 1959) bears on this problem, but his proposed and experimental devices do not yet clearly show how to avoid exponential growth.[11]

3.6.3 Articulation and Attention—Limitations of the Property-list Method

Because of its fixed size, the property-list scheme is limited (for any given set of properties) in the detail of the distinctions it can make. Its ability to deal with a compound scene containing several objects is critically weak, and its direct extensions are unwieldy and unnatural. If a machine can recognize a chair and a table, it surely should be able to tell us that "there is a chair and

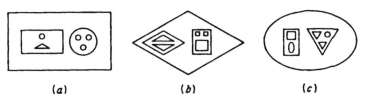

Figure 7. The picture (*a*) is first described verbally in the text. Then, by introducing notation for the relations "inside of," "to the left of" and "above," we construct a symbolic description. Such descriptions can be formed and manipulated by machines. By abstracting out of the complex relation between the parts of the figure we can use the same formula to describe the related pictures (*b*) and (*c*), changing only the list of primitive parts. It is up to the programmer to decide at just what level of complexity a part of a picture should be considered "primitive," this will depend on what the description is to be used for. We could further divide the drawings into vertices, lines, and arcs. Obviously, for some applications the relations would need more metrical information, e.g., specification of lengths or angles.

a table." To an extent, we can invent properties which allow some capacity for super position of object characters.[12] But there is no way to escape the information limit.

What is required is clearly (1) a *list* (of whatever length is necessary) of the primitive objects in the scene and (2) a statement about the relations among them. Thus we say of Figure 7a, "A rectangle (1) contains two subfigures disposed horizontally. The part on the left is a rectangle (2) which contains two subfigures disposed vertically; the upper a circle (3) and the lower a triangle (4). The part on the right... etc." Such a description entails an ability to separate or "articulate" the scene into parts. (Note that in this example the articulation is essentially *recursive;* the figure is first divided into two parts; then each part is described using the same machinery.) We can formalize this kind of description in an expression language whose fundamental grammatical form is a pair (R,L) whose first member R names a relation and whose second member L is an ordered list $(x_1, x_2, \ldots , x_n)$ of the objects or subfigures which bear that relation to one another. We obtain the required flexibility by allowing the members of the list L to contain not only the names of "elementary" figures but also "subexpressions" of the form (R,L) designating complex subfigures. Then our scene above may be described by the expression

$$[O, ([\square, (\rightarrow ,\{(O, (\square, (\downarrow, (O, \triangle)))), (O, (O, (\triangledown, (O, O, O))))\}))]$$

where $(O, (x,y))$ means that y is contained in x; $(\rightarrow,(x,y))$ means that y is to the right of x; $(\downarrow, (x,y))$ means that y is below x, and $(\triangle ,(x,y,z))$ means that y is to the right of x and z is underneath and between them. The symbols $\square$, O, and $\triangle$ represent the indicated kinds of primitive geometric objects. This expression-pair description language may be regarded as a simple kind of "list-structure" language. Powerful computer techniques have been developed, originally by Newell, Shaw and Simon, for manipulating symbolic expressions in such languages for purposes of heuristic programming. (See the remarks at the end of Section 5. If some of the members of a list are themselves lists, they must be surrounded by exterior parentheses, and this accounts for the accumulation of parentheses.)

It may be desirable to construct descriptions in which the complex relation is extracted, e.g., so that we have an expression of the form FG where F is an expression which at once denotes the composite relation between all the primitive parts listed in G. A complication arises in connection with the "binding" of variables, i.e., in specifying the manner in which the elements of G participate in the relation F. This can be handled in general by the "λ" notation (McCarthy 1960) but here we can just use integers to order the variables.

For the given example, we could describe the relational part F by an expression $\Theta(1,\rightarrow (\Theta(2,\downarrow(3,4)),\Theta(5,\nabla(6,7,8))))$ in which we now use a "functional notation;" "$(\Theta, (x,y))$" is replaced by "$(\Theta\ (x,y))$," etc., making for better readability. To obtain the desired description, this expression has to be applied to an ordered list of primitive objects, which in this case is ($\square$, $\square$, O, $\triangle$, O, O, O, O). This composite functional form allows us to abstract the composite relation. By changing only the object list we can obtain descriptions also of the objects in Figure 7b and c.

The important thing about such "articular" descriptions is that they can be obtained by *repeated application of a fixed set of pattern-recognition techniques*. Thus we can obtain *arbitrarily complex* descriptions from a fixed complexity classification mechanism. The new element required in the mechanism (beside the capacity to manipulate the list structures) is the ability to articulate—to "attend fully" to a selected part of the picture and bring all one's resources to bear on that part. In efficient problem solving programs, we will not usually complete such a description in a single operation. Instead, the depth or detail of description will be under the control of other processes. These will reach deeper, or look more carefully, only when they have to, e.g., when the presently available description is inadequate for a current goal. The author, together with L. Hodes, is working on pattern-recognition schemes using articular descriptions. By manipulating the formal descriptions we can deal with overlapping and incomplete figures, and several other problems of the "Gestalt" type.

It seems likely that as machines are turned toward more difficult problem areas, *passive* classification systems will become less adequate, and we may have to turn toward schemes which are based more on internally generated hypotheses, perhaps "error-controlled" along the lines proposed by MacKay (1956).

Space requires us to terminate this discussion of pattern-recognition and description. Among the important works not reviewed here should be mentioned those of Bomba (1959) and Grimsdale et al. (1959), which involve elements of description, Unger (1959) and Holland (1960) for parallel processing schemes, Hebb (1949) who is concerned with physiological description models, and the work of the Gestalt psychologists, notably Kohler (1947), who have certainly raised, if not solved, a number of important questions. Sherman (1959), Haller (1959) and others have completed programs using line-tracing operations for topological classification. The papers of Selfridge (1955, 1956) have been a major influence on work in this general area.

See also Kirsch et al. (1957) for discussion of a number of interesting computer image processing techniques, and see Minot (1959) and Stevens (1957) for reviews of the reading machine and related problems. One should also examine some biological work, e.g., Tinbergen (1951) to see instances in which some discriminations which seem, at first glance very complicated are explained on the basis of a few apparently simple properties arranged in simple decision trees.

4. Learning Systems

In order to solve a new problem, one should first try using methods similar to those that have worked on similar problems. To implement this "basic learning heuristic" one must generalize on past experience, and one way to do this is to use success-reinforced decision models. These learning systems are shown to be averaging devices. Using devices which learn also which events are associated with reinforcement, i.e., reward, we can build more autonomous "secondary reinforcement" systems. In applying such methods to complex problems, one encounters a serious difficulty—in distributing credit for success of a complex strategy among the many decisions that were involved. This problem can be managed by arranging for local reinforcement of partial goals within a hierarchy, and by grading the training sequence of problems to parallel a process of maturation of the machine's resources.

In order to solve a new problem one uses what might be called the basic learning heuristic—first try using methods similar to those which have worked, in the past, on similar problems. We want our machines, too, to benefit from their past experience. Since we cannot expect new situations to be precisely the same as old ones, any useful learning will have to involve generalization techniques. There are too many notions associated with "learning" to justify defining the term precisely. But we may be sure that any useful learning system will have to use records of the past as evidence for more general propositions; it must thus entail some commitment or other about "inductive inference." (See Section 6.2.) Perhaps the simplest way of generalizing about a set of entities is through constructing a new one which is an "ideal," or rather, a typical member of that set; the usual way to do this is to smooth away variation by some sort of averaging technique. And indeed we find that most of the simple learning devices do incorporate some averaging technique—often that of averaging some sort of product, thus obtaining a sort of correlation. We shall discuss this family of devices here, and some more abstract schemes in Section 6.

4.1 Reinforcement

A reinforcement process is one in which some aspects of the behavior of a system are caused to become more (or less) prominent in the future as a consequence of the application of a "reinforcement operator" Z. This operator is required to affect only those aspects of behavior for which instances have actually occurred recently.

The analogy is with "reward" or "extinction" (not punishment) in animal behavior. The important thing about this kind of process is that it is "operant" [a term of Skinner (1953)]; the reinforcement operator does not initiate behavior, but merely selects that which the trainer likes from that which has occurred. Such a system must then contain a device M which generates a variety of behavior (say, in interacting with some environment) and a trainer who makes critical judgments in applying the available reinforcement operators. (See Figure 8.)

Let us consider a very simple reinforcement model. Suppose that on each presentation of a stimulus S an animal has to make a choice, e.g., to turn left or right, and that its probability of turning right, at the nth trial, is p_n. Suppose that we want it to turn right. Whenever it does this we might "reward" it by applying the operator $Z+$;

$$p_{n+1} = Z_+(p_n) = \theta p_n + (1 - \theta) \quad 0 < \theta < 1$$

which moves p a fraction $(1 - \theta)$ of the way toward unity.[13] If we dislike what it does we apply negative reinforcement,

$$p_{n+1} = Z_-(p_n) = \theta p_n$$

moving p the same fraction of the way toward 0. Some theory of such "linear" learning operators, generalized to several stimuli and responses, will be found in Bush and Mosteller (1955). We can show that the learning result is an average weighted by an exponentially-decaying time factor: Let Z_n be ± 1 according to whether the nth event is rewarded or extinguished and replace p_n by $c_n = 2p_n - 1$ so that $-1 \leq c_n \leq 1$, as for a correlation coefficient. Then (with $c_0 = 0$) we obtain by induction

$$c_{n+1} = (1 - \theta) \sum_{i=0}^{n} \theta^{n-1} Z_i$$

and since

$$\frac{1}{1 - \theta} \approx \sum_{0}^{n} \theta^{n-i}$$

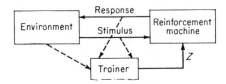

Figure 8. Parts of an "operant reinforcement" learning system. In response to a stimulus from the environment, the machine makes one of several possible responses. It remembers what decisions were made in choosing this response. Shortly thereafter, the trainer sends to the machine positive or negative reinforcement (reward) signal; this increases or decreases the tendency to make the same decisions in the future. Note that the trainer need not know how to solve problems, but only how to detect success or failure, or relative improvement; his function is selective. The trainer might be connected to observe the actual stimulus-response activity, or, in a more interesting kind of system, just some function of the state of the environment.

we can write this as

$$c_{n+1} \approx \frac{\Sigma \theta^{n-i} Z_i}{}$$

(1)

If the term Z_i is regarded as a product of (i) how the creature responded and (ii) which kind of reinforcement was given, then c_n is a kind of correlation function (with the decay weighting) of the joint behavior of these quantities. The ordinary, uniformly weighted average has the same general form but with time-dependent θ:

$$c_{n+1} = \left(1 - \frac{1}{N}\right) c_n + \frac{1}{N} Z_n$$

(2)

In (1) we have again the situation described in Section 3.7; a small value of θ gives fast learning, and the possibility of quick adaptation to a changing environment. A near-unity value of θ gives slow learning, but also smooths away uncertainties due to noise. As noted in Section 3.7, the response distribution comes to approximate the probabilities of rewards of the alternative responses. (The importance of this phenomenon has, I think, been overrated; it is certainly not an especially rational strategy. One reasonable alternative is that of computing the numbers p_{ij} as indicated, but actually playing at each trial the "most likely" choice. Except in the presence of a hostile opponent, there is usually no reason to play a "mixed" strategy.[14])

In Samuel's coefficient-optimizing program (1959b) [see Section 4.3.1], there is a most ingenious compromise between the exponential and the uniform averaging methods: the value of N in (2) above begins at 16 and so remains until $n = 16$, then N is 32 until $n = 32$, and so on until $n = 256$. Thereafter N remains fixed at 256. This nicely prevents violent fluctuations in c_n at the start, approaches the uniform weighting for a while, and finally approaches the exponentially weighted correlation, all in a manner that requires very little computation effort! Samuel's program is at present the outstanding example of a game-playing program which matches average human ability, and its success (in real time) is attributed to a wealth of such elegancies, both in heuristics and in programming.

The problem of extinction or "unlearning" is especially critical for complex, hierarchical, learning. For, once a generalization about the past has been made, one is likely to build upon it. Thus, one may come to select certain properties as important and begin to use them in the characterization of experience, perhaps storing one's memories in terms of them. If later it is discovered that some other properties would serve better, then one must face the problem of translating, or abandoning, the records based on the older system. This may be a very high price to pay. One does not easily give up an old way of looking at things, if the better one demands much effort and experience to be useful. Thus the *training sequences* on which our machines will spend their infancies, so to speak, must be chosen very shrewdly to insure that early abstractions will provide a good foundation for later difficult problems.

Incidentally, in spite of the space given here for their exposition, I am not convinced that such "incremental" or "statistical" learning schemes should play a central role in our models. They will certainly continue to appear as components of our programs but, I think, mainly by default. The more intelligent one is, the more often he should be able to learn from an experience something rather definite; e.g., to reject or accept a hypothesis, or to change a goal. (The obvious exception is that of a truly statistical environment in which averaging is inescapable. But the heart of problem-solving is always, we think, the combinatorial part that gives rise to searches, and we should usually be able to regard the complexities caused by "noise" as mere annoyances, however irritating they may be.) In this connection we can refer to the discussion of memory in Miller, Galanter and Pribram (1960).[15] This seems to be the first major work in psychology to show the influence of work in the artificial intelligence area, and its program is generally quite sophisticated.

4.2 Secondary Reinforcement and Expectation Models

The simple reinforcement system is limited by its dependence on the trainer. If the trainer can detect only the *solution* of a problem, then we may encounter "mesa" phenomena which will limit performance on difficult problems. (See Section 2.3.) One way to escape this is to have the machine learn to generalize on what the trainer does. Then, in difficult problems, it may be able to give itself partial reinforcements along the way, e.g., upon the solution of relevant subproblems. The machine in Figure 9 has some such ability.

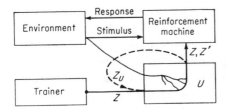

Figure 9. An additional device U gives the machine of Figure 8 the ability to learn which signals from the environment have been associated with reinforcement. The primary reinforcement signals Z are routed through U. By a Pavlovian conditioning process (not described here), external signals come to produce reinforcement signals like those that have frequently succeeded them in the past. Such signals might be abstract, e.g., verbal encouragement. If the "secondary reinforcement" signals are allowed, in turn, to acquire further external associations (through, e.g., a channel Z_u as shown) the machine might come to be able to handle chains of subproblems. But something must be done to stabilize the system against the positive symbolic feedback loop formed by the path Z_u. The profound difficulty presented by this stabilization problem may be reflected in the fact that, in lower animals, it is very difficult to demonstrate such chaining effects.

The new unit U is a device that learns which external stimuli are strongly correlated with the various reinforcement signals, and responds to such stimuli by reproducing the corresponding reinforcement signals. (The device U is not itself a reinforcement learning device; it is more like a "Pavlovian" conditioning device, treating the Z signals as "unconditioned" stimuli and the S signals as conditioned stimuli.) The heuristic idea is that any signal from the environment which in the past has been well correlated with (say) positive reinforcement is likely to be an indication that something good has just happened. If the training on early problems was such that this is realistic, then the system eventually should be able to detach itself from the trainer, and become autonomous. If we further permit "chaining" of the "secondary reinforcers," e.g., by admitting the connection shown as a dotted line in Figure 9, the scheme becomes quite powerful, in principle. There are obvious pitfalls in admitting such a degree of autonomy; the values of the system may drift to a "nonadaptive" condition.

4.3 Prediction and Expectation

The evaluation unit U is supposed to acquire an ability to tell whether a situation is good or bad. This evaluation could be applied to *imaginary* situations as well as to real ones. If we could estimate the consequences of a proposed action (without its actual execution), we could use U to evaluate the (estimated) resulting situation. This could help in reducing the effort in search, and we would have in effect a machine with some ability to look ahead, or *plan*.

In order to do this we need an additional device P which, given the description of a situation and an action, will predict a description of the likely result. (We will discuss schemes for doing this in Section 5.3.) The device P might be constructed along the lines of a reinforcement learning device. In such a system the required reinforcement signals would have a very attractive character. For the machine must reinforce P positively when the actual outcome resembles that which was predicted—accurate expectations are rewarded. If we could further add a premium to reinforcement of those predictions which have a novel aspect, we might expect to discern behavior motivated by a sort of curiosity. In the reinforcement of mechanisms for confirmed novel expectations (or new explanations) we may find the key to simulation of intellectual motivation.[16]

4.3.1 Samuel's Program for Checkers

In Samuel's "generalization learning" program for the game of checkers (1959a) we find a novel heuristic technique which could be regarded as a simple example of the "expectation reinforcement" notion. Let us review very briefly the situation in playing two-person board games of this kind. As noted by Shannon (1956) such games are in principle finite, and a best strategy can be found by following out all possible continuations—if he goes there I can go there, or there, etc.—and then "backing up" or "minimaxing" from the terminal positions, won, lost, or drawn. But in practice the full exploration of the resulting colossal "move tree" is out of the question. No doubt, some exploration will always be necessary for such games. But the tree must be pruned. We might simply put a limit on depth of exploration—the number of moves and replies. We might also limit the number of alternatives explored from each position—this requires some heuristics for selection of "plausible moves."[17] Now, if the backing-up technique is still to be used (with the incomplete move tree) one has to substitute for the absolute "win, lose, or draw" criterion some other "static" way of evaluating nonterminal positions.[18] (See Figure 10.) Perhaps the simplest scheme is to use a weighted sum of some selected set of "property" functions of the positions—mobility, advancement, center control, and the like. This is done in Samuel's program, and in most of its predecessors. Associated with this is a multiple-simultaneous-optimizer method for discovering a good coefficient assignment (using the correlation technique noted in Section 4.1). But the source of reinforcement signals in Samuel (1959a) is novel. One cannot afford to play out one or more entire games for each single learning step. Samuel measures instead *for each move* the difference between what the evaluation function yields *directly* of a position and what it *predicts* on the basis of an extensive continuation exploration, i.e., backing up. The sign of this error, "Delta," is used for reinforcement; thus the system may learn something at each move.[19]

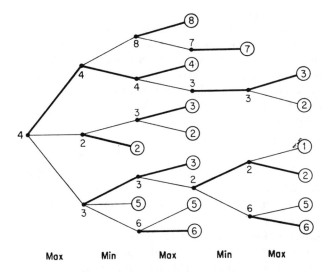

Figure 10. "Backing up" the static evaluations of proposed moves in a game tree. From the vertex at the left, representing the present position in a board game, radiate three branches, representing the *player's* proposed moves. Each of these might be countered by a variety of *opponent* moves, and so on. According to some program, a finite tree is generated. Then the worth to the player of each terminal board position is estimated (see text). If the opponent has the same values, he will choose to minimize the score, while the player will always try to maximize. The heavy lines show how this minimaxing process backs up until a choice is determined for the present position.

The full tree for chess has the order of 10^{120} branches—beyond the reach of any man or computer. There is a fundamental heuristic exchange between the effectiveness of the evaluation function and the extent of the tree. A very weak evaluation (e.g., one which just compares the players' values of pieces) would yield a devastating game if the machine could explore all continuations out to, say, 20 levels. But only 6 levels, roughly within the range of our presently largest computers, would probably not give a brilliant game; less exhaustive strategies, perhaps along the lines of Newell, Shaw, and Simon (1958b), would be more profitable.

4.4 The Basic Credit-Assignment Problem for Complex Reinforcement Learning Systems

In playing a complex game such as chess or checkers, or in writing a computer program, one has a definite success criterion—the game is won or lost. But in the course of play, each ultimate success (or failure) is associated with a vast number of internal decisions. If the run is successful, how can we assign credit for the success among the multitude of decisions? As Newell noted,

> It is extremely doubtful whether there is enough information in "win lose, or draw" when referred to the whole play of the game to permit any learning at all over available time scales.... For learning to take place, each play of the game must yield much more information. This is... achieved by breaking the problem

into components. The unit of success is the goal. If a goal is achieved, its sub-goals are reinforced; if not they are inhibited. (Actually, what is reinforced is the transformation rule that provided the subgoal.)... This also is true of the other kinds of structure: every tactic that is created provides information about the success or failure of tactic search rules; every opponent's action provides information about success or failure of likelihood inferences; and so on. The amount of information relevant to learning increases directly with the number of mechanisms in the chess-playing machine.[20]

We are in complete agreement with Newell on this approach to the problem.[21]

It is my impression that many workers in the area of "self-organizing" systems and "random neural nets" do not feel the urgency of this problem. Suppose that one million decisions are involved in a complex task (such as winning a chess game). Could we assign to each decision element one-millionth of the credit for the completed task? In certain special situations we can do just this—e.g., in the machines of Rosenblatt (1958), Roberts (1960), and Farley and Clark (1954), etc., where the connections being reinforced are to a sufficient degree independent. But the problem-solving ability is correspondingly weak.

For more complex problems, with decisions in hierarchies (rather than summed on the same level) and with increments small enough to assure probable convergence, the running times would become fantastic. For complex problems we will have to define "success" in some rich local sense. Some of the difficulty may be evaded by using carefully graded "training sequences" as described in the following section.

4.4.1 Friedberg's Program-Writing Program

An important example of comparative failure in this credit-assignment matter is provided by the program of Friedberg (1958, 1959) to solve program-writing problems. The problem here is to write programs for a (simulated) very simple digital computer. A simple problem is assigned, e.g., "compute the AND of two bits in storage and put the result in an assigned location." A generating device produces a random (64-instruction) program. The program is run and its success or failure is noted. The success information is used to reinforce *individual instructions* (in fixed locations) so that each success tends to increase the chance that the instructions of successful programs will appear in later trials. (We lack space for details of how this is done.) Thus the program tries to find "good" instructions, more or less independently, for each location in program memory. The machine did learn to solve some extremely simple problems. But it took of the order of 1000 times longer than pure chance would expect. In part II of Friedberg et al. (1959), this failure is discussed, and attributed in part to what we called (Section 2.3) the "mesa phenomena." In changing just one instruction at a time the machine had not taken large enough steps in its search through program space.

The second paper goes on to discuss a sequence of modifications in the program generator and its reinforcement operators. With these, and with some "priming" (starting the machine off on the right track with some useful instructions), the system came to be only a little worse than chance. Friedberg et al. (1959) conclude that with these improvements "the generally superior performance of those machines with a success number reinforcement mechanism over those without does serve to indicate that such a mechanism can provide a basis for constructing a learning machine." I disagree with this conclusion. It seems to me that each of the "improvements" can be interpreted as serving only to increase the step size of the search, that is, the randomness of the mechanism; this helps to avoid the mesa phenomenon and thus approach chance behavior. But it certainly does not show that the "learning mechanism" is working—one would want at least to see some better than chance results before arguing this point. The trouble, it seems, is with credit-assignment. The credit for a working program can only be assigned to functional groups of instructions, e.g., subroutines, and as these operate in hierarchies we should not expect individual instruction reinforcement to work well.[22] It seems surprising that it was not recognized in Friedberg et al. (1959) that the doubts raised earlier were probably justified! In the last section of Friedberg et al. (1959) we see some real success obtained by breaking the problem into parts and solving them sequentially. (This successful demonstration using division into subproblems does not use any reinforcement mechanism at all.) Some experiments of similar nature are reported in Kilburn, Grimsdale and Sumner (1959).

It is my conviction that no scheme for learning, or for pattern recognition, can have very general utility unless there are provisions for recursive, or at least hierarchical, use of previous results. We cannot expect a learning system to come to handle very hard problems without preparing it with a reasonably graded sequence of problems of growing difficulty. The first problem must be one which can be solved in reasonable time with the initial resources. The next must be capable of solution in reasonable time by using reasonably simple and accessible combinations of methods developed in the first, and so on. The only alternatives to this use of an adequate "training sequence" are (1) advanced resources, given initially, or (2) the fantastic exploratory processes found perhaps only in the history of organic evolution.[23] And even there, if we accept the general view of Darlington (1958) who emphasizes the heuristic aspects of genetic systems, we must have developed early (in, e.g., the phenomena of meiosis and crossing-over) quite highly specialized mechanisms providing for the segregation of groupings related to solutions of subproblems. Recently, much effort has been devoted to the construction of training sequences in connection with programming "teaching machines." Naturally, the psychological literature abounds with theories of how complex behavior is built up from simpler. In our own area, perhaps the work of Solomonoff (1957), while overly cryptic, shows the most thorough consideration of this dependency on *training sequences*.

5. Problem-Solving and Planning

The solution, by machine, of really complex problems will require a variety of administration facilities. During the course of solving a problem, one becomes involved with a large assembly of interrelated subproblems. From these, at each stage, a very few must be chosen for investigation. This decision must be based on (1) estimates of relative difficulties and (2) estimates of centrality of the different candidates for attention. Following subproblem selection (for which several heuristic methods are proposed), one must choose methods appropriate to the selected problems. But for really difficult problems, even these step-by-step heuristics for reducing search will fail, and the machine must have resources for analyzing the problem structure in the large—in short, for "planning." A number of schemes for planning are discussed, among them the use of models — analogous, semantic, and abstract. Certain abstract models, "character algebras," can be constructed by the machine itself, on the basis of experience or analysis. For concreteness, the discussion begins with a description of a simple but significant system (LT) which encounters some of these problems.

5.1 The "Logic Theory" Program of Newell, Shaw and Simon

It is not surprising that the testing grounds for early work on mechanical problem-solving have usually been areas of mathematics, or games, in which the rules are defined with absolute clarity. The "Logic Theory" machine of Newell and Simon (1956a, 1957a), called "LT" below, was a first attempt to prove theorems in logic, by frankly heuristic methods. Although the program was not by human standards a brilliant success (and did not surpass its designers), it stands as a landmark both in heuristic programming and also in the development of modern automatic programming.

The problem domain here is that of discovering proofs in the Russell Whitehead system for the propositional calculus. That system is given as a set of (five) axioms and (three) rules of inference; the latter specify how certain transformations can be applied to produce new theorems from old theorems and axioms.

The LT program is centered around the idea of "working backward" to find a proof. Given a theorem T to be proved, LT searches among the axioms and previously established theorems for one from which T can be deduced by a single application of one of three simple "methods" (which embody the given rules of inference). If one is found, the problem is solved. Or the search might fail completely. But finally, the search may yield one or more "problems" which are usually propositions from which T may be deduced directly. If one of these can, in turn, be proved a theorem the main problem will be solved. (The situation is actually slightly more complex.) Each such subproblem is adjoined to the "subproblem list" (after a limited preliminary attempt) and LT works around to it later. The full power of LT, such as it is, can be applied to each subproblem, for LT can use itself as a subroutine in a recursive fashion.

The heuristic technique of working backward yields something of a teleological process, and LT is a forerunner of more complex systems which construct hierarchies of goals and subgoals. Even so, the basic administrative structure of the program is no more than a nested set of searches through lists in memory. We shall first outline this structure and then mention a few heuristics that were used in attempts to improve performance.

1. Take the next problem from problem list.
   (If there are no more problems, EXIT with total failure.)

2. Choose the next of the three basic methods.
   (If no more methods, go to 1.)

3. Choose the next member of the list of axioms and previous theorems.
   (If no more, go to 2.)
   Then apply the method to the problem, using the chosen theorem or axiom.
   If problem is solved, EXIT with complete proof.
   If no result, go to 3.
   If new subproblem arises, go to 4.

4. Try the special (substitution) method on the subproblem
   If problem is solved, EXIT with complete proof.
   If no result, put the subproblem at the end of the problem list and go to 3.

Among the heuristics that were studied were (1) *a similarity test* to reduce the work in step 4 (which includes another search through the theorem list), (2) *a simplicity test* to select apparently easier problems from the problem list, and (3) *a strong nonprovability test* to remove from the problem list expressions which are probably false and hence not provable. In a series of experiments "learning" was used to find which earlier theorems had been most useful and should be given priority in step 3. We cannot review the effects of these changes in detail. Of interest was the balance between the extra cost for administration of certain heuristics and the resultant search reduction; this balance was quite delicate in some cases when computer memory became saturated. The system seemed to be quite sensitive to the training sequence—the order in which problems were given. And some heuristics which gave no significant over-all improvement did nevertheless affect the class of solvable problems. Curiously enough, the general efficiency of LT was not greatly improved by any or all of these devices. But all this practical experience is reflected in the design of the much more sophisticated "GPS" system described briefly in Section 5.4.2.

Wang (1960) has criticized the LT project on the grounds that there exist, as he and others have shown, mechanized proof methods which, for the particular run of problems considered, use far less machine effort than does LT and which have the advantage that they will ultimately find a proof for any provable proposition. (LT does not have this exhaustive "decision procedure" character and can fail ever to find proofs for some theorems.) The authors of "Empirical Explorations of the Logic Theory Machine," perhaps unaware of the existence of even moderately efficient exhaustive methods, supported their arguments by comparison with a particularly inefficient exhaustive procedure. Nevertheless, I feel that some of Wang's criticisms are misdirected. He does not seem to recognize that the authors of LT are not so much interested in proving these theorems as they are in the general problem of solving difficult problems. The combinatorial system of Russell and Whitehead (with which LT deals) is far less simple and elegant than the system used by Wang.[24] [Note, e.g., the emphasis in Newell, Shaw and Simon (1958a, 1958b).] Wang's problems, while logically equivalent, are formally much simpler. His methods do not include any facilities for using previous results (hence they are sure to degrade rapidly at a certain level of problem complexity), while LT is fundamentally oriented around this problem. Finally, because of the very effectiveness of Wang's method on the particular set of theorems in question, he simply did not have to face the fundamental heuristic problem of *when to decide to give up on a line of attack.* Thus the formidable performance of his program (1960) perhaps diverted his attention from heuristic problems that must again spring up when real mathematics is ultimately encountered.

This is not meant as a rejection of the importance of Wang's work and discussion. He and others working on "mechanical mathematics" have discovered that there are proof procedures which are much more efficient than has been suspected. Such work will unquestionably help in constructing intelligent machines, and these procedures will certainly be preferred, when available, to "unreliable heuristic methods." Wang, Davis and Putnam, and several others are now pushing these new techniques into the far more challenging domain of theorem proving in the predicate calculus (for which exhaustive decision procedures are no longer available). We have no space to discuss this area,[25] but it seems clear that a program to solve real mathematical problems will have to combine the mathematical sophistication of Wang with the heuristic sophistication of Newell, Shaw and Simon.[26]

5.2 Heuristics for Subproblem Selection

In designing a problem-solving system, the programmer often comes equipped with a set of more or less distinct "methods"—his real task is to find an efficient way for the program to decide where and when the different methods are to be used.

Methods which do not dispose of a problem may still transform it to create new problems or subproblems. Hence, during the course of solving one problem we may become involved with a large assembly of interrelated subproblems. A "parallel" computer, yet to be conceived, might work on many at a time. But even the parallel machine must have procedures to allocate its resources because it cannot simultaneously apply all its methods to all the problems. We shall divide this administrative problem into two parts: the selection of those subproblem(s) which seem most critical, attractive, or otherwise immediate, and, in the next section, the choice of which method to apply to the selected problem.

In the basic program for LT (Section 5.1), subproblem selection is very simple. New problems are examined briefly and (if not solved at once) are placed at the end of the (linear) problem list. The main program proceeds along this list (step 1), attacking the problems in the order of their generation. More powerful systems will have to be more judicious (both in generation and selection of problems) for only thus can excessive branching be restrained.[27] In more complex systems we can expect to consider for each subproblem, at least these two aspects: (1) its apparent "centrality"—how will its solution promote the main goal, and (2) its apparent "difficulty"—how much effort is it liable to consume. We need heuristic methods to estimate each of these quantities and, further, to select accordingly one of the problems and allocate to it some reasonable quantity of effort.[28] Little enough is known about these matters, and so it is not entirely for lack of space that the following remarks are somewhat cryptic.

Imagine that the problems and their relations are arranged to form some kind of directed-graph structure (Minsky, 1956b; Newell and Simon, 1956b; Gelernter and Rochester, 1958). The main problem is to establish a "valid" path between two initially distinguished nodes. Generation of new problems is represented by the addition of new, not-yet-valid paths, or by the insertion of new nodes in old paths. Then problems are represented by not-yet-valid paths, and "centrality" by location in the structure. Associate with each connection, quantities describing its current validity state (solved, plausible, doubtful, etc.) and its current estimated difficulty.

5.2.1. Global Methods

The most general problem-selection methods are "global"—at each step they look over the entire structure. There is one such simple scheme which works well on at least one rather degenerate interpretation of our problem graph. This is based on an electrical analogy suggested to us by a machine designed by Shannon [related to one described in Shannon (1955) which describes quite a variety of interesting game-playing and learning machines] to play a variant of the game marketed as "Hex" (and known among mathematicians as "Nash"). The initial board position can be represented as a certain network of resistors. (See Figure 11.) One player's goal is to construct a *short-circuit* path between two given boundaries; the opponent tries to open the circuit between them.

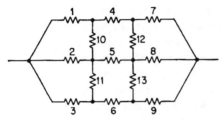

Figure 11. This board game (due to C. E. Shannon) is played on a network of equal resistors. The first player's goal is to open the circuit between the end points; the second player's goal is to short the circuit. A move consists of opening or shortening a resistor. If the first player begins by opening resistor 1, the second player might counter by shorting resistor 4, following the strategy described in the text. The remaining move pairs (if both players use that strategy) would be (5, 8) (9, 13) (12, 10 or 2) (2 or 10 *win*). In this game the first player should be able to force a win, and the maximum-current strategy seems always to do so, even on larger networks.

Each move consists of shorting (or opening), irreversibly, one of the remaining resistors. Shannon's machine applies a potential between the boundaries and selects that resistor which carries the largest current. Very roughly speaking, this resistor is likely to be most critical because changing it will have the largest effect on the resistance of the net and, hence, in the goal direction of shorting (or opening) the circuit. And although this argument is not perfect, nor is this a perfect model of the real combinatorial situation, the machine does play extremely well. (It can make unsound moves in certain artificial situations, but no one seems to have been able to force this during a game.)

The use of such a global method for problem selection requires that the available "difficulty estimates" for related subproblems be arranged to combine in roughly the manner of resistance values. Also, we could regard this machine as using an "analog model" for "planning." (See Section 5.4.)[29]

5.2.2. Local and "Hereditary" Methods

The prospect of having to study at each step the whole problem structure is discouraging, especially since the structure usually changes only slightly after each attempt. One naturally looks for methods which merely update or modify a small fragment of the stored record. Between the extremes of the "first-come-first-served" problem-list method and the full global-survey methods, lie a variety of compromise techniques. Perhaps the most attractive of these are what we will call the *inheritance* methods—essentially recursive devices.

In an inheritance method, the effort assigned to a subproblem is determined only by its immediate ancestry; at the time each problem is created it is assigned a certain total quantity Q of time or effort. When a problem is later split into subproblems, such quantities are assigned to them by some local process which *depends only on their relative merits and on what remains of Q.* Thus the centrality problem is managed implicitly. Such schemes are quite easy to program, especially with the new programming systems such as IPL (Newell and Tonge, 1960c) and LISP (McCarthy, 1960) (which are themselves based on certain hereditary or recursive operations). Special cases of the inheritance method arise when one can get along with a simple all-or-none Q. e.g., a "stop condition"—this yields the exploratory method called "backtracking" by Golumb (1961). The decoding procedure of Wozencraft (1961) is another important variety of inheritance method.

In the complex exploration process proposed for chess by Newell, Shaw, and Simon (1958b) we have a form of inheritance method with a *non-numerical stop condition*. Here, the subproblems inherit *sets of goals to be achieved*. This teleological control has to be administered by an additional goal-selection system and is further complicated by a global (but reasonably simple) stop rule of the back-up variety (Section 4.3). (Note: we are identifying here the move-tree-limitation problem with that of problem selection.) Even though extensive experimental results are not yet available, we feel that the scheme of Newell, Shaw, and Simon (1958b) deserves careful study by anyone planning serious work in this area. It shows only the beginning of the complexity sure to come in our development of intelligent machines.[30]

5.3 "Character-Method" Machines

Once a problem is selected, we must decide which method to try first. This depends on our ability to classify or characterize problems. We first compute the character of our problem (by using some pattern recognition technique) and then consult a "character method" table or other device which is supposed to tell us which method(s) are most effective on problems of that character. This information might be built up from experience, given initially by the programmer, deduced from "advice" (McCarthy, 1959), or obtained as the solution to some other problem, as suggested in the GPS proposal (Newell, Shaw and Simon, 1959a). In any case, this part of the machine's behavior, regarded from the outside, can be treated as a sort of stimulus-response, or "table look-up," activity.

If the characters (or descriptions) have too wide a variety of values, there will be a serious problem of filling a character-method table. One might then have to reduce the detail of information, e.g., by using only a few important properties. Thus the *differences* of GPS (see Section 5.4.2) describe no more than is necessary to define a single goal, and a priority scheme selects just one of these to characterize the situation. Gelernter and Rochester (1958) suggest using a property-weighting scheme, a special case of the "Bayes net" described in Section 3.7.

5.4 Planning

Ordinarily one can solve a complicated problem only by dividing it into a

number of parts, each of which can be attacked by a smaller search (or be further divided). Generally speaking, a successful division will reduce the search
time not by a mere fraction, but by a *fractional exponent.* In a graph with 10
branches descending from each node, a 20-step search might involve 10^{20} trials, which is out of the question, while the insertion of just four *lemmas* or *sequential subgoals* might reduce the search to only 5×10^4 trials, which is
within reason for machine exploration. Thus it will be worth a relatively enormous effort to find such "islands" in the solution of complex problems.[31] Note
that even if one encountered, say, 10^6 failures of such procedures before success, one would still have gained a factor of perhaps 10^{10} in over-all trial reduction! Thus practically *any ability at all* to "plan," or "analyze," a problem
will be profitable if the problem is difficult. It is safe to say that all simple,
unitary, notions of how to build an intelligent machine will fail, rather sharply,
for some modest level of problem difficulty. Only schemes which actively
pursue an analysis toward obtaining a set of *sequential goals* can be expected
to extend smoothly into increasingly complex problem domains.

Perhaps the most straight-forward concept of planning is that of using a
simplified model of the problem situation. Suppose that there is available, for
a given problem, some other problem of "essentially the same character" but
with less detail and complexity. Then we could proceed first to solve the simpler problem. Suppose, also, that this is done using a second set of methods,
which are also simpler, but in some correspondence with those for the original. The solution to the simpler problem can then be used as a "plan" for the
harder one. Perhaps each step will have to be expanded in detail. But the
multiple searches will add, not multiply, in the total search time. The situation would be ideal if the model were, mathematically, a homomorphism of
the original. But even without such perfection the model solution should be a
valuable guide. In mathematics one's proof procedures usually run along
these lines: one first assumes, e.g., that integrals and limits always converge,
in the planning stage. Once the outline is completed, in this simpleminded
model of mathematics, then one goes back to try to "make rigorous" the
steps of the proof, i.e., to replace them by chains of argument using genuine
rules of inference. And even if the plan fails, it may be possible to patch it by
replacing just a few of its steps.

Another aid to planning is the *semantic,* as opposed to the homomorphic,
model (Minsky, 1956a, 1959a). Here we may have an *interpretation* of the current problem within another system, not necessarily simpler, but with which
we are more familiar and have already more powerful methods. Thus, in connection with a plan for the proof of a theorem, we will want to know whether
the proposed lemmas, or islands in the proof, are actually true; if not, the plan
will surely fail. We can often easily tell if a proposition is true by looking at an
interpretation. Thus the truth of a proposition from plane geometry can be supposed, at least with great reliability, by actual measurement of a few construct-

ed drawings (or the analytic geometry equivalent). The geometry machine of Gelernter and Rochester (1958, 1959) uses such a semantic model with excellent results; it follows closely the lines proposed in Minsky (1956a).

5.4.1 The "Character-Algebra" Model

Planning with the aid of a model is of the greatest value in reducing search. Can we construct machines which find their own models? I believe the following will provide a general, straightforward way to construct certain kinds of useful, abstract models. The critical requirement is that we be able to compile a "character-method matrix" (in addition to the simple character-method table in Section 5.3). The CM matrix is an array of entries which predict with some reliability what will happen when methods are applied to problems. Both of the matrix dimensions are indexed by problem characters; if there is a method which usually transforms problems of character C_i into problems of character C_j then let the matrix entry C_{ij} be the name of that method (or a list of such methods). If there is no such method the corresponding entry is null.

Now suppose that there is no entry for C_{ij}—meaning that we have no direct way to transform a problem of type C_i into one of type C_j. Multiply the matrix by itself. If the new matrix has a non-null (i,j) entry then there must be a sequence of two methods which effects the desired transformation. If that fails, we may try higher powers. Note that [if we put unity for the (i,i) terms] we can reach the 2^n matrix power with just n multiplications. We don't need to define the symbolic multiplication operation; one may instead use arithmetic entries—putting unity for any non-null entry and zero for any null entry in the original matrix. This yields a simple connection, or flow diagram, matrix, and its nth power tells us something about its set of paths of length 2^n.[32] [Once a non-null entry is discovered, there exist efficient ways to find the corresponding sequences of methods. The problem is really just that of finding paths through a maze, and the method of Moore (1959) would be quite efficient. Almost any problem can be converted into a problem of finding a chain between two terminal expressions in some formal system.] If the characters are taken to be abstract representations of the problem expressions, this "character algebra" model can be as abstract as are the available pattern-recognition facilities. See Minsky (1956a, 1959a).

The critical problem in using the character-algebra model for planning is, of course, the *prediction reliability of the matrix entries.* One cannot expect the character of a result to be strictly determined by the character of the original and the method used. And the reliability of the predictions will, in any case, deteriorate rapidly as the matrix power is raised. But, as we have noted, any plan at all is so much better than none that the system should do very much better than exhaustive search, even with quite poor prediction quality.

This matrix formulation is obviously only a special case of the character planning idea. More generally, one will have descriptions, rather than fixed characters, and one must then have more general methods to calculate from a description what is likely to happen when a method is applied.

5.4.2. Characters and Differences

In the GPS (general problem solver) proposal of Newell, Shaw, and Simon (1959a, 1960a) we find a slightly different framework: they use a notion of difference between two problems (or expressions) where we speak of the character of a single problem. These views are equivalent if we take our problems to be links or connections between expressions. But this notion of difference (as the character of a pair) does lend itself more smoothly to teleological reasoning. For what is the goal defined by a problem but to *reduce the "difference" between the present state and the desired state?* The underlying structure of GPS is precisely what we have called a "character-method machine" in which each kind of difference is associated in a table with one or more methods which are known to "reduce" that difference. Since the characterization here depends always on (1) the current problem expression and (2) the desired end result, it is reasonable to think, as its authors suggest, of GPS as using "means-end" analysis.

To illustrate the use of Differences, we shall review an example (Newell, Shaw, and Simon, 1960a). The problem, in elementary propositional calculus, is to prove that from $S \wedge (- P \supset Q)$ we can deduce $(Q \vee P) \wedge S$. The program looks at both of these expressions with a recursive matching process which branches out from the main connectives. The first difference it encounters is that S occurs on different sides of the main connective "$\wedge$." It therefore looks in the difference-method table under the heading "change position." It discovers there a method which uses the theorem $(A \wedge B) \equiv (B \wedge A)$ which is obviously useful for removing, or "reducing," differences of position. GPS applies this method, obtaining $(- P \supset Q) \wedge S$. GPS now asks what is the difference between this new expression and the goal. This time the matching procedure gets down into the connectives inside the left-hand members and finds a difference between the connectives "$\supset$" and "$\vee$." It now looks in the CM table under the heading "change connective" and discovers the appropriate method using $(- A \supset B) \equiv (A \vee B)$. It applies this method, obtaining $(P \vee Q) \wedge S$. In the final cycle, the difference-evaluating procedure discovers the need for a "change position" inside the left member, and applies a method using $(A \vee B) \equiv (B \vee A)$. This completes the solution of the problem.[33]

Evidently, the success of this "means-end" analysis in reducing general search will depend on the degree of specificity that can be written into the difference-method table—basically the same requirement for an effective character-algebra.

It may be possible to plan using differences, as well. One might imagine a "difference-algebra" in which the predictions have the form $D = D'D''$. One must construct accordingly a difference factorization algebra for discovering longer chains $D = D_1 \cdots D_n$ and corresponding method plans. We should note that one cannot expect to use such planning methods with such primitive differences as are discussed in Newell, Shaw, and Simon (1960a); for these cannot form an adequate difference-algebra (or character-algebra). Unless the characterizing expressions have many levels of descriptive detail, the matrix powers will too swiftly become degenerate. This degeneracy will ultimately limit the capacity of any formal planning device.

One may think of the general planning heuristic as embodied in a recursive process of the following form. Suppose we have a problem P:

1. Form a plan for problem P.

2. Select first (next) step of the plan. (If no more steps, exit with "success.")

3. Try the suggested method(s):
   Success: return to (2), i.e., try next step in the plan.
   Failure: return to (1), i.e., form new plan, or perhaps change current plan to avoid this step.
   Problem judged too difficult: *Apply this entire procedure to the problem of the current step.*

Observe that such a program schema is essentially recursive; it uses itself as a subroutine (explicitly, in the last step) in such a way that its current state has to be stored, and restored when it returns control to itself.[34]

Miller, Galanter and Pribram[35] discuss possible analogies between human problem-solving and some heuristic planning schemes. It seems certain that, for at least a few years, there will be a close association between theories of human behavior and attempts to increase the intellectual capacities of machines. But, in the long run, we must be prepared to discover profitable lines of heuristic programming which do not deliberately imitate human characteristics.[36]

6. Induction and Models

6.1 Intelligence

In all of this discussion we have not come to grips with anything we can isolate as "intelligence." We have discussed only heuristics, shortcuts, and classification techniques. Is there something missing? I am confident that sooner or later we will be able to assemble programs of great problem solving ability from complex combinations of heuristic devices—multiple optimizers, pattern-recognition tricks, planning algebras, recursive administration procedures, and the like. In no one of these will we find the seat of intelligence.

Should we ask what intelligence "really is"? My own view is that this is more of an aesthetic question, or one of sense of dignity, than a technical matter! To me "intelligence" seems to denote little more than the complex of performances which we happen to respect, but do not understand. So it is, usually, with the question of "depth" in mathematics. Once the proof of a theorem is really understood its content seems to become trivial. (Still, there may remain a sense of wonder about how the proof was discovered.)

Programmers, too, know that there is never any "heart" in a program. There are high-level routines in each program, but all they do is dictate that "if such and such, then transfer to such and such a subroutine." And when we look at the low-level subroutines, which "actually do the work," we find senseless loops and sequences of trivial operations, merely carrying out the dictates of their superiors. The intelligence in such a system seems to be as intangible as becomes the meaning of a single common word when it is thoughtfully pronounced over and over again.

But we should not let our inability to discern a locus of intelligence lead us to conclude that programmed computers therefore cannot think. For it may be so with *man,* as with *machine,* that, when we understand finally the structure and program, the feeling of mystery (and self-approbation) will weaken.[37] We find similar views concerning "creativity" in Newell, Shaw, and Simon (1958c). The view expressed by Rosenbloom (1951) that minds (or brains) can transcend machines is based, apparently, on an erroneous interpretation of the meaning of the "unsolvability theorems" of Godel.[38]

6.2 Inductive Inference

Let us pose now for our machines, a variety of problems more challenging than any ordinary game or mathematical puzzle. Suppose that we want a machine which, when embedded for a time in a complex environment or "universe," will essay to produce a description of that world—to discover its regularities or laws of nature. We might ask it to predict what will happen next. We might ask it to predict what would be the likely consequences of a certain action or experiment. Or we might ask it to formulate the laws governing some class of events. In any case, our task is to equip our machine with *inductive ability*—with methods which it can use to construct general statements about events beyond its recorded experience. Now, there can be no system for inductive inference that will work well in all possible universes. But given a universe, or an ensemble of universes, and a criterion of success, this (epistemological) problem for machines becomes technical rather than philosophical. There is quite a literature concerning this subject, but we shall discuss only one approach which currently seems to us the most promising; this is what we might call the "grammatical induction" schemes of Solomonoff (1957, 1958, 1959a), based partly on work of Chomsky and Miller (1957b, 1958) .

We will take *language* to mean the set of expressions formed from some given set of primitive symbols or expressions, by the repeated application of some given set of rules; the primitive expressions plus the rules is the grammar of the language. Most induction problems can be framed as problems in the *discovery of grammars*. Suppose, for instance, that a machine's prior experience is summarized by a large collection of statements, some labelled "good" and some "bad" by some critical device. How could we generate selectively more good statements? The trick is to find some relatively simple (formal) language in which the good statements are grammatical, and in which the bad ones are not. Given such a language, we can use it to generate more statements, and presumably these will tend to be more like the good ones. The heuristic argument is that if we can find a relatively simple way to separate the two sets, the discovered rule is likely to be useful beyond the immediate experience. If the extension fails to be consistent with new data, one might be able to make small changes in the rules and, generally, one may be able to use many ordinary problem-solving methods for this task.

The problem of finding an efficient grammar is much the same as that of finding efficient *encodings,* or programs, for machines; in each case, one needs to discover the important regularities in the data, and exploit the regularities by making shrewd *abbreviations*. The possible importance of Solomonoff's work (1960) is that, despite some obvious defects, it may point the way toward systematic mathematical ways to explore this discovery problem. He considers the class of all programs (for a given general-purpose computer) which will produce a certain given output (the body of data in question). Most such programs, if allowed to continue, will add to that body of data. By properly weighting these programs, perhaps by length, we can obtain corresponding weights for the different possible continuations, and thus a basis for prediction. If this prediction is to be of any interest, it will be necessary to show some independence of the given computer; it is not yet clear precisely what form such a result will take.

6.3 Models of Oneself

If a creature can answer a question about a hypothetical experiment, without actually performing that experiment, then the answer must have been obtained from some submachine inside the creature. The output of that submachine (representing a correct answer) as well as the input (representing the question) must be coded descriptions of the corresponding external events or event classes. Seen through this pair of encoding and decoding channels, the internal submachine acts like the environment, and so it has the character of a "model." The inductive inference problem may then be regarded as the problem of constructing such a model.

To the extent that the creature's actions affect the environment, this internal model of the world will need to include some representation of the creature itself. If one asks the creature "why did you decide to do such and such" (or if it asks this of itself), any answer must come from the internal model. Thus the evidence of introspection itself is liable to be based ultimately on the processes used in constructing one's image of one's self. Speculation on the form of such a model leads to the amusing prediction that intelligent machines may be reluctant to believe that they are just machines. The argument is this: our own self-models have a substantially "dual" character; there is a part concerned with the physical or mechanical environment—with the behavior of inanimate objects—and there is a part concerned with social and psychological matters. It is precisely because we have not yet developed a satisfactory mechanical theory of mental activity that we have to keep these areas apart. We could not give up this division even if we wished to—until we find a unified model to replace it. Now, when we ask such a creature what sort of being it is, it cannot simply answer "directly;" it must inspect its model(s). And it must answer by saying that it seems to be a dual thing—which appears to have two parts—a "mind" and a "body." Thus, even the robot, unless equipped with a satisfactory theory of artificial intelligence, would have to maintain a dualistic opinion on this matter.[39]

7. Conclusion

In attempting to combine a survey of work on "artificial intelligence" with a summary of our own views, we could not mention every relevant project and publication. Some important omissions are in the area of "brain models"; the early work of Farley and Clark (1954) [also Farley's paper in Yovitts and Cameron (1960), often unknowingly duplicated, and the work of Rochester (1956) and Milner (1960)]. The work of Lettvin et al. (1959) is related to the theories in Selfridge (1959). We did not touch at all on the problems of logic and language, and of information retrieval, which must be faced when action is to be based on the contents of large memories; see, e.g., McCarthy (1959). We have not discussed the basic results in mathematical logic which bear on the question of what can be done by machines. There are entire literatures we have hardly even sampled—the bold pioneering work of Rashevsky (c. 1929) and his later co-workers (Rashevsky 1960); Theories of Learning, e.g., Gorn (1959); Theory of Games, e.g., Shubik (1960); and Psychology, e.g., Bruner et al. (1956). And everyone should know the work of Polya (1945, 1954) on how to solve problems. We can hope only to have transmitted the flavor of some of the more ambitious projects *directly* concerned with getting machines to take over a larger portion of problem-solving tasks.

One last remark: we have discussed here only work concerned with more or less self-contained problem-solving programs. But as this is written, we are at last beginning to see vigorous activity in the direction of constructing usable *time-sharing* or *multiprogramming* computing systems. With these systems, it will at last become economical to match human beings in real time with really large machines. This means that we can work toward programming what will be, in effect, "thinking aids." In the years to come, we expect that these man-machine systems will share, and perhaps for a time be dominant, in our advance toward the development of "artificial intelligence."

Notes

1. The adjective "heuristic," as used here and widely in the literature, means related to *improving problem-solving performance;* as a noun it is also used in regard to any method or trick used to improve the efficiency of a problem-solving system. A "heuristic program," to be considered successful, must work well on a variety of problems, and may often be excused if it fails on some. We often find it worthwhile to introduce a heuristic method which happens to cause occasional failures, if there is an over-all improvement in performance. But imperfect methods are not necessarily heuristic, nor vice versa. Hence "heuristic" should not be regarded as opposite to "foolproof;" this has caused some confusion in the literature.

2. McCarthy (1956) has discussed the enumeration problem from a recursive function-theory point of view. This incomplete but suggestive paper proposes, among other things, that "the enumeration of partial recursive functions should give an early place to compositions of functions that have already appeared."

I regard this as an important notion, especially in the light of Shannon's results (1949) on two-terminal switching circuits—that the "average" n-variable switching function requires about $2^n/n$ contacts. This disaster does not usually strike when we construct "interesting" large machines, presumably because they are based on composition of functions already found useful. One should not overlook the pioneering paper of Newell (1955), and Samuel's discussion of the minimaxing process in (1959a).

3. In 1952 and especially in 1956, Ashby has an excellent discussion of the search problem. (However, I am not convinced of the usefulness of his notion of "ultrastability," which seems to be little more than the property of a machine to search until something stops it.)

4. In the case studied in Pitts and McCulloch (1947) the transformation space is a *group* with a uniquely defined measure: the set $[F]$ can be computed without repetitions by scanning through the application of all the transforms T_a to the given figure so that the invariant property can be defined by

$$P*(F) = \int_{\alpha \in G} P(T_\alpha(F)) \, d\mu$$

where G is the group and μ the measure. By substituting $T_\beta(F)$ for F in this, one can see that the result is independent of choice of p since we obtain the same integral over $G\beta^{-1} = G$.

5. See pp. 160ff. of Wiener (1948).

6. See p. 93 of Selfridge (1955).

7. At the cost of an additional network layer, we may also account for the possible cost g_{jk} that would be incurred if we were to assign to F_k a figure really in class F_j; in this case the minimum cost decision is given by the k for which

$$\sum_j g_{jk}\phi_j \prod_{i \in v} p_{ij} \prod_{i \in v} q_{ij}$$

is the least. $\overline{V}$ is the complement set to V. q_{ij} is $(1 - p_{ij})$.

8. See also the report in Selfridge and Neisser (1960) .

9. See also Minsky and Selfridge (1960), and Papert (1961).

10. See also Roberts (1960), Papert (1961), and Hawkins (1958). We can find nothing resembling an analysis in Rosenblatt (1958) or his subsequent publications.

11. See also Papert (1961).

12. Cf. Mooers' technique of zatocoding (1956a, 1956b).

13. Properly, the reinforcement functions should depend both on the p's and on the previous reaction—reward should decrease p if our animal has just turned to the left. The notation in the literature is also somewhat confusing in this regard.

14. The question of just how often one should play a strategy different from the estimated optimum, in order to gain information, is an underlying problem in many fields. See, e.g., Shubik (1960).

15. See especially Chapter 10.

16. See also Chapter 6 of Minsky (1954).

17. See the discussion of Bernstein (1958) and the more extensive review and discussion in the very suggestive paper of Newell, Shaw and Simon (1958b).

18. In some problems the backing-up process can be handled in closed analytic form so that one may be able to use such methods as Bellman's "Dynamic Programming" (1957). Freimer (1960) gives some examples for which limited "look ahead" doesn't work.

19. It should be noted that Samuel (1959a) describes also a rather successful checker-playing program based on recording and retrieving information about positions encountered in the past, a less abstract way of exploiting past experience. Samuel's work is notable in the variety of experiments that were performed, with and without various heuristics. This gives an unusual opportunity to really find out how different heuristic methods compare. More workers should choose (other things being equal) problems for which such variations are practicable.

20. See p. 108 of Newell (1955).

21. See also the discussion in Samuel (p. 22, 1959a) on assigning credit for a change in "Delta."

22. See the introduction to Friedberg (1958) for a thoughtful discussion of the plausibility of the scheme.

23. It should, however, be possible to construct learning mechanisms which can select for themselves reasonably good training sequences (from an always complex environment) by prearranging a relatively slow development (or "maturation") of the system's facilities. This might be done by prearranging that sequence of goals attempted by the primary trainer to match reasonably well, at each stage, the complexity of performance mechanically available to the pattern-recognition and other parts of the system. One might be able to do much of this by simply limiting the depth of hierarchical activity perhaps only later permitting limited recursive activity.

24. Wang's procedure (1960a), too, works backward, and can be regarded as a generalization of the method of "falsification" for deciding truth functional tautology. In Wang (1960b) and its unpublished sequel, he introduces more powerful methods (for much more difficult problems).

25. See Davis and Putnam (1960), and Wang (1960b).

26 All these efforts are directed toward the reduction of search effort. In that sense they are all heuristic programs. Since practically no one still uses "heuristic" in a sense opposed to "algorithmic," serious workers might do well to avoid pointless argument on this score. The real problem is to find methods which significantly delay the apparently inevitable exponential growth of search trees.

27. Note that the simple scheme of LT has the property that each generated problem will eventually get attention, even if several are created in a step 3. If one were to turn *full* attention to each problem, as generated, one might never return to alternate branches.

28. One will want to see if the considered problem is the same as one already considered, or very similar. See the discussion in Gelernter and Rochester (1958). This problem might be handled more generally by simply remembering the (characters of) problems that have been attacked, and checking new ones against this memory, e.g., by methods of Mooers (1956), looking more closely if there seems to be a match.

29. A variety of combinatorial methods will be matched against the network-analogy opponent in a program being completed by R. Silver, Lincoln Laboratory, MIT, Lexington, Mass.

30. Some further discussion of this question may be found in Slagle (1961).

31. See Section 10 of Ashby (1956).

32. See, e.g., Hohn, Seshu, and Aufenkamp (1957).

33. Compare this with the "matching" process described in Newell and Simon (1956). The notions of "character," "character-algebra," etc., originate in Minsky (1956) but seem useful in describing parts of the "GPS" system of Newell and Simon (1956) and Newell, Shaw, and Simon (1960a). The latter contains much additional material we cannot survey here. Essentially, GPS is to be self-applied to the problem of discovering sets of differences appropriate for given problem areas. This notion of "bootstrapping"—applying a problem solving system to the task of improving some of its own methods—is old and familiar, but in Newell, Shaw, and Simon (1960a) we find perhaps the first specific proposal about how such an advance might be realized.

34. This violates, for example, the restrictions on "DO loops" in programming systems such as Fortran. Convenient techniques for programming such processes were developed by Newell, Shaw and Simon (1960b); the program state variables are stored in "pushdown lists" and both the program and the data are stored in the form of "list structures." Gelernter (1959) extended Fortran to manage some of this. McCarthy has extended these notions in Lisp (1960) to permit explicit recursive definitions of programs in a language based on recursive functions of symbolic expressions; here the management of program state variables is fully automatic. See also Orchard-Hays (1960).

35. See Chapters 12 and 13 of Miller, Galanter, and Pribram (1960).

36 Limitations of space preclude detailed discussion here of theories of self-organizing neural nets, and other models based on brain analogies. [Several of these are described or cited in *Proceedings of a Symposium on Mechanization of Thought Processes,* London: H. M. Stationery Office, 1959, and *Self Organizing Systems,* M. T. Yovitts and S. Cameron (eds.), New York: Pergamon Press, 1960.] This omission is not too serious, I feel, in connection with the subject of heuristic programming, because the motivation and methods of the two areas seem so different. Up to the present time, at least, research on neural-net models has been concerned mainly with the attempt to show that certain rather simple heuristic processes, e.g., reinforcement learning, or property-list pattern recognition, can be realized or evolved by collections of simple elements without very highly organized interconnections. Work on heuristic programming is characterized quite differently by the search for new, more powerful heuristics for solving very complex problems, and by very little concern for what hardware (neuronal or otherwise) would minimally suffice for its realization. In short, the work on "nets" is concerned with how far one can get with a small initial endowment; the work on "artificial intelligence" is concerned with using all we know to build the most powerful systems that we can. It is my expectation that, in problem-solving power, the (allegedly brainlike) minimal-structure systems will never threaten to compete with their more deliberately designed contemporaries; nevertheless, their study should prove profitable in the development of component elements and subsystems to be used in the

construction of the more systematically conceived machines.

37. See Minsky (1956, 1959)

38. On problems of volition we are in general agreement with McCulloch (1954) that our *freedom of will* "presumably means no more than that we can distinguish between what we intend (i.e., our *plan),* and some intervention in our action." See also MacKay (1959) and [the] references; we are, however, unconvinced by his eulogization of "analog" devices. Concerning the "mind-brain" problem, one should consider the arguments of Craik (1952), Hayek (1952), and Pask (1959). Among the active leaders in modern heuristic programming, perhaps only Samuel (1960b) has taken a strong position against the idea of machines thinking. His argument, based on the fact that reliable computers do only that which they are instructed to do, has a basic flaw; it does not follow that the programmer therefore has full knowledge (and therefore full responsibility and credit for) what will ensue. For certainly the programmer may set up an evolutionary system whose limitations are for him unclear and possibly incomprehensible. No better does the mathematician know all the consequences of a proposed set of axioms. Surely a machine has to be in order to perform. But we cannot assign all the credit to its programmer if the operation of a system comes to reveal structures not recognizable or anticipated by the programmer. While we have not yet seen much in the way of intelligent activity in machines, Samuel's arguments (circular in that they are based on the presumption that machines do not have minds) do not assure us against this. Turing (1956) gives a very knowledgeable discussion of such matters.

39. There is a certain problem of infinite regression in the notion of a machine having a *good* model of itself: of course, the nested models must lose detail and finally vanish. But the argument, e.g., of Hayek (see 8.69 and 8.79, 1952) that we cannot "fully comprehend the unitary order" (of our own minds) ignores the power of recursive description as well as Turing's demonstration that (with sufficient external writing space) a "general-purpose" machine can answer any question about a description of itself that any larger machine could answer.

4

Computer Science as Empirical Inquiry
Symbols and Search

Allen Newell and Herbert A. Simon

1. Introduction

Computer science is the study of the phenomena surrounding computers. The founders of this society understood this very well when they called themselves the Association for Computing Machinery. The machine—not just the hardware, but the programmed, living machine—is the organism we study.

This is the tenth Turing Lecture. The nine persons who preceded us on this platform have presented nine different views of computer science, for our organism, the machine, can be studied at many levels and from many sides. We are deeply honored to appear here today and to present yet another view, the one that has permeated the scientific work for which we have been cited. We wish to speak of computer science as empirical inquiry.

Our view is only one of many; the previous lectures make that clear. However, even taken together the lectures fail to cover the whole scope of our science. Many fundamental aspects of it have not been represented in these ten awards. And if the time ever arrives, surely not soon, when the compass has been boxed, when computer science has been discussed from every side, it will be time to start the cycle again. For the hare as lecturer will have to make an annual sprint to overtake the cumulation of small, incremental gains that the tortoise of scientific and technical development has achieved in his steady march. Each year will create a new gap and call for a new sprint, for in science there is no final word.

Computer science is an empirical discipline. We would have called it an experimental science, but like astronomy, economics, and geology, some of its unique forms of observation and experience do not fit a narrow stereotype of the experimental method. None the less, they are experiments. Each new machine that is built is an experiment. Actually constructing the machine poses a question to nature; and we listen for the answer by observing the machine in operation and analyzing it by all analytical and measurement means available. Each new program that is built is an experiment. It poses a question to nature, and its behavior offers clues to an answer. Neither machines nor programs are black boxes; they are artifacts that have been designed, both hardware and software, and we can open them up and look inside. We can relate their structure to their behavior and draw many lessons from a single experiment. We don't have to build 100 copies of, say, a theorem prover, to demonstrate statistically that it has not overcome the combinatorial explosion of search in the way hoped for. Inspection of the program in the light of a few runs reveals the flaw and lets us proceed to the next attempt.

We build computers and programs for many reasons. We build them to serve society and as tools for carrying out the economic tasks of society. But as basic scientists we build machines and programs as a way of discovering new phenomena and analyzing phenomena we already know about. Society often becomes confused about this, believing that computers and programs are to be constructed only for the economic use that can be made of them (or as intermediate items in a developmental sequence leading to such use). It needs to understand that the phenomena surrounding computers are deep and obscure, requiring much experimentation to assess their nature. It needs to understand that, as in any science, the gains that accrue from such experimentation and understanding pay off in the permanent acquisition of new techniques; and that it is these techniques that will create the instruments to help society in achieving its goals.

Our purpose here, however, is not to plead for understanding from an outside world. It is to examine one aspect of our science, the development of new basic understanding by empirical inquiry. This is best done by illustrations. We will be pardoned if, presuming upon the occasion, we choose our examples from the area of our own research. As will become apparent, these examples involve the whole development of artificial intelligence, especially in its early years. They rest on much more than our own personal contributions. And even where we have made direct contributions, this has been done in cooperation with others. Our collaborators have included especially Cliff Shaw, with whom we formed a team of three through the exciting period of the late fifties. But we have also worked with a great many colleagues and students at Carnegie Mellon University.

Time permits taking up just two examples. The first is the development of the notion of a symbolic system. The second is the development of the notion of heuristic search. Both conceptions have deep significance for understanding how information is processed and how intelligence is achieved. However, they do not come close to exhausting the full scope of artificial intelligence, though they seem to us to be useful for exhibiting the nature of fundamental knowledge in this part of computer science.

2. Symbols and Physical Symbol Systems

One of the fundamental contributions to knowledge of computer science has been to explain, at a rather basic level, what symbols are. This explanation is a scientific proposition about nature. It is empirically derived, with a long and gradual development.

Symbols lie at the root of intelligent action, which is, of course, the primary topic of artificial intelligence. For that matter, it is a primary question for all of computer science. All information is processed by computers in the service of ends, and we measure the intelligence of a system by its ability to achieve stated ends in the face of variations, difficulties and complexities posed by the task environment. This general investment of computer science in attaining intelligence is obscured when the tasks being accomplished are limited in scope, for then the full variations in the environment can be accurately foreseen. It becomes more obvious as we extend computers to more global, complex and knowledge-intensive tasks—as we attempt to make them our agents, capable of handling on their own the full contingencies of the natural world.

Our understanding of the systems requirements for intelligent action emerges slowly. It is composite, for no single elementary thing accounts for intelligence in all its manifestations. There is no "intelligence principle," just as there is no "vital principle" that conveys by its very nature the essence of life. But the lack of a simple *deus ex machina* does not imply that there are no structural requirements for intelligence. One such requirement is the ability to store and manipulate symbols. To put the scientific question, we may paraphrase the title of a famous paper by Warren McCulloch (1961): What is a symbol, that intelligence may use it, and intelligence, that it may use a symbol?

2.1 Laws of Qualitative Structure

All sciences characterize the essential nature of the systems they study. These characterizations are invariably qualitative in nature, for they set the terms within which more detailed knowledge can be developed. Their essence can often be captured in very short, very general statements. One might judge these general laws, due to their limited specificity, as making relatively little contribution to the sum of a science, were it not for the historical evidence that shows them to be results of the greatest importance.

2.1.1 The Cell Doctrine in Biology.

A good example of a law of qualitative structure is the cell doctrine in biology, which states that the basic building block of all living organisms is the cell. Cells come in a large variety of forms, though they all have a nucleus surrounded by protoplasm, the whole encased by a membrane. But this internal structure was not, historically, part of the specification of the cell doctrine; it was subsequent specificity developed by intensive investigation. The cell doctrine can be conveyed almost entirely by the statement we gave above, along with some vague notions about what size a cell can be. The impact of this law on biology, however, has been tremendous, and the lost motion in the field prior to its gradual acceptance was considerable.

2.1.2 Plate Tectonics in Geology

Geology provides an interesting example of a qualitative structure law, interesting because it has gained acceptance in the last decade and so its rise in status is still fresh in memory. The theory of plate tectonics asserts that the surface of the globe is a collection of huge plates—a few dozen in all—which move (at geological speeds) against, over, and under each other into the center of the earth, where they lose their identity. The movements of the plates account for the shapes and relative locations of the continents and oceans, for the areas of volcanic and earthquake activity, for the deep sea ridges, and so on. With a few additional particulars as to speed and size, the essential theory has been specified. It was of course not accepted until it succeeded in explaining a number of details, all of which hung together (e.g., accounting for flora, fauna, and stratification agreements between West Africa and Northeast South America). The plate tectonics theory is highly qualitative. Now that it is accepted, the whole earth seems to offer evidence for it everywhere, for we see the world in its terms.

2.1.3 The Germ Theory of Disease

It is little more than a century since Pasteur enunciated the germ theory of disease, a law of qualitative structure that produced a revolution in medicine. The theory proposes that most diseases are caused by the presence and multiplication in the body of tiny single-celled living organisms, and that contagion consists in the transmission of these organisms from one host to another. A large part of the elaboration of the theory consisted in identifying the organisms associated with specific diseases, describing them, and tracing their life histories. The fact that the law has many exceptions—that many diseases are not produced by germs—does not detract from its importance. The law tells us to look for a particular kind of cause; it does not insist that we will always find it.

2.1.4 The Doctrine of Atomism

The doctrine of atomism offers an interesting contrast to the three laws of qualitative structure we have just described. As it emerged from the work of Dalton and his demonstrations that the chemicals combined in fixed proportions, the law provided a typical example of qualitative structure: the elements are composed of small, uniform particles, differing from one element to another. But because the underlying species of atoms are so simple and limited in their variety, quantitative theories were soon formulated which assimilated all the general structure in the original qualitative hypothesis. With cells, tectonic plates, and germs, the variety of structure is so great that the underlying qualitative principle remains distinct, and its contribution to the total theory clearly discernible.

2.1.5 Conclusion

Laws of qualitative structure are seen everywhere in science. Some of our greatest scientific discoveries are to be found among them. As the examples illustrate, they often set the terms on which a whole science operates.

2.2 Physical Symbol Systems

Let us return to the topic of symbols, and define a *physical symbol system.* The adjective "physical" denotes two important features: (1) Such systems clearly obey the laws of physics—they are realizable by engineered systems made of engineered components; (2) although our use of the term "symbol" prefigures our intended interpretation, it is not restricted to human symbol systems.

A physical symbol system consists of a set of entities, called symbols, which are physical patterns that occur as components of another type of entity called an expression (or symbol structure). Thus, a symbol structure is composed of a number of instances (or tokens) of symbols related in some physical way (such as one token being next to another). At any instant of time the system will contain a collection of these symbol structures. Besides these structures, the system also contains a collection of processes that operate on expressions to produce other expressions: processes of creation, modification, reproduction and destruction. A physical symbol system is a machine that produces through time an evolving collection of symbol structures. Such a system exists in a world of objects wider than just these symbolic expressions themselves.

Two notions are central to this structure of expressions, symbols, and objects: designation and interpretation.

> *Designation.* An expression designates an object if, given the expression, the system can either affect the object itself or behave in ways dependent on the object.

In either case, access to the object via the expression has been obtained, which is the essence of designation.

> *Interpretation.* The system can interpret an expression if the expression designates a process and if, given the expression, the system can carry out the process.

Interpretation implies a special form of dependent action: given an expression the system can perform the indicated process, which is to say, it can evoke and execute its own processes from expressions that designate them.

A system capable of designation and interpretation, in the sense just indicated, must also meet a number of additional requirements, of completeness and closure. We will have space only to mention these briefly; all of them are important and have far-reaching consequences.

- A symbol may be used to designate any expression whatsoever. That is, given a symbol, it is not prescribed a priori what expressions it can designate. This arbitrariness pertains only to symbols; the symbol tokens and their mutual relations determine what object is designated by a complex expression.

- There exist expressions that designate every process of which the machine is capable.

- There exist processes for creating any expression and for modifying any expression in arbitrary ways.

- Expressions are stable; once created they will continue to exist until explicitly modified or deleted.

- The number of expressions that the system can hold is essentially unbounded.

The type of system we have just defined is not unfamiliar to computer scientists. It bears a strong family resemblance to all general purpose computers. If a symbol manipulation language, such as Lisp, is taken as defining a machine, then the kinship becomes truly brotherly. Our intent in laying out such a system is not to propose something new. Just the opposite: it is to show what is now known and hypothesized about systems that satisfy such a characterization.

We can now state a general scientific hypothesis—a law of qualitative structure for symbol systems:

> *The Physical Symbol System Hypothesis.* A physical symbol system has the nec-

essary and sufficient means for general intelligent action.

By "necessary" we mean that any system that exhibits general intelligence will prove upon analysis to be a physical symbol system. By "sufficient" we mean that any physical symbol system of sufficient size can be organized further to exhibit general intelligence. By "general intelligent action" we wish to indicate the same scope of intelligence as we see in human action: that in any real situation behavior appropriate to the ends of the system and adaptive to the demands of the environment can occur, within some limits of speed and complexity.

The physical symbol system hypothesis clearly is a law of qualitative structure. It specifies a general class of systems within which one will find those capable of intelligent action.

This is an empirical hypothesis. We have defined a class of systems; we wish to ask whether that class accounts for a set of phenomena we find in the real world. Intelligent action is everywhere around us in the biological world, mostly in human behavior. It is a form of behavior we can recognize by its effects whether it is performed by humans or not. The hypothesis could indeed be false. Intelligent behavior is not so easy to produce that any system will exhibit it willy nilly. Indeed, there are people whose analysis lead them to conclude either on philosophical or on scientific grounds that the hypothesis is false. Scientifically, one can attack or defend it only by bringing forth empirical evidence about the natural world.

We now need to trace the development of this hypothesis and look at the evidence for it.

2.3 Development of the Symbol System Hypothesis

A physical symbol system is an instance of a universal machine. Thus the symbol system hypothesis implies that intelligence will be realized by a universal computer. However, the hypothesis goes far beyond the argument, often made on general grounds of physical determinism, that any computation that is realizable can be realized by a universal machine, provided that it is specified. For it asserts specifically that the intelligent machine is a symbol system, thus making a specific architectural assertion about the nature of intelligent systems. It is important to understand how this additional specificity arose.

2.3.1 Formal Logic

The roots of the hypothesis go back to the program of Frege and of Whitehead and Russell for formalizing logic: capturing the basic conceptual notions of mathematics in logic and putting the notions of proof and deduction on a secure footing. This effort culminated in mathematical logic—our familiar propositional, first-order, and higher-order logics. It developed a characteristic view, often referred to as the "symbol game." Logic, and by incorporation all of mathematics, was a game played with meaningless tokens according to certain purely syntactic rules. All meaning had been purged. One had a mechanical, though permissive (we would now say nondeterministic), system about which various things could be proved. Thus progress was first made by walking away from all that seemed relevant to meaning and human symbols. We could call this the stage of formal symbol manipulation.

This general attitude is well reflected in the development of information theory. It was pointed out time and again that Shannon had defined a system that was useful only for communication and selection, and which had nothing to do with meaning. Regrets were expressed that such a general name as "information theory" had been given to the field, and attempts were made to rechristen it as "the theory of selective information"—to no avail, of course.

2.3.2 Turing Machines and the Digital Computer

The development of the first digital computers and of automata theory, starting with Turing's own work in the '30s, can be treated together. They agree in their view of what is essential. Let us use Turing's own model, for it shows the features well.

A Turing machine consists of two memories: an unbounded tape and a finite state control. The tape holds data, i.e., the famous zeroes and ones. The machine has a very small set of proper operations— read, write, and scan operations—on the tape. The read operation is not a data operation, but provides conditional branching to a control state as a function of the data under the read head. As we all know, this model contains the essentials of all computers, in terms of what they can do, though other computers with different memories and operations might carry out the same computations with different requirements of space and time. In particular, the model of a Turing machine contains within it the notions both of what cannot be computed and of universal machines—computers that can do anything that can be done by any machine.

We should marvel that two of our deepest insights into information processing were achieved in the thirties, before modern computers came into being. It is a tribute to the genius of Alan Turing. It is also a tribute to the development of mathematical logic at the time, and testimony to the depth of computer science's obligation to it. Concurrently with Turing's work appeared the work of the logicians Emil Post and (independently) Alonzo Church. Starting from independent notions of logistic systems (Post productions and recursive functions, respectively) they arrived at analogous results on undecidability and universality—results that were soon shown to imply that all three systems were equivalent. Indeed, the convergence of all these attempts to define the most general class of information processing systems provides some of the force of our conviction that we have captured the essentials of information processing in these models.

In none of these systems is there, on the surface, a concept of the symbol

as something that *designates*. The data are regarded as just strings of zeroes
and ones—indeed that data be inert is essential to the reduction of computation to physical process. The finite state control system was always viewed as
a small controller, and logical games were played to see how small a state
system could be used without destroying the universality of the machine. No
games, as far as we can tell, were ever played to add new states dynamically
to the finite control—to think of the control memory as holding the bulk of
the system's knowledge. What was accomplished at this stage was half the
principle of interpretation—showing that a machine could be run from a description. Thus, this is the state of automatic formal symbol manipulation.

2.3.3 The Stored Program Concept

With the development of the second generation of electronic machines in the
mid-forties (after the Eniac) came the stored program concept. This was
rightfully hailed as a milestone, both conceptually and practically. Programs
now can be data, and can be operated on as data. This capability is, of course,
already implicit in the model of Turing: the descriptions are on the very same
tape as the data. Yet the idea was realized only when machines acquired
enough memory to make it practicable to locate actual programs in some internal place. After all, the Eniac had only twenty registers.

The stored program concept embodies the second half of the interpretation
principle, the part that says that the system's own data can be interpreted. But
it does not yet contain the notion of designation—of the physical relation that
underlies meaning.

2.3.4 List Processing

The next step, taken in 1956, was list processing. The contents of the data
structures were now symbols, in the sense of our physical symbol system:
patterns that designated, that had referents. Lists held addresses which permitted access to other lists—thus the notion of list structures. That this was a
new view was demonstrated to us many times in the early days of list processing when colleagues would ask where the data were—that is, which list
finally held the collections of bits that were the content of the system. They
found it strange that there were no such bits, there were only symbols that
designated yet other symbol structures.

List processing is simultaneously three things in the development of computer science. (1) It is the creation of a genuine dynamic memory structure in
a machine that had heretofore been perceived as having fixed structure. It
added to our ensemble of operations those that built and modified structure in
addition to those that replaced and changed content. (2) It was an early
demonstration of the basic abstraction that a computer consists of a set of
data types and a set of operations proper to these data types, so that a computational system should employ whatever data types are appropriate to the ap-

plication, independent of the underlying machine. (3) List processing produced a model of designation, thus defining symbol manipulation in the sense in which we use this concept in computer science today.

As often occurs, the practice of the time already anticipated all the elements of list processing: addresses are obviously used to gain access, the drum machines used linked programs (so-called one-plus-one addressing), and so on. But the conception of list processing as an abstraction created a new world in which designation and dynamic symbolic structure were the defining characteristics. The embedding of the early list processing systems in languages (the IPLs, Lisp) is often decried as having been a barrier to the diffusion of list processing techniques throughout programming practice; but it was the vehicle that held the abstraction together.

2.3.5 Lisp

One more step is worth noting: McCarthy's creation of Lisp in 1959-60 (McCarthy 1960). It completed the act of abstraction, lifting list structures out of their embedding in concrete machines, creating a new formal system with S-expressions, which could be shown to be equivalent to the other universal schemes of computation.

2.3.6 Conclusion

That the concept of the designating symbol and symbol manipulation does not emerge until the mid-fifties does not mean that the earlier steps were either inessential or less important. The total concept is the join of computability, physical realizability (and by multiple technologies), universality, the symbolic representation of processes (i.e., interpretability), and, finally, symbolic structure and designation. Each of the steps provided an essential part of the whole.

The first step in this chain, authored by Turing, is theoretically motivated, but the others all have deep empirical roots. We have been led by the evolution of the computer itself. The stored program principle arose out of the experience with Eniac. List processing arose out of the attempt to construct intelligent programs. It took its cue from the emergence of random access memories, which provided a clear physical realization of a designating symbol in the address. Lisp arose out of the evolving experience with list processing.

2.4 The Evidence

We come now to the evidence for the hypothesis that physical symbol systems are capable of intelligent action, and that general intelligent action calls for a physical symbol system. The hypothesis is an empirical generalization and not a theorem. We know of no way of demonstrating the connection between symbol systems and intelligence on purely logical grounds. Lacking such a demonstration, we must look at the facts. Our central aim, however, is not to review the evidence in detail, but to use the example before us to illustrate the proposition that computer science is a field of empirical inquiry. Hence, we will only indicate what kinds of evidence there is, and the general nature of the testing process.

The notion of physical symbol system had taken essentially its present form by the middle of the 1950's, and one can date from that time the growth of artificial intelligence as a coherent subfield of computer science. The twenty years of work since then has seen a continuous accumulation of empirical evidence of two main varieties. The first addresses itself to the *sufficiency* of physical symbol systems for producing intelligence, attempting to construct and test specific systems that have such a capability. The second kind of evidence addresses itself to the *necessity* of having a physical symbol system wherever intelligence is exhibited. It starts with Man, the intelligent system best known to us, and attempts to discover whether his cognitive activity can be explained as the working of a physical symbol system. There are other forms of evidence, which we will comment upon briefly later, but these two are the important ones. We will consider them in turn. The first is generally called artificial intelligence, the second, research in cognitive psychology.

2.4.1 Constructing Intelligent Systems

The basic paradigm for the initial testing of the germ theory of disease was: identify a disease; then look for the germ. An analogous paradigm has inspired much of the research in artificial intelligence: identify a task domain calling for intelligence; then construct a program for a digital computer that can handle tasks in that domain. The easy and well-structured tasks were looked at first: puzzles and games, operations research problems of scheduling and allocating resources, simple induction tasks. Scores, if not hundreds, of programs of these kinds have by now been constructed, each capable of some measure of intelligent action in the appropriate domain.

Of course intelligence is not an all-or-none matter, and there has been steady progress toward higher levels of performance in specific domains, as well as toward widening the range of those domains. Early chess programs, for example, were deemed successful if they could play the game legally and with some indication of purpose; a little later, they reached the level of human beginners; within ten or fifteen years, they began to compete with serious amateurs. Progress has been slow (and the total programming effort invested small) but continuous, and the paradigm of construct-and-test proceeds in a regular cycle—the whole research activity mimicking at a macroscopic level the basic generate-and-test cycle of many of the AI programs.

There is a steadily widening area within which intelligent action is attainable. From the original tasks, research has extended to building systems that handle and understand natural language in a variety of ways, systems for interpreting visual scenes, systems for hand-eye coordination, systems that design, systems that write computer programs, systems for speech understanding—the list is, if not endless, at least very long. If there are limits beyond which the hypothesis will not carry us, they have not yet become apparent. Up to the present, the rate of progress has been governed mainly by the rather modest quantity of scientific resources that have been applied and the inevitable requirement of a substantial system building effort for each new major undertaking.

Much more has been going on, of course, than simply a piling up of examples of intelligent systems adapted to specific task domains. It would be surprising and unappealing if it turned out that the AI programs performing these diverse tasks had nothing in common beyond their being instances of physical symbol systems. Hence, there has been great interest in searching for mechanisms possessed of generality, and for common components among programs performing a variety of tasks. This search carries the theory beyond the initial symbol system hypothesis to a more complete characterization of the particular kinds of symbol systems that are effective in artificial intelligence. In the second section of the paper, we will discuss one example of a hypothesis at this second level of specificity: the heuristic search hypothesis.

The search for generality spawned a series of programs designed to separate out general problem-solving mechanisms from the requirements of particular task domains. The General Problem Solver (GPS) was perhaps the first of these, while among its descendants are such contemporary systems as PLANNER and CONNIVER. The search for common components has led to generalized schemes of representation for goals and plans, methods for constructing discrimination nets, procedures for the control of tree search, pattern-matching mechanisms, and language-parsing systems. Experiments are at present under way to find convenient devices for representing sequences of time and tense, movement, causality and the like. More and more, it becomes possible to assemble large intelligent systems in a modular way from such basic components.

We can gain some perspective on what is going on by turning, again, to the analogy of the germ theory. If the first burst of research stimulated by that theory consisted largely in finding the germ to go with each disease, subsequent effort turned to learning what a germ was—to building on the basic qualitative law a new level of structure. In artificial intelligence, an initial burst of activity aimed at building intelligent programs for a wide variety of almost randomly selected tasks is giving way to more sharply targeted research aimed at understanding the common mechanisms of such systems.

2.4.2 The Modeling of Human Symbolic Behavior

The symbol system hypothesis implies that the symbolic behavior of man arises because he has the characteristics of a physical symbol system. Hence, the results of efforts to model human behavior with symbol systems become an important part of the evidence for the hypothesis, and research in artificial intelligence goes on in close collaboration with research in information processing psychology, as it is usually called.

The search for explanations of man's intelligent behavior in terms of symbol systems has had a large measure of success over the past twenty years, to the point where information processing theory is the leading contemporary point of view in cognitive psychology. Especially in the areas of problem solving, concept attainment, and long-term memory, symbol manipulation models now dominate the scene.

Research in information processing psychology involves two main kinds of empirical activity. The first is the conduct of observations and experiments on human behavior in tasks requiring intelligence. The second, very similar to the parallel activity in artificial intelligence, is the programming of symbol systems to model the observed human behavior. The psychological observations and experiments lead to the formulation of hypotheses about the symbolic processes the subjects are using, and these are an important source of the ideas that go into the construction of the programs. Thus, many of the ideas for the basic mechanisms of GPS were derived from careful analysis of the protocols that human subjects produced while thinking aloud during the performance of a problem-solving task.

The empirical character of computer science is nowhere more evident than in this alliance with psychology. Not only are psychological experiments required to test the veridicality of the simulation models as explanations of the human behavior, but out of the experiments come new ideas for the design and construction of physical symbol systems.

2.4.3 Other Evidence

The principal body of evidence for the symbol system hypothesis that we have not considered is negative evidence: the absence of specific competing hypotheses as to how intelligent activity might be accomplished—whether by man or machine. Most attempts to build such hypotheses have taken place within the field of psychology. Here we have had a continuum of theories from the points of view usually labeled "behaviorism" to those usually labeled "Gestalt theory." Neither of these points of view stands as a real competitor to the symbol system hypothesis, and this for two reasons. First, neither behaviorism nor Gestalt theory had demonstrated, or even shown how to demonstrate, that the explanatory mechanisms it postulates are sufficient to account for intelligent behavior in complex tasks. Second, neither theory has been formulated with anything like the specificity of artificial programs. As a matter of fact, the alternative theories are sufficiently vague so that it is not terribly difficult to give them information processing interpretations, and thereby assimilate them to the symbol system hypothesis.

2.5 Conclusion

We have tried to use the example of the physical symbol system hypothesis to illustrate concretely that computer science is a scientific enterprise in the usual meaning of that term: that it develops scientific hypotheses which it then seeks to verify by empirical inquiry. We had a second reason, however, for choosing this particular example to illustrate our point. The physical symbol system hypothesis is itself a substantial scientific hypothesis of the kind that we earlier dubbed "laws of qualitative structure." It represents an important discovery of computer science, which if borne out by the empirical evidence, as in fact appears to be occurring, will have major continuing impact on the field. We turn now to a second example, the role of search in intelligence. This topic and the particular hypothesis about it that we shall examine have also played a central role in computer science, in general, and artificial intelligence, in particular.

3. Heuristic Search

Knowing that physical symbol systems provide the matrix for intelligent action does not tell us how they accomplish this. Our second example of a law of qualitative structure in computer science addresses this latter question, asserting that symbol systems solve problems by using the processes of heuristic search. This generalization, like the previous one, rests on empirical evidence, and has not been derived formally from other premises. However, we shall see in a moment that it does have some logical connection with the symbol system hypothesis, and perhaps we can look forward to formalization of the connection at some time in the future. Until that time arrives, our story must again be one of empirical inquiry. We will describe what is known about heuristic search and review the empirical findings that show how it enables action to be intelligent. We begin by stating this law of qualitative structure, the heuristic search hypothesis.

> *Heuristic Search Hypothesis.* The solutions to problems are represented as symbol structures. A physical symbol system exercises its intelligence in problem solving by search—that is, by generating and progressively modifying symbol structures until it produces a solution structure.

Physical symbol systems must use heuristic search to solve problems because such systems have limited processing resources; in a finite number of steps, and over a finite interval of time, they can execute only a finite number of processes. Of course that is not a very strong limitation, for all universal Turing machines suffer from it. We intend the limitation, however, in a stronger sense: we mean practically limited. We can conceive of systems that are not limited in a practical way, but are capable, for example, of searching in parallel the nodes of an exponentially expanding tree at a constant rate for each unit advance in depth. We will not be concerned here with such systems, but with systems whose computing resources are scarce relative to the complexity of the situations with which they are confronted. The restriction will not exclude any real symbol systems, in computer or man, in the context of real tasks. The fact of limited resources allows us, for most purposes, to view a symbol system as though it were a serial, one-process-at-a-time device. If it can accomplish only a small amount of processing in any short time interval, then we might as well regard it as doing things one at a time. Thus "limited resource symbol system" and "serial symbol system" are practically synonymous. The problem of allocating a scarce resource from moment to moment can usually be treated, if the moment is short enough, as a problem of scheduling a serial machine.

3.1 Problem Solving

Since ability to solve problems is generally taken as a prime indicator that a system has intelligence, it is natural that much of the history of artificial intelligence is taken up with attempts to build and understand problem-solving systems. Problem solving has been discussed by philosophers and psychologists for two millenia, in discourses dense with the sense of mystery. If you think there is nothing problematic or mysterious about a symbol system solving problems, then you are a child of today, whose views have been formed since mid-century. Plato (and, by his account, Socrates) found difficulty understanding even how problems could be *entertained,* much less how they could be solved. Let me remind you of how he posed the conundrum in the *Meno:*

> Meno: And how will you inquire, Socrates, into that which you know not? What will you put forth as the subject of inquiry? And if you find what you want, how will you ever know that this is what you did not know?

To deal with this puzzle, Plato invented his famous theory of recollection: when you think you are discovering or learning something, you are really just recalling what you already knew in a previous existence. If you find this explanation preposterous, there is a much simpler one available today, based upon our understanding of symbol systems. An approximate statement of it is:

> To state a problem is to designate (1) a *test* for a class of symbol structures solutions of the problem), and (2) a *generator* of symbol structures (potential solutions). To solve a problem is to generate a structure, using (2), that satisfies the test of (1).

We have a problem if we know what we want to do (the test), and if we don't know immediately how to do it (our generator does not immediately produce a symbol structure satisfying the test). A symbol system can state and solve problems (sometimes) because it can generate and test.

If that is all there is to problem solving, why not simply generate at once an expression that satisfies the test? This is, in fact, what we do when we wish and dream. "If wishes were horses, beggars might ride." But outside the world of dreams, it isn't possible. To know how we would test something, once constructed, does not mean that we know how to construct it—that we have any generator for doing so.

For example, it is well known what it means to "solve" the problem of playing winning chess. A simple test exists for noticing winning positions, the test for checkmate of the enemy King. In the world of dreams one simply generates a strategy that leads to checkmate for all counter strategies of the opponent. Alas, no generator that will do this is known to existing symbol systems (man or machine). Instead, good moves in chess are sought by generating various alternatives, and painstakingly evaluating them with the use of approximate, and often erroneous, measures that are supposed to indicate the likelihood that a particular line of play is on the route to a winning position. Move generators there are; winning move generators there are not.

Before there can be a move generator for a problem, there must be a problem space: a space of symbol structures in which problem situations, including the initial and goal situations, can be represented. Move generators are processes for modifying one situation in the problem space into another. The basic characteristics of physical symbol systems guarantee that they can represent problem spaces and that they possess move generators. How, in any concrete situation they synthesize a problem space and move generators appropriate to that situation is a question that is still very much on the frontier of artificial intelligence research.

The task that a symbol system is faced with, then, when it is presented with a problem and a problem space, is to use its limited processing resources to generate possible solutions, one after another, until it finds one that satisfies the problem-defining test. If the system had some control over the order in which potential solutions were generated, then it would be desirable to arrange this order of generation so that actual solutions would have a high likelihood of appearing early. A symbol system would exhibit intelligence to the extent that it succeeded in doing this. Intelligence for a system with limited processing resources consists in making wise choices of what to do next.

3.2 Search in Problem Solving

During the first decade or so of artificial intelligence research, the study of problem solving was almost synonymous with the study of search processes. From our characterization of problems and problem solving, it is easy to see why this was so. In fact, it might be asked whether it could be otherwise. But before we try to answer that question, we must explore further the nature of search processes as it revealed itself during that decade of activity.

3.2.1 Extracting Information from the Problem Space

Consider a set of symbol structures, some small subset of which are solutions to a given problem. Suppose, further, that the solutions are distributed randomly through the entire set. By this we mean that no information exists that would enable any search generator to perform better than a random search. Then no symbol system could exhibit more intelligence (or less intelligence) than any other in solving the problem, although one might experience better luck than another.

A condition, then, for the appearance of intelligence is that the distribution of solutions be not entirely random, that the space of symbol structures exhibit at least some degree of order and pattern. A second condition is that pattern in the space of symbol structures be more or less detectable. A third condition is that the generator of potential solutions be able to behave differentially, depending on what pattern it detected. There must be information in the problem space, and the symbol system must be capable of extracting and using it. Let us look first at a very simple example, where the intelligence is easy to come by.

Consider the problem of solving a simple algebraic equation:

$$AX + B = CX + D$$

The test defines a solution as any expression of the form, $X = E$, such that $AE + B = CE + D$. Now one could use as generator any process that would produce numbers which could then be tested by substituting in the latter equation. We would not call this an intelligent generator.

Alternatively, one could use generators that would make use of the fact that the original equation can be modified—by adding or subtracting equal quantities from both sides, or multiplying or dividing both sides by the same quantity—without changing its solutions. But, of course, we can obtain even more information to guide the generator by comparing the original expression with the form of the solution, and making precisely those changes in the equation that leave its solution unchanged, while at the same time, bringing it into the desired form. Such a generator could notice that there was an unwanted CX on the right-hand side of the original equation, subtract it from both sides and collect terms again. It could then notice that there was an unwanted B on the left-hand side and subtract that. Finally, it could get rid of the unwanted coefficient $(A - C)$ on the left-hand side by dividing.

Thus by this procedure, which now exhibits considerable intelligence, the generator produces successive symbol structures, each obtained by modifying the previous one; and the modifications are aimed at reducing the differences between the form of the input structure and the form of the test expression, while maintaining the other conditions for a solution. This simple example already illustrates many of the main mechanisms that are used by symbol systems for intelligent problem solving. First, each successive expression is not generated independently, but is produced by modifying one produced previously. Second, the modifications are not haphazard, but depend upon two kinds of information. They depend on information that is constant over this whole class of algebra problems, and that is built into the structure of the generator itself: all modifications of expressions must leave the equation's solution unchanged. They also depend on information that changes at each step: detection of the differences in form that remain between the current expression and the desired expression. In effect, the generator incorporates some of the tests the solution must satisfy, so that expressions that don't meet these tests will never be generated. Using the first kind of information guarantees that only a tiny subset of all possible expressions is actually generated, but without losing the solution expression from this subset. Using the second kind of information arrives at the desired solution by a succession of approximations, employing a simple form of means-ends analysis to give direction to the search.

There is no mystery where the information that guided the search came from. We need not follow Plato in endowing the symbol system with a previous existence in which it already knew the solution. A moderately sophisticated generator-test system did the trick without invoking reincarnation.

3.2.2 Search Trees

The simple algebra problem may seem an unusual, even pathological, example of search. It is certainly not trial-and-error search, for though there were a few trials, there was no error. We are more accustomed to thinking of problem-solving search as generating lushly branching trees of partial solution possibilities which may grow to thousands, or even millions, of branches, before they yield a solution. Thus, if from each expression it produces, the generator creates B new branches, then the tree will grow as B^D, where D is its depth. The tree grown for the algebra problem had the peculiarity that its branchiness, B, equaled unity.

Programs that play chess typically grow broad search trees, amounting in some cases to a million branches or more. (Although this example will serve to illustrate our points about tree search, we should note that the purpose of search in chess is not to generate proposed solutions, but to evaluate (test) them.) One line of research into game playing programs has been centrally concerned with improving the representation of the chess board, and the processes for making moves on it, so as to speed up search and make it possible to search larger trees. The rationale for this direction, of course, is that the deeper the dynamic search, the more accurate should be the evaluations at the end of it. On the other hand, there is good empirical evidence that the strongest human players, grandmasters, seldom explore trees of more than one hundred branches. This economy is achieved not so much by searching less deeply than do chess-playing programs, but by branching very sparsely and selectively at each node. This is only possible, without causing a deterioration of the evaluations, by having more of the selectivity built into the generator itself, so that it is able to select for generation just those branches that are very likely to yield important relevant information about the position.

The somewhat paradoxical-sounding conclusion to which this discussion leads is that search—successive generation of potential solution structures—is a fundamental aspect of a symbol system's exercise of intelligence in problem solving but that amount of search is not a measure of the amount of intelligence being exhibited. What makes a problem a problem is not that a large amount of search is required for its solution, but that a large amount would be required if a requisite level of intelligence were not applied. When the symbolic system that is endeavoring to solve a problem knows enough about what to do, it simply proceeds directly towards its goal; but whenever its knowledge becomes inadequate, when it enters terra incognita, it is faced with the threat of going through large amounts of search before it finds its way again.

The potential for the exponential explosion of the search tree that is present in every scheme for generating problem solutions warns us against depending on the brute force of computers—even the biggest and fastest computers—as a compensation for the ignorance and unselectivity of their generators. The hope is still periodically ignited in some human breasts that a computer can be found that is fast enough, and that can be programmed cleverly enough, to play good chess by brute-force search. There is nothing known in theory about the game of chess that rules out this possibility. Empirical studies on the management of search in sizable trees with only modest results make this a much less promising direction than it was when chess was first chosen as an appropriate task for artificial intelligence. We must regard this as one of the important empirical findings of research with chess programs.

3.2.3 The Forms of Intelligence

The task of intelligence, then, is to avert the ever-present threat of the exponential explosion of search. How can this be accomplished? The first route, already illustrated by the algebra example, and by chess programs that only generate "plausible" moves for further analysis, is to build selectivity into the generator: to generate only structures that show promise of being solutions or of being along the path toward solutions. The usual consequence of doing this is to decrease the rate of branching, not to prevent it entirely. Ultimate exponential explosion is not avoided—save in exceptionally highly structured situations like the algebra example—but only postponed. Hence, an intelligent system generally needs to supplement the selectivity of its solution generator with other information-using techniques to guide search.

Twenty years of experience with managing tree search in a variety of task environments has produced a small kit of general techniques which is part of the equipment of every researcher in artificial intelligence today. Since these techniques have been described in general works like that of Nilsson (1971), they can be summarized very briefly here.

In serial heuristic search, the basic question always is: what shall be done next? In tree search, that question, in turn, has two components: (1) from what node in the tree shall we search next, and (2) what direction shall we take from that node? Information helpful in answering the first question may be interpreted as measuring the relative distance of different nodes from the goal. Best-first search calls for searching next from the node that appears closest to the goal. Information helpful in answering the second question—in what direction to search—is often obtained, as in the algebra example, by detecting specific differences between the current nodal structure and the goal structure described by the test of a solution, and selecting actions that are relevant to reducing these particular kinds of differences. This is the technique known as means-ends analysis, which plays a central role in the structure of the General Problem Solver.

The importance of empirical studies as a source of general ideas in AI research can be demonstrated clearly by tracing the history, through large numbers of problem-solving programs, of these two central ideas: best-first search and means-ends analysis. Rudiments of best-first search were already present, though unnamed, in the Logic Theorist in 1955. The General Problem Solver, embodying means-ends analysis, appeared about 1957—but combined it with modified depth-first search rather than best-first search. Chess programs were generally wedded, for reasons of economy of memory, to depth-first search, supplemented after about 1958 by the powerful alpha-beta pruning procedure. Each of these techniques appears to have been reinvented a number of times, and it is hard to find general, task-independent theoretical discussions of problem solving in terms of these concepts until the middle or late 1960's. The amount of formal buttressing they have received from mathematical theory is still miniscule: some theorems about the reduction in search that can be secured from using the alpha-beta heuristic, a couple of theorems (reviewed by Nilsson [1971]) about shortest-path search, and some very recent theorems on best-first search with a probabilistic evaluation function.

3.2.4 "Weak" and "Strong" Methods

The techniques we have been discussing are dedicated to the control of exponential expansion rather than its prevention. For this reason, they have been properly called "weak methods"—methods to be used when the symbol system's knowledge or the amount of structure actually contained in the problem space is inadequate to permit search to be avoided entirely. It is instructive to contrast a highly structured situation, which can be formulated, say, as a linear programming problem, with the less structured situations of combinatorial problems like the traveling salesman problem or scheduling problems. ("Less structured" here refers to the insufficiency or nonexistence of relevant theory about the structure of the problem space.)

In solving linear programming problems, a substantial amount of computation may be required, but the search does not branch. Every step is a step along the way to a solution. In solving combinatorial problems or in proving theorems, tree search can seldom be avoided, and success depends on heuristic search methods of the sort we have been describing.

Not all streams of AI problem-solving research have followed the path we have been outlining. An example of a somewhat different point is provided by the work on theorem-proving systems. Here, ideas imported from mathematics and logic have had a strong influence on the direction of inquiry. For example, the use of heuristics was resisted when properties of completeness could not be proved (a bit ironic, since most interesting mathematical systems are known to be undecidable). Since completeness can seldom be proved for best-first search heuristics, or for many kinds of selective generators, the effect of this requirement was rather inhibiting. When theorem-proving programs were continually incapacitated by the combinatorial explosion of their search trees, thought began to be given to selective heuristics, which in many cases proved to be analogues of heuristics used in general problem solving programs. The set-of-support heuristic, for example, is a form of working backwards, adapted to the resolution theorem proving environment.

3.2.5 A Summary of the Experience

We have now described the workings of our second law of qualitative structure, which asserts that physical symbol systems solve problems by means of heuristic search. Beyond that, we have examined some subsidiary characteristics of heuristic search, in particular the threat that it always faces of exponential explosion of the search tree, and some of the means it uses to avert that threat. Opinions differ as to how effective heuristic search has been as a problem-solving mechanism—the opinions depending on what task domains are considered and what criterion of adequacy is adopted. Success can be guaranteed by setting aspiration levels low—or failure by setting them high. The evidence might be summed up about as follows. Few programs are solving problems at "expert" professional levels. Samuel's checker program and Feigenbaum and Lederberg's DENDRAL are perhaps the best-known exceptions, but one could point also to a number of heuristic search programs for such operations research problem domains as scheduling and integer programming. In a number of domains, programs perform at the level of competent amateurs: chess, some theorem-proving domains, many kinds of games and puzzles. Human levels have not yet been nearly reached by programs that have a complex perceptual "front end": visual scene recognizers, speech understanders, robots that have to maneuver in real space and time. Nevertheless, impressive progress has been made, and a large body of experience assembled about these difficult tasks.

We do not have deep theoretical explanations for the particular pattern of performance that has emerged. On empirical grounds, however, we might draw two conclusions. First, from what has been learned about human expert performance in tasks like chess, it is likely that any system capable of matching that performance will have to have access, in its memories, to very large stores of semantic information. Second, some part of the human superiority in tasks with a large perceptual component can be attributed to the special-purpose built-in parallel processing structure of the human eye and ear.

In any case, the quality of performance must necessarily depend on the characteristics both of the problem domains and of the symbol systems used to tackle them. For most real-life domains in which we are interested, the domain structure has not proved sufficiently simple to yield (so far) theorems about complexity, or to tell us, other than empirically, how large real-world problems are in relation to the abilities of our symbol systems to solve them. That situation may change, but until it does, we must rely upon empirical explorations, using the best problem solvers we know how to build, as a principal source of knowledge about the magnitude and characteristics of problem difficulty. Even in highly structured areas like linear programming, theory has been much more useful in strengthening the heuristics that underlie the most powerful solution algorithms than in providing a deep analysis of complexity.

3.3 Intelligence Without Much Search

Our analysis of intelligence equated it with ability to extract and use information about the structure of the problem space, so as to enable a problem solution to be generated as quickly and directly as possible. New directions for improving the problem-solving capabilities of symbol systems can be equated, then, with new ways of extracting and using information. At least three such ways can be identified.

3.3.1 Nonlocal Use of Information

First, it has been noted by several investigators that information gathered in the course of tree search is usually only used *locally*, to help make decisions at the specific node where the information was generated. Information about a chess position, obtained by dynamic analysis of a subtree of continuations, is usually used to evaluate just that position, not to evaluate other positions that may contain many of the same features. Hence, the same facts have to be rediscovered repeatedly at different nodes of the search tree. Simply to take the information out of the context in which it arose and use it generally does not solve the problem, for the information may be valid only in a limited range of contexts. In recent years, a few exploratory efforts have been made to transport information from its context of origin to other appropriate contexts. While it is still too early to evaluate the power of this idea, or even exactly how it is to be achieved, it shows considerable promise. An important line of investigation that Berliner (1975) has been pursuing is to use causal analysis to determine the range over which a particular piece of information is valid. Thus if a weakness in a chess position can be traced back to the move that made it, then the same weakness can be expected in other positions descendant from the same move.

The HEARSAY speech understanding system has taken another approach to making information globally available. That system seeks to recognize speech strings by pursuing a parallel search at a number of different levels: phonemic, lexical, syntactic, and semantic. As each of these searches provides and evaluates hypotheses, it supplies the information it has gained to a common "blackboard" that can be read by all the sources. This shared information can be used, for example, to eliminate hypotheses, or even whole classes of hypotheses, that would otherwise have to be searched by one of the processes. Thus, increasing our ability to use tree-search information nonlocally offers promise for raising the intelligence of problem-solving systems.

3.3.2 Semantic Recognition Systems

A second active possibility for raising intelligence is to supply the symbol system with a rich body of semantic information about the task domain it is dealing with. For example, empirical research on the skill of chess masters shows that a major source of the master's skill is stored information that enables him to recognize a large number of specific features and patterns of features on a chess board, and information that uses this recognition to propose actions appropriate to the features recognized. This general idea has, of course, been incorporated in chess programs almost from the beginning. What is new is the realization of the number of such patterns and associated information that may have to be stored for master-level play: something of the order of 50,000.

The possibility of substituting recognition for search arises because a particular, and especially a rare, pattern can contain an enormous amount of information, provided that it is closely linked to the structure of the problem space. When that structure is "irregular," and not subject to simple mathematical description, then knowledge of a large number of relevant patterns may be the key to intelligent behavior. Whether this is so in any particular task domain is a question more easily settled by empirical investigation than by theory. Our experience with symbol systems richly endowed with semantic information and pattern-recognizing capabilities for accessing it is still extremely limited. The discussion above refers specifically to semantic information associated with a recognition system. Of course, there is also a whole large area of AI research on semantic information processing and the organization of semantic information of semantic memories that falls outside the scope of the topics we are discussing in this chapter.

3.3.3 Selecting Appropriate Representations

A third line of inquiry is concerned with the possibility that search can be reduced or avoided by selecting an appropriate problem space. A standard example that illustrates this possibility dramatically is the mutilated checkerboard problem. A standard 64 square checkerboard can be covered exactly with 32 tiles, each 1 x 2 rectangle covering exactly two squares. Suppose, now, that we cut off squares at two diagonally opposite corners of the checkerboard, leaving a total of 62 squares. Can this mutilated board be covered exactly with 31 tiles? With (literally) heavenly patience, the impossibility of achieving such a covering can be demonstrated by trying all possible arrangements. The alternative, for those with less patience, and more intelligence, is to observe that the two diagonally opposite corners of a checkerboard are of the same color. Hence, the mutilated checkerboard has two less squares of one color than of the other. But each tile covers one square of one color and one square of the other, and any set of tiles must cover the same number of squares of each color. Hence, there is no solution. How can a symbol system discover this simple inductive argument as an alternative to a hopeless attempt to solve the problem by search among all possible coverings? We would award a system that found the solution high marks for intelligence.

Perhaps, however, in posing this problem we are not escaping from search processes. We have simply displaced the search from a space of possible problem solutions to a space of possible representations. In any event, the whole process of moving from one representation to another, and of discovering and evaluating representations, is largely unexplored territory in the domain of problem-solving research. The laws of qualitative structure governing representations remain to be discovered. The search for them is almost sure to receive considerable attention in the coming decade.

4. Conclusion

That is our account of symbol systems and intelligence. It has been a long road from Plato's *Meno* to the present, but it is perhaps encouraging that most of the progress along that road has been made since the turn of the twentieth century, and a large fraction of it since the midpoint of the century. Thought was still wholly intangible and ineffable until modern formal logic interpreted it as the manipulation of formal tokens. And it seemed still to inhabit mainly the heaven of Platonic ideals, or the equally obscure spaces of the human mind, until computers taught us how symbols could be processed by machines. A. M. Turing, whom we memorialize this morning, made his great contributions at the mid-century crossroads of these developments that led from modern logic to the computer.

4.1 Physical Symbol Systems

The study of logic and computers has revealed to us that intelligence resides in physical symbol systems. This is computer science's most basic law of qualitative structure.

Symbol systems are collections of patterns and processes, the latter being capable of producing, destroying and modifying the former. The most important properties of patterns is that they can designate objects, processes, or other patterns, and that, when they designate processes, they can be interpreted. Interpretation means carrying out the designated process. The two most significant classes of symbol systems with which we are acquainted are human beings and computers.

Our present understanding of symbol systems grew, as indicated earlier, through a sequence of stages. Formal logic familiarized us with symbols, treated syntactically, as the raw material of thought, and with the idea of manipulating them according to carefully defined formal processes. The Turing machine made the syntactic processing of symbols truly machine-like, and affirmed the potential universality of strictly defined symbol systems. The stored-program concept for computers reaffirmed the interpretability of symbols, already implicit in the Turing machine. List processing brought to the forefront the denotational capacities of symbols, and defined symbol processing in ways that allowed independence from the fixed structure of the underlying physical machine. By 1956 all of these concepts were available, together with hardware for implementing them. The study of the intelligence of symbol systems, the subject of artificial intelligence, could begin.

4.2 Heuristic Search

A second law of qualitative structure for AI is that symbol systems solve problems by generating potential solutions and testing them, that is, by searching. Solutions are usually sought by creating symbolic expressions and modifying them sequentially until they satisfy the conditions for a solution. Hence symbol systems solve problems by searching. Since they have finite resources, the search cannot be carried out all at once, but must be sequential. It leaves behind it either a single path from starting point to goal or, if correction and backup are necessary, a whole tree of such paths.

Symbol systems cannot appear intelligent when they are surrounded by pure chaos. They exercise intelligence by extracting information from a problem domain and using that information to guide their search, avoiding wrong turns and circuitous bypaths. The problem domain must contain information, that is, some degree of order and structure, for the method to work. The paradox of the *Meno* is solved by the observation that information may be remembered, but new information may also be extracted from the domain that the symbols designate. In both cases, the ultimate source of the information is the task domain.

4.3 The Empirical Base

Artificial intelligence research is concerned with how symbol systems must be organized in order to behave intelligently. Twenty years of work in the area has accumulated a considerable body of knowledge, enough to fill several books (it already has), and most of it in the form of rather concrete experience about the behavior of specific classes of symbol systems in specific task domains. Out of this experience, however, there have also emerged some generalizations, cutting across task domains and systems, about the general characteristics of intelligence and its methods of implementation.

We have tried to state some of these generalizations in this chapter. They are mostly qualitative rather than mathematical. They have more the flavor of geology or evolutionary biology than the flavor of theoretical physics. They are sufficiently strong to enable us today to design and build moderately intelligent systems for a considerable range of task domains, as well as to gain a rather deep understanding of how human intelligence worked in many situations.

4.4 What Next?

In this account, we have mentioned open questions as well as settled ones; there are many of both. We see no abatement of the excitement of exploration that has surrounded this field over the past quarter century. Two resource limits will determine the rate of progress over the next such period. One is the amount of computing power that will be available. The second, and probably the more important, is the number of talented young computer scientists who will be attracted to this area of research as the most challenging they can tackle.

A. M. Turing concluded his famous paper on "Computing Machinery and Intelligence" with the words: "We can only see a short distance ahead, but we can see plenty there that needs to be done."

Many of the things Turing saw in 1950 that needed to be done have been done, but the agenda is as full as ever. Perhaps we read too much into his simple statement above, but we like to think that in it Turing recognized the fundamental truth that all computer scientists instinctively know. For all physical symbol systems, condemned as we are to serial search of the problem environment, the critical question is always: What to do next?

Postscript: Reflections on the Tenth Turing Award Lecture

Our Turing Award lecture was given in 1975, two decades after the beginnings of artificial intelligence in the mid-fifties. Another decade has now passed. The lecture mostly avoided prophecy and agenda building, choosing rather to assert a verity—that computer science is an empirical science. It did that by looking backward at the development of two general principles that underlie the theory of intelligent action—the requirements for physical symbol systems and for search. It might be interesting to ask whether the intervening decade has added to or subtracted from the stance and assessments set forth then.

A lot has happened in that decade. Both computer science and artificial intelligence have continued to grow, scientifically, technologically, and economically. A point implicit but deliberate in the lecture was that artificial intelligence is a part of computer science, both rising from the same intellectual ground. Social history has continued to follow logic here (it does not always do so), and artificial intelligence continues to be a part of computer science. If anything, their relations are becoming increasingly intimate as the application of intelligent systems to software engineering in the guise of expert systems becomes increasingly attractive.

The main point about empirical inquiry is reflected throughout computer science. A lot has happened everywhere, but let us focus on artificial intelligence. The explosion of work in expert systems, the developments in learning systems, and the work on intelligent tutoring provide significant examples of areas that have blossomed since the lecture (and received no recognition in it). All of them have been driven by empirical inquiry in the strongest way. Even the emergence of the work on logic programming, which is an expression of the side of artificial intelligence that is most strongly identified with formal procedures and theorem proving, has attained much of its vitality from being turned into a programming enterprise—in which, thereby, experience leads the way.

There have, of course, been significant developments of theory. Particularly pertinent to the content of our lecture has been work in the complexity analysis of heuristic search, as exemplified in the recent book by Pearl (1984). But this too illustrates the standard magic cycle of science, where theory finally builds up when analyzed experience has sufficiently accumulated. We are still somewhat shy of closing that cycle by getting theory to the point where it provides the routine framework within which further experience is planned so that henceforth data and theory go hand in hand. That time will surely come, although it is still a little distant.

We chose the forum of an award lecture to give voice to two fundamental principles (about symbols and search) that seemed to us to be common currency in the practice and understanding of artificial intelligence, but which needed to be recognized for what they were—the genuine foundations of intelligent action. Their histories in the meantime have been somewhat different, though both remain on paths we interpret as supporting their essential correctness.

Bringing to the fore the physical symbol system hypothesis has proved useful to the field, although we did find it worthwhile subsequently to set out the hypothesis in more detail (Newell 1980). The hypothesis is taken rather generally to express the view of mind that has arisen from the emergence of the computer. However, that does not mean it is not controversial. There remain intellectual positions that stand outside the entire computational view and regard the hypothesis as undoubtedly false (Dreyfus 1979, Searle 1980). More to the point are two other positions. One is found among the philosophers, many of whom believe that the central problem of semantics or intentionality—how symbols signify their external referents—is not addressed by physical symbol systems. The other position is found among some of the connectionists within artificial intelligence and cognitive science, who believe there are forms of processing organization (wrought in the image of neural systems) that will accomplish all that symbol systems do, but in which symbols will not be identifiable entities. In both cases more investigation is clearly needed and will no doubt be forthcoming. The case for symbols still seems clear to us, so our bets remain on the side of the symbol system hypothesis.

A development related to the physical symbol system hypothesis is worth noting. It is the practice in computer science and artificial intelligence to describe systems simply in terms of the knowledge they have, presuming that there exist processing mechanisms that will cause the system to behave as if it could use the knowledge to attain the purposes the system is supposed to serve. This practice extends to design, where stipulating the knowledge a system is to have is a specification for what mechanisms are to be constructed. We took an opportunity, analogous to that of the Turing Award, namely, the presidential address of the American Association for Artificial Intelligence (AAAI), to also cast this.practice in crisp terms (Newell 1982). We defined another computer-system level above the symbol level, called the knowledge level. This corresponds pretty clearly to what Dan Dennett in philosophy had come to call the intentional stance (Dennett 1978). Its roots, of course, lie in that remarkable characteristic of adaptive systems that they behave solely as a function of the task environment, hiding therewith the nature of their internal mechanisms (Newell 1972, Simon 1969). Again, our motives in identifying the knowledge level were the same as in the Turing Award lecture— to articulate what every good computer-science practitioner knows in a form that admits further technical expansion. There are some small signs that this expansion is beginning for the knowledge level (Levesque 1984).

Turning to the second hypothesis, that of heuristic search, recognition of its importance was explicit and abundant in the early years of artificial intelligence. Our aim in the Turing Award lecture was to emphasize that search is essential to all intelligent action, rather than just one interesting mechanism among many. As it happened, the year of the lecture, 1975, just preceded the efflorescence of the view that knowledge is of central importance to intelligence. The trend had been building from the early 1970s. The sign of this new view was the emergence of the field of expert systems and the new role of the knowledge engineer (Feigenbaum 1977). The exuberance of this movement can be seen in the assertion that there had been a paradigm shift in artificial intelligence, which had finally abandoned search and would henceforth embrace knowledge as its guiding principle (Goldstein and Papert 1977).

An alternative interpretation (and the one we hold) is that no revolution occurred, but something more akin to the cycle of accommodation, assimilation, and equilibration that Piaget describes as the normal process of development (although he was talking of children and not scientific fields). Science works by expanding each new facet of understanding as it emerges—it accommodates to new understanding by an extended preoccupation to assimilate it. The late 1970s and early 1980s were devoted to exploring what it meant for systems to have enough knowledge about their task to dispense with much search of the problem space, and yet to do tasks that demanded intelligence, as opposed to just implementing small algorithms. (As the amount of knowledge increased, of course, these systems did require search of the rules in the knowledge base.) Concomitantly, the tasks performed by these systems, although taken from the real world, were also of little intellectual (i.e., inferential) difficulty. The role of search in difficult intellectual tasks remained apparent to those who continued to work on programs to accomplish them—it is hard to avoid when the threat of combinatorial explosion lurks around every corner. Having now assimilated some of the mechanisms for bringing substantial amounts of knowledge to bear, the field seems to have reached an understanding that both search and knowledge play an essential role.

A last reflection concerns chess, which runs like a thread through the whole lecture, providing (as it always does) clear examples for many points. The progress of a decade is apparent in the current art, where the Hitech chess machine (Berliner and Ebeling 1986) has now attained high master ratings (2340, where masters range from 2200 to 2400). It is still climbing, although no one knows how long it can continue to rise. Hitech, itself, illustrates many things. First, it brings home the role of heuristic search. Second, it is built upon massive search (200,000 positions a second) so that it shows that progress has moved in exactly the direction we asserted in the lecture to be wrong. It is fun to be wrong, when the occasion is one of new scientific knowledge. But third, the basic theoretical lesson from the machine is still the one emphasized in the lecture: namely, intelligent behavior involves the interplay of knowledge obtained through search and knowledge obtained from stored recognitional structure. For the last 200 points of Hitech's improvement—and the gains that have propelled it to fame—have come entirely from the addition of knowledge to a machine with fixed, albeit large, search capabilities. Fourth and finally, the astounding performance of Hitech and the new phenomena it generates bears witness once more, if more is needed, that progress in computer science and artificial intelligence occurs by empirical inquiry.

Acknowledgment

The authors research over the years have been supported in part by the Advanced Research Projects Agency of the Department of Defense (monitored by the Air Force Office of Scientific Research) and in part by the National Institutes of Mental Health.

PART TWO

Knowledge Representation

To build a computational account of intelligence requires a specification language along with an associated set of search algorithms. Representation and search are usually tightly coupled in that the commitment to one determines limits for the other. AI workers often call the selection of entities from a problem domain for representation the *ontology* of the modeling process and the choices for representation/search mechanisms offer an *inductive bias* for problem solving analysis.

The wealth of programming skill and ontological analysis within the AI community is no better seen than in the various representations proposed for intelligent problem solving. Part II presents a broad introduction to these representational mechanisms, many of which are presented by their original designers. These representations include rules, semantic networks, frames, conceptual dependencies, connectionist networks, and genetic algorithms. It is only appropriate that the final chapter questions the need for ANY explicit representational scheme for intelligence!

In the first chapter, Newell describes *The Knowledge Level* problem representation. Newell's analysis is built on years of use of a production system accounting of behavior in their Carnegie Mellon research labs (Newell & Simon 1972). This work is a precursor of the SOAR architecture (Newell 1990).

During the late 1970s and 1980s there was a strong movement away from rules and predicate logic as a representation language. We present both sides of this controversy, Hayes's *In Defense of Logic* (Chapter 10) is contrasted with Minsky's *Framework for Representing Knowledge* (Chapter 6) and Collins & Quillian's semantic network analyses (Chapter 7). Winograd and

Schank (Chapters 8 and 9) add their comments to this controversy.

Winograd, in Chapter 8, proposes a procedural representation for natural language analysis. Winograd uses explicit domain representation for disambiguation of language queries and pronoun reference. His procedural approach proved an important starting point for much of the AI natural language analysis of the subsequent twenty years.

Also working in the area of natural language understanding, Schank proposes conceptual dependency theory (Chapter 9) to reflect the semantic meaning in language structures. Schank proposes scripts to represent the meaning of typical event sequences, such as going to a restaurant or attending a birthday party.

Even more diverse representational proposals are made by Holland in Chapter 11 with classifier systems based on genetic algorithms. Holland suggests simple bit level representations with search based on genetic operators, including mutation and crossover, producing new offspring at any generation that are then selected for their fitness. Descendents of Holland's original research include the extension of classifier systems and the study of emergent computation.

McClelland, Rumelhardt, & Hinton (Chapter 12) propose a parallel distributed processing approach to problem solving. Their paradigm is sometimes called *subsymbolic representation,* or *connectionism.* Rumelhardt & McClelland's two volume presentation (1986) was pivotal in calling attention to connectionist approaches, first suggested in AI's earliest years (McCulloch & Pitts 1943, Rosenblatt 1958). Many new research initiatives now use connectionist systems to model perception, language, and learning.

In the final chapter of Part II, Brooks proposes that intelligence may indeed not require any a priori representational commitment. Brooks suggests that the phenomena of intelligence emerges as an artifact of societies of interactive individually determined entities. Brooks approach has led to a number of researchers rethinking the representational aspects of intelligence and with proposals such as distributed semi-autonomous agents whose combined interactions produce intelligent behavior (Agre, Ch 28).

There are a number of other important readings supporting the issues and possible answers of Part II. Especially important is Bartlett's (1932) description of psychological phenomena supporting frame and schema based representations, Woods (1985) questioning of the ontology often implicit in creating semantic nets, and McCarthy's (1977, 1980) continued argument regarding the essential role of logic in AI representations.

A number of computer languages, quite often reflecting representational commitments, emerged during the 1960-1980 time period. Papers on these issues include Lisp and McCarthy's (1960) *Recursive Functions of Symbolic Expressions and their Computation by Machine,* logic programming with PROLOG and Kowalski's (1979) *Logic for Problem Solving,* and Bobrow and Winograd's (1977) creation of KRL, a knowledge representation language that integrated procedural specifications with a richly structured declarative semantics.

5

The Knowledge Level

Allen Newell

1. Introduction

This is the first presidential address of AAAI, the American Association for Artificial Intelligence.[1,2] In the grand scheme of history, even the history of artificial intelligence (AI), this is surely a minor event. The field this scientific society represents has been thriving for quite some time. No doubt the society itself will make solid contributions to the health of our field. But it is too much to expect a presidential address to have a major impact.

So what is the role of the presidential address and what is the significance of the first one? I believe its role is to set a tone, to provide an emphasis. I think the role of the *first* address is to take a stand about what that tone and emphasis should be, to set expectations for future addresses and to communicate to my fellow presidents.

Only two foci are really possible for a presidential address: the state of the society or the state of the science. I believe the latter to be the correct focus. AAAI itself, its nature and its relationship to the larger society that surrounds it, are surely important.[3] However, our main business is to help AI become a science—albeit a science with a strong engineering flavor. Thus, though a president's address cannot be narrow or highly technical, it can certainly address a substantive issue. That is what I propose to do.

I wish to address the question of knowledge and representation. That is a little like a physicist wishing to address the question of radiation and matter. Such broad terms designate a whole arena of phenomena and a whole armada of questions. But comprehensive treatment is neither possible nor intended. Rather, such broad phrasing indicates an intent to deal with the subject in some basic way. Thus, the first task is to make clear the aspect of knowledge and representation of concern, namely, what is the nature of knowledge. The second task will be to outline an answer to this question. As the title indicates I will propose the existence of something called the *knowledge level.* The third task will be to describe the knowledge level in as much detail as time and my own understanding permits. The final task will be to indicate some consequences of the existence of a knowledge level for various aspects of AI.

2. The Problem of Representation and Knowledge

2.1 The Standard View

Two orthogonal and compatible basic views of the enterprise of AI serve our field, beyond all theoretical quibbles. The first is a geography of task areas. There is puzzle solving, theorem proving, game-playing, induction, natural language, medical diagnosis, and on and on, with subdivisions of each major territory. AI, in this view, is an exploration, in breadth and in depth, of new territories of tasks with their new patterns of intellectual demands. The second view is the functional components that comprise an intelligent system. There is a perceptual system, a memory system, a processing system, a motor system, and so on. It is this second view that we need to consider to address the role of representation and knowledge.

Figure 1 shows one version of the functional view, taken from Newell and Simon (1972), neither better nor worse than many others. An intelligent agent is embedded in a *task environment;* a *task statement* enters via a *perceptual* component and is encoded in an initial *representation.* Whence starts a cycle of activity in which a recognition occurs (as indicated by the eyes) of a method to use to attempt the problem. The method draws upon a memory of *general world knowledge.* In the course of such cycles, new methods and new representations may occur, as the agent attempts to solve the problem. The *goal structure,* a component we all believe to be important, does not receive its due in this figure, but no matter. Such a picture represents a convenient and stable decomposition of the *functions* to be performed by an intelli-

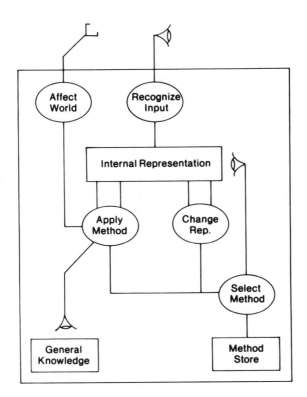

Figure 1. Functional diagram of general intelligent agent (after Newell and Simon [1972]).

gent agent, quite independent of particular implementations and anatomical arrangements. It also provides a convenient and stable decomposition of the entire scientific field into subfields. Scientists specialize in perception, or problem solving methods, or representation, etc.

It is clear to us all what *representation* is in this picture. It is the data structures that hold the problem and will be processed into a form that makes the solution available. Additionally, it is the data structures that hold the world knowledge and will be processed to acquire parts of the solution or to obtain guidance in constructing it. The first data structures represent the problem, the second represent world knowledge.

A data structure by itself is impotent, of course. We have learned to take the representation to include the basic operations of reading and writing, of access and construction. Indeed, as we know, it is possible to take a pure process view of the representation and work entirely in terms of the inputs and outputs to the read and write processes, letting the data structure itself fade into a mythical story we tell ourselves to make the memory-dependent behavior of the read and write processes coherent.

We also understand, though not so transparently, why the representation represents. It is because of the totality of procedures that process the data structure. They transform it in ways consistent with an interpretation of the data structure as representing something. We often express this by saying that a data structure requires an *interpreter,* including in that term much more than just the basic read/write processes, namely, the whole of the active system that uses the data structure.

The term *representation* is used clearly (almost technically) in AI and computer science. In contrast, the term *knowledge* is used informally, despite its prevalence in such phrases as knowledge engineering and knowledge sources. It seems mostly a way of referring to whatever it is that a representation has. If a system has (and can use) a data structure which can be said to represent something (an object, a procedure, ... whatever), then the system itself can also be said to have knowledge, namely the knowledge embodied in that representation about that thing.

2.2 Why Is There a Problem?

This seems to be a reasonable picture, which is serving us well. Why then is there a problem? Let me assemble some contrary indicators from our current scene.

A first indicator comes from our continually giving to representation a somewhat magical role.[4] It is a cliche of AI that representation is the *real* issue we face. Though we have programs that search, it is said, we do not have programs that determine their own representations or invent new representations. There is of course some substance to such statements. What is indicative of underlying difficulties is our inclination to treat representation like a *homunculus,* as the locus of *real* intelligence.

A good example is our fascination with problems such as the *mutilated checkboard* problem (Newell 1965). The task is to cover a checkboard with two-square dominoes. This is easy enough to do with the regular board and clearly impossible to do if a single square is removed, say from the upper right corner. The problem is to do it on a (mutilated) board which has two squares removed, one from each of two opposite corners. This task also turns out to be impossible. The actual task, then, is to show the impossibility. This goes from apparently intractable combinatorially, if the task is represented as all ways of laying down dominoes, to transparently easy, if the task is represented as just the *numbers* of black and white squares that remain to be covered. Now, the crux for AI is that no one has been able to formulate in a reasonable way the problem of finding the good representation, so it can be tackled by an AI system. By implication—so goes this view—the capability to invent such appropriate representations requires intelligence of some new and different kind.

A second indicator is the great theorem-proving controversy of the late sixties and early seventies. Everyone in AI has some knowledge of it, no doubt, for its residue is still very much with us. It needs only brief recounting.

Early work in theorem proving programs for quantified logics culminated in 1965 with Alan Robinson's development of a machine-oriented formulation of first-order logic called *Resolution* (Robinson 1965). There followed an immensely productive period of exploration of resolution-based theorem-proving. This was fueled, not only by technical advances, which occurred rapidly and on a broad front (Loveland 1978), but also by the view that we had a general purpose reasoning engine in hand and that doing logic (and doing it well) was a foundation stone of all intelligent action. Within about five years, however, it became clear that this basic engine was not going to be powerful enough to prove theorems that are hard on a human scale, or to move beyond logic to mathematics, or to serve other sorts of problem solving, such as robot planning.

A reaction set in, whose slogan was "uniform procedures will not work." This reaction itself had an immensely positive outcome in driving forward the development of the second generation of AI languages: Planner, Microplanner, QA4, Conniver, POP2, etc. (Bobrow and Raphael 1974). These unified some of the basic mechanisms in problem solving—goals, search, pattern matching, and global data bases—into a programming language framework, with its attendant gains of involution.

However, this reaction also had a negative residue, which still exists today, well after these new AI languages have come and mostly gone, leaving their own lessons. The residue in its most stereotyped form is that logic is a bad thing for AI. The stereotype is not usually met with in pure form, of course. But the mat of opinion is woven from a series of strands that amount to as much: uniform proof techniques have been proven grossly inadequate; the failure of resolution theorem proving implicates logic generally; logic IS permeated with a static view, and logic does not permit control. Any doubts about the reality of this residual reaction can be stilled by reading Pat Hayes's attempt to counteract it in Hayes (1977).

A third indicator is the recent SIGART "Special issue of knowledge representation" (Brachman and Smith 1980). This consisted of the answers (plus analysis) to an elaborate questionnaire developed by Ron Brachman of BBN and Brian Smith of MIT, which was sent to the AI research community working on knowledge representation. In practice, this meant work in natural language, semantic nets, logical formalisms for representing knowledge, and in the third generation of programming and representation systems, such as AIMDS, KRL, and KLONE. The questionnaire not only covered the basic demography of the projects and systems, but also the position of the respondent (and his system) on many critical issues of representation—quantification, quotation, self-description, evaluation vs. reference-finding, and so on.

The responses were massive, thoughtful and thorough, which was impressive given that the questionnaire took well over an hour just to read, and that answers were of the order of ten single-spaced pages. A substantial fraction of the field received coverage in the 80 odd returns since many of them represented entire projects. Although the questionnaire left much to be desired in terms of the precision of its questions, the *Special Issue* still provides an extremely interesting glimpse of how AI sees the issues of knowledge representation. The main result was overwhelming diversity—a veritable jungle of opinions. There was no consensus on any question of substance. Brachman and Smith themselves highlight this throughout the issue, for it came as a major surprise to them. Many (but of course not all!) respondents themselves felt the same way. As one said, "Standard practice in the representation of knowledge is the scandal of AI."

What is so overwhelming about the diversity is that it defies characterization. The role of logic and theorem proving, just described above, are in evidence but there is much else besides. There is no tidy space of underlying issues in which respondents, hence the field, can be plotted to reveal a pattern of concerns or issues. Not that Brachman and Smith could see. Not that this reader could see.

2.3 A Formulation of the Problem

These three items—mystification of the role of representation, the residue of the theorem-proving controversy, and the conflicting webwork of opinions on knowledge representation—are sufficient to indicate that our views on representation and knowledge are not in satisfactory shape. However, they hardly indicate a crisis, much less a scandal. At least not to me. Science easily inhabits periods of diversity; it tolerates bad lessons from the past in concert with good ones. The chief signal these three send is that we must redouble our efforts to bring some clarity to the area. Work on knowledge and representation should be a priority item on the agenda of our science.

No one should have any illusions that clarity and progress will be easy to achieve. The diversity that is represented in the SIGART special issue is highly articulate and often highly principled. Viewed from afar, any attempt to clarify the issues is simply one more entry into the cacophony—possibly treble, possibly bass, but in any case a note whose first effect will be to increase dissonance, not diminish it.

Actually, these indicators send an ambiguous signal. An alternative view of such situations in science is that effort is premature. Only muddling can happen for the next while—until more evidence accumulates or conceptions ripen elsewhere in AI to make evident patterns that now seem only one possibility among many. Work should be left to those already committed to the area; the rest of us should make progress where progress can clearly be made.

Still, though not compelled, I wish to have a go at this problem.

I wish to focus attention on the question: *What is knowledge?* In fact, knowledge gets very little play in the three indicators just presented. Representation occupies center stage, with logic in the main supporting role. I could claim that this is already the key—that the conception of knowledge is logically prior to that of representation, and until a clear conception of the former exists, the latter will remain confused. In fact, this is not so. Knowledge is simply one particular entry point to the whole tangled knot. Ultimately, clarity will be attained on all these notions together. The path through which this is achieved will be grist for those interested in the history of science, but is unlikely to affect our final understanding.

To reiterate: What is the nature of knowledge? How is it related to representation? What is it that a system has, when it has knowledge? Are we simply dealing with redundant terminology, not unusual in natural language, which is better replaced by building on the notions of data structures, interpreters, models (in the strict sense used in logic), and the like? I think not. I think knowledge is a distinct notion, with its own part to play in the nature of intelligence.

2.4 The Solution Follows from Practice

Before starting on matters of substance, I wish to make a methodological point. The solution I will propose follows from the practice of AI. Although the formulation I present may have some novelty, it should be basically familiar to you, for it arises from how we in AI treat knowledge in our work with intelligent systems. Thus, your reaction may (perhaps even should) be "But that is just the way I have been thinking about knowledge all along. What is this man giving me?" On the first part, you are right. This is indeed the way AI has come to use the concept of knowledge. However, this is not the way the rest of the world uses the concept. On the second part, what I am giving you is a directive that your practice represents an important source of knowledge about the nature of intelligent systems. It is to be taken seriously.

This point can use expansion. Every science develops its own ways of finding out about its subject matter. These get tidied up in metamodels about scientific activity, e.g., the so called *scientific method* in the experimental sciences. But these are only models; in reality, there is immense diversity in how scientific progress is made.

For instance, in computer science many fundamental conceptual advances occur by (scientifically) uncontrolled experiments in our own style of computing.[5] Three excellent examples are the developments of time-sharing, packet switched networks, and locally-networked personal computing. These are major conceptual advances that have broadened our view of the nature of computing. Their primary validation is entirely informal. Scientific activity of a more traditional kind certainly takes place—theoretical development with careful controlled testing and evaluation of results. But it happens on the details, not on the main conceptions. Not everyone understands the necessary scientific role of such experiments in computational living, nor that standard experimental techniques cannot provide the same information. How else to explain, for example, the calls for controlled experimental validation that speech understanding will be useful to computer science? When that experiment of style is finally performed there will be no doubt at all. No standard experiment will be necessary. Indeed, none could have sufficed.

As an example related to the present chapter, I have spent some effort recently in describing what Herb Simon and I have called the "physical symbol system hypothesis" (Newell 1980, Newell and Simon 1976). This hypothesis identifies a class of systems as embodying the essential nature of symbols and as being the necessary and sufficient condition for a generally intelligent agent. Symbol systems turn out to be universal computational systems, viewed from a different angle. For my point here, the important feature of this hypothesis is that it grew out of the practice in AI—out of the development of list processing languages and Lisp, and out of the structure adopted in one AI program after another. We in AI were led to an adequate notion of a symbol by our practice. In the standard catechism of science, this is not how great ideas develop. Major ideas occur because great scientists discover (or invent) them, introducing them to the scientific community for testing and elaboration. But here, working scientists have evolved a new major scientific concept, under partial and alternative guises. Only gradually has it acquired its proper name.

The notions of knowledge and representation about to be presented also grow out of our practice. At least, so I assert. That does not give them immunity from criticism, for in listening for these lessons I may have a tin ear. But in so far as they are wanting, the solution lies in more practice and more attention to what emerges there as pragmatically successful. Of course, the message will be distorted by many things, e.g., peculiar twists in the evolution of computer science hardware and software, our own limitations of view, etc. But our practice remains a source of knowledge that cannot be obtained from anywhere else. Indeed, AI as a field is committed to it. If it is fundamentally flawed, that will just be too bad for us. Then, other paths will have to be found from elsewhere to discover the nature of intelligence.

3. The Knowledge Level

I am about to propose the existence of something called the knowledge level within which knowledge is to be defined. To state this clearly, requires first reviewing the notion of computer systems levels.

Aspects	Register-transfer level	Symbol level
Systems	Digital systems	Computers
Medium	Bit vectors	Symbols, expressions
Components	Registers	
	Functional units	Operations
Composition laws	Transfer path	Designation, association
Behavior laws	Logical operations	Sequential interpretation

Table 1. Defining aspects of a computer system level

3.1 Computer System Levels

Figure 2 shows the standard hierarchy, familiar to everyone in computer science. Conventionally, it starts at the bottom with the *device level,* then up to the *circuit level,* then the *logic level,* with its two sublevels, *combinatorial* and *sequential circuits,* and the *register-transfer level,* then the *program level* (referred to also as the *symbolic level)* and finally, at the top, the *configuration level* (also called the *PMS* or *processor-memory-switch level).* We have drawn the configuration level to one side, since it lies directly above both the symbol level and the register-transfer level.

The notion of levels occurs repeatedly throughout science and philosophy, with varying degrees of utility and precision. In computer science, the notion is quite precise and highly operational. Table 1 summarizes its essential attributes. A level consists of a *medium* that is to be processed, *components* that provide primitive processing, *laws of composition* that permit components to be assembled into systems, and *laws of behavior* that determine how system behavior depends on the component behavior and the structure of the system. There are many variant instantiations of a given level, e.g., many programming systems and machine languages and many register-transfer systems.[6]

Each level is defined in two ways. First, it can be defined autonomously, without reference to any other level. To an amazing degree, programmers need not know logic circuits, logic designers need not know electrical circuits, managers can operate at the configuration level with no knowledge of programming, and so forth. Second, each level can be reduced to the level below. Each aspect of a level—medium, components, laws of composition and behavior—can be defined in terms of systems at the level next below. The *architecture* is the name we give to the register-transfer level system that defines a symbol (programming) level, creating a machine language and making it run as described in the programmers manual for the machine. Neither of these two definitions of a level is the more fundamental. It is essential that they both exist and agree.

Some intricate relations exist between and within levels. Any instantiation

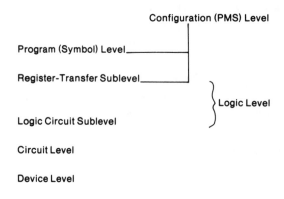

Figure 2. Computer system levels.

of a level can be used to create any instantiation of the next higher level. Within each level, systems hierarchies are possible, as in the subroutine hierarchy at the programming level. Normally, these do not add anything special in terms of the computer system hierarchy itself. However, as we all know, at the program level it is possible to construct any instantiation within any other instantiation (mudulo some rigidity in encoding one data structure into another), as in creating new programming languages.

There is no need to spin out the details of each level. We live with them every day and they are the stuff of architecture textbooks (Bell and Newell 1971), machine manuals and digital component catalogues, not research papers. However, it is noteworthy how radically the levels differ. The medium changes from electrons and magnetic domains at the device level, to current and voltage at the circuit level, to bits at the logic level (either single bits at the logic circuit level or bit vectors at the register-transfer level), to symbolic expressions at the symbol level, to amounts of data (measured in data bits) at the configuration level. System characteristics change from continuous to discrete processing, from parallel to serial operation, and so on.

Despite this variety, all levels share some common features. Four of these, though transparently obvious, are important to us.

Point 1. Specification of a system at a level always determines completely a definite behavior for the system at that level (given initial and boundary conditions).

Point 2. The behavior of the total system results from the local effects of each component of the system processing the medium at its inputs to produce its outputs.

Point 3. The immense variety of behavior is obtained by system structure, i.e., by the variety of ways of assembling a small number of component types (though perhaps a large number of instances of each type).

Point 4. The medium is realized by state-like properties of matter, which remain passive until changed by the components.

Computer systems levels are not simply levels of abstraction. That a system has a description at a given level does not necessarily imply it has a description at higher levels. There is no way to abstract from an arbitrary electronic circuit to obtain a logic-level system. There is no way to abstract from an arbitrary register-transfer system to obtain a symbol-level system. This contrasts with many types of abstraction which can be uniformly applied, and thus have a certain optional character (as in abstracting away from the visual appearance of objects to their masses). Each computer system level is a *specialization* of the class of systems capable of being described at the next lower level. Thus, it is a priori open whether a given level has any physical realizations.

In fact, computer systems at all levels are realizable, reflecting indirectly the structure of the physical world. But more holds than this. Computer systems levels are realized by *technologies*. The notion of a technology has not received the conceptual attention it deserves. But roughly, given a specification of a particular system at a level, it is possible to construct by *routine* means a physical system that realizes that specification. Thus, systems can be obtained to specification within limits of time and cost. It is not possible to invent arbitrarily additional computer system levels that nestle between existing levels. Potential levels do not become technologies, just by being thought up. Nature has a say in whether a technology can exist.

Computer system levels are *approximations.* All of the above notions are realized in the real world only to various degrees. Errors at lower levels propagate to higher ones, producing behavior that is not explicable within the higher level itself. Technologies are imperfect, with constraints that limit the size and complexity of systems that can actually be fabricated. These constraints are often captured in design rules (e.g., fan-out limits, stack-depth limits, etc.), which transform system design from routine to problem solving. If the complexities become too great, the means of system creation no longer constitute a technology, but an arena of creative invention.

We live quite comfortably with imperfect system levels, especially at the extremes of the hierarchy. At the bottom, the device level is not complete, being used only to devise components at the circuit level. Likewise, at the top, the configuration level is incomplete, not providing a full set of behavioral laws. In fact, it is more nearly a pure level of abstraction than a true system level. This accounts for both symbol level and register transfer level systems having configuration (PMS) level abstractions (see Bell, Grason, and Newell [1972] for a PMS approach to the register-transfer level).

These levels provide ways of describing computer systems; they do not provide ways of describing their environments. This may seem somewhat unsatisfactory, because a level does not then provide a general closed description of an entire universe, which is what we generally expect (and get) from a level of scientific description in physics or chemistry. However, the situation is understandable enough. System design and analysis requires only that the interface between the environment and the system (i.e., the inner side of the transducers) be adequately described in terms of each level, e.g., as electrical signals, bits, symbols or whatever. Almost never does the universe of system plus environment have to be modeled in toto, with the structure and dynamics of the environment described in the same terms as the system itself. Indeed, in general no such description of the environment in the terms of a given computer level exists. For instance, no register-transfer level description exists of the airplane in which an airborne computer resides. Computer system levels describe the internal structure of a particular class of systems, not the structure of a total world.

To sum up, computer system levels are a reflection of the nature of the physical world. They are not just a point of view that exists solely in the eye of the beholder. This reality comes from computer system levels being genuine specializations, rather than being just abstractions that can be applied uniformly.

3.2 A New Level

I now propose that there does exist yet another system level, which I will call the *knowledge level*. It is a true systems level, in the sense we have just reviewed. The thrust of this chapter is that distinguishing this level leads to a simple and satisfactory view of knowledge and representation. It dissolves some of the difficulties and confusions we have about this aspect of artificial intelligence.

A quick overview of the knowledge level, with an indication of some of its immediate consequences, is useful before entering into details.

The system at the knowledge level is the *agent*. The components at the knowledge level are *goals, actions,* and *bodies*. Thus, an agent is composed of a set of actions, a set of goals and a body. The medium at the knowledge level is *knowledge* (as might be suspected). Thus, the agent processes its knowledge to determine the actions to take. Finally, the behavior law is the *principle of rationality:* actions are selected to attain the agent's goals.

To treat a system at the knowledge level is to treat it as having some knowledge and some goals, and believing it will do whatever is within its power to attain its goals, in so far as its knowledge indicates. For example:

- "She knows where this restaurant is and said she'd meet me here. I don't know why she hasn't arrived."
- "Sure, he'll fix it. He knows about cars."
- "If you know that $2 + 2 = 4$, why did you write 5?"

The knowledge level sits in the hierarchy of systems levels immediately

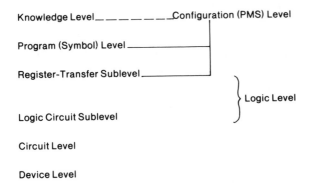

Figure 3. New version of computer system levels.

above the symbol level, as Figure 3 shows. Its components (actions, goals, body) and its medium (knowledge) can be defined in terms of systems at the symbol level, just as any level can be defined by systems at the level one below. The knowledge level has been placed side by side with the configuration level. The gross anatomical description of a knowledge-level system is simply (and only) that the agent has as parts bodies of knowledge, goals and actions. They are all connected together in that they enter into the determination of what actions to take. This structure carries essentially no information; the specification at the knowledge level is provided entirely by the content of the knowledge and the goals, not by any structural way they are connected together. In effect, the knowledge level can be taken to have a degenerate configuration level.

As is true of any level, although the knowledge level can be constructed from the level below (i.e., the symbol level), it also has an autonomous formulation as an independent level. Thus, knowledge can be defined independent of the symbol level, but can also be reduced to symbol systems.

As the Figure 3 makes evident, the knowledge level is a separate level from the symbol level. Relative to the existing view of the computer systems hierarchy, the symbol level has been split in two, one aspect remaining as the symbol level proper and another aspect becoming the knowledge level. The description of a system as exhibiting intelligent behavior still requires both levels, as we shall see. Intelligent systems are not to be described exclusively in terms of the knowledge level.

To repeat the final remark of the prior section: computer system levels really exist, as much as anything exists. They are not just a point of view. Thus, to claim that the knowledge level exists is to make a scientific claim, which can range from dead wrong to slightly askew, in the manner of all scientific claims. Thus, the matter needs to be put as a hypothesis:

The Knowledge Level Hypothesis: There exists a distinct computer systems level, lying immediately above the symbol level, which is characterized by knowledge as the medium and the principle of rationality as the law of behavior.

Some preliminary feeling for the nature of knowledge according to this hypothesis can be gained from the following remarks.

- Knowledge is intimately linked with rationality. Systems of which rationality can be posited can be said to have knowledge. It is unclear in what sense other systems can be said to have knowledge.

- Knowledge is a competence-like notion, being a potential for generating action.[7]

- The knowledge level is an approximation. Nothing guarantees how much of a system's behavior can be viewed as occurring at the knowledge level. Although extremely useful, the approximation is quite imperfect, not just in degree but in scope.

- Representations exist at the symbol level, being systems (data structures and processes) that realize a body of knowledge at the knowledge level.

- Knowledge serves as the specification of what a symbol structure should be able to do.

- Logics are simply one class of representations among many, though uniquely fitted to the analysis of knowledge and representation.

4. The Details of the Knowledge Level

We begin by defining the knowledge level autonomously, i.e., independently of lower system levels. Table 1 lists what is required, though we will take up the various aspects in a different order: first, the structure, consisting of the system, components and laws for composing systems; second, the laws of behavior (the law of rationality); and third, the medium (knowledge). After this we will describe how the knowledge level reduces to the symbol level.

Against the background of the common features of the familiar computer system levels listed earlier (Section 3.1), there will be four surprises in how the knowledge level is defined. These will stretch the notion of system level somewhat, but will not break it.

4.1 The Structure of the Knowledge Level

An agent (the system at the knowledge level), has an extremely simple structure, so simple there is no need even to picture it.

First, the agent has some *physical body* with which it can act in the environment (and be acted upon). We talk about the body as if it consists of a set of *actions,* but that is only for simplicity. It can be an arbitrary physical system with arbitrary modes of interaction with its environment. Though this body can be arbitrarily complex, its complexity lies external to the system described at the knowledge level, which simply has the power to evoke the behavior of this physical system.

Second, the agent has a body of knowledge. This body is like a memory. Whatever the agent knows at some time, it continues to know. Actions can add knowledge to the existing body of knowledge. However, in terms of structure, a body of knowledge is extremely simple compared to a memory, as defined at lower computer system levels. There are no structural constraints to the knowledge in a body, either in capacity (i.e., the amount of knowledge) or in how the knowledge is held in the body. Indeed, there is no notion of how knowledge is held (*encoding* is a notion at the symbol level, not knowledge level). Also, there are no well-defined structural properties associated with access and augmentation. Thus, it seems preferable to avoid calling the body of knowledge a memory. In fact, referring to a 'body of knowledge,' rather than just to 'knowledge,' is hardly more than a manner of speaking, since this body has no function except to be the physical component which has the knowledge.

Third, and finally, the agent has a *set of goals*. A goal is a body of knowledge of a state of affairs in the environment. Goals are structurally distinguished from the main body of knowledge. This permits them to enter into the behavior of the agent in a distinct way, namely, that which the organism strives to realize. But, except for this distinction, goal components are structurally identical to bodies of knowledge. Relationships exist between goals, of course, but these are not realized in the structure of the system, but in knowledge.

There are no laws of composition for building a knowledge level system out of these components. An agent always has just these components. They all enter directly into the laws of behavior. There is no way to build up complex agents from them.

This complete absence of significant structure in the agent is the first surprise, running counter to the common feature at all levels that variety of behavior is realized by variety of system structure (Section 3.1, Point 3). This is not fortuitous, but is an essential feature of the knowledge level. The focus for determining the behavior of the system rests with the knowledge, i.e., with the *content* of what is known. The internal structure of the system is defined exactly so that nothing need be known about it to predict the agent's behavior. The behavior is to depend only on what the agent knows, what it wants and what means it has for interacting physically with the environment.

4.2 The Principle of Rationality

The behavioral law that governs an agent, and permits prediction of its behavior, is the rational principle that knowledge will be used in the service of goals.[8] This can be formulated more precisely as follows:

Principle of rationality. If an agent has knowledge that one of its actions will lead to one of its goals, then the agent will select that action.

This principle asserts a connection between knowledge and goals, on the one hand, and the selection of actions on the other, without specification of any mechanism through which this connection is made. It connects all the components of the agent together directly.

This direct determination of behavior by a global principle is the second surprise, running counter to the common feature at all levels that behavior is determined bottom-up through the local processing of components (Section 3.1, Point 2). Such global principles are not incompatible with systems whose behavior is also describable by mechanistic causal laws, as testified by various global principles in physics, e.g., Fermat's principle of least time in geometrical optics, or the principle of least effort in mechanics. The principles in physics are usually optimization (i.e., extremum) principles. However, the principle of rationality does not have built into it any notion of optimal or best, only the automatic connection of actions to goals according to knowledge.

Under certain simple conditions, the principle as stated permits the calculation of a system's trajectory, given the requisite initial and boundary conditions (i.e., goals, actions, initial knowledge, and acquired knowledge as determined by actions). However, the principle is not sufficient to determine the behavior in many situations. Some of these situations can be covered by adding *auxiliary* principles. Thus, we can think of an extended principle of *rationality,* building out from the *central* or *main* principle, given above.

To formulate additional principles, the phrase *selecting an action* is taken to mean that the action becomes a member of a candidate set of actions, the *selected set,* rather than being the action that actually occurs. When all principles are taken into account, if only one action remains in the selected set, that action actually taken is determined; if several candidates remain, then the action actually taken is limited to these possibilities. An action can actually be taken only if it is physically possible, given the situation of the agent's body and the resources available. Such limits to action will affect the actions selected only if the agent has knowledge of them.

The main principle is silent about what happens if the principle applies for more than one action for a given goal. This can be covered by the following auxiliary principle.

Equipotence of acceptable actions. For given knowledge, if action A_1 and action A_2 both lead to goal G, then both actions are selected.[9]

This principle simply asserts that all ways of attaining the goal are equally acceptable from the standpoint of the goal itself. There is no implicit optimality principle that selects among such candidates.

The main principle is also silent about what happens if the principle applies to several goals in a given situation. A simple auxiliary principle is the following.

Preference of joint goal satisfaction. For given knowledge, if goal G_1 has the set of selected actions $\{A_{1,i}\}$ and goal G_2 has the set of selected actions $\{A_{2,j}\}$, then the elective set of selected actions is the intersection of $\{A_{1,i}\}$ and $\{A_{2,j}\}$.

It is better to achieve both of two goals than either alone. This principle determines behavior in many otherwise ambiguous situations. If the agent has general goals of minimizing effort, minimizing cost, or doing things in a simple way, these general goals select out a specific action from a set of otherwise equipotent task-specific actions.

However, this principle of joint satisfaction still goes only a little ways further towards obtaining a principle that will determine behavior in all situations. What if the intersection of selected action sets is null? What if there are several mutually exclusive actions leading to several goals? What if the attainment of two goals is mutually exclusive no matter through what actions they are attained? These types of situations too can be dealt with by extending the concept of a goal to include *goal preferences,* that is, specific preferences for one state of the affairs over another that are not grounded in knowledge of how these states differentially aid in reaching some common superordinate.

Even this extended principle of rationality does not cover all situations. The central principle refers to an action leading to a goal. In the real world it as often not clear whether an action will attain a specific goal. The difficulty is not just one of the possibility of error. The actual outcome may be truly probabilistic, or the action may be only the first step in a sequence that depends on other agents' moves, etc. Again, extensions exist to deal with uncertainty and risk, such as adopting expected value calculations and principles of minimizing maximum loss.

In proposing each of these solutions, I am not inventing anything. Rather, this growing extension of rational behavior moves along a well-explored path, created mostly by modern day game theory, econometrics and decision theory (Luce and Raiffa 1957, Von Neumann and Morgenstern 1947). It need not be retraced here. The exhibition of the first few elementary extensions can serve to indicate the total development to be taken in search of a principle of rationality that always determines the action to be taken.

Complete retracing is not necessary because the path does not lead, even ultimately, to the desired principle. No such principle exists.[10] Given an agent in the real world, there is no guarantee at all that his knowledge will determine which actions realize which goals. Indeed, there is no guarantee even that the difficulty resides in the incompleteness of the agent's knowledge. There need not exist any state of knowledge that would determine the action.

The point can be brought home by recalling Frank Stockton's famous short story, "The lady or the tiger?" (Stockton 1895). The upshot has the lover of a beautiful princess caught by the king. He now faces the traditional ordeal of judgment in this ancient and barbaric land: in the public arena he must choose to open one of two utterly indistinguishable doors. Behind one is a ferocious tiger and death; behind the other a lovely lady, life and marriage. Guilt or innocence is determined by fate. The princess alone, spurred by her love, finds out the secret of the doors on the night before the trial. To her consternation she finds that the lady behind the door is to be her chief rival in loveliness. On the judgment day, from her seat in the arena beside the king, she indicates by a barely perceptible nod which door her lover should open. He, in unhesitating faithfulness, goes directly to that door. The story ends with a question. Did the princess send her lover to the lady or the tiger?

Our knowledge-level model of the princess, even if it were to include her complete knowledge, would not tell us which she chose. But the failure of determinancy is not the model's. Nothing says that multiple goals need be compatible, nor that the incompatibility be resolvable by any higher principles. The dilemma belongs to the princess, not to the scientist attempting to formulate an adequate concept of the knowledge level. That she resolved it is clear, but that her behavior in doing so was describable at the knowledge level does not follow.

This failure to determine behavior uniquely is the third surprise, running counter to the common feature at all levels that a system is a determinate machine (Section 3.1, Point 1). A complete description of a system at the program, logic or circuit level yields the trajectory of the system's behavior over time, given initial and boundary conditions. This is taken to be one of its important properties, consistent with being the description of a deterministic (macro) physical system. Yet, *radical* incompleteness characterizes the knowledge level. Sometimes behavior can be predicted by the knowledge level description; often it cannot. The incompleteness is not just a failure in certain special situations or in some small departures. The term radical is used to indicate that entire ranges of behavior may not be describable at the knowledge level, but only in terms of systems at a lower level (namely, the symbolic level). However, the necessity of accepting this incompleteness is an essential aspect of this level.

4.3. The Nature of Knowledge

The ground is now laid to provide the definition of knowledge. As formulated so far, knowledge is defined to be the medium at the knowledge level, something to be processed according to the principle of rationality to yield behavior. We wish to elevate this into a complete definition:

> *Knowledge.* Whatever can be ascribed to an agent, such that its behavior can be computed according to the principle of rationality.

Knowledge is to be characterized entirely *functionally*, in terms of what it does, not structurally, in terms of physical objects with particular properties and relations. This still leaves open the requirement for a physical structure for knowledge that can fill the functional role. In fact, that key role is never filled directly. Instead, it is filled only indirectly and approximately by *symbol systems* at the next lower level. These are total systems, not just symbol structures. Thus, knowledge, though a medium, is embodied in no medium-like passive physical structure.

This failure to have the medium at the knowledge level be a statelike physical structure is the fourth surprise, running counter to the common feature at all levels of a passive medium (Section 3.1, Point 4). Again, it is an essential feature of the knowledge level, giving knowledge its special abstract and competence-like character. One can see on the blackboard a symbolic expression (say a list of theorem names). Though the actual seeing is a tad harder, yet there is still no difficulty seeing this same expression residing in a definite set of memory cells in a computer. The same is true at lower levels—the bit vectors at the register-transfer level—marked on the blackboard or residing in a register as voltages. Moreover, the medium at one level plus additional static structure defines the medium at the next level up. The bit plus its organization into registers provides the bit-vector; collections of bit vectors plus functional specialization to link fields, type fields, etc., defines the symbolic expression. All this fails at the knowledge level. The knowledge cannot so easily be seen, only imagined as the result of interpretive processes operating on symbolic expressions. Moreover, knowledge is not just a collection of symbolic expressions plus some static organization; it requires both processes and data structures.

The definition above may seem like a reverse, even perverse, way of defining knowledge. To understand it—to see how it works, why it is necessary, why it is useful, and why it is effective—we need to back off and examine the situation in which knowledge is used.

4.3.1 How It Works

Figure 4 shows the situation, which involves an observer and an agent. The observer treats the agent as a system at the knowledge level, i.e., ascribes knowledge and goals to it. Thus, the observer knows the agent's knowledge (K) and goals (G), along with his possible actions and his environment (these latter by direct observation, say). In consequence, the observer can make predictions of the agent's actions using the principle of rationality.

Assume the observer ascribes correctly, i.e., the agent behaves as if he has knowledge K and goals G. What the agent really has is a symbol system, S. that permits it to carry out the calculations of what actions it will take, because it has K and G (with the given actions in the given environment).

The observer is itself an agent, i.e., is describable at the knowledge level. There is no way in this theory of knowledge to have a system that is not an agent have knowledge or ascribe knowledge to another system. Hence, the

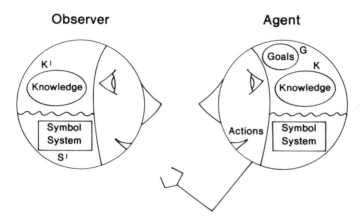

Figure 4. The situation in which knowledge is used.

observer has all this knowledge (i.e., K', consisting of knowledge K, knowledge that K is the agent's knowledge, knowledge G, knowledge that these are the agent's goals, knowledge of the agent's actions etc.). But what the observer really has, of course, is a symbol system, S', that lets it calculate actions on the basis of K, goals, etc., i.e., calculate what the agent would do if it had K and G.

Thus, as the figure shows, each agent (the observer and the observed) has knowledge by virtue of a symbol system that provides the ability to act as if it had the knowledge. The total system (i.e., the dyad of the observing and observed agents) runs without there being any physical structure that is the knowledge.

4.3.2 Why It Is Necessary

Even granting the scheme of Figure 4 to be possible, why cannot there simply be some physical structure that corresponds to knowledge? Why are not S and S' simply the knowledge? The diagram seems similar to what could be drawn between any two adjacent system levels, and in these other cases corresponding structures do exist at each level. For example, the medium at the symbol level (the symbolic expressions) corresponds to the medium at the register-transfer level (the bit vectors). The higher medium is simply a specialized use of the lower medium, but both are physical structures. The same holds when we descend from the register-transfer level (bit vectors) to the logic circuit level (single bits); the relationship is simply one of aggregation. Descending to the circuit level again involves specialization in which some feature of the circuit level medium (e.g., voltage) is taken to define the bit (e.g., a high and a low voltage level).

The answer in a nutshell is that knowledge of the world cannot be captured in a finite structure. The world is too rich and agents have too great a capability for responding.[11] Knowledge is about the world. Insofar as an agent can select actions based on some truth about the world, any candidate structure for knowledge must contain that truth. Thus knowledge as a structure must contain at least as much variety as the set of all truths (i.e., propositions) that the agent can respond to.

A representation of any fragment of the world (whether abstract or concrete), reveals immediately that the knowledge is not finite. Consider our old friend, the chess position. How many propositions can be stated about the position? For a given agent, only propositions need be considered that could materially affect an action of the agent relative to its goal. But given a reasonably intelligent agent who desires to win, the list of aspects of the position is unbounded. Can the Queen take the Pawn? Can it take the Pawn next move? Can it if the Bishop moves? Can it if the Rook is ever taken? Is a pin possible that will unblock the Rook attacker before a King side attack can be mounted? And so on.

A seemingly appropriate objection is: (1) the agent is finite so can't actually have an unbounded anything; and (2) the chess position is also just a finite structure. However, the objection fails, because it is not possible to state from afar (i.e., from the observer's viewpoint) a bound on the set of propositions about the position that will be available. Of course, if the observer had a model of the agent at the symbolic process level, then a (possibly accurate) prediction might be made. But the knowledge level is exactly the level that abstracts away from symbolic processes. Indeed, the way the observer determines what the agent might know is to consider what he (the observer) can find out. And this he cannot determine in advance.

The situation here is not really strange. The underlying phenomenon is the generative ability of computational systems, which involves an active process working on an initially given data structure. Knowledge is the posited extensive form of all that be obtained potentially from the process. This potential is unbounded when the details of processing are unknown and the gap is closed by assuming (from the principle of rationality) the processing to be whatever makes the correct selection. Of course, there are limits to this processing, namely, that it cannot go beyond the knowledge given.

What the computational system generates are selections of actions for goals conditioned on states of the world. Each such basic means-ends relation may be taken as an element of knowledge. To have the knowledge available in extension would be to have all these possible knowledge elements for all the goals, actions and states of the world discriminable to the agent at the given moment. The knowledge could then be thought of as a giant table full of these knowledge elements, but it would have to be an infinite table. Consequently, this knowledge (i.e., these elements) can only be created dynamical-

ly in time. If generated by some simple procedure, only relatively uninterest-
ing knowledge can be found. Interesting knowledge requires generating only
what is relevant to the task at hand, i.e., generating intelligently.

4.3.3 Why It Is Useful

The knowledge level permits predicting and understanding behavior without
having an operational model of the processing that is actually being done by
the agent. The utility of such a level would seem clear, given the widespread
need in life's affairs for distal prediction, and also the paucity of knowledge
about the internal workings of humans. (And animals, some of which are
usefully described at the knowledge level.) The utility is also clear in designing AI systems, where the internal mechanisms are still to be specified. To
the extent that AI systems successfully approximate rational agents, it is also
useful for predicting and understanding them. Indeed, the usefulness extends
beyond AI systems to all computer programs.

Prediction of behavior is not possible without knowing something about
the agent. However, what is known is not the processing structure, but the
agent's knowledge of its external environment, which is also accessible to the
observer directly (to some extent). The agent's goals must also be known, of
course, and these certainly are internal to the agent. But they are relatively
stable characteristics that can be inferred from behavior and (for human
adults) can sometimes be conveyed by language. One way of viewing the
knowledge level is as the attempt to build as good a model of an agent's behavior as possible based on formation external to the agent, hence permitting
distal prediction. This standpoint makes understandable why such a level
might exist even though it is radically incomplete. If such incompleteness is
the best that can be done, it must be tolerated.

4.3.4 Why It Is Effective

The knowledge level, being indirect and abstract, might be thought to be excessively complex, even abstruse. It could hardly have arisen naturally. On the
contrary, given the situation of Figure 4, it arises as day follows night. The
knowledge attributed by the observer to the agent is knowledge about the external world. If the observer takes to itself the role of the other (i.e., the agent), assuming the agent's goals and attending to the common external environment,
then the actions it determines for itself will be those that the agent should take.
Its own computational mechanisms (i.e., its symbolic system) will produce the
predictions that flow from attributing the appropriate knowledge to the agent.

This scheme works for the observer without requiring the development of
any explicit theory of the agent or the construction of any computational
model. To be more accurate, all that is needed is a single general purpose
computational mechanism; namely, creating an *embedding content* that
posits the agent's goals and symbolizes (rather than executes) the resulting

actions.[12] Thus, *simulation* turns out to be a central mechanism that enables the knowledge level and makes it useful.

4.4 Solutions to the Representation of Knowledge

The principle of rationality provides, in effect, a general functional equation for knowledge. The problem for agents is to find systems at the symbol level that are solutions to this functional equation, and hence can serve as representations of knowledge. That, of course, is also our own problem, as scientists of the intelligent. If we wish to study the knowledge of agents we must use representations of that knowledge. Little progress can be made given only abstract characterizations. The solutions that agents have found for their own purposes are also potentially useful solutions for scientific purposes, quite independently of their interest, *because* they are used by agents whose intelligent processing we wish to study.

Knowledge, in the principle of rationality, is defined entirely in terms of the *environment* of the agent, for it is the environment that is the object of the agent's goals, and whose features therefore bear on the way actions can attain goals. This is true even if the agent's goals have to do with the agent itself as a physical system. Therefore, the solutions are ways to say things about the environment, not ways to say things about reasoning, internal information processing states, and the like. (However, control over internal processing does require symbols that designate internal processing states and structures.)

Logics are obvious candidates. They are, exactly, refined means for saying things about environments. Logics certainly provide solutions to the functional equation. One can find many situations in which the agent's knowledge can be characterized by an expression in a logic, and from which one can go through in mechanical detail all the steps implied in the principle, deriving ultimately the actions to take and linking them up via a direct semantics so the actions actually occur. Examples abound. They do not even have to be limited to mathematics and logic, given the work in AI to use predicate logic (e.g., resolution) as the symbol level structures for robot tasks of spatial manipulation and movement, as well as for many other sorts of tasks (Nilsson 1980).

A logic is just a representation of knowledge. It is not the knowledge itself but a structure at the symbol level. If we are given a set of logical expressions, say $\{L_i\}$, of which we are willing to say that the agent "knows $\{L_i\}$," then the knowledge K that we ascribe to the agent is:

The agent knows all that can be inferred from the conjunction of $\{L_i\}$.

This statement simply expresses for logic what has been set out more generally above. There exists a symbol system in the agent that is able to bring any inference from $\{L_i\}$ to bear to select the actions of the agent as appropriate (i.e., in the services of the agent's goals). If this symbol system uses the clauses themselves as a representation, then presumably the active processes would consist of a theorem prover on the logic, along with sundry heuristic devices to aid the agent in arriving at the implications in time to perform the requisite action selections.

This statement should bring to prominence an important question, which, if not already at the forefront of concern, should be.

> Given that a human cannot know all the implications of an (arbitrary) set of axioms, how can such a formulation of knowledge be either correct or useful?

Philosophy has many times explicitly confronted the proposition that knowledge is the logical closure of a set of axioms. It has seemed so obvious. Yet the proposal has always come to grief on the rocky question above. It is trivial to generate counterexamples that show a person cannot possibly know all that is implied. In a field where counterexamples are a primary method for making progress, this has proved fatal and the proposal has little standing.[13] Yet, the theory of knowledge being presented here embraces that the knowledge to be associated with a conjunction of logical expressions is its logical closure. How can that be?

The answer is straightforward. The knowledge level is only an *approximation,* and a relatively poor one on many occasions—we called it radically incomplete. It is poor for predicting whether a person remembers a telephone number just looked up. It is poor for predicting what a person knows given a new set of mathematical axioms with only a short time to study them. And so on, through whole meadows of counterexamples. Equally, it is a good approximation in many other cases. It is good for predicting that a person can find his way to the bedroom of his own house, for predicting that a person who knows arithmetic will be able to add a column of numbers. And so on, through much of what is called common sense knowledge.

This *move* to appeal to approximation (as the philosophers are wont to call such proposals) seems weak, because declaring something an approximation seems a general purpose dodge, applicable to dissolving every difficulty, hence clearly dispelling none. However, an essential part of the current proposal is the existence of the second level of approximation, namely, the symbol level. We now have models of the symbol level that describe how information processing agents arrive at actions by means of search—search of problem spaces and search of global data bases—and how they map structures that are representations of given knowledge to structures that are representations of task-state knowledge in order to create representations of solutions. The discovery, development and elaboration of this second level of approximation to describing and predicting the behavior of an intelligent agent has been what AI has been all about in the quarter century of its existence. In sum, given a theory of the symbol level, we can finally see that the knowledge level is just about what seemed obvious all along.

Returning to the search for solutions to the functional equation expressed by the principle of rationality, logics are only one candidate. They are in no way privileged.[14] There are many other systems (i.e., combinations of symbol structures and processes) that can yield useful solutions. To be useful an observer need only use it to make predictions according to the principle of rationality. If we consider the problem from the point of view of agents, rather than of AI scientists, then the fundamental principle of the observer must be:

To ascribe to an agent the structure S is to ascribe whatever the observer can know from structure S.

Theories, models, pictures, physical views, remembered scenes, linguistic texts and utterances, etc., etc.: all these are entirely appropriate structures for ascribing knowledge. They are appropriate because for an observer to have these structures is also for it to have means (i.e., the symbolic processes) for extracting knowledge from them.

Not only are logics not privileged, there are difficulties with them. One already mentioned in connection with the resolution controversy, is processing inefficiency. Another is the problem of contradiction. From an inconsistent conjunction of propositions, any proposition follows. Further, in general, the contradiction cannot be detected or extirpated by any finite amount of effort. One response to this latter difficulty takes the form of developing new logics or logic-like representations, such as non-monotonic logics (Bobrow 1977). Another is to treat the logic as only an approximation, with a limited scope, embedding its use in a larger symbol processing system. In any event, the existence of difficulties does not distinguish logics from other candidate representations. It just makes them one of the crowd.

When we turn from the agents themselves and consider representations from the view-point of the AI scientist, many candidates become problems rather than solutions. If the data structures alone are known (the pictures, language expressions, and so on), and not the procedures used to generate the knowledge from them, they cannot be used in engineered AI systems or in theoretical analyses of knowledge. The difficulty follows simply from the fact that we do not know the entire representational system.[15] As a result representations, such as natural language, speech and vision, become arenas for research, not tools to be used by the AI scientist to characterize the knowledge of agents under study. Here, logics have the virtue that the entire system of data structure and processes (i.e., rules of inference) has been externalized and is well understood.

The development of AI is the story of constructing many other systems that are not logics, but can be used as representations of knowledge. Furthermore the development of mathematics, science and technology is in part the story of bringing representational structures to a degree of explicitness very close to what is needed by AI. Often only relatively modest effort has been needed to extend such representations to be useful for AI systems. Good examples are algebraic mathematics and chemical notations.

4.5 Relation of the Knowledge Level to the Symbol Level

Making clear the nature of knowledge has already required discussing the central core of the reduction of the knowledge level to the symbol level. Hence the matter can be summarized briefly.

Table 2 lists the aspects of the knowledge level and shows to what each corresponds at the symbol level. Starting at the top, the agent corresponds to the total system at the symbol level. Next, the actions correspond to systems that include external transducers, both input and output. An arbitrary amount of programmed system can surround and integrate the operations that are the actual primitive transducers at the symbolic level.

As we have seen, knowledge, the medium at the knowledge level, corresponds at the symbol level to data structures plus the processes that extract from these structures the knowledge they contain. To 'extract knowledge' is to participate with other symbolic processes in executing actions, just to the extent that the knowledge leads to the selection of these actions at the knowledge level. The total body of knowledge corresponds, then, to the sum total of the memory structure devoted to such data and processes.

A goal is simply more knowledge, hence corresponds at the symbol level to data structures and processes, just as does any body of knowledge. Three sorts of knowledge are involved: knowledge of the desired state of affairs; knowledge that the state of affairs is desired; and knowledge of associated concerns, such as useful methods, prior attempts to attain the goals, etc. It is of little moment whether these latter items are taken as part of the goal or as part of the body of knowledge of the world.

The principle of rationality corresponds at the symbol level to the processes (and associated data structures) that attempt to carry out problem solving to attain the agent's goals. There is more to the total system than just the separate symbol systems that correspond to the various bodies of knowledge. As repeatedly emphasized, the agent cannot generate at any instant all the knowledge that it has encoded in its symbol systems that correspond to its bodies of knowledge. It must generate and bring to bear the knowledge that, in fact, is relevant to its goals in the current environment.

At the knowledge level, the principle of rationality and knowledge present a seamless surface: a uniform principle to be applied uniformly to the content of what is known (i.e., to whatever is the case about the world). There is no reason to expect this to carry down seamlessly to the symbolic level, with (say) separate subsystems for each aspect and a uniform encoding of knowledge. Decomposition must occur, of course, but the separation into processes and data structures is entirely a creation of the symbolic level, which is governed by processing and encoding considerations that have no existence at the knowl-

Knowledge level	Symbol level
Agent	Total symbol system
Actions	Symbol systems with transducers
Knowledge	Symbol structure plus its processes
Goals	(Knowledge of goals)
Principle of rationality	Total problem solving process

Table 2. Reduction of the knowledge level to the symbol level.

edge level. The interface between the problem solving processes and the knowledge extraction processes is as diverse as the potential ways of designing intelligent systems. A look at existing AI programs will give some idea of the diversity, though no doubt we still are only at the beginnings of exploration of potential mechanisms. In sum, the seamless surface at the knowledge level is most likely a pastiche of interlocked intricate structures when seen from below „much like the smooth skin of a baby when seen under a microscope.

The theory of the knowledge level provides a definition of representation, namely, a symbol system that encodes a body of knowledge. It does not provide a *theory* of representation, which properly exists only at the symbol level and which tells how to create representations with particular properties, how to analyze their efficiency, etc. It does suggest that a useful way of thinking about representation is according to the slogan equation

Representation = Knowledge + Access

The representation consists of a system for providing access to a body of knowledge, i.e., to the knowledge in a form that can be used to make selections of actions in the service of goals. The access function is not a simple generator, producing one knowledge element (i.e., means-end relation) after another. Rather, it is a system for delivering the knowledge encoded in a data structure that can be used by the larger system that represents the knowledge about goals, actions, etc. Access is a computational process, hence has associated costs. Thus, a representation imposes a profile of computational costs on delivering different parts of the total knowledge encoded in the representation.

4.5.1 Mixed Systems

The classic relationship between computer system levels is that, once a level is adopted, useful analysis and synthesis can proceed exclusively in terms of that level, with only side studies on how lower level behavior might show as errors or lower level constraints might condition the types of structures that are efficient. The radical incompleteness of the knowledge level leads to a different relationship between it and the symbol level. Mixed systems are often considered, even becoming the norm on occasions.

One way this happens is in the distal prediction of human behavior, in which it often pays to mix a few processing notions along with the pure knowledge considerations. This is what is often called man-in-the-street psychology. We recognize that forgetting is possible, and so we do not assume that knowledge once obtained is forever. We know that inferences are available only if the person thinks it through, so we don't assume that knowing X means knowing all the remote consequences of X, though we have no good way of determining exactly what inferences will be known. We know that people can only do a little processing in a short time, or do less processing when under stress. Having only crude models of the processing at the symbol level, these mixed models are neither very tidy nor uniformly effective. The major tool is the use of self as simulator for the agent. But mixed models are often better than pure knowledge-level models.

Another important case of mixed models—especially for AI and computer science—is the use of the knowledge level to characterize components in a symbol-level description of a system. Memories are described as having a given body of knowledge and messages are described as transferring knowledge from one memory to another. This carries all the way to design philosophies that work in terms of a 'society of minds' (Minsky 1977) and to executive systems that oversee and analyze the operation of other internal processing. The utility of working with such mixed-level systems is evident for both design and analysis. For design, it permits specifications of the behavior of components to be given prior to specifying their internal structure. For analysis, it lets complex behavior be summarized in terms of the external environments of the components (which comprises the other internal parts of the system).

Describing a component at the knowledge level treats it as an intelligent agent. The danger in this is well known; it is called the problem of the homunculus. If an actual system is produced, all knowledge-level descriptions must ultimately be replaced by symbol-level descriptions and there is no problem. As such replacement proceeds, the internal structure of the components becomes simpler, thus moving further away from a structure that could possibly realize an intelligent agent. Thus, the interesting question is how the knowledge-level description can be a good approximation even though the subsystem being so described is quite simple. The answer turns on the limited nature of the goals and environments of such agents, whose specification is also under the control of the system designer.

5. Consequences and Relationships

We have set out the theory in sufficient outline to express its general nature. Here follows some discussion of its consequences, its relations to other aspects of AI, and its relations to conceptions in other fields.

5.1 The Practice of AI

At the beginning I claimed that this theory of knowledge derived from our practice in AI. Some of its formal aspects clearly do not, especially positing a distinct systems level, which splits apart the symbol and the knowledge level. Thus, it is worth exploring the matter of our practice briefly.

When we say, as we often do in explaining an action of a program, that "the program knows K" (e.g., "the theorem prover knows the distributive law"), we mean that there is some structure in the program that we view as holding K and also that this structure was involved in selecting the action in exactly the manner claimed by the principle of rationality, namely, the encoding of that knowledge is related to the goal the action is to serve, etc.

More revealing, when we talk, as we often do during the design of a program, about a proposed data structure having or holding knowledge K (e.g., "this table holds the knowledge of co-articulation effects"), we imply that some processes must exist that takes that data structure as input and make selections of which we can say, "The program did action A because it knew K." Those processes may not be known to the system's designer yet, but the belief exists that they can be found. They may not be usable when found, because they take too much time or space. Such considerations do not affect whether "knowledge K is there," only whether it can be extracted usefully. Thus, our notion of knowledge has precisely a competence-like character. Indeed, one of its main uses is to let us talk about what can be done, before we have found out how to do it.

Most revealingly of all, perhaps, when we say, as we often do, that a program "can't do action A, because it doesn't have knowledge K," we mean that no amount of processing by the processes now in the program on the data structures now in the program can yield the selection of A. (E.g., "This chess program can't avoid the tie, because it doesn't know about repetition of positions.") Such a statement presupposes that the principle of rationality would lead to A given K, and no way to get A selected other than having K satisfies the principle of rationality. If in fact some rearrangement of the processing did lead to selecting A, then additional knowledge can be expected to have been imported, e.g., from the mind of the programmer who did the rearranging (though accident can confound expectation on occasion, of course).

The Hearsay II speech understanding system (Erman, Hayes-Roth, Lesser, and Reddy 1980) provides a concrete example of how the concept of knowledge is used. Hearsay has helped to make widespread a notion of a system composed of numerous *sources of knowledge,* each of which is associated with a separate module of the program (called, naturally enough, a *knowledge source),* and all of which act cooperatively and concurrently to attain a solution. What makes this idea so attractive—indeed, seductive—is that such a system seems a close approximation to a system that operates purely at the knowledge level, i.e., purely in terms of simply having knowledge and bringing it to bear. It permits design by identifying first a source of knowledge in the abstract—e.g., syntax, phonology, coarticulation, etc.—and then designing representations and processes that encode that knowledge and provide for its extraction against a common representation of the task in the blackboard (the working memory).

This theory of knowledge has not arisen sui generis from unarticulated practice. On the contrary, the fundamental insights on which the theory draws have been well articulated and are part of existing theoretical notions, not only in AI but well beyond, in psychology and the social sciences. That an adaptive organism, by the very act of adapting, conceals its internal structure from view and makes its behavior solely a function of the task environment, has been a major theme in the artificial sciences. In the work of my colleague, Herb Simon, it stretches back to the 1940s (Simon 1947), with a concern for the nature of *administrative man* versus *economic man*. In our book *Human Problem Solving* (Newell and Simon 1972) we devoted an entire chapter to an analysis of the task environment, which turned on precisely this point. And Herb Simon devoted his recent talk at the formative meeting of the Cognitive Science Society to a review of this same topic (Simon 1980), to which I refer you for a wider discussion and references. In sum, the present theory is to be seen as a refinement of this existing view of adaptive systems, not as a new theory.

5.2 Contributions to the Knowledge Level Versus the Symbol Level

By distinguishing sharply between the knowledge level and the symbol level the theory implies an equally sharp distinction between the knowledge required to solve a problem and the processing required to bring that knowledge to bear in real time and real space. Contributions to AI may be of either flavor, i.e., either to the knowledge level or to the symbol level. Both aspects always occur in particular studies, because experimentation always occurs in total AI systems. But looking at the major contribution to science, it is usually toward one pole or the other, only rarely is a piece of research innovative enough to make both types of contributions. For instance, the major thrust of the work on MYCIN (Shortliffe 1976) was fundamentally to the knowledge level in capturing the knowledge used by medical experts. The processing, an adaptation of well understood notions of backward chaining, played a much smaller role. Similarly, the SNAC procedure used by Berliner (1980) to improve radically his Backgammon program was primarily a contribution to our understanding of the symbol level, since it discovered (and ameliorated) the effects of discontinuities in global evaluation functions patched together from many local ones. It did not add to our formulation of our knowledge about Backgammon.

This proposed separation immediately recalls the well-known distinction of John McCarthy and Pat Hayes (1969) between *epistemological adequacy* and *heuristic adequacy*. Indeed, they would seem likely to be steadfast supporters of the theory presented here, perhaps even claiming much of it to be at most a refinement on their own position. I am not completely against such an interpretation, for I find considerable merit in their position. In fact, a recent essay by McCarthy on ascribing mental qualities to machines (McCarthy 1979) makes many points similar to those of the present paper (though without embracing the notion of a new computer systems level).

However, all is not quite so simple. I once publicly put to John McCarthy (McCarthy 1977) the proposition that the role of logic was as a tool for the analysis of knowledge, not for reasoning by intelligent agents, and he denied it flat out.

The matter is worth exploring briefly. It appears to be a prime plank in McCarthy's research program that the appropriate representation of knowledge is with a logic. The use of other forms plays little role in his analyses. Thus, the fundamental question of epistemological adequacy, namely, whether there exists an adequate explicit representation of some knowledge is conflated with how to represent the knowledge in a logic. As observed earlier, there are many other forms in which knowledge can be represented, even setting entirely to one side forms whose semantics are not yet well enough understood scientifically, such as natural language and visual images.

Let us consider a simple example (McCarthy 1977, p. 987), shown in Figure 5, one of several that McCarthy has used to epitomize various problems in representation within logic. This one is built to show difficulties in transparency of reference. In obvious formulations, having identified Mary's and Mike's telephone numbers, it is difficult to retain the distinction between what Pat knows and what is true in fact.

However, the difficulty simply does not exist if the situation is represented by an appropriate model. Let Pat and the program be modeled as agents who have knowledge, with the knowledge localized inside the agent and associated with definite data structures, with appropriate input and output actions, etc.— i.e., a simple version of an information processing system. Then, there is no difficulty in keeping knowledges straight, as well as what can be and cannot be inferred.

The example exhibits a couple of wrinkles, but they do not cause conceptual problems. The program must model itself, if it is to talk about what it doesn't know. That is, it must circumscribe the data structures that are the source of its knowledge about Pat. Once done, however, its problem of ascertaining its own knowledge is no different from its problem of ascertaining Pat's knowledge. Also, one of its utterances depends on whether from its representation of the knowledge of Pat, it can infer some other knowledge. But the difficulties of deciding whether a fact cannot be inferred from a given

When program is told:
"Mary has the same telephone number as Mike."
"Pat knows Mike's telephone number."
"Pat dialed Mike's telephone number."

Program should assert:
"Pat dialed Mary's telephone number."
"I do not know if Pat knows Mary's telephone number."

Figure 5. Example from McCarthy (1977).

finite base, seem no different from deciding any issue of failure to infer from given premises.

To be sure, my treatment here is a little cavalier, given existing analyses. It has been pointed out that difficulties emerge in the model-based solution, if it is known only that either Pat knows Mike's telephone number or his address; and that even worse difficulties ensue from knowing that Pat doesn't know Mike's telephone number (e.g., see Moore [1980], Chapter 2). Without pretending to an adequate discussion, it does not seem to me that the difficulties here are other than those in dealing with knowing only that a box is painted red or blue inside, or knowing that your hen will not lay a golden egg. In both cases, the representation of this knowledge by the observer must be in terms of descriptions of the model, not of an instance of the model. But knowledge does not pose special difficulties.[16]

As one more example of differences between contributions to the knowledge level and the symbol level, consider a well-known albeit somewhat controversial case, namely, Schank's work on *conceptual dependency structures* (Schank 1974). I believe its main contribution to AI has been at the knowledge level. That such a view is not completely obvious, can be seen by the contrary stance of Pat Hayes in his already mentioned piece, "In defense of logic" (Hayes 1977). Though not much at variance from the present paper in its basic theme, his paper exhibits Figure 6, classifies it as *pretend-it's-English,* and argues that there is no effective way to know its meaning.

On the contrary, I claim that conceptual dependency structures made a real contribution to our understanding at the knowledge level. The content of this contribution lies in the model indicated in Figure 7, taken rather directly from Schank and Ableson (1977). The major claim of conceptual dependency is that the simplest causal model is adequate to give first approximation semantics of a certain fragment of natural language. This model, though really only sketched in the figure, is not in itself very problematical, though as with all formalization it is an important act to reduce it to a finite apparatus. There is a world of states filled with objects that have attributes and whose

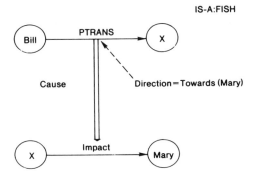

Figure 6. A Conceptual dependency diagram from Patrick Hayes (1977).

dynamics occur through actions. Some objects, called actors, have a mentality, which is to say they have representations in a long term memory and are capable of mental acts. The elementary dynamics of this world, in terms of what can produce or inhibit what, are indicated in the figure.

The claim in full is that if sentences are mapped into a model of this sort in the obvious way, an interpretation of these sentences is obtained that captures a good deal of its meaning. The program Margie (Schank 1973) provided the initial demonstration, using paraphrase and inference as devices to provide explicit evidence. The continued use of these mechanisms as part of the many programs that have followed Margie has added to the evidence implicitly, as it gradually has become part of the practice in AI.

Providing a simple model such as this constitutes a contribution to the knowledge level—to how to encode knowledge of the world in a representation. It is a quite general contribution, expressed in a way that makes it adaptable to a wide variety of intelligent systems.[17] On the other hand, this work made relatively little contribution to the symbol level, i.e., to our notions of symbolic processing. The techniques that were used were essentially state of the art. This can be seen in the relative lack of emphasis or discussion of the internal mechanics of the program. For many of us, the meaning of conceptual dependency seemed undefined without a process that created conceptual dependency structures from sentences. Yet, when this was finally forthcoming (in Margie), there was nothing there except a large AI program containing the usual sorts of things, e.g., various ad hoc mechanisms within a familiar framework (a parser, etc.). What was missed was that the program was simply the implementation of the model in the obvious, i.e., straightforward, way. The program was not supposed to add significantly to the specification of the mapping. There would have been trouble if additions had been required, just as a computer program for partial differential equations is not

World: states, actions, objects, attributes

Actors: objects With mentality (central processor plus long-term memory)

↑ Cause

↑ **r**   An act results in a state.

↑ **E**   A state enables an act.

↑ **I**   A state or act initiates a mental state.

↑ **R**   A mental act is the reason for a physical act.

↑ **dE**   A state disables an act.

Figure 7. Conceptual dependency model (after Schank and Ableson 1976).

supposed to add to the mathematics.

5.3 Laying to Rest the Predicate Calculus Phobia

Let us review the theorem proving controversy of the sixties. From all that has been said earlier, it is clear that the residue can be swept aside. Logic is the appropriate tool for analyzing the knowledge level, though it is often not the preferred representation to use for a given domain. Indeed, given a representation—e.g., a semantic net, a data structure for a chess position, a symbolic structure for some abstract problem space, a program, or whatever— to determine exactly what knowledge is in the representation and to characterize it requires the use of logic. Whatever the detailed differences represented in my discussion in the last section of the Pat and Mike example, the types of analysis being performed by McCarthy, Moore and Konolige (to mention only the names that arose there) are exactly appropriate. Just as talking of programmerless programming violates truth in packaging, so does talking of a nonlogical analysis of knowledge.

Logic is of course a representation (actually, a family of them), and is therefore a candidate (along with its theorem proving engine) for the representation to be used by an intelligent agent. Its use in such a role depends strongly on computational considerations, for the agent must gain access to very large amounts of encoded knowledge, swiftly and reliably. The lessons of the sixties taught us some things about the limitations of using logics for this role. However, these lessons do not touch the role of logic as the essential language of analysis at the knowledge level.

Let me apply this view to Nilsson's new textbook in AI (Nilsson 1980). Now, I am an admirer of Nilsson's book (Newell 1981).[18] It is the first attempt to transform textbooks in AI into the mold of basic texts in science and engineering. Nilsson's book uses the first order predicate calculus as the lingua franca for presenting and discussing representation throughout the book. The theory developed here says that is just right; I think it is an important position for the book to have adopted. However, the book also introduces logic in intimate connection with resolution theorem proving, thus asserting to the reader that logic is to be seen as a representation for problem solving systems. That seems to me just wrong. Logic as a representation for problem solving rates only a minor theme in our textbooks. One consequence of the present theory of knowledge will be to help assign logic its proper role in AI.

5.4 The Relationship with Philosophy

The present theory bears some close and curious relationships with philosophy, though only a few preliminary remarks are possible here. The nature of mind and the nature of knowledge have been classical concerns in philosophy, forming major continents of its geography. There has been increasing contact between philosophy and AI in the last decade, focussed primarily in the area of knowledge representation and natural language. Indeed, the respondents to the Brachman and Smith questionnaire, reflecting exactly this group, opined that philosophy was more relevant to AI than psychology.

Philosophy's concern with knowledge centers on the issue of certainty. When can knowledge be trusted? Does a person have privileged access to his subjective awareness, so his knowledge of it is infallible? This is ensconced in the distinction in philosophy between knowledge and belief, as indicated in the slogan phrase, *knowledge is justified true belief.* AI, taking all knowledge to be errorful, has seen fit to call all such systems *knowledge systems.* It uses the term belief only informally when the lack of veridicality is paramount, as in political belief systems. From philosophy's standpoint, AI deals only in belief systems. Thus, the present theory of knowledge, sharing as it does AI's view of general indifference to the problems of absolute certainty, is simply inattentive to some central philosophical concerns.

An important connection appears to be with the notion of *intentional* systems. Starting in the work of Brentano (1973), the notion was of a class of systems capable of having desires, expectations, etc.—all things that were *about* the external world. The major function of the formulation was to provide a way of distinguishing the physical from the mental, i.e., of providing a characterization of the mental. A key result of this analysis was to open an unbridgeable gap between the physical and the mental. Viewing a system as physical precluded being able to ascribe intentionality to it. The enterprise seems at opposite poles from work in AI, which is devoted precisely to realizing mental functions in physical systems.

In the hands of Daniel Dennett (1978), a philosopher who has concerned himself rather deeply with AI, the doctrine of intentional systems has taken a form that corresponds closely to the notion of the knowledge level, as developed here. He takes pains to lay out an *intentional stance,* and to relate it to what he calls the *subpersonal stance.* His notion of *stance* is a system level, but ascribed entirely to the observer, i.e., to he who takes the stance. The subpersonal stance corresponds to the symbolic or programming level, being illustrated repeatedly by Dennett with the gross flow diagrams of AI programs. The intentional stance corresponds to the knowledge level. In particular, Dennett takes the important step of jettisoning the major result-cum-assumption of the original doctrine, to wit, that the intentional is unalterably separated from the physical (i.e., subpersonal).

Dennett's formulation differs in many details from the present one. It does not mention knowledge at all, but focuses on intentions. It does not provide (in the papers I have seen) a technical analysis of intentions—one understands this class of systems more by intent than by characterization. It does not deal with the details of the reduction. It does not, as noted, assign reality to the different system levels, but keeps them in the eye of the beholder. Withal, there is little doubt that both Dennett and myself are reaching for the characterization of exactly the same class of systems. In particular, the role of rationality is central to both, and in the same way. A detailed examination of the relation of Dennett's theory with the present one is in order, though it cannot be accomplished here.

However, it should at least be noted that the knowledge level does not itself explain the notion of *aboutness;* rather, it assumes it. The explanation occurs partly at the symbol level, in terms of what it means for symbols to designate external situations, and partly at lower levels, in terms of the mechanisms that permit designation to actually occur (Newell 1980).

5.5 A Generative Space of Rational Systems

My talk on physical symbol systems to the La Jolla Cognitive Science Conference last year (Newell 1980), employed a frame story that decomposed the attempt to understand the nature of mind into a large number of constraints—universal flexibility of response, use of symbols, use of language, development, real time response, and so on. The importance of physical symbol systems was underscored by its being a single class of systems that embodied two distinct constraints, universality of functional response and symbolic behavior, and was intimately tied to a third, goal-directed behavior, as indicated by the experience in AI.

An additional indicator that AI is on the right track to understanding mind came from the notion of a *generative class* of systems, in analogy with the use of the term in *generate and test.* Designing a system is a problem precisely because there is in general no way simply to generate a system with specified properties. Always the designer must back off to some class of encompassing systems that can be generated, and then test (intelligently) whether generated candidate systems have desirable properties. The game, as we all know, is to embody as many constraints as possible in the generators leaving as few as possible to be dealt with by testing.

Now, the remarkable property about universal, symbolic systems is that they are generative in this sense. We have fashioned a technology that lets us take for granted that whatever system we construct will be universal and will have full symbolic capability. Anyone who works in Lisp, or other similar systems, gets these constraints satisfied automatically. Effort is then devoted to contriving designs to satisfy additional constraints—real time, or learning, or whatnot.

For most constraints we do not have generative classes of systems— for real-time, for development, for goal-directedness, etc. There is no way to explore spaces of systems that automatically satisfy these constraints, looking for instances with additional important properties. An interesting question is whether the present theory offers some hope of building a generative class of rational goal-directed systems. It would perforce also need to be universal and symbolic, but that can be taken for granted.

It seems to me possible to glimpse what such a class might be like, though the idea is fairly speculative. First, implicit in all that has gone before, the class of rational goal-directed systems is the class of systems that has a knowledge level. Second, though systems only approximate a knowledge level description, they are rational systems precisely to the extent they do. Thus, the design form for all intelligent systems is in terms of the body of knowledge that they contain and the approximation they provide to being a system describable at the knowledge level. If the technology of symbol systems can be developed in this factored form, then it may be possible to remain always within the domain of rational systems, while exploring variants that meet the additional constraints of real time, learnability, and so forth.

6. Conclusion

I have presented a theory of the nature of knowledge and representation. Knowledge is the medium of a systems level that resides immediately above the symbol level. A representation is the structure at the symbol level that realizes knowledge, i.e., it is the reduction of knowledge to the next lower computer systems level. The nature of the approximation is such that the representation at the symbol level can be seen as knowledge plus the access structure to that knowledge.

This new level fits into the existing concept of computer systems levels. However, it has several surprising features:

1) a complete absence of structure, as characterized at the configuration level;

2) no specification of processing mechanisms, only a global principle to be

satisfied by the system behavior;

3) a radical degree of approximation that does not guarantee a deterministic machine; and

4) a medium that is not realized in physical space in a passive way, but only in an active process of selection.

Both little and much flow from this theory. This notion of knowledge and representation corresponds to how we in AI already use these terms in our (evolving) everyday scientific practice. Also, it is a refinement of some fundamental features of adaptive systems that have been well articulated and it has nothing that is incompatible with foundation work in logic. To this extent not much change will occur, especially in the short run. We already have assimilated these notions and use them instinctively. In this respect, my role in this paper is merely that of reporter.

However, as I emphasized at the beginning, I take this close association with current practice as a source of strength, not an indication that the theory is not worthwhile, because it is not novel enough. Observing our own practice—that is, seeing what the computer implicitly tells us about the nature of intelligence as we struggle to synthesize intelligent systems—is a fundamental source of scientific knowledge for us. It must be used wisely and with acumen, but no other source of knowledge comes close to it in value.

Making the theory explicit will have many consequences. I have tried to point out some of these, ranging from fundamental issues to how some of my colleagues should do their business. Reiteration of that entire list would take too long. Let me just emphasize those that seem most important, in my current view.

- Knowledge is that which makes the principle of rationality work as a law of behavior. Thus, knowledge and rationality are intimately tied together.

- Splitting what was a single level (symbol) into two (knowledge plus symbol) has immense long-term implications for the development of AI. It permits each of the separate aspects to be adequately developed technically.

- Knowledge is not representable by a structure at the symbol level. It requires both structures and processes. Knowledge remains forever abstract and can never be actually in hand.

- Knowledge is a radical approximation, failing on many occasions to be an adequate model of an agent. It must be coupled with some symbol level representation to make a viable view.

- Logic is fundamentally a tool for analysis at the knowledge level. Logical formalisms with theorem-proving can certainly be used as a representation in an intelligent agent, but it is an entirely separate issue (though one we already know much about, thanks to the investigations in AI and mechanical mathematics over the last fifteen years).

- The separate knowledge level may lead to constructing a generative class of rational systems, although this is still mostly hope.

As stated at the beginning, I have no illusions that yet one more view on the nature of knowledge and representation will serve to quiet the cacophony revealed by the noble surveying efforts of Brachman and Smith. Indeed, amid the din, it may not even be possible to hear another note being played. However, I know of no other way to proceed. Of greater concern is how to determine whether this theory of knowledge is correct in its essentials, how to find the bugs in it, how to shake them out, and how to turn it to technical use.

Acknowledgements

This research was sponsored by the Defense Advanced Research Projects Agency (DOD), ARPA Order No.3597, monitored by the Air Force Avionics Laboratory under contract F336157X-C-1551.

I am grateful for extensive comments on an earlier draft provided by Jon Bentley, Danny Bobrow, H.T. Kung, John McCarthy, John McDermott, Greg Harris, Zenon Pylyshyn, Mike Rychener and Herbert Simon. They all tried in their several (not necessarily compatible) ways to keep me from error.

Notes

1. Presidential Address, American Association for Artificial Intelligence, AAA180, Stanford University, 19 Aug 1980. Also published in the *AI Magazine* 2(2)1981.

2. The views and conclusions contained in this document are those of the authors and should not be interpreted as representing the official policies, either expressed or implied, of the Defense Advanced Research Projects Agency or the US Government.

3. I have already provided some comments, as president, on such matters (Newell 1980).

4. Representation is not the only aspect of intelligent systems that has a magical quality; learning is another. But that is a different story for a different time.

5. Computer science is not unique in having modes of progress that don't fit easily into the standard frames. In the heyday of paleontology, major conceptual advances occurred by stumbling across the bones of immense beasties. Neither controlled experimentation nor theoretical prediction played appreciable roles.

6. Though currently dominated by electrical circuits, variant circuit level instantiations also exist, e.g., fluidic circuits.

7. How almost interchangeable the two notions might be can be seen from a quotation from Chomsky (1975, p. 315): "In the past I have tried to avoid, or perhaps evade the problem of explicating the notion 'knowledge of language' by using an invented technical term, namely the term 'competence' in place of 'knowledge.'"

8. This principle is not intended to be directly responsive to all the extensive philosophical discussion on rationality, e g., the notion that rationality implies the ability for an agent to give *reasons* for what it does.

9. For simplicity, in this principle and others, no explicit mention is made of the agent whose goals, knowledge and actions are under discussion.

10. An adequate critical recounting of this intellectual development is not possible here. Formal systems (utility fields) can be constructed that appear to have the right property. But they work,

not by connecting actions with goals via knowledge of the task environment, but by positing of the agent a complete set of goals (actually, preferences) that directly specify all action selections over all combinations of task states (or probabilistic options over task states). Such a move actually abandons the enterprise.

11. Agents with finite knowledge are certainly possible, but would be extraordinarily limited.

12. However, obtaining this is still not a completely trivial cognitive accomplishment, as indicated by the emphasis on egocentrism in the early work of Piaget and the significance of *taking the role of the other* in the work of the social philosopher, George H. Meade (1934), who is generally credited with originating the phrase.

13. For example, both the beautiful formal treatment of knowledge by Hintikka (1962) and the work in AI by Moore (1980) continually insist that knowing P and knowing that P implies Q need not lead to knowing Q.

14. Although the contrary might seem the case. The principle of rationality might seem to presuppose logic, or at least its formulation might. Untangling this knot requires more care than can be spent here. Note only that it is we, the observer, who formulates the principle of rationality (in some representation). Agents only use it: indeed, only approximate it.

15. It is irrelevant that each of us, as agents rather than AI scientists, happens to embody some of the requisite procedures, so long as we, as AI scientists, cannot get them externalized appropriately.

16. Indeed, two additional recent attempts on this problem, though cast as logical systems, seem essentially to adopt a model view. One is by McCarthy himself (1979), who introduces the concept of a number as distinct from the number. Concepts seem just to be a way to get data structures to talk about. The other attempt (Konolige 1980) uses expressions in two languages, again with what seems the same effect.

17. This interpretation of conceptual dependency in terms of a model is my own; Schank and Abelson (1977) prefer to cast it as a *causal syntax*. This latter may mildly obscure its true nature, for it seems to beg for a *causal semantics* as well.

18. Especially so, because Nils and I both set out at the same time to write textbooks of AI. His is now in print and I am silent about mine.

6

A Framework for Representing Knowledge

Marvin Minsky

1. Frames

It seems to me that the ingredients of most theories both in artificial intelligence and in psychology have been on the whole too minute, local, and unstructured to account—either practically or phenomenologically—for the effectiveness of common-sense thought. The "chunks" of reasoning, language, memory, and perception ought to be larger and more structured; their factual and procedural contents must be more intimately connected in order to explain the apparent power and speed of mental activities.

Similar feelings seem to be emerging in several centers working on theories of intelligence. They take one form in the proposal of Papert and myself (1972) to divide knowledge into substructures, "micro-worlds." Another form is in the "problem-spaces" of Newell and Simon (1972), and yet another is in the new, large structures that theorists like Schank (1973), Abelson

(1973), and Norman (1973) assign to linguistic objects. I see all these as moving away from the traditional attempts both by behavioristic psychologists and by logic-oriented students of artificial intelligence in trying to represent knowledge as collections of separate, simple fragments.

I try here to bring together several of these issues by pretending to have a unified, coherent theory. The chapter raises more questions than it answers, and I have tried to note the theory's deficiencies.

Here is the essence of the theory: When one encounters a new situation (or makes a substantial change in one's view of the present problem), one selects from memory a structure called a *frame*. This is a remembered framework to be adapted to fit reality by changing details as necessary.

A *frame* is a data-structure for representing a stereotyped situation, like being in a certain kind of living room, or going to a child's birthday party. Attached to each frame are several kinds of information. Some of this information is about how to use the frame. Some is about what one can expect to happen next. Some is about what to do if these expectations are not confirmed.

We can think of a frame as a network of nodes and relations. The top levels of a frame are fixed, and represent things that are always true about the supposed situation. The lower levels have many *terminals*—slots that must be filled by specific instances or data. Each terminal can specify conditions its assignments must meet. (The assignments themselves are usually smaller subframes.) Simple conditions are specified by *markers* that might require a terminal assignment to be a person, an object of sufficient value, or a pointer to a subframe of a certain type. More complex conditions can specify relations among the things assigned to several terminals.

Collections of related frames are linked together into *frame systems*. The effects of important actions are mirrored by *transformations* between the frames of a system. These are used to make certain kinds of calculations economical, to represent changes of emphasis and attention, and to account for the effectiveness of imagery.

For visual scene analysis, the different frames of a system describe the scene from different viewpoints, and the transformations between one frame and another represent the effects of moving from place to place. For nonvisual kinds of frames, the differences between the frames of a system can represent actions, cause-effect relations, or changes in conceptual viewpoint. *Different frames of a system share the same terminals;* this is the critical point that makes it possible to coordinate information gathered from different viewpoints.

Much of the phenomenological power of the theory hinges on the inclusion of expectations and other kinds of presumptions. *A frame's terminals are normally already filled with "default" assignments.* Thus a frame may contain a great many details whose supposition is not specifically warranted by the situation. These have many uses in representing general information, most likely cases, techniques for bypassing "logic," and ways to make useful generalizations.

The default assignments are attached loosely to their terminals, so that they can be easily displaced by new items that fit better the current situation. They thus can serve also as variables or as special cases for reasoning by example, or as textbook cases, and often make the use of logical quantifiers unnecessary.

The frame-systems are linked, in turn, by an *information retrieval network.* When a proposed frame cannot be made to fit reality—when we cannot find terminal assignments that suitably match its terminal marker conditions—this network provides a replacement frame. These interframe structures make possible other ways to represent knowledge about facts, analogies, and other information useful in understanding.

Once a frame is proposed to represent a situation, a *matching* process tries to assign values to each frame's terminals, consistent with the markers at each place. The matching process is partly controlled by information associated with the frame (which includes information about how to deal with surprises) and partly by knowledge about the system's current goals. There are important uses for the information, obtained when a matching process fails. I will discuss how it can be used to select an alternative frame that better suits the situation.

An apology: The schemes proposed herein are incomplete in many respects. First, I often propose representations without specifying the processes that will use them. Sometimes I only describe properties the structures should exhibit. I talk about markers and assignments as though it were obvious how they are attached and linked; it is not.

Besides the technical gaps, I will talk as though unaware of many problems related to "understanding" that really need much deeper analysis. I do not claim that the ideas proposed here are enough for a complete theory, only that the frame-system scheme may help explain a number of phenomena of human intelligence. The basic frame idea itself is not particularly original—it is in the tradition of the "schemata" of Bartlett and the "paradigms" of Kuhn; the idea of a frame-system is probably more novel. Winograd (1974) discusses the recent trend, in theories of AI, toward frame-like ideas.

In the body of the paper, I discuss different kinds of reasoning by analogy, and ways to impose stereotypes on reality and jump to conclusions based on partial-similarity matching. These are basically uncertain methods. Why not use methods that are more logical and certain? Section 6 is a sort of appendix which argues that traditional logic cannot deal very well with realistic, complicated problems because it is poorly suited to represent approximations to solutions—and these are absolutely vital.

Thinking always begins with suggestive but imperfect plans and images; these are progressively replaced by better—but usually still imperfect—ideas.

1.1 Artificial Intelligence and Human Problem Solving

In this essay I draw no boundary between a theory of human thinking and a scheme for making an intelligent machine; no purpose would be served by separating them today, since neither domain has theories good enough to explain, or produce, enough mental capacity. There is, however, a difference in professional attitudes. Workers from psychology inherit stronger desires to minimize the variety of assumed mechanisms. I believe this leads to attempts to extract more performance from fewer "basic mechanisms" than is reasonable. Such theories especially neglect mechanisms of procedure control and explicit representations of processes. On the other side, workers in AI have perhaps focused too sharply on just such questions. Neither has given enough attention to the structure of knowledge, especially procedural knowledge.

It is understandable that psychologists are uncomfortable with complex proposals not based on well-established mechanisms, but I believe that parsimony is still inappropriate at this stage, valuable as it may be in later phases of every science. There is room in the anatomy and genetics of the brain for much more mechanism than anyone today is prepared to propose, and we should concentrate for a while longer on *sufficiency* and *efficiency* rather than on *necessity*.

1.2 Default Assignment

Although both seeing and imagining result in assignments to frame terminals, imagination leaves us wider choices of detail and variety of such assignments. I conjecture that frames are never stored in long-term memory with unassigned terminal values. Instead, what really happens is that frames are stored with weakly bound default assignments at every terminal! These manifest themselves as often useful but sometimes counterproductive stereotypes.

Thus if I say, "John kicked the ball," you probably cannot think of a purely abstract ball, but must imagine characteristics of a vaguely particular ball; it probably has a certain default size, default color, default weight. Perhaps it is a descendant of one you first owned or were injured by. Perhaps it resembles your latest one. In any case your image lacks the sharpness of presence because the processes that inspect and operate upon the weakly bound default features are very likely to change, adapt, or detach them.

Such default assignments would have subtle, idiosyncratic influences on the paths an individual would tend to follow in making analogies, generalizations, and judgements, especially when the exterior influences on such choices are weak. Properly chosen, such stereotypes could serve as a storehouse of valuable heuristic plan skeletons; badly selected, they could form paralyzing collections of irrational biases. Because of them one might expect, as reported by Freud, to detect evidences of early cognitive structures in free association thinking.

2 Language, Understanding, and Scenarios

2.1 Words, Sentences, and Meanings

The device of images has several defects that are the price of its peculiar excellences. Two of these are perhaps the most important: the image, and particularly the visual image, is apt to go farther in the direction of the individualization of situations than is biologically useful; and the principles of the combination of images have their own peculiarities and result in constructions which are relatively wild, jerky and irregular, compared with the straightforward unwinding of a habit, or with the somewhat orderly march of thought.

—F. C. Bartlett (1932)

The concepts of frame and default assignment seem helpful in discussing the phenomenology of "meaning." Chomsky (1957) points out that such a sentence as

A) colorless green ideas sleep furiously

is treated very differently from the nonsentence

B) furiously sleep ideas green colorless

and suggests that because both are "equally nonsensical," what is involved in the recognition of sentences must be quite different from what is involved in the appreciation of meanings.

There is no doubt that there are processes especially concerned with grammar. Since the meaning of an utterance is encoded as much in the positional and structural relations between the words as in the word choices themselves, there must be processes concerned with analyzing those relations in the course of building the structures that will more directly represent the meaning. What makes the words of (A) more effective and predictable than (B) in producing such a structure—putting aside the question of whether that structure should be called semantic or syntactic—is that the word order relations in (A) exploit the (grammatical) conventions and rules people usually use to induce others to make assignments to terminals of structures. This is entirely consistent with theories of grammar. A generative grammar would be a summary description of the *exterior* appearance of those frame rules—or their associated processes—while the operators of transformational grammars seem similar enough to some of our frame transformations.

But one must also ask: to what degree does grammar have a separate identity in the actual working of a human mind? Perhaps the rejection of an utterance (either as nongrammatical, as nonsensical, or, most important, as *not understood*) indicates a more complex failure of the semantic process to arrive at any usable representation; I will argue now that the grammar-meaning distinction may illuminate two extremes of a continuum but obscures its all-important interior.

We certainly cannot assume that logical meaninglessness has a precise psychological counterpart. Sentence (A) can certainly generate an image! The dominant frame (in my case) is that of someone sleeping; the default system assigns a particular bed, and in it lies a mummy-like shape-frame with a translucent green color property. In this frame there is a terminal for the character of the sleep—restless, perhaps—and "furiously" seems somewhat inappropriate at that terminal, perhaps because the terminal does not like to accept anything so "intentional" for a sleeper. "Idea" is even more disturbing, because a person is expected, or at least something animate. I sense frustrated procedures trying to resolve these tensions and conflicts more properly, here or there, into the sleeping framework that has been evoked.

Utterance (B) does not get nearly so far because no subframe accepts any substantial fragment. As a result no larger frame finds anything to match its terminals, hence, finally, no top level "meaning" or "sentence" frame can organize the utterance as either meaningful or grammatical. By combining this "soft" theory with gradations of assignment tolerances, I imagine one could develop systems that degrade properly for sentences with poor grammar rather than none; if the smaller fragments—phrases and subclauses —satisfy subframes well enough, an image adequate for certain kinds of comprehension could be constructed anyway, even though some parts of the top level structure are not entirely satisfied. Thus we arrive at a qualitative theory of "grammatical":

> If the top levels are satisfied but some lower terminals are not, we have a meaningless sentence; if the top is weak but the bottom solid, we can have an ungrammatical but meaningful utterance.

I do not mean to suggest that sentences must evoke visual images. Some people do not admit to assigning a color to the ball in "he kicked the ball." But everyone admits (eventually) to having assumed, if not a size or color, at least some purpose, attitude, or other elements of an assumed scenario. When we go beyond vision, terminals and their default assignments can represent purposes and functions, not just colors, sizes and shapes.

2.2 Scenarios

> Thinking... is biologically subsequent to the image-forming process. It is possible only when a way has been found of breaking up the 'massed' influence of past stimuli and situations, only when a device has already been discovered for conquering the sequential tyranny of past reactions. But though it is a later and a higher development, it does not supercede the method of images. It has its own drawbacks. Contrasted with imaging it loses something of vivacity, of vividness, of variety. Its prevailing instruments are words, and, not only because these are social, but also because in use they are necessarily strung out in sequence, they drop into habit reactions even more readily than images do. [With thinking] we

run greater and greater risk of being caught up in generalities that may have little to do with actual concrete experience. If we fail to maintain the methods of thinking, we run the risks of becoming tied to individual instances and of being made sport of by the accidental circumstances belonging to these.

—F. C. Bartlett (1932)

We condense and conventionalize, in language and thought, complex situations and sequences into compact words and symbols. Some words can perhaps be "defined" in elegant, simple structures, but only a small part of the meaning of "trade" is captured by:

first frame	second frame
$\rightarrow$	
A has X B has Y	B has X A has Y

Trading normally occurs in a social context of law, trust, and convention. Unless we also represent these other facts, most trade transactions will be almost meaningless. It is usually essential to know that each party usually wants both things but has to compromise. It is a happy but unusual circumstance in which each trader is glad to get rid of what he has. To represent trading strategies, one could insert the basic maneuvers right into the above frame-pair scenario: in order for A to make B want X more (or want Y less) we expect him to select one of the familiar tactics:

- Offer more for Y.
- Explain why X is so good.
- Create favorable side effect of B having X.
- Disparage the competition.
- Make B think C wants X.

These only scratch the surface. Trades usually occur within a scenario tied together by more than a simple chain of events each linked to the next. No single such scenario will do; when a clue about trading appears, it is essential to guess which of the different available scenarios is most likely to be useful.

Charniak's thesis (1972) studies questions about transactions that seem easy for people to comprehend yet obviously need rich default structures. We find in elementary school reading books such stories as:

Jane was invited to Jack's Birthday Party.
She wondered if he would like a kite.
She went to her room and shook her piggy bank.
It made no sound.

Most young readers understand that Jane wants money to buy Jack a kite for a present but that there is no money to pay for it in her piggy bank. Charniak proposes a variety of ways to facilitate such inferences—a "demon" for *present* that looks for things concerned with *money*, a demon for "piggy bank" which knows that shaking without sound means the bank is empty, etc. But although *present* now activates *money,* the reader may be surprised to find that neither of those words (nor any of their synonyms) occurs in the story. "Present" is certainly associated with "party" and "money" with "bank," but how are the longer chains built up? Here is another problem raised by Charniak. A friend tells Jane:

> He already has a Kite.
> He will make you take it back.

Take *which* kite back? We do not want Jane to return Jack's old kite. To determine the referent of the pronoun "it" requires understanding a lot about an assumed scenario. Clearly, "it" refers to the proposed *new* kite. How does one know this? (Note that we need not agree on any single explanation.) Generally, pronouns refer to recently mentioned things, but as this example shows, the referent depends on more than the local syntax.

Suppose for the moment we are already trying to instantiate a "buying a present" default subframe. Now, the word "it" alone is too small a fragment to deal with, but "take it back" could be a plausible unit to match a terminal of an appropriately elaborate *buying* scenario. Since that terminal would be constrained to agree with the assignment of "present" itself, we are assured of the correct meaning of it in "take X back." Automatically, the correct kite is selected. Of course, that terminal will have its own constraints as well; a subframe for the "take it back" idiom should know that "take X back" requires that:

> X was recently purchased.
> The return is to the place of purchase.
> You must have your sales slip.
> Etc.

If the current scenario does not contain a "take it back" terminal, then we have to find one that does and substitute it, maintaining as many prior assignments as possible. Notice that if things go well, the question of it being the old kite never even arises. *The sense of ambiguity arises only when a "near miss" mismatch is tried and rejected.*

Charniak's proposed solution to this problem is in the same spirit but emphasizes understanding that because Jack already has a kite, he may not want another one. He proposes a mechanism associated with "present":

> A) If we see that a person *P* might not like a present *X,* then look for *X* being returned to the store where it was bought.

> B) If we see this happening, or even being suggested, assert that the reason why is that *P* does not like *X.*

This statement of "advice" is intended by Charniak to be realized as a production-like entity to be added to the currently active database whenever a certain kind of context is encountered. Later, if its antecedent condition is satisfied, its action adds enough information about Jack and about the new kite to lead to a correct decision about the pronoun.

Charniak in effect proposes that the system should watch for certain kinds of events or situations and inject proposed reasons, motives, and explanations for them. The additional interconnections between the story elements are expected to help bridge the gaps that logic might find it hard to cross, because the additions are only "plausible" default explanations, assumed without corroborative assertions. By assuming (tentatively) "does not like X" when X is taken back, Charniak hopes to simulate much of ordinary "comprehension" of what is happening. We do not yet know how complex and various such plausible inferences must be to get a given level of performance, and the thesis does not answer this because it did not include a large simulation. Usually he proposes terminating the process by asserting the allegedly plausible motive without further analysis unless necessary. To understand why Jack might return the additional kite, it should usually be enough to assert that he does not like it. A deeper analysis might reveal that Jack would not really mind having two kites but he probably realizes that he will get only one present; his utility for two different presents is probably higher.

2.3 Scenarios and "Questions"

The meaning of a child's birthday party is very poorly approximated by any dictionary definition like "a party assembled to celebrate a birthday," where a party would be defined, in turn, as "people assembled for a celebration." This lacks all the flavor of the culturally required activities. Children know that the "definition" should include more specifications, the particulars of which can normally be assumed by way of default assignments:

```
DRESS.........................SUNDAY BEST.
PRESENT...................MUST PLEASE HOST.
.....................................MUST BE BOUGHT AND GIFT-WRAPPED.
GAMES.......................HIDE AND SEEK. PIN TAIL ON DONKEY.
DECOR .......................BALLOONS. FAVORS. CREPE-PAPER.
PARTY-MEAL ............CAKE. ICE-CREAM. SODA. HOTDOGS.
CAKE..........................CANDLES. BLOW-OUT. WISH. SING BIRTHDAY SONG.
ICE-CREAM...............STANDARD THREE-FLAVOR.
```

These ingredients for a typical American birthday party must be set into a larger structure. Extended events take place in one or more days. A party takes place in a day, of course, and occupies a substantial part of it, so we locate it in an appropriate day frame. A typical day has main events, such as

Get-up Dress Eat-1 Go-to-Work Eat-2

but a School-Day has more fixed detail:

Get-up Dress
   Eat-1 Go-to-School Be-in-School
      Home-Room Assembly English   Math (arrgh)
        Eat-2 Science   Recess Sport
          Go-Home Play
            Eat-3   Homework Go-To-Bed

Birthday parties obviously do not fit well into school-day frames. Any parent knows that the Party-Meal is bound to Eat-2 of its Day. I remember a child who did not seem to realize this. Absolutely stuffed after the Party-Meal, he asked when he would get lunch.

Returning to Jane's problem with the kite, we first hear that she is invited to Jack's birthday party. Without this party scenario, or at least an invitation scenario, the second line seems rather mysterious:

She wondered if he would like a kite.

To explain one's rapid comprehension of this, I will make a somewhat radical proposal: *to represent explicitly, in the frame for a scenario structure, pointers to a collection of the most serious problems and questions commonly associated with it.* In fact we shall consider the idea that the frame terminals are exactly those questions. Thus, for the birthday party:

Y must get P for X . . . . . . .Choose $P!$
X must like P . . . . .Will X like P?
Buy P . . . . .Where to buy P?
Get money to buy P . . . . .Where to get money?
(Sub-question of the "present" frame?)
Y must dress up . . . . .What should Y wear?

Certainly these are one's first concerns, when one is invited to a party.

The reader is free to wonder, with the author, whether this solution is acceptable. The question, "Will X like P?" certainly matches "She wondered if he would like a kite?" and correctly assigns the kite to P. But is our world regular enough that such question sets could be precompiled to make this mechanism often work smoothly? I think the answer is mixed. We do indeed expect many such questions; we surely do not expect all of them. But surely "expertise" consists partly in not having to realize ab initio what are the outstanding problems and interactions in situations. Notice, for example, that there is *no* default assignment for the present in our party-scenario frame. This mandates attention to that assignment problem and prepares us for a possible thematic concern. In any case, we probably need a more active mechanism for understanding "wondered" which can apply the information currently in the frame to produce an expectation of what Jane will think about.

The third line of our story, about shaking the bank, should also eventually match one of the present-frame questions, but the unstated connection between Money and Piggy-Bank is presumably represented in the piggy-bank frame, not the party frame, although once it is found, it will match our Get-Money question terminal. The primary functions and actions associated with piggy banks are Saving and Getting-Money-Out, and the latter has three principal methods:

1. Using a key. Most piggy banks don't offer this option.
2. Breaking it. Children hate this.
3. Shaking the money out, or using a thin slider.

In the fourth line does one know specifically that a *silent* Piggy Bank is empty, and hence out of money (I think, yes), or does one use general knowledge that a hard container which makes no noise when shaken is empty? I have found quite a number of people who prefer the latter. Logically the "general principle" would indeed suffice, but I feel that this misses the important point that a specific scenario of this character is engraved in every child's memory. The story is instantly intelligible to most readers. If more complex reasoning from general principles were required, this would not be so, and more readers would surely go astray. It is easy to find more complex problems:

A goat wandered into the yard where Jack was painting. The goat got the paint all over himself. When Mother saw the goat, she asked, "Jack, did you do that?"

There is no one word or line, which is the referent of "that." It seems to refer, as Charniak notes, to "cause the goat to be covered with paint." Charniak does not permit himself to make a specific proposal to handle this kind of problem, remarking only that his "demon" model would need a substantial extension to deal with such a poorly localized "thematic subject." Consider how much one has to know about our culture, to realize that *that* is not the *goat-in-the-yard* but the *goat-covered-with-paint*. Charniak's thesis—basically a study rather than a debugged system—discusses issues about the activation, operation, and dismissal of expectation and default-knowledge demons. Many of his ideas have been absorbed into this essay.

In spite of its tentative character, I will try to summarize this image of language understanding as somewhat parallel to seeing. The key words and ideas of a discourse evoke substantial thematic or scenario structures, drawn from memory with rich default assumptions. The individual statements of a discourse lead to temporary representations—which seem to correspond to what contemporary linguists call "deep structures"—which are then quickly rearranged or consumed in elaborating the growing scenario representation. In order of "scale," among the ingredients of such a structure there might be these kinds of levels:

Surface Syntactic Frames. Mainly verb and noun structures. Prepositional and word-order indicator conventions.

Surface Semantic Frames. Action-centered meanings of words. Qualifiers and relations concerning participants, instruments, trajectories and strategies, goals, consequences and side effects.

Thematic Frames. Scenarios concerned with topics, activities, portraits, setting. Outstanding problems and strategies commonly connected with topic.

Narrative Frames. Skeleton forms for typical stories, explanations, and arguments. Conventions about foci, protagonists, plot forms, development, etc., designed to help a listener construct a new, instantiated Thematic Frame in his own mind.

A single sentence can assign terminals, attach subframes, apply a transformation, or cause a gross replacement of a high level frame when a proposed assignment no longer fits well enough. A pronoun is comprehensible only when general linguistic conventions, interacting with defaults and specific indicators, determine a terminal or subframe of the current scenario.

In *vision* the transformations usually have a simple grouplike structure, in *language* we expect more complex, less regular systems of frames. Nevertheless, because *time, cause,* and *action* are so important to us, we often use sequential transformation pairs that replace situations by their temporal or causal successors.

Because syntactic structural rules direct the selection and assembly of the transient sentence frames, research on linguistic structures should help us understand how our frame systems are constructed. One might look for such structures specifically associated with assigning terminals, selecting emphasis or attention viewpoints (transformations), inserting sentential structures into thematic structures, and changing gross thematic representations.

Finally, just as there are familiar "basic plots" for stories, there must be basic superframes for discourses, arguments, narratives, and so forth. As with sentences, we should expect to find special linguistic indicators for operations concerning these larger structures; we should move beyond the grammar of sentences to try to find and systematize the linguistic conventions that, operating across wider spans, must be involved with assembling and transforming scenarios and plans.

2.4 Questions, Systems, and Cases

Questions arise from a point of view—from something that helps to structure what is problematical, what is worth asking, and what constitutes an answer (or progress). It is not that the view determines reality, only what we accept from reality and how we structure it. I am realist enough to believe that in the long run reality gets its own chance to accept or reject our various views.

—A. Newell (1973a)

Examination of linguistic discourse leads thus to a view of the frame concept in which the "terminals" serve to represent the questions most likely to arise in a situation. To make this important viewpoint more explicit, we will spell out this reinterpretation.

A Frame is a collection of questions to be asked about a hypothetical situation: it specifies issues to be raised and methods to be used in dealing with them.

The terminals of a frame correspond perhaps to what Schank (1973) calls "conceptual cases," although I do not think we should restrict them to as few types as Schank suggests. To understand a narrated or perceived action, one often feels compelled to ask such questions as

What caused it (agent)?
What was the purpose (intention)?
What are the consequences (side-effects)?
Whom does it affect (recipient)?
How is it done (instrument)?

The number of such "cases" or questions is problematical. While we would like to reduce meaning to a very few "primitive" concepts, perhaps in analogy to the situation in traditional linguistic analysis, I know of no reason to suppose that that goal can be achieved. My own inclination is to side with such workers as W. Martin (1974), who look toward very large collections of "primitives," annotated with comments about how they are related. Only time will tell which is better.

For entities other than actions one asks different questions; for thematic topics the questions may be much less localized, e.g.,

Why are they telling this to me?
How can I find out more about it?
How will it help with the "real problem"?

and so forth. In a "story" one asks what is the topic, what is the author's attitude, what is the main event, who are the protagonists, and so on. As each question is given a tentative answer, the corresponding subframes are attached and the questions they ask become active in turn.

The "markers" we proposed for vision-frames become more complex in this view. If we adopt for the moment Newell's larger sense of "view," it is not enough simply to ask a question; one must indicate how it is to be answered. Thus a terminal should also contain (or point to) suggestions and recommendations about how to find an assignment. Our "default" assignments then become the simplest special cases of such recommendations, and one certainly could have a hierarchy in which such proposals depend on features of the situation, perhaps along the lines of Wilks's (1973) "preference" structures.

For syntactic frames, the drive toward ritualistic completion of assignments is strong, but we are more flexible at the conceptual level. As Schank (1973a) says,

People do not usually state all the parts of a given thought that they are trying to communicate because the speaker tries to be brief and leaves out assumed or unessential information [...]. The conceptual processor makes use of the unfilled slots to search for a given type of information in a sentence or a larger unit of discourse that will fill the needed slot.

Even in physical perception we have the same situation. A box will not present all of its sides at once to an observer, and although this is certainly not because it wants to be brief, the effect is the same; the processor is prepared to find out what the missing sides look like and (if the matter is urgent enough) to move around to find answers to such questions.

Frame-*Systems,* in this view, become choice-points corresponding (on the conceptual level) to the mutually exclusive choice "Systems" exploited by Winograd (1975). The different frames of a system represent different ways of using the same information, located at the common terminals. As in the grammatical situation, one has to choose one of them at a time. On the conceptual level, this choice becomes: *what questions shall I ask about this situation?*

View-changing, as we shall argue, is a problem-solving technique important in representing, explaining, and predicting. In the rearrangements inherent in the frame-system representation (for example, of an action), we have a first approximation to Simmons' (1973) idea of "procedures which in some cases will change the contextual definitional structure to reflect the action of a verb."

Where do the "questions" come from? That is not in the scope of this paper, really, but we can be sure that the frame-makers (however they operate) must use some principles. The methods used to generate the questions ultimately shape each person's general intellectual style. People surely differ in details of preferences for asking "Why?" "How can I find out more?" "What's in it for me?" "How will this help with the current higher goals?" and so forth.

Similar issues about the style of *answering* must arise. In its simplest form the drive toward instantiating empty terminals would appear as a variety of hunger or discomfort, satisfied by any default or other assignment that does not conflict with a prohibition. In more complex cases we should perceive less animalistic strategies for acquiring deeper understandings.

It is tempting, then, to imagine varieties of frame-systems that span from simple template-filling structures to implementations of the "views" of Newell—with all their implications about coherent generators of issues with which to be concerned, ways to investigate them, and procedures for evaluating proposed solutions. But I feel uncomfortable about any superficially coherent synthesis in which one expects the same kind of theoretical framework to function well on many different levels of scale or concept. We should expect very different question-processing mechanisms to operate our low-level stereotypes and our most comprehensive strategic overviews.

3. Learning, Memory, and Paradigms

To the child, Nature gives various means of rectifying any mistakes he may commit respecting the salutary or hurtful qualities of the objects which surround him. On every occasion his judgements are corrected by experience; want and pain are the necessary consequences arising from false judgement; gratification and pleasure are produced by judging aright. Under such masters, we cannot fail but to become well informed; and we soon learn to reason justly, when want and pain are the necessary consequences of a contrary conduct.

In the study and practice of the sciences it is quite different: the false judgements we form neither affect our existence nor our welfare; and we are not forced by any physical necessity to correct them. Imagination, on the contrary, which is ever wandering beyond the bounds of truth, joined to self-love and that self-confidence we are so apt to indulge, prompt us to draw conclusions that are not immediately derived from facts.

—A. Lavoisier (1949)

How does one locate a frame to represent a new situation? Obviously, we cannot begin any complete theory outside the context of some proposed global scheme for the organization of knowledge in general. But if we imagine working within some bounded domain, we can discuss some important issues:

Expectation: How to select an initial frame to meet some given conditions.

Elaboration: How to select and assign subframes to represent additional details.

Alteration: How to find a frame to replace one that does not fit well enough.

Novelty: What to do if no acceptable frame can be found. Can we modify an old frame or must we build a new one?

Learning: What frames should be stored, or modified, as a result of the experience?

In popular culture, memory is seen as separate from the rest of thinking: but finding the right memory—it would be better to say: finding a *useful* memory—needs the same sorts of strategies used in other kinds of thinking!

We say someone is "clever" who is unusually good at quickly locating highly appropriate frames. His information-retrieval systems are better at making good hypotheses, formulating the conditions the new frame should meet, and exploiting knowledge gained in the "unsuccessful" part of the search. Finding the right memory is no less a problem than solving any other kind of puzzle! Because of this a good retrieval mechanism can be based only in part upon basic "innate" mechanisms. It must also depend largely on (learned) knowledge about the structure of one's own knowledge! Our proposal will combine several elements—a pattern matching process, a clustering theory, and a similarity network.

In seeing a room or understanding a story, one assembles a network of frames and subframes. Everything noticed or guessed, rightly or wrongly, is represented in this network. We have already suggested that an active frame cannot be maintained unless its terminal conditions are satisfied.

We now add the postulate that *all satisfied frames must be assigned to terminals of superior frames.* This applies, as a special case, to any substantial fragments of "data" that have been observed and represented.

Of course, there must be an exception! We must allow a certain number of items to be attached to something like a set of "short term memory" registers. But the intention is that very little can be remembered unless embedded in a suitable frame. This, at any rate, is the conceptual scheme; in certain domains we would, of course, admit other kinds of memory "hooks" and special sensory buffers.

3.1 Requests to Memory

We can now imagine the memory system as driven by two complementary needs. *On one side are items demanding to be properly represented by being embedded into larger frames; on the other side are incompletely filled frames demanding terminal assignments.* The rest of the system will try to placate these lobbyists, but not so much in accord with general principles as in accord with special knowledge and conditions imposed by the currently active goals.

When a frame encounters trouble—when an important condition cannot be satisfied—something must be done. We envision the following major kinds of accommodation to trouble:

Matching: When nothing more specific is found, we can attempt to use some "basic" associative memory mechanism. This will succeed by itself only in relatively simple situations, but should play a supporting role in the other tactics.

Excuse: An apparent misfit can often be excused or explained. A "chair" that meets all other conditions but is much too small could be a "toy."

Advice: The frame contains explicit knowledge about what to do about the trouble. Below, we describe an extensive, learned, "Similarity Network" in which to embed such knowledge.

Summary: If a frame cannot be completed or replaced, one must give it up. But first one must construct a well-formulated complaint or summary to help whatever process next becomes responsible for reassigning the subframes left in limbo.

In my view, all four of these are vitally important. I discuss them in the following sections.

3.2 Excuses

We can think of a frame as describing an "ideal." If an ideal does not match reality because it is "basically" wrong, it must be replaced. *But it is in the nature of ideals that they are really elegant simplifications; their attractiveness derives from their simplicity, but their real power depends upon additional knowledge about interactions between them!* Accordingly we need not abandon an ideal because of a failure to instantiate it, provided one can explain the discrepancy in terms of such an interaction. Here are some examples in which such an "excuse" can save a failing match:

Occlusion: A table, in a certain view, should have four legs, but a chair might occlude one of them. One can look for things like T-joints and shadows to support such an excuse.

Functional Variant: A chair-leg is usually a stick, geometrically; but more important, it is *functionally* a support. Therefore, a strong center post, with an adequate base plate, should be an acceptable replacement for all the legs. Many objects are multiple purpose and need functional rather than physical descriptions.

Broken: A visually missing component could be explained as in fact physically missing, or it could be broken. Reality has a variety of ways to frustrate ideals.

Parasitic Contexts: An object that is just like a chair, except in size, could be (and probably is) a toy chair. The complaint "too small" could often be so interpreted in contexts with other things too small, children playing, peculiarly large "grain," and so forth.

In most of those examples, the kinds of knowledge to make the repair— and thus salvage the current frame—are "general" enough usually to be attached to the thematic context of a superior frame. In the remainder of this essay, I will concentrate on types of more sharply localized knowledge that would naturally be attached to a frame itself, for recommending its own replacement.

3.3 Clusters, Classes, and a Geographic Analogy

Though a discussion of *some* of the attributes shared by a number of games or chairs or leaves often helps us to learn how to employ the corresponding term, there is no set of characteristics that is simultaneously applicable to all members of the class and to them alone. Instead, confronted with a previously unobserved activity, we apply the term 'game' because what we are seeing bears a close 'family resemblance' to a number of the activities we have previously learned to call by that name. For Wittgenstein, in short, games, chairs, and leaves are natural families, each constituted by a network of overlapping and crisscross resemblances. The existence of such a network sufficiently accounts for our success in identifying the corresponding object or activity.

—T. Kuhn (1970)

To make the similarity network act more "complete," consider the following analogy. In a city, any person should be able to visit any other; but we do not build a special road between each pair of houses; we place a group of houses on a "block." We do not connect roads between each pair of blocks, but have them share streets. We do not connect each town to every other, but construct main routes, connecting the centers of larger groups. Within such an organization, each member has direct links to some other individuals at his own "level," mainly to nearby, highly similar ones; but each individual has also at least a few links to "distinguished" members of higher level groups. The result is that there is usually a rather short sequence between any two individuals, if one can but find it.

To locate something in such a structure, one uses a hierarchy like the one implicit in a mail address. Everyone knows something about the largest categories, in that he knows where the major cities are. An inhabitant of a city knows the nearby towns, and people in the towns know the nearby villages. No person knows all the individual routes between pairs of houses; but, for a particular friend, one may know a special route to his home in a nearby town that is better than going to the city and back. *Directories* factor the problem, basing paths on standard routes between major nodes in the network. Personal shortcuts can bypass major nodes and go straight between familiar locations. Although the standard routes are usually not quite the very best possible, our stratified transport and communication services connect everything together reasonably well, with comparatively few connections.

At each level, the aggregates usually have distinguished foci or *capitals.* These serve as elements for clustering at the next level of aggregation. There is no nonstop airplane service between New Haven and San Jose because it is more efficient overall to share the trunk route between New York and San Francisco, which are the capitals at that level of aggregation.

As our memory networks grow, we can expect similar aggregations of the destinations of our similarity pointers. Our decisions about what we consider to be primary or trunk difference features and which are considered subsidiary will have large effects on our abilities. Such decisions eventually accumulate to become epistemological commitments about the conceptual cities of our mental universe.

The nonrandom convergences and divergences of the similarity pointers, for each difference d, thus tend to structure our conceptual world around:

1) the aggregation into d-clusters, and
2) the selection of d-capitals.

Note that it is perfectly all right to have *several capitals in a cluster,* so that there need be no one attribute common to them all. The "crisscross resemblances" of Wittgenstein are then consequences of the local connections in our similarity network, which are surely adequate to explain how we can feel as though we know what a chair or a game is—yet cannot always define it in a logical way as an element in some class-hierarchy or by any other kind of compact, formal, declarative rule. The apparent coherence of the conceptual aggregates need not reflect explicit definitions, but can emerge from the success-directed sharpening of the difference describing processes.

The selection of capitals corresponds to selecting stereotypes or typical elements whose default assignments are unusually useful. There are many forms of chairs, for example, and one should choose carefully the chair-description frames that are to be the major capitals of chair-land. These are used for rapid matching and assigning priorities to the various differences. The lower priority features of the cluster center then serve either as default properties of the chair types or, if more realism is required, as dispatch pointers to the local chair villages and towns. Difference pointers could be "functional" as well as geometric. Thus after rejecting a first try at "chair," one might try the functional idea of "something one can sit on" to explain an un-conventional form. This requires a deeper analysis in terms of forces and strengths. Of course, that analysis would fail to capture toy chairs, or chairs of such ornamental delicacy that their actual use would be unthinkable. These would be better handled by the method of excuses, in which one would bypass the usual geometrical or functional explanations in favor of re-sponding to contexts involving art or play.

It is important to reemphasize that there is no reason to restrict the memory structure to a single hierarchy; the notions of "level" of aggregation need not coincide for different kinds of differences. The d-capitals can exist, not only by explicit declarations, but also implicitly by their focal locations in the structure defined by convergent d-pointers. (In the Newell-Simon GPS framework, the "differences" are ordered into a fixed hierarchy. By making the priorities depend on the goal, the same memories could be made to serve more purposes; the resulting problem-solver would lose the elegance of a single, simple-ordered measure of "progress," but that is the price of moving from a first-order theory.)

Finally, we should point out that we do not need to invoke any mysterious additional mechanism for *creating* the clustering structure. Developmentally, one would assume, the earliest frames would tend to become the capitals of their later relatives, unless this is firmly prevented by experience, because each time the use of one stereotype is reasonably successful, its centrality is reinforced by another pointer from somewhere else. Otherwise, *the acquisition of new centers is in large measure forced upon us from the outside by the words available in one's language; by the behavior of objects in one's environment; by what one is told by one's teachers, family, and general culture.* Of course, at each step the structure of the previous structure dominates the acquisition of the later. But in any case such forms and clusters should emerge from the interactions between the world and almost any memory-using mechanism; it would require more explanation were they *not* found!

3.4 Analogies and Alternative Descriptions

We have discussed the use of different frames of the same system to describe the same situation in different ways: for change of position in vision and for change of emphasis in language. Sometimes, in "problem-solving" we use two or more descriptions in a more complex way to construct an analogy or to apply two radically *different* kinds of analysis to the same situation. *For hard problems, one "problem space" is usually not enough!*

Suppose your car battery runs down. You believe that there is an electricity shortage and blame the generator.

The generator can be represented as a mechanical system: the rotor has a pulley wheel driven by a belt from the engine. Is the belt tight enough? Is it even there? The output, seen mechanically, is a cable to the battery or whatever. Is it intact? Are the bolts tight? Are the brushes pressing on the commutator?

Seen electrically, the generator is described differently. The rotor is seen as a flux-linking coil, rather than as a rotating device. The brushes and commutator are seen as electrical switches. The output is current along a pair of conductors leading from the brushes through control circuits to the battery.

We thus represent the situation in two quite different frame systems. In one, the armature is a mechanical rotor with pulley; in the other, it is a conductor in a changing magnetic field. The same—or analogous—elements share terminals of different frames, and the frame-transformations apply only to some of them.

The differences between the two frames are substantial. The entire mechanical chassis of the car plays the simple role, in the electrical frame, of one of the battery connections. The diagnostician has to use both representations. A failure of current to flow often means that an intended conductor is not acting like one. For this case, the basic transformation between the frames depends on the fact that electrical continuity is in general equivalent to firm mechanical attachment. Therefore, any conduction disparity revealed by electrical measurements should make us look for a corresponding disparity in the mechanical frame. In fact, since "repair" in this universe is synonymous with "mechanical repair," the diagnosis *must* end in the mechanical frame. Eventually, we might locate a defective mechanical junction and discover a loose connection, corrosion, wear, or whatever.

Why have two separate frames, rather than one integrated structure to represent the generator? I believe that in such a complex problem, one can never cope with many details at once. At each moment one must work within a reasonably simple framework. I contend that any problem that a person can solve at all is worked out at each moment in a small context and that the key operations in problem-solving are concerned with finding or constructing these working environments.

Indeed, finding an electrical fault requires moving between at least three frames: a visual one along with the electrical and mechanical frames. If electrical evidence suggests a loose mechanical connection, one needs a visual frame to guide one's self to the mechanical fault.

Are there general methods for constructing adequate frames? The answer is both yes and no! There are some often-useful strategies for adapting old frames to new purposes; but I should emphasize that humans certainly have no magical way to solve *all* hard problems! One must not fall into what Papert calls the Superhuman-Human Fallacy and require a theory of human behavior to explain even things that people cannot really do!

One cannot expect to have a frame exactly right for any problem or expect always to be able to invent one. But we do have a good deal to work with, and it is important to remember the contribution of one's culture in assessing the complexity of problems people seem to solve. *The experienced mechanic need not routinely invent;* he already has engine representations in terms of ignition, lubrication, cooling, timing, fuel mixing, transmission, compression, and so forth. Cooling, for example, is already subdivided into fluid circulation, air flow, thermostasis, etc. Most "ordinary" problems are presumably solved by systematic use of the analogies provided by the transformations between pairs of these structures. The huge network of knowledge, acquired from school, books, apprenticeship, or whatever is interlinked by difference and relevancy pointers. No doubt the culture imparts a good deal of this structure by its conventional use *of the same words* in explanations of different views of a subject.

3.5 Frames and Paradigms

Until that scholastic paradigm (the medieval 'impetus' theory) was invented, there were no pendulums, but only swinging stones, for scientists to see. Pendulums were brought into the world by something very like a paradigm-induced gestalt switch.

Do we, however, really need to describe what separates Galileo from Aristotle, or Lavoisier from Priestly, as a transformation of vision? Did these men really see different things when looking at the same sorts of objects? Is there any legitimate sense in which we can say they pursued their research in different worlds?

[I am] acutely aware of the difficulties created by saying that when Aristotle and Galileo looked at swinging stones, the first saw constrained fall, the second a pendulum. Nevertheless, I am convinced that we must learn to make sense of sentences that at least resemble these.

–T. Kuhn (1970)

According to Kuhn's model of scientific evolution, normal science proceeds by using established descriptive schemes. Major changes result from new paradigms, new ways of describing things that lead to new methods and techniques. Eventually there is a redefining of "normal."

Now while Kuhn prefers to apply his own very effective redescription paradigm at the level of major scientific revolutions, it seems to me that the same idea applies as well to the microcosm of everyday thinking. Indeed, in that last sentence quoted, we see that Kuhn is seriously considering that the paradigms play a substantive rather than metaphorical role in visual perception, just as we have proposed for frames.

Whenever our customary viewpoints do not work well, whenever we fail to find effective frame systems in memory, we must construct new ones that bring out the right features. Presumably, the most usual way to do this is to build some sort of pair-system from two or more old ones and then edit or debug it to suit the circumstances. How might this be done? It is tempting to formulate the requirements, and then solve the construction problem.

But that is certainly not the usual course of ordinary thinking! Neither are requirements formulated all at once, nor is the new system constructed entirely by deliberate preplanning. Instead we recognize unsatisfied requirements, one by one, as deficiencies or "bugs," in the course of a sequence of modifications made to an unsatisfactory representation.

I think Papert (1972; see also Minsky, 1970) is correct in believing that the ability to diagnose and modify one's own procedures is a collection of specific and important "skills." *Debugging,* a fundamentally important component of intelligence, has its own special techniques and procedures. Every normal person is pretty good at them; or otherwise he would not have learned to see and talk! Although this essay is already speculative, I would like to point here to the theses of Goldstein (1974) and Sussman (1973) about the explicit use of *knowledge about debugging* in learning symbolic representations. They build new procedures to satisfy multiple requirements by such elementary but powerful techniques as:

1) Make a crude first attempt by the first order method of simply putting together procedures that separately achieve the individual goals.

2) If something goes wrong, try to characterize one of the defects as a specific (and undesirable) kind of interaction between two procedures.

3) Apply a debugging technique that, according to a record in memory, is good at repairing that *specific kind* of interaction.

4) Summarize the experience, to add to the "debugging techniques library" in memory.

These might seem simple-minded, but if the new problem is not too radically different from the old ones, they have a good chance to work, especially if one picks out the right first-order approximations. If the new problem *is* radically different, one should not expect *any* learning theory to work well. Without a structured cognitive map—without the "near misses" of Winston or a cultural supply of good training sequences of problems, we should not expect radically new paradigms to appear magically whenever we need them.

What are "kinds of interactions," and what are "debugging techniques?" The simplest, perhaps, are those in which the result of achieving a first goal interferes with some condition prerequisite for achieving a second goal. The simplest repair is to reinsert that prerequisite as a new condition. There are examples in which this technique alone cannot succeed because a prerequisite for the second goal is incompatible with the first. Sussman presents a more sophisticated diagnosis and repair method that recognizes this and exchanges the order of the goals. Goldstein considers related problems in a multiple description context.

If asked about important future lines of research on artificial or natural intelligence, I would point to the interactions between these ideas and the problems of using multiple representations to deal with the same situation from several viewpoints. To carry out such a study, we need better ideas about interactions among the transformed relationships. Here the frame-system idea by itself begins to show limitations. Fitting together new representations from parts of old ones is clearly a complex process itself, and one that could be solved within the framework of our theory (if at all) only by an intricate bootstrapping. This, too, is surely a special skill with its own techniques. I consider it a crucial component of a theory of intelligence.

We must not expect complete success in the above enterprise; there is a difficulty, as Newell (1973) notes in a larger context:

> 'Elsewhere' is another view—possibly from philosophy—or other 'elsewheres' as well, since the views of man are multiple. Each view has its own questions. Separate views speak mostly past each other. Occasionally, of course, they speak to the same issue and then comparison is possible, but not often and not on demand.

4. Criticism of the Logistic Approach

> If one tries to describe processes of genuine thinking in terms of formal traditional logic, the result is often unsatisfactory; one has, then, a series of correct operations, but the sense of the process and what was vital, forceful, creative in it seems somehow to have evaporated in the formulations.
>
> –M. Wertheimer (1959)

I here explain why I think more "logical" approaches will not work. There have been serious attempts, from as far back as Aristotle, to represent common sense reasoning by a "logistic" system—that is, one that makes a complete separation between

1) "propositions" that embody specific information, and
2) "syllogisms" or general laws of proper inference.

No one has been able successfully to confront such a system with a realistically large set of propositions. I think such attempts will continue to fail, because of the character of logistic in general rather than from defects of particular formalisms. (Most recent attempts have used variants of "first order predicate logic," but I do not think *that* is the problem.)

A typical attempt to simulate common-sense thinking by logistic systems begins in a microworld of limited complication. At one end are high-level goals such as "I want to get from my house to the Airport." At the other end we start with many small items—the *axioms*—like "The car is in the garage," "One does not go outside undressed," "To get to a place one should (on the whole) move in its direction," etc. To make the system work, one designs heuristic search procedures to "prove" the desired goal, or to produce a list of actions that will achieve it.

I will not recount the history of attempts to make both ends meet—but merely summarize my impression: in simple cases one can get such systems to "perform," but as we approach reality, the obstacles become overwhelming. The problem of finding suitable axioms—the problem of "stating the facts" in terms of always-correct, logical assumptions—is very much harder than is generally believed.

Formalizing the Required Knowledge: Just constructing a knowledge base is a major intellectual research problem. Whether one's goal is logistic or not, we still know far too little about the contents and structure of common-sense knowledge. A "minimal" common-sense system must "know" something about cause and effect, time, purpose, locality, process, and types of knowledge. It also needs ways to acquire, represent, and use such knowledge. We need a serious epistemological research effort in this area. The essays of McCarthy (1969) and Sandewall (1970) are steps in that direction. I have no easy plan for this large enterprise; but the magnitude of the task will certainly depend strongly on the representations chosen, and I think that "Logistic" is already making trouble.

Relevancy: The problem of selecting relevance from excessive variety is a key issue! A modern epistemology will not resemble the old ones! Computational concepts are necessary and novel. Perhaps the better part of knowledge is not propositional in character, but interpropositional. For each "fact" one needs meta-facts about how it is to be used and when it should not be used. In McCarthy's "Airport" paradigm we see ways to deal with some interactions between "situations, actions, and causal laws" within a restricted microworld of things and actions. But though the system can make deductions implied by its axioms, it cannot be told when it should or should not make such deductions.

For example, one might want to tell the system to "not cross the road if a car is coming." But one cannot demand that the system "prove" no car is coming, for there will not usually be any such proof. In PLANNER, one can direct an *attempt* to prove that a car IS coming, and if the (limited) deduction attempt ends with "failure," one can act. This cannot be done in a pure logistic system. "Look right, look left" is a first approximation. But if one tells the system the real truth about speeds, blind driveways, probabilities of racing cars whipping around the corner, proof becomes impractical. If it reads in a physics book that intense fields perturb light rays, should it fear that a mad scientist has built an invisible car? We need to represent "usually!" Eventually it must understand the trade-off between mortality and accomplishment, for one can do nothing if paralyzed by fear.

Monotonicity: Even if we formulate relevancy restrictions, logistic systems have a problem in using them. In any logistic system, all the axioms are necessarily "permissive"—they all help to permit new inferences to be drawn. Each added axiom means more theorems; none can disappear. There simply is no direct way to add information to tell such a system about kinds of conclusions that should not be drawn! To put it simply: if we adopt enough axioms to deduce what we need, we deduce far too simply: if we adapt enough axioms to deduce what we need, we deduce far too many other things. But if we try to change this by adding axioms about relevancy, we still produce all the unwanted theorems, plus annoying statements about their irrelevancy.

Because logicians are not concerned with systems that will later be enlarged, they can design axioms that permit only the conclusions they want. In the development of intelligence the situation is different. One has to learn which features of situations are important and which kinds of deductions are not to be regarded seriously. The usual reaction to the "liar's paradox" is, after a while, to laugh. The conclusion is not to reject an axiom, but to reject the deduction itself! This raises another issue:

Procedure-Controlling Knowledge: The separation between axioms and deduction makes it impractical to include classificational knowledge about propositions. Nor can we include knowledge about management of deduction. A paradigm problem is that of axiomatizing everyday concepts of approximation or nearness. One would like nearness to be transitive:

(A near B) AND (B near C) $\Rightarrow$ (A near C)

but unrestricted application of this rule would make everything near everything else. One can try technical tricks like

(A near *1 B) AND (B near *1 C) $\Rightarrow$ (A near *2 C)

and admit only (say) five grades of near *1, near *2, near *3, etc. One might invent analog quantities or parameters. But one cannot (in a Logistic system) decide to make a new kind of "axiom" to prevent applying transitivity after (say) three chained uses, conditionally, unless there is a "good excuse." I do not mean to propose a particular solution to the transitivity of nearness. (To my knowledge, no one has made a creditable proposal about it.) My complaint is that because of acceptance of Logistic, no one has freely explored this kind of procedural restriction.

Combinatorial Problems: I see no reason to expect these systems to escape combinatorial explosions when given richer knowledge bases. Although we see encouraging demonstrations in microworlds, from time to time, it is common in AI research to encounter high-grade performance on hard puzzles—given just enough information to solve the problem—but this does not often lead to good performance in larger domains.

Consistency and Completeness: A human thinker reviews plans and goallists as he works, revising his knowledge and policies about using it. One can program some of this into the theorem proving program itself—but one really wants also to represent it directly, in a natural way, in the declarative corpus—for use in further introspection. Why then do workers try to make Logistic systems do the job? A valid reason is that the systems have an attractive simple elegance; if they worked, this would be fine. An invalid reason is more often offered: that such systems have a mathematical virtue because they are

1) Complete—"All true statements can be proven"; and
2) Consistent—"No false statements can be proven."

It seems not often realized that completeness is no rare prize. It is a trivial consequence of any exhaustive search procedure, and any system can be "completed" by adjoining to it any other complete system and interlacing the computational steps. Consistency is more refined; it requires one's axioms to imply no contradictions. But I do not believe that consistency is necessary or even desirable in a developing intelligent system. No one is ever completely consistent. What is important is how one handles paradox or conflict, how one learns from mistakes, how one turns aside from suspected inconsistencies.

Because of this kind of misconception, Godel's Incompleteness Theorem has stimulated much foolishness about alleged differences between machines and men. No one seems to have noted its more "logical" interpretation: that enforcing consistency produces limitations. Of course there will be differences between humans (who are demonstrably inconsistent) and machines whose designers have imposed consistency. But it is not inherent in machines that they be programmed only with consistent logical systems. Those "philosophical" discussions all make these quite unnecessary assumptions! (I regard the recent demonstration of the consistency of modern set-theory, thus, as indicating that set-theory is probably inadequate for our purposes—not as reassuring evidence that set theory is safe to use!)

A famous mathematician, warned that his proof would lead to a paradox if he took one more logical step, replied "Ah, but I shall not take that step." He was completely serious. A large part of ordinary (or even mathematical) knowledge resembles that in dangerous professions: When are certain actions unwise? When are certain approximations safe to use? When do various measures yield sensible estimates? Which self-referent statements are permissible if not carried too far? Concepts like "nearness" are too valuable to give up just because no one can exhibit satisfactory axioms for them. To summarize:

1) "Logical" reasoning is not flexible enough to serve as a basis for thinking: I prefer to think of it as a collection of heuristic methods, effective only when applied to starkly simplified schematic plans. The Consistency that Logic absolutely demands is not otherwise usually available—*and probably not even desirable!*—because consistent systems are likely to be too weak.

2) I doubt the feasibility of representing ordinary knowledge effectively in the form of many small, independently true propositions.

3) The strategy of complete separation of specific knowledge from general rules of inference is much too radical. We need more direct ways for linking fragments of knowledge to advice about *how* they are to be used.

4) It was long believed that it was crucial to make all knowledge accessible to deduction in the form of declarative statements; but this seems less urgent as we
learn ways to manipulate structural and procedural descriptions.

I do not mean to suggest that "thinking" can proceed very far without
something like "reasoning." We certainly need (and use) something like syllogistic deduction; but I expect mechanisms for doing such things to emerge
in any case from processes for "matching" and "instantiation" required for
other functions. Traditional formal logic is a technical tool for discussing either everything that can be deduced from some data or whether a certain consequence can be so deduced; it cannot discuss at all what *ought* to be deduced under ordinary circumstances. Like the abstract theory of syntax,
formal logic without a powerful procedural semantics cannot deal with
meaningful situations.

I cannot state strongly enough my conviction that the preoccupation with
consistency, so valuable for mathematical logic, has been incredibly destruc-
tive to those working on models of mind. At the popular level it has produced
a weird conception of the potential capabilities of machines in general. At
the "logical" level it has blocked efforts to represent ordinary knowledge, by
presenting an unreachable image of a corpus of context-free "truths" that can
stand almost by themselves. And at the intellect-modeling level it has
blocked the fundamental realization that *thinking begins first with suggestive
but defective plans and images that are slowly (if ever) refined and replaced
by better ones.*

Retrieval Time from Semantic Memory

Allan M. Collins and M. Ross Quillian

1. Introduction

Quillian (1967, 1969) has proposed a model for storing semantic information in a computer memory. In this model each word has stored
with it a configuration of pointers to other words in the memory; this
configuration-represents the word's meaning. Figure 1 illustrates the organization of such a memory structure. If what is stored with canary is "a yellow
bird that can sing" then there is a pointer to bird, which is the category name
or *superset* of canary, and pointers to two *properties,* that a canary is yellow
and that it can sing. Information true of birds in general (such as that they
can fly, and that they have wings and feathers) need not be stored with the
memory node for each separate kind of bird. Instead, the fact that a canary
can fly can be inferred by retrieving that a canary is a bird and that birds can
fly. Since an ostrich cannot fly, we assume this information is stored as a
property with the node for ostrich, just as is done in a dictionary, to preclude
the inference that an ostrich can fly. By organizing the memory in this way,
the amount of space needed for storage is minimized.

If we take this as a model for the structure of human memory, it can lead to testable predictions about retrieving information. Suppose a person has only the information shown in Figure 1 stored on each of the nodes. Then to decide "A canary can sing," the person need only start at the node canary and retrieve the properties stored there to find the statement is true. But, to decide that "A canary can fly," the person must move up one level to bird before he can retrieve the property about flying. Therefore, the person should require more *time* to decide that "A canary can fly" than he does to decide that "A canary can sing." Similarly, the person should require still longer to decide that "A canary has skin," since this fact is stored with his node for animal, which is yet another step removed from canary. More directly, sentences which themselves assert something about a node's supersets, such as "A canary is a bird," or "A canary is an animal," should also require decision times that vary directly with the number of levels separating the memory nodes they talk about.

A number of assumptions about the retrieval process must be made before predictions such as those above can be stated explicitly. First, we need to assume that both retrieving a property from a node and moving up a level in a hierarchy take a person time. Second, we shall assume that the times for these two processes are additive, whenever one step is dependent on completion of another step. This assumption is equivalent to Donders' assumption of additivity (Smith 1968) for the following two cases: (a) When moving up a level is followed by moving up another level, and (b) when moving up a level is followed by retrieving a property at the higher level. Third, we assume that the time to retrieve a property from a node is independent of the level of the node, although different properties may take different times to retrieve from the same node. It also seems reasonable to assume that searching properties at a node and moving up to the next level occur in a parallel rather than a serial manner, and hence are not additive. However, this assumption is not essential, and our reasons for preferring it are made clear in the discussion section (3).

We have labeled sentences that state property relations P sentences, and those that state superset relations S sentences. To these labels numbers are appended. These indicate the number of levels the model predicts it would be necessary to move through to decide the sentence is true. Thus, "A canary can sing" would be a P0 sentence, "A canary can fly" would be a P1 sentence, and "A canary has skin" would be a P2 sentence. Similarly, "A canary is a canary" would be an S0 sentence, "A canary is a bird" would be an S1 sentence, and "A canary is an animal" would be an S2 sentence.

It follows from the assumptions above that the time differences predicted for P0, P1, and P2 sentences are entirely a result of moving from one level in the hierarchy to the next. Thus, the increase in time from S0 to S1 should be the same as from P0 to P1 since both increases are a result of moving from level 0 to level 1. Likewise, the time increase from S1 to S2 should equal the

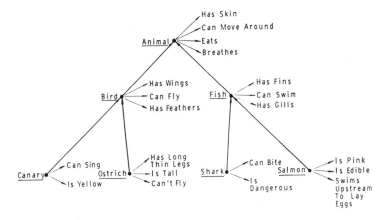

Figure 1. Illustration of the hypothetical memory structure for a 3-level hierarchy.

time increase from P1 to P2. In fact, if we assume that the time to move from one level to the next is not dependent on which levels are involved, all the time increases (from PO to P1, P1 to P2, SO to S1, and S1 to S2) should be equal.

Recently, reaction time (RT) has been used as a measure of the time it takes people to retrieve information from memory. By constructing a large number of true sentences of the six types discussed and interspersing these with equal numbers of false sentences, we can measure the reaction time for subjects (Ss) to decide which sentences are true and which are false. Thus, this method can be used to test the prediction we have derived from the model and our assumptions about the retrieval process.

A caution is in order here: Dictionary definitions are not very orderly and we doubt that human memory, which is far richer, is even as orderly as a dictionary. One difficulty is that hierarchies are not always clearly ordered, as exemplified by dog, mammal, and animal. Subjects tend to categorize a dog as an animal, even though a stricter classification would interpose the category mammal between the two. A second difficulty is that people surely store certain properties at more than one level in the hierarchy. For example, having leaves is a general property of trees, but many people must have information stored about the maple leaf directly with maple, because of the distinctiveness of its leaf. In selecting examples, such hierarchies and instances were avoided. However, there will always be Ss for whom extensive familiarity will lead to the storing of many more properties (and sometimes supersets) than we have assumed. By averaging over different examples and different subjects, the effect of such individual idiosyncrasies of memory can be minimized.

2. Method

Three experiments were run, with eight Ss used in each experiment. The Ss were all employees of Bolt Beranek and Newman, Inc. who served voluntarily and had no knowledge of the nature of the experiment. Because of a faulty electrical connection, only three Ss gave usable data in Experiment 3. The same general method was used for all three experiments, except in the way the false sentences were constructed.

2.1 Apparatus

The sentences were displayed one at a time on the cathode ray tube (CRT) of a DEC PDP-1 computer. The timing and recording of responses were under program control. Each sentence was centered vertically on one line. The length of line varied from 10 to 34 characters (approximately 4-11° visual angle). The S sat directly in front of the CRT with his two index fingers resting on the two response buttons. These each required a displacement of 1/4 inch to trigger a microswitch.

2.2 Procedure

The sentences were grouped in runs of 32 or 48, with a rest period of approximately 1 minute between runs. Each sentence appeared on the CRT for 2 seconds and was followed by a blank screen for 2 seconds before the next sentence. The subject (S) was instructed to press one button if the sentence was generally true and the other button if it was generally false, and he was told to do so as accurately and as quickly as possible. The S could respond anytime within the 4 seconds between sentences, but his response did not alter the timing of the sentences. Each S was given a practice run of 32 sentences similarly constructed.

2.3 Sentences

There were two kinds of semantic hierarchies used in constructing sentences for the experiments, 2-level and 3-level. In Figure 1, a 2-level hierarchy might include bird, canary, and ostrich and their properties, whereas the whole diagram represents a 3-level hierarchy. A 2-level hierarchy included true PO, P1, SO and S1 sentences; a 3-level hierarchy included true P2 and S2 sentences as well. Examples of sentence sets with 2-level and 3-level hierarchies are given in Table 1. As illustrated in Table 1, equal numbers of true and false sentences were always present (but in random sequence) in the sentences an S read. Among both true and false sentences, there are the two general kinds: Property relations (P), ant superset relations (S).

In Experiment 1, each S read 128 two-level sentences followed by 96 three-level sentences. In Experiment 2, each S read 128 two-level sentences, but dif-

Sentence type	True Sentence	Sentence type*	False Sentences
Experiment 1, 2-level			
PO	Baseball has innings	P	Checkers has pawns
P1	Badminton has rules	P	Ping pong has baskets
SO	Chess is chess	S	Hockey is a race
S1	Tennis is a game	S	Football is a lottery
Experiment 1, 3-level			
PO	An oak has acorns	P	A hemlock has buckeyes
P1	A spruce has branches	P	A poplar has thorns
P2	A birch has seeds	P	A dogwood is lazy
SO	A maple is a maple	S	A pine is barley
S1	A cedar is a tree	S	A juniper is grain
S2	An elm is a plant	S	A willow is grass
Experiment 2, 2-level			
PO	Seven-up is colorless	PO	Coca-cola is blue
P1	Ginger ale is carbonated	P1	Lemonade is alcoholic
SO	Pepsi-cola is Pepsi-cola	SO	Bitter lemon is orangeade
Sl	Root beer is a soft drink	S1	Club soda is wine

*There were no distinctions as to level made for false sentences in Experiment 1.

Table 1. Illustrative sets of stimulus sentences.

ferent sentences from those used in Experiment 1. In Experiment 3, a different group of *S*s read the same 96 three-level sentences used in Experiment 1. Each run consisted of sentences from only four subject-matter hierarchies.

To generate the sentences we first picked a hierarchical group with a large set of what we shall call *instances* at the lowest level. For example, baseball, badminton, etc. are instances of the superset game. Different instances were used in each sentence, because repetition of a word is known to have substantial effects in reducing RT (Smith 1967). In constructing S1 and S2 sentences, the choice of the category name or superset was in most cases obvious though in a case such as the above 2-level example, sport might have been used as the superset rather than game. To assess how well our choices corresponded with the way most people categorize, two individuals who did not serve in any of the three experiments were asked to generate a category name for each S1 and S2 sentence we used, e.g., "tennis is—." These two individuals generated the category names we used in about 3/4 of their choices, and only in one case, "wine is a drink" instead of "liquid," was their choice clearly not synonymous.

In generating sentences that specified properties, only the verbs "is," "has," and "can" were used, where "is" was always followed by an adjective, "has" by a noun, and "can" by a verb. To produce the PO sentence one of the instances such as baseball was chosen that had a property (in this case innings) which was clearly identifiable with the instance and not the superset. To generate a P1 or P2 sentence, we took a salient property of the superset that could be expressed with the restriction to "is," "has," or "can." In the first example of Table 1, rules were felt to be a very salient property of games. Then an instance was chosen, in this case badminton, to which the P1 property seemed not particularly associated. Our assumption was that, if the model is correct, a typical S should decide whether badminton has rules or not by the path, badminton is a game and games have rules.

In Experiment 1, false sentences were divided equally between supersets and properties. No systematic basis was used for constructing false sentences beyond an attempt to produce sentences that were not unreasonable or semantically anomalous, and that were always untrue rather than usually untrue. In Experiment 2, additional restrictions were placed on the false sentences. The properties of the false PO sentences were chosen so as to contradict a property of the instance itself. In example 3 of Table 1, "Coca-cola® is blue" contradicts a property of Coca-cola®, that it is brown or caramel-colored. In contrast, the properties of false P1 sentences were chosen so as to contradict a property of the superset. In the same example, alcoholic was chosen, because it is a contradiction of a property of soft drinks in general. The relation of elements in the false SO and S1 sentences can be illustrated by reference to Figure 1. The false SO sentences were generated by stating that one instance of a category was equivalent to another, such as "A canary is an ostrich." The false S1 sentence was constructed by choosing a category one level up from the instance, but in a different branch of the structure, such as "A canary is a fish."

The sequence of sentences the S saw was randomly ordered, except for the restriction to four hierarchies in each run. The runs were counterbalanced over Ss with respect to the different sentence types, and each button was assigned true for half the Ss, and false for the other half.

3. Results and Discussion

In analyzing the data from the three experiments we have used the mean RT for each S's correct responses only. Error rates were on the average about 8 percent and tended to increase where RT increased.

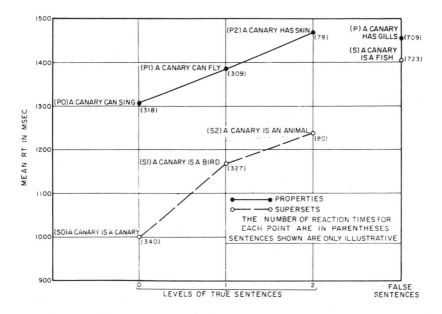

Figure 2. Average reaction times for different types of sentences in three experiments.

3.1 Deciding a Sentence is True

The data from all three experiments have been averaged in Figure 2. To evaluate the differences shown there for true sentences, two separate analyses of variance were performed: One for the 2-level runs and one for the 3-level runs. For the 2-level data the difference between P sentences and S sentences was significant $F(1, 60) = 19.73$, $p < .01$, the difference between levels was significant $F(1, 60) = 7.74$, $p < .01$, but the interaction was not quite significant, $F(1, 60) = 2.06$. For the 3-level data, the difference between P and S sentences was significant, $F(1, 60) = 27.02$, p < .01, the difference between levels was significant, $F(2, 60) = 5.68$, p < .01, and the interaction was not significant, $F < 1$.

Our prediction was that the RT curves for PO, P1, and P2 sentences and for SO, S1, and S2 sentences should be two parallel straight lines. The results are certainly compatible with this prediction, except for the SO point, which is somewhat out of line. It was anticipated that presenting the entire sentence on the CRT at one time would permit the Ss to answer the SO sentences, e.g., "A maple is a maple," by pattern matching. That they did so was substantiated by spontaneous reports from several Ss that on the SO sentences they often did not even think what the sentence said. Overall, the underlying model is supported by these data.

It can also be concluded, if one accepts the model and disregards the SO point as distorted by pattern matching, that the time to move from a node to its superset is on the order of 75 milliseconds, this figure being the average RT increase from PO to P1, P1 to P2, and S1 to S2. The differences between S1 and P1 and between S2 and P2, which average to about 225 milliseconds, represent the time it takes to retrieve a property from the node at the level where we assume it is stored.

We have assumed that retrieval of properties at a node and moving up to the superset of the node are parallel processes, but this was not a necessary assumption. In actual fact the computer realization of the model completes the search for properties at a node before moving up one level to its superset. If the property search is assumed to be complete *before* moving up to the next level, then the 75 milliseconds would have to be divided into two processes: (a) The time spent searching for properties, and (b) the time to move up to the superset. If such an assumption is made, then there is no clear prediction as to whether the increases for P sentences should parallel the increases for S sentences. If, given an S-type sentence, the S could dispense with process (a) above, then the slope of the curve for S sentences would be less than for P sentences; if he could not, then the prediction of two parallel lines would still hold. However, the fact that the time attributable to retrieving a property from a node is much longer than the time to move from one node to the next suggests that the processing is in fact parallel. It is unlikely that a search of all the properties at a node could be completed before moving up to the next level in less than 75 milliseconds, if it takes some 225 milliseconds actually to retrieve a property when it is found at a node. This might be reasonable if most of the 225 milliseconds was spent in verification or some additional process necessary when the search at a node is successful, but attributing most of the 225 milliseconds to such a process involves the unlikely assumption that this process takes much longer for P sentences than for S sentences. If it were the same for both sentence types, then it would not contribute to the difference (the 225 milliseconds) between their RTs.

Since any other systematic differences between sentence types might affect RTs, we did three further checks. We computed the average number of letters for each sentence type and also weighted averages of the word-frequencies based on the Thorndike and Lorge (1944) general count. Then we asked four Ss to rate how important each property was for the relevant instance or superset, e.g., how important it is for birds that they can fly. In general, we found no effects that could account for the differences in Figure 2 on the basis of sentence lengths, frequency counts, or subject ratings of importance. The only exception to this is that the higher frequency of superset words such as bird and animal in the predicates of S1 and S2 sentences may have lowered the averages for S1 and S2 sentences relative to those for P sentences.

3.2 Deciding a Sentence Is False

There are a number of conceivable strategies or processes by which a person might decide a sentence is false. All of these involve a search of memory; they fall into two classes on the basis of how the search is assumed to terminate.

3.2.1 The Contradiction Hypothesis

Under this hypothesis, false responses involve finding a contradiction between information stored in memory and what the statement says. For example, if the sentence is "Coca-cola® is blue," the S searches memory until he finds a property of Coca-cola® (that it is brown or caramel colored) which contradicts the sentence.

The contradiction hypothesis was tested by the construction of false sentences for Experiment 2. We predicted that the RT increase from PO to P1 found for true sentences might also be found for false sentences. The difference found was in the right direction, but it was negligibly small (7 milliseconds). Similarly, it was thought that if Ss search for a contradiction, false SO sentences should produce faster times than the false S1 sentences since there is one less link in the path between the two nodes for an SO sentence. (This can be seen by comparing the path in Figure 1 between canary and ostrich as in SO sentences to the path between canary and fish as in S1 sentences.) The difference turned out to be in the opposite direction by 59 milliseconds on the average, $t(7) = 2.30$, p < .1. If anything, one should conclude from the false SO and S1 sentences in Experiment 2 that the closer two nodes are in memory, the longer it takes to decide that they are not related in a stated manner.

3.2.2 The Unsuccessful Search Hypothesis

This is a generalization of what Sternberg (1966) calls the "self-terminating search," one of the two models he considered with regard to his RT studies of short-term memory search. Under this hypothesis an S would search for information to decide that a given sentence is true, and, when the search fails, as determined by some criterion, he would respond false. One possible variation, suggested by the longer RTs for false responses, would be that Ss search memory for a fixed period of time, responding true at any time information is found that confirms the statement is true, and responding false if nothing is found by the end of the time period. Such a hypothesis should lead to smaller standard deviations for false sentences than for true sentences, but the opposite was found for Experiment 2, where it could be checked most easily.

3.2.3 The Search and Destroy Hypothesis

We developed another variation of the unsuccessful search hypothesis after the contradiction hypothesis proved unsatisfactory and Ss had been interrogated as to what they thought they were doing on false sentences. Under this hypothesis we assume the S tries to find paths through his memory which connect the subject and predicate of the sentence (e.g., the path "canary → bird → animal → has skin" connects the two parts of "A canary has skin"). Whenever he finds such a path he must check to see if it agrees with what is stated in the sentence. When the S has checked to a certain number of levels or "depth" (Quillian 1967), all connections found having been rejected, the S will then respond false. Under this hypothesis, the times for false sentences will be longer, in general, and highly variable depending upon how many connective paths the S has to check out before rejecting the statement. For instance, assuming people know Coca-Cola® comes in green bottles, a statement such as "Coca-cola® is blue" would on the average take less time than "Coca-Cola® is green." This is because the S would have to spend time checking whether or not the above path between Coca-cola® and green (i.e., that its bottles are green) corresponds to the relation stated in the sentence.

This hypothesis would explain the longer times in Experiment 2 for sentences such as "A canary is an ostrich" as compared with "A canary is a fish" in terms of the greater number of connections between canary and ostrich that presumably would have to be checked out. This difference in the number of connections would derive from the greater number of properties that are common to two nodes close together in the network, such as canary and ostrich, than are common to nodes further apart and at different levels, such as canary and fish.

Finding contradictions can be included in this hypothesis, as is illustrated with "Gin is wet." Here the S might make a connection between gin and wet through the path "gin is dry and dry is the opposite of wet." Seeing the contradiction, he rejects this as a basis for responding true, but continues to search for an acceptable path. In this example, if he searches deep enough, he will find the path "gin is liquor, and liquor is liquid, and liquid is wet" which is, in fact, what the sentence requires. The point we want to emphasize here is that even though a contradiction can be used to reject a path, it cannot be used to reject the truth of a statement.

There are certainly other possible hypotheses, and it is possible that a combination of this hypothesis with the contradiction hypothesis may be necessary to explain false judgments. Needless to say, the process by which a person decides that a statement is false does not seem to be very simple.

4. Conclusion

In a computer system designed for the storage of semantic information, it is more economical to store generalized information with superset nodes, rather than with all the individual nodes to which such a generalization might apply.

But such a storage system incurs the cost of additional processing time in retrieving information. When the implications of such a model were tested for human Ss using well-ordered hierarchies that are part of the common culture, there was substantial agreement between the predictions and the data.

There is no clear picture that emerges as to how people decide a statement is false. Our current hypothesis, that people must spend time checking out any interpretations that are possible (see the discussion of the search and destroy hypothesis), should be testable, but even corroborative evidence would not clear up many of the questions about such decisions.

The model also makes predictions for other RT tasks utilizing such hierarchies. For instance, if Ss are given the task of deciding what common category two instances belong to, then RT should reflect the number of supersets the S must move through to make the decision. (Consider fish and bird, vs. shark and bird, vs. shark and canary; see Figure 1). Such RT differences should parallel those in our data. Furthermore, if utilizing a particular path in retrieval increases its accessibility temporarily, then we would expect prior exposure to "A canary is a bird" to have more effect in reducing RT to "A canary can fly" than to "A canary can sing." There are many similar experiments which would serve to pin down more precisely the structure and processing of human semantic memory.

Acknowledgements

This research was supported by the Aerospace Medical Research Laboratories, Aerospace Medical Division, Air Force Systems Command, Wright-Patterson Air Force Base, Ohio, under Contract No. F33615-67-C-1982 with Bolt Beranek and Newman, Inc. and also partly by Advanced Research Projects Agency, monitored by the Air Force Cambridge Research Laboratories, under Contract No. F1962868-C0125.

The authors thank Ray Nickerson for the use of his program and for his help in modifying it to run on BBN's PDP-1.

8

A Procedural Model of
Language Understanding

Terry Winograd

1. Introduction

Much of the research on language is based on an attempt to separate it into distinct components, components that can then be studied independently. Modern syntactic theoreticians have been tremendously successful at setting up complex rules which describe in detail the possible orderings of syntactic constituents; at the same time other researchers are trying to define semantic relations and to model the cognitive structures underlying language use.

Most attempts to model language understanding on the computer have followed this strategy of dealing with a single component of language. They are constructed primarily as a syntactic program (Kuno 1965), a model of semantic connections (Schank 1971), or an attempt to model the memory structures (Quillian 1967).

Question-answering systems have had to deal with the entire language process but they have been severely limited in the breadth of their language ability. The only attempt to handle large portions of language data was the machine translation effort, and it soon became obvious that the methods were not up to the requirements of the task. Language translation could not be treated as a problem of rearranging syntactic structures and words, because attention to meaning was required even to achieve moderately acceptable results.

One basic limitation of those programs that have tried to handle the problems of meaning is that they have dealt almost exclusively with the understanding of single sentences, when in fact almost no human use of language takes place in such an artificial setting. We are always in a context, and in that context we make use of what has gone on to help interpret what is coming. Much of the structure of language comes from its being a process of communication between an intelligent speaker and hearer, occurring in a setting. The setting includes not only a physical situation and a topic of discourse, but also the knowledge each participant has about the world and the other's ideas.

This chapter describes an attempt to explore the interconnections between the different types of knowledge required for language understanding. It is based on a computer program that "understands" language in a limited domain by including a model of the subject being talked about and a context of discourse. As an example of the interactions between the different sorts of knowledge the system must have, let us look first at the use of pronouns.

Our syntactic knowledge of English enables us to know that in the sentence "Arthur wants to see him," the word "him" must refer to someone other than Arthur (otherwise we would have used "himself"). In "Arthur wants somebody to see him," "him" might or might not refer to Arthur. The distribution of reflexive pronouns like "himself" depends in a complex way on the syntactic structure of the sentences in which they appear, and a language understander must have this knowledge. As a semantic fact, we know that "him" must refer to something which the speaker is characterizing as animate and male.

At another level, we know that the referent is likely to occur in the preceding sentence, or earlier in the sentence being interpreted, that it is more likely to refer to the topic or the subject of the previous sentence, and is much more likely to refer to a major constituent than to one deeply embedded in the structure. This type of heuristic knowledge about the organization of discourse also plays a part in our understanding.

Finally, there is a level based on knowledge of the world. In the sentence "Sam and Bill wanted to take the girls to the movies, but they didn't have any money," we understand "they" as referring to Sam and Bill. This doesn't involve syntactic or general semantic knowledge, but depends on our knowledge of our social culture. When someone takes someone else to the movies, it is the inviter who pays, and it is his or her financial situation that is relevant.

Whenever we look into realistic language use, these types of interaction play a large role, not only with pronouns, but in deciding on the structures of sentences and meanings of individual words as well. We assign different structures to sentences like "He gave the house plants to charity," and "He gave the boy plants to water," on the basis of our syntactic and semantic knowledge. Even the most common words have multiple meanings, and we must bring a variety of facts to bear in deciding, for example, the meaning of "had" in "Mary had a little lamb, but I preferred the baked lobster."

In discourse, people take advantage of a variety of mechanisms that depend on the existence of an intelligent hearer who will use all sorts of knowledge to fill in any necessary information. In making a computer model of language use, this presents a serious problem. On the one hand, it is impossible to isolate one aspect of language from the others, or to separate a person's use of linguistic knowledge from his use of other knowledge. On the other hand, it is clearly folly at this point to think of giving the program all the knowledge a person brings into a conversation. In our program, we choose to resolve the dilemma by picking a tiny bit of the world to talk about. Within this mini-world, we can give the computer a deep kind of knowledge, including the equivalent of "Who would pay for a movie?"

The subject chosen was the world of a toy robot with a simple arm. It can manipulate toy blocks on a table containing simple objects like a box. In the course of a dialogue, it can be asked to manipulate the objects, doing such things as building stacks and putting things into the box. It can be questioned about the current configurations of blocks on the table, about the events that have gone on during the discussion, and to a limited extent about its reasoning. It can be told simple facts which are added to its store of knowledge for use in later reasoning. The conversation goes on within a dynamic framework—one in which the computer is an active participant, doing things to change his toy world, and discussing them.

The program was written in Lisp on the PDP-10 ITS time-sharing system of the Artificial Intelligence Laboratory at MIT.[1] It displays a simulated robot world on a television screen and converses with a human on a teletype. It was not written for any particular use with a real robot and does not have a model of language based on peculiarities of the robot environment. Rather, it is precisely by limiting the subject matter to such a small area that we can address the general issues of how language is used in a framework of physical objects, events, and a continuing discourse.

The programs can be roughly divided into the three domains mentioned above: There is a syntactic parser which works with a large-scale grammar of English; there is a collection of semantic routines that embody the kind of knowledge needed to interpret the meanings of words and structures; and there is a cognitive deductive system for exploring the consequences of facts, making plans to carry out commands and finding the answers to questions. There is also a comparatively simple set of programs for generating appropriate English responses.

In designing these pieces, the main emphasis was on the interaction of the three domains. The form in which we want to state a syntactic theory or a type of deduction must take into account the fact that it is only a part of a larger system. One of the most useful organizing principles was the representation of much of the knowledge as procedures. Many other theories of language state their rules in a form modelled on the equations of mathematics or the rules of symbolic logic. These are static rules that do not explicitly describe the process involved in using them, but are instead manipulated by some sort of uniform deduction procedure. By writing special languages suited to the various types of knowledge (semantic, syntactic, deductive), we are able to preserve the simplicity of these systems. This is accomplished by putting the knowledge in the form of programs in which we can explicitly express the connections between the different parts of the system's knowledge, thus enriching their possibilities for interaction.

The rest of this chapter illustrates the capabilities of the system and explains in some detail how it works. The second section presents a sample of a dialogue with the program, along with comments describing some of the features being demonstrated. The third section gives a closer view of the program itself, and the final section discusses some of its basic limitations.

2. Sample Dialogue

This section contains a sample dialogue with the language-understanding system. This system carries out actions and answers questions about a simple scene containing a table, hand, and box, and several blocks and pyramids. The numbered lines in lower case were typed in by a person, and the lines in upper case are the computer's response. Other lines are comments describing some of the features being exhibited.

The dialogue was carried out in real time with the response of the "robot" displayed on a television screen. Figures are included to show the state of the scene at various points.

1. pick up a big red block.

OK.

The system answers "OK" when it carries out a command. In order to pick up the red block, it had to clear it off by finding a space for the green one and moving the green one away. The initial situation is shown in Figure 1, and the result in Figure 2.

2. grasp the pyramid.

I DON'T UNDERSTAND WHICH PYRAMID YOU MEAN.

There are three pyramids in the scene, and the program knows that phrases

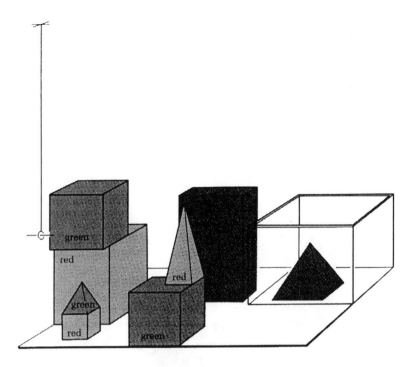

Figure 1. The physical environment of the robot.

beginning with "the" are intended to refer to a specific object the speaker has in mind.

3. find a block which is taller than the one you are holding and put it into the box.

The system has to figure out what is meant by "one" and "it," as well as using deduction to decide which block it is holding.

BY "IT," I ASSUME YOU MEAN THE BLOCK WHICH IS TALLER THAN THE ONE I AM HOLDING.

There were two possible referents for "it": the one selected, and "the one you are holding." The program has heuristics for choosing between them.

OK.

The hand has to set down the red block to pick up the taller blue one. Figure 3 shows the result of the system's manipulations so far.

4. what does the box contain?

THE BLUE PYRAMID AND THE BLUE BLOCK.

5. what is the pyramid supported by?

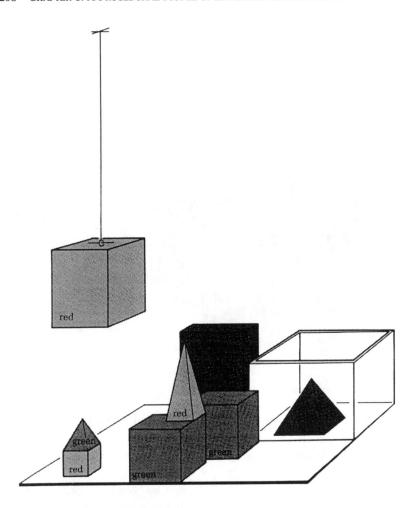

Figure 2. "Pick up a big red block."

Earlier the system responded to "the pyramid" by saying "I DON'T UN-DERSTAND WHICH PYRAMID YOU MEAN." Now, it assumes that we mean the one just mentioned.

THE BOX.

6. how many blocks are not in the box?

Negatives such as "not" and "no" are handled whether they appear in clauses or noun groups (such as "no boxes").

FOUR OF THEM.

7. is at least one of them narrower then the one which I told you to pick up?

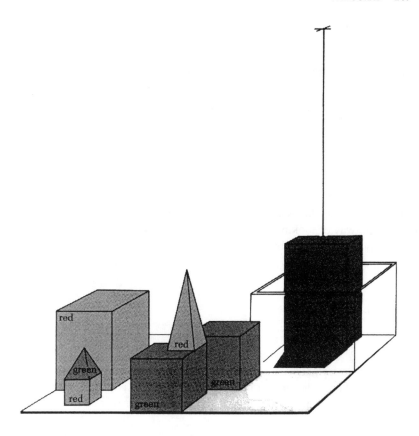

Figure 3. "Find a block which is taller than the one you are holding and put it into the box."

The phrase "at least one of them" must be analyzed to refer back to the previous question, and 'the one which...'" must also refer to blocks. Noun groups can have complicated numbers such as "at least one," "more than three," "exactly seven," etc. The memory of past events is used to deduce which block is "the one which I told you to pick up." Notice the complicated syntactic structure in which "the one" is actually the object of a clause embedded two levels deeper. The parser incorporates a grammar that handles this kind of complexity in a general way.

YES, THE RED CUBE.

8. is it supported?

YES, BY THE TABLE.

The system has heuristics about what information is relevant to a person who asks a question, even if he does not request that information specifically.

9. can the table pick up blocks?

NO.

The semantic rules include the knowledge that "picking up" must be done by an animate object, and that the table is not animate.

10. can a pyramid be supported by a block?

YES.

The deductive system finds an actual example, so it knows this is possible.

11. can a pyramid support a pyramid?

I DON'T KNOW.

The question makes sense, but there is no example in the scene. The system has no way of looking into the details of its programs, even though these ultimately define its capabilities.

12. stack up two pyramids.

I CAN'T.

The robot tries and fails.

13. the blue pyramid is mine.

I UNDERSTAND.

All of the information about colors, shapes, sizes and locations of the objects is known to the program initially. Possession is left as an unknown property of objects about which it can be told. It stores this information in its data base.

14. I own all blocks which are not red, but I don't own anything which supports a pyramid.

I UNDERSTAND.

The result of understanding these sentences is the creation of new procedures within the robot for deducing whether I own something.

15. do I own the box?

NO.

The box supports whatever it contains, including a pyramid.

16. do I own anything in the box?

YES, TWO THINGS: THE BLUE BLOCK AND THE BLUE PYRAMID.

17. will you please stack up both of the red blocks and either a green cube or a pyramid?

OK.

Logical connectives, such as "and," "or," "either," etc., are handled in both

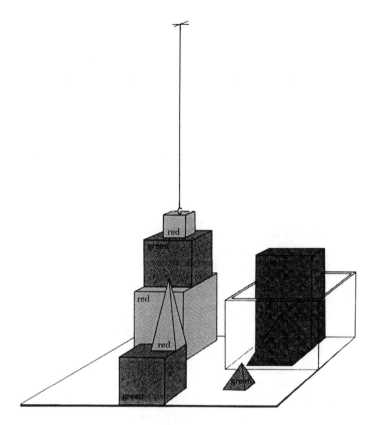

Figure 4. "Will you please stack up both of the red blocks and either a green cube or a pyramid."

the grammar and semantics. A command is executed even if it looks like a question. The command is carried out by the following series of steps: It puts a green cube on the large red block (it chooses the green cube with nothing on it), then removes the small pyramid from the little red cube, so that it can use that cube to complete the stack as specified, resulting in what is described in Figure 4.

18. which cube is sitting on the table?

THE LARGE GREEN ONE WHICH SUPPORTS THE RED PYRAMID.

Ordinarily the system would be satisfied with calling this "a big green cube," but since we asked "which cube" it has to be more specific in naming it. It has procedures for using substitute nouns (such as "one") and pronouns in answers to make the discourse more natural.

19. is there a large block behind a pyramid?

YES, THREE OF THEM: A LARGE RED ONE, A LARGE GREEN CUBE
AND THE BLUE ONE.

20. put a small one onto the green cube which supports a pyramid.

"A small one" must contrast with the person's earlier phrase "a large
block," so this means "a small block."

OK.

21. put the littlest pyramid on top of it.

Words like "littlest" are not in the dictionary but are interpreted from the
root forms like "little." The program compares the sizes of all the pyramids
to carry out the action.

OK.

22. how many things are on top of green cubes?

I'M NOT SURE WHAT YOU MEAN BY "ON TOP OF" IN THE PHRASE
"ON TOP OF GREEN CUBES" DO YOU MEAN:
1—DIRECTLY ON THE SURFACE
2—ANYWHERE ON TOP OF?

In the previous sentence, the phrase "on top of" was interpreted without
trouble because the context made it clear what was meant. In this one, the
heuristics for disambiguation do not come up with a clear-cut decision, so the
system has to ask the user for more information. The paraphrases were included with the dictionary definition of "on." A request like this can also
occur when the meaning of a pronoun such as "it" or "they" is unclear.

23. had you touched any pyramid before you put the green one on the little cube?

YES, THE GREEN ONE.

The system deduces from its memory what event is being referred to, and
can relate other events to it in time. The analysis includes complex tenses of
verb groups, and there are special facilities for keeping track of the various
forms of irregular verbs like "have."

24. when did you pick it up?

WHILE I WAS STACKING UP THE RED CUBE, A LARGE RED BLOCK
AND A LARGE GREEN CUBE.

A time is described by naming the main goal which was being worked on.

25. why?

The system remembers immediately previous sentences to understand
questions like this and the following ones.

TO GET RID OF IT.

By keeping track of selected parts of the original subgoal tree, the system
has some understanding of its own motives.

26. why did you do that?

TO CLEAN OFF THE RED CUBE.

"That" refers to the action mentioned in the system's last answer.

27. why did you clear off that cube?

Here, "that" means the one just referred to.

TO PUT IT ON A LARGE GREEN CUBE.

28. why did you do that?

TO STACK UP THE RED CUBE, A LARGE RED BLOCK AND A LARGE GREEN CUBE.

29. why did you do that?

BECAUSE YOU ASKED ME TO.

It remembers what it did, not how the request was worded.

30. how did you do it?

"It" refers to the action mentioned in the last question, rather than the answer.

BY PUTTING A LARGE RED BLOCK ON THE TABLE; THEN LETTING GO OF IT; THEN PUTTING A LARGE GREEN CUBE ON IT; THEN LETTING GO OF THAT CUBE; THEN PUTTING THE RED CUBE ON THAT CUBE; THEN LETTING GO OF THAT CUBE.

This is a description of the top-level subgoals used to achieve the goal.

31. how many objects did you touch while you were doing it?

Time references can refer to a time span, using words like "while."

FOUR OF THEM.

32. what did the red cube support before you started to clean it off?

THE GREEN PYRAMID.

By remembering what has been moved, it is possible to deduce things about earlier states of the scene. We can use complex nestings of clauses like "before you started to clean it off."

33. there were five blocks to the left of the box then.

"Then" must refer to the time mentioned in the last sentence.

NO, ONLY FOUR OF THEM: THE RED CUBE, TWO LARGE GREEN CUBES AND A LARGE RED BLOCK.

Earlier in the dialogue, information about "owning" was accepted at face value. But the system knows that it has complete information about the basic properties of objects, including location. It checks any statements about these to see whether it agrees or disagrees.

34. put the blue pyramid on the block in the box.

This is syntactically ambiguous, but is understood without ambiguity since the parsing corresponding to "put the blue pyramid which is on the block into the box" does not make sense in the current scene, whereas "put the blue pyramid onto the block which is in the box" does.

OK.

35. is there anything which is bigger than every pyramid but is not as wide as the thing that supports it?

The system understands quantifiers such as "every," "any," "some," etc., and structures such as "bigger than," "as wide as," etc. Here "it" refers to a noun group within the same sentence but two levels up in the parsing tree.

YES, THE BLUE BLOCK.

36. does a steeple

SORRY, I DON'T KNOW THE WORD "STEEPLE."

The system interrupts immediately when it sees a word it doesn't know.

37. a "steeple" is a stack which contains two green cubes and a pyramid.

The quote marks indicate that we are defining a new word. The definition is added to the dictionary in a form compatible with all the words it already knows.

I UNDERSTAND.

38. are there any steeples now?

NO.

The new definition is used as a description to recognize steeples.

39. build one.

OK.

The description given in the definition is enough to deduce a plan for building new objects as well as recognizing them. The word "one" means "a steeple," and the plan is carried out. First, one of the large green cubes is cleared off by removing the red cube and two pyramids. Then the two green cubes and the tall red pyramid are stacked up to fit the description.

40. call the biggest block "superblock."

OK.

We can also give objects names.

41. have you picked up superblock since we began?

YES.

42. why did you drop it?

BY "IT," I ASSUME YOU MEAN THE SUPERBLOCK. I CAN'T EXPLAIN

A NON-EXISTENT EVENT.

There is no record in memory of any block being dropped. The answer routines have special checks for this type of "loaded question" which presupposes things which aren't true.

43. is there anything to the right of the red pyramid?

YES, FOUR THINGS: THE BOX, THE RED CUBE, THE BLUE PYRAMID AND THE BLOCK NAMED SUPERBLOCK.

Once an object has a name, the name is used to help identify it in responses.

44. thank you.

YOU'RE WELCOME!

The grammar is written as a procedure, which gives it the capability to carry out special sorts of parsing for idioms.

3. Details of the Model

In this section we go into some detail about the various parts of the language understanding program and its operation. This type of analysis is important for understanding any computer model, since the surface appearance of its output can be deceptive. A program may succeed by carefully choosing the problem it will attack, so that some simple special-purpose solution will work. Eliza (Weizenbaum 1965) and Student (Bobrow 1967) are examples of programs which give impressive performances owing to a severe and careful restriction of the kind of understanding they try to achieve. If a model is to be of broader significance, it must be designed to cover a large range of the things we mean when we talk of understanding. The principles should derive from an attempt to deal with the basic cognitive structures.

On the other hand, it is possible to devise abstract ideas of the logical structure of language—ideas which seem in theory to be applicable. Often, such systems, although interesting mathematically, are not valid as psychological models of human language, since they have not concerned themselves with the operational problems of a mental procedure. They often include types of representation and processes which are highly implausible, and which may be totally inapplicable in complex situations because their very nature implies astronomically large amounts of processing for certain kinds of computations. Transformational grammar and resolution theorem proving (Green 1969) are examples of such approaches.

3.1 The Representation of Meaning

Our program makes use of a detailed world model, describing both the cur-

```
(IS B1 BLOCK)
(IS B2 PYRAMID)
(AT B1 (LOCATION 1OO 1OO O))
(SUPPORT B1 B2)
(CLEARTOP B2)
(MANIPULABLE B1)
(CONTAIN BOX1 B4)
(COLOR-OF B1 RED)
(SHAPE-OF B2 POINTED)
(IS BLUE COLOR)
(CAUSE EVENT27 EVENT29)
```

Box 1. Typical data expressions.

rent state of the blocks world environment and its knowledge of procedures for changing that state and making deductions about it. This model is not in spatial or analog terms, but is a symbolic description, abstracting those aspects of the world which are relevant to the operations used in working with it and discussing it. First there is a data base of simple facts like those shown in Box 1, describing what is true at any particular time. There we see, for example, that B1 is a block, B1 is red, B2 supports B3, blue is a color, EVENT 27 caused EVENT 29, etc. The notation simply involves indicating relationships between objects by listing the name of the relation (such as IS or SUPPORT) followed by the things being related.[2] These include both concepts (like BLOCK or BLUE) and proper names of individual objects and events (indicated with numbers, like B1 and TABLE2).[3] The symbols used in these expressions represent the concepts (or conceptual categories) that form the vocabulary of the language user's cognitive model. A concept corresponds vaguely to what we might call a single meaning of a word, but the connection is more complex. Underlying the organization is a belief that meanings cannot be reduced to any set of pure "elements" or components from which everything else is built. Rather, a person categorizes his experience along lines which are relevant to the thought processes he will use, and his categorization is generally neither consistent, nor parsimonious, nor complete. A person may categorize a set of objects in his experience into, for example "chair," "stool," "bench," etc. If pushed, he cannot give an exact definition for any of these, and in naming some objects he will not be certain how to make the choice between them. This is even clearer if we consider words like "truth," "virtue," and "democracy." The meaning of any concept depends on its interconnection with all of the other concepts in the model.

Most formal approaches to language have avoided this characterization of meaning even though it seems close to our intuitions about how language is used. This is because the usual techniques of logic and mathematics are not easily applicable to such "holistic" models. With such a complex notion of

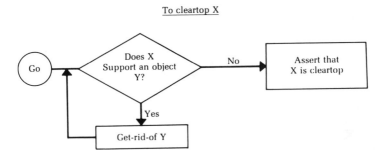

To cleartop X

Figure 5. Procedural description for the concept CLEARTOP .

"concept," we are unable to prove anything about meaning in the usual mathematical notion of proof. One important aspect of computational approaches to modelling cognitive processes is their ability to deal with this sort of formalism. Rather than trying to prove things about meaning we can design procedures which can operate with the model and simulate the processes involved in human use of meaning. The justification for the formalism is the degree to which it succeeds in providing a model of understanding.

What is important then, is the part of the system's knowledge which involves the interconnections between the concepts. In our model, these are in the form of procedures written in the PLANNER language (Hewitt 1971). For example, the concept CLEARTOP (which might be expressed in English by a phrase like "clear off") can be described by the procedure diagrammed in Figure 5. The model tells us that to clear off an object X, we start by checking to see whether X supports an object Y. If so, we GET-RID-OF Y, and go check again. When X does not support any object, we can assert that it is CLEARTOP. In this operational definition, we call on other concepts like GET-RID-OF and SUPPORT. Each of these in turn is a procedure, involving other concepts like PICKUP and GRASP. This representation is oriented to a model of deduction in which we try to satisfy some goal by setting up successive subgoals, which must be achieved in order to eventually satisfy the main goal. Looking at the flow chart for GRASP in Figure 6, we can see the steps the program would take if asked to grasp an object B1 while holding a different object B2. It would be called by setting up a goal of the form (GRASP B1), so when the GRASP program ran, X would represent the object B1. First it checks to see whether B1 is a manipulable object, since if not the effort must fail. Next it sees if it is already grasping B1, since this would satisfy the goal immediately. Then, it checks to see if it is holding an object other than B1, and if so tries to GET-RID-OF it. The program for GET-RID-OF tries to put the designated object on the table by calling a program for

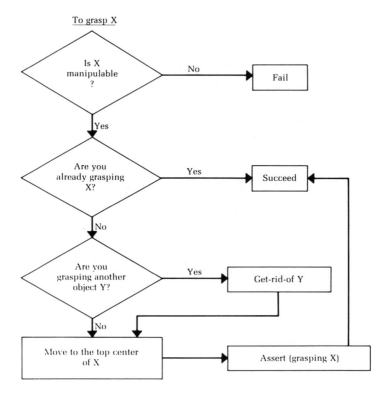

Figure 6. Procedural description of GRASP.

PUTON, which in turn looks for an empty location and calls PUT. PUT deduces where the hand must be moved and calls MOVEHAND. If we look at the set of currently active goals at this point, we get the stack in Box 2.

Notice that this subgoal structure provides the basis for asking "why" questions, as in sentences 25 through 29 of the dialog in Section 2. If asked "Why did you put B2 on the table?," the program would look to the goal that called PUTON, and say "To get rid of it." If asked "Why did you get rid of it?" it would go up one more step to get "To grasp B1." (Actually, it would generate an English phrase describing the object B1 in terms of its shape, size, and color.) "How" questions are answered by looking at the set of subgoals called directly in achieving a goal, and generating descriptions of the actions involved.

These examples illustrate the use of procedural descriptions of concepts for

```
(GRASP B1)
    (GET-RID-OF B2)
        (PUTON B2 TABLE1)
            (PUT B2 (453 201 O))
                (MOVEHAND (553 301 100))
```

```
(GOAL (IS ?X1 BLOCK))
(GOAL (COLOR-OF ?X1 RED))
(GOAL (EQUIDIMENSIONAL ?X1))
(GOAL (IS ?X2 PYRAMID))
(GOAL (SUPPORT ?X1 ?X2))
```

Box 3 Planner program for description of "a red cube which supports a pyramid."

carrying out commands, but they can also be applied to other aspects of language, such as questions and statements. One of the basic viewpoints underlying the model is that all language use can be thought of as a way of activating procedures within the hearer. We can think of any utterance as a program—one that indirectly causes a set of operations to be carried out within the hearer's cognitive system. This "program writing" is indirect in the sense that we are dealing with an intelligent interpreter who may take a set of actions which are quite different from those the speaker intended. The exact form is determined by his knowledge of the world, his expectations about the person talking to him, his goals, etc. In this program we have a simple version of this process of interpretation as it takes place in the robot. Each sentence interpreted by the robot is converted to a set of instructions in PLANNER. The program that is created is then executed to achieve the desired effect. In some cases the procedure invoked requires direct physical actions like the aforementioned. In others, it may be a search for some sort of information (perhaps to answer a question), whereas in others it is a procedure which stores away a new piece of knowledge or uses it to modify the knowledge it already has. Let us look at what the system would do with a simple description like "a red cube which supports a pyramid." The description will use concepts like BLOCK, RED, PYRAMID, and EQUIDIMENSIONAL—all parts of the system's underlying categorization of the world. The result can be represented in a flow chart like that of Figure 7. Note that this is a program for finding an object fitting the description. It would then be incorporated into a command for doing something with the object, a question asking something about it, or, if it appeared in a statement, it would become part of the program which was generated to represent the meaning for

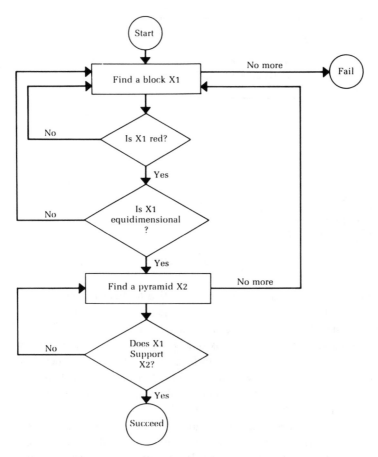

Figure 7. Procedural representation of "a red cube which supports a pyramid."

later use. Note that this bit of program could also be used as a test to see whether an object fit the description, if the first FIND instruction were told in advance to look only at that particular object.

At first glance, it seems that there is too much structure in this program, as we don't like to think of the meaning of a simple phrase as explicitly containing loops, conditional tests, and other programming details. The solution is to provide an internal language that contains the appropriate looping and checking as its primitives, and in which the representation of the process is as simple as the description. PLANNER provides these primitives in our system. The program described in Figure 7 would be written in PLANNER looking something like Box 3.[4] The loops of the flow chart are implicit in PLANNER's backtrack control structure. The description is evaluated by proceeding down the list until some goal fails, at which time the system backs up auto-matically to the last point where a decision was made, trying a different pos-sibility. A decision can be made whenever a new object name or variable (in-dicated by the prefix ?) such as ?Xl or ?X2 appears. The variables are used by a pattern matcher. If they have already been assigned to a particular item, it checks to see whether the GOAL is true for that item. If not, it checks for all possible items which satisfy the GOAL, by choosing one, and then taking successive ones whenever backtracking occurs to that point. Thus, even the distinction between testing and choosing is implicit. Using other primitives of PLANNER, such as NOT and FIND (which looks for a given number of ob-jects fitting a description), we can write procedural representations for a vari-ety of descriptions, as shown in Box 4.

3.2 Semantic Analysis

When we have decided how the system will represent meanings internally, we must deal with the way in which it creates a program when it is given an En-glish input. There must be ways to interpret the meanings of individual words and the syntactic structures in which they occur. First, let us look at how we can define simple words like "cube," and "contain." The definitions in Box 5 are completely equivalent to those used in the program with a straightforward interpretation.[5] The first says that a cube is an object that is RECTANGULAR and MANIPULABLE, and can be recognized by the fact that it is a BLOCK and EQUIDIMENSIONAL. The first part of this definition is based on the use of se-mantic markers and provides for efficiency in choosing interpretations. By

```
        (GOAL (IS ?X2 PYRAMID))
        (GOAL (SUPPORT  ?Xl ?X2))
        "which supports a pyramid"
        ***************
        (GOAL (SUPPORT ?Xl B3))
        "which supports the pyramid"
    B3 is the name of the object referred to by "the pyramid,"
        which is determined earlier in the analysis
        **************
    (FIND 3 ?X2 (GOAL (IS ?X2 PYRAMID))
                (GOAL (SUPPORT ?X1 ?X2)))
        "which supports three pyramids"
        **************
    (NOT (FIND ?X2  (GOAL (IS ?X2 PYRAMID))
                    (GOAL (SUPPORT ?X1 ?X2))))
        "which supports no pyramids"
        **************

    . .
    (NOT (FIND SX2    (GOAL (IS ?X2 PYRAMID))
                      (NOT (GOAL (SUPPORT ?X1 ?X2)))))
        "which supports every pyramid"
        **************
```

Box 4. Planner programs for some quantified modifiers describing the object X1.

```
(CUBE
    ((NOUN  (OBJECT
                ((MANIPULABLE RECTANGULAR)
                    ((IS ? BLOCK)
                        (EQUIDIMENSIONAL ?)))))))

(CONTAIN
    ((VERB  ((TRANSITIVE      (RELATION
                (((CONTAINER)) ((PHYSICAL-OBJECT))
                    (CONTAIN #1 #2))
                (((CONSTRUCT)) ((PHYSICAL-OBJECT))
                    (PART-OF #2 #1)))))))))
```

Box 5. Dictionary definitions for "cube" and "contain."

making a rough categorization of the objects in the model, the system can make quick checks to see whether certain combinations are ruled out by simple tests like "this meaning of the adjective applies only to words which represent physical objects." Chomsky's famous sentence "Colorless green ideas sleep furiously" would be eliminated easily by such markers. The system uses this information, for example, in answering question 9 in the dialogue, "Can the table pick up blocks?," as "pick up" demands a subject that is ANIMATE, whereas "table" has the marker INANIMATE. These markers are a useful but rough approximation to human deductions.

The definition for "contain" shows how they might be used to choose between possible word meanings. If applied to a CONTAINER and a PHYSICAL-OBJECT, as in "The box contains three pyramids," the word implies the usual relationship we mean by CONTAIN. If instead, it applies to a CONSTRUCT (like "stack," "pile," or "row") and an object, the meaning is different. "The stack contains a cube" really means that a cube is PART of the stack, and the system will choose this meaning by noting that CONSTRUCT is one of the semantic markers of the word "stack" when it applies the definition.

One important aspect of these definitions is that although they look like static rule statements, they are actually calls to programs (OBJECT and RELATION) which do the appropriate checks and build the semantic structures. Once we get away from the simplest words, these programs need to be more flexible in what they look at. For example, in the robot world, the phrase "pick up" has different meanings depending on whether it refers to a single object or several. In sentence 1, the system interprets "Pick up the big red block," by grasping it and raising the hand. If we said "Pick up all of your toys," it would interpret "pick up" as meaning "put away," and would pack them all into the box. The program for checking to see whether the object is singular or plural is simple, and any semantic system must have the flexibility to incorporate such things in the word definitions. We do this by having the definition of every word be a program which is called at an appropriate point in the analysis, and which can do arbitrary computations involving the sentence and the present physical situation.

This flexibility is even more important once we get beyond simple words. In defining words like "the," or "of," or "one" in "Pick up a green one," we can hardly make a simple list of properties and descriptors as in Figure 12. The presence of "one" in a noun group must trigger a program which looks into the previous discourse to see what objects have been mentioned, and can apply various rules and heuristics to determine the appropriate reference. For example it must know that in the phrase "a big red block and a little one," we are referring to "a little red block," not "a little big red block" or simply "a little block." This sort of knowledge is part of a semantic procedure attached to the word "one" in the dictionary.

Words like "the" are more complex. When we use a definite article like "the" or "that" in English, we have in mind a particular object or objects which we expect the hearer to know about. I can talk about "the moon" since there is only one moon we usually talk about. In the context of this article, I can talk about "the dialogue," and the reader will understand from the context which dialogue I mean. If I am beginning a conversation, I will say "Yesterday I met a strange man" even though I have a particular man in mind, since saying "Yesterday I met the strange man' would imply that the hearer already knows of him. Elsewhere, "the" is used to convey the information that the object being referred to is unique. If I write "The reason I wrote this paper was...," it implies that there was a single reason, whereas "A reason I wrote this paper was..." implies that there were others. In generic statements, "the" may be used to refer to a whole class, as in "The albatross is a strange bird." This is a quite different use from the single referent of "The albatross just ate your lunch."

A model of language use must be able to account for the role this type of knowledge plays in understanding. In the procedural model, it is a part of the process of interpretation for the structure in which the relevant word is embedded. The different possibilities for the meaning of "the" are procedures which check various facts about the context, then prescribe actions such as "Look for a unique object in the data base which fits this description." or "Assert that the object being described is unique as far as the speaker is concerned." The program incorporates a variety of heuristics for deciding what part of the context is relevant. For example, it keeps track of when in the dialogue something has been mentioned. In sentence 2 of the dialogue, "Grasp the pyramid" is rejected since there is no particular pyramid which the system can see as distinguished. However, in sentence 5 it accepts the question "What is the pyramid supported by?" since in the answer to sentence 4 it mentioned a particular pyramid.

This type of knowledge plays a large part in understanding the things that hold a discourse together, such as pronouns, adverbs like "then and "there," substitute nouns such as "one," phrases beginning with "that" and ellipses. The system is structured in such a way that the heuristics for handling mechanisms like these can be expressed as procedures in a straightforward way.

3.3 The Role of Syntax

In describing the process of semantic interpretation, we stated that part of the relevant input was the syntactic structure of the sentence. In order to provide this, the program contains a parser and a fairly comprehensive grammar of English.[6] The approach to syntax is based on a belief that the form of syntactic analysis must be usable by a realistic semantic system, and the emphasis of the resulting grammar differs in several ways from traditional transformational approaches.

First, it is organized around looking for syntactic units which play a primary role in determining meaning. A sentence such as "The three big red dogs ate a raw steak" will be parsed to generate the structure in Figure 8. The noun groups (NG) correspond to descriptions of objects, whereas the clause is a description of a relation or event. The semantic programs are organized into groups of procedures, each of which is used for interpreting a certain type of unit.

For each unit, there is a syntactic program (written in a language called Programmer, especially designed for the purpose) which operates on the input string to see whether it could represent a unit of that type. In doing this, it will call on other such syntactic programs (and possibly on itself recursively). It embodies a description of the possible orderings of words and other units, for example, the scheme for a noun group, as shown in Figure 9. The presence of an asterisk after a symbol means that that function can be filled more than once. The figure shows that we have a determiner (such as "the") followed by an ordinal (such as "first"), then a number ("three") followed by one or more adjectives ("big," "red") followed by one or more nouns being used as classifiers ("fire hydrant") followed by a noun ("covers") followed by qualifying phrases which are preposition groups or clauses ("without han-

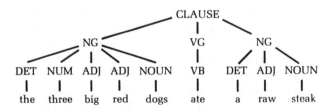

Figure 8. Syntactic parse tree.

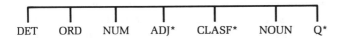

DET   ORD   NUM   ADJ*   CLASF*   NOUN   Q*

Figure 9. Structure of noun groups.

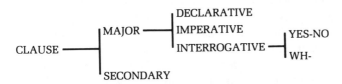

Figure 10. Simple system network for clauses.

dles" "which you can find"). Of course many of the elements are optional, and there are restriction relations between the various possibilities. If we choose an indefinite determiner such as "a," we cannot have an ordinal and number, as in the illegal string "a first three big red fire hydrant covers without handles you can find." The grammar must be able to express these rules in a way which is not simply an ad hoc set of statements. Our grammar takes advantage of some of the ideas of Systemic Grammar (Halliday 1970).

Systemic theory views a syntactic structure as being made up of units, each of which can be characterized in terms of the features describing its form, and the functions it fills in a larger structure or discourse. In the sentence in Figure 8, the noun group "three big red dogs" can be described as exhibiting features such as DETERMINED, INDEFINITE, PLURAL, etc. It serves the function SUBJECT in the clause of which it is a part, and various discourse functions, such as THEME as well. It in turn is made up of other units—the individual words—which fill functions in the noun group, such as DETERMINER and HEAD. A grammar must include a specification of the possible features a unit can have, and the relation of these to both the functions it can play, and the functions and constituents it controls.

These features are not haphazard bits of information we might choose to notice about units, but form a highly structured system (hence the name systemic grammar). As an example, we can look at a few of the features for the CLAUSE in Figure 10. The vertical lines represent sets from which a single feature must be selected and horizontal lines indicate logical dependency. Thus, we must first choose whether the clause is MAJOR which corresponds to the function of serving as an independent sentence or SECONDARY, which corresponds to the various functions a clause can serve as a constituent of another unit (for example as a QUALIFIER in the noun group "the ball which is on the table"). If a clause is MAJOR, it is either DECLARATIVE ("She went"), IMPERATIVE ("Go"), or INTERROGATIVE ("Did she go?"). If it is INTER-ROGATIVE, there is a further choice between YES-NO ("Did she go?") and WH- ("Where did she go?").

It is important to note that these features are syntactic, not semantic. They do not represent the use of a sentence as a question, statement, or command, but are rather a characterization of its internal structure—which words follow in what order. A DECLARATIVE can be used as a question by giving it a ris-ing intonation, or even as a command, as in "You're going to give that to me," spoken in an appropriate tone. A question may be used as a polite form of a command, as in "Can you give me a match?" and so on. Any language understander must know the conventions of the language for interpreting such utterances in addition to its simpler forms of syntactic knowledge. To do this, it must have a way to state things like "If something is syntactically a question but involves an event which the hearer could cause in the immediate future, it may be intended as a request." Syntactic features are therefore basic to the description of the semantic rules. The actual features in a comprehen-sive grammar are related in a more complex way than the simple example of Figure 10, but the basic ideas of logical dependency are the same.

In the foregoing we stated that there is a choice between certain features, and that depending on the selection made from one set, we must then choose between certain others. In doing this we are not postulating a psychological model for the order of making choices. The networks are an abstract charac-terization of the possibilities, and form only a part of a grammar. In addition we need realization and interpretation rules. Realization rules describe how a given set of choices would be expressed in the form of surface syntactic structures, whereas interpretation rules describe how a string of words is ana-lyzed to find its constituents and their features.

Our grammar is an interpretation grammar for accepting grammatical sen-tences. It differs from more usual grammars by being written explicitly in the form of a program. Ordinarily, grammars are stated in the form of rules, which are applied in the framework of a special interpretation process. This may be very complex in some cases (such as transformational grammars) with separate phases, special "traffic rules" for applying the other rules in the right order, cy-cles of application, and other sorts of constraints. In our system, the sequence of the actions is represented explicitly in the set of rules. The process of under-standing an utterance is basic to the organization of the grammar.[7]

In saying that grammars are programs, it is important to separate the proce-dural aspect from the details usually associated with programming. If we say to a linguist "Here is a grammar of English," he can rightfully object if it be-gins "Take the contents of location 177 and put them into register 2, adding the index..." The formalization of the syntax should include only those operations and concepts that are relevant to linguistic analysis, and should not be burdened with paraphernalia needed for programming details. Our model is based on the belief that the basic ideas of programming such as procedure and subprocedure, iteration, recursion, etc. are central to all cognitive processes, and in particular to the theory of language. What is needed is a formalism for describing syntactic processes. Our grammar is written in a language which was designed specifically for the purpose. It is a system built in Lisp, called Programmar, and its primitive operations are those involving the building of syntactic structures, and the generation of systemic descriptions of their parts.

The set of typical grammar rules shown in Box 6 would be expressed in Programmar by the program diagrammed in Figure 11. For such a simplified bit of grammar, there isn't much difference between the two formulations, except that the Programmar representation is more explicit in describing the flow of control. When we try to deal with more complex parts of syntax, the ability to specify procedures becomes more important. For example the word "and" can be associated with a program that can be diagrammed as shown in Figure 12. Given the sentence, "The giraffe ate the apples and peaches," it would first encounter "and" after parsing the noun "apples." It would then try to parse a second noun, and would succeed, resulting in the structure shown in Figure 13. If we had the sentence "The giraffe ate the apples and drank the vodka," the parser would have to try several different things. The "and" appears at a point which represents boundaries between several units. It is after the noun "apples," and the NP, "the apples." It is also after the entire VP "ate the apples." The parser, however, cannot find a noun or NP beginning with the following word "drank." It therefore tries to parse a VP and would successfully find "drank the vodka." A CONJOINED VP would be created, producing the final result shown in Figure 14. Of course the use of conjunctions is more complex than this, and the actual program must take into account such things as lists and branched structures in addition to the problems of backing up if a wrong possibility has been tried. But the basic operation of "look for another one like the one you just found" seems both practical and intuitively plausible as a description of how conjunction works. The ability to write the rules as procedures leaves us the flexibility to extend and refine it.

Viewing "and" as a special program that interrupts the normal parsing sequence also gives us a sort of explanation for some puzzling syntactic facts. The statement "I saw Ed with Steve" has a corresponding question, "Whom did you see Ed with?" But "I saw Ed and Steve" cannot be turned into "Whom did you see Ed and?" The "and" program cannot be called when there is no input for it to work with.

3.4 Program Organization

So far, we have described how three different types of knowledge are repre-

DEFINE program SENTENCE

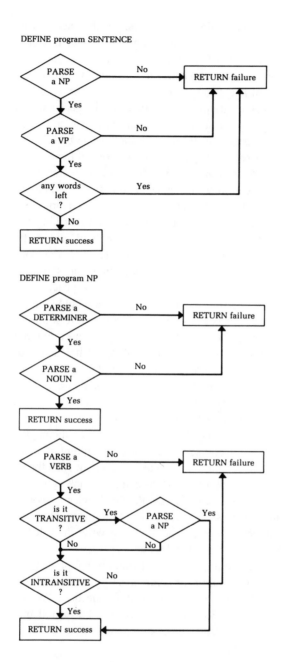

DEFINE program NP

Figure 11. PROGRAMMAR Grammar from Winograd, T. "Understanding Natural Language." *Cognitive Psychology,* 3:1-191. Copyright © by Academic Press.

```
S   →   NP VP
NP  →   DETERMINER NOUN
VP  →   VERB/TRANSITIVE NP
VP  →   VERB/INTRANSITIVE
```

Box 6. Simple grammar in replacement rule form.

sented and used. There is the data base of assertions and PLANNER procedures which represent the knowledge of the physical world; there are semantic analysis programs which know about such problems as reference; and there is a grammar which determines the syntactic structure. The most important element, however, is the interaction between these components. Language cannot be reduced into separate areas such as "syntax, semantics, and pragmatics" in hopes that by understanding each of them separately, we have understood the whole. The key to the function of language as a means of communication is in the way these areas interact.

Our program does not operate by first parsing a sentence, then doing semantic analysis, and finally by using deduction to produce a response. These three activities go on concurrently throughout the understanding of a sen-

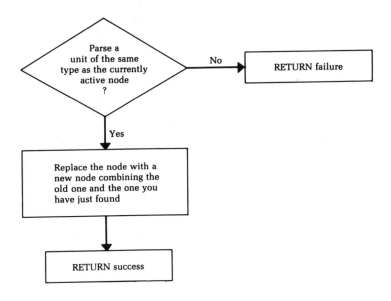

Figure 12. Conjunction program. from Winograd, T., "Understanding Natural Language." *Cognitive Psychology,* 3:1-191. Copyright © by Academic Press.

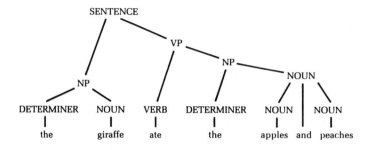

Figure 13. Conjoined noun structure. From Winograd, T., Understanding Natural Languages *Cognitive Psychology,* 3:1-191. Copyright © by Academic Press.

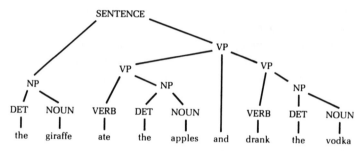

Figure 14. Conjoined VP structure. From Winograd, T., "Understanding Natural Language." *Cognitive Psychology,* 3:1-191. Copyright © by Academic Press.

tence. As soon as a piece of syntactic structure begins to take shape, a semantic program is called to see whether it might make sense, and the resultant answer can direct the parsing. In deciding whether it makes sense, the semantic routine may call deductive processes and ask questions about the real world. As an example, in sentence 36 of the dialogue ("Put the blue pyramid on the block in the box"), the parser first comes up with "the blue pyramid on the block" as a candidate for a noun group. At this point, semantic analysis is begun, and since "the" is definite, a check is made in the data base for the object being referred to. When no such object is found, the parsing is redirected to find the noun group "the blue pyramid." It will then go on to find "on the block in the box" as a single phrase indicating a location. In other examples the system of semantic markers may reject a possible interpretation on the basis of conflicting category information. Thus, there is a continuing interplay between the different sorts of analysis, with the results of one affecting the others.

The procedure as a whole operates in a left to right direction through the sentence. It does not carry along multiple possibilities for the syntactic analysis, but instead has ways of going back and doing something different if it runs into trouble. It does not use the general backup mechanism of PLANNER, but decides what to do on the basis of exactly what sort of problem arose. In the sentences like those of the dialogue, very little backup is ever used, since the combination of syntactic and semantic information usually guides the parser quite efficiently.

4. Limitations of the Approach

The program we are describing does not purport to be a point by point model of psychological processes at a detailed level. Rather, it is an attempt to show how a general view of language can really be filled in with enough detail to provide a working model. The importance from a psychological point of view is the approach to language as a process which can be modeled within the context of a procedural description of cognitive processes. Rather than trying to attach psychological meaning to isolated components into which language has been divided for abstract study, it attempts to relate the various types of knowledge and procedures involved in intelligent language use.

Looking into the specific capabilities of the system, we can find many places where the details seem inadequate, or whole areas are missing. The program does not attempt to handle hypothetical or counterfactual statements; it only accepts a limited range of declarative information, it cannot talk about verbal acts, and the treatment of "the" is not as general as the description above, and so on. These deficiencies, however, seem to be more a matter of what has been tackled so far, rather than calling into question the underlying model. Looking deeper, we can find two basic ways in which it seems an inadequate model of human language use. The first is the way in which the process is directed, and the second is concerned with the interaction of the context of the conversation and the understanding of its content.

We can think of a program for understanding a sentence as having two kinds of operations—coming up with possible interpretations, and choosing between them. Of course, these are not separate psychologically, but in the organization of computer programs, the work is divided up.

In our program, the syntactic analysis is in charge of coming up with possibilities. The basic operation requires that we find a syntactically acceptable phrase, and then do a semantic interpretation on it to decide whether to continue along that line of parsing. Other programs such as Schank (1971) and Quillian (1967) use the semantic information contained in the definitions of the words to provide an initial set of possibilities, then use syntactic information in a secondary way to check whether the hypothesized underlying semantic structure is in accord with the arrangement of the words. By observing human language use, it seems clear that no single approach is really correct. On the one hand, people are able to interpret utterances which are not syntactically well formed, and can even assign meanings to collections of words without use of syntax. The list "skid, crash, hospitals" presents a certain image even though two of the words are both nouns and verbs and there are no explicit syntactic connections. It is therefore wrong to insist that some sort of complete parsing is a prerequisite to semantic analysis.

On the other hand, people are able to interpret sentences syntactically even when they do not know the meanings of the individual words. Most of our vocabulary (beyond a certain age) is learned by hearing sentences in which unfamiliar words appear in syntactically well-defined positions. We process the sentence without knowing any category information for the words, and in fact use the results of that processing to discover the semantic meaning. In addition, much of our normal conversation is made up of sentences like, "Then the other one did the same thing to it" in which the words taken individually do not provide clues to enable us to determine the conceptual structure without a complete syntactic analysis.

What really seems to be going on is a coordinated process in which a variety of syntactic and semantic information can be relevant, and in which the hearer takes advantage of whatever is more useful in understanding a given part of a sentence. Our system models this coordination in its order of doing things, by carrying on all of the different levels of analysis concurrently, although it does not model it in the control structure.

Much remains to be done in understanding how to write computer programs in which a number of concurrent processes are working in a coordinated fashion without being under the primary hierarchical control of one of them. A language model able to implement the sort of "heterarchy" found in biological systems (like the coordination between different systems of an organism) will be much closer to a valid psychological theory.

The second basic shortcoming is in not dealing with all the implications of viewing language as a process of communication between two intelligent people. A human language user is always engaged in a process of trying to understand the world around him, including the person he is talking to. He is actively constructing models and hypotheses, and he makes use of them in the process of language understanding. As an example, let us consider again the use of pronouns. In Section 1, we described some of the knowledge involved in choosing referents. It included syntax, semantic categories, and heuristics about the structure of discourse.

But all of these heuristics are really only a rough approximation to what is really going on. The reason that the focus of the previous sentence is more likely to be the referent of "it" is because a person generally has a continuity in his conversation, which comes from talking about a particular object or event. The focus (or subject) is more likely just because that is the thing he is talking about, and he is likely to go on talking about it. Certain combinations of conceptual category markers are more plausible than others because the speaker is probably talking about the real world, where certain types of events are more sensible than others. If we prefix almost any sentence with "I just had the craziest dream..." the whole system of plausible conceptual relations is turned topsy-turvy.

If someone says "I dropped a bottle of Coke® on the table and it broke," there are two obvious interpretations. The semantic categories and the syntactic heuristics make it slightly more plausible that it was the bottle that broke. But consider what would happen if we heard "Where is the tool box? I dropped a bottle of Coke® on the table and it broke" or, "Where is the furniture polish? I dropped a bottle of Coke® on the table and it broke." The referent is now perfectly clear—only because we have a model of what is reasonable in the world, and what a person is likely to say. We know that there is nothing in the tool box to help fix a broken Coke® bottle and that nobody would be likely to try fixing one. It would be silly to polish a table that just got broken, while it would be logical to polish one that just had a strong corrosive spilled on it. Of course, all this must be combined with deductions based on other common sense knowledge, such as the fact that when a bottle containing a liquid breaks, the liquid in it spills.

Even more important, we try to understand what the speaker is "getting at." We assume that there is a meaningful connection between his sentences, and that his description of what happened is probably intended as an explanation for why he wants the polish or toolbox. More subtle deductions are implied here as well. It is possible that he broke the table and fixed it, and now wants the polish to cover the repair marks. If this were the case, he would almost surely have mentioned the repair to allow us to follow that chain of logic.

Our system makes only the most primitive use of this sort of deduction. Since it keeps track of when things have been mentioned, it can check a possible interpretation of a question to see whether the asker could answer it himself from his previous sentences. If so, it assumes that he probably means something else. We could characterize this as containing two sorts of knowledge. First, it assumes that a person asks questions for the purpose of getting information he doesn't already have, and second, it has a very primitive model of what information he has on the basis of what he has said. A realistic view of language must have a complex model of this type, and the heuristics in our system touch only the tiniest bit of the relevant knowledge.

It is important to recognize that this sort of interaction does not occur only with pronouns and explicit discourse features, but in every part of the understanding process. In choosing between alternative syntactic structures for a sentence, or picking between multiple meanings of words, we continually use this sort of higher level deduction. We are always basing our understanding on the answer to questions like "Which interpretation would make sense given what I already know?" and "What is he trying to communicate?"

Any attempt to model human language with simple semantic rules and heuristics like those described above is a bit like an attempt to model the behavior of a complex system by using unrelated mathematical formulas whose results are a general approximation to its output. The results may be of interest, and the resulting equations may have a high correlation with what is going on, but it is not a model in the true sense of reflecting the underlying process.

It seems likely that more advanced computational models will move towards overcoming these deficiencies. As we learn more about the organization of large complex systems, we may well be able to model language in ways which are more complete, clearer, and closer to psychological reality.

Notes

1. For more details on the entire system, see Winograd (1972). The actual program is written in Lisp, occupies about 100K of storage on the PDP-10, and operates in approximately real time, responding to a sentence in an average of 10 or 15 seconds.

2. The fact that B1 is a block could be represented in more usual predicate notation as (BLOCK B1). We have chosen to associate with each object or concept a property describing its most relevant category for the purpose of generating an English phrase for it. Thus (IS B1 BLOCK) is used to describe B1 as a block. Similarly, properties like colors are represented (COLOR B1 BLUE) instead of (BLUE B1). This allows for more efficiency in the operation of the deduction system, without changing its logical characteristics.

3. The notation does not correspond exactly to that in the original program, as mnemonics have been used here to increase readability

4. The system actually uses MICRO-PLANNER (Sussman et. al. 1970) a partial implementation of PLANNER. In this presentation we have slightly simplified the details of its syntax.

5. Again, in comparing this with the details in Winograd (1972), note that some of the symbols have been replaced with more understandable mnemonic versions.

6. It is of course impossible to provide a complete grammar of English, and often difficult to evaluate a partial one. The dialogue of Section 2 gives a sample of the constructions which can be handled, and does not make use of specially included patterns. Winograd (1972) gives a full description of the grammar used.

7. For a discussion of the psycholinguistic relevance of such interpretive grammars see Kaplan (1971). He describes a similar formulation of procedural grammar, represented as a transition network.

9

The Structure of Episodes in Memory

Roger C. Schank

1. Introduction

The past few years have significantly altered the direction of research in computer processing of natural language. For nearly the entire history of the field, parsing and generating have been the major preoccupations of researchers. The realization that meaning representation is a crucial issue that cannot be divorced from the above two problems, leads to a concern with the following two questions:

- How much information must be specified, and at what level, in a meaning representation?
- To what extent can problems of inference be simplified or clarified by the choice of meaning representation?

2. Conceptual Dependency

These are the principal issues we have been concerned with in our work on conceptual dependency: (1) It is useful to restrict severely the concepts of action such that actions are separated from the states that result from those actions. (2) Missing information can be as useful as given information. It is thus the responsibility of the meaning representation to provide a formalism with requirements on items which must be associated with a concept. If a slot for an item is not filled, requirements for the slot are useful for making predictions about yet to be received information. (3) Depending on the purposes of the understanding processes, inferences must be made that will (a) fill in slots that are left empty after a sentence is completed and (b) tie together single actor-action complexes (called "conceptualizations") with other such complexes in order to provide higher-level structures.

Throughout our research it was our goal to solve the paraphrase problem. We wanted our theory to explain how sentences which were constructed differently lexically could be identical in meaning. To do this we used the consequence of (1) and (2) to derive a theory of primitive ACTs. Simply stated, the theory of primitive ACTs states that within a well-defined meaning representation it is possible to use as few as eleven ACTs as building blocks which can combine with a larger number of states to represent the verbs and abstract nouns in a language. For more detail on these acts, the reader is referred to the Appendix and to Schank (1973a) and Schank (1975). We claim that no information is lost using these ACTs to represent actions. The advantage of such a system is this:

1. Paraphrase relations are made clearer.
2. Similarity relations are made clearer.
3. Inferences that are true of various classes of verbs can be treated as coming from the individual ACTs. All verbs map into a combination of ACTs and states. The inferences come from the ACTs and states rather than from words.
4. Organization in memory is simplified because much information need not be duplicated. The primitive ACTs provide focal points under which information is organized.

2.1 Some Caveats about Oversimplification

The simplest view of a system which uses primitive ACTs gives rise to a number of misconceptions. The following caveats, which we subscribe to, must be observed.

1. There is no right number of ACTs. It would be possible to map all of language into combinations of mental and physical MOVE. This would, however, be extremely cumbersome to deal with in a computer system. A larger set (several hundred) would overlap tremendously causing problems in paraphrase recognition and inference organization. The set we have chosen is small enough not to cause these problems without being too small. Other sets on the same order of magnitude might do just as well.

2. The primitive ACTs overlap. That is, some ACTs nearly always imply others either as results or as instruments. Our criteria for selecting a given ACT is that it must have inferences which are unique and separate from the set of already existing ACTs.

3. Information can be organized under each primitive ACT, but it is definitely necessary to organize information around certain standard combinations of these ACTs. Such "super predicates" should be far fewer than those presented by other researchers, but they certainly must exist. Many inferences come from "kiss" for example that are in addition to those for MOVE. Organizing information under super predicates such as "prevent" is, however, misguided since prevent is no more than the sum of its individual parts.

4. Information is not lost by the use of primitive ACTs, nor is operating with them cumbersome in a computer program. Goldman (in Schank 1975) has shown that it is possible to read combinations of ACTs into words very easily. Rieger (1974) has written a program to do inferences based on a memory that uses only those ACTs. Riesbeck (1974) has shown that predictions made from the ACTs can be used as the basis of a parsing program that can bypass syntactic analysis. The MARGIE program (see Schank, Goldman, Rieger, & Riesbeck 1973) would seem to indicate that objections to ACTs on computational grounds are misguided at the current level of technology.

2.2 Toward Episode Representation

This chapter outlines our assumptions about how people tie together episodes or stories. We use the notions of conceptual dependency and primitive ACTs to represent and paraphrase entire episodes. We assume that knowing how to build larger structures bears upon the problem of how to use context to direct inferencing, and when to stop making inferences. The program of Goldman and Riesbeck (1973) paraphrased sentences semantically but did not go beyond the level of the sentence. The solution that we will present is meant to be a partial solution to the paraphrase problem.

Our goal is to combine input sentences which are part of a paragraph into one or more connected structures which represent the meaning of the paragraph as a whole. While doing this we want to bear in mind the following: (1) A good paraphrase of a paragraph may be longer or shorter (in terms of the number of sentences in it) than the original. (2) Humans have little trouble picking out the main "theme" of the paragraph. (3) Knowing what is nonessential or readily inferable from the sentences of a paragraph is crucial in paraphrasing it as well as parsing it.

We pose the question of exactly how units larger than the sentence are understood. That is, what would the resulting structure in intermediate memory look like after a six-sentence episode or story had been input? Obviously, there must be more stored than just the conceptual dependency representation for each of the six sentences, but we could not store all possible inferences for each of the six sentences. Ideally what we want is to store the six sentences in terms of the conceptualizations that underlie them as an interconnected chain. That is, we shall claim that the amount of inferencing which is useful to represent the meaning of a paragraph of six sentences in length is precisely as much as will allow for the creation of a causal chain between the original conceptualizations.

Finally we shall address the question of creating the best model to explain how information is stored in human memory. We do not believe that people remember everything that they hear, but rather that forgetting can be explained partially in terms of what information is crucial to a text as a whole and what information can be easily rediscovered.

2.3 Causal Links

We shall claim here that the causal chain is the means for connecting the conceptualizations underlying sentences in a text. Conceptual dependency allows for four kinds of causal links. These are:

Result Causation: An action causes a state change. The potential results for a given action can be enumerated according to the nature of that action. Consider some illustrative examples: *John hurt Mary.* John did something which *resulted in* Mary suffering a negative physical state change. *John chopped the wood*—John propelled something into wood which resulted in the wood being in pieces.

Enable Causation: A state allows for an action to have the potential of taking place. Here too, the states necessary for an action to occur can be enumerated. *John read a book*—John's having access to the book and eyes, etc. *enabled* John to read. *John helped Mary hit Bill*—John did something which *resulted* in a state which enabled Mary to hit Bill. *John prevented Bill* from leaving—John did something which ended the conditions which enabled Bill to go. (This is *unenable* causation.)

Initiation Causation: Any act or state change can cause an individual to think about (MBUILD) that or any other event. *John reminds me of Peter*—when I think of John it initiates a thought of Peter. *When John heard the footsteps he got scared*—hearing the footsteps *initiated* a thought about some harm that might befall John.

Reason Causation: An MBUILD of a new thought can usually serve as the reason for an action. Reason causation is the interface between mental decisions and their physical effects. *John hit Mary because he hated her*—John thought about his feelings about Mary which made him decide to hit her which was the *reason* he hit her.

In this chapter causality will be denoted by a line from cause (top) to effect (bottom). A label will indicate which causal it is. Sometimes two or more labels will appear at once, which indicates that all the intermediate conceptualizations exist, but that we simply choose not to write them.

3. Understanding Paragraphs

Consider the following three paragraphs constructed from three different introductions (S1, S2 and S3) followed by a paragraph (BP). The base paragraph is:

(BP) John began to mow his lawn. Suddenly his toe started bleeding. He turned off the motor and went inside to get a bandage. When he cleaned off his foot, he discovered that he had stepped in tomato sauce.

(S1) It was a warm June day. (followed by) BP.

(S2) It was a cold December day. (followed by) BP.

(S3) John was eating a pizza outside on his lawn. He noticed the grass was very long so he got out his lawn mower. (followed by) BP.

We will refer to S1 (S2, S3) followed by BP as paragraph I (II, III).

Within the context of a paragraph, a sentence has a dual role. It has the usual role of imparting information or giving a meaning. In addition, it serves to set up the conditions by which sentences that follow it in the paragraph can be coherent. Thus in general, in order for sentence Y to follow sentence X and be understood in a paragraph, the conditions for Y must have been set up. Often these conditions will have been set up by X, but this is by no means necessarily the case. The conditions for Y might be generally understood, that is, part of everyday knowledge, so that they need not be set up at all. If this is not the case, then it is irrelevant that X precedes Y.

3.1 Necessary Conditions

By a *necessary condition,* we mean a state (in conceptual dependency terms) that enables an ACT. Thus one cannot play baseball unless one has access to a ball, a bat, a field to play on, etc. The conditions that are necessary in order to do a given ACT must be present before that ACT can occur.

It is thus necessary, in order to understand that a given ACT has occurred, to satisfy oneself that its necessary conditions have been met. Often this requires finding a causal chain that would lead to that condition being present. That is, if we cannot establish that John has a bat, but we can establish that he had some money and was in a department store, we can infer that he bought one there if we know that he has one now. Obviously there are many possible ways to establish the validity of a necessary condition. Often, it is all right just to assume that it is "normally" the case that this condition holds. Rieger (1975) makes extensive use of this kind of assumption in his inference program. Establishing or proving necessary conditions is an important part of tying diverse sentences together in a story. (John wanted to play baseball on Saturday. He went to the department store.). It is also, as we shall see, an important part of knowing when a paragraph does not make sense.

Thus the problem of representing a paragraph conceptually is at least in part the problem of tying together the conditions set up by sentences with the sentences that required those conditions to be set up. In the base paragraph (BP), no conditions have been set up under which tomato sauce could reasonably be considered to be present. Thus BP does not hang together very well as a paragraph. With S3, however, the conditions for tomato sauce being present are set up, the last sentence of BP can be tied to those conditions, and this is an integral paragraph. Note that there is no need to set up "bandage's" existence, since people can normally be assumed to have a bandage in a medicine cabinet in a bathroom in their house. If the third sentence were replaced by: "He took a bandage off of his lawn mower," however, there would be problems.

What we are seeking to explain then is what the entire conceptual representation of a paragraph must be. It can be seen from the above that in our representation of BP, it might well be argued that "bathroom" and "medicine cabinet" are rightfully part of the representation. The representation of a paragraph is a combination of the conceptualizations underlying the individual sentences of the paragraph plus the inferences about the necessary conditions that tie one conceptualization to another or to a given normality condition.

Let us consider the connectivity relationships with S1. We shall do this by looking at the necessary conditions required for each conceptualization and established by that conceptualization for subsequent conceptualizations.

S1, *It was a warm June day,* consists of two details. One is that the time of some unspecified conceptualization was a day in June. The other is that the temperature for that day was warm (or to be more precise greater than the norm for that season). These two states enable all warm weather activities. That is, the established conditions invalidate any activities for which contradictory conditions would be necessary.

Consider as an example S1 followed by an S4 such as: S2. *John began to build a snowman.* The fact that people would find such sequences bothersome, if not absurd, indicates that part of the process of understanding is the tying together of *necessary conditions* and *established conditions*. Necessary conditions are backward looking inferences that must be generated for each input conceptualization. For S4 we would have something like "check to see if the necessary condition for this action (coldness) has been established. If it has not been, then infer it unless a contradictory condition has been established in which case there is an anomaly."

Established conditions are forward-looking inferences. These are states which are inferable from an input conceptualization. Often established conditions are input directly and need not be inferred at all. Thus S1 provides two established conditions. Neither of these conditions are called into play until a request for their existence is received from a following input conceptualization.

Now the actual S2 in paragraph I is *John began to mow his lawn.* S2 requires appropriate necessary conditions to be satisfied. Some of these are: (a) John has a lawn; (b) John has a lawn mower; (c) John's lawn has grown to a length such that it might be mowed; (d) It is a pleasant day for being outside. (Obviously, there is an extremely large set of conditions to be satisfied. Part of the problem is knowing how to reduce the search space.)

It can be seen from these four conditions that they are not all equal. That is (a) and (b) are of the class of necessary conditions that we shall call "absolutely necessary conditions" (ANCs). An ANC is a state which must be present in order to enable a given ACT to take place. If an ANC is violated, a sentence sequence is construed to be anomalous. Conditions (c) and (d), however, are the more interesting. They are what we shall call "reasonable necessary conditions" (RNCs). An RNC is a state which is usually a prerequisite for a given ACT. If an RNC is violated, the story sequence is not interrupted. Rather a peculiarity marking is made. These peculiarity markings turn out to be a crucial part of story understanding because they are predictive. That is, the sequence "It was a cold December day. John walked outside in his bathing suit." predicts a to-be-related consequence which is likely the point of the story. What makes this prediction is the peculiarity marking that would be generated from the established violation of the RNC involving warm weather necessary for walking outside scantily clad.

Necessary conditions are thus a subset of the set of possible inferences. They are precisely the set which is commonly used to connect isolated conceptualizations together. Necessary conditions are checked by means of establishing whether there exist records of them in memory. First, there is an attempt to tie them to information already present from previous sentences. This is done by use of the general facts in memory (e.g., about warm weather and lawns) including normality conditions. If such facts are present or can be established, an enable causation link is established between the previously input or inferred state and the new input conceptualization. That is, it is quite usual for people to possess lawns and lawn mowers so the fact that nobody told us this about John is not upsetting. (Of course, if we knew that John lived in an apartment then an ANC would be violated and there would be trouble.) If the connection can be established from normality information, then the new states involving this normality information are inferred as being the case in this particular instance (i.e., John has a lawn is inferred). When none of this can be done, a severe problem in the cohesion of the story (for the listener) exists.

The interesting part of paragraph connectivity comes when we examine the sentence "Suddenly his toe started bleeding." How can we connect this sentence to previous information? In fact humans do it with little trouble. A question is generated, "what can cause bleeding in people?" This question is coupled with an inquiry as to whether the established conditions demandable from any previous information in the text result in "a human bleeding" under the right circumstances. Working in both directions at once, we can establish a chain from "lawn mowing" to "blades turning" to "toe bleeding" if we hypothesize contact between blade and toe. The syntax for causality in this chain follows exactly the same lines as proposed by Schank (1973b). The kind of inference outlined previously has been considered in some detail (including programming some examples on the order of complexity shown here) by Rieger (1975). Let us now consider what the final representation of paragraph I should be.

In our representation we shall use a simplified conceptual dependency diagram, consisting of a parenthesized expression in the order: (ACTOR ACTION OBJECT X) where X is any other relevant case which we choose to include which we make explicit there. State diagrams are written: (OBJECT NEW-STATE). Necessary conditions are abbreviated as ANCs or RNCs. Ss designate input sentences. INFs designate inferences needed to complete causal chains. The time of an event or state is relative to the others around it with earlier events higher on the page; story (for the listener) exists. Figure 1 is the final representation of the paragraph except for the following:

1. Normally the initiation reason causation (from ANC/3) would have to be expanded. In this case there would have to be a belief about what bandages had to do with bleeding body parts. This belief would be part of the MBUILD structure that supplied the reason for going in the house.

2. All the ANCs would have to be accounted for. This would be done as the paragraph was being processed.

The ANCs for the above paragraph are as follows:

ANC/1, ANC/2,....: These specify that John has a lawn and a lawn mower and can push it, etc.

ANC/3: John has a toe and he was not wearing shoes, etc.

ANC/4: John has a house, it is nearby and he can get in, etc.

ANC/5: John has a bandage in his house, and he can find and get it.

ANC/6: This is provided by "John cleaned his toe." Thus the entire structure causally related to ANC/6 established another chain apart from the actual story.

ANC/7: This is specified by the next part of the last sentence.

ANC/8: This is the condition that tomato sauce be in a place where John might have stepped in it.

Two important things are illustrated in this diagram of paragraph I: (1) Conceptually, a paragraph is essentially a set of causal chains, some leading to dead ends and at least one carrying on the theme and point of the story. (2) As long as required necessary conditions can be established and inferences necessary to complete causal chains can be resolved, a paragraph is coherent and understandable. When these processes are too difficult or impossible problems result.

In paragraph I, ANCs 1-5 are easily satisfied by everyday normality conditions, but ANCs 6-8 are more of a problem. ANC/6 is provided by the story in C15, but C17 which is initiated by ANC/6 requires John himself to establish (in an MBUILD) ANC/7. In trying to establish ANC/7, John concludes that C19 is true. This leaves the reader with the problem of verifying ANC/8, which is not possible under these conditions. The rest of the story thus remains incomplete and can never really get to C14 and C20.

Now, in paragraph III on the other hand, ANC/8, when it is discovered, is easily resolvable. (PIZZA LOC (LAWN)) is a possible result of the first sentence (John was eating a pizza outside on his lawn). If the problem of knowing that a pizza contains tomato sauce is resolvable, then so is ANC/8. In that case, an ANC would be resolved from within the given paragraph as was done for ANC/6 and ANC/7 in paragraph I.

Some additional comments that can be made about the representation of paragraph I are:

1. C5 is a deadend. Short grass may be the condition for something, but this story does not tell us nor make use of it. Dead-end paths in a story indicate items of less importance in the story. This information is crucial in the problem of paraphrase of paragraphs since it tells you what you can leave out.

2. The inference of the result link between C4 and C6 is one of the most important inferences in the story. It serves to tie together two apparently unrelated events into a contiguous whole.

3. The information about turning the lawn mower off is another dead end. In fact, there was no reason for this information to be in the story at all.

4. C14 and C20 are crucial to a story that has not been told. What has happened is that the attempted resolution of ANC/6 has interrupted the flow of the story. Inside the resolution of ANC/6 we have had to resolve ANC/8 which causes us to quit.

Diagrammatically we can view the story as in Figure 2 which shows a version of the story structure with only concept labels. From various sources of information we can construct a path that sets up C4. One of the inferences from C4 is fruitful in that it provides a chain to C7. Two paths come from C7, one is fruitful in leading us to C10 (whose conditions can be explained by ANC/4). On our way to C14, we try to establish ANC/6. Doing so leads to a direct path to C18. In order to prove the conditions for C18, however, we need ANC/8 which cannot be determined.

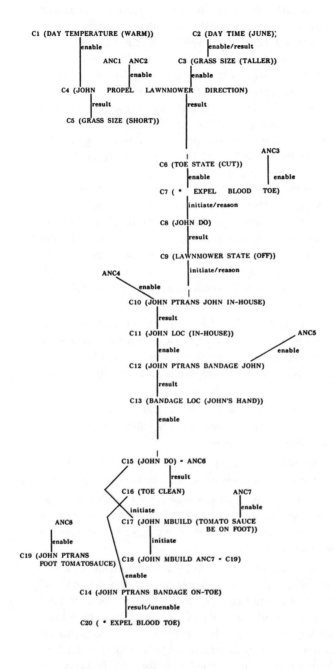

Figure 1. Conceptual dependency representation of the paragraph.

3.2 Remembering Paragraphs

We have established in the previous section some basic principles regarding what we would expect to be the result in memory after a paragraph has been input. (1) The conceptual dependency representation of each input sentence is included. (2) The conceptualizations that underlie the sentences should connect to each other conceptually. (3) The basic means of connecting the conceptualizations underlying the input sentences to each other is the causal chain. (4) Inferences from the input conceptualizations are part of the representation of the total paragraph if they are used in order to connect input conceptualizations into a causal chain. (5) The necessary conditions must be satisfied for every represented conceptualization. This is done by inferring facts both from inside and outside the paragraph. Inferences made from outside the paragraph proper are still part of the representation of the total paragraph. (6) Stories can be viewed as the joining together of various causal chains that culminate in the "point" of the story. Dead end paths that lead away from the main flow of the story can thus be considered to be of lesser importance.

From the point of view of paraphrasing tasks or the problem of remembering, the things most likely to be left out in a recall task are: the dead end paths; the easily satisfied necessary conditions, whether they were explicit in the original paragraph or not; and the inferences that make up the causal chain that are "obvious" and easy to recover at any time.

In order to better examine the validity of our predictions about memory and the usefulness of our representation for stories, we diagrammed the well known "The War of the Ghosts," a story used by Bartlett (1932) for experiments in memory. We are not interested here in all the facets of memory that Bartlett considered, but some of the problems that he concerned himself with can be handled more easily using our representation. The story is:

> One night two young men from Egulac went down to the river to hunt seals, and while they were there it became foggy and calm. Then they heard war-cries, and they thought: "Maybe this is a war-party." They escaped to the shore, and hid behind a log. Now canoes came up, and they heard the noise of paddles, and saw one canoe coming up to them. There were five men in the canoe, and they said:
>
> "What do you think? We wish to take you along. We are going up the river to make war on the people."
>
> One of the young men said: "I have no arrows."
>
> "Arrows are in the canoe," they said.
>
> "I will not go along. I might be killed. My relatives do not know where I have gone. But you," he said, turning to the other, "may go with them."
>
> So one of the young men went, but the other returned home.
>
> And the warriors went on up the river to a town on the other side of Kalama. The people came down to the water, and they began to fight, and many were killed. But presently the young man heard one of the warriors say: "Quick, let us

go home; that Indian has been hit." Now he thought: "Oh, they are ghosts." He did not feel sick, but they said he had been shot.

So the canoes went back to Egulac, and the young man went ashore to his house, and made a fire. And he told everybody and said: "Behold I accompanied the ghosts, and we went to fight. Many of our fellows were killed, and many of those who attacked us were killed. They said I was hit, and I did not feel sick."

He told it all, and then he became quiet. When the sun rose he fell down. Something black came out of his mouth. His face became contorted. The people jumped up and cried.

He was dead.

Using a diagram for this story based on causal chains, we followed the rules given below to prune the causal chains to create a summary diagram which would allow a paraphrase to be generated on later remembering. We have not worked out a complete set of rules, but the following give a reasonable first approximation:

1. Dead end chains will be forgotten.

2. Sequential flows (correct chains) may be shortened.

   (a) The first link in the chain is most important.

   (b) Resolution of questions or problems is too.

3. Disconnected pieces will be either connected correctly or forgotten.

4. Pieces that have many connections are crucial.

Using a diagram with only the causal connections (as shown in Figure 2 for paragraph I) and the above rules, we derived a paraphrase which was:

Two men went to the river. While they were there they heard some noises and hid. Some men approached them in canoes. They asked them if they would go on a war party with them. One man went. He got shot. The men took him home. He told the people what happened and then he died.

The reasonableness of this paraphrase suggests that the above procedural outline for paragraph paraphrase is a good one.

If one compares our paraphrase with the output of Bartlett's subjects, the one striking difference is that the two conceptualizations missing necessary conditions are present in his subjects' output. We hypothesized that peculiarity markings would be generated for violation of necessary conditions. C37 and C52 ("They are ghosts," and "Something black came out of his mouth.") would have generated peculiarity markings. If Bartlett's output is examined, it can be seen that his subjects handled these peculiarity markings in various ways. They were made part of the causal chain in entirely different ways for each speaker and were hardly ever forgotten.

Paraphrases can be generated from meaning representations of text by procedures that read out the conceptualizations which are central to the flow of the diagram. Paraphrases longer than the original text would be generated by realizing all the conceptualizations in the final meaning representation. Para-

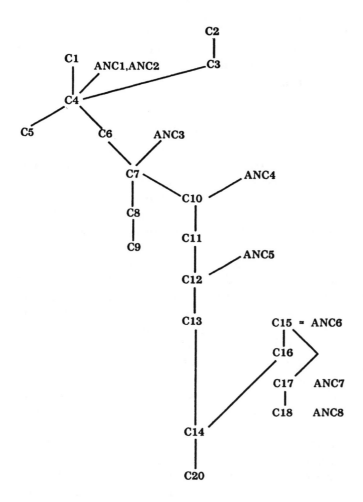

Figure 2. A diagrammatic version of the paragraph.

phrases shorter than the text would be generated by various means. Among these are: (a) leaving out dead end paths, (b) only realizing conceptualizations that have more than two pointers to them in the text, (c) reading out only starting and ending points of the subchains in a text. Summaries would be developed in similar ways.

The main problem in building a computer program to do paraphrases is, at this point, not the generation aspect, but the problem of actually being able to make the crucial inferences that connect texts together. In the base paragraph the inference that the lawn mower may have cut John's toe is difficult to make. In "The War of the Ghosts" the crucial inference that the notion of ghosts somehow resolves the unconnectable causal chain at the end of the story is too difficult for humans to figure out.

4. Long-Term Memory

Text is not really remembered verbatim. At some point there must be an integration of new input information within the long-term store. We have outlined some forgetting heuristics above, but they are only part of the issue. We must investigate as well, what we imagine long-term memory to look like, or, with respect to what we have just done here, how would the conceptual content in "The War of the Ghosts" be stored in long-term memory?

We shall advance the view here that a story is stored as a whole (albeit partially forgotten) unit, not decomposed. Such a view claims that any sequence of new information forms an episode in memory and any piece of information within an episode can be accessed only by referencing the episode in which it occurs. This view is similar to the view of memory expressed by using frames. We will contrast this with the view that most information is stored in a hierarchically organized semantic memory.

As originally proposed by Quillian (1968), semantic memory was an associative network of words which were intended to represent the meaning of sentences as well as the knowledge used in understanding sentences. More recent modifications to Quillian's ideas on semantic memory have suggested network models which were both better structured in terms of the kinds of associative links allowed as well as more representative of the meaning of sentences. For example, Rumelhart, Lindsay, and Norman (1972) and Anderson and Bower (1973) each proposed a semantic memory which relates words together, and this same semantic memory was intended to account for meaning and world knowledge. Tulving (1972) proposed that this memory ought to be divided into two distinct pieces: a hierarchical portion containing static knowledge about relations between "words, concepts, and classification of concepts;" and an episodic portion which contains information gained through personal experience.

What we shall argue in the remainder of this chapter is that the distinction between semantic memory and episodic memory is a false one. We shall argue that what must be present is a lexical memory which contains all of the information about words, idioms, common expressions, etc., and which links these to nodes in a conceptual memory, which is language free. We believe that it is semantic memory rather than episodic which is the misleading notion. Once we change semantic memory by separating out lexical memory, we are left with a set of associations and other relations between concepts that could only have been acquired by personal experience. We claim that conceptual memory, therefore, is episodic in nature.

4.1 Supersets in Memory

The case of much of semantic memory work relies on the notion of superset to organize the lexical data. Is there any reason to believe that humans really use supersets in their memories? To some extent the Collins and Quillian (1969) experiments indicate that some supersets are used by people. But it is important to point out where they are probably not used.

The 50 States Problem: A classic barroom bet involves asking someone to name all 50 states in the U.S. Very few people can actually name all 50 of them (including professors). It is not that they do not really "know" all 50. That is, they can recognize each of them as well as produce the names of each of them in response to specific queries (e.g., What state is Baltimore in?), but in the task of naming all 50, people find that their method for organizing the data is not a simple list called "States of the U.S." under which all 50 are stored. Some people try to visualize a map and read off the names. Others associate specific experiences with each.

The point is this: The information about states is organized around experiences. People probably have a marker after their memory token for a state saying that it is a state. They have no effective procedure that can "get all the tokens that have state on their property list." Rather, they try to find other pieces of their memory that have pointers to the tokens for the states (i.e., "places I went on my trip in 1971"). Not all the states can be located in this fashion and they are left out. Conrad's (1972) experiments suggest that such information is not necessarily stored in the most economical fashion possible. In other words, while general information exists, it is not part of the actual day to day working part of memory. Thus certain superset information may well exist in memory, but as part of an infrequently used general knowledge store, rather than as part of the core of working memory.

4.1.1 The Rabbit Problem

Suppose you wanted to code in your memory that "Rabbits eat carrots." A hierarchical organization suggests that carrots should be listed under the node "food." It is plain, however that carrots are only food for some animals, not all. The best organization would be one where experience codes static information. That is, "carrot is a potential food for rabbits" is more optimally coded with what we might call a "FOOD" link. That is, there is an associative link from carrot to rabbit. This link has a name which we can write as FOOD.

We are introducing here two concepts: (1) Links can themselves be linked to conceptualizations that describe the nature of the link. There are as many types of associations between concepts as there are conceptualizations in which they could possibly occur. (2) Hierarchical superset nodes are eliminated for functional supersets like food since information about food would be bound under particular instances of animals eating what is good for them. (This says nothing about nonfunctional supersets such as "bird.")

4.1.2 Contextual Organization

Naive organization of superset relationships fails to group contextually related entities. Thus while hammer, saw, and plunger all are tools, the first two are certainly more closely related to each other than they are to the third. This can be handled by having subheadings in the hierarchical tree, but this merely worsens an already mistaken notion. Concepts which have no place under an organizing node such as "tool" would still be closer to some tools than some tools would be to other tools. Thus we propose that "wood" is closer to "saw" than "plunger" is to "saw," even though the latter two are both tools. Hammers and nails and saws and wood only relate to each other through the conceptualization that involves their function and is part of various episodes. Thus "tool" is not a category name, but rather the specific instance of a tool is its relationship to an episode of its use.

In memory I propose that we might have an abstract conceptualization C1 with variables O1, O2, D1, and D2:

C1:   ACTOR: ONE
       ACTION: PROPEL
       OBJECT: O1
       DIRECTION: D1
       INSTRUMENT: ACTOR: ONE
                      ACTION: PROPEL
                      OBJECT: O2
                      DIRECTION: D2

In episodic memory, a particular instance of C1 might contain O1= NAIL, D1=WOOD, O2=HAMMER, and D2=NAIL to describe a nail propelled toward wood by the act of propelling a hammer toward the nail. Other less filled instances of C1 might contain only

O1=NAIL   O2=HAMMER   (Hammering a nail)
D1=WOOD   O2=HAMMER   (Hammering wood)

Another instance of C1 might contain

D1=WOOD   O2=SAW   (Sawing wood)

There is no conceptualization containing both hammer and plunger. Thus the relationship between these objects is not direct; both occur in instances of

C1 as object O2. I predict that finding these relations by analogy is a more difficult (and hence time-consuming) process than finding relations within a single instance of a conceptualization. I believe that the definition of a nominal concept (e.g., "tool") is a functional description of its use within an episode in memory (e.g., O2 in C1). Hammer and saw are closer than hammer and plunger because the former share a common element, D1=WOOD, in instances of C1.

4.1.3 Nonstatic Context

Going on with our discussion of what is likely to be close to what is in memory, we would claim that it is shorter from goulash to chicken paprikash than it is from goulash to spaghetti. This is a general statement that could be wrong for any particular individual. That is, someone who ate goulash only once and at the time had the best spaghetti of his life is likely to have a different organization.

For our average person we are again faced with the seemingly simplest choice of having a subset entitled "Hungarian food." The enticing properties of this are that things which are like each other would be grouped together. We would claim, however, that "the time I was in Budapest" and "the gypsy band that played while I ate goulash" are still closer to goulash than goulash is to spaghetti (where closeness is defined with respect to the number of links separating two concepts).

We are claiming, then, that in an actual memory, experiential groupings are the core of organization. Supersets give way in the memory to organizing contexts and, once a context is entered, a person is more likely to think of another item in that context than an item from a different context that might be classed in the same superset.

4.2 Associative Links

We claim that the basis of human memory is the conceptualization. Internally the conceptualization is action-based with certain specified associative links between actions and objects. Externally, conceptualizations can relate to other conceptualizations within a context or episodic sequence. Objects are related to other objects only by the internal or external associations within the conceptualizations of which they are both part. That is, objects cannot be separated from the action sequences in which they are encountered. Objects relate to the episodes in which they occur, which may include other objects.

We classify the links in a memory to be of two kinds, intercontextual and intracontextual. The intracontextual links have as a subset all the links of conceptual dependency. Since the elements that make up a context are episodes which are coded into conceptualizations, this follows directly.

We define a context as any group of links which do not include intercontextual links. The intercontextual links are:

1. ISA: superset
2. PROPS: shares properties with.

An example of a natural path within a context would be, "Going to the museum in Berlin reminded me of going to the museum in Boston." An example of a jump between contexts would be "The museum in Berlin reminded me of an old hotel."

In the former example it is important to point out that the relation is between the *events* of going to the museum, not the museums themselves. Thus a memory should have in it the general paradigm of "museum going" and relate together the two instantiations of that paradigm simply because they both are connected to that paradigm. Thus the two particular events are related to each other directly through the paradigm of the event that they each represent.

In the second example, the museum only reminds one of the hotel because of shared properties. This represents a shift in contexts and is in fact likely to get one thinking about something that happened in that hotel which would be quite unrelated to the museum. This is where the *PROPS* link comes in. A context can be left (the museum) by going to another context which is related to it by a set of shared properties.

4.3 Rules of Association

What constitutes a reasonable path in memory? People usually agree that (A) is reasonable:

(A) First I thought of a pen, and then I thought of the paper I was writing.

A deviant path would be (B):

(B) First I thought of a watermelon, and then I thought of the paper I was writing.

What are the rules for reasonable paths? The last example is, of course, an unreasonable path as long as there are no intermediate steps to be filled in. We could argue that there must be a certain kind of path that a person follows to get from "watermelon" to "paper." For example, if there were watermelon stains on his paper, or the paper was about watermelon production, or first he ate a watermelon and then he wrote the paper, these would all be considered reasonable paths.

We wish to do more than just be able to point out when a statement seems well structured. We are concerned with finding the rules which allow a person to identify unacceptable structures and fill in for himself what he considers possible explanations of what the speaker "must have meant." Guessing the speaker's intent is of less importance than being able to ask a speaker for clarification at a particular point in a conversation.

With respect to causality we have listed the specific causal rules that allow one to fill in gaps in causality statements. We would claim that memory is structured using the same causal rules as stories. To this it is necessary to add rules which allow for tying together of statements that are not causally related. Consider the following sentence:

Seeing my mother reminded me of ice cream.

It is a usual inference to assume that this person had, according to some prescribed rules of concept organization, a relatively short path between these two concepts. People, in hearing the above sentence, can make guesses about what that path might be, for example:

a) perhaps his mother used to make ice cream for him;

b) perhaps he and his mother used to go to an ice cream store together;

c) perhaps his mother told him to stop eating so much ice cream;

d) perhaps his mother worked in an ice cream factory.

What is important about the above guesses is that to most people they would account for the path between the two concepts. That is, people can recognize (as well as generate) possible conceptualizations which relate two concepts. They do this in order to make sense of relatedness statements, or more importantly, to know when some idea "follows" from another. This latter is important in listening to a discourse in order to know that it is necessary to infer a connection between thoughts that were not explicitly stated or to question the lack of cohesion of a string of ideas. We establish a set of rules for this linking. The first rule is:

I. Conceptualizations connect together the individual concepts that make them up.

That is, in order to get from one concept to another in memory, there must be a conceptualization of which they are both a part. The above rule is incomplete in that there is perhaps a more important corollary to it:

II. If two concepts do not exist in one conceptualization in memory, there must exist a causal chain between two separate conceptualizations in which they occur in order to associate them in memory.

What we are doing, then, is defining the notion *association*. We are establishing that an associative conceptual memory is made up of the links that exist within a conceptualization. Tokens of a concept type can lead to tokens of another concept type by means of the conceptualizations that connect them. Such linkages explain associations and eliminate the need for supersets and other artificial relationships.

There is one further corollary:

III. Two concepts can be related by their occurrence in separate conceptualizations which are part of the same episode in memory.

These three rules indicate that an association in memory must be initiated by conceptualizations which are part of episodes. Thus conceptual memory can be considered to be a series of conceptualizations linked together causally or temporally in episodic sequences.

4.4 Discussion

We have been arguing for a combination of the notions of semantic memory and episodic memory. In particular, we have said that all semantic information is encoded in episodes in the memory. We have further argued that the notion of superset in memory is vastly overused and that much superset information can be better stored as episodes.

Although the Collins and Quillian (1969) experiments have met with some dispute, we feel that the basic idea is correct. That is, some supersets must be used which store the features of the class. This is done in order to save space, but more importantly, it is necessary for information which was derived from sources other than direct experience. If you have never seen an orangutan, it still is easy to know that it must breathe because we know it is an animal.

We would propose that very few supersets (maybe no more than 10) would actually be used in the memory as nodes under which information is stored. Thus "food" above has a definition but is only a lexical entry, not really a node in memory. This is because no information is actually stored under "food" per se. Likewise, "mammal" is only a dictionary entry which calls up the superset "animal." and makes a feature distinction within that class. This explains why people have trouble remembering if a whale is a fish or a mammal. A whale would be considered to be a fish in our memory, but one that might have information stored with it that related it to the feature change produced by "mammal" under "animal."

Thus we hold the view that semantic memory really is a misnomer and furthermore that the distinction between semantic memory and episodic memory is wrong. Once lexical memory is separated out, the resulting conceptual memory is basically episodic in nature. Definitions of words are part of lexical memory. Consequences of events involving concepts are part of episodic conceptual memory. Associations between concepts are limited to the way concepts can relate within complete action-based conceptualizations. Supersets are mostly artificial constructs with definitions in lexical memory and without a place in the episodic conceptual memory.

4.5 Scripts

Some of the episodes which occur in memory serve to organize and make sense of new inputs. These episodic sequences we call *scripts*. A script is an elaborate causal chain which provides world knowledge about an often experienced situation. Specifically, scripts are associated as the definitions of certain situational nouns. Words whose definitions are scripts are, for example, restaurant, football game, birthday party, classroom, meeting. Some words that have scriptal definitions have physical senses as well, of course. "Restaurant," for example, has a physical sense which is only partially related to its scriptal sense.

The notion of scripts has been proposed generally and specifically in different forms by Minsky (1975), Abelson (1973), and Charniak (1974). What we call scripts represent only a small subset of the concept as used by others. For our purposes, scripts are predetermined sequences of actions that define a situation. Scripts have entering conditions (how you know you are in one), reasons (why you get into one), and crucial conceptualizations (without which the script would fall apart and no longer be that script). In addition, scripts allow, between each causal pair, the possibility for the lack of realization of that causation and some newly generated behavior to remedy the problem. In general, scripts are nonplanful behavior except when problems occur within a script or when people are planning to get into a script.

Scripts are recognizable partially by the fact that, after they have been entered, objects that are part of the script may be referenced as if they had been mentioned before. For example:

I. John went into a restaurant. When he looked at the menu he complained to the waitress about the lack of choice. Later he told the chef that if he could not make much, at least he could make it right.

II. We saw the Packers-Rams game yesterday. The Packers won on a dive play from the two with three seconds left. Afterwards they gave the game ball to the fullback.

These paragraphs have in common that they set up a script in the first sentence. This script then sets up a set of roles which are implicitly referenced and a set of props which are implicitly referenced. From that point, roles and props can be referenced as if they had already been mentioned. (Actually, we would claim that they have been mentioned by the definition of the script word.)

The script also sets up a causal chain with the particulars left blank. The hearer goes through a process of taking new input conceptualizations previously predicted by the script that has been entered. As before, pieces that are not specifically mentioned are inferred. Now, however, we are going further than we went in the first part of this chapter, in saying that the sequences implicitly referenced by the script are inferred and treated as if they were actually input. This is intended to account for problems in memory recognition tasks that occur with paragraphs such as these.

Let us consider the restaurant script in some more detail.

Script: restaurant
Roles: customer, waitress, chef, cashier
Reason: hunger for customer, money for others

Part 1: Entering

*PTRANS	(into restaurant)
MBUILD	(where is table)
ATTEND	(find table)
PTRANS	(to table)
MOVE	(sit down)

Part 2: Ordering

ATRANS	(receive menu)
ATTEND	(look at it)
MBUILD	(decide)
MTRANS	(tell waitress)
MTRANS	(waitress tells chef)
DO	(chef prepares food)

Part 3: Eating

ATRANS	(waitress gets food)
*ATRANS	(receive food)
*INGEST	(eat food)

Part 4: Leaving

MTRANS	(ask for check)
ATRANS	(leave tip)
PTRANS	(to cashier)
*ATRANS	(pay bill)
PTRANS	(exit)

In the restaurant script given above, we have oversimplified the issue as well as arbitrarily decided the kind of restaurant we are dealing with. Basically, a restaurant is defined by a script that has only the starred ACTs. Restaurants exist where the maitre d' must be tipped in order to get a table, where you get your own food, and so on. The sequence of ACTs above is meant only to suggest the abstract form of a script. A complete script would have at each juncture a set of "what-ifs" which would serve as options for the customer if some sequence did not work out. In addition, other kinds of restaurants could have been accounted for in one script by having choice points in the script. A still further issue is that this is how the restaurant looks from the customer's point of view. Other things happen in restaurants that have nothing to do with restaurants per se and other participants see them differently.

With all these disclaimers aside, the restaurant script predicts all the conceptualizations whose ACTs are listed above, and in a manner quite similar to the functioning of our language analysis program (Riesbeck 1975): it is necessary in understanding to go out and look for them.

Stories, fortunately for the hearer, unfortunately for us, usually convey information which is out of the ordinary mundane world. The first paragraph tells that the customer did not like the restaurant. His complaining behavior is part of the "what-if" things which we mentioned earlier. The purpose of the script is to answer questions like "Did he eat?" and "Why did he complain to the chef?" These are trivial questions as long as one understands implicitly the script that is being discussed. Otherwise they are rather difficult.

It is perhaps simplest to point out that the second paragraph is incomprehensible to someone who does not know football yet makes perfect sense to someone who does. In fact, football is never mentioned, yet questions like "What kind of ball was given to the fullback?" and "Why was it given?" are simple enough to answer, as long as the script is available.

5. Summary

We are saying that the process of understanding is, in large part, the assigning of new input conceptualizations to causal sequences and the inference of remembered conceptualizations which will allow for complete causal chains. To a large extent, the particular chains which result are tied up in one's personal experience with the world. Information is organized within episodic sequences and these episodic sequences serve to organize understanding. The simplest kind of episodic sequence is the script that organizes information about everyday causal chains that are part of a shared knowledge of the world.

Human understanding, then, is a process by which new information gets treated in terms of the old information already present in memory. We suspect that mundane observations such as this will serve as the impetus for building programs that understand paragraphs.

6. Addendum: Conceptual Dependency

We regard language as being a multi-leveled system, and the problem of understanding as being the process of mapping linear strings of words into well formed conceptual structures. A conceptual structure is defined as a network of concepts, where certain classes of concepts can be related to other classes of concepts. The rules by which classes of concepts combine are called the conceptual syntax rules. Since the conceptual level is considered to underlie language it is also considered to be apart from language. Thus the conceptual syntax rules are organizing rules of thought as opposed to rules of a language.

Crucial to all this is the notion of category of a concept. We allow the following categories:

PP—a conceptual nominal, restricted to physical objects only,
PA—a state which together with a value for that state describes a PP,
ACT—something that a PP can do to another PP (or conceptualization for mental ACTs),

LOC—a location in the coordinates of the universe,
T—a time on the time line of eternity, either a point or a segment on the line or relative to some other point or segment on the line,
AA— a modification of some aspect of an ACT,
VAL—a value for a state.

In conceptual dependency, a conceptualization consists of an actor (an animate PP), an ACT, an object (a PP or another conceptualization in the case of three mental ACTs) a direction or a recipient (two PPs indicating the old and new possessors or two LOCs indicating the old and new directions—often PPs are used to denote LOCs in which case the LOC of that PP is what is meant) and an instrument (defined as a conceptualization itself). A conceptualization can also be an object and a value for an attribute of that object. Conceptualizations can relate in certain causality relations.

We have required of our representation that if two sentences, whether in the same or different languages, are agreed to have the same meaning, they must have identical representations. That requirement, together with the requirement that ACTs can only be things that animate objects can do to physical objects severely restricts what can be an ACT in this representation. We have found that it is possible to build an adequate system (that is, one that functions on a computer for a general class of sentences and that has no obvious deficiencies in hand analysis) using only eleven ACTs.

The eleven ACTs that are used are:

ATRANS: The transfer of an abstract relationship such as possessions, ownership or control. Thus one sense of *give* is: ATRANS something to oneself. *Buy* is made up of two conceptualizations that cause each other, one an ATRANS of money, the other an ATRANS of the object being bought.

PTRANS: The transfer of the physical location of an object. Thus *go* is PTRANS oneself to a place, *put* is PTRANS of an object to a place. Certain words only infer PTRANS. Thus *throw* will be referred to as PROPEL below, but most things that are PROPELed are also PTRANSed. Deciding whether PTRANS is true for these is the job of the inference program.

PROPEL: The application of a physical force to an object. PROPEL is used whenever any force is applied regardless of whether a movement (PTRANS) took place. In English, *push, pull, throw, kick,* have PROPEL as part of them. "John pushed the table to the wall" is a PROPEL that causes a PTRANS. "John threw the ball" is a PROPEL that involves an ending of a GRASP ACT at the same time. Often words that do not necessarily mean PROPEL can probably infer PROPEL. Thus *break* means to DO something that causes a change in physical state of a specific sort (where DO indicates an unknown ACT). Most of the time the ACT that fills in the DO is PROPEL although this is certainly not necessarily the case.

MOVE: The movement of a body part of an animal by that animal. MOVE is nearly always the ACT of an instrumental conceptualization for other ACTs. That is, in order to *throw,* it is necessary to MOVE one's arm. Likewise MOVE foot is often the instrument of hand. MOVE is less frequently used noninstrumentally, but *kiss, raise your hand, scratch* are examples.

GRASP: The grasping of an object by an actor. The verbs *hold, grab, let go,* and *throw* involve GRASP or the ending of a GRASP.

INGEST: The taking in of an object by an animal to the inside of that animal. Most commonly the semantics for the objects of INGEST (that is, what is usually INGESTed) are food, liquid, and gas. Thus *eat, drink, smoke, breathe,* are common examples of INGEST.

EXPEL: The expulsion of an object from the body of an animal into the physical world. Whatever is EXPELed is very likely to have been previously INGESTed. Words for excretion and secretion are described by EXPEL. Among them are *sweat, spit,* and *cry.*

MTRANS: The transfer of mental information between animals or within an animal. We partition memory into three pieces: The CP (conscious processor where something is thought of), the LTM (where things are stored) and, IM (intermediate memory, where current context is stored). The various sense organs can also serve as the originators of an MTRANS. Thus *tell* is MTRANS between people, *see* is MTRANS from eyes to CP, *remember* is MTRANS from LTM to CO, *forget* is the inability to do that, *learn* is the MTRANSing of new information to LTM.

MBUILD: The construction by an animal of new information from old information. Thus *decide, conclude, imagine, consider,* are common examples of MBUILD.

SPEAK: The actions of producing sounds. Many objects can SPEAK, human ones usually are SPEAKing as an instrument of MTRANSing. The words *say, play, music, purr, scream* involve SPEAK.

ATTEND: The action of attending or focusing a sense organ towards a stimulus. ATTEND ear is *listen,* ATTEND eye is *see* and so on. ATTEND is nearly always referred to in English as the instrument of MTRANS. Thus in conceptual dependency, *see* is treated as MTRANS to CP from eye by instrument of ATTEND to eye to object.

The states that are used in this chapter are ad hoc. A more adequate treatment can be found in Schank (1975).

Acknowledgments

The research described here was done partially while the author was at the Institute for Semantic and Cognitive Studies, Castagnola, Switzerland, partially while the author was at Bolt Beranek and Newman, Cambridge, Massachusetts, and partially at Yale University.

10

In Defense of Logic

Patrick J. Hayes

1. Introduction

Modern formal logic is the most successful precise language ever developed to express human thought and inference. Measured across any reasonably broad spectrum, including philosophy, linguistics, computer science, mathematics and artificial intelligence, no other formalism has been anything like so successful. And yet recent writers in the AI field have been almost unanimous in their condemnation of logic as a representational language, and other formalisms are in a state of rapid development.

I will argue that most of this criticism misses the point, and that the real contribution of logic is not its usual rather sparse syntax, but the semantic theory which it provides. AI is as much in need now of good semantic theories with which to compare formalisms as it always has been. I will also re-examine the procedural/declarative controversy and show how regarding representational languages as programming languages has, ironically, made procedural ideas as vulnerable to the old proceduralists' criticisms as the classical theorem-proving paradigm was. I will argue that the contrast be-

tween assertional and procedural languages is false: we have rather two kinds
of subject-matter than two kinds of language.

This chapter is deliberately polemical in tone. Much has been written from
the proceduralist point of view. It's time the other arguments were put.

2. Logic Is Not a Programming System

It will, and has been, said that to defend logic is to adopt a reactionary position. Logic has been tried (in the late sixties) and found wanting: now it has
been superseded by better systems, in particular, procedural languages such
as μPLANNER (Sussman 1970), CONNIVER (Sussman and McDermott 1972)
and more recently KRL (Bobrow and Winograd 1976).

But logic is not a *system* in this sense. It's not a style of programming. It
entails no commitment to the use of any particular process organization or
technique of coding. To think that it does is to make a category error.

Logic is a collection of ideas on how to express a certain kind of knowledge
about a certain kind of world. The metatheory of logic is a collection of mathematical tools for analyzing representational languages of this class. What these
tools analyze is not the behavior of an interpreter, or the structure of processes
in some running system, but rather, the extensional meaning of expressions of a
language, when these are taken to be making claims about some external world.

These two distinct topics—the meaning of a language and the behavior of
an interpreter for it—are related in various ways. They meet in particular, in
the notion of inference. Logical meaning *justifies* inferences. A running system *performs* inferences: some of its processes are the making of inferences.

But two different systems may be based on the same notion of inference
and the same representational language. The *inference structure* of the language used by a system does not depend on the process structure. In particular, a system may have a logical inference structure—may be making deductively valid inferences—without being a classical uniform theorem-prover
which just "grinds lists of clauses together."

3. What Logic Is: The Extensional Analysis of Meaning

One of the first tasks which faces a theory of representation is to give some
account of what a representation or representational language *means*. Without such an account, comparisons between representations or languages can
only be very superficial. Logical model theory provides such an analysis.

Suppose it is claimed that:

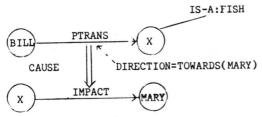

means that Bill hit Mary with a fish (to take a representative example), or that:

((DO#AGENT)#$BADTHING))CAUSE(#AGENT)DISPLAY
(#NEGATIVEEMOTION)))

means that people often seem upset when bad things happen (to take another). How could one judge whether they really do mean those things? What would count as a specification of their meanings? Several answers can be suggested.

The first might be called "pretend-it's-English." Here, one takes the primitive symbols to stand for their ordinary English meaning, and gives a way of translating the grammar of the representation into English surface syntax (this is often left implicit but fairly obvious). The first example above then is to be read as something like "Bill moved some object—which was a fish—in the direction of Mary, thus causing the object to make an impact upon Mary." One now has to judge whether this English sentence has the same meaning as the original English sentence "Bill hit Mary with a fish". The English rendering of the second example is even more obvious.

This way of analyzing meaning has the virtue of simplicity, and it also requires very little technical expertise. It is widely used in modern linguistics, where it often goes hand in hand with the assumption there is some finite collection of *basic* words in terms of which the meanings of all sentences can be explained.

But there are many problems with this simple idea. For a start, it's perilously vague. It's always hard to judge whether two English sentences have the same meaning. It depends what you mean by "meaning"—with a very tight sense of "meaning," the sentences "John hit Mary" and "Mary was hit by John" are different in meaning. Second, it's an essentially *linguistic* view of meaning. While this doesn't bother many workers in the natural language area, it should bother anyone who believes that at least some knowledge representations need to be independent of any particular sensory bias. (We can all look at a scene and describe what we see. How is information transferred from the visual recognition process to the linguistic representation?) Much of what a vision program needs to represent may not be readily expressible in English (e.g., two-dimensional patterns of light and shade). Third, it provides no useful guidelines for how a system might *use* the representation. Given that the network of the first example is supposed to mean the same as its anglicisation, does anything follow concerning what inferences can or should be made from the network?

This last point is really a symptom of the most basic problem, which is that on this account we could just as well use the English sentences themselves as their own representations. The symbols in the formalism might as well be English words. (Wilks [1975] states this explicitly.) Until some independent account of the formalism is provided, no actual *analysis* of meaning is forthcoming.

The model-theoretic approach to meaning interprets an expression of a formalism as making a claim about the way the world is. Suppose we give some criteria by which we can judge whether a suggested possible world satisfies the expression, or whether on the contrary it is a *counterexample* to the claim made by the expression. Then these criteria can be used as an account of meaning. An expression means what it claims about a possible world. Two expressions which are satisfied by the same possible worlds are identical in meaning. A natural notion of inference follows also. If every counterexample to E_1 is also a counterexample to E_2, then we can infer E_1 from E_2: for then all the possible worlds which are consistent with the claim we make when E_2 is asserted also satisfy E_1.

Notice that on this account an expression can usually not be said to definitely correspond to anything in the *actual* world. Its meaning is fixed only with respect to a *possible* world. In order to pin down its meaning (we should say "referent") more precisely in the actual world, we must add more assertions so as to cut down the set of possible example worlds. Take for example the expression "MARY," which is intended to denote a particular lady in the real world. In order to achieve this identification, we would have to assert enough axioms containing the expression "MARY" to ensure that in any possible world satisfying them, the denotation of "MARY" corresponded to the particular lady in question in the actual world. These axioms will contain other names and relations symbols, and we cannot in general say conclusively that any of these is defined in terms of some particular subset of the others. The entire web of logically connected assertions is presumably tied down to the actual world by some of them having an interpretation as observations, in the case of an actual robot with these beliefs in its head. On this account, perception is a form of inference: inference which involves observational assertions. (This is not to say that we can *deductively* derive beliefs from observations, which is of course not time in general. The required relationship is *consistency:* beliefs must be kept consistent with observations.)

This model-theoretic account of meaning corresponds exactly to Bobrow and Winograd's (1976) view that "a description ... cannot be broken down into a single set of primitives, but must be expressed through multiple views" and "...there would be no simple sense in which the system contains a 'definition' of the object, or a complete description in terms of its structure." Their subsequent remarks suggest, however, a confusion between the logical notion of meaning and the pretend-it's-English notion using "primitives."

The problem with this approach to meaning is, of course, to specify what we mean by a possible world in such a way that we can state the meaning criteria—the truth-conditions as they are usually and somewhat misleadingly called. First-order logic makes only very elementary assumptions. A logically-possible world is a set of individuals (each name denotes some individual) and a set of relations between them (each relation symbol denotes some relation). The rules for deciding which worlds are examples for an expression and which are counterexamples, are well known, yielding the usual notion of deductive inference.

Model theory, unlike pretend-it's-English, gives an account of extensional meaning relative to an exact notion of possible world. One might object that this notion is mistaken. Perhaps the real world isn't like that, does not consist of individuals with relations between them. Certainly this notion of world seems too simple. Are liquids individuals, for example? Either answer (yes or no) gives rise to certain problems. There is much scope for ingenuity in giving precise descriptions of more interesting classes of possible worlds. It would be interesting to see a class of worlds in which there was a fixed notion of causality, for example Hayes (1971). Notice how such an enterprise would differ from the 'analysis' of CAUSE provided by pretend-it's-English. The latter yields no account of what a causally possible world would be like, nor does it explain what constitutes causally valid inference.

An important property of the model-theoretic account is that it enables one to judge a proposed representation by imagining the circumstances which would render it true. Of course this is only a heuristic remark, but I find that it is an important feature. One way to test a proposed representation is to run it, if possible on a computer, but perhaps only in a pencil and paper sense, i.e., write down some formal consequences of it using whatever inference structure comes with the representational language. But this does not always generate insight into errors or inadequacies of the representation, because a characteristic symptom of such a situation is that nonsense becomes derivable, or alternatively that nothing useful is derivable at all, neither of which is very much help. Another way to test it, however, is to attempt to understand it as a description of a world, and to imagine what the world would have to be like to make it false. I find the latter the most useful.

For example, suppose one is trying to formalize knowledge about liquids, and one writes something like

IN(LIQUID,CONTAINER)&MOVES(CONTAINER)
⇒ IN(LIQUID,CONTAINER)

Is this a reasonable assertion? In order to answer that question, one would at least have to say whether it were usually true. What would the world have to be like to render it false: what would be a counterexample? Well, what does it *mean?* It's not clear, since we have no model theory. Presumably IN is a relation, but is MOVES then a relation? The intention behind this semiformal axiom can be crudely expressed thus:

IN(LIQUID,CONTAINER,STATE)
⇒ IN(LIQUID,CONTAINER,MOVE(STATE))

where MOVE is a function from states to states. Now the ontology is clear, anyone who has picked up an overfull cup of coffee can easily imagine a counterexample. Without a model theory—albeit perhaps an informal one—we would not be able to so connect expressions of the formalism to possible configurations of a world that it would even be possible to imagine such counterexamples. A formalism without a model theory can hardly be said to constitute a representational language at all.

None of these basic semantic ideas say anything about the syntax of the expressions used to encode facts. The same meanings can be expressed in a wide variety of syntactic forms. There is thus an a priori possibility that some already existing language may be best interpreted as another syntax for predicate (or even propositional) calculus. "Semantic networks" are a good example, as several recent writers have observed (see for example Woods [1975] and Schubert [1975]). If someone argues for the superiority of semantic networks over logic, he must be referring to some other property of the former than their meaning (for example, their usefulness for retrieving relevant facts from a database—an aspect of a possible process structure—or their attractive appearance on a printed page). A more recent example is KRL. Virtually the whole of KRL-0 can be regarded as merely a new syntax for first-order predicate logic.

Now it must be admitted that sometimes semantic networks (for example) are used in ways which do not reflect their obvious logical meaning. For example, there is often a sort of implicit uniqueness condition which prevents two nodes from denoting the same entity in any interpretation. Without such a condition, for example, the 'pedestal' network of Figure 1 would be merely an instance of the 'arch' network, got by identifying B2 and B3 (much as $P(x, x)$ is an instance of $P(x, y)$ in the usual syntax).

Similarly, frames are a syntax which have been used to convey a variety of meanings. They can be understood as a strange syntax for logic in at least two distinct ways (either frames are objects and slots 2-place relations, or frames are n-place relations), they are used in GUS (Bobrow 1976) to represent conversational sequencing, in EVIL (Brooks and Rowbury 1976) to represent perceptual hypotheses. One syntax, four different meanings.

4. Representation and Control

Almost every idea on representation in AI has eventually appeared in the guise of a programming language. This is in part the legacy of the procedu-

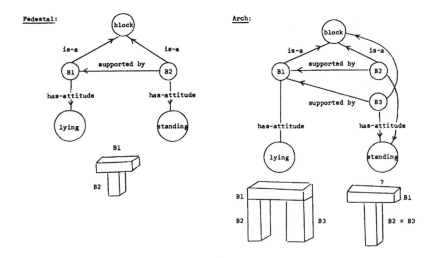

Figure 1. A pedestal is an arch.

ral/assertional debate, which was won fairly conclusively by the procedural-ists. It is worth, however, going back over the old history of this dispute rather carefully, as the ground of the argument has shifted subtly but significantly over the years.

Classical theorem-proving operated in the general problem-solver paradigm. This takes the form of a competitive game between he who de-signs the theorem-prover and he who provides the axioms on which they are tested. The aim of the game is to write theorem provers which can solve *re-ally hard* problems, and which are *general*. To cunningly adapt the axioms so that the theorem-prover is able to prove the theorem is *cheating* and is frowned upon, like cheating at cards. Moreover, the theorem-prover, being general purpose, has no bias to any particular domain. The result is that clas-sical theorem provers know very little about what to do, and are incapable of being told it.

This was the position the proceduralists attacked, and their argument was, I think, conclusive. It has to be possible to tell a system what to *do: what* infer-ences to make and *when* to make them (and not to make them), as well as what is true. In a word, a system has to be programmable.

Contrast the problem-solver methodology with the programming language designer's methodology. The latter does his best to make the workings of the language interpreter available, or at least visible, to the user, even to the extent in some cases of writing a manual (the ultimate anathema for problem solvers: a handbook for cheats). The difference is ultimately one of where the *respon-sibility* for a system's behavior lies: the problem solving system designer retains it, the programming language designer gives it to the user, to the person who composes the knowledge representations. What is more natural, then, than to regard a representation language as a programming language?

It is important to emphasize this contrast of methodologies because it is the *only* significant difference between the proceduralist position, as it was argued in the early seventies, and the traditional theorem proving view. In particular, the procedural languages, offered in this period as replacements for logic, have very similar inference structures to predicate calculus. The proceduralist's own remarks about how to represent facts reiterate the basic semantic intuitions of formal logic (see Winograd [1972] for example). The inference structure of μPLANNER is a subset of predicate calculus, augmented with THNOT. Even the newer languages, such as KRL, based on different and apparently rival intuitions (see Minsky's broadside in Minsky [1974]) display some remarkably logical features.

Nor is there any important difference in underlying mechanisms of implementation. The basic, and quite old, mechanism of an *and/or* tree with variable-sharing across *and* nodes, implemented using invocation records with separate access and control links and local environment bindings, underlies theorem-proving programs, AI programming interpreters, production systems and ACTORS (Hewitt and Steiger 1973).

But this methodological difference runs very deep, and does have technical consequences. A *procedural* language to *represent knowledge* has two distinct tasks to perform. It must encode facts and inferences about external domains (and hence have some kind of inference structure which we might try to analyze using logical tools); and it must also express strategies of behavior for its interpreter to obey, some of which will presumably be strategies of inference. It will have both an inference structure and a process structure, both usable by the programmer. This is a tall order, and nobody has managed to build a satisfactory such language yet. There have been essentially three ideas on how to do it.

The first idea is to specify control *by the way in which one states the facts.* Supposing that there are a few predefined strategies which the interpreter can use to process an assertion: then one provides the user with just enough syntactic variants for stating facts to enable him to implicitly tell the interpreter which strategy to use. This is the μPLANNER idea (THCONSE and THASSERT), also underlies Kowalski's more recent proposal to treat predicate logic as a programming language (Kowalski 1975), and has been used by some "natural deduction" theorem-provers which find it much easier to prove A⊃B than ¬ A ∨ B. But this idea is far too inflexible: one rapidly finds that one wants to specify behaviors which cannot be encoded as some simple combination of the predefined strategies.

The natural reaction to this situation is to build systems which provide the necessary machinery but make few commitments as to how it should be used.

To build systems, that is, in which specialist interpreters can be implemented. This is the second idea. CONNIVER has just this relationship to μPLANNER, for example. CONNIVER was a toolkit for implementing PLANNER-like systems and, more usefully, for experimenting with routine control structures. The KRL authors similarly insist that a representation language "must provide a flexible set of underlying tools, rather than embody specific commitments about either processing strategies or the representation of specific areas of knowledge," (Bobrow and Winograd 1976, page 4).

But what then happens to the inference structure of the representational language? We have now moved to a lower conceptual level, the level of the interpreter rather than the level at which substantive claims about some domain are made. What we now have is purely a programming language, and not a descriptive language. The objects which, in a descriptive language, would be meaningful assertions or descriptions or names—meaningful in the exact sense that their relationship to a possible external world was defined by the *meaning of the language*—these objects appear merely as data structures in an interpreter implementing language. And of course it is part of the philosophy of programming language design that the interpretation of what a data structure means must be left to the programmer.

Going down a level thus renders vacuous the original claims of the proceduralists with regard to representation. To argue that CONNIVER is better than predicate calculus is to compare incomparables. CONNIVER is about processes and their behavior: logic is about assertions and their meaning. CONNIVER is one of the programming languages one might use to implement a system with a logical inference structure (or indeed any other structure).

There is still a procedural problem, in any case. The interpreter defining language has to be based on some control regime. CONNIVER and INTERLISP use coroutineing, for example. But whatever control regime is used, at this level it is deterministic code—a sequence of instructions—which actually runs.

A widespread dissatisfaction with purely procedural languages stems from the feeling that procedural code is too rigid a language to express interesting behaviors (see Bobrow and Winograd 1976, page 36, for example). One can use "pattern-directed invocation" (i.e., resolution[1]), or "procedural attachment," or whatever, to make a more sensitive choice of which procedure to run: but when that choice has been made, deterministic code is found in its body. It all gets down to Lisp in the end. Using the CONNIVER (GEDANKEN, PAL...) idea of frozen process states allows a certain amount of freedom: but still we have the feeling that control is like a baton being passed from hand to hand. If one process doesn't know who to hand it to, everything comes unstuck. All runnable code, while running, has total responsibility for keeping the whole system alive.

While this does make some ingenious programming possible, especially when combined with a database of assertions used to "simulate" a world (see Fahlman 1974 for a beautiful example), it still lacks the flexibility and opportunism which we need.

We need to have several coexisting processes, each acting for itself without needing to be explicitly called from some other process. The obvious idea then is some form of multiprocessing, where the interpreter maintains a queue of processes and runs them all from time to time, according to some strategy. This is the third idea. Calling a process is putting it on the queue. This makes apparently hard code, like: *beginF()*; *G()*; *H() end;* into something much softer, since exactly what will happen depends on what other processes there are around. When *F* is called, that doesn't mean that it's actually called, only that it's put on the agenda.[2] Maybe some other process will run first and flush *F* before it has a chance to run, for example.

This very old (c.f., Elcock and Foster 1969) idea is currently popular. But we have now come full circle, to a classical problem-solving situation. How can the interpreter decide what order to run the processes in? It doesn't know anything about any particular domain, so it can't decide. So we have to be able to tell it. But how?

This is exactly the situation with which we began, the situation the proceduralists attacked. In removing the decision to actually run from the code and placing in in the interpreter, advocates of multiprocessing systems have re-created the uniform black-box problem-solver.

The next step then is to design a language in which the programmer can control the agenda. The simplest such idea is to use numbers: the agenda has levels numbered from zero, and process calls specify their level. This is used by KRL-0 and the Graph Traverser (Doran and Michie 1966). A somewhat more sophisticated idea is to allow descriptors for subqueues and allow processes to access these descriptors, as in POPEYE (Sloman 1976) . But none of these ideas seem very convincing. And we have now moved down another level, to the interpreter of the interpreter-writing language of the representational language.

The only way out of this descending spiral is upwards. We need to be able to describe processing strategies in a language at least as rich as that in which we describe the external domains: and for good engineering, it should be the *same* language. The aspects of procedural languages—THNOT of μPLAN-NER, passing context frames as parameters in CONNIVER, defaults in KRL—which resist simple syntactic mappings into logic, are all places where the languages refer to their own interpreter's behavior. THNOT means not *provable* (from current resources): passing a context frame is proving something *about another proof:* a default value is one which is taken unless *there is a proof* that its value is different. It is this reflexive nature of these languages which gives them their "non-logical" features.

But this is a question of what knowledge is represented, not of what language it is represented in. These reflexive assertions, referring to the system's own internal states, can also be expressed in logic, with the same gains in ontological clarity as are realized in other areas. This distinction between logic and procedures is then seen as a distinction between kinds of domain rather than kinds of language: the proceduralist position leads one to envisage a system which can describe its own inferential processes and thus make inferences about its own behavior.

In order to design the interpreter for such a system, one needs a framework in which these behaviors can be adequately described. Logic provides—in the notion of proof—a richer such framework than any of the usual procedural ideas.

5. What Logic Isn't

It's worth spending a little time laying to rest some misunderstandings I've met about logic.

1. Logic isn't a programming system.

2. Logic isn't a particular syntax.

3. Logic does not assume that the world is made up of concrete physical individuals without "abstract" individuals such as properties, events, nations or feelings. This view is *nominalism,* and leads to a quite different sort of semantic intuition, in which, for example, *red* denotes not a property of physical individuals, but the (rather disconnected) individual consisting of all pieces of red stuff in the world.

Other similar confusions are also made. For example, logic is no worse (and no better) than a conceptual dependency at representing warm, human facts about people hitting each other.

4. Logic doesn't give "the ultimate in decomposition of knowledge."
Winograd, in his widely cited discussion (Winograd 1975) of the assertional/procedural controversy, draws a distinction between logic's atomistic view of knowledge, in which a representation is seen as a set of separate disconnected facts, and the proceduralist's holistic view in which interactions between procedures have prominence. But this is exactly the opposite of the truth. The interactions sanctioned by logic between assertions are far richer and more complicated than the interactions between procedures in a procedural language (any procedural language). Thus, explicit recursive procedure calls (Lisp) are more restricted than explicit routine calls (SIMULA), these more restricted than pattern-directed coroutineing (CONNIVER), these more restricted than resolution (which allows both caller and callee to have variables bound during the matching process) and finally resolution itself is a special case of general logic inference rules of instantiation and cut. In each

case, one pattern of interactions is a special case of, and can be imitated by, the next. In each case, the more general interaction pattern allows more inter- actions and hence yields a more complex search space, and a more difficult search problem. It is precisely the restrictions on interactions in procedural languages which make them so useful.

Again, Winograd claims that procedures, unlike assertions, mean very little in isolation but acquire meaning from their interactions with other proce- dures; and again has got it exactly the wrong way round. A procedure may well mean a lot in isolation. RANDOM(), for example, or PRINT(X): any pro- cedure whose body contains code but no calls of other procedures. Whereas the function and predicate symbols in a logical axiomatisation, like the to- kens at nodes of a semantic net, *literally* mean nothing unless their meaning is specified by axioms. The model-theoretic account of meaning makes this absolutely precise: as one conjoins assertions, so the set of interpretations possible for the symbols occurring in them is restricted, and the set of possi- ble inferences from them is enlarged. Their meaning is progressively tight- ened, as more facts involving them become inferrable.

5. The tendency to replace representational languages by purely procedural languages goes hand in hand with a tendency to judge representational issues in computational terms. Thus Minsky (1974) in attacking what he sees as the malevolent influence of logic, dismisses predicate calculus by observing that the machinery of P.C. inference—instantiation and tree-growing, basically—is available as a simple by-product of the more sophisticated sym- bol manipulation operations needed for analogical reasoning. But this, while perhaps true, misses the point: it is the meaning of those operations, inter- preted as inferences, of which logic provides an analysis.

Again, Winograd (1975) identifies the procedural/assertional distinction with the program/datastructure distinction, a completely false analogy. The latter distinction is to do with two different relationships a piece of data can have to an interpreter (including, ultimately, the hardware CPU): the former with the meanings of those structures. An assertion can be treated as a data structure or interpreted as a program, just as a procedure can. The distinc- tions are orthogonal.

6. Last Word

I have argued the case for taking logic's notion of meaning seriously. I do not, however, wish to argue that this is the only important issue in consider- ing representational languages. Process control is important, of course: ques- tions of ease of retrieval, of focusing of attention, of relevance, are also of great significance. Neither is syntactic convenience completely unimportant.

These issues are however all receiving considerable attention already. Semantics—questions of meaning—tend to be discussed less.

Acknowledgements

I have had helpful conversations and correspondence with Bruce Anderson, Richard Bornat, Eugene Charniak, Jack Lang, Bob Wielinga and Yorick Wilks. Alan Bundy, Aaron Sloman and Terry Winograd made useful comments on the first draft of the chapter. This work was supported in part by the Science Research Council.

Notes

1. Resolution is an inference rule, not a "strategy" or a "method."

2. Agenda = queue. A lot of impressive renaming goes on in this business. For example, good old environments appear in KRL under the titles "procedure directory" and "signal path."

11

Escaping Brittleness:
The Possibilities of General-Purpose Learning Algorithms Applied to Parallel Rule-Based Systems

John H. Holland

1. Introduction

The research that has culminated in the design of expert systems is a solid achievement for artificial intelligence: Given appropriately re-stricted domains, expert systems display the reasoned consideration of alternatives that one expects of an expert. The source of this success, the do-main-specific character of the systems, is also a source of limitations. The systems are *brittle* in the sense that they respond appropriately only in nar-row domains and require substantial human intervention to compensate for even slight shifts in domain (see Duda and Shortliffe 1983). This problem of brittleness and ways to temper it are the main concern of this chapter. The overall theme is that *induction* is the basic—and perhaps only—way of mak-ing large advances in this direction.

To gain a clearer idea of the scope of the overall problem, consider some of the specific problems induction faces in this context. At the top of the list is the task of generating useful ways of categorizing input. In complex domains there is a perpetual novelty to the input so that experience can guide future action only if the system discovers regularities or recurrences in the input. The categories induced must be broad enough to "cover" the likely possibilities parsimoniously; at the same time they must be specific enough to distinguish situations requiring different behaviors. Categories must be incorporated into rules that "point" both to actions and to an aura of associated categories. That is, as the categories are induced, they must be arranged in a "tangled hierarchy" (see Fahlman 1979) that enables the system to model its environment appropriately.

On a larger scale induction must provide plausible alternatives and changes in the hierarchies and models based upon these categories. In this structure, credit must be apportioned to the all-important categories that point to "stage-setting" actions necessary for later success. Because of the uncertainty of any induction, the process must be carried out in such a way that the system can absorb new, tentative rules without destroying capabilities in well-practiced situations. In all but the simplest situations a complex combination of competing rules will be activated so that the system must select a subset of rules that provides a coherent "picture" (model) of the situation. This picture in turn directs behavior and attempts at confirmation. At the highest level, the system must make effective use of metaphor and analogy to transfer inferences from familiar to unfamiliar situations (a capacity only touched upon in this chapter). The first two sections of the chapter will expand upon these problems. Section 2 takes a closer look at the notions of domain and environment, and Section 3 examines (informal) criteria bearing on the escape from brittleness.

The approach advocated in this chapter is based upon a class of message passing, rule-based systems, called *classifier systems,* in which large numbers of rules can be active simultaneously. Individual rules can be kept simple and standardized because combinations of rules are used to define complex situations. This approach results in both parsimony and flexibility, because the same rule can be used in many contexts (see criterion 1 in Section 3). Moreover, it gives a different slant to the induction task—the object becomes that of finding rules that serve well in a variety of tasks.

All rules are in condition/action form. Each condition specifies the set of messages satisfying it, and each action specifies the message sent when the condition part is satisfied. Because messages are kept to a standard length, it is possible to define conditions using strings of standard length, and this is done in such a way that it is simple to set the generality of a condition. As a consequence default hierarchies are easy to generate and use. Rules can be tied together into networks of various kinds by appropriate use of tagging. Section 4 describes classifier systems in detail.

Simplicity of the component rules also eases the tasks of the learning algorithms. First among these tasks is that of rating the usefulness of existing rules. This is the task of the *bucket-brigade* algorithm; it assigns a *strength* to each individual rule, modifying the strength on the basis of the rule's overall usefulness as the system accumulates experience. In effect the algorithm treats each rule as a middleman in a complex economy, its survival being dependent upon "making a profit" in its local interactions. In the long run, such profits will recur only if the rule is tied into chains of interactions leading to successful actions. Bucket-brigade algorithms are defined and described in the first part of Section 5.

The most difficult inductive task is that of generating plausible new rules. Here that task is carried out by a *genetic algorithm*. It uses high-strength classifiers as the "parents" of new classifiers to be tested under the bucket brigade. Although the genetic algorithm acts directly upon the strings defining classifiers, it can be shown that it is implicitly searching and using a space of "building blocks." Moreover, it is searching this space orders of magnitude more rapidly than would be indicated by the rate at which it is processing strings. Rules generated by the genetic algorithm do not displace their parents; rather they displace low-strength rules, entering into competition with the other rules in the system. This competition gives the overall system a graceful way of handling conflicts and tentative hypotheses. The latter part of Section 5 describes genetic algorithms and their effects upon classifiers.

Systems organized along these lines have been tested successfully in a variety of contexts. For example, a poker-playing version of the system (Smith 1980), starting with classifiers embodying only the rules of the game, competed with overwhelming success against Waterman's learning poker player (Waterman and Hayes-Roth,1978). Recently, Goldberg (1983) tested a system that, starting with a clean slate (randomly generated classifiers), confronted a gas pipeline transmission problem involving diurnal variation, seasonal variation, and leaks. The system generated successful control procedures embedded in a (discovered) default hierarchy distinguishing normal operation from "leaky" operation. Additional tests are discussed in Section 6.

2. Domains and Environments

A closer look at the role of induction begins with a closer look at the domains—the *environment*—in which the system is to operate. The environment provides the grist for the inductive mill, thereby setting the possibilities for, and the ultimate limitations on, the inductive process. An environment with no regularities (however defined) offers no opportunities for induction. Human experience indicates that real environments abound in regularities. The problem is to uncover and exploit them.

This chapter will restrict itself to environments that, implicitly or explicitly, present problems in terms of goals to be attained. In this context the system "closes the loop" through the environment, receiving information from the environment and acting upon the environment to bring about changes therein. The environment signals the solution of a problem by feeding back a quantity called *payoff*. (This term from game theory, chosen for its neutrality is the cognate of *utility* in economics, *error signals* in control theory, *fitness* in genetics, *reward* in psychology, and so on.) This format cleanly exposes most of the difficult problems in planning and problem solving, ranging from game playing though the design of mobile robots to abstract tasks such as the production of a corpus of useful theorems. The system uses the states of the environment as "stepping stones" to reach goal states that feed back payoff. The problem, simply, is to go efficiently from "here," a nongoal state, to "there," a goal state. The subtleties underlying this simple statement increase rapidly as the complexity of the state graph of the environment increases. One need go no further than the game trees and simply defined goals of chess or go to see deep subtleties; real-world situations typified by the design of flexible robots or interactive information retrieval systems offer even deeper problems.

The system can be thought of as receiving information about the current state of its environment in the form of *messages* generated by an input interface. The input interface typically consists of a set of feature detectors, and the message consists of a string of feature values. The systems dealt with here generally do *not* have high-level interpreters for these messages. That is, the rules of the system work directly on the message strings, acting on the presence or absence of certain bits. Whatever meanings there are, are supplied by the actions of the rules and, ultimately, by the effects produced on the environment.

The contrast between this "environment-oriented" approach and a "language-oriented" approach is worth pointing up. Consider the game Checkers. A language-oriented approach would use a language (symbols, grammar, etc., based, say, on standard checkers move notation) to specify legal moves, desirable configurations, and so on. The language, with an interpreter providing properties of board configurations and the like, would then be used, along with deductive inference, to develop a goal-oriented plan. The environment-oriented approach uses detectors (cf. the "parameters" used by Samuel 1959) to generate bit strings based on the checkerboard configuration. These messages are processed by rules (arranged in a complex default hierarchy; see below) to determine plans and moves. An environment-oriented approach does not explicitly assign abstract symbols to board configurations, nor does it explicitly search for and apply grammatical rules to such symbols.

Note that the environment-oriented approach is not more restricted in its powers of definition than the language-oriented approach. The ultimate limits on the definitional powers of either approach are set by the input interface. The system cannot distinguish environmental state configurations assigned identical values by the input interface, be they symbols or feature strings. (This sets aside certain sequential tests, but the argument remains the same even if these are used. More formally, the input interface groups environmental states into equivalence classes; elements of the same equivalence class are the same as far as the system is concerned.) All that definition can do under either approach is to categorize the distinguishable. It divides the distinguishable elements into two classes—those that satisfy the definition and those that do not.

If the system is computationally complete (can define any procedure) with respect to sorting the input messages into classes, then it has reached the limits of what definition can do for it relative to distinguishability. Stated another way, if two systems are computationally complete with respect to input interfaces that set identical restrictions on distinguishability, then the systems have the same limits on their powers of definition. This is true even if one system is language-oriented and the other is environment-oriented. The environment-oriented systems that will be examined shortly accomplish definition by a combination of conditions, tags, and recoding (see Section 4.3); they are computationally complete relative to the set of messages produced by any input interface.

3. Criteria

This investigation of ways of avoiding brittleness has been guided by several informal criteria derived primarily from ruminations about flexible natural systems and consideration of various landmarks in machine learning. The systems defined in the next Section are intended as procedural implementations of these criteria, which are as follows:

3.1. Recombination and Parallelism

In order to avoid a distinct rule for each situation (a "visiting grandmother" rule, a "yellow Volkswagon® with a flat tire" rule, etc.), it is imperative that the system's response to any situation be mediated by the concurrent activation of a set of relevant rules. By activating several elementary rules in response to a complex set of conditions, rather than relying on anticipation of the overall situation by provision of a single preformed rule, the system sets combinatorics to work for it rather than against it. As a simple example, by selecting one each from ten hairlines, ten eye configurations, ten noses, ten mouths, and ten jaw lines, the system can match any one of one hundred thousand distinct-faces at the cost of retaining only fifty elementary rules.

Under this criterion, it is incumbent upon induction and learning to search for rules that are useful "building blocks" in a variety of contexts. If the building blocks are well chosen, the system may be able to function well in situations not previously encountered. For instance, if the system has rules categorizing and handling input messages according to the usual notions of hooved, four-legged, and horned, it is conceivable that it would infer that a unicorn (observed for the first time) is *herbivorous*.

3.2 Categorization and Default Hierarchies

Categorization is the system's major weapon for combating the environment's perpetual novelty. The system must readily generate categories for input messages, and it must be able to generate categories relevant to its internal processes. These candidates must be tested repeatedly for usefulness and used with increasing or decreasing frequency in accord with the outcome (see criterion 3.5).

Moreover, there must be some criterion of plausibility so that the system is not overwhelmed with poor candidates. Appropriate bottom-up procedures (e.g., generalization of input messages) and top-down procedures (e.g., recombination of parts of the definitions of extant categories) can go far toward implementing this constraint. The categories generated should spontaneously arrange themselves into a default hierarchy (much like the skeleton of Fahlman's NETL 1979), so that details invoke "sketches" of the situations, allowing transfer of information between experiences activating similar sketches. (The more rules held in common by the clusters of rules defining two sketches, the more similar they are.) High-level interpreters for determining categories should be avoided where possible because they impose complex relations between syntax and semantics, greatly complicating the induction of categories.

3.3 Association

The use of categories as building blocks is much enhanced if, as the categories develop, an aura of associations with other categories also develops. Various "triggers," such as the co-occurrence of a pair of categories in a given environmental situation, can limit the formation of associations to plausible candidates. Associations are recorded by *synchronic pointers*— pointers that do not imply temporal sequence—and these pointers must be tested repeatedly for usefulness (see criterion 3.5). The generation and selection of the categories and pointers that serve as building blocks are processes that provide the system with a wide range of structures that act much like *virtual copies* (Fahlman 1979). To use a biological analogy, these virtual copies play the role of "species" filling the "niches" defined by the regularities (opportunities for exploitation) uncovered in the system's experience.

The meaning of the virtual copies stems from the process of competition and selection that determines their emergence. This contrasts strongly with attempts to arrive at such structures a priori, which is much like attempting to develop a taxonomy for species without understanding their ontogeny.

3.4 Diachronic Pointing, Models, and Prediction

Although Samuel's paper (1959) is often cited in machine learning, his use of model building to solve problems is almost always overlooked. (This may be because he modeled strategies by using linear forms, forms that typically serve only as linear pattern recognition devices.) Because of the model building, Samuel's checkers player can refine its strategy while playing the game, when there is no payoff from the environment. This greatly enhances the system's flexibility. When a system uses a model to generate expectations or predictions, it can use subsequent verification or falsification of the predictions to guide revisions of the model (toward better prediction) even in the absence of payoff.

In the present context, the construction of a model requires that the system include a second kind of pointer—the *diachronic pointers*—to indicate temporal sequences of categories. In short, the system forms temporal associations. Trigger conditions serve to restrict the generation of candidates, as they did in the case of synchronic pointers. For example, if a well-established category *Y* consistently follows well-established category *X* when the system makes response *R*, then it is plausible to induce a diachronic pointer between *X* and *Y*. (Note that a general category will often describe an environmental situation that persists over an extended period, as in the case of a *going home* or *pursuit of prey* category, allowing the trigger to link categories well separated in time.) As in the case of synchronic pointers, the diachronic pointers must be subjected to continued selection for usefulness.

3.5 Competition, Confirmation, and Gracefulness

The previous criteria have exploited parallelism to provide clusters of rules that serve both as virtual copies and as models. Parallelism neatly sidesteps the priority issues of one-rule-at-a-time systems but leaves open questions concerning conflict and consistency. Of all the elementary rules that are candidates for activation in a given situation, which ones get the nod? The foundation for an answer is set by an effective apportionment-of-credit algorithm. Strengths must be assigned to rules in accord with their past usefulness in the situations in which they have been invoked. Once again Samuel (1959) leads the way. The problem is one of strengthening stage-setting rules that make possible later actions yielding payoff. The exploitation of predictions provides a mechanism. Let us assume, following Samuel, that the strength of a rule amounts to a prediction of the average payoff the system will receive later if the rule is invoked concurrently as part of a cluster. Assume further that a second rule is coupled to the given rule by a diachronic pointer. If this second rule has a strength (prediction) very different from that of the first rule, then the strength of the first rule can be revised to bring it into line with the later prediction (see discussion in Samuel 1959, and the definition of the bucket-brigade algorithm in Section 5). When the system has such an algorithm for revising strengths, then the invocation of rules can be decided by a competition based on strength and the degree to which the rule's conditions are satisfied by the current situation.

In effect the various rules held by the system are treated as competing hypotheses. The winners are the system's estimate of the current situation. It is critical to the system's performance and flexibility that its rules represent a wide range of competing, even conflicting, hypotheses. The competition replaces a criterion of global consistency—a criterion that is infeasible for any very large system of rules—with one of progressive confirmation under the apportionment-of-credit algorithm. With this outlook, rules that consistently make poor predictions when invoked have their strength steadily decreased to the point that they are displaced by newer candidates. The newer candidates must in turn compete, usually doing well in "niches" not well handled by rules already in the system. The combination of competition and confirmation contributes to the system's *gracefulness:* Large numbers of new candidates can be injected without disturbing performance in well-practiced domains.

4. Classifier Systems

4.1 Overview

Classifier systems are general-purpose programming systems designed to meet the objectives and criteria set forth in Sections 2 and 3. They have been designed from the outset to be amenable to modification by learning algorithms. Particular attention has been given to questions of gracefulness and to the provision of "natural" building blocks. The systems have already been tested in a variety of contexts (see Section 6).

Classifier systems have many affinities to the rule-based (production system) approach to expert systems (see, for example, Davis and King 1977, or Waterman and Hayes-Roth 1978) but with the following major differences:

1. Any number of rules, called *classifiers,* can be active at the same time. There can be no direct conflict between classifiers because the only action of a classifier is to post a message to a global message list—the more classifiers activated, the more messages on the message list. The

resulting conflict-free concurrency sidesteps the difficult conflict resolution problems of one-rule-at-a-time systems (see McDermott and Forgy 1978), allowing the system to use many rules concurrently to summarize and act upon a situation. The rules become building blocks that can be combined to handle a wide variety of situations. Moreover, the parallelism makes it easier to specify and control the parallel processes that pervade the real world.

2. Messages are strings of fixed length k over a fixed alphabet, taken to be $\{1,0\}$ in the definitions that follow. Classifiers, as is usual with production systems, consist of a *condition* part and an *action* part, but the conditions are all specified by strings of length k over the alphabet $\{1,0,\#\}$. With this provision it is possible to use a simple matching operator to test whether or not some message satisfies a condition. From the architectural viewpoint, the fixed lengths encourage organizations exploiting fixed-length registers, an important consideration in simulations or physical realizations.

3. When the condition part of a classifier is satisfied by some message on the message list, the action part uses the message to form a new message, which is posted on the new message list. Thus the basic procedure of the *system* is a simple loop in which all classifiers access the current message list, determine if their conditions have been satisfied, and if so, post messages to the message list for the next time-step. As mentioned earlier, any number of classifiers can be active simultaneously without conflict, because actions only add messages to the new message list.

4. All external communication (input and output) is via messages to the message list. As a result, all internal control information and external communication reside in the same data structure.

5. Because the order in which classifiers are executed is independent of the order in which the classifiers are stored, and because satisfaction of conditions is determined by a simple matching operation, there is no need for an interpreter. This makes it possible to design local syntactic operators that modify systems of classifiers ("programs") in useful ways, something difficult to do for standard languages or production systems but very important if the system is to be modified by learning algorithms or expert advice.

6. Because of the global nature of the message list, tagging and related techniques become efficient ways of "coupling" classifiers, forcing predetermined execution sequences, and so on. The combination of concurrency and a global list avoids the limitations on tagging discussed by Davis and King (1977) in their review of production systems.

4.2 Definition of the Basic Elements: Classifiers and Messages

Classifiers have the same role in classifier systems that instructions have in computer language. They are called classifiers because they can be used to classify messages into general sets, but they are broader in concept and application than this name would indicate, providing both processing and recoding. The message specified by the action part of the classifier changes the internal state of the system, thereby influencing later action, and it may cause external (effecter) action. Provided with some simple message-processing capabilities, classifiers can carry out arbitrary operations on messages, including recursions. It follows that there are classifier systems that are computationally universal.

The major technical hurdle in implementing a message-processing version of a production system is that of providing a simple way of defining conditions in terms of messages. Each condition specifies a subset of the set of all possible messages—the set of messages that *satisfies* the condition. There is no simple and compact way of specifying an arbitrary subset of a large set; that is, most subsets must be specified element by element. Nevertheless there is one large and important class of subsets that can be simply specified, and any other subset can be defined as a union of these subsets. Each subset in this special class is specified by a string of length k over the three-letter alphabet $\{1,0,\#\}$. (Recall that messages, for present purposes, are strings of length k over the alphabet $\{1,0\}$.) The # symbol plays the role here of a "don't care" in the sense that wherever a # occurs in the specifying string one can substitute either a 1 or a 0 and still have a member of the subset. For example, the string 11 ... 1# specifies the subset of exactly two elements, namely, the messages $\{11 ... 11, 11 ... 10\}$, and the string 1##... ## specifies the subset consisting of all messages that start with a 1.

More formally, let

$$<s_1, s_2, \dots , s_j, \dots s_k>, s_j \varepsilon \ \{1,0,\#\}$$

be a string of k symbols specifying a subset, and let

$$<m_1, m_2, \dots m_k>, m_j \varepsilon \{1,0\}$$

be a k-bit message. The message belongs to the specified subset just in case

1. if $s_j = 1$ or $s_j = 0$, then $m_j = s_j$

2. if $s_j = \#$, then m_j can be either 1 or 0.

The subset consists of all messages satisfying this requirement; that is, each subset is a hyperplane in the space of messages.

In this notation, classifier conditions are specified using strings of length k over the alphabet $\{1,0,\#\}$. We extend the notation by allowing the string to be prefixed by a minus sign (–), with the intended interpretation that the prefixed condition is satisfied only if *no* message of the given subset is present on the message list. That is, if string c specifies subset S of the set of all messages, the condition $-c$ is *not* satisfied just in case the message list contains a message belonging to S. Combinations of classifiers can be used to implement conditions over arbitrary subsets in much the same way that AND, OR, and NOT can be combined to yield arbitrary Boolean functions (see Section 4.3).

When the condition part of a classifier is satisfied, it produces a message specified by its action (or message specification) part. The action part, like the condition part, is specified by a string of length k that contains the # symbol, but the # has a different meaning. Now it plays the role of a "pass through" in the sense that wherever the # symbol occurs in the action part, the corresponding bit in a message satisfying the condition part is passed through into the outgoing message. For example, consider the message specification 11... 1# in the action part of the classifier, and assume the message 00 ... 00 satisfies the condition part of the classifier. Then the outgoing message will be 11 ... 10.

More formally, let

$$<a_1, a_2, ..., a_j,... a_k>, a_j \; \varepsilon \; \{1,0,\#\}$$

be a string of k symbols in the action part of a classifier, and let

$$<m_1, m_2,..., m_j,..., m_k>, m_j \; \varepsilon \; \{1,0\}$$

be a message satisfying the condition part of the classifier. Then the outgoing message, at position j, has value

1. a_j, if $a_j = 1$ or 0

2. m_j, if $a_j = \#$.

In brief, if a message satisfies the condition of a classifier, a new message is generated from the action portion of the classifier by using the 1's and 0's of the action part and passing through bits of the satisfying message at the pass through positions of the action part.

It is useful to generalize the notion of a classifier to allow an arbitrary number of conditions. Condition i of an r-condition classifier C is specified by a string c_i of length k over the symbols $\{1,0,\#\}$, possibly prefixed by a $-$; the action part is specified by a single string a of a length k over the symbols $\{1,0,\#\}$. Notationally, the conditions in the condition part are separated by ";" and the action part is separated from the condition part by "/". Thus the specification of an r-condition classifier will have the form $c_1, c_2,..., c_r/a$.

The condition part of the classifier C is *satisfied* if each condition c_j is satisfied by some message M_j on the current message list. When the classifier is satisfied, an outgoing message M^* is generated as before using the message M_j satisfying condition c_1 and the action part a. At each position where a has a bit 0 or 1, M^* gets that bit; at each position where a has a pass through #, M^* gets the corresponding bit of M_j.

These definitions are sufficient to define the basic elements of a classifier system. A *classifier system* consists of a list of classifiers $\{C_1, C_2, ... C_n\}$, a message list, an input interface, and an output interface. The basic execution cycle of this system proceeds as follows:

1. Place all messages from the input interface on the current message list.

2. Compare all messages to all conditions and record all matches.

3. For each match generate a message for the new message list.

4. Replace the current message list by the new message list.

5. Process the new message list through the output interface to produce system output.

6. Return to step 1.

A classifier system may be augmented by algorithms for "look-ahead," inference, and learning. Several methods for doing these things will be described in the next two subsections and in Section 5. For some of these, weights are associated with classifiers and messages, and wherever a match is made a record is kept of the classifier that is satisfied and of the combinations of messages that satisfied it so that these weights can be modified periodically. Such enriched systems will still be called classifier systems unless there is some distinction to be pointed up by using a different name.

Because matching messages against conditions is a simple process, the central loop of the process (step 2 above) proceeds rapidly even on standard von Neumann architectures. One simulation currently in operation executes a time-step involving 256 conditions and thirty-two messages in less than 0.1 second. Parallel architectures offer speedups in proportion to the parallelism.

4.3 Tagging and Networks

Pointers, action sequences, and other processes dependent upon "addressing" are attained using *tags* to *couple* classifiers.

A classifier C_2 is coupled to a classifier C_1 if some condition of C_2 is satisfied by the message(s) generated by the action part of C_1. Note that a classifier with very specific conditions (few #'s) will typically be coupled to only a few other classifiers, and a classifier with very general conditions (many #'s) will be coupled to many other classifiers. When used to implement part of a "semantic network" or neural network, a classifier with very specific conditions has few incoming branches, and a classifier with very general conditions has many incoming branches.

Tags are a simple way of providing coupling. For example, any message with the prefix 1101 will satisfy a condition of the form 1101 # ... #, so a classifier with this condition in effect has an address: to send a message to this classifier one employs the prefix 1l0l. Since b bits yield 2^b tags and tags can be placed anywhere in a condition, a great number of conditions can be addressed uniquely.

By using appropriate prefixes, one can define a classifier that attends to a specific set of classifiers. Consider a pair of classifiers C_1 and C_2 that send messages tagged with 1101 and 1001, respectively. A classifier with the condition 1101## ... ## will attend only to C_1, whereas a classifier with the configuration 1#01## ... ## will attend to both C_1 and C_2. Using a combination of pass throughs (#'s in the action parts) and recodings (in which the prefix on the outgoing message differs from that of the satisfying messages), one can circumvent, usually with little effort, the limitation that the conditions be hyperplanes in the message space.

Boolean compounds of conditions—and hence the specification of conditions satisfied by arbitrarily chosen subsets of messages—are readily achieved by tags. An AND-condition is expressed by a single multicondition classifier such as M_1, M_2/M, for M is only added to the list if both M_1 and M_2 are satisfied. An OR-condition is expressed by a set of classifiers such as $\{M_1/M; M_2/M\}$, for M is added to the list if either M_1 or M_2 is satisfied. With these primitives, any Boolean form can be expressed by a set of classifiers. For example, $(M_1 \& M_2) \lor [(M_3 \& (-M_4)]$ is achieved by the classifiers

$$\{M_1, M_2/M_5 ; M_3 - M_4/M_5\}.$$

The judicious use of #'s and recoding again reduces the number of classifiers required when the Boolean expressions are complex. By assigning tags to the input, internal, and output states of a finite system, one can realize arbitrary state transition diagrams.

The use of tags to couple classifiers for purposes of control and sequencing is illustrated in detail in the next subsection. The example also illustrates the use of concurrency and distributed control in classifier systems.

4.4 A Simple Classifier Control System

Figure 1 gives the schematic of a simple control routine for a classifier system operating in a two-dimensional environment. When there is an object of a specified type anywhere in the system's field of vision, this classifier routine acts to bring the system next to the object and hold it there.

The environment contains objects distributed over a planar surface. The input interface produces a message for an object in the field of vision. This message indicates the relative position of the object in the field of vision (left-of-center, center, right-of-center) and whether it is distant from or adjacent to the system. The classifiers process this information and issue commands to the output interface (ROTATE VISION VECTOR [LEFT, RIGHT], COUPLE MOTION VECTOR TO VISION VECTOR, MOVE FORWARD, STOP). The control routine proceeds by stages, first centering the object, then aligning the direction of motion to that vision direction, next moving forward in that direction, and finally stopping when adjacent to the object. The operations of the system take place over successive execution cycles or time-steps.

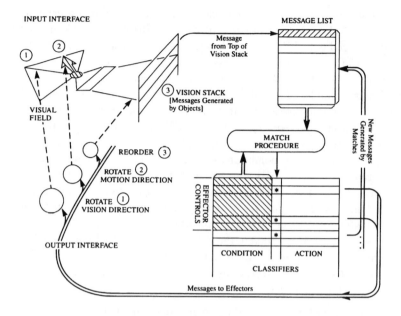

Figure 1. Schematic for a classifier-based cognitive system.

To define the classifier system, one first defines the input messages, then the condition parts of classifiers, and then the action parts of classifiers. Each of these is 16 bits long, though the present example is based on actual simulation in which they are 32 bits long.

The left-most bit of a message is a tag, 1 for an input message and 0 for any other kind of message. The next 12 bits of an input message specify the properties of an object. (Note that these 12 bits can be used for entirely different purposes for messages with initial tag 0.) There are twelve independent properties, with 1 indicating the presence and 0 indicating the absence of a property in an object. For concreteness we will stipulate that the system is searching for objects—goal objects—that satisfy the condition #111000#########. That is, it is searching for objects that have the first three properties and lack the next three, whether or not they have the remaining six properties.

The last 3 bits in an interface message give information about the relative position of the object in the field of vision. They are interpreted as follows:

    bits 14, 15:   1,0 object left-of-center
                    0,1 object right-of-center
                    0,0 object centered
    bit 16:   1 object adjacent
                    0 object not adjacent.

Thus, the message <u>11110</u>001 01011<u>100</u> indicates the presence in the visual field of a goal object that is left-of center and not adjacent, only the underlined bits being relevant to this interpretation.

Classifier *conditions* will be abbreviated as follows:

x = desired object x is present in the field of vision
c = object is centered
l = object is left-of-center
r = object is right-of-center
a = object is adjacent
$-a$ = object is not adjacent

Following these conventions, $[x,l,-a]$ specifies the condition 1111000# #####100, and so on.

The action part of each classifier specifies a 16-bit message issued when the conditions of the classifier are satisfied. Each such message will simply be abbreviated as the corresponding 16-bit integer. That is, "[4]" abbreviates the *message* 00000000 00000100, the tag 0 at the first position indicating that this is *not* an input message.

The classifier routine controls three effectors: an effector to move the direction of vision incrementally (15 degrees in the simulation) to the led or right, a second effector to set the direction of motion parallel to the direction of vision, and a third effector to cause the system to move forward one unit in the direction of motion. If no command is issued to a given effector during an execution cycle, that effecter retains its last setting. In presenting the action effected by messages to effecters we will use

L = rotate vision vector 15 degrees to the left
R = rotate vision vector 15 degrees to the right
P = set the move vector parallel to the vision vector
G = move one unit forward in the move vector direction

There are nine classifiers in this illustrative system. The first four lead to operations by the remaining five, the next three cause output actions, the eighth causes the system to halt, and the ninth will be explained shortly.

C1 $[x,l]$/[4]
C2 $[x,r]$/[5]
C3 $[x,c, -a]$/[6]
C4 $[x,c,a]$/[7]
C5 [4]/[8]   [8] causes effector action L
C6 [5]/[9]   [9] causes effector action R
C7 [6]/[10]   [10] causes effecter actions P and G
C8 [7]/[11]   [11] causes the cycling to halt
C9 [4or5or6or7]/[0]
(Note that the condition [4or5or6or7] is specified by the string 00000000 000001##.)

If an object of the desired type x appears at the far left of the field of vision at execution cycle t, classifier $C1$ is activated, placing message [4] on the message list at cycle $t + 1$. Assuming the object x is still left-of-center, the classifiers $C1$, $C5$, and $C9$ become active at cycle $t + 1$ and the message list consists of 4 messages: [4], [8], [0], and the message from the input interface. This list of messages continues until x is centered as a result of the repetitions of the L command, whereupon $C3$ would be activated, and so on (see Table 1).

Note that message [4] provides a recording of the message from the input interface, coupling this information to the classifier $C5$ ([4]/[8]), which causes effecter action L. Any message [m] could have been used for this purpose; for example, the pair of classifiers [x, 1]/[m] and [m]/[8] would have produced the same action L. It is this "internal" recoding that permits the classifier systems to carry out arbitrary computations, so that formally speaking classifier languages are computationally complete.

In detail, the execution sequence of the classifier system proceeds as shown in Table 1. It is clear that the classifier [4or5or6or7]/[0] plays no role in this example. It is inserted to illustrate the concept of a *support* classifier, which is useful when the bucket-brigade algorithm (see Section 5) is incorporated into this classifier system. In that case the classifier [4or5or6or7]/[0] serves to reinforce the whole set of classifiers. With further additions such a classifier can be used to call the whole routine when an object x appears.

4.5 Use of Classifiers to Define Complex Entities and Hierarchies

The introduction to this chapter made the point that the ultimate limitations on definition are no greater for the environment-oriented approach than for the language-oriented approach, that limit being set by distinguishability. Section 4.3 showed that clusters of coupled classifiers can be arranged to respond to any chosen subset of the set of possible messages. Because messages are the unifying element of classifier systems—providing internal communication as well as communication from the environment—this capability provides broad powers of definition. There is not room here for a detailed exposition, but the possibility of defining objects involving complex combinations of categories and relations—Winston's definition of an *arch* (1975) is a simple example—can at least be made plausible.

First, networklike interactions of coupled classifiers, through the use of tags and conditions of varying generality, have already been discussed (Section 4.3). When the condition part of a rule is satisfied and it is coupled into such array, it acts by pointing to other classifiers that are to have their condition parts tested in turn. That is, the outgoing message is tagged so that it is attended to by the classifiers to which the rule is to be coupled. This operation is quite analogous to passing a marker over a link in NETL (Fahlman 1979) or to moving down one of the links in a linked list.

Major Cycle (Time)	Active Classifiers	Message List
t	C1	11110001 10000100
		[4]
$t+1$	C1, C5, C9	11110001 10000100
		[4]
		[8]
		[0]
$t+2$	C1, C5, C9	11110001 10000100
		[4]
		[8]
		[0]
:		

($t + c$ is the time at which object x is first centered.)

$t+c$	C3, C9	11110001 10000000
		[6]
		[0]
$t + c + 1$	C3, C7, C9	11110001 10000000
		[6]
		[10]
		[0]
:		

(t + a is the time at which the system is first adjacent to object x.)

$t + a$	C4, C9	11110001 10000001
		[7]
		[0]
$t + a + 1$	C4, C8, C9	11110001 10000001
		[7]
		11]
		[0]

(The system has now halted adjacent to object x.)

Table 1. Example of a typical execution sequence.

Because messages are involved, not just markers, a great deal of information can be carried from point to point in the network. For instance, the tag of a message can indicate its point of origin, and other bits carry information passed through or recoded (see Section 4.2). Because of the parallelism of classifier systems, clusters of coactive rules can be used to define categories and objects (see Section 4.3 and 4.4). The pointing technique can be extended to include relations, coupling some classifiers in a cluster to other related clusters. Finally, default hierarchies develop naturally under the bidding process discussed in Section 5. Under the bidding process, when two classifiers are satisfied, say by the same message, the one with the more specific condition (fewer #'s) usually becomes active. As the induction procedures add new candidates to the system (see Section 5), the "specialists" (fewer #'s) serve as exceptions to the "generalists" (more #'s) under the competition induced by the bidding process. A specialist may in turn serve as a default for a still more specific classifier, whence the developing default hierarchy arises.

The combination of the default hierarchy, so realized, with the clusters of coupled classifiers provides an effect much like Fahlman's virtual copy (1979). Environmental messages cause the activation of a cluster of classifiers that provides the "frame" and specifics wherein the system builds its responses to the situation. The tag on the outgoing message from a cluster can indicate the presence of some complex object, such as an *arch,* while the pass through bits (see Section 4.2) carry incidental information (color, size, etc.) possibly relevant to further processing. The processing can include expectations (classifiers satisfied by messages from the virtual copy but not yet supported by messages from the environment) and plans (coupled sequences of classifiers wherein only the first element of the sequence is activated by messages from the environment).

The object of the next section is to show how such structures can emerge, in response to experience, under the impetus of competition and learning and induction rules. Some early uses of classifier systems for realistic problems (Wilson 1982, Goldberg 1983) show that default hierarchies do emerge and that sequences of coupled classifiers sensitive to stage-setting situations do develop.

5. Learning and Induction

The essence of classifier systems is a parallelism and a standardization that permit both a "building block" approach to the processing of information and the use of competition to resolve conflicts. It is the latter property, competition, that makes possible an approach to learning that is both general and powerful.

Two kinds of learning algorithms are required if a classifier system is to adapt to changes in the domains and goals presented to it. The first is an algorithm that reinforces or apportions credit to rules already available to the system. (Samuel's 1959 paper is full of insights concerning this problem.) The second is an algorithm for generating new, plausible rules when the rules available prove inadequate. (Samuel calls this "the parameter problem," and it is the one problem on which he did not really make progress. Recently both Lenat (1983) and Hofstadter (1983) have offered interesting approaches to it.) Here, in order to exploit competition between classifiers, two new kinds of algorithm are introduced. The first, the apportionment-of-credit algorithm, is called a *bucket-brigade algorithm.* The second, the rule generation algorithm, is called a *genetic algorithm.*

5.1 Bucket Brigade Algorithms

The bucket-brigade algorithm is designed to assign credit to each classifier in the system according to its overall usefulness in attaining system goals. To this end, each classifier in the system is assigned a value, called its *strength*, and it is this value that the bucket-brigade algorithm adjusts. The problem is easy enough when a classifier participates directly in goal-achieving action that produces payoff, but it is quite difficult to decide which of the classifiers active early in a sequence sets the stage for later successful actions. (In Samuel's terms, it is easy enough to credit classifiers that combine to produce a triple jump at some point in the game; it is much harder to decide which classifiers active earlier were responsible for changes that made the later jump possible.) By a combination of analysis, and simulation (Wilson 1982, Goldberg 1983), we can show that the bucket-brigade algorithm actually accomplishes this task.

The algorithm works, via a modification of the basic execution cycle, by introducing a competition between classifiers. Recall that, during the execution cycle, each classifier scans all the messages on the global message list, producing a new message from each message satisfying its conditions. That procedure is now modified so that satisfied classifiers must compete to get their messages on the message list. Each satisfied classifier makes a *bid* based on its strength, and only the highest bidding classifiers get their messages on the list. The size of the bid depends not only on the classifier's strength but also on its specificity. (Recall that the specificity of a classifier is measured by the number of non-#'s in its condition part.) Specifically, the bid produced by a classifier is proportional to the product of its strength ("past usefulness") and its specificity ("relevance"—the amount of information about the current situation incorporated in its condition part).

Formally, when the condition part of a classifier C is satisfied, it makes a bid

$$\text{Bid}(C,t) = cR(C)\text{Strength}(C,t)$$

where $R(C)$ is the specificity, equal to the number of non-#'s in the condition part of C divided by the length thereof; $S(C,t)$ is the strength of C at time t, and c is a constant considerably less than 1 (e.g., 1/8 or 1/16).

The *winning* (high) bidders place their messages on the message list and have their strength *reduced* by the amount of the bid (they are paying for the privilege of posting a new message):

$$\text{Strength}(C,t + 1) = \text{Strength}(C,t) - B(C,t)$$

for a winning classifier C. The classifiers $\{C'\}$ that sent the messages matched by this winner have their strengths *increased* by the amount of the bid (it is shared among them in the simplest version):

$$\text{Strength}(C't + 1) = \text{Strength}(C't) + a\text{Bid}(C,t)$$

where $a = 1/(\text{number of members of } \{C'\})$. (The senders are rewarded for setting up a situation usable by C.)

The bucket-brigade algorithm treats each classifier as a kind of middleman in a complex economy, the strength of a classifier measuring its ability to turn a "profit." As a middleman, the classifier only deals with its suppliers —the classifiers that send messages satisfying its conditions—and its consumers—the classifiers that are in turn satisfied by the messages it sends. Whenever a classifier wins a bidding competition, it initiates a transaction in which it pays out part of its strength to its suppliers and then receives similar payments from its consumers.

The classifier's strength is a kind of capital. If a classifier receives more from its consumers than it paid out, it has made a profit, that is, its strength is increased. This is likely to occur only if the consumer in turn is profitable. This chain leads to the ultimate consumers, the classifiers that attain goals directly and receive payoff directly from the environment. That is, certain actions are immediately rewarded or reinforced by the environment; this payoff for goal attainment is added to the strengths of all classifiers active at that time. The profitability of other classifiers depends upon their being coupled into sequences leading to payoff. Thus, the bucket brigade assures that early-acting, stage-setting classifiers receive credit if they (on average) make possible later, overtly rewarding acts.

It is worth noting that some of the fixed-point theorems of mathematical economics provide a way of proving the above for environments that have "stable" statistics.

5.2 Genetic Algorithms

Once strengths can be assigned to classifiers, a basis exists for generating new classifiers to enter the competition. In broadest terms the genetic algorithm uses high-strength classifiers as progenitors for new classifiers to be tested under the bucket brigade. Because of the parallelism of classifier systems, newly generated classifiers can be inserted into the "population" without the system's repertoire in well-practiced situations being seriously disrupted (see below). It is vital to the understanding of genetic algorithms to know that even the simplest versions act much more subtly than "random search with preservation of the best" (contrary to common misreading of genetics as a process primarily driven by mutation). Genetic algorithms have been studied intensively through analysis (Holland 1975, Bethke 1980) and simulation (DeJong 1980, Smith 1980, Booker 1982, and others).

Although genetic algorithms act subtly, the basic execution cycle (the "central loop") is quite simple:

1. Select pairs from the set of classifiers according to strength—the stronger the classifier, the more likely its selection.

2. Apply genetic operators to the pairs, creating "offspring." Chief among the genetic operators is crossover, which simply exchanges a randomly selected segment between the pairs (see Figure 3).

3. Replace the weakest classifiers with the offspring.

The effect of this procedure is to emphasize various combinations of defining elements—schemata—as building blocks for the construction of new classifiers. The tentative nature of the classifiers constructed in this way is pointed up by step 3 above. They will be displaced if they do not acquire strength under the bucket brigade algorithm. Note that a newly constructed classifier gains or loses strength (aside from certain "taxations") only when its condition is satisfied and it wins the bidding competition to become active. As will be seen, this has much to do with the overall system's gracefulness relative to the insertion of new rules.

5.2.1 Definitions

To begin, let us consider the set $\mathbf{C}$ of all strings of length k over an alphabet of n letters. For example, the alphabet could be $\{1,0,\#\}$ so that the strings designate condition parts or message parts for classifiers. In the standard terminology of genetics these strings would be called *genotypes* and the values for individual letters in a string would be called *alleles*. The set of strings being tested at a given time (e.g., a classifier system) is called a *population*. In brief, and very roughly, a genetic algorithm can be looked upon as a sampling procedure that draws samples from the set $\mathbf{C}$; each sample drawn has a value, the fitness of the corresponding genotype. From this viewpoint, the classifier system at time t—call it $B(t)$—is a set of classifiers drawn from $\mathbf{C}$, and the fitness of each classifier is its strength. The genetic algorithm uses the fitnesses of the genotypes in $B(t)$ to generate new genotypes for test.

As will soon be seen in detail, the genetic algorithm uses the familiar "reproduction according to fitness" in combination with certain genetic operators (e.g., crossover; see below) to generate the new genotypes (classifiers). This process progressively biases the sampling procedure toward the use of *combinations* of alleles (building blocks) associated with above-average fitness. Surprisingly, in a population of size M, the algorithm effectively exploits some multiple of M^3 combinations in exploring $\mathbf{C}$. (How this happens will be seen in a moment.) For populations of more than a few individuals this number, M^3, is vastly greater than the total number of alleles in the population. The corresponding speedup in the rate of searching $\mathbf{C}$, a property called *implicit parallelism,* makes possible very high rates of adaptation. Moreover, because a genetic algorithm uses a distributed database (the population) to generate new samples, it is all but immune to some of the difficulties—false peaks, discontinuities, high-dimensionality, and so on—that commonly attend complex problems.

The task now is to give some substance—and intuition—to this outline. An understanding of some of the advantages and limitations of genetic algorithms can be reached via three short steps. First, in order to describe the nonuniform sampling procedure generated by a genetic algorithm, a special class of subsets of **C** is defined. Then, in the second step, an explicit sampling procedure emphasizing the sampling of combinations is used to examine the role of these special subsets in the nonuniform sampling procedure. The final step is to show how the genetic algorithm accomplishes implicitly and rapidly what is an intolerable computational burden for the explicit procedure.

For the first step, the subsets (combinations) of interest, called *schemata,* can be characterized as follows: Much as in the definition of conditions for classifiers (see Section 4.2), values are first fixed at a selected set of positions in the k-position strings. Note that for classifiers the strings are over the alphabet $\{1,0,\#\}$ rather than the alphabet $\{1,0\}$. By using a (new) "don't care" symbol * for positions not fixed, one can specify schemata quite compactly. Thus *0**#**... ** is the set of *all* conditions (or actions) having a 0 at position 2 and a # at position 5. The set of schemata is the set of all collections that can be defined in this way. Note that schemata for classifiers define subsets of the *space of possible conditions* (or actions), in contrast to the conditions themselves, which define subsets of the *space of messages.* Thus a schema constitutes a building block from which one can construct classifiers.

Parenthetically, schemata can also be characterized in a way familiar to mathematicians: If we look upon the k-position strings as vectors in a k-dimensional space (each component having one of n values $0, 1,..., n-1$), then the schemata are hyperplanes of the k-dimensional space. Schemata name particular subsets of the set **C** of k-position strings. These subsets are of interest because they correspond to particular combinations of letters and because they are easily and compactly defined by strings on an $n + 1$-letter alphabet $\{0, 1,..., n-1, *\}$.

(For simplicity, $n = 2$, implying binary strings, will be used throughout the rest of this subsection. For theoretical reasons it is usually advantageous to recode strings over large alphabets, $n > 2$, into binary strings. To apply the discussion directly to classifiers, simply increase n to 3, using the particular alphabet $\{1,0,\#\}$.)

Now it is time for the second step. For a better illustration of the way in which schemata can aid a search, an algorithm will be considered that manipulates schemata explicitly. Although this algorithm is an aid to understanding, it is impractical from the computational point of view because of the enormous amounts of time and storage it would require. The genetic algorithm, to be described in the third step accomplishes the same actions concisely and rapidly via an implicit manipulation. The explicit version involves the following steps:

1. Set $t = 0$ and generate, at random, a set $B(t)$ of M strings.

2. Observe the value of v(**C**), the "fitness," of each string **C** in $B(t)$. (From

a more formal point of view, steps 1 and 2 amount to sampling the random variable v, using a sample of size M taken from **C**.)

3. Let $M(s, t)$ be the number of strings in $B(t)$ belonging to the schema **s** (i.e., the strings are instances of **s**). If $M(s, t) > 0$ for **s**, calculate the average value $\hat{v}(s, t)$ of the strings in $B(t)$ belonging to that schema. Calculate, also, the average value $\hat{v}(t)$ of the set of M samples. (There will be somewhere between 2^k and $M*2^k$ schemata with one or more instances in $B(t)$. More formally, $\hat{v}(s, t)$ is the marginal sample average of v over the subset **s**.)

4. Select a new set $B(t + 1)$ of M strings so that the number of instances of each schema s in the new set is equal to

$$M(s, t + 1) = [\, \hat{v}(s, t) \,/\, \hat{v}(t)]*M(s, t)$$

for as many schemata as possible. (Informally, this recursion says that schemata observed to be above average, $\hat{v}(s, t) > \hat{v}(t)$, receive more samples on the next time-step. Similarly, below-average schemata receive fewer samples. At first sight it may seem impossible to meet this requirement in any meaningful way because there are so many schemata, but see below.)

5. Set t to $t + 1$ and return to step 2.

It is difficult to satisfy the requirement of step 4 because the schemata (hyperplanes) intersect each other over and over again. In fact there are so many intersections that *each* string belongs to 2^k distinct schemata. Thus any sample allocated to one schema is as well a sample of $2^k - 1$ other schemata. However, a little thought and some calculation show that it is possible to distribute M new samples so that all schemata *with more than a few elements* receive the requisite number of samples. (Note that this means that schemata with more than a few *'s in their defining strings can be sampled according to the dictates of step 4.) Actually to carry out the distribution explicitly, allocating samples schema by schema so that step 4 is satisfied, would require an enormous amount of computation.

Setting aside the difficulties of implementation, we find that the algorithm uses very plausible inferences in generating "fit" strings. Most importantly, it samples with increasing intensity schemata that contain strings of above-average strength. The net effect of increasing the proportion of samples allocated to above-average schemata is to move the overall average $\hat{v}(t)$ upward. Because the average $\hat{v}(t)$ increases with time, this sampling procedure is a global "force" driving the search into subsets observed to contain valuable strings. Moreover, because the algorithm works from a database of M points distributed over **C**, it is not easily caught on "false peaks" (local optima). (Standard optimization procedures work well only with single-peak func-

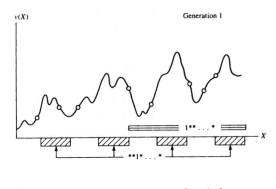

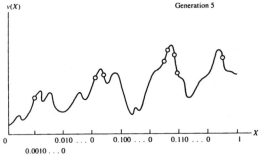

Figure 2. Example of function optimization by genetic algorithm.

tions, relying on a uniform random search for "starting points" when there are multiple peaks.) Overall, this algorithm is much more globally oriented than standard optimization procedures, searching through a great many schemata for regularities and interactions that can be exploited. This point has been established, for the algorithm described next, by extensive experimental comparisons between that algorithm and standard procedures (Bethke 1980, DeJong 1980).

Figure 2 illustrates the use of schemata to locate the global optimum of a function $v(x)$ on the interval [0,1]. The arguments of the function are represented as binary fractions so that, for example, the argument $x = 1/2$ is represented as 0.100 ... 0. If we look upon the binary representations as strings, then the schema 1** ... * is the subset of all arguments greater than or equal to 1/2, that is, the interval [1/2,1]. Similarly, the schema **1* ... * is a set of intervals (see top half of Figure 2) corresponding to all the binary fractions that have a 1 in the third place. Other schemata are determined accordingly. Regularities of the function, such as periodicities, trends, and so on, are readily exploited by the biasing of samples toward appropriate schemata. The ge-

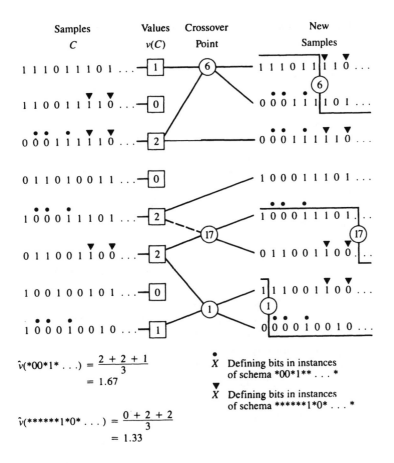

$$\hat{v}(*00*1* \ldots) = \frac{2 + 2 + 1}{3}$$
$$= 1.67$$

$\overset{\bullet}{X}$ Defining bits in instances
of schema *00*1** . . . *

$\overset{\blacktriangledown}{X}$ Defining bits in instances
of schema ******1*0* . . . *

$$\hat{v}(******1*0* \ldots) = \frac{0 + 2 + 2}{3}$$
$$= 1.33$$

Figure 3. Example of the genetic algorithm's effect on schemata

netic algorithm automatically takes advantage of such schemata, as will be seen in a moment.

From an intuitive point of view, good schemata (schemata containing strings of above-average fitness) can be thought of as useful building blocks for constructing new strings. For example, if the schemata 1*0** ... ** and ***001** ... ** are both good, then it seems reasonable to investigate strings constructed with these building blocks, namely, strings belonging to the schema 1*0001** ... **. The power of this kind of algorithm lies in its rapid accumulation of large numbers of better-than average building blocks—building blocks that exploit regularities and interactions in the sample space *C*. By carefully choosing *TM* samples over *T* iterations, the algorithm accumulates information about a large number of potential building blocks, a number somewhere between 2^k and $TM2^k$.

Our objective now is to see how we can obtain the effects of this direct algorithm without paying the tremendous computational costs. This third step of the explanation involves, first, a specification of the genetic algorithm and, second, an explanation of its implicit manipulation of schemata (see Figure 3). The specification is as follows:

1. Set $t = 0$ and generate, at random, a set $B(t)$ of M strings.
2. Observe the value $v(C)$ of each string C in $B(t)$.
3. Compute the average strength $\hat{v}$ of the M strings in the database $B(t)$ and assign a normalized value $v(C)/\hat{v}$ to each string C in $B(t)$.
4. Assign each string in $B(t)$ a probability proportional to its normalized value and then select n, $n < < M$, pairs of strings from $B(r)$ using this probability distribution.
5. Apply genetic operators to each pair, forming $2n$ new strings. The most important of the genetic operators is crossover (see Figure 3): A position along the string is selected at random, and then, in the pair being operated upon, the segments to the left of this position are exchanged. This simple operation has subtle effects when used in combination with the "emphasis" provided by step 3 as will be seen shortly. The other operators, such as *mutation* and *inversion,* have lesser roles in this use of the algorithm, mainly providing "insurance" against overemphasis of a given kind of schema. (See Holland 1975, Chapter 6, Sections 2, 3, and 4 for details.)
6. Select $2n$ strings from $B(t)$ and replace them with the $2n$ new strings resulting from step 4. (There are some technical issues involved in the selection of the strings to be replaced. These issues primarily concern limitations on the portion of the database allocated to strings of a given type. In effect each string belongs to a niche in the database and its spread is to be limited to the size—i.e., carrying capacity—of that niche. See Bethke 1980, and DeJong 1980, for details.)
7. Set t to $t + 1$ and return to step 2.

Unlike the earlier direct algorithm, the genetic algorithm never deals directly with schemata—it only manipulates the strings in B(t). If one wishes to explore the action of the algorithm relative to schemata, it is helpful to divide the algorithm's action into two phases: Phase 1 consists of steps 2-4; phase 2 consists of steps 5-6.

Consider first what would happen if phase 1 were iterated without the execution of phase 2 (but with the replacement of strings in $B(t)$). In particular, let phase 1 be iterated $M/2n$ times (assuming for convenience that M is a multiple of $2n$). It is not difficult to show that the expected number of instances of a schema **s** at the end of this iteration is just $\hat{v}(s)$ times the number of instances at the outset (see Holland 1975). This is true of *every* schema with instances in *B*, and this is just what was required of the direct algorithm in step 4.

What, then, is accomplished by phase 2? The problem is that phase 1 introduces no new strings into *B*; it merely introduces additional copies of strings already there. Phase I provides emphasis, but no new trials. The genetic operators, applied in phase 2, obviously modify the strings in *B*. It is a fundamental property of genetic algorithms (Theorem 6.2.3, Holland 1975) that the emphasis provided by phase 1 is little disturbed by phase 2. That is, after phase 2, schemata with instances in *B* will largely have the *number* of instances provided by phase 1 *but they will be new instances*.

Thus the genetic algorithm as a whole generates new samples of *schemata* already present, increasing or decreasing the sampling rate according to the multiplier $\hat{v}(s,t)/\hat{v}(t)$, as desired. From the point of view of sampling theory, these new samples increase confidence in the estimates $\hat{v}(s)$ for each above-average schema s in B. Some calculation (Holland 1975, chap. 4) shows that considerably more than M^3 schemata are so treated every $M/2n$ time steps. Moreover, samples are generated for schemata not previously tried without this procedure being disrupted. All of this comes about through simple—and fast—manipulations of $2n$ strings per step. This implicit manipulation of a great many schemata via operations on relatively few strings is called *implicit parallelism*.

5.2.2 Application to Classifiers

How does all this apply to the generation of new classifiers? As mentioned, the strengths assigned by the bucket-brigade algorithm serve as the fitnesses of the classifiers. Because the parts of the classifier are strings of standard length k over a fixed alphabet $\{1,0,\#\}$, three possible alleles per locus, the procedures of the genetic algorithm are directly applicable. A combination of alleles that occurs in several strong classifiers—for example, a particular tag, or part of a message, or a combination of properties—automatically becomes a building block for the construction of new classifiers. Such combinations amount to schemata that are subject to the theorems concerning implicit parallelism.

If the classifier system is using *M* classifiers, it can be shown that, as the genetic algorithm generates new classifiers, it is effectively selecting amongst more than M^3 building blocks, each rated on the basis of past experience! The building blocks so manipulated determine important properties, such as classifier coupling and control sequencing (see Section 4.3 and 4.4). Thus the genetic algorithm can encourage variants of useful subroutines, and it can generate hierarchical substructures for testing. In sum, the genetic algorithm offers an inductive procedure that is (1) fast (because of the implicit parallelism), (2) relatively immune to misdirection (because of the distributed database provided by the population), and (3) capable of sophisticated transfer of knowledge from one situation to another (because of the role of schemata).

It is important to note that in general, the candidate rules generated by the genetic algorithm do *not* displace the parent rules. The parent rules simply supply copies of their parts for use by the genetic operators (such as crossover); they remain in the system in their original form. The offspring rules typically displace rules of low strength, thus eliminating rules that have not proved valuable to the system. As a consequence the parent rules, because of their high strength, will tend to remain in control of situations in which they acquired their strength. New rules typically get their chance in situations where none of the high-strength rules have their conditions satisfied. That is, they tend to fill new niches corresponding to domains in which the system has inadequate sets of rules. (This feature goes hand in hand with Scott's (1983) use of "play" as a means of reducing uncertainty about the environment.)

Ultimately, of course, new rules may out compete their parents (or other relatives) if they prove superior under the bucket-brigade algorithm. The *explicit* parallelism, under which a variety of rules is active simultaneously, encourages the competition. The result is a system that can explore without disturbing well-established capabilities. In short, the system is graceful rather than brittle.

6. Tests and Prospects

Several years ago a series of tests of simplified classifier systems (Holland and Reitman 1978) demonstrated simple transfer of learning from problem to problem and showed that the genetic algorithm yielded learning, in that context, an order of magnitude faster than weight-changing techniques alone. The results were encouraging enough to spark a variety of subsequent tests at several places. Smith (then at the University of Pittsburgh, now at Carnegie Mellon University) completed a classifier system (1980) that competed against Waterman's poker player (Waterman and Hayes-Roth 1978)—also a learning program—with overwhelming success. Wilson (then at Polaroid, now at the Rowland Institute) used a classifier system (1982) with a genetic algorithm in a series of experiments involving TV-camera-mechanical-arm coordination, culminating in a successful demonstration of the segregation of the classifiers, under learning, into sets (Wilson calls them *demes)* corresponding to control subroutines. Booker has done an in-depth simulation study (1982) of classifier systems as cognitive models, with particular emphasis on the generation of cognitive maps under experience. More recently, Goldberg (1983) has demonstrated emergence of a default hierarchy in a study of the use of classifiers, under the genetic algorithm, as adaptive controls for gas pipeline transmission. There are several ongoing projects, including one that uses a classifier system to deal with the classification problem in KL-ONE (Forrest 1982).

The more advanced properties of classifier systems are being tested with the help of a program, CS1, that is both a "compiler," allowing design and simulation of classifier systems on a serial computer, and a "test-bed," providing the means of simulating a wide range of environments for testing the learning algorithms. The current version provides the following facilities:

1. Simulation of a task environment consisting of up to 256 objects, each with up to thirty-two distinct features, emplaced on a 65,000 by 65,000 grid. Any or all of the objects may be mobile.

2. An input interface that consist of an arbitrarily shaped "vision cone" that views a local part of the surface (typically less than 1000 grid points) and uses feature detectors to generate an input message for each object in the vision cone.

3. An emulator for the classifier system that can retain, in random access memory, the description of over 1000 classifiers and a message list of up to thirty-two messages. This part of the system is written in machine language and can execute a basic time-step (all classifiers matched against all messages) in about 0.1 second. The overall system runs in close to real time, making it convenient to run long learning sequences in the simulated environment.

4. An output interface that permits manipulation of objects on the grid, movement over the grid, rotation of a visual cone, and in fact any other effector action conveniently specifiable by a subroutine.

5. Parameterized versions of both the bucket-brigade and genetic algorithms, including provisions for contingent activation of these algorithms (such as activation of the genetic algorithm when no classifier responds to an input message).

Studying full-fledged classifier systems is much like studying an ecology. There are niches, adaptations exploiting them, and shifting hierarchies of interaction—the emergence of parasitic classifiers has even been observed! Questions abound. Most pressing is the question of limitations. What is it that such systems cannot learn from experience? The author's observations to date indicate that general-purpose learning algorithms, given the right grist, can produce organizations that are detailed, appropriate, and subtle. This contradicts accepted wisdom in AI; somewhere there is a boundary (or set of them) that marks the limits of what can be accomplished reasonably with so-called weak methods. The author's impression is that the domain of-such methods is *much* larger than is usually believed. Within this domain brittleness is no longer a bête noire.

Although most of the studies to date have dealt with systems that start with a tabula rasa—the most difficult test for a general purpose learning procedure—this would not be the typical use of such systems. Classifier systems are general-purpose systems that can be programmed initially to implement whatever expert knowledge is available to the designers and their consultants. Learning then allows the system to expand, correct errors, and transfer information from one domain to another. In this context the question becomes one of how flexible and graceful such a system can be. It is important to provide ways of instructing such systems so that they can generate rules—hypotheses to be held tentatively—on the basis of advice. Little has been done in this direction.

Much more remains to be discovered about conditions that induce a classifier system to construct models of its environment for purposes of planning and look-ahead. It is particularly important to understand how look-ahead and virtual explorations can be incorporated without other activities of the system being disturbed. Ultimately the question is whether such systems can develop symbols (cf. Hofstadter 1983) and use them, via abstract models, to generate plans and expectations.

Acknowledgements

This research was supported in part by the National Science Foundation under grants IST-8018043, MCS-7826016, and MCS8305830.

12

The Appeal of
Parallel Distributed Processing

J. L. McClelland, D. E. Rumelhart, and G. E. Hinton

1. Introduction

W
hat makes people smarter than machines? They certainly are not
quicker or more precise. Yet people are far better at perceiving objects in natural scenes and noting their relations, at understanding
language and retrieving contextually appropriate information from memory, at
making plans and carrying out contextually appropriate actions, and at a wide
range of other natural cognitive tasks. People are also far better at learning to
do these things more accurately and fluently through processing experience.

What is the basis for these differences? One answer, perhaps the classic
one we might expect from artificial intelligence, is "software." If we only had
the right computer program, the argument goes, we might be able to capture
the fluidity and adaptability of human information processing.

Certainly this answer is partially correct. There have been great breakthroughs in our understanding of cognition as a result of the development of expressive high-level computer languages and powerful algorithms. No doubt there will be more such breakthroughs in the future. However, we do not think that software is the whole story.

In our view, people are smarter than today's computers because the brain employs a basic computational architecture that is more suited to deal with a central aspect of the natural information processing tasks that people are so good at. In this chapter, we will show through examples that these tasks generally require the simultaneous consideration of many pieces of information or constraints. Each constraint may be imperfectly specified and ambiguous, yet each can play a potentially decisive role in determining the outcome of processing. After examining these points, we will introduce a computational framework for modeling cognitive processes that seems well suited to exploiting these constraints and that seems closer than other frameworks to the style of computation as it might be done by the brain. We will review several early examples of models developed in this framework, and we will show that the mechanisms these models employ can give rise to powerful emergent properties that begin to suggest attractive alternatives to traditional accounts of various aspects of cognition. We will also show that models of this class provide a basis for understanding how learning can occur spontaneously, as a by-product of processing activity.

1.1 Multiple Simultaneous Constraints

1.1.1 Reaching and Grasping

Hundreds of times each day we reach for things. We nearly never think about these acts of reaching. And yet, each time, a large number of different considerations appear to jointly determine exactly how we will reach for the object. The position of the object, our posture at the time, what else we may also be holding, the size, shape, and anticipated weight of the object, any obstacles that may be in the way—all of these factors jointly determine the exact method we will use for reaching and grasping.

Consider the situation shown in Figure 1. Figure 1A shows Jay McClelland's hand, in typing position at his terminal. Figure 1B indicates the position his hand assumed in reaching for a small knob on the desk beside the terminal. We will let him describe what happened in the first person:

> On the desk next to my terminal are several objects—a chipped coffee mug, the end of a computer cable, a knob from a clock radio. I decide to pick the knob up. At first I hesitate, because it doesn't seem possible. Then I just reach for it, and find myself grasping the knob in what would normally be considered a very awkward position—but it solves all of the constraints. I'm not sure what all the details of the movement were, so I let myself try it a few times more. I observe that my right hand is carried up off the keyboard, bent at the elbow, until my forearm is at

A

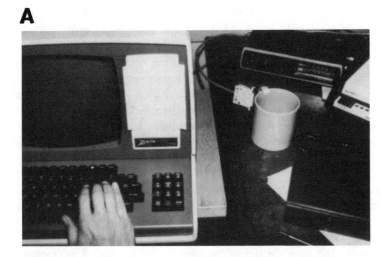

B

Figure 1. A: An everyday situation in which it is necessary to take into account a large number of constraints to grasp a desired object. In this case the target object is the small knob to the left of the cup. **B:** The posture the arm arrives at in meeting these constraints.

about a 30° angle to the desk top and parallel to the side of the terminal. The palm is facing downward through most of this. Then, my arm extends and lowers down more or less parallel to the edge of the desk and parallel to the side of the terminal and, as it drops, it turns about 90° so that the palm is facing the cup and the thumb and index finger are below. The turning motion occurs just in time, as my hand drops, to avoid hitting the coffee cup. My index finger and thumb close in on the knob and grasp it, with my hand completely upside down.

Though the details of what happened here might be quibbled with, the broad outlines are apparent. The shape of the knob and its position on the table; the starting position of the hand on the keyboard; the positions of the terminal, the cup, and the knob; and the constraints imposed by the structure of the arm and the musculature used to control it—all these things conspired to lead to a solution which exactly suits the problem. If any of these constraints had not been included, the movement would have failed. The hand would have hit the cup or the terminal—or it would have missed the knob.

1.1.2 The Mutual Influence of Syntax and Semantics

Multiple constraints operate just as strongly in language processing as they do in reaching and grasping. Rumelhart (1977) has documented many of these multiple constraints. Rather than catalog them here, we will use a few examples from language to illustrate the fact that the constraints tend to be reciprocal: The example shows that they do not run only from syntax to semantics—they also run the other way.

It is clear, of course, that syntax constrains the assignment of meaning. Without the syntactic rules of English to guide us, we cannot correctly understand who has done what to whom in the following sentence:

The boy the man chased kissed the girl.

But consider these examples (Rumelhart 1977, Schank 1973):

I saw the grand canyon flying to New York.
I saw the sheep grazing in the field.

Our knowledge of syntactic rules alone does not tell us what grammatical role is played by the prepositional phrases in these two cases. In the first, "flying to New York" is taken as describing the context in which the speaker saw the Grand Canyon—while he was flying to New York. In the second, "grazing in the field" could syntactically describe an analogous situation, in which the speaker is grazing in the field, but this possibility does not typically become available on first reading. Instead we assign "grazing in the field" as a modifier of the sheep (roughly, "who were grazing in the field"). The syntactic structure of each of these sentences, then, is determined in part by the semantic relations that the constituents of the sentence might plausibly bear to one another. Thus, the influences appear to run both ways, from the syntax to the semantics and from the semantics to the syntax.

In these examples, we see how syntactic considerations influence semantic ones and how semantic ones influence syntactic ones. We cannot say that one kind of constraint is primary.

Mutual constraints operate, not only between syntactic and semantic processing, but also within each of these domains as well. Here we consider an example from syntactic processing, namely, the assignment of words to syntactic categories. Consider the sentences:

I like the joke.
I like the drive.
I like to joke.
I like to drive.

In this case it looks as though the words *the* and *to* serve to determine whether the following word will be read as a noun or a verb. This, of course, is a very strong constraint in English and can serve to force a verb interpretation of a word that is not ordinarily used this way:

I like to mud.

On the other hand, if the information specifying whether the function word preceding the final word *to* or *the* is ambiguous, then the typical reading of the word that follows it will determine which way the function word is heard. This was shown in an experiment by Isenberg, Walker, Ryder, and Schweikert (1980). They presented sounds halfway between *to* (actually /t^/) and *the* (actually /d^/) and found that words like *joke*, which we tend to think of first as nouns, made subjects hear the marginal stimuli as *the*, while words like *drive*, which we tend to think of first as verbs, made subjects hear the marginal stimuli as *to*. Generally, then, it would appear that each word can help constrain the syntactic role, and even the identity, of every other word.

1.1.3 Simultaneous Mutual Constraints in Word Recognition

Just as the syntactic role of one word can influence the role assigned to another in analyzing sentences, so the identity of one letter can influence the identity assigned to another in reading. A famous example of this, from Selfridge, is shown in Figure 2. Along with this is a second example in which none of the letters, considered separately, can be identified unambiguously, but in which the possibilities that the visual information leaves open for each so constrain the possible identities of the others that we are capable of identifying all of them.

At first glance, the situation here must seem paradoxical: The identity of each letter is constrained by the identities of each of the others. But since in general we cannot know the identities of any of the letters until we have established the identities of the others, how can we get the process started?

The resolution of the paradox, of course, is simple. One of the different possible letters in each position fits together with the others. It appears then that our perceptual system is capable of exploring all these possibilities without committing itself to one until all of the constraints are taken into account.

1.1.4 Understanding through the Interplay of Multiple Sources of Knowledge

It is clear that we know a good deal about a large number of different standard situations. Several theorists have suggested that we store this knowledge in terms of structures called variously: *scripts* (Schank 1976), *frames* (Min-

Figure 2. Some ambiguous displays. The first one is from Selfridge, 1955. The second line shows that three ambiguous characters can each constrain the identity of the others. The third, fourth, and fifth lines show that these characters are indeed ambiguous in that they assume other identities in other contexts. (The ink-blot technique of making letters ambiguous is due to Lindsay and Norman, 1972).

sky 1975), or *schemata* (Norman and Bobrow 1976; Rumelhart 1975). Such knowledge structures are assumed to be the basis of comprehension. A great deal of progress has been made within the context of this view.

However, it is important to bear in mind that most everyday situations cannot be rigidly assigned to just a single script. They generally involve an interplay between a number of different sources of information. Consider, for example, a child's birthday party at a restaurant. We know things about birthday parties, and we know things about restaurants, but we would not want to assume that we have explicit knowledge (at least, not in advance of our first restaurant birthday party) about the conjunction of the two. Yet we can imagine what such a party might be like. The fact that the party was being held in a restaurant would modify certain aspects of our expectations for birthday parties (we would not expect a game of Pin-the-Tail-on-the-Donkey, for example), while the fact that the event was a birthday party would inform our expectations for what would be ordered and who would pay the bill.

Representations like scripts, frames, and schemata are useful structures for encoding knowledge, although we believe they only approximate the underlying structure of knowledge representation. Our main point here is that any theory that tries to account for human knowledge using scriptlike knowledge structures will have to allow them to interact with each other to capture the generative capacity of human understanding in novel situations. Achieving such interactions has been one of the greatest difficulties associated with implementing models that really think generatively using script or framelike representations.

2. Parallel Distributed Processing

In the examples we have considered, a number of different pieces of information must be kept in mind at once. Each plays a part, constraining others and being constrained by them. What kinds of mechanisms seem well suited to these task demands? Intuitively, these tasks seem to require mechanisms in which each aspect of the information in the situation can act on other aspects, simultaneously influencing other aspects and being influenced by them. To articulate these intuitions, we and others have turned to a class of models we call *parallel distributed processing* (PDP) models. These models assume that information processing takes place through the interactions of a large number of simple processing elements called units, each sending excitatory and inhibitory signals to other units. In some cases, the units stand for possible hypotheses about such things as the letters in a particular display or the syntactic roles of the words in a particular sentence. In these cases, the activations stand roughly for the strengths associated with the different possible hypotheses, and the interconnections among the units stand for the constraints the system knows to exist between the hypotheses. In other cases, the units stand for possible goals and actions, such as the goal of typing a particular letter, or the action of moving the left index finger, and the connections relate goals to subgoals, subgoals to actions, and actions to muscle movements. In still other cases, units stand not for particular hypotheses or goals, but for aspects of these things. Thus a hypothesis about the identity of a word, for example, is itself distributed in the activations of a large number of units.

2.1 PDP Models: Cognitive Science or Neuroscience?

One reason for the appeal of PDP models is their obvious "physiological" flavor: They seem so much more closely tied to the physiology of the brain than are other kinds of information-processing models. The brain consists of a large number of highly interconnected elements (Figure 3) which apparently send very simple excitatory and inhibitory messages to each other and update their excitations on the basis of these simple messages. The properties of the units in many of the PDP models we will be exploring were inspired by basic properties of the neural hardware. In Rumelhart (1986) we examine in some detail the relation between PDP models and the brain.

Though the appeal of PDP models is definitely enhanced by their physiological plausibility and neural inspiration, these are not the primary bases for their appeal to us. We are, after all, cognitive scientists, and PDP models appeal to us for psychological and computational reasons. They hold out the hope of offering computationally sufficient and psychologically accurate mechanistic accounts of the phenomena of human cognition which have eluded successful explication in conventional computational formalisms; and

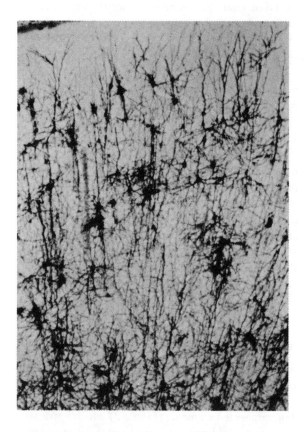

Figure 3. The arborizations of about 1 percent of the neurons near a vertical slice through the cerebral cortex. The full height of the figure corresponds to the thickness of the cortex, which is in this instance about 2 mm. (From Mechanics of the Mind, p. 84, by C. Blakemore 1977, Reprinted by permission.)

they have radically altered the way we think about the time course of processing, the nature of representation, and the mechanisms of learning.

2.1 The Microstructure of Cognition

The process of human cognition, examined on a time scale of seconds and minutes, has a distinctly sequential character to it. Ideas come, seem promising, and then are rejected; leads in the solution to a problem are taken up, then abandoned and replaced with new ideas. Though the process may not be discrete, it has a decidedly sequential character, with transitions from state-to-state occurring, say, two or three times a second. Clearly, any useful description of the overall organization of this sequential flow of thought will necessarily describe a sequence of states.

But what is the internal structure of each of the states in the sequence, and how do they come about? Serious attempts to model even the simplest macrosteps of cognition—say, recognition of single words—require vast numbers of microsteps if they are implemented sequentially. As Feldman and Ballard (1982) have pointed out, the biological hardware is just too sluggish for sequential models of the microstructure to provide a plausible account, at least of the microstructure of *human* thought. And the time limitation only gets worse, not better, when sequential mechanisms try to take large numbers of constraints into account. Each additional constraint requires more time in a sequential machine, and, if the constraints are imprecise, the constraints can lead to a computational explosion. Yet people get faster not slower, when they are able to exploit additional constraints.

Parallel distributed processing models offer alternatives to serial models of the microstructure of cognition. They do not deny that there is a macrostructure, just as the study of subatomic particles does not deny the existence of interactions between atoms. What PDP models do is describe the internal structure of the larger units, just as subatomic physics describes the internal structure of the atoms that form the constituents of larger units of chemical structure.

We shall show as we proceed through this chapter that the analysis of the microstructure of cognition has important implications for most of the central issues in cognitive science. In general, from the PDP point of view, the objects referred to in macrostructural models of cognitive processing are seen as approximate descriptions of emergent properties of the microstructure. Sometimes these approximate descriptions may be sufficiently accurate to capture a process or mechanism well enough but many times, we will argue, they fail to provide sufficiently elegant or tractable accounts that capture the very flexibility and open endedness of cognition that their inventors had originally intended to capture. We hope that our analysis of PDP models will show how an examination of the microstructure of cognition can lead us closer to an adequate description of the real extent of human processing and learning capacities.

The development of PDP models is still in its infancy. Thus far the models which have been proposed capture simplified versions of the kinds of phenomena we have been describing rather than the full elaboration that these phenomena display in real settings. But we think there have been enough steps forward in recent years to warrant a concerted effort at describing where the approach has gotten and where it is going now, and to point out some directions for the future.

3. Examples of PDP Models

In what follows, we review a number of recent applications of PDP models to problems in motor control, perception, memory, and language. In many cases, as we shall see, parallel distributed processing mechanisms are used to provide natural accounts of the exploitation of multiple, simultaneous, and often mutual constraints. We will also see that these same mechanisms exhibit emergent properties which lead to novel interpretations of phenomena which have traditionally been interpreted in other ways.

3.1 Motor Control

Having started with an example of how multiple constraints appear to operate in motor programming, it seems appropriate to mention two models in this domain. These models have not developed far enough to capture the full details of obstacle avoidance and multiple constraints on reaching and grasping, but there have been applications to two problems with some of these characteristics.

3.1.1 Finger Movements in Skilled Typing

One might imagine, at first glance, that typists carry out keystrokes successively, first programming one stroke and then, when it is completed, programming the next. However, this is not the case. For skilled typists, the fingers are continually anticipating upcoming keystrokes. Consider the word vacuum. In this word, the *v, a,* and *c* are all typed with the left hand, leaving the right hand nothing to do until it is time to type the first *u*. However, a high speed film of a good typist shows that the right hand moves up to anticipate the typing of the *u*, even as the left hand is just beginning to type the *v*. By the time the *c* is typed the right index finger is in position over the *u* and ready to strike it.

When two successive key strokes are to be typed with the fingers of the same hand, concurrent preparation to type both can result in similar or conflicting instructions to the fingers and/or the hand. Consider, in this light, the difference between the sequence *ev* and the sequence *er.* The first sequence requires the typist to move up from home row to type the *e* and to move down from the home row to type the *v,* while in the second sequence, both the *e* and the *r* are above the home row.

The hands take very different positions in these two cases. In the first case, the hand as a whole stays fairly stationary over the home row. The middle

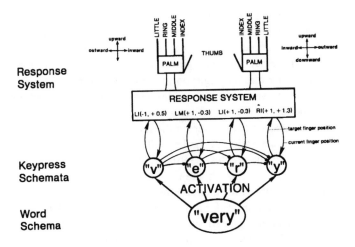

Figure 4. The interaction of activations in typing the word *very.* The *very* unit is activated from outside the model. It in turn activates the units for each of the component letters. Each letter unit specifies the target finger positions, specified in a keyboard coordinate system. L and R stand for the left and right hands, and I and M for the index and middle fingers. The letter units receive information about the current finger position from the response system. Each letter unit inhibits the activation of all letter units that follow it in the word: inhibitory connections are indicated by the lines with solid dots at their terminations (From Rumelhart and Norman 1982; Copyright 1982 by Ablex Publishing. Reprinted by permission.)

finger moves up to type the *e,* and the index finger moves down to type the *v.* In the second case, the hand as a whole moves up, bringing the middle finger over the *e* and the index finger over the *r.* Thus, we can see that several letters can simultaneously influence the positioning of the fingers and the hands.

From the point of view of optimizing the efficiency of the typing motion, these different patterns seem very sensible. In the first case, the hand as a whole is maintained in a good compromise position to allow the typist to strike both letters reasonably efficiently by extending the fingers up or down. In the second case, the need to extend the fingers is reduced by moving the whole hand up, putting it in a near optimal position to strike either key.

Rumelhart and Norman (1982) have simulated these effects using PDP mechanisms. Figure 4 illustrates aspects of the model as they are illustrated in typing the word *very.* In brief, Rumelhart and Norman assumed that the decision to type a word caused activation of a unit for that word. That unit, in turn, activated units corresponding to each of the letters in the word. The unit for the first letter to be typed was made to inhibit the units for the second and following letters, the unit for the second to inhibit the third and following letters, and so on. As a result of the interplay of activation and inhibition among these units, the unit for the first letter was at first the most strongly active, and the units for the other letters were partially activated.

Each letter unit exerts influences on the hand and finger involved in typing the letter. The v unit, for example, tends to cause the index finger to move down and to cause the whole hand to move down with it. The e unit, on the other hand, tends to cause the middle finger on the left hand to move up and to cause the whole hand to move up also. The r unit also causes the left index finger to move up and the left hand to move up with it.

The extent of the influences of each letter on the hand and finger it directs depends on the extent of the activation of the letter. Therefore, at first, in typing the word *very*, the v exerts the greatest control. Because the e and r are simultaneously pulling the hand up, though, the v is typed primarily by moving the index finger, and there is little movement on the whole hand.

Once a finger is within a certain striking distance of the key to be typed, the actual pressing movement is triggered, and the keypress occurs. The keypress itself causes a strong inhibitory signal to be sent to the unit for the letter just typed, thereby removing this unit from the picture and allowing the unit for the next letter in the word to become the most strongly activated.

This mechanism provides a simple way for all of the letters to jointly determine the successive configurations the hand will enter into in the process of typing a word. This model has shown considerable success predicting the time between successive keystrokes as a function of the different keys involved. Given a little noise in the activation process, it can also account for some of the different kinds of errors that have been observed in transcription typing.

The typing model represents an illustration of the fact that serial behavior—a succession of key strokes—is not necessarily the result of an inherently serial processing mechanism. In this model, the sequential structure of typing emerges from the interaction of the excitatory and inhibitory influences among the processing units.

3.1.2 Reaching for an Object without Falling Over

Similar mechanisms can be used to model the process of reaching for an object without losing one's balance while standing, as Hinton (1984) has shown. He considered a simple version of this task using a two-dimensional "person" with a foot, a lower leg, an upper leg, a trunk, an upper arm, and a lower arm. Each of these limbs is joined to the next at a joint which has a single degree of rotational freedom. The task posed to this person is to reach a target placed somewhere in front of it, without taking any steps and without falling down. This is a simplified version of the situation in which a real person has to reach out in front for an object placed somewhere in the plane that vertically bisects the body. The task is not as simple as it looks, since if we just swing an arm out in front of ourselves, it may shift our center of gravity so far forward that we will lose our balance. The problem, then, is to find a set of joint angles that simultaneously solves the two constraints on the task.

First, the tip of the forearm must touch the object. Second, to keep from falling down, the person must keep its center of gravity over the foot.

To do this, Hinton assigned a single processor to each joint. On each computational cycle, each processor received information about how far the tip of the hand was from the target and where the center of gravity was with respect to the foot. Using these two pieces of information, each joint adjusted its angle so as to approach the goals of maintaining balance and bringing the tip closer to the target. After a number of iterations, the stick-person settled on postures that satisfied the goal of reaching the target and the goal of maintaining the center of gravity over the "feet."

Though the simulation was able to perform the task, eventually satisfying both goals at once, it had a number of inadequacies stemming from the fact that each joint processor attempted to achieve a solution in ignorance of what the other joints were attempting to do. This problem was overcome by using additional processors responsible for setting combinations of joint angles. Thus, a processor for flexion and extension of the leg would adjust the knee, hip, and ankle joints synergistically, while a processor for flexion and extension of the arm would adjust the shoulder and elbow together. With the addition of processors of this form, the number of iterations required to reach a solution was greatly reduced, and the form of the approach to the solution looked very natural. The sequence of configurations attained in one processing run is shown in Figure 5.

Explicit attempts to program a robot to cope with the problem of maintaining balance as it reaches for a desired target have revealed the difficulty of deriving explicitly the right combinations of actions for each possible starting state and goal state. This simple model illustrates that we may be wrong to seek such an explicit solution. We see here that a solution to the problem can emerge from the action of a number of simple processors each attempting to honor the constraints independently.

3.2 Perception

3.2.1 Stereoscopic Vision

One early model using parallel distributed processing was the model of stereoscopic depth perception proposed by Marr and Poggio (1976). Their theory proposed to explain the perception of depth in random-dot stereograms (Julesz 1971, see Figure 6) in terms of a simple distributed processing mechanism.

Random-dot stereograms present interesting challenges to mechanisms of depth perception. A stereogram consists of two random-dot patterns. In a simple stereogram such as the one shown here, one pattern is an exact copy of the other except that the pattern of dots in a region of one of the patterns is

Figure 5. A sequence of configurations assumed by the stick "person" performing the reaching task described in the text, from Hinton (1984). The small circle represents the center of gravity of the whole stick-figure, and the cross represents the goal to be reached The configuration is shown on every second iteration.

Figure 6. Random-dot stereograms. The two patterns are identical except that the pattern of dots in the central region of the left pattern are shifted over with respect to those in the right. When viewed stereoscopically such that the left pattern projects to the left eye and the right pattern to the right eye, the shifted area appears to hover above the page. Some readers may be able to achieve this by converging to a distant point (e.g., a far wall) and then interposing the figure into the line of sight. (From Julesz 1971, Copyright 1971 by Bell Telephone Laboratories. Inc. Reprinted by permission.)

shifted horizontally with respect to the rest of the pattern. Each of the two patterns—corresponding to two retinal images—consists entirely of a pattern of random dots, so there is no information in either of the two views considered alone that can indicate the presence of different surfaces, let alone depth relations among those surfaces. Yet, when one of these dot patterns is projected to the left eye and the other to the right eye, an observer sees each region as a surface, with the shifted region hovering in front of or behind the other, depending on the direction of the shift.

What kind of a mechanism might we propose to account for these facts? Marr and Poggio (1976) began by explicitly representing the two views in two arrays, as human observers might in two different retinal images. They noted that corresponding black dots at different perceived distances from the observer will be offset from each other by different amounts in the two views. The job of the model is to determine which points correspond. This task is, of course, made difficult by the fact that there will be a very large number of spurious correspondences of individual dots. The goal of the mechanism, then, is to find those correspondences that represent real correspondences in depth and suppress those that represent spurious correspondences.

To carry out this task, Marr and Poggio assigned a processing unit to each possible conjunction of a point in one image and a point in the other. Since the eyes are offset horizontally, the possible conjunctions occur at various offsets or disparities along the horizontal dimension. Thus, for each point in one eye, there was a set of processing units with one unit assigned to the conjunction of that point and the point at each horizontal offset from it in the other eye.

Each processing unit received activation whenever both of the points the unit stood for contained dots. So far, then, units for both real and spurious correspondences would be equally activated. To allow the mechanism to find the right correspondences, they pointed out two general principles about the visual world: (a) Each point in each view generally corresponds to one and only one point in the other view, and (b) neighboring points in space tend to be at nearly the same depth and therefore at about the same disparity in the two images. While there are discontinuities at the edges of things, over most of a two-dimensional view of the world there will be continuity. These principles are called the *uniqueness* and *continuity* constraints, respectively.

Marr and Poggio incorporated these principles into the interconnections between the processing units. The uniqueness constraint was captured by inhibitory connections among the units that stand for alternative correspondences of the same dot. The continuity principle was captured by excitatory connections among the units that stand for similar offsets of adjacent dots.

These additional connections allow the Marr and Poggio model to "solve" stereograms like the one shown in the figure. At first, when a pair of patterns is presented, the units for all possible correspondences of a dot in one eye with a dot in the other will be equally excited. However, the excitatory connections cause the units for the correct conjunctions to receive more excitation than units for spurious conjunctions, and the inhibitory connections allow the units for the correct conjunctions to turn off the units for the spurious connections. Thus, the model tends to settle down into a stable state in which only the correct correspondence of each dot remains active.

There are a number of reasons why Marr and Poggio (1979) modified this model (see Marr 1982, for a discussion), but the basic mechanisms of mutual excitation between units that are mutually consistent and mutual inhibition between units that are mutually incompatible provide a natural mechanism for settling on the right conjunctions of points and rejecting spurious ones. The model also illustrates how general principles or rules such as the uniqueness and continuity principles may be embodied in the connections between processing units, and how behavior in accordance with these principles can emerge from the interactions determined by the pattern of these interconnections.

3.2.2 Perceptual Completion of Familiar Patterns

Perception, of course, is influenced by familiarity. It is a well-known fact that we often misperceive unfamiliar objects as more familiar ones and that we can get by with less time or with lower-quality information in perceiving familiar items than we need for perceiving unfamiliar items. Not only does familiarity help us determine what the higher-level structures are when the lower-level information is ambiguous; it also allows us to fill in missing lower-level information within familiar higher-order patterns. The well-known *phonemic restoration effect* is a case in point. In this phenomenon, perceivers hear sounds that have been cut out of words as if they had actually been present. For example, Warren (1970) presented *legi#lature* to subjects, with a click in the location marked by the #. Not only did subjects correctly identify the word legislature; they also heard the missing /s/ just as though it had been presented. They had great difficulty localizing the click, which they tended to hear as a disembodied sound. Similar phenomena have been observed in visual perception of words since the work of Pillsbury (1897).

Two of us have proposed a model describing the role of familiarity in perception based on excitatory and inhibitory interactions among units standing for various hypotheses about the input at different levels of abstraction (McClelland and Rumelhart 1981, Rumelhart and McClelland 1982). The model has been applied in detail to the role of familiarity in the perception of letters in visually presented words, and has proved to provide a very close account of the results of a large number of experiments.

The model assumes that there are units that act as detectors for the visual features which distinguish letters, with one set of units assigned to detect the features in each of the different letter positions in the word. For four-letter words, then, there are four such sets of detectors. There are also four sets of detectors for the letters themselves and a set of detectors for the words.

In the model, each unit has an activation value, corresponding roughly to the strength of the hypothesis that what that unit stands for is present in the perceptual input. The model honors the following important relations which hold between these "hypotheses" or activations: First, to the extent that two hypotheses are mutually consistent, they should support each other. Thus, units that are mutually consistent, in the way that the letter T in the first position is consistent with the word TAKE, tend to excite each other. Second, to the extent that two hypotheses are mutually inconsistent, they should weaken each other. Actually, we can distinguish two kinds of inconsistency: The first kind might be called between-level inconsistency. For example, the hypothesis that a word begins with a T is inconsistent with the hypothesis that the word is MOVE. The second might be called mutual exclusion. For example, the hypothesis that a word begins with T excludes the hypothesis that it begins with R since a word can only begin with one letter. Both kinds of inconsistencies operate in the word perception model to reduce the activations of units. Thus, the letter units in each position compete with all other letter units in the same position, and the word units compete with each other. This type of inhibitory interaction is often called *competitive inhibition*. In addition, there are inhibitory interactions between incompatible units on different levels. This type of inhibitory interaction is simply called *between-level inhibition*.

The set of excitatory and inhibitory interactions between units can be diagrammed by drawing excitatory and inhibitory links between them. The whole picture is too complex to draw, so we illustrate only with a fragment: Some of the interactions between some of the units in this model are illustrated in Figure 7.

Let us consider what happens in a system like this when a familiar stimulus is presented under degraded conditions. For example, consider the display shown in Figure 8. This display consists of the letters W, O, and R, completely visible, and enough of a fourth letter to rule out all letters other than R and K. Before onset of the display, the activations of the units are set at or below 0. When the display is presented, detectors for the features present in each position become active (i.e., their activations grow above 0). At this point, they begin to excite and inhibit the corresponding detectors for letters. In the first three positions, W, O, and R are unambiguously activated, so we will focus our attention on the fourth position where R and K are both equally consistent with the active features. Here, the activations of the detectors for R and K start out growing together, as the feature detectors below them become activated. As these detectors become active, they and the active letter detectors for W, O, and R in the other positions start to activate detectors for words which have these letters in them and to inhibit detectors for words which do not have these letters. A number of words are partially consistent with the active letters, and receive some net excitation from the letter level, but only the word *WORK* matches one of the active letters in all four positions. As a result, *WORK* becomes more active than any other word and inhibits the other words, thereby successfully dominating the pattern of activation among the word units. As it grows in strength, it sends feedback to the letter level, reinforcing the activations of the W, O, R, and K in the corre-

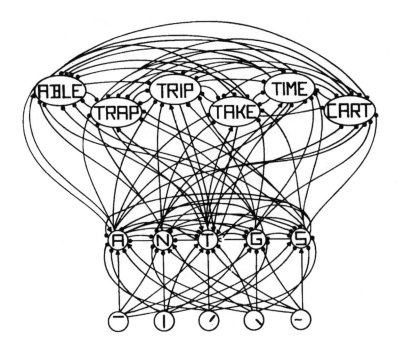

Figure 7. The unit for the letter T in the first position of a Fourier array and some of its neighbors. Note that the feature and letter units stand only for the first position; in a complete picture of the units needed from processing four-letter displays, there would be four full sets of feature detectors and four full sets of letter detectors. (From McClelland and Rumelhart 1981, Copyright 1981 by the American Psychological Association. Reprinted by permission.)

sponding positions. In the fourth position, this feedback gives *K* the upper hand over *R,* and eventually the stronger activation of the *K* detector allows it to dominate the pattern of activation, suppressing the *R* detector completely.

This example illustrates how PDP models can allow knowledge about what letters go together to form words to work together with natural constraints on the task (i.e., that there should only be one letter in one place at one time), to produce perceptual completion in a simple and direct way.

3.2.3 Completion of Novel Patterns

However, the perceptual intelligence of human perceivers far exceeds the ability to recognize familiar patterns and fill in missing portions. We also show facilitation in the perception of letters in unfamiliar letter strings which are wordlike but not themselves actually familiar.

One way of accounting for such performances is to imagine that the per-

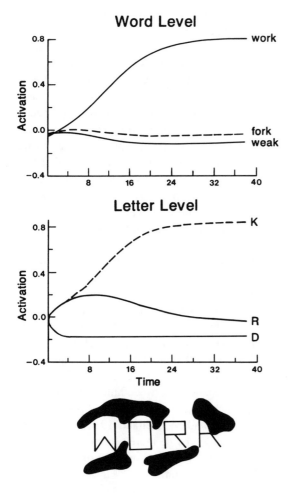

Figure 8. A possible display which might be presented to the interactive activation model of word recognition, and the resulting activations of selected letter and word units. The letter units are for the letters indicated in the fourth position of a four-letter display.

ceiver possesses, in addition to detectors for familiar words, sets of detectors for regular subword units such as familiar letter clusters, or that they use abstract rules, specifying which classes of letters can go with which others in different contexts. It turns out, however, that the model we have already described needs no such additional structure to produce perceptual facilitation for word-like letter strings; to this extent it acts as if it "knows" the orthographic structure of English. We illustrate this feature of the model with the example shown in Figure 9, where the nonword *YEAD* is shown in degraded form so that the second letter is incompletely visible. Given the information about this letter, considered alone, either *E* or *F* would be possible in the second position. Yet our model will tend to complete this letter as an *E*.

The reason for this behavior is that, when *YEAD* is shown, a number of words are partially activated. There is no word consistent with *Y, E,* or *F, A,* and *D,* but there are words which match *YEA_* (*YEAR,* for example) and others which match *_EAD* (*BEAD, DEAD, HEAD,* and *READ,* for example). These and other near misses are partially activated as a result of the pattern of activation at the letter level. While they compete with each other, none of these words gets strongly enough activated to completely suppress all the others. Instead, these units act as a group to reinforce particularly the letters *E* and *A.* There are no close partial matches which include the letter *F* in the second position, so this letter receives no feedback support. As a result, *E* comes to dominate, and eventually suppress, the *F* in the second position.

The fact that the word perception model exhibits perceptual facilitation to pronounceable nonwords as well as words illustrates once again how behavior in accordance with general principles or rules can emerge from the interactions of simple processing elements. Of course, the behavior of the word perception model does not implement exactly any of the systems of orthographic rules that have been proposed by linguists (Chomsky and Halle 1968, Venesky 1970) or psychologists (Spoehr and Smith 1975). In this regard, it only approximates such rule-based descriptions of perceptual processing. However, rule systems such as Chomsky and Halters or Venesky's appear to be only approximately honored in human performance as well (Smith and Baker 1976). Indeed, some of the discrepancies between human performance data and rule systems occur in exactly the ways that we would predict from the word perception model (Rumelhart and McClelland 1982). This illustrates the possibility that PDP models may provide more accurate accounts of the details of human performance than models based on a set of rules representing human competence—at least in some domains.

3.3 Retrieving Information From Memory

3.3.1 Content Addressability

One very prominent feature of human memory is that it is content addressable. It seems fairly clear that we can access information in memory based on nearly any attribute of the representation we are trying to retrieve.

Of course, some cues are much better than others. An attribute which is shared by a very large number of things we know about is not a very effective retrieval cue, since it does not accurately pick out a particular memory representation. But, several such cues, in conjunction, can do the job. Thus, if we ask a friend who goes out with several women, "Who was that woman I saw you with?" he may not know which one we mean—but if we specify

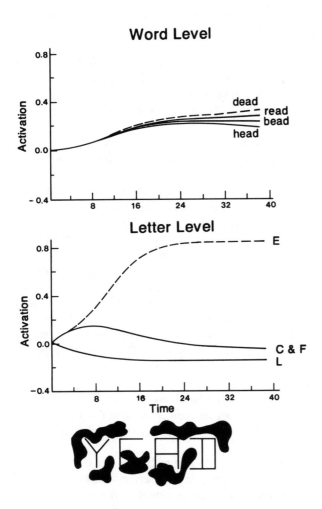

Figure 9. An example of a nonword display that might be presented to the interactive activation model of word recognition and the response of selected units at the letter and word levels. The letter units illustrated are detectors for letters in the second input position.

something else about her—say the color of her hair, what she was wearing (in so far as he remembers this at all), where we saw him with her—he will likely be able to hit upon the right one.

It is, of course, possible to implement some kind of content addressability of memory on a standard computer in a variety of different ways. One way is to search sequentially, examining each memory in the system to find the memory or the set of memories which has the particular content specified in the cue. An alternative, somewhat more efficient, scheme involves some form of indexing—keeping a list, for every content a memory might have, of which memories have that content.

Such an indexing scheme can be made to work with error-free probes, but it will break down if there is an error in the specification of the retrieval cue. There are possible ways of recovering from such errors, but they lead to the kind of combinatorial explosions which plague this kind of computer implementation.

But suppose that we imagine that each memory is represented by a unit which has mutually excitatory interactions with units standing for each of its properties. Then, whenever any property of the memory became active, the memory would tend to be activated, and whenever the memory was activated, all of its contents would tend to become activated. Such a scheme would automatically produce content addressability for us. Though it would not be immune to errors, it would not be devastated by an error in the probe if the remaining properties specified the correct memory.

As described thus far, whenever a property that is a part of a number of different memories is activated, it will tend to activate all of the memories it is in. To keep these other activities from swamping the "correct" memory unit, we simply need to add initial inhibitory connections among the memory units. An additional desirable feature would be mutually inhibitory interactions among mutually incompatible property units. For example, a person cannot both be single and married at the same time, so the units for different marital states would be mutually inhibitory.

McClelland (1981) developed a simulation model that illustrates how a system with these properties would act as a content addressable memory. The model is obviously oversimplified, but it illustrates many of the characteristics of more complex models.

Consider the information represented in Figure 10, which lists a number of people we might meet if we went to live in an unsavory neighborhood, and some of their hypothetical characteristics. A subset of the units needed to represent this information is shown in Figure 11. In this network, there is an "instance unit" for each of the characters described in Figure 10, and that unit is linked by mutually excitatory connections to all of the units for the fellow's properties. Note that we have included property units for the names of the characters, as well as units for their other properties.

Now, suppose we wish to retrieve the properties of a particular individual, say Lance. And suppose that we know Lance's name. Then we can probe the network by activating Lance's name unit, and we can see what pattern of activation arises as a result. Assuming that we know of no one else named Lance, we can expect the Lance name unit to be hooked up only to the instance unit for Lance. This will in turn activate the property units for Lance, thereby creating the pattern of activation corresponding to Lance. In effect,

The Jets and The Sharks

Name	Gang	Age	Edu	Mar	Occupation
Art	Jets	40's	J.H.	Sing.	Pusher
Al	Jets	30's	J.H.	Mar.	Burglar
Sam	Jets	20's	COL.	Sing.	Bookie
Clyde	Jets	40's	J.H.	Sing.	Bookie
Mike	Jets	30's	J.H.	Sing.	Bookie
Jim	Jets	20's	J.H.	Div.	Burglar
Greg	Jets	20's	H.S.	Mar.	Pusher
John	Jets	20's	J.H.	Mar.	Burglar
Doug	Jets	30's	H.S.	Sing.	Bookie
Lance	Jets	20's	J.H.	Mar.	Burglar
George	Jets	20's	J.H.	Div.	Burglar
Pete	Jets	20's	H.S.	Sing.	Bookie
Fred	Jets	20's	H.S.	Sing.	Pusher
Gene	Jets	20's	COL.	Sing.	Pusher
Ralph	Jets	30's	J.H.	Sing.	Pusher
Phil	Sharks	30's	COL.	Mar.	Pusher
Ike	Sharks	30's	J.H .	Sing.	Bookie
Nick	Sharks	30's	H.S.	Sing.	Pusher
Don	Sharks	30's	COL.	Mar.	Burglar
Ned	Sharks	30's	COL.	Mar.	Bookie
Karl	Sharks	40's	H.S.	Mar.	Bookie
Ken	Sharks	20's	H.S.	Sing.	Burglar
Earl	Sharks	40's	H.S.	Mar.	Burglar
Rick	Sharks	30's	H.S.	Div.	Burglar
Ol	Sharks	30's	COL.	Mar.	Pusher
Neal	Sharks	30's	H.S.	Sing.	Bookie
Dave	Sharks	30's	H.S.	Div.	Pusher

Figure 10. Characteristics of a number of individuals belonging to two gangs, the Jets and the Sharks. (From McClelland 1981. Copyright 1981 by J. L. McClelland. Reprinted by permission.)

we have retrieved a representation of Lance. More will happen than just what we have described so far, but for the moment let us stop here.

Of course, sometimes we may wish to retrieve a name, given other information. In this case, we might start with some of Lance's properties, effectively asking the system, say "Who do you know who is a Shark and in his 20s?" by activating the Shark and 20s units. In this case it turns out that there is a single individual, Ken, who fits the description. So, when we activate these two properties, we will activate the instance unit for Ken, and this in

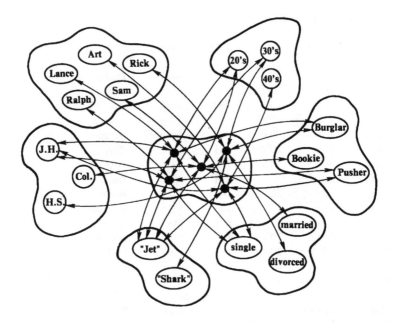

Figure 11. Some of the units and interconnections needed to represent the individuals shown in Figure 10. The units connected with double-headed arrows are mutually excitatory. All the units within the same cloud are mutually inhibitory. (From McClelland 1981, Copyright 1981 by J. L. McClelland. Reprinted by permission.)

turn will activate his name unit, and fill in his other properties as well.

3.3.2 Graceful Degradation

A few of the desirable properties of this kind of model are visible from considering what happens as we vary the set of features we use to probe the memory in an attempt to retrieve a particular individual's name. Any set of features which is sufficient to uniquely characterize a particular item will activate the instance node for that item more strongly than any other instance node. A probe which contains misleading features will most strongly activate the node that it matches best. This will clearly be a poorer cue than one which contains no misleading information—but it will still be sufficient to activate the "right answer" more strongly than any other, as long as the introduction of misleading information does not make the probe closer to some other item. In general, though the degree of activation of a particular instance node and of the corresponding name nodes varies in this model as a function of the exact content of the probe, errors in the probe will not be fatal unless they make the probe point to the wrong memory. This kind of model's handling of incomplete or partial probes also requires no special error-recovery scheme to work—it is a natural by-product of the nature of the retrieval mechanism that it is capable of graceful degradation.

These aspects of the behavior of the Jets and Sharks model deserve more detailed consideration than the present space allows. One reason we do not go into them is that we view this model as a stepping stone in the development of other models, such as the models using more distributed representations, that occur in Rumelhart (1986). We do, however, have more to say about this simple model, for like some of the other models we have already examined, this model exhibits some useful properties which emerge from the interactions of the processing units.

3.3.3 Default Assignment

It probably will have occurred to the reader that in many of the situations we have been examining, there will be other activations occurring which may influence the pattern of activation which is retrieved. So, in the case where we retrieved the properties of Lance, those properties, once they become active, can begin to activate the units for other individuals with those same properties. The memory unit for Lance will be in competition with these units and will tend to keep their activation down, but to the extent that they do become active, they will tend to activate their own properties and therefore fill them in. In this way, the model can fill in properties of individuals based on what it knows about other, similar instances.

To illustrate how this might work we have simulated the case in which we do not know that Lance is a Burglar as opposed to a Bookie or a Pusher. It turns out that there are a group of individuals in the set who are very similar to Lance in many respects. When Lance's properties become activated, these other units become partially activated, and they start activating their properties. Since they all share the same "occupation," they work together to fill in that property for Lance. Of course, there is no reason why this should necessarily be the right answer, but generally speaking, the more similar two things are in respects that we know about, the more likely they are to be similar in respects that we do not, and the model implements this heuristic.

3.3.4 Spontaneous Generalization

The model we have been describing has another valuable property as well—it tends to retrieve what is common to those memories which match a retrieval cue which is too general to capture any one memory. Thus, for example, we could probe the system by activating the unit corresponding to membership in the Jets. This unit will partially activate all the instances of the Jets, thereby causing each to send activations to its properties. In this way the model can retrieve the typical values that the members of the Jets have on each dimension—even though there is no one Jet that has these typical values. In the example, 9 of 15 Jets are single, 9 of 15 are in their 20s, and 9 of 15 have only a Junior High School education; when we probe by activating the Jet unit, all three of these properties dominate. The Jets are evenly divided between the three occupations, so each of these units becomes partially activated. Each has a different name, so that each name unit is very weakly activated, nearly cancelling each other out.

In the example just given of spontaneous generalization, it would not be unreasonable to suppose that someone might have explicitly stored a generalization about the members of a gang. The account just given would be an alternative to "explicit storage" of the generalization. It has two advantages, though, over such an account. First, it does not require any special generalization formation mechanism. Second, it can provide us with generalizations on unanticipated lines, on demand. Thus, if we want to know, for example, what people in their 20s with a junior high school education are like, we can probe the model by activating these two units. Since all such people are Jets and Burglars, these two units are strongly activated by the model in this case; two of them are divorced and two are married, so both of these units are partially activated.[1]

The sort of model we are considering, then, is considerably more than a content addressable memory. In addition, it performs default assignment, and it can spontaneously retrieve a general concept of the individuals that match any specifiable probe. These properties must be explicitly implemented as complicated computational extensions of other models of knowledge retrieval, but in PDP models they are natural by-products of the retrieval process itself.

4. Representation and Learning In PDP Models

In the Jets and Sharks model, we can speak of the model's active *representation* at a particular time, and associate this with the pattern of activation over the units in the system. We can also ask: What is the stored knowledge that gives rise to that pattern of activation? In considering this question, we see immediately an important difference between PDP models and other models of cognitive processes. In most models, knowledge is stored as a static copy of a pattern. Retrieval amounts to finding the pattern in long-term memory and copying it into a buffer or working memory. There is no real difference between the stored representation in long-term memory and the active representation in working memory. In PDP models, though, this is not the case. In these models, the patterns themselves are not stored. Rather, what is stored is the *connection strengths* between units that allow these patterns to be re-created. In the Jets and Sharks model, there is an instance unit assigned to each individual, but that unit does not contain a copy of the representation of that individual. Instead, it is simply the case that the connections between it and the other units in the system are such that activation of the unit will cause the pattern for the individual to be reinstated on the property units.

This difference between PDP models and conventional models has enormous implications, both for processing and for learning. We have already seen some of the implications for processing. The representation of the knowledge is set up in such a way that the knowledge necessarily influences the course of processing. Using knowledge in processing is no longer a matter of finding the relevant information in memory and bringing it to bear; it is part and parcel of the processing itself.

For learning, the implications are equally profound. For if the knowledge is the strengths of the connections, learning must be a matter of finding the right connection strengths so that the right patterns of activation will be produced under the right circumstances. This is an extremely important property of this class of models, for it opens up the possibility that an information processing mechanism could learn, as a result of tuning its connections, to capture the interdependencies between activations that it is exposed to in the course of processing.

In recent years, there has been quite a lot of interest in learning in cognitive science. Computational approaches to learning fall predominantly into what might be called the "explicit rule formulation" tradition, as represented by the work of Winston (1975), the suggestions of Chomsky and the ACT* model of J. R. Anderson (1983). All of this work shares the assumption that the goal of learning is to formulate explicit rules (propositions, productions, etc.) which capture powerful generalizations in a succinct way. Fairly powerful mechanisms, usually with considerable innate knowledge about a domain, and/or some starting set of primitive propositional representations, then formulate hypothetical general rules, e.g., by comparing particular cases and formulating explicit generalizations.

The approach that we take in developing PDP models is completely different. First, we do not assume that the goal of learning is the formulation of explicit rules. Rather, we assume it is the acquisition of connection strengths which allow a network of simple units to act *as though* it knew the rules. Second, we do not attribute powerful computational capabilities to the learning mechanism. Rather, we assume very simple connection strength modulation mechanisms which adjust the strength of connections between units based on information locally available at the connection.

These issues will be addressed at length in Rumelhart (1986). For now, our purpose is to give a simple, illustrative example of the connection strength modulation process, and how it can produce networks which exhibit some interesting behavior.

4.1 Local Versus Distributed Representation

Before we turn to an explicit consideration of this issue, we raise a basic question about representation. Once we have achieved the insight that the knowledge is stored in the strengths of the interconnections between units, a question arises. Is there any reason to assign one unit to each pattern that we wish to learn? Another possibility—one that we explore extensively in Rumelhart (1986)—is the possibility that the knowledge about any individual pattern is not stored in the connections of a special unit reserved for that pattern, but is distributed over the connections among a large number of processing units. On this view, the Jets and Sharks model represents a special case in which separate units are reserved for each instance.

Models in which connection information is explicitly thought of as distributed have been proposed by a number of investigators. The units in these collections may themselves correspond to conceptual primitives, or they may have no particular meaning as individuals. In either case, the focus shifts to patterns of activation over these units and to mechanisms whose explicit purpose is to learn the right connection strengths to allow the right patterns of activation to become activated under the right circumstances.

In the rest of this section, we will give a simple example of a PDP model in which the knowledge is distributed. We will first explain how the model would work, given pre-existing connections, and we will then describe how it could come to acquire the right connection strengths through a very simple learning mechanism. A number of models which have taken this distributed approach have been discussed in this book's predecessor, Hinton and J. A. Anderson's (1981) *Parallel Models of Associative Memory*. We will consider a simple version of a common type of distributed model, a pattern associator.

Pattern associators are models in which a pattern of activation over one set of units can cause a pattern of activation over another set of units without any intervening units to stand for either pattern as a whole. Pattern associators would, for example, be capable of associating a pattern of activation on one set of units corresponding to the appearance of an object with a pattern on another set corresponding to the aroma of the object, so that, when an object is presented visually, causing its visual pattern to become active, the model produces the pattern corresponding to its aroma.

4.2 How a Pattern Associator Works

For purposes of illustration, we present a very simple pattern associator in Figure 12. In this model, there are four units in each of two pools. The first pool, the A units, will be the pool in which patterns corresponding to the sight of various objects might be represented. The second pool, the B units, will be the pool in which the pattern corresponding to the aroma will be represented. We can pretend that alternative patterns of activation on the A units

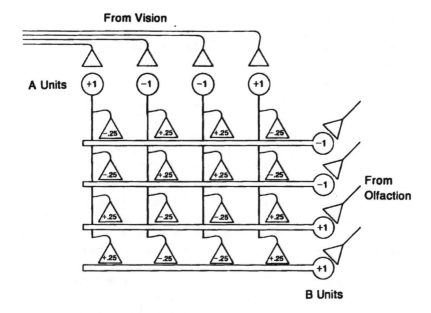

Figure 12. A simple pattern associator. The example assumes that patterns of activation in the A units can be produced by the visual system and patterns in the B units can be produced by the olfactory system. The synaptic connections allow the outputs of the A units to influence the activations of the B units. The synaptic weights linking the A units to the B units were selected so as to allow the pattern of activation shown on the A units to reproduce the pattern of activation shown on the B units without the need for any olfactory input.

are produced upon viewing a rose or a grilled steak, and alternative patterns on the B units are produced upon sniffing the same objects. Figure 13 shows two pairs of patterns, as well as sets of interconnections necessary to allow the A member of each pair to reproduce the B member.

The details of the behavior of the individual units vary among different versions of pattern associators. For present purposes, we'll assume that the units can take on positive or negative activation values, with 0 representing a kind of neutral intermediate value. The strengths of the interconnections between the units can be positive or negative real numbers.

The effect of an A unit on a B unit is determined by multiplying the activation of the A unit times the strength of its synaptic connection with the B unit. For example, if the connection from a particular A unit to a particular B unit has a positive sign, when the A unit is excited (activation greater than 0), it will excite the B unit. For this example, we'll simply assume that the activation of each unit is set to the sum of the excitatory and inhibitory effects operating on it. This is one of the simplest possible cases.

Suppose, now, that we have created on the A units the pattern correspond-

+1   −1   −1   +1   −1   +1   −1   +1

−.25	+.25	+.25	−.25	−1
−.25	+.25	+.25	−.25	−1
+.25	−.25	−.25	+.25	+1
+.25	−.25	−.25	+.25	+1

+.25	−.25	+.25	−.25	−1
−.25	+.25	−.25	+.25	+1
−.25	+.25	−.25	+.25	+1
+.25	−.25	+.25	−.25	−1

Figure 13. Two simple associators represented as matrices. The weights in the two matrices allow the A pattern shown above the matrix to produce the B pattern shown to the right of it. Note that the weights in the first matrix are the same as those shown in the diagram in Figure 12.

ing to the first visual pattern shown in Figure 13, the rose. How should we arrange the strengths of the interconnections between the A units and the B units to reproduce the pattern corresponding to the aroma of a rose? We simply need to arrange for each A unit to tend to excite each B unit which has a positive activation in the aroma pattern and to inhibit each B unit which has a negative activation in the aroma pattern. It turns out that this goal is achieved by setting the strength of the connection between a given A unit and a given B unit to a value proportional to the product of the activation of the two units. In Figure 12, the weights on the connections were chosen to allow the A pattern illustrated there to produce the illustrated B pattern according to this principle. The actual strengths of the connections were set to ±.25, rather than ± 1, so that the A pattern will produce the right magnitude, as well as the right sign, for the activations of the units in the B pattern. The same connections are reproduced in matrix form in Figure 13 (left).

Pattern associators like the one in Figure 12 have a number of nice properties. One is that they do not require a perfect copy of the input to produce the correct output, though its strength will be weaker in this case. For example, suppose that the associator shown in Figure 12 were presented with an A pattern of (1,—1,0,1). This is the A pattern shown in the figure, with the activation of one of its elements set to 0. The B pattern produced in response will have the activations of all of the B units in the right direction; however, they will be somewhat weaker than they would be, had the complete A pattern been shown. Similar effects are produced if an element of the pattern is distorted—or if the model is damaged, either by removing whole units, or random sets of connections, etc. Thus, the pattern retrieval performance of the model degrades gracefully both under degraded input and under damage.

4.3 How a Pattern Associator Learns

So far, we have seen how we as model builders can construct the right set of weights to allow one pattern to cause another. The interesting thing, though, is that we do not need to build these interconnection strengths in by hand. Instead, the pattern associator can teach itself the right set of interconnections through experience processing the patterns in conjunction with each other.

A number of different rules for adjusting connection strengths have been proposed. One of the first—and definitely the best known—is due to D. O. Hebb (1949). Hebb's actual proposal was not sufficiently quantitative to build into an explicit model. However, a number of different variants can trace their ancestry back to Hebb. Perhaps the simplest version is:

When unit A and unit B are simultaneously excited, increase the strength of the connection between them.

A natural extension of this rule to cover the positive and negative activation values allowed in our example is:

Adjust the strength of the connection between units A and B in proportion to the product of their simultaneous activation.

In this formulation, if the product is positive, the change makes the connection more excitatory, and if the product is negative, the change makes the connection more inhibitory. For simplicity of reference, we will call this the Hebb rule, although it is not exactly Hebb's original formulation.

With this simple learning rule, we could train a "blank copy" of the pattern associator shown in Figure 12 to produce the B pattern for rose when the A pattern is shown, simply by presenting the A and B patterns together and modulating the connection strengths according to the Hebb rule. The size of the change made on every trial would, of course, be a parameter. We generally assume that the changes made on each instance are rather small, and that connection strengths build up gradually. The values shown in Figure 13 (left), then, would be acquired as a result of a number of experiences with the A and B pattern pair.

It is very important to note that the information needed to use the Hebb rule to determine the value each connection should have is locally available at the connection. All a given connection needs to consider is the activation of the units on both sides of it. Thus, it would be possible to actually implement such a connection modulation scheme locally, in each connection, without requiring any programmer to reach into each connection and set it to just the right value.

It turns out that the Hebb rule as stated here has some serious limitations, and, to our knowledge, no theorists continue to use it in this simple form. More sophisticated connection modulation schemes have been proposed by other workers; most important among these are the delta rule, the competitive learning rule, and the rules for learning in stochastic parallel models. All of these learning rules have the property that they adjust the strengths of connections between units on the basis of information that can be assumed to be locally available to the unit. Learning, then, in all of these cases, amounts to a very simple process that can be implemented locally at each connection without the need for any overall supervision. Thus, models which incorpo-

$$\begin{bmatrix} - & + & + & - \\ - & + & + & - \\ + & - & - & + \\ + & - & - & + \end{bmatrix} + \begin{bmatrix} + & - & + & - \\ - & + & - & + \\ - & + & - & + \\ + & - & + & - \end{bmatrix} = \begin{bmatrix} & & ++ & -- \\ -- & ++ & & \\ & & -- & ++ \\ ++ & -- & & \end{bmatrix}$$

Figure 14. The weights in the third matrix allow either A pattern shown in Figure 13 to recreate the corresponding B pattern. Each weight in this case is equal to the sum of the weight for the A pattern and the weight for the B pattern, as illustrated.

rate these learning rules train themselves to have the right interconnections in the course of processing the members of an ensemble of patterns.

4.4 Learning Multiple Patterns in the Same Set of Interconnections

Up to now, we have considered how we might teach our pattern associator to associate the visual pattern for one object with a pattern for the aroma of the same object. Obviously, different patterns of interconnections between the A and B units are appropriate for causing the visual pattern for a different object to give rise to the pattern for its aroma. The same principles apply, however, and if we presented our pattern associator with the A and B patterns for steak, it would learn the right set of interconnections for that case instead (these are shown in Figure 13, right). In fact, it turns out that we can actually teach the same pattern associator a number of different associations. The matrix representing the set of interconnections that would be learned if we taught the same pattern associator both the rose association and the steak association is shown in Figure 14. The reader can verify this by adding the two matrices for the individual patterns together. The reader can also verify that this set of connections will allow the rose A pattern to produce the rose B patterns and the steak A pattern to produce the steak B pattern: when either input pattern is presented, the correct corresponding output is produced.

The examples used here have the property that the two different visual patterns are completely uncorrelated with each other. This being the case, the rose pattern produces no effect when the interconnections for the steak have been established, and the steak pattern produces no effect when the interconnections for the rose association are in effect. For this reason, it is possible to add together the pattern of interconnections for the rose association and the pattern for the steak association, and still be able to associate the sight of the steak with the smell of a steak and the sight of a rose with the smell of a rose. The two sets of interconnections do not interact at all.

One of the limitations of the Hebbian learning rule is that it can learn the connection strengths appropriate to an entire ensemble of patterns only when all the patterns are completely uncorrelated. This restriction does not, however, apply to pattern associators which use more sophisticated learning schemes.

4.5 Attractive Properties of Pattern Associator Models

Pattern associator models have the property that uncorrelated patterns do not interact with each other, but more similar ones do. Thus, to the extent that a new pattern of activation on the A units is similar to one of the old ones, it will tend to have similar effects. Furthermore, if we assume that learning the interconnections occurs in small increments, similar patterns will essentially reinforce the strengths of the links they share in common with other patterns. Thus, if we present the same pair of patterns over and over, but each time we add a little random noise to each element of each member of the pair, the system will automatically learn to associate the central tendency of the two patterns and will learn to ignore the noise. What will be stored will be an average of the similar patterns with the slight variations removed. On the other hand, when we present the system with completely uncorrelated patterns, they will not interact with each other in this way. Thus, the same pool of units can extract the central tendency of each of a number of pairs of unrelated patterns.

4.6 Extracting the Structure of an Ensemble of Patterns

The fact that similar patterns tend to produce similar effects allows distributed models to exhibit a kind of spontaneous generalization, extending behavior appropriate for one pattern to other similar patterns. This property is shared by other PDP models, such as the word perception model and the Jets and Sharks model described above; the main difference here is in the existence of simple, local, learning mechanisms that can allow the acquisition of the connection strengths needed to produce these generalizations through experience with members of the ensemble of patterns. Distributed models have another interesting property as well: If there are regularities in the correspondences between pairs of patterns, the model will naturally extract these regularities. This property allows distributed models to acquire patterns of interconnections that lead them to behave in ways we ordinarily take as evidence for the use of linguistic rules.

Here, we describe the model very briefly. The model is a mechanism that learns how to construct the past tenses of words from their root forms through repeated presentations of examples of root forms paired with the corresponding past-tense form. The model consists of two pools of units. In one pool, patterns of activation representing the phonological structure of the root form of the verb can be represented, and, in the other, patterns representing the phonological structure of the past tense can be represented. The goal of the model is simply to learn the right connection strengths between the root units and the past-tense units, so that whenever the root form of a verb is presented the model will construct the corresponding past-tense form. The model is trained by presenting the root form of the verb as a pattern of activation over the root units, and then using a simple, local, learning rule to adjust the connection strengths so that this root form will tend to produce the correct pattern of activation over the past-tense units. The model is tested by simply presenting the root form as a pattern of activation over the root units and examining the pattern of activation produced over the past-tense units.

The model is trained initially with a small number of verbs children learn early in the acquisition process. At this point in learning, it can only produce appropriate outputs for inputs that it has explicitly been shown. But as it learns more and more verbs, it exhibits two interesting behaviors. First, it produces the standard *ed* past tense when tested with pseudo-verbs or verbs it has never seen. Second, it "overregularizes" the past tense of irregular words it previously completed correctly. Often, the model will blend the irregular past tense of the word with the regular *ed* ending, and produce errors like *CAMED* as the past of *COME*. These phenomena mirror those observed in the early phases of acquisition of control over past tenses in young children.

The generativity of the child's responses—the creation of regular past tenses of new verbs and the overregularization of the irregular verbs—has been taken as strong evidence that the child has induced the rule which states that the regular correspondence for the past tense in English is to add a final *ed* (Berko 1958). On the evidence of its performance, then, the model can be said to have acquired the rule. However, no special rule-induction mechanism is used, and no special language-acquisition device is required. The model learns to behave in accordance with the rule, not by explicitly noting that most words take *ed* in the past tense in English and storing this rule away explicitly, but simply by building up a set of connections in a pattern associator through a long series of simple learning experiences. The same mechanisms of parallel distributed processing and connection modification which are used in a number of domains serve, in this case, to produce implicit knowledge tantamount to a linguistic rule. The model also provides a fairly detailed account of a number of the specific aspects of the error patterns children make in learning the rule. In this sense, it provides a richer and more detailed description of the acquisition process than any that falls out naturally from the assumption that the child is building up a repertoire of explicit but inaccessible rules.

There is a lot more to be said about distributed models of learning, about their strengths and their weaknesses, than we have space for in this preliminary consideration. For now we hope mainly to have suggested that they provide dramatically different accounts of learning and acquisition than are offered by traditional models of these processes. We saw in earlier sections of this chapter that performance in accordance with rules can emerge from the interactions of simple, interconnected units. Now we can see how the aquisition of performance that conforms to linguistic rules can emerge from a simple, local, connection strength modulation process.

We have seen what the properties of PDP models are in informal terms, and we have seen how these properties operate to make the models do many of the kinds of things that they do. Now we wish to describe some of the major sources of inspiration for the PDP approach.

5. Origins of Parallel Distributed Processing

The ideas behind the PDP approach have a history that stretches back indefinitely. In this section, we mention briefly some of the people who have thought in these terms, particularly those whose work has had an impact on our own thinking. This section should not been seen as an authoritative review of the history, but only as a description of our own sources of inspiration.

Some of the earliest roots of the PDP approach can be found in the work of the unique neurologists, Jackson (1869/1958) and Luria (1966). Jackson was a forceful and persuasive critic of the simplistic localizationist doctrines of late nineteenth century neurology, and he argued convincingly for distributed, multilevel conceptions of processing systems. Luria, the Russian psychologist and neurologist, put forward the notion of the *dynamic functional system*. On this view, every behavioral or cognitive process resulted from the coordination of a large number of different components, each roughly localized in different regions of the brain, but all working together in dynamic interaction. Neither Hughlings-Jackson nor Luria is noted for the clarity of his views, but we have seen in their ideas a rough characterization of the kind of parallel distributed processing system we envision.

Two other contributors to the deep background of PDP were Hebb (1949) and Lashley (1950). We already have noted Hebb's contribution of the Hebb rule of synaptic modification; he also introduced the concept of cell assemblies—a concrete example of a limited form of distributed processing—and discussed the idea of reverberation of activation within neural networks. Hebb's ideas were cast more in the form of speculations about neural functioning than in the form of concrete processing models, but his thinking captures some of the flavor of parallel distributed processing mechanisms. Lashley's contribution was to insist upon the idea of distributed representation. Lashley may have been too radical and too vague, and his doctrine of equipotentiality of broad regions of cortex clearly overstated the case. Yet many of his insights into the difficulties of storing the "engram" locally in the brain are telling, and he seemed to capture quite precisely the essence of distributed representation in insisting that "there are no special cells reserved for special memories" (Lashley 1950, p. 500).

In the 1950s, there were two major figures whose ideas have contributed to the development of our approach. One was Rosenblatt (1959, 1962) and the other was Selfridge (1955). In his *Principles of Neurodynamics* (1962), Rosenblatt articulated clearly the promise of a neurally inspired approach to computation, and he developed the perceptron convergence procedure, an important advance over the Hebb rule for changing synaptic connections. Rosenblatt's work was very controversial at the time, and the specific models he proposed were not up to all the hopes he had for them. But his vision of the human information processing system as a dynamic, interactive, self-organizing system lies at the core of the PDP approach. Selfridge's contribution was his insistence on the importance of interactive processing, and the development of *Pandemonium,* an explicitly computational example of a dynamic, interactive mechanism applied to computational problems in perception.

In the late 1960s and early 1970s, serial processing and the von Neumann computer dominated both psychology and artificial intelligence, but there were a number of researchers who proposed neural mechanisms which capture much of the flavor of PDP models. Among these figures, the most influential in our work have been J. A. Anderson, Grossberg, and Longuet-Higgins. Grossberg's mathematical analysis of the properties of neural networks led him to many insights we have only come to appreciate through extensive experience with computer simulation, and he deserves credit for seeing the relevance of neurally inspired mechanisms in many areas of perception and memory well before the field was ready for these kinds of ideas (Grossberg 1978). Grossberg (1976) was also one of the first to analyze some of the properties of the competitive learning mechanism. Anderson's work differs from Grossberg's in insisting upon distributed representation, and in showing the relevance of neurally inspired models for theories of concept learning (Anderson 1973, 1977). Anderson's work also played a crucial role in the formulation of the cascade model (McClelland 1979), a step away from serial processing down the road to PDP. Longuet-Higgins and his group at Edinburgh were also pursuing distributed memory models during the same period, and David Willshaw, a member of the Edinburgh group, provided some very elegant mathematical analyses of the properties of various distributed representation schemes (Willshaw 1981). Many of the contributions of Anderson, Willshaw, and other distributed modelers may be found in Hinton and Anderson (1981). Others who have made important contributions to learning in PDP models include Amari (1977a), Bienenstock, Cooper, and Munro (1982), Fukushima (1975), Kohonen (1977, 1984), and von der Malsburg (1973).

Toward the middle of the 1970s, the idea of parallel processing began to have something of a renaissance in computational circles. We have already mentioned the Marr and Poggio (1976) model of stereoscopic depth perception. Another model from this period, the HEARSAY model of speech understanding, played a prominent role in the development of our thinking. Unfortunately, HEARSAY's computational architecture was too demanding for the available computational resources, and so the model was not a computational success. But its basically parallel, interactive character inspired the interactive model of reading (Rumelhart 1977), and the interactive activation model of word recognition (McClelland and Rumelhart 1981, Rumelhart and McClelland 1982).

The ideas represented in the interactive activation model had other precursors as well. Morton's *logogen* model (Morton 1969) was one of the first models to capture concretely the principle of interaction of different sources of information, and Marslen-Wilson (e.g., Marslen-Wilson and Welsh 1978) provided important empirical demonstrations of interaction between different levels of language processing. Levin's (1976) *Proteus* model demonstrated the virtues of activation-competition mechanisms, and Glushko (1979) helped us see how conspiracies of partial activations could account for certain aspects of apparently rule-guided behavior.

Our work also owes a great deal to a number of colleagues who have been working on related ideas in recent years. Feldman and Ballard (1982) laid out many of the computational principles of the PDP approach (under the name of *connectionism*), and stressed the biological implausibility of most of the prevailing computational models in artificial intelligence. Hofstadter (1979, 1985) deserves credit for stressing the existence of a subcognitive—what we call microstructural—level, and pointing out how important it can be to delve into the microstructure to gain insight. A sand dune, he has said, is not a gram of sand. Others have contributed crucial technical insights. Sutton and Barto (1981) provided an insightful analysis of the connection modification scheme we call the *delta rule* and illustrated the power of the rule to account for some of the subtler properties of classical conditioning. And Hopfield's (1982) contribution of the idea that network models can be seen as seeking minima in energy landscapes played a prominent role in the development of the Boltzmann machine, and in the crystallization of ideas on harmony theory and schemata.

The power of parallel distributed processing is becoming more and more apparent, and many others have recently joined in the exploration of the capabilities of these mechanisms. We hope this chapter represents the nature of the enterprise we are all involved in, and that it does justice to the potential of the PDP approach.

Acknowledgments

This research was supported by Contract N00014-79-C-0323, NR 667-437 with the Personnel and Training Research Programs of the Office of Naval Research, by grants from the System Development Foundation, and by an NIMH Career Development Award (MH00385) to the first author.

Notes

1. In this and all other cases, there is a tendency for the pattern of activation to be influenced by partially activated, near neighbors, which do not quite match the probe. Thus, in this case, there is a Jet Al, who is a Married Burglar. The unit for Al gets slightly activated; giving Married a slight edge over Divorced in the simulation.

13

Intelligence Without Representation

Rodney A. Brooks

1. Introduction

Artificial intelligence started as a field whose goal was to replicate human level intelligence in a machine. Early hopes diminished as the magnitude and difficulty of that goal was appreciated. Slow progress was made over the next 25 years in demonstrating isolated aspects of intelligence. Recent work has tended to concentrate on commercializable aspects of "intelligent assistants" for human workers.

No one talks about replicating the full gamut of human intelligence any more. Instead we see a retreat into specialized subproblems, such as ways to represent knowledge, natural language understanding, vision or even more specialized areas such as truth maintenance systems or plan verification. All the work in these subareas is benchmarked against the sorts of tasks humans do within those areas. Amongst the dreamers still in the field of AI (those not dreaming about dollars, that is), there is a feeling that one day all these pieces will all fall into place and we will see "truly" intelligent systems emerge.

However, I, and others, believe that human level intelligence is too complex and little understood to be correctly decomposed into the right sub-pieces at the moment and that even if we knew the subpieces we still wouldn't know the right interfaces between them. Furthermore, we will never understand how to decompose human level intelligence until we've had a lot of practice with simpler level intelligences.

In this chapter I therefore argue for a different approach to creating artificial intelligence:

- We must incrementally build up the capabilities of intelligent systems, having complete systems at each step of the way and thus automatically ensure that the pieces and their interfaces are valid.

- At each step we should build complete intelligent systems that we let loose in the real world with real sensing and real action. Anything less provides a candidate with which we can delude ourselves.

We have been following this approach and have built a series of autonomous mobile robots. We have reached an unexpected conclusion (C) and have a rather radical hypothesis (H).

C. When we examine very simple level intelligence we find that explicit representations and models of the world simply get in the way. It turns out to be better to use the world as its own model.

H. Representation is the wrong unit of abstraction in building the bulkiest parts of intelligent systems.

Representation has been the central issue in artificial intelligence work over the last 15 years only because it has provided an interface between otherwise isolated modules and conference papers.

2. The Evolution of Intelligence

We already have an existence proof of the possibility of intelligent entities: human beings. Additionally, many animals are intelligent to some degree. (This is a subject of intense debate, much of which really centers around a definition of intelligence.) They have evolved over the 4.6 billion year history of the earth.

It is instructive to reflect on the way in which earth-based biological evolution spent its time. Single-cell entities arose out of the primordial soup roughly 3.5 billion years ago. A billion years passed before photosynthetic plants appeared. After almost another billion and a half years, around 550 million years ago, the first fish and vertebrates arrived, and then insects 450 million years ago. Then things started moving fast. Reptiles arrived 370 million years ago, followed by dinosaurs at 330 and mammals at 250 million years ago. The first primates appeared 120 million years ago and the immediate predecessors to the great apes a mere 18 million years ago. Man arrived in roughly his present form 2.5 million years ago. He invented agriculture a mere 19,000 years ago, writing less than 5000 years ago and "expert" knowledge only over the last few hundred years.

This suggests that problem solving behavior, language, expert knowledge and application, and reason, are all pretty simple once the essence of being and reacting are available. That essence is the ability to move around in a dynamic environment, sensing the surroundings to a degree sufficient to achieve the necessary maintenance of life and reproduction. This part of intelligence is where evolution has concentrated its time—it is much harder.

I believe that mobility, acute vision and the ability to carry out survival-related tasks in a dynamic environment provide a necessary basis for the development of true intelligence. Moravec (1984) argues this same case rather eloquently.

Human level intelligence has provided us with an existence proof but we must be careful about what the lessons are to be gained from it.

2.1. A Story

Suppose it is the 1890s. Artificial flight is the glamour subject in science, engineering, and venture capital circles. A bunch of AF researchers are miraculously transported by a time machine to the 1980s for a few hours. They spend the whole time in the passenger cabin of a commercial passenger Boeing 747 on a medium duration flight.

Returned to the 1890s they feel vigorated, knowing that AF is possible on a grand scale. They immediately set to work duplicating what they have seen. They make great progress in designing pitched seats, double pane windows, and know that if only they can figure out those weird "plastics" they will have their grail within their grasp. (A few connectionists amongst them caught a glimpse of an engine with its cover off and they are preoccupied with inspirations from that experience.)

3. Abstraction as a Dangerous Weapon

Artificial intelligence researchers are fond of pointing out that AI is often denied its rightful successes. The popular story goes that when nobody has any good idea of how to solve a particular sort of problem (e.g., playing chess) it is known as an AI problem. When an algorithm developed by AI researchers successfully tackles such a problem, however, AI detractors claim that since the problem was solvable by an algorithm, it wasn't really an AI problem after all. Thus AI never has any successes. But have you ever heard of an AI failure?

I claim that AI researchers are guilty of the same (self) deception. They

partition the problems they work on into two components. The AI component, which they solve, and the non-AI component which they don't solve.
Typically, AI "succeeds" by defining the parts of the problem that are un-
solved as not AI. The principal mechanism for this partitioning is abstraction. Its application is usually considered part of good science, not, as it is in
fact used in AI, as a mechanism for self-delusion. In AI, abstraction is usually used to factor out all aspects of perception and motor skills. I argue below
that these are the hard problems solved by intelligent systems, and further
that the shape of solutions to these problems constrains greatly the correct
solutions of the small pieces of intelligence which remain.

Early work in AI concentrated on games, geometrical problems, symbolic
algebra, theorem proving, and other formal systems (e.g., Feigenbaum and
Feldman 1963, and Minsky 1968). In each case the semantics of the domains
were fairly simple.

In the late 1960s and early 1970s the blocks world became a popular domain for AI research. It had a uniform and simple semantics. The key to success was to represent the state of the world completely and explicitly. Search
techniques could then be used for planning within this well-understood
world. Learning could also be done within the blocks world; there were only
a few simple concepts worth learning and they could be captured by enumerating the set of subexpressions which must be contained in any formal description of a world including an instance of the concept. The blocks world
was even used for vision research and mobile robotics, as it provided strong
constraints on the perceptual processing necessary (Nilsson 1984).

Eventually criticism surfaced that the blocks world was a "toy world" and
that within it there were simple special purpose solutions to what should be
considered more general problems. At the same time there was a funding crisis within AI (both in the US and the UK, the two most active places for AI
research at the time). AI researchers found themselves forced to become relevant. They moved into more complex domains, such as trip planning, going
to a restaurant, medical diagnosis, etc.

Soon there was a new slogan: "Good representation is the key to AI" (e.g.,
conceptually efficient programs in Bobrow and Brown 1975). The idea was
that by representing only the pertinent facts explicitly, the semantics of a
world (which on the surface was quite complex) were reduced to a simple
closed system once again. Abstraction to only the relevant details thus simplified the problems.

Consider a chair for example. While the following two characterizations
are true:

(CAN (SIT-ON PERSON CHAIR)), (CAN (STAND-ON PERSON CHAIR)),

there is much more to the concept of a chair. Chairs have some flat (maybe)
sitting place, with perhaps a back support. They have a range of possible

sizes, requirements on strength, and a range of possibilities in shape. They often have some sort of covering material, unless they are made of wood, metal or plastic. They sometimes are soft in particular places. They can come from a range of possible styles. In particular the concept of what is a chair is hard to characterize simply. There is certainly no AI vision program which can find arbitrary chairs in arbitrary images; they can at best find one particular type of chair in carefully selected images.

This characterization, however, is perhaps the correct AI representation of solving certain problems; e.g., a person sitting on a chair in a room is hungry and can see a banana hanging from the ceiling just out of reach. Such problems are never posed to AI systems by showing them a photo of the scene. A person (even a young child) can make the right interpretation of the photo and suggest a plan of action. For AI planning systems however, the experimenter is required to abstract away most of the details to form a simple description in terms of atomic concepts such as PERSON, CHAIR and BANANAS.

But this abstraction is the essence of intelligence and the hard part of the problems being solved. Under the current scheme the abstraction is done by the researchers leaving little for the AI programs to do but search. A truly intelligent program would study the photograph, perform the abstraction and solve the problem.

The only input to most AI programs is a restricted set of simple assertions deduced from the real data by humans. The problems of recognition, spatial understanding, dealing with sensor noise, partial models, etc. are all ignored. These problems are relegated to the realm of input black boxes. Psychophysical evidence suggests they are all intimately tied up with the representation of the world used by an intelligent system.

There is no clean division between perception (abstraction) and reasoning in the real world. The brittleness of current AI systems attests to this fact. For example, MYCIN (Shortliffe 1976) is an expert at diagnosing human bacterial infections, but it really has no model of what a human (or any living creature) is or how they work, or what are plausible things to happen to a human. If told that the aorta is ruptured and the patient is losing blood at the rate of a pint every minute, MYCIN will try to find a bacterial cause of the problem.

Thus, because we still perform all the abstractions for our programs, most AI work is still done in the blocks world. Now the blocks have slightly different shapes and colors, but their underlying semantics have not changed greatly.

It could be argued that performing this abstraction (perception) for AI programs is merely the normal reductionist use of abstraction common in all good science. The abstraction reduces the input data so that the program experiences the same perceptual world (*Merkwelt* in von Uexküll 1921) as humans. Other (vision) researchers will independently fill in the details at some other time and place. I object to this on two grounds. First, as von Uexküll and others have pointed out, each animal species, and clearly each robot species with their own distinctly non-human sensor suites, will have their own different *Merkwelt*. Second, the *Merkwelt* we humans provide our programs is based on our own introspection. It is by no means clear that such a *Merkwelt* is anything like what we actually use internally—it could just as easily be an output coding for communication purposes (e.g., most humans go through life never realizing they have a large blind spot almost in the center of their visual fields).

The first objection warns of the danger that reasoning strategies developed for the human-assumed *Merkwelt* may not be valid when real sensors and perception processing is used. The second objection says that even with human sensors and perception the *Merkwelt* may not be anything like that used by humans. In fact, it may be the case that our introspective descriptions of our internal representations are completely misleading and quite different from what we really use.

3.1. A Continuing Story

Meanwhile our friends in the 1890s are busy at work on their AF machine. They have come to agree that the project is too big to be worked on as a single entity and that they will need to become specialists in different areas. After all, they had asked questions of fellow passengers on their flight and discovered that the Boeing Company employed over 6000 people to build such an airplane.

Everyone is busy but there is not a lot of communication between the groups. The people making the passenger seats used the finest solid steel available as the framework. There was some muttering that perhaps they should use tubular steel to save weight, but the general consensus was that if such an obviously big and heavy airplane could fly then clearly there was no problem with weight.

On their observation flight none of the original group managed to get a glimpse of the driver's seat, but they have done some hard thinking and think they have established the major constraints on what should be there and how it should work. The pilot, as he will be called, sits in a seat above a glass floor so that he can see the ground below so he will know where to land. There are some side mirrors so he can watch behind for other approaching airplanes. His controls consist of a foot pedal to control speed (just as in these newfangled automobiles that are starting to appear), and a steering wheel to turn left and right. In addition, the wheel stem can be pushed forward and back to make the airplane go up and down. A clever arrangement of pipes measures airspeed of the airplane and displays it on a dial. What more could one want? Oh yes. There's a rather nice setup of louvers in the windows so that the driver can get fresh air without getting the full blast of the wind in his face. An interesting sidelight is that all the researchers have by now abandoned the study of aerodynamics. Some of them had intensely questioned their fellow passengers on this subject and not one of the modern flyers had known a thing about it. Clearly the AF researchers had previously been wasting their time in its pursuit.

4. Incremental Intelligence

I wish to build completely autonomous mobile agents that co-exist in the world with humans, and are seen by those humans as intelligent beings in their own right. I will call such agents *Creatures*. This is my intellectual motivation. I have no particular interest in demonstrating how human beings work, although humans, like other animals, are interesting objects of study in this endeavor as they are successful autonomous agents. I have no particular interest in applications; it seems clear to me that if my goals can be met then the range of applications for such Creatures will be limited only by our (or their) imagination. I have no particular interest in the philosophical implications of Creatures, although clearly there will be significant implications.

Given the caveats of the previous two sections and considering the parable of the AF researchers, I am convinced that I must tread carefully in this endeavor to avoid some nasty pitfalls.

For the moment then, consider the problem of building Creatures as an engineering problem. We will develop an *engineering methodology* for building Creatures.

First, let us consider some of the requirements for our Creatures.

- A Creature must cope appropriately and in a timely fashion with changes in its dynamic environment.

- A Creature should be robust with respect to its environment; minor changes in the properties of the world should not lead to total collapse of the Creature's behavior; rather one should expect only a gradual change in capabilities of the Creature as the environment changes more and more.

- A Creature should be able to maintain multiple goals and, depending on the circumstances it finds itself in, change which particular goals it is actively pursuing; thus it can both adapt to surroundings and capitalize on fortuitous circumstances.

- A Creature should do something in the world; it should have some purpose in being.

Now, let us consider some of the valid engineering approaches to achieving these requirements. As in all engineering endeavors it is necessary to decompose a complex system into parts, build the parts, then interface them into a complete system.

4.1. Decomposition by Function

Perhaps the strongest traditional notion of intelligent systems (at least implicitly among AI workers) has been of a central system, with perceptual modules as inputs and action modules as outputs. The perceptual modules deliver a symbolic description of the world and the action modules take a symbolic description of desired actions and make sure they happen in the world. The central system then is a symbolic information processor.

Traditionally, work in perception (and vision is the most commonly studied form of perception) and work in central systems has been done by different researchers and even totally different research laboratories. Vision workers are not immune to earlier criticisms of AI workers. Most vision research is presented as a transformation from one image representation (e.g., a raw grey scale image) to another registered image (e.g., an edge image). Each group, AI and vision, makes assumptions about the shape of the symbolic interfaces. Hardly anyone has ever connected a vision system to an intelligent central system. Thus the assumptions independent researchers make are not forced to be realistic. There is a real danger from pressures to neatly circumscribe the particular piece of research being done.

The central system must also be decomposed into smaller pieces. We see subfields of artificial intelligence such as "knowledge representation," "learning," "planning," "qualitative reasoning," etc. The interfaces between these modules are also subject to intellectual abuse.

When researchers working on a particular module get to choose both the inputs and the outputs that specify the module requirements I believe there is little chance the work they do will fit into a complete intelligent system.

This bug in the functional decomposition approach is hard to fix. One needs a long chain of modules to connect perception to action. In order to test any of them they all must first be built. But until realistic modules are built it is highly unlikely that we can predict exactly what modules will be needed or what interfaces they will need.

4.2. Decomposition by Activity

An alternative decomposition makes no distinction between peripheral systems, such as vision, and central systems. Rather the fundamental slicing up of an intelligent system is in the orthogonal direction dividing it into *activity* producing subsystems. Each activity, or behavior producing system individually connects sensing to action. We refer to an activity producing system as a *layer.* An activity is a pattern of interactions with the world. Another name for our activities might well be *skill,* emphasizing that each activity can, at least post facto, be rationalized as pursuing some purpose. We have chosen the word activity, however, because our layers must decide when to act for themselves, not be some subroutine to be invoked at the beck and call of some other layer. The advantage of this approach is that it gives an incremental path from very simple systems to complex autonomous intelligent systems. At each step of the way it is only necessary to build one small piece, and interface it to an existing, working, complete intelligence.

The idea is to first build a very simple complete autonomous system, and *test it in the real world*. Our favorite example of such a system is a Creature, actually a mobile robot, which avoids hitting things. It senses objects in its immediate vicinity and moves away from them, halting if it senses something in its path. It is still necessary to build this system by decomposing it into parts, but there need be no clear distinction between a "perception subsystem," a "central system" and an "action system." In fact, there may well be two independent channels connecting sensing to action (one for initiating motion, and one for emergency halts), so there is no single place where "perception" delivers a representation of the world in the traditional sense.

Next we build an incremental layer of intelligence which operates in parallel to the first system. It is pasted on to the existing debugged system and tested again in the real world. This new layer might directly access the sensors and run a different algorithm on the delivered data. The first-level autonomous system continues to run in parallel, and unaware of the existence of the second level. For example, in Brooks (1986) we reported on building a first layer of control which let the Creature avoid objects and then adding a layer which instilled an activity of trying to visit distant visible places. The second layer injected commands to the motor control part of the first layer directing the robot towards the goal, but independently the first layer would cause the robot to veer away from previously unseen obstacles. The second layer monitored the progress of the Creature and sent updated motor commands, thus achieving its goal without being explicitly aware of obstacles, which had been handled by the lower level of control.

5. Who Has the Representations?

With multiple layers, the notion of perception delivering a description of the world gets blurred even more as the part of the system doing perception is spread out over many pieces which are not particularly connected by data paths or related by function. Certainly there is no identifiable place where the "output" of perception can be found. Furthermore, totally different sorts of processing of the sensor data proceed independently and in parallel, each affecting the overall system activity through quite different channels of control.

In fact, not by design, but rather by observation we note that a common theme in the ways in which our layered and distributed approach helps our Creatures meet our goals is that there is no central representation.

- Low-level simple activities can instill the Creature with reactions to dangerous or important changes in its environment. Without complex representations and the need to maintain those representations and reason about them, these reactions can easily be made quick enough to serve their purpose. The key idea is to sense the environment often, and so have an up-to-date idea of what is happening in the world.

- By having multiple parallel activities, and by removing the idea of a central representation, there is less chance that any given change in the class of properties enjoyed by the world can cause total collapse of the system. Rather one might expect that a given change will at most incapacitate some but not all of the levels of control. Gradually as a more alien world is entered (alien in the sense that the properties it holds are different from the properties of the world in which the individual layers were debugged), the performance of the Creature might continue to degrade. By not trying to have an analogous model of the world, centrally located in the system, we are less likely to have built in a dependence on that model being completely accurate. Rather, individual layers extract only those *aspects* (Agre and Chapman 1986) of the world which they find relevant—projections of a representation into a simple subspace, if you like. Changes in the fundamental structure of the world have less chance of being reflected in every one of those projections than they would have of showing up as a difficulty in matching some query to a central single world model.

- Each layer of control can be thought of as having its own implicit purpose (or goal if you insist). Since they are *active* layers, running in parallel and with access to sensors, they can monitor the environment and decide on the appropriateness of their goals. Sometimes goals can be abandoned when circumstances seem unpromising, and other times fortuitous circumstances can be taken advantage of. The key idea here is to be using the world as its own model and to continuously match the preconditions of each goal against the real world. Because there is separate hardware for each layer we can match as many goals as can exist in parallel, and do not pay any price for higher numbers of goals as we would if we tried to add more and more sophistication to a single processor, or even some multiprocessor with a capacity-bounded network.

- The purpose of the Creature is implicit in its higher-level purposes, goals or layers. There need be no explicit representation of goals that some central (or distributed) process selects from to decide what is most appropriate for the Creature to do next.

5.1. No Representation Versus No Central Representation

Just as there is no central representation there is not even a central system. Each activity producing layer connects perception to action directly. It is only the observer of the Creature who imputes a central representation or central control. The Creature itself has none; it is a collection of competing behaviors. Out of the local chaos of their interactions there emerges, in the eye of an observer, a coherent pattern of behavior. There is no central purposeful locus of control. Minsky (1986) gives a similar account of how human behavior is generated.

Note carefully that we are not claiming that chaos is a necessary ingredient of intelligent behavior. Indeed, we advocate careful engineering of all the interactions within the system (evolution had the luxury of incredibly long time scales and enormous numbers of individual experiments and thus perhaps was able to do without this careful engineering).

We do claim however, that there need be no explicit representation of either the world or the intentions of the system to generate intelligent behaviors for a Creature. Without such explicit representations, and when viewed locally, the interactions may indeed seem chaotic and without purpose.

I claim there is more than this, however. Even at a local level we do not have traditional AI representations. We never use tokens which have any semantics that can be attached to them. The best that can be said in our implementation is that one number is passed from a process to another. But it is only by looking at the state of both the first and second processes that that number can be given any interpretation at all. An extremist might say that we really do have representations, but that they are just implicit. With an appropriate mapping of the complete system and its state to another domain, we could define a representation that these numbers and topological connections between processes somehow encode.

However we are not happy with calling such things a representation. They differ from standard representations in too many ways.

There are no variables (e.g., see Agre and Chapman [1986] for a more thorough treatment of this) that need instantiation in reasoning processes. There are no rules which need to be selected through pattern matching. There are no choices to be made. To a large extent the state of the world determines the action of the Creature. Simon (1969) noted that the complexity of behavior of a system was not necessarily inherent in the complexity of the creature, but perhaps in the complexity of the environment. He made this analysis in his description of an ant wandering the beach, but ignored its implications in the next paragraph when he talked about humans. We hypothesize (following Agre and Chapman) that much of even human level activity is similarly a reflection of the world through very simple mechanisms without detailed representations.

6. The Methodology in Practice

In order to build systems based on an activity decomposition so that they are truly robust we must rigorously follow a careful methodology.

6.1. Methodological Maxims

First, it is vitally important to test the Creatures we build in the real world; i.e., in the same world that we humans inhabit. It is disastrous to fall into the temptation of testing them in a simplified world first, even with the best intentions of later transferring activity to an unsimplified world. With a simplified world (matte painted walls, rectangular vertices everywhere, colored blocks as the only obstacles) it is very easy to accidentally build a submodule of the system which happens to rely on some of those simplified properties. This reliance can then easily be reflected in the requirements on the interfaces between that submodule and others. The disease spreads and the complete system depends in a subtle way on the simplified world. When it comes time to move to the unsimplified world, we gradually and painfully realize that every piece of the system must be rebuilt. Worse than that we may need to rethink the total design as the issues may change completely. We are not so concerned that it might be dangerous to test simplified Creatures first and later add more sophisticated layers of control because evolution has been successful using this approach.

Second, as each layer is built it must be tested extensively in the real world. The system must interact with the real world over extended periods. Its behavior must be observed and be carefully and thoroughly debugged. When a second layer is added to an existing layer there are three potential sources of bugs: the first layer, the second layer, or the interaction of the two layers. Eliminating the first of these source of bugs as a possibility makes finding bugs much easier. Furthermore, there is only one thing possible to vary in order to fix the bugs—the second layer.

6.2. An Instantiation of the Methodology

We have built a series of four robots based on the methodology of task decomposition. They all operate in an unconstrained dynamic world (laboratory and office areas in the MIT Artificial Intelligence Laboratory). They successfully operate with people walking by, people deliberately trying to confuse them, and people just standing by watching them. All four robots are Creatures in the sense that on power-up they exist in the world and interact with it, pursuing multiple goals determined by their control layers implementing different activities. This is in contrast to other mobile robots that are given programs or plans to follow for a specific mission.

The four robots are shown in Figure 1. Two are identical, so there are real-

Figure 1. The four MIT AI laboratory Mobots. Left-most is the first built Allen, which relies on an offboard LISP machine for computation support. The right-most one is Herbert, shown with a 24 node CMOS parallel processor surrounding its girth. New sensors and fast early vision processors are still to be built and installed. In the middle are Tom and Jerry, based on a commercial toy chassis, with single PALs (Programmable Array of Logic) as their controllers.

ly three designs. One uses an offboard Lisp machine for most of its computations, two use onboard combinational networks, and one uses a custom onboard parallel processor. All the robots implement the same abstract architecture, which we call the *subsumption architecture,* which embodies the fundamental ideas of decomposition into layers of task achieving behaviors, and incremental composition through debugging in the real world. Details of these implementations can be found in Brooks (1986).

Each layer in the subsumption architecture is composed of a fixed topology network of simple finite state machines. Each finite state machine has a handful of states, one or two internal registers, one or two internal timers, and access to simple computational machines, which can compute things such as vector sums. The finite state machines run asynchronously, sending and receiving fixed length messages (1-bit messages on the two small robots, and 24-bit messages on the larger ones) over *wires*. On our first robot these were virtual wires; on our later robots we have used physical wires to connect computational components.

There is no central locus of control. Rather, the finite state machines are data-driven by the messages they receive. The arrival of messages or the expiration of designated time periods cause the finite state machines to change state. The finite state machines have access to the contents of the messages and might output them, test them with a predicate and conditionally branch to a different state, or pass them to simple computation elements. There is no possibility of access to global data, nor of dynamically established communications links. There is thus no possibility of global control. All finite state machines are equal, yet at the same time they are prisoners of their fixed topology connections.

Layers are combined through mechanisms we call *suppression* (whence the name subsumption architecture) and *inhibition*. In both cases as a new layer is added, one of the new wires is side-tapped into an existing wire. A pre-defined time constant is associated with each side-tap. In the case of suppression the side-tapping occurs on the input side of a finite state machine. If a message arrives on the net wire it is directed to the input port of the finite state machine as though it had arrived on the existing wire. Additionally, any new messages on the existing wire are suppressed (i.e., rejected) for the specified time period. For inhibition the sidetapping occurs on the output side of a finite state machine. A message on the new wire simply inhibits messages being emitted on the existing wire for the specified time period. Unlike suppression the new message is not delivered in their place.

As an example, consider the three layers of Figure 2. These are three layers of control that we have run on our first mobile robot for well over a year. The robot has a ring of twelve ultrasonic sonars as its primary sensors. Every second these sonars are run to give twelve radial depth measurements. Sonar is extremely noisy due to many objects being mirrors to sonar. There are thus problems with specular reflection and return paths following multiple reflections due to surface skimming with low angles of incidence (less than thirty degrees) .

In more detail the three layers work as follows:

(1) The lowest-level layer implements a behavior which makes the robot (the physical embodiment of the Creature) avoid hitting objects. It both avoids static objects and moving objects, even those that are actively attacking it. The finite state machine labeled *sonar* simply runs the sonar devices and every second emits an instantaneous map with the readings converted to polar coordinates. This map is passed on to the *collide* and *feelforce* finite state machine. The first of these simply watches to see if there is anything dead ahead, and if so sends a *halt* message to the finite state machine in charge of running the robot forwards—if that finite state machine is not in the correct state the message may well be ignored. Simultaneously, the other finite state machine computes a repulsive force on the robot, based on an inverse square law, where each sonar return is considered to indicate the presence of a repulsive object. The contributions from each sonar are added to produce an overall force acting on the robot. The output is passed to the *runaway* machine which thresh-

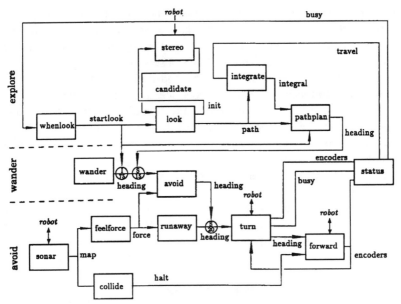

Figure 2. We wire finite state machines together into layers of control. Each layer is built on top of existing layers. Lower level layers never rely on the existence of higher level layers.

olds it and passes it on to the *turn* machine which orients the robot directly away from the summed repulsive force. Finally, the *forward* machine drives the robot forward. Whenever this machine receives a halt message while the robot is driving forward, it commands the robot to halt.

This network of finite state machines generates behaviors which let the robot avoid objects. If it starts in the middle of an empty room it simply sits there. If someone walks up to it, the robot moves away. If it moves in the direction of other obstacles it halts. Overall, it manages to exist in a dynamic environment without hitting or being hit by objects.

(2) The next layer makes the robot wander about, when not busy avoiding objects. The *wander* finite state machine generates a random heading for the robot every ten seconds or so. The *avoid* machine treats that heading as an attractive force and sums it with the repulsive force computed from the sonars. It uses the result to suppress the lower-level behavior, forcing the robot to move in a direction close to what *wander* decided but at the same time avoid any obstacles. Note that if the *turn* and *forward* finite state machines are busy running the robot the new impulse to wander will be ignored.

(3) The third layer makes the robot try to explore. It looks for distant places, then tries to reach them. This layer suppresses the wander layer, and observes how the bottom layer diverts the robot due to obstacles (perhaps dynamic). It corrects for any divergences and the robot achieves the goal.

The *whenlook* finite state machine notices when the robot is not busy moving, and starts up the free space finder (labeled stereo in the diagram) finite state machine. At the same time it inhibits wandering behavior so that the observation will remain valid. When a path is observed it is sent to the *pathplan* finite state machine, which injects a commanded direction to the *avoid* finite state machine. In this way, lower-level obstacle avoidance continues to function. This may cause the robot to go in a direction different to that desired by *pathplan*. For that reason the actual path of the robot is monitored by the *integrate* finite state machine, which sends updated estimates to the *pathplan* machine. This machine then acts as a difference engine forcing the robot in the desired direction and compensating for the actual path of the robot as it avoids obstacles.

These particular layers were implemented on our first robot. See Brooks (1986) for more details. Brooks and Connell (1986) report on another three layers implemented on that particular robot.

7. What This Is Not

The subsumption architecture with its network of simple machines is reminiscent, at the surface level at least, with a number of mechanistic approaches to intelligence, such as connectionism and neural networks. But it is different in many respects for these endeavors, and also quite different from many other post-Dartmouth traditions in artificial intelligence. We very briefly explain those differences in the following sections.

7.1. It Isn't Connectionism

Connectionists try to make networks of simple processors. In that regard, the things they build (in simulation only—no connectionist has ever driven a real robot in a real environment, no matter how simple) are similar to the subsumption networks we build. However, their processing nodes tend to be uniform and they are looking (as their name suggests) for revelations from understanding how to connect them correctly (which is usually assumed to mean richly at least). Our nodes are all unique finite state machines and the density of connections is very much lower, certainly not uniform, and very low indeed between layers. Additionally, connectionists seem to be looking for explicit distributed representations to spontaneously arise from their networks. We harbor no such hopes because we believe representations are not necessary and appear only in the eye or mind of the observer.

7.2. It Isn't Neural Networks

Neural networks is the parent discipline of which connectionism is a recent incarnation. Workers in neural networks claim that there is some biological significance to their network nodes, as models of neurons. Most of the models seem wildly implausible given the paucity of modeled connections relative to the thousands found in real neurons. We claim no biological significance in our choice of finite state machines as network nodes.

7.3. It Isn't Production Rules

Each individual activity producing layer of our architecture could be viewed as an implementation of a production rule. When the right conditions are met in the environment a certain action will be performed. We feel that analogy is a little like saying that any Fortran program with IF statements is implementing a production rule system. A standard production system really is more—it has a rule base, from which a rule is selected based on matching preconditions of all the rules to some database. The preconditions may include variables which must be matched to individuals in the database. Our layers run in parallel and have no variables or need for matching. Instead, aspects of the world are extracted and these directly trigger or modify certain behaviors of the layer.

7.4. It Isn't a Blackboard

If one really wanted, one could make an analogy of our networks to a blackboard control architecture. Some of the finite state machines would be localized knowledge sources. Others would be processes acting on these knowledge sources by finding them on the blackboard. There is a simplifying point in our architecture however: all the processes know exactly where to look on the blackboard as they are hard-wired to the correct place. I think this forced analogy indicates its own weakness. There is no flexibility at all on where a process can gather appropriate knowledge. Most advanced blackboard architectures make heavy use of the general sharing and availability of almost all knowledge. Furthermore, in spirit at least, blackboard systems tend to hide from a consumer of knowledge who the particular producer was. This is the primary means of abstraction in blackboard systems. In our system we make such connections explicit and permanent.

7.5. It Isn't German Philosophy

In some circles much credence is given to Heidegger as one who understood the dynamics of existence. Our approach has certain similarities to work inspired by this German philosopher (e.g., Agre and Chapman 1986) but our work was not so inspired. It is based purely on engineering considerations. That does not preclude it from being used in philosophical debate as an example on any side of any fence, however.

8. Limits to Growth

Since our approach is a performance-based one, it is the performance of the systems we build which must be used to measure its usefulness and to point to its limitations.

We claim that as of mid-1987 our robots, using the subsumption architecture to implement complete Creatures, are the most reactive real-time mobile robots in existence. Most other mobile robots are still at the stage of individual "experimental runs" in static environments, or at best in completely mapped static environments. Ours, on the other hand, operate completely autonomously in complex dynamic environments at the flick of their on switches, and continue until their batteries are drained. We believe they operate at a level closer to simple insect level intelligence than to bacteria level intelligence. Our goal (worth nothing if we don't deliver) is simple insect level intelligence within two years. Evolution took 3 billion years to get from single cells to insects, and only another 500 million years from there to humans. This statement is not intended as a prediction of our future performance, but rather to indicate the nontrivial nature of insect level intelligence.

Despite this good performance to date, there are a number of serious questions about our approach. We have beliefs and hopes about how these questions will be resolved, but under our criteria only performance truly counts. Experiments and building more complex systems take time, so with the caveat that the experiments described below have not yet been performed we outline how we currently see our endeavor progressing. Our intent in discussing this is to indicate that there is at least a plausible path forward to more intelligent machines from our current situation.

Our belief is that the sorts of activity producing layers of control we are developing (mobility, vision and survival related tasks) are necessary prerequisites for higher-level intelligence in the style we attribute to human beings.

The most natural and serious questions concerning limits of our approach are:

- How many layers can be built in the subsumption architecture before the interactions between layers become too complex to continue?

- How complex can the behaviors be that are developed without the aid of central representations?

- Can higher-level functions such as learning occur in these fixed topology networks of simple finite state machines?

We outline our current thoughts on these questions.

8.1. How Many Layers?

The highest number of layers we have run on a physical robot is three. In simulation we have run six parallel layers. The technique of completely debugging the robot on all existing activity producing layers before designing and adding a new one seems to have been practical till now at least.

8.2. How Complex?

We are currently working towards a complex behavior pattern on our fourth robot which will require approximately fourteen individual activity producing layers.

The robot has infrared proximity sensors for local obstacle avoidance. It has an onboard manipulator which can grasp objects at ground and table-top levels, and also determine their rough weight. The hand has depth sensors mounted on it so that homing in on a target object in order to grasp it can be controlled directly. We are currently working on a structured light laser scanner to determine rough depth maps in the forward looking direction from the robot.

The high-level behavior we are trying to instill in this Creature is to wander around the office areas of our laboratory, find open office doors, enter, retrieve empty soda cans from cluttered desks in crowded offices and return them to a central repository.

In order to achieve this overall behavior a number of simpler task achieving behaviors are necessary. They include: avoiding objects, following walls, recognizing doorways and going through them, aligning on learned landmarks, heading in a homeward direction, learning homeward bearings at landmarks and following them, locating table-like objects, approaching such objects, scanning table tops for cylindrical objects of roughly the height of a soda can, serving the manipulator arm, moving the hand above sensed objects, using the hand sensor to look for objects of soda can size sticking up from a background, grasping objects if they are light enough, and depositing objects.

The individual tasks need not be coordinated by any central controller. Instead they can index off of the state of the world. For instance the grasp behavior can cause the manipulator to grasp any object of the appropriate size seen by the hand sensors. The robot will not randomly grasp just any object however, because it will only be when other layers or behaviors have noticed an object of roughly the right shape on top of a table-like object that the grasping behavior will find itself in a position where its sensing of the world tells it to react. If, from above, the object no longer looks like a soda can, the grasp reflex will not happen and other lower-level behaviors will cause the robot to look elsewhere for new candidates.

8.3. Is Learning and Such Possible?

Some insects demonstrate a simple type of learning that has been dubbed "learning by instinct" (Gould and Marler 1986). It is hypothesized that honey bees for example are pre-wired to learn how to distinguish certain classes of flowers, and to learn routes to and from a home hive and sources of nectar.

Other insects, butterflies, have been shown to be able to learn to distinguish flowers, but in an information limited way (Lewis 1986). If they are forced to learn about a second sort of flower, they forget what they already knew about the first, in a manner that suggests the total amount of information which they know, remains constant.

We have found a way to build fixed topology networks of our finite state machines which can perform learning, as an isolated subsystem, at levels comparable to these examples. At the moment of course we are in the very position we lambasted most AI workers for earlier in this chapter. We have an isolated module of a system working, and the inputs and outputs have been left dangling.

We are working to remedy this situation, but experimental work with physical Creatures is a nontrivial and time consuming activity. We find that almost any pre-designed piece of equipment or software has so many preconceptions of how they are to be used built in to them, that they are not flexible enough to be a part of our complete systems. Thus, as of mid-1987, our work in learning is held up by the need to build a new sort of video camera and high-speed low-power processing box to run specially developed vision algorithms at 10 frames per second. Each of these steps is a significant engineering endeavor which we are undertaking as fast as resources permit.

Of course, talk is cheap.

8. 4 The Future

Only experiments with real creatures in real worlds can answer the natural doubts about our approach. Time will tell.

Acknowledgement

This chapter describes research done at the Artificial Intelligence Laboratory of the Massachusetts Institute of Technology. Support for the research is provided in part by an IBM Faculty Development Award, in part by a grant from the Systems Development Foundation, in part by the University Research Initiative under Office of Naval Research contract N00014-86-K-0685 and in part by the Advanced Research Projects Agency under Office of Naval Research contract N00014-85-K-0124.

Phil Agre, David Chapman, Peter Cudhea, Anita Flynn, David Kirsh and Thomas Marill made many helpful comments on earlier drafts of this chapter.

PART THREE

Weak Method Problem Solving

In the late 1950s and early 1960s Allen Newell and Herbert Simon wrote several computer programs to test the hypothesis that intelligent behavior resulted from heuristic search. Their first major program, the *Logic Theorist* (Chapter 14) developed in conjunction with J.C. Shaw, proved theorems in elementary logic, using the axiomatization of Russell and Whitehead's *Principia Mathematica*. The authors describe their research as being:

> aimed at understanding the complex processes (heuristics) that are effective in problem solving. Here we are not interested in methods that guarantee solutions, but which require vast amounts of computation. Rather we wish to understand how a mathematician, for example, is able to prove a theorem even though he does not know when he starts how, or if, he is going to succeed.

In later work Newell and Simon (Chapter 16) continued this search for general principles for intelligent problem solving. GPS, the *General Problem Solver*, used a technique the authors called *means-ends-analysis* to reduce differences between states of the problem domain. Programs like GPS, which focus on the syntactic structure of problem descriptions, are commonly called *weak method solvers* and make up the content of Part III.

Several chapters from Part II, including the work on genetic algorithms and parallel distributed processing, could equally well have been placed in Part III. We place them in Part II because these approaches also offered insight into the diversity of representational schemes that make up AI.

Arthur Samuel, in Chapter 15, designed the first program that could learn. Samuel's checker playing program had two approaches: *rote learning*, based on a scheme that used saved states to recognize desired situations as well as to extend search, and *generalization learning*, where an evaluation polynomial with look-ahead could recognize promising states of the problem. In retrospect, Samuel's use of 1950s computing technology was an impressive accomplishment, leading to much subsequent research in machine learning.

Following the early successes of programs by Newell and Simon, theorem proving became an important subarea of AI research. An important breakthrough in this research was Alan Robinson's (1965) identification of the *resolution inference rule* and some very efficient strategies for its use in a clause based refutation logic. Resolution is a generalization of modus ponens and a refutation system uses an assumed negation of the desired goal to show a contradiction in the axiom system. Resolution thus offers a powerful tool for weak method pattern analysis (Luger and Stubblefield 1993, chapter. 12). Resolution is employed in STRIPS plan formation to generate moves for a robot problem solver (Chapter 17).

The *blackboard* is another weak method AI architecture that emerged from early research at Carnegie Mellon, a derivative of the Hearsay language understanding project (Reddy 1976). A global database, the *blackboard*, is used as a communication link between several *knowledge sources*, each operating independently, and posting their results back to the blackboard. The history and development of blackboards is presented in Chapter 18.

Some of the other important work in the weak method tradition and not mentioned in Part III includes that of Slagle (1963) on symbolic integration. This work led to the important numerical programs of the later MACSYMA project at MIT. Another project was the geometry program of Galernter (1963), which proved many of the theorems of high school geometry. Finally, Evans (1964) wrote a program to solve simple analogy problems, such as those found in IQ tests. Evans solved problems of the form: A is to B as C is to ... where the program could select from several options. Evans built descriptions of A and B and then applied the differences noted between A and B to C, in an attempt to find the best finish for the analogy.

Several architectures for weak method problem solving emerged from this period. These include the *production system*, a generalization of the GPS approach and based on a computational formalism originally proposed by Post (1943). The first use of the production system was in the research of Newell and Simon at Carnegie Mellon University. Here it served both as a AI tool for effective problem solving but also fit nicely into their description of human performance. In fact GPS was a precursor of the Cognitive Science research area, many of whose accomplishments are summarized by Simon in Chapter 30.

14

Empirical Explorations with the Logic Theory Machine:

A Case Study in Heuristics

Allen Newell, J. C. Shaw, and Herbert A. Simon

1. Introduction

This is a case study in problem-solving, representing part of a program of research on complex information-processing systems. We have specified a system for finding proofs of theorems in elementary symbolic logic, and by programming a computer to these specifications, have obtained empirical data on the problem-solving process in elementary logic. The program is called the Logic Theory Machine (LT); it was devised to learn how it is possible to solve difficult problems such as proving mathematical theorems, discovering scientific laws from data, playing chess, or understanding the meaning of English prose.

The research reported here is aimed at understanding the complex processes (heuristics) that are effective in problem-solving. Hence, we are not interested in methods that guarantee solutions, but which require vast amounts of computation. Rather, we wish to understand how a mathematician, for example, is able to prove a theorem even though he does not know when he starts how, or if, he is going to succeed.

This focuses on the pure theory of problem-research solving (Newell and Simon 1956a). Previously we specified in detail a program for the Logic Theory Machine; and we shall repeat here only as much of that specification as is needed so that the reader can understand our data. In a companion study (Newell and Shaw 1957) we consider how computers can be programmed to execute processes of the kinds called for by LT, a problem that is interesting in its own right. Similarly, we postpone to later papers a discussion of the implications of our work for the psychological theory of human thinking and problem-solving. Other areas of application will readily occur to the reader, but here we will limit our attention to the nature of the problem-solving process itself.

Our research strategy in studying complex systems is to specify them in detail, program them for digital computers, and study their behavior empirically by running them with a number of variations and under a variety of conditions. This appears at present the only adequate means to obtain a thorough understanding of their behavior. Although the problem area with which the present system, LT, deals is fairly elementary, it provides a good example of a difficult problem—logic is a subject taught in college courses, and is difficult enough for most humans.

Our data come from a series of programs run on the JOHNNIAC, one of RAND's high-speed digital computers. We will describe the results of these runs, and analyze and interpret their implications for the problem solving process.

2. The Logic Theory Machine in Operation

We shall first give a concrete picture of the Logic Theory Machine in operation. LT, of course, is a program, written for the JOHNNIAC, represented by marks on paper or holes in cards. However, we can think of LT as an actual physical machine and the operation of the program as the behavior of the machine. One can identify LT with JOHNNIAC after the latter has been loaded with the basic program, but before the input of data.

LT's task is to prove theorems in elementary symbolic logic, or more precisely, in the sentential calculus. The sentential calculus is a formalized system of mathematics, consisting of expressions built from combinations of basic symbols. Five of these expressions are taken as axioms, and there are rules of inference for generating new theorems from the axioms and from other theorems. In flavor and form elementary symbolic logic is much like abstract algebra.

Normally the variables of the system are interpreted as sentences, and the axioms and rules of inference as formalizations of logical operations, e.g., deduction. However, LT deals with the system as a purely formal mathematics, and we will have no further need of the interpretation. We need to introduce a smattering of the sentential calculus to understand LT's task.

There is postulated a set of variables p, q, r, ...A, B, C, ..., with which the sentential calculus deals. These variables can be combined into expressions by means of connectives. Given any variable p, we can form the expression "not-p." Given any two variables p and q, we can form the expression "p or q," or the expression "p implies q," where "or" and "implies" are the connectives. There are other connectives, for example "and," but we will not need them here. Once we have formed expressions, these can be further combined into more complicated expressions. For example, we can form:[1]

"$(p$ implies not-$p)$ implies not-p." (2.01)

There is also given a set of expressions that are axioms. These are taken to be the universally true expressions from which theorems are to be derived by means of various rules of inference. For the sake of definiteness in our work with LT, we have employed the system of axioms, definitions, and rules that is used in the *Principia Mathematica,* which lists five axioms:

$(p$ or $p)$ implies p (1.2)

p implies $(q$ or $p)$ (1.3)

$(p$ or $q)$ implies $(q$ or $p)$ (1.4)

$[p$ or $(q$ or $r)]$ implies $[q$ or $(p$ or $r)]$ (1.5)

$(p$ implies $q)$ implies $[(r$ or $p)$ implies $(r$ or $q)]$ (1.6)

Given some true theorems one can derive new theorems by means of three rules of inference: *substitution, replacement,* and *detachment.*

1. By the rule of substitution, any expression may be substituted for any variable in any theorem, provided the substitution is made throughout the theorem wherever that variable appears. For example, by substitution of "p or q" for "p," in the second axiom we get the new theorem:

$(p$ or $q)$ implies $[q$ or $(p$ or $q)]$.

2. By the rule of replacement, a connective can be replaced by its definition, and vice versa, in any of its occurrences. By definition "p implies q" means the same as "not-p or q." Hence the former expression can always be replaced by the latter and vice versa. For example from axiom 1.3, by replacing "implies" with "or," we get the new theorem:

not-p or $(q$ or $p)$.

3. By the rule of detachment, if "A" and "A implies B" are theorems, then "B" is a theorem. For example, from:

(p or p) implies *p*,

and [*(p or p)* implies *p*] implies *(p* implies *p)*,

we get the new theorem:

p implies *p*.

Given an expression to prove, one starts from the set of axioms and theorems already proved, and applies the various rules successively until the desired expression is produced. The proof is the sequence of expressions, each one validly derived from the previous ones, that leads from the axioms and known theorems to the desired expression.

This is all the background in symbolic logic needed to observe LT in operation. LT "understands" expressions in symbolic logic—that is, there is a simple code for punching expressions on cards so they can be fed into the machine. We give LT the five axioms, instructing it that these are theorems it can assume to be true. LT already knows the rules of inference and the definitions—how to substitute, replace, and detach. Next we give LT a single expression, say expression 2.01, and ask LT to find a proof for it. LT works for about 10 seconds and then prints out the following proof:

(p implies not-*p)* implies not-*p*	(theorem 2.01, to be proved)
1. *(A or A)* implies *A*	(axiom 1.2)
2. (not-*A* or not-*A*) implies not-*A*	(subs. of not-*A* for *A*)
3. *(A* implies not-*A)* implies not-*A*	(repl. of "or" with "implies")
4. *(p* implies not-*p)* implies not-*p*	(subs. of *p* for *A*; QED).

Next we ask LT to prove a fairly advanced theorem (Whitehead and Russell 1935), theorem 2.45; allowing it to use all 38 theorems proved prior to 2.45. After about 12 minutes, LT produces the following proof:

not *(p or q)* implies not-*p*	(theorem 2.45, to be proved)
1. *A* implies *(A or B)*	(theorem 2.2)
2. *p* implies *(p or q)*	(subs. *P* for *A*, *q* for *B* in 1)
3. *(A* implies *B)* implies (not-*B* implies not-*A*)	(theorem 2.16)
4. [*p* implies *(p or q)*] implies [not *(p or q)* implies not-*p*]	[subs. *p* for A, *(p or q)* for *B* in 3]
5. not *(p or q)* implies not-*p*	(detach right side of 4, using 2; QED)

Finally, all the theorems prior to (2.31) are given to LT (a total of 28); and then LT is asked to prove:

[*p* or *(q* or *r)*] implies [*(p or q)* or *r*].   (2.31)

LT works for about 23 minutes and then reports that it cannot prove (2.31), that it has exhausted its resources.

Now, what is there in this behavior of LT that needs to be explained? The specific examples given are difficult problems for most humans, and most humans do not know what processes they use to find proofs, if they find them. There is no known simple procedure that will produce such proofs. Various methods exist for verifying whether any given expression is true or false; the best known procedure is the method of truth tables. But these procedures do not produce a proof in the meaning of Whitehead and Russell. One can invent "automatic" procedures for producing proofs. We will look at one briefly later, but these turn out to require computing times of the orders of thousands of years for the proof of (2.45).

We must clarify why such problems are difficult in the first place, and then show what features of LT account for its successes and failures. These questions will occupy the rest of this study.

3. Problems, Algorithms, and Heuristics

In describing LT, its environment, and its behavior we will make repeated use of three concepts. The first of these is the concept of *problem*. Abstractly, a person is given a problem if he is given a set of possible solutions, and a test for verifying whether a given element of this set is in fact a solution to his problem.

The reason why problems are problems is that the original set of possible solutions given to the problem-solver can be very large, the actual solutions can be dispersed very widely and rarely throughout it, and the cost of obtaining each new element and of testing it can be very expensive. Thus the problem-solver is not really "given" the set of possible solutions; instead he is given some process for generating the elements of that set in some order. This generator has properties of its own, not usually specified in stating the problem; e.g., there is associated with it a certain cost per element produced, it may be possible to change the order in which it produces the elements, and so on. Likewise the verification test has costs and times associated with it. The problem can be solved if these costs are not too large in relation to the time and computing power available for solution.

One very special and valuable property that a generator of solutions sometimes has is a guarantee that if the problem has a solution, the generator will, sooner or later, produce it. We will call a process that has this property for some problem an *algorithm* for that problem. The guarantee provided by an algorithm is not an unmixed blessing, of course, since nothing has been specified about the cost or time required to produce the solutions. For example, a simple algorithm for opening a combination safe is to try all combinations, testing each one to see if it opens the safe. This algorithm is a typical problem-solving process: there is a generator that produces new combinations in some order, and there is a verifier that determines whether each new combination is in fact a solution to the problem. This search process is an algorithm because it is known that some combination will open the safe, and because the generator will exhaust all combinations in a finite interval of time. The algorithm is sufficiently expensive, however, that a combination safe can be used to protect valuables even from people who know the algorithm.

A process that *may* solve a given problem, but offers no guarantees of doing so, is called a *heuristic*[2] for that problem. This lack of a guarantee is not an unmixed evil. The cost inflicted by the lack of guarantee depends on what the process costs and what algorithms are available as alternatives. For most run-of-the-mill problems we have only heuristics, but occasionally we have both algorithms and heuristics as alternatives for solving the same problem. Sometimes, as in the problem of finding maxima for simple differentiable functions, everyone uses the algorithm of setting the first derivative equal to zero; no one sets out to examine all the points on the line one by one as if it were possible. Sometimes, as in chess, everyone plays by heuristic, since no one is able to carry out the algorithm of examining all continuations of the game to termination.

4. The Problem of Proving Theorems in Logic

Finding a proof for a theorem in symbolic logic can be described as selecting an element from a generated set, as shown by Figure 1. Consider the set of *all* possible sequences of logic expressions—call it E. Certain of these sequences, a very small minority, will be proofs. A proof sequence satisfies the following test:

Each expression in the sequence is either

1. One of the accepted theorems or axioms, or

2. Obtainable from one or two previous expressions in the sequence by application of one of the three rules of inference.

Call the set of sequences that are proofs P. Certain of the sequences in E have the expression to be proved—call it X, as their final expression. Call this set of sequences T_x. Then, to find a proof of a given theorem X means to select an element of E that belongs to the intersection of P and T_x. The set E is given implicitly by rules for generating new sequences of logic expressions.

The difficulty of proving theorems depends on the scarcity of elements in the intersection of P and T_x, relative to the number of elements in E. Hence, it depends on the cost and speed of the available generators that produce elements of E, and on the cost and speed of making tests that determine whether an element belongs to T_x or P. The difficulty also depends on whether gener-

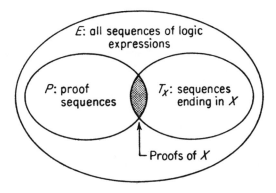

Figure 1. Relationships between E, P, and T_X.

ators can be found that guarantee that any element they produce automatically satisfies some of the conditions. Finally, as we shall see, the difficulty depends heavily on what heuristics can be found to guide the selection.

A little reflection, and experience in trying to prove theorems, make it clear that proof sequences for specified theorems are rare indeed. To reveal more precisely why proving theorems is difficult, we will construct an algorithm for doing this. The algorithm will be based only on the tests and definitions given above, and not on any "deep" inferred properties of symbolic logic. Thus it will reflect the basic nature of theorem proving; that is, its nature prior to building up sophisticated proof techniques. We will call this algorithm the British Museum algorithm, in recognition of the supposed originators of procedures of this type.

4.1 The British Museum Algorithm

The algorithm constructs all possible proofs in a systematic manner, checking each time (1) to eliminate duplicates, and (2) to see if the final theorem in the proof coincides with the expression to be proved. With this algorithm the set of one-step proofs is identical with the set of axioms (i.e., each axiom is a one-step proof of itself). The set of n-step proofs is obtained from the set of $(n - 1)$-step proofs by making all the permissible substitutions and replacements in the expressions of the $(n - 1)$-step proofs, and by making all the permissible detachments of pairs of expressions as permitted by the recursive definition of proof.[3]

Figure 2 shows how the set of n-step proofs increases with n at the very start of the proof-generating process. This enumeration only extends to replacements of "or" with "implies," "implies" with "or," and negation of vari-

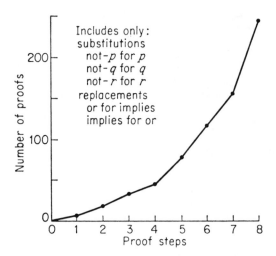

Figure 2. Number of proofs generated by first few steps of British Museum algorithm.

ables (e.g., "not-*p*" for "p"). No detachments and no complex substitutions (e.g., "*q* or *r*" for "*p*") are included. No specializations have been made (e.g., substitution of *p* for *q* in "*p* or *q*"). If we include the specializations, which take three more steps, the algorithm will generate an (estimated) additional 600 theorems, thus providing a set of proofs of 11 steps or less containing almost 1000 theorems, none of them duplicates.

In order to see how this algorithm would provide proofs of specified theorems, we can consider its performance on the sixty-odd theorems of Chapter 2 of *Principia*. One theorem (2.01) is obtained in step (4) of the generation, hence is among the first 42 theorems proved. Three more (2.02, 2.03, and 2.04) are obtained in step (6), hence among the first 115. One more (2.05) is obtained in step (8), hence in the first 246. Only one more is included in the first 1000, theorem 2.07. The proofs of all the remainder require complex substitutions or detachment.

We have no way at present to estimate how many proofs must be generated to include proofs of all theorems of Chapter 2 of *Principia*. Our best guess is that it might be a hundred million. Moreover, apart from the six theorems listed, there is no reason to suppose that the proofs of these theorems would occur early in the list.

Our information is too poor to estimate more than very roughly the times required to produce such proofs by the algorithm; but we can estimate times of about 16 minutes to do the first 250 theorems of Figure 2 [i.e., through step (8)] assuming processing times comparable with those in LT. The first part of the algorithm has an additional special property, which holds only to the point where detachment is first used; that no check for duplication is necessary. Thus the time of computing the first few thousand proofs only increases linearly with the number of theorems generated. For the theorems requiring detachments, duplication checks must be made, and the total computing time increases as the square of the number of expressions generated. At this rate it would take hundreds of thousands of years of computation to generate proofs for the theorems in Chapter 2.

The nature of the problem of proving theorems is now reasonably clear. When sequences of expressions are produced by a simple and cheap (per element produced) generator, the chance that any particular sequence is the desired proof is exceedingly small. This is true even if the generator produces sequences that always satisfy the most complicated and restrictive of the solution conditions: that each is a proof of something. The set of sequences is so large, and the desired proof so rare, that no practical amount of computation suffices to find proofs by means of such an algorithm.

5. The Logic Theory Machine

If LT is to prove any theorems at all it must employ some devices that alter radically the order in which possible proofs are generated, and the way in which they are tested. To accomplish this, LT gives up almost all the guarantees enjoyed by the British Museum algorithm. Its procedures guarantee neither that its proposed sequences are proofs of something, nor that LT will ever find the proof, no matter how much effort is spent. However, they *often* generate the desired proof in a reasonable computing time.

5.1 Methods

The major type of heuristic that LT uses we call a *method*. As yet we have no precise definition of a method that distinguishes it from all the other types of routines in LT. Roughly, a method is a reasonably self-contained operation that, if it works, makes a major and permanent contribution toward finding a proof. It is the largest unit of organization in LT, subordinated only to the executive routines necessary to coordinate and select the methods.

5.1.1 The Substitution Method

This method seeks a proof for the problem expression by finding an axiom or previously proved theorem that can be transformed, by a series of substitutions for variables and replacements of connectives, into the problem expression.

5.1.2 The Detachment Method

This method attempts, using the rule of detachment, to substitute for the problem expression a new subproblem which, if solved, will provide a proof for the problem expression. Thus, if the problem expression is *B*, the method of detachment searches for an axiom or theorem of the form "*A* implies *B*." If one is found, *A* is set up as a new subproblem. If *A* can be proved, then, since "*A* implies *B*" is a theorem, *B* will also be proved.

5.1.3 The Chaining Methods

These methods use the transitivity of the relation of implication to create a new subproblem which, if solved, will provide a proof for the problem expression. Thus, if the problem expression is "*a* implies *c*," the method of forward chaining searches for an axiom or theorem of the form "*a* implies *b*." If one is found, "*b* implies *c*" is set up as a new subproblem. Chaining backward works analogously: it seeks a theorem of the form "*b* implies *c*," and if one is found, "*a* implies *b*" is set up as a new subproblem.

Each of these methods is an independent unit. They are alternatives to one another, and can be used in sequence, one working on the subproblems generated by another. Each of them produces a major part of a proof. Substitution actually proves theorems, and the other three generate subproblems, which can become the intermediate expressions in a proof sequence.

These methods give no guarantee that they will work. There is no guarantee that a theorem can be found that can be used to carry out a proof by the substitution method, or a theorem that will produce a subproblem by any of the other three methods. Even if a subproblem is generated, there is no guarantee that it is part of the desired proof sequence, or even that it is part of any proof sequence (e.g., it can be false). On the other hand, the generated methods do guarantee that any subproblem generated is part of a sequence of expressions that ends in the desired theorem (this is one of the conditions that a sequence be a proof). The methods also guarantee that each expression of the sequence is derived by the rules of inference from the preceding ones (a second condition of proof). What is not guaranteed is that the beginning of the sequence can be completed with axioms or previously proved theorems.

There is also no guarantee that the combination of the four methods, used in any fashion whatsoever and with unlimited computing effort, comprises a sufficient set of methods to prove all theorems. In fact, we have discovered a theorem [(2.13), "*p* or not-not-not-*p*"] which the four methods of LT cannot prove. All the subproblems generated for (2.13) after a certain point are false, and therefore cannot lead to a proof.

We have yet no general theory to explain why the methods transform LT into an effective problem-solver. That they do, in conjunction with the other mechanisms to be described shortly, will be demonstrated amply in the remainder of this study. Several factors may be involved. First, the methods organize the sequences of individual processing steps into larger units that can be handled as such. Each processing step can be oriented toward the special

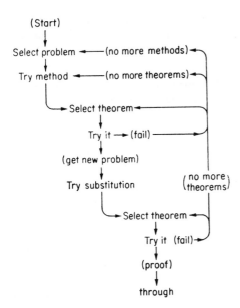

Figure 3. General flow diagram of LT.

function it performs in the unit as a whole, and the units can be manipulated and organized as entities by the higher-level routines.

Apart from their "unitizing" effect, the methods that generate subproblems work "backward" from the desired theorem to axioms or known theorems rather than "forward" as did the British Museum algorithm. Since there is only one theorem to be proved, but a number of known true theorems, the efficacy of working backward may be analogous to the ease with which a needle can find its way out of a haystack, compared with the difficulty of someone finding the lone needle in the haystack.

5.2 The Executive Routine

In LT, the four methods are organized by an executive routine, whose flow diagram is shown in Figure 3.

1. When a new problem is presented to LT, the substitution method is tried first, using all the axioms and theorems that LT has been told to assume, and that are now stored in a *theorem list*.

2. If substitution fails, the detachment method is tried, and as each new subproblem is created by a successful detachment, an attempt is made to prove the new subproblem by the substitution method. If substitution fails again, the subproblem is added to a *subproblem list*.

3. If detachment fails for all the theorems in the theorem list, the same cycle is repeated with forward chaining, and then with backward chaining:

try to create a subproblem; try to prove it by the substitution method; if unsuccessful, put the new subproblem on the list. By the nature of the methods, if the substitution method ever succeeds with a single subproblem, the original theorem is proved.

4. If all the methods have been tried on the original problem and no proof has been produced, the executive routine selects the next untried subproblem from the subproblem list, and makes the same sequence of attempts with it. This process continues until (1) a proof is found, (2) the time allotted for finding a proof is used up, (3) there is no more available memory space in the machine, or (4) no untried problems remain on the subproblem list.

In the three examples cited earlier, the proof of (2.01) [(*p* implies not-*p*) implies not-*p*] was obtained by the substitution method directly, hence did not involve use of the subproblem list.

The proof of (2.45) [not (*p* or *q*) implies not-*p*] was achieved by an application of the detachment method followed by a substitution. This proof required LT to create a subproblem, and to use the substitution method on it. It did not require LT ever to select any subproblem from the subproblem list, since the substitution was successful. Figure 4 shows the *tree of subproblems* corresponding to the proof of (2.45). The subproblems are given in the form of a downward branching tree. Each node is a subproblem, the original problem being the single node at the top. The lines radiating down from a node lead to the new subproblems generated from the subproblem corresponding to the node. The proof sequence is given by the dashed line; the top link was constructed by the detachment method, and the bottom link by the substitution method. The other links extending down from the original problem lead to other subproblems generated by the detachment method (but not provable by direct substitution) prior to the time LT tried the theorem that leads to the final proof.

LT did not prove theorem 2.31, also mentioned earlier, and gave as its reason that it could think of nothing more to do. This means that LT had considered all subproblems on the subproblem list (there were six in this case) and had no new subproblems to work on. In none of the examples mentioned did LT terminate because of time or space limitations; however, this is the most common result in the cases where LT does not find a proof. Only rarely does LT run out of things to do.

This section has described the organization of LT in terms of methods. We have still to examine in detail why it is that this organization, in connection with the additional mechanisms to be described below, allows LT to prove theorems with a reasonable amount of computing effort.

5.5 The Matching Process

The times required to generate proofs for even the simplest theorems by the British Museum algorithm are larger than the times required by LT by factors

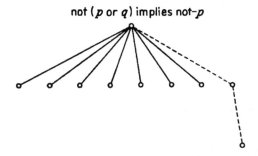

not $(p$ or $q)$ implies not-p

Figure 4. Subproblem tree of proof by LT of (2.45) (all previous theorems available).

ranging from five (for one particular theorem) to a hundred and upward. Let us consider an example from the earliest part of the generation, where we have detailed information about the algorithm. The seventy-ninth theorem generated by the algorithm (see Figure 2) is theorem 2.02 of *Principia,* one of the theorems we asked LT to prove. This theorem, "*p* implies (*q* implies *p*)," is generated by the algorithm in about 158 seconds with a sequence of substitutions and replacements; it is proved by LT in about 10 seconds with the method of substitution. The reason for the difference becomes apparent if we focus attention on axiom 1.3, "*p* implies (*q* or *p*)," from which the theorem is derived in either scheme.

Figure 5 shows the tree of proofs of the first twelve theorems obtained from (1.3) by the algorithm. The theorem 2.02 is node (9) on the tree and is obtained by substitution of "not-*q*" for "*q*" in axiom 1.3 to reach node (5); and then by replacing the "(not-*q* or *p*)" by "(*q* implies *p*)" in (5) to get (9). The ninth theorem generated from axiom 1.3 is the seventy-ninth generated from the five axioms considered together.

This proof is obtained directly by LT using the following matching procedure. We compare the axiom with (9), the expression to be proved:

p implies $(q$ or $p)$ (1.3)

p implies $(q$ implies $p)$ (9)

First, by a direct comparison, LT determines that the main connectives are identical. Second, LT determines that the variables to the left of the main connectives are identical. Third, LT determines that the connectives within parentheses on the right hand sides are different. It is necessary to replace the "or" with "implies," but in order to do this (in accordance with the definition of implies) there must be a negation sign before the variable that precedes the "or." Hence, LT first replaces the "*q*" on the right-hand side with "not-*q*" to get the required negation sign, obtaining (5). Now LT can change the "or" to "implies," and determines that the resulting expression is identical with (9).

The matching process allowed LT to proceed directly down the branch

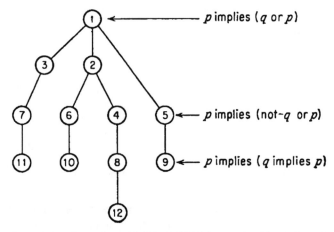

Figure 5. Proof tree of proof 2.02 by British Museum algorithm (using axion 1.3).

from (1) through (5) to (9) without even exploring the other branches. Quantitatively, it looked at only two expressions instead of eight, thus reducing the work of comparison by a factor of four. Actually, the saving is even greater, since the matching procedure does not deal with whole expressions, but with a single pair of elements at a time.

An important source of efficiency in the matching process is that it proceeds component-wise, obtaining at each step a feedback of the results of a substitution or replacement that can be used to guide the next step. This feedback keeps the search on the right branch of the tree of possible expressions. It is not important for an efficient search that the goal be known from the beginning; it is crucial that hints of "warmer" or "colder" occur as the search proceeds.[4] Closely related to this feedback is the fact that where LT is called on to make a substitution or replacement at any step, it can determine immediately what variable or connective to substitute or replace by direct comparison with the problem expression, and without search.

Thus far we have assumed that LT knows at the beginning that (1.3) is the appropriate axiom to use. Without this information, it would begin matching with each axiom in turn, abandoning it for the next one if the matching should prove impossible. For example, if it tries to match the theorem against axiom 1.2, it determines almost immediately (on the second test) that "p or p" cannot be made into "p" by substitution. Thus, the matching process permits LT to abandon unprofitable lines of search as well as guiding it to correct substitutions and replacements.

5.5.1 Matching in the Substitution Methods

The matching process is an essential part of the substitution method. Without it, the substitution method is just that part of the British Museum algorithm that uses only replacements and substitutions. With it, LT is able, either directly or in combination with the other methods, to prove many theorems with reasonable effort.

To obtain data on its performance, LT was given the task of proving in sequence the first 52 theorems of *Principia*. In each case, LT was given the axioms plus all the theorems previously proved in Chapter 2 as the material from which to work (regardless of whether LT had proved the theorems itself).[5]

Of the 52 theorems, proofs were found for a total 38 (73 percent). These proofs were obtained by various combinations of methods, but the substitution method was an essential component of all of them. Seventeen of these proofs, almost a half, were accomplished by the substitution method alone. Subjectively evaluated, the theorems that were proved by the substitution method alone have the appearance of "corollaries" of the theorems they are derived from; they occur fairly close to them in the chapter, generally requiring three or fewer attempts at matching per theorem proved (54 attempts for 17 theorems).

The performance of the substitution method on the subproblems is somewhat different, due, we think, to the kind of selectivity implicit in the order of theorems in *Principia*. In 338 attempts at solving subproblems by substitution, there were 21 successes (6.2 percent). Thus, there was about one chance in three of proving an original problem directly by the substitution method, but only about one chance in 16 of so proving a subproblem generated from the original problem.

5.5.2 Matching in Detachment and Chaining

So far the matching process has been considered only as a part of the substitution method, but it is also an essential component of the other three methods. In detachment, for example, a theorem of form "A implies B" is sought, where B is identical with the expression to be proved. The chances of finding such a theorem are negligible unless we allow some modification of B to make it match the theorem to be proved. Hence, once a theorem is selected from the theorem list, its right-hand subexpression is matched against the expression to be proved. An analogous procedure is used in the chaining methods.

We can evaluate the performance of the detachment and chaining methods with the same sample of problems used for evaluating the substitution method. However, a successful match with the former three methods generates a subproblem and does not directly prove the theorem. With the detachment method, an average of three new subproblems were generated for each application of the method; with forward chaining the average was 2.7; and with backward chaining the average was 2.2. For all the methods, this represents about one subproblem per 7½ theorems tested (the number of theorems available varied slightly).

As in the case of substitution, when these three methods were applied to the original problem, the chances of success were higher than when they were applied to subproblems. When applied to the original problem, the number of subproblems generated averaged eight to nine; when applied to subproblems derived from the original, the number of subproblems generated fell to an average of two or three.

In handling the first 52 problems in Chapter 2 of *Principia,* 17 theorems were proved in one step—that is, in one application of substitution. Nineteen theorems were proved in two steps, 12 by detachment followed by substitution, and seven by chaining forward followed by substitution. Two others were proved in three steps. Hence, 38 theorems were proved in all. There are no two-step proofs by backward chaining, since, for two-step proofs only, if there is a proof by backward chaining, there is also one by forward chaining. In 14 cases LT failed to find a proof. Most of these unsuccessful attempts were terminated by time or space limitations. One of these 14 theorems we know LT cannot prove, and one other we believe it cannot prove. Of the remaining twelve, most of them can be proved by LT if it has sufficient time and memory (see section on subproblems, however).

5.6 Similarity Tests and Descriptions

Matching eliminates enough of the trial and error in substitutions and replacements to make LT into a successful problem solver. Matching permeates all of the methods, and without it none of them would be useful within practical amounts of computing effort. However, a large amount of search is still used in finding the correct theorems with which matching works. Returning to the performance of LT in Chapter 2, we find that the over-all chances of a particular match being successful are 0.3 percent for substitution, 13.4 percent for detachment, 13.8 percent for forward chaining, and 9.4 percent for backward chaining.

The amount of search through the theorem list can be reduced by interposing a screening process that will reject any theorem for matching that has low likelihood of success. LT has such a screening device, called the *similarity test.* Two logic expressions are defined to be similar if both their left-hand and right-hand sides are equal, with respect to, (1) the maximum number of levels from the main connective to any variable; (2) the number of distinct variables; and (3) the number of variable places. Speaking intuitively, two logic expressions are "similar" if they look alike, and look alike if they are similar. Consider for example:

(p or q) implies *(q or p)*	(1)
p implies *(q or p)*	(2)
r implies *(m* implies *r)*	(3)

By the definition of similarity, (2) and (3) are similar, but (1) is not similar to either (2) or (3).

Method	Theorems considered	Theorems similar	Theorems matched	% similar of theorems considered	% matched of theorems similar
Substitution	11,298	993	37	8.8	3.7
Detachment	1,591	406	210	25.5	51.7
Chain. forward	869	200	120	23.0	60.0
Chain. backward	673	146	63	21.7	43.2

Table 1. Statistics of similarity tests and matching.

In all of the methods LT applies the similarity tests to all expressions to be matched, and only applies the matching routine if the expressions are similar; otherwise it passes on to the next theorem in the theorem list. The similarity test reduces substantially the number of matchings attempted as the numbers in Table 1 show, and correspondingly raises the probability of a match if the matching is attempted. The effect is particularly strong in substitution, where the similarity test reduces the matchings attempted by a factor of ten, and increases the probability of a successful match by a factor of ten. For the other methods attempted matchings were reduced by a factor of four or five, and the probability of a match increased by the same factor.

These figures reveal a gross, but not necessarily a net, gain in performance through the use of the similarity test. There are two reasons why all the gross gain may not be realized. First, the similarity test is only a heuristic. It offers no guarantee that it will let through only expressions that will subsequently match. The similarity test also offers no guarantee that it will not reject expressions that would match if attempted. The similarity test does not often commit this type of error (corresponding to a type II statistical error), as will be shown later. However, even rare occurrences of such errors can be costly. One example occurs in the proof of theorem 2.07:

p implies *(p or p)*. (2.07)

This theorem is proved simply by substituting *p* for *q* in axiom 1.3:

p implies *(q or p)*. (1.3)

However, the similarity test, because it demands equality in the number of distinct variables on the right-hand side, calls (2.07) and (1.3) dissimilar because (2.07) contains only *p* while (1.3) contains *p* and *q*. LT discovers the proof through chaining forward, where it checks for a direct match before creating the new subproblem, but the proof is about five times as expensive as when the similarity test is omitted.

The second reason why the gross gain will not all be realized is that the similarity test is not costless, and in fact for those theorems which pass the test the cost of the similarity test must be paid in addition to the cost of the matching. We will examine these costs in the next section when we consider the effort LT expends.

Experiments have been carried out with a weaker similarity test, which compares only the number of variable places on both sides of the expression. This test will not commit the particular type II error cited above, and (2.07) is proved by substitution using it. Apart from this, the modification had remarkably little effect on performance. On a sample of ten problems it admitted only 10 percent more similar theorems and about 10 percent more subproblems. The reason why the two tests do not differ more radically is that there is a high correlation among the descriptive measures.

5.7 Effort in LT

So far we have focused entirely on the performance characteristics of the heuristics in LT, except to point out the tremendous difference between the computing effort required by LT and by the British Museum algorithm. However, it is clear that each additional test, search, description, and the like, has its costs in computing effort as well as its gains in performance. The costs must always be balanced against the performance gains, since there are always alternative heuristics which could be added to the system in place of those being used. In this section we will analyze the computing effort used by LT. The memory space used by the various processes also constitutes a cost, but one that will not be discussed in this study.

5.7.1 Measuring Efforts

LT is written in an interpretive language or pseudocode, which is described in Newell and Shaw (1957). LT is defined in terms of a set of primitive operations, which, in turn, are defined by subroutines in JOHNNIAC machine language. These primitives provide a convenient unit of effort, and all effort measurements will be given in terms of total number of primitives executed. The relative frequencies of the different primitives are reasonably constant, and, therefore, the total number of primitives is an adequate index of effort. The average time per primitive is quite constant at about 30 milliseconds, although for very low totals (less than 1000 primitives) a figure of about 20 milliseconds seems better.

5.7.2 Computing Effort and Performance

On a priori grounds we would expect the amount of computing effort required to solve a logic problem to be roughly proportional to the total number of theorems examined (i.e., tested for similarity, if there is a similarity routine; or tested for matching, if there is not) by the various methods in the course of solving the problem. In fact, this turns out to be a reasonably good predictor of effort; but the fit to data is much improved if we assign greater weight to theorems considered for detachment and chaining than to theorems considered for substitution.

Actual and predicted efforts are compared below (with the full similarity

Total primitives, thousands

Theorem	Actual	Estimate
2.06	3.2	0.8
2.07	4.3	4.4
2.08	3.5	3.3
2.11	2.2	2.2
2.13	24.5	24.6
2.14	3.3	3.2
2.15	15.8	13.6
2.18	34.1	35.8
2.25	11.1	11.5

Table 2. Effort statistics with "Precompute Description" routine.

test included, and excluding theorems proved by substitution) on the assumption that the number of primitives per theorem considered is twice as great for chaining as for substitution, and three times as great for detachment. About 45 primitives are executed per theorem considered with the substitution method (hence 135 with detachment and 90 with chaining). As Table 2 shows, the estimates are generally accurate within a few percent, except for theorem 2.06, for which the estimate is too low.

There is an additional source of variation not shown in the theorems selected for Table 2. The descriptions used in the similarity test must be computed from the logic expressions. Since the descriptions of the theorems are used over and over again, LT computes these at the start of a problem and stores the values with the theorems, so they do not have to be computed again. However, as the number of theorems increases, the space devoted to storing the precomputed descriptions becomes prohibitive, and LT switches to recomputing them each time it needs them. With recomputation, the problem effort is still roughly proportional to the total number of theorems considered, but now the number of primitives per theorem is around 70 for the substitution method, 210 for detachment, and 140 for chaining.

Our analysis of the effort statistics shows, then, that in the first approximation the effort required to prove a theorem is proportional to the number of theorems that have to be considered before a proof is found; the number of theorems considered is an effort measure for evaluating a heuristic. A good heuristic, by securing the consideration of the "right" theorems early in the proof, reduces the expected number of theorems to be considered before a proof is found.

5.7.3 Evaluation of the Similarity Test

As we noted in the previous section, to evaluate an improved heuristic, account must be taken of any additional computation that the improvement introduces. The net advantage may be less than the gross advantage, or the extra computing effort may actually cancel out the gross gain in selectivity. We are now in a position to evaluate the similarity routines as preselectors of theorems for matching.

A number of theorems were run, first with the full similarity routine, then with the modified similarity routine (which tests only the number of variable places), and finally with no similarity test at all. We also made some comparisons with both precomputed and recomputed descriptions.

When descriptions are precomputed, the computing effort is less with the full similarity test than without it; the factor of saving ranged from 10 to 60 percent (e.g., 3534/5206 for theorem 2.08). However, if LT must recompute the descriptions every time, the full similarity test is actually more expensive than no similarity test at all (e.g., 26,739/22,914 for theorem 2.45).

The modified similarity test fares somewhat better. For example, in proving (2.45) it requires only 18,035 primitives compared to the 22,914 for no similarity test (see the paragraph above). These comparisons involve recomputed descriptions; we have no figures for precomputed descriptions, but the additional saving appears small since there is much less to compute with the abridged than with the full test.

Thus the similarity test is rather marginal, and does not provide anything like the factors of improvement achieved by the matching process, although we have seen that the performance figures seem to indicate much more substantial gains. The reason for the discrepancy is not difficult to find. In a sense, the matching process consists of two parts. One is a testing part that locates the differences between elements and diagnoses the corrective action to be taken. The other part comprises the processes of substituting and replacing. The latter part is the major expense in a matching that works, but most of this effort is saved when the matching fails. Thus matching turns out to be inexpensive for precisely those expressions that the similarity test excludes.

6. Subproblems

LT can prove a great many theorems in symbolic logic. However, there are numerous theorems that LT cannot prove, and we may describe LT as having reached a plateau in its problem solving ability.

Figure 6 shows the amount of effort required for the problems LT solved out of the sample of 52. Almost all the proofs that LT found took less than 30,000 primitives of effort. Among the numerous attempts at proofs that went beyond this effort limit, only a few succeeded, and these required a total effort that was very much greater.

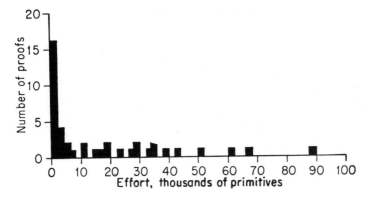

Figure 6. Distribution of LT's proofs by effort. Data include all proofs from attempts on the first 52 theorems in Chapter 2 of *Principia*.

The predominance of short proofs is even more striking than the approximate upper limit of 30,000 primitives suggests. The proofs by substitution—almost half of the total—required about 1000 primitives or less each. The effort required for the longest proof—89,000 primitives—is some 250 times the effort required for the short proofs. We estimate that to prove the 12 additional theorems that we believe LT can prove requires the effort limit to be extended to about a million primitives.

From these data we infer that LT's power as a problem solver is largely restricted to problems of a certain class. While it is logically possible for LT to solve others by large expenditures of effort, major adjustments are needed in the program to extend LT's powers to essentially new classes of problems. We believe that this situation is typical: good heuristics produce differences in performance of large orders of magnitude, but invariably a "plateau" is reached that can be surpassed only with quite different heuristics. These new heuristics will again make differences of orders of magnitude. In this section we shall analyze LT's difficulties with those theorems it cannot prove, with a view to indicating the general type of heuristic that might extend its range of effectiveness.

6.1 The Subproblem Tree

Let us examine the proof of theorem 2.17 when all the preceding theorems are available. This is the proof that cost LT 89,000 primitives. It is reproduced below, using chaining as a rule of inference (each chaining could be expanded into two detachments, to conform strictly to the system of *Principia*).

(not-*q* implies not-*p*) implies (*p*-implies *q*)   (theorem 2.17, to be proved)

   1. *A* implies not-not-*A*   (theorem 2.12)

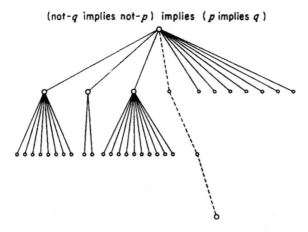

(not-*q* implies not-*p*) implies (*p* implies *q*)

Figure 7. Subproblem tree of proof by LT of (2.17) (all previous theorems available).

2. *p* implies not-not-*p*   (subs. *p* for *A* in 1)

3. (*A* implies *B*) implies [(*B* implies *C*)   (theorem 2.06)
   implies (*A* implies *C*)]

4. *(p* implies not-not-*p)* implies   (subs. *p* for A, not-not-*p* for *B*,
   [(not-not-*p* implies *q*) implies (*p* implies *q*)]   *q* for *C* in 3)

5. (not-not-*p* implies *q*) implies *(p* implies *q*)   (det. 4 from 3)

6. (not-*A* implies *B*) implies (not-*B* implies *A*)   (theorem 2.15)

7. (not-*q* implies not-*p)* implies   (subs. *q* for *A*, not-*p* for *B*)
   (not-not-*p* implies *q*)

8. (not-*q* implies not-*p*) implies *(p* implies *q*)   (chain 7 and 5; QED)

The proof is longer than either of the two given earlier. In terms of LT's methods it takes three steps instead of two or one: a forward chaining, a detachment, and a substitution. This leads to the not surprising notion, given human experience, that length of proof is an important variable in determining total effort: short proofs will be easy and long proofs difficult and difficulty will increase more than proportionately with length of proof. Indeed, all the one-step proofs require 500 to 1500 primitives, while the number of primitives for two-step proofs ranges from 3000 to 50,000. Further, LT has obtained only six proofs longer than two steps, and these require from 10,000 to 90,000 primitives.

The significance of length of proof can be seen by comparing Figure 7 which gives the proof tree for (2.17), with Figure 4, which gives the proof tree for (2.45), a two-step proof. In going one step deeper in the case of (2.17), LT had to generate and examine many more subproblems. A compari-

p implies $[(p$ implies $q)$ implies $q]$

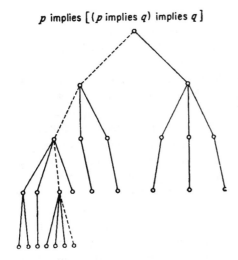

Figure 8. Subproblem tree of proof by LT of (2.27) (using the axioms).

son of the various statistics of the proofs confirms this statement: the problems are roughly similar in other respects (e.g., in effort per theorem considered); hence the difference in total effort can be attributed largely to the difference in number of subproblems generated.

Let us examine some more evidence for this conclusion. Figure 8 shows the subproblem tree for the proof of (2.27) from the axioms, which is the only four-step proof LT has achieved to date. The tree reveals immediately why LT was able to find the proof. Instead of branching widely at each point, multiplying rapidly the number of subproblems to be looked at, LT in this case only generates a few subproblems at each point. It thus manages to penetrate to a depth of four steps with a reasonable amount of effort (38,367 primitives). If this tree had branched as the other two did. LT would have had to process about 250 subproblems before arriving at a proof, and the total effort would have been at least 250,000 primitives. The statistics quoted earlier on the effectiveness of subproblem generation support the general hypothesis that the number of subproblems to be examined increases more or less exponentially with the depth of the proof.

The difficulty is that LT uses an algorithmic procedure to govern its generation of subproblems. Apart from a few subproblems excluded by the type II errors of the similarity test, the procedure guarantees that all subproblems that can be generated by detachment and chaining will in fact be obtained (duplications are eliminated). LT also uses an algorithm to determine the order in which it will try to solve subproblems. The subproblems are considered in order of generation, so that a proof will not be missed through failure to consider a subproblem that has been generated.

Because of these systematic principles incorporated in the executive program, and because the methods, applied to a theorem list averaging 30 expressions in length, generate a large number of subproblems, LT must find a rare sequence that leads to a proof by searching through a very large set of such sequences. For proofs of one step, this is no problem at all; for proofs of two steps, the set to be examined is still of reasonable size in relation to the computing power available. For proofs of three steps, the size of the search already presses LT against its computing limits; and if one or two additional steps are added the amount of search required to find a proof exceeds any amount of computer power that could practically be made available.

The set of subproblems generated by the Logic Theory Machine, however large it may seem, is exceedingly selective and rich in proofs compared with the set through which the British Museum algorithm searches. Hence, the latter algorithm could find proofs in a reasonable time for only the simplest theorems, while proofs for a much larger number are accessible with LT. The line dividing the possible from the impossible for any given problem-solving procedure is relatively sharp; hence a further increase in problem-solving power, comparable to that obtained in passing from the British Museum algorithm to LT, will require a corresponding enrichment of the heuristic.

6.2 Modification of the Logic Theory Machine

There are many possible ways to modify LT so that it can find proofs of more than two steps in a way which has reason and insight, instead of by brute force. First, the unit cost of processing subproblems can be substantially reduced so that a given computing effort will handle many more subproblems. (This does not, perhaps, change the "brute force" character of the process, but makes it feasible in terms of effort.) Second, LT can be modified so that it will select for processing only subproblems that have a high probability of leading to a proof. One way to do this is to screen subproblems before they are put on the subproblem list, and eliminate the unlikely ones altogether. Another way is to reduce selectively the number of subproblems generated.

For example, to reduce the number of subproblems generated, we may limit the lists of theorems available for generating them. That this approach may be effective is suggested by the statistics we have already cited, which show that the number of subproblems generated by a method per theorem examined is relatively constant (about one subproblem per seven theorems).

An impression of how the number of available theorems affects the generation of subproblems may be gained by comparing the proof trees of (2.17) (Figure 7) and (2.27) (Figure 8). The broad tree for (2.17) was produced with a list of twenty theorems, while the deep tree for (2.27) was produced with a list of only five theorems. The smaller theorem list in the latter case generated fewer subproblems at each application of one of the methods.

Another example of the same point is provided by two proofs of theorem 48 obtained with different lists of available theorems. In the one case, (2.48) was proved starting with all prior theorems on the theorem list; in the other case it was proved starting only with the axioms and theorem 2.16. We had conjectured that the proof would be more difficult to obtain under the latter conditions, since a longer proof chain would have to be constructed than under the former. In this we were wrong: with the longer theorem list, LT proved theorem 2.48 in two steps, employing 51,450 primitives of effort. With the shorter list, LT proved the theorem in three steps, but with only 18,558 primitives, one-third as many as before. Examination of the first proof shows that the many "irrelevant" theorems on the list took a great deal of processing effort. The comparison provides a dramatic demonstration of the fact that a problem solver may be encumbered by too much information, just as he may be handicapped by too little.

We have only touched on the possibilities for modifying LT, and have seen some hints in LT's current behavior about their potential effectiveness. All of the avenues mentioned earlier appear to offer worthwhile modifications of the program. We hope to report on these explorations at a later time.

7. Conclusion

We have provided data on the performance of a complex information processing system that is capable of finding proofs for theorems in elementary symbolic logic. We have used these data to analyze and illustrate the difference between systematic, algorithmic processes, on the one hand, and heuristic, problem-solving processes, on the other. We have shown how heuristics give the program power to solve problems in a reasonable computing time that could be solved algorithmically only in large numbers of years. Finally, we have assessed the limitations of the present program of the Logic Theory Machine and have indicated some of the directions that improvement would have to take to extend its powers to problems at new levels of difficulty.

Our explorations of the Logic Theory Machine represent a step in a program of research on complex information processing systems that is aimed at developing a theory of such systems and applying that theory to such fields as computer programming and human learning and problem solving.

Notes

1. For easy reference we have numbered axioms and theorems to correspond to their numbers in *Principia Mathematica*, second edition, volume 1, New York: by A. N. Whitehead and B. Russell, 1935.

2. As a noun, "heuristic" is rare and generally means the art of discovery. The adjective "heuris-

tic" is defined by Webster as: serving to discover or find out. It is in this sense that it is used in the phrase "heuristic process" or "heuristic method." For conciseness, we will use "heuristic" as a noun synonymous with "heuristic process." No other English word appears to have this meaning.

3. A number of fussy but not fundamental points must be taken care of in constructing the algorithm. The phrase "all permissible substitutions" needs to be qualified, for there is an infinity of these. Care must be taken not to duplicate expressions that differ only in the names of their variables. We will not go into details here, but simply state that these difficulties can be removed. The essential feature in constructing the algorithm is to allow only one thing to happen in generating each new expression, i.e., one replacement, substitution of "not-p" for "p," etc.

4 The following analogy may be instructive. Changing the symbols in a logic expression until the "right" expression is obtained is like turning the dials on a safe until the right combination is obtained. Suppose two safes, each with ten dials and ten numbers on a dial. The first safe gives a signal (a "click") when any given dial is turned to the correct number; the second safe clicks only when all ten dials are correct. Trial-and-error search will open the first safe, on the average, in 50 trials; the second safe, in five billion trials.

5. The version of LT used for seeking solutions of the 52 problems included a similarity test (see next section). Since the matching process is more important than the similarity test, we have presented the facts about matching first, using adjusted statistics. A notion of the sample sizes can be gained from Table 1. The sample was limited to the first 52 of the 67 theorems in Chapter 2 of *Principia* because of memory limitations of JOHNNIAC.

15

Some Studies in Machine Learning Using the Game of Checkers

Arthur L. Samuel

1. Introduction

The studies reported here have been concerned with the programming of a digital computer to behave in a way which, if done by human beings or animals, would be described as involving the process of learning. While this is not the place to dwell on the importance of machine-learning procedures, or to discourse on the philosophical aspects,[1] there is obviously a very large amount of work, now done by people, which is quite trivial in its demands on the intellect but does, nevertheless, involve some learning. We have at our command computers with adequate data-handling ability and with sufficient computational speed to make use of machine-learning techniques, but our knowledge of the basic principles of these techniques is still rudimentary. Lacking such knowledge, it is necessary to specify methods of problem solution in minute and exact detail, a time consuming and costly procedure.

Programming computers to learn from experience should eventually eliminate the need for much of this detailed programming effort.

1.1 General Methods of Approach

At the outset it might be well to distinguish sharply between two general approaches to the problem of machine learning. One method, which might be called the *neural-net approach,* deals with the possibility of inducing learned behavior into a randomly connected switching net (or its simulation on a digital computer) as a result of a reward-and-punishment routine. A second, and much more efficient approach, is to produce the equivalent of a highly organized network which has been designed to learn only certain specific things. The first method should lead to the development of general-purpose learning machines. A comparison between the size of the switching nets that can be reasonably constructed or simulated at the present time and the size of the neural nets used by animals, suggests that we have a long way to go before we obtain practical devices.[2] The second procedure requires reprogramming for each new application, but it is capable of realization at the present time. The experiments to be described here were based on this second approach.

1.2 Choice of Problem

For some years the writer has devoted his spare time to the subject of machine learning and has concentrated on the development of learning procedures as applied to games.[3] A game provides a convenient vehicle for such study as contrasted with a problem taken from life, since many of the complications of detail are removed. Checkers, rather than chess (Shannon 1950, Bernstein and Roberts 1958b, Kister et al. 1957, Newell, Shaw, and Simon 1958b), was chosen because the simplicity of its rules permits greater emphasis to be placed on learning techniques. Regardless of the relative merits of the two games as intellectual pastimes, it is fair to state that checkers contains all of the basic characteristics of an intellectual activity in which heuristic procedures and learning processes can play a major role and in which these processes can be evaluated.

Some of these characteristics might well be enumerated. They are:

1. The activity must not be deterministic in the practical sense. There exists no known algorithm which will guarantee a win or a draw in checkers, and the complete explorations of every possible path through a checker game would involve perhaps 10^{40} choices of moves which, at 3 choices per millimicrosecond, would still take 10^{21} centuries to consider.

2. A definite goal must exist—the winning of the game—and at least one criterion or intermediate goal must exist which has a bearing on the achievement of the final goal and for which the sign should be known. In checkers the goal is to deprive the opponent of the possibility of moving, and the

dominant criterion is the number of pieces of each color on the board. The importance of having a known criterion will be discussed later.

3. The rules of the activity must be definite and they should be known. Games satisfy this requirement. Unfortunately, many problems of economic importance do not. While in principle the determination of the rules can be a part of the learning process, this is a complication which might well be left until later.

4. There should be a background of knowledge concerning the activity against which the learning progress can be tested.

5. The activity should be one that is familiar to a substantial body of people so that the behavior of the program can be made understandable to them. The ability to have the program play against human opponents (or antagonists) adds spice to the study and, incidentally, provides a convincing demonstration for those who do not believe that machines can learn.

Having settled on the game of checkers for our learning studies, we must, of course, first program the computer to play legal checkers; that is, we must express the rules of the game in machine language and we must arrange for the mechanics of accepting an opponent's moves and of reporting the computer's moves, together with all pertinent data desired by the experimenter. The general methods for doing this were described by Shannon in 1950 as applied to chess rather than checkers. The basic program used in these experiments is quite similar to the program described by Strachey in 1952. The availability of a larger and faster machine (the IBM 704), coupled with many detailed changes in the programming procedure, leads to a fairly interesting game, even without any learning. The basic forms of the program will now be described.

2. The Basic Checker-Playing Program

The computer plays by looking ahead a few moves and by evaluating the resulting board positions much as a human player might do. Board positions are stored by sets of machine words, four words normally being used to represent any particular board position. Thirty-two bit positions (of the 36 available in an IBM 704 word) are, by convention, assigned to the 32 playing squares on the checkerboard, and pieces appearing on these squares are represented by 1's appearing in the assigned bit positions of the corresponding word. "Looking ahead" is prepared for by computing all possible next moves, starting with a given board position. The indicated moves are explored in turn by producing new board-position records corresponding to the conditions after the move in question (the old board positions being saved to facilitate a return to the starting point) and the process can be repeated. This

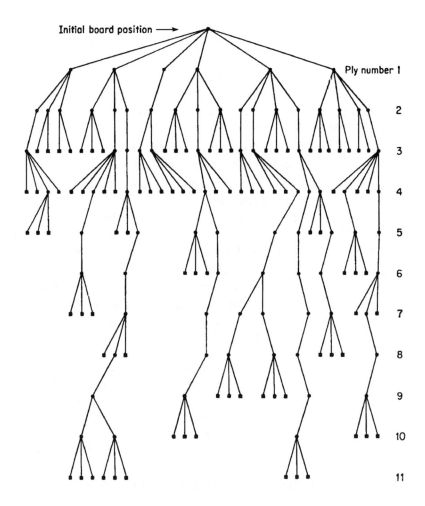

Figure 1. A "tree" of moves which might be investigated during the look-ahead procedure. The actual branchings are much more numerous than those shown, and the "tree" is apt to extend to as many as 20 levels.

look-ahead procedure is carried several moves in advance, as illustrated in Figure 1. The resulting board positions are then scored in terms of their relative value to the machine.

The standard method of scoring the resulting board positions has been in terms of a linear polynomial. A number of schemes of an abstract sort were tried for evaluating board positions without regard to the usual checker concepts, but none of these was successful.[4] One way of looking at the various terms in the scoring polynomial is that those terms with numerically small coefficients should measure criteria related as intermediate goals to the criteria measured by the larger terms. The achievement of these intermediate goals indicates that the machine is going in the right direction, such that the larger terms will eventually increase. If the program could look far enough ahead we need only ask, "Is the machine still in the game?"[5] Since it cannot look this far ahead in the usual situation, we must substitute something else, say the piece ratio, and let the machine continue the look-ahead until one side has gained a piece advantage. But even this is not always possible, so we have the program test to see if the machine has gained a positional advantage, et cetera. Numerical measures of these various properties of the board positions are then added together (each with an appropriate coefficient which defines its relative importance) to form the evaluation polynomial.

More specifically, as defined by the rules for checkers, the dominant scoring parameter is the inability for one side or the other to move.[6] Since this can occur but once in any game, it is tested for separately and is not included in the scoring polynomial as tabulated by the computer during play. The next parameter to be considered is the relative piece advantage. It is always assumed that it is to the machine's advantage to reduce the number of the opponent's pieces as compared to its own. A reversal of the sign of this term will, in fact, cause the program to play "giveaway" checkers, and with learning it can only learn to play a better and better giveaway game. Were the sign of this term not known by the programmer it could, of course, be determined by tests, but it must be fixed by the experimenter and, in effect, it is one of the instructions to the machine defining its task. The numerical computation of the piece advantage has been arranged in such a way as to account for the well-known property that it is usually to one's advantage to trade pieces when one is ahead and to avoid trades when behind. Furthermore, it is assumed that kings are more valuable than pieces, the relative weights assigned to them being three to two.[7] This ratio means that the program will trade three men for two kings, or two kings for three men, if by so doing it can obtain some positional advantage.

The choice for the parameters to follow this first term of the scoring polynomial and their coefficients then becomes a matter of concern. Two courses are open—either the experimenter can decide what these subsequent terms are to be, or he can arrange for the program to make the selection. We will discuss the first case in some detail in connection with the rote-learning studies and leave for a later section the discussion of various program methods of selecting parameters and adjusting their coefficients.

It is not satisfactory to select the initial move which leads to the board position with the highest score, since to reach this position would require the cooperation of the opponent. Instead, an analysis must be made proceeding *backward* from the evaluated board positions through the "tree" of possible moves, each time with consideration of the intent of the side whose move is being ex-

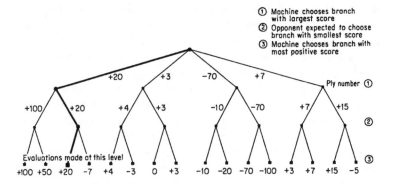

Figure 2. Simplified diagram showing how the evaluations are backed up through the tree of possible moves to arrive at the best next move. The evaluation process starts at (3).

amined, assuming that the opponent would always attempt to minimize the machine's score while the machine acts to maximize its score. At each branch point, then, the corresponding board position is given the score of the board position which would result from the most favorable move. Carrying this "minimax" procedure back to the starting point results in the selection of a "best move." The score of the board position at the end of the most likely chain is also brought back and for learning purposes this score is now assigned to the present board position. This process is shown in Figure 2. The best move is executed, reported on the console lights, and tabulated by the printer.

The opponent is then permitted to make his move, which can be communicated to the machine either by means of console switches or by means of punched cards. The computer verifies the legality of the opponent's move, rejecting[8] or accepting it, and the process is repeated. When the program can look ahead and predict a win, this fact is reported on the printer. Similarly, the program concedes when it sees that it is going to lose.

2.1 Ply Limitations

Playing-time considerations make it necessary to limit the look ahead distance to some fairly small value. This distance is defined as the ply (a ply of 2 consisting of one proposed move by the machine and the anticipated reply by the opponent). The ply is not fixed but depends upon the dynamics of the situation, and it varies from move to move and from branch to branch during the move analysis. A great many schemes of adjusting the look-ahead distance have been tried at various times, some of them quite complicated. The most effective one, although quite detailed, is simple in concept and is as follows. The program always looks ahead a minimum distance, which for the opening game and without learning is usually set at three moves. At this minimum ply the program will evaluate the board position if none of the following conditions occurs: (1) the next move is a jump, (2) the last move was a jump, or (3) an exchange offer is possible. If any one of these conditions exists, the program continues looking ahead. At a ply of 4 the program will stop and evaluate the resulting board position if conditions (1) and (3) above are not met. At a ply of 5 or greater, the program stops the look ahead whenever the next ply level does not offer a jump. At a ply of 11 or greater, the program will terminate the look-ahead, even if the next move is to be a jump, should one side at this time be ahead by more than two kings (to prevent the needless exploration of obviously losing or winning sequences). The program stops at a ply of 20 regardless of all conditions (since the memory space for the look-ahead moves is then exhausted) and an adjustment in score is made to allow for the pending jump. Finally, an adjustment is made in the levels of the break points between the different conditions when time is saved through rote learning (see below) and when the total number of pieces on the board falls below an arbitrary number. All break points are determined by single data words which can be changed at any time by manual intervention.

This tying of the ply with board conditions achieves three desired results. In the first place, it permits board evaluations to be made under conditions of relative stability for so-called dead positions, as defined by Turing (Bowden 1953). Secondly, it causes greater surveillance of those paths which offer better opportunities for gaining or losing an advantage. Finally, since branching is usually seriously restricted by a jump situation, the total number of board positions and moves to be considered is still held down to a reasonable number and is more equitably distributed between the various possible initial moves.

As a practical matter, machine playing time usually has been limited to approximately 30 seconds per move. Elaborate table look-up procedures, fast sorting and searching procedures, and a variety of new programming tricks were developed, and full use was made of all of the resources of the IBM 704 to increase the operating speed as much as possible. One can, of course, set the playing time at any desired value by adjustments of the permitted ply; too small a ply results in a bad game and too large a ply makes the game unduly costly in terms of machine time.

2.2 Other Modes of Play

For study purposes the program was written to accommodate several variations of this basic plan. One of these permits the program to play against itself, that is, to play both sides of the game. This mode of play has been found to be especially good during the early stages of learning.

The program can also follow book games presented to it either on cards or on magnetic tape. When operating in this mode, the program decides at each point in the game on its next move in the usual way and reports this proposed move. Instead of actually making this move, the program refers to the stored record of a book game and makes the book move. The program records its evaluation of the two moves, and it also counts and reports the number of possible moves which the program rates as being better than the book move and the number it rates as being poorer. The sides are then reversed and the process is repeated. At the end of a book game a correlation coefficient is computed, relating the machine's indicated moves to those moves adjudged best by the checker masters.[9]

It should be noted that the emphasis throughout all of these studies has been on learning techniques. The temptation to improve the machine's game by giving it standard openings or other man-generated knowledge of playing techniques has been consistently resisted. Even when book games are played, no weight is given to the fact that the moves as listed are presumably the best possible moves under the circumstances.

For demonstration purposes, and also as a means of avoiding lost machine time while an opponent is thinking, it is sometimes convenient to play several simultaneous games against different opponents. With the program in its present form the most convenient number for this purpose has been found to be six, although eight have been played on a number of occasions.

Games may be started with any initial configuration for the board position so that the program may be tested on end games, checker puzzles, et cetera. For nonstandard starting conditions, the program lists the initial piece arrangement. From time to time, and at the end of each game, the program also tabulates various bits of statistical information which assist in the evaluation of playing performance.

Numerous other features have also been added to make the program convenient to operate (for details see Section 7), but these have no direct bearing on the problem of learning, to which we will now turn our attention.

3. Rote Learning and Its Variants

Perhaps the most elementary type of learning worth discussing would be a form of rote learning in which the program simply saved all of the board positions encountered during play, together with their computed scores. Reference could then be made to this memory record and a certain amount of computing time might be saved. This can hardly be called a very advanced form of learning; nevertheless, if the program then utilizes the saved time to compute further in depth it will improve with time.

Fortunately, the ability to store board information at a ply of 0 and to look up boards at a larger ply provides the possibility of looking much farther in advance than might otherwise be possible. To understand this, consider a very simple case where the look ahead is always terminated at a fixed ply, say 3. Assume further that the program saves only the board positions encountered during the actual play with their associated backed-up scores. Now it is this list of previous board positions that is used to look up board positions while at a ply level of 3 in the subsequent games. If a board position is found, its score has, in effect, already been backed up by three levels, and if it becomes effective in determining the move to be made, it is a 6-ply score rather than a simple 3-ply score. This new initial board position with its 6-ply score is, in turn, saved and it may be encountered in a future game and the score backed up by an additional set of three levels, et cetera. This procedure is illustrated in Figure 3. The incorporation of this variation, together with the simpler rote-learning feature, results in a fairly powerful learning technique which has been studied in some detail.

Several additional features had to be incorporated into the program before it was practical to embark on learning studies using this storage scheme. In the first place, it was necessary to impart a sense of direction to the program in order to force it to press on toward a win. To illustrate this, consider the situation of two kings against one king, which is a winning combination for practically all variations in board positions. In time, the program can be assumed to have stored all of these variations, each associated with a winning score. Now, if such a situation is encountered, the program will look ahead along all possible paths and each path will lead to a winning combination, in spite of the fact that only one of the possible initial moves may be along the direct path toward the win while all of the rest may be wasting time. How is the program to differentiate between these?

A good solution is to keep a record of the ply value of the different board positions at all times and to make a further choice between board positions on this basis. If ahead, the program can be arranged to push directly toward the win while, if behind, it can be arranged to adopt delaying tactics. The most recent method used is to carry the effective ply along with the score by simply decreasing the magnitude of the score a small amount each time it is backed up a ply level during the analyses. If the program is now faced with a choice of board positions whose scores differ only by the ply number, it will automatically make the most advantageous choice, choosing a low-ply alternative if winning and a high-ply alternative if losing. The significance of this concept of a direction sense should not be overlooked. Even without "learning," it is very important. Several of the early attempts at learning failed because the direction sense was not properly taken into account.

3.1 Cataloging and Culling Stored Information

Since practical considerations limit the number of board positions which can be saved, and since the time to search through those that are saved can easily become unduly long, one must devise systems (1) to catalog boards that are

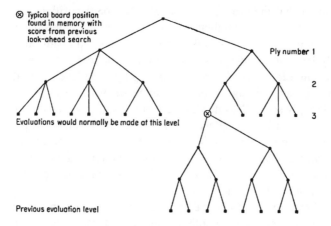

Figure 3. Simplified representation of the rote-learning process, in which information saved from a previous game is used to increase the effective ply of the backed-up score.

saved, (2) to delete redundancies, and (3) to discard board positions which are not believed to be of much value. The most effective cataloging system found to date starts by standardizing all board positions, first by reversing the pieces and piece positions if it is a board position in which White is to move, so that all boards are reported as if it were Black's turn to move. This reduces, by nearly a factor of two, the number of boards which must be saved. Board positions, in which all of the pieces are kings, can be reflected about the diagonals with a possible fourfold reduction in the number which must be saved. A more compact board representation than the one employed during play is also used so as to minimize the storage requirements.

After the board positions are standardized, they are grouped into records on the basis of (1) the number of pieces on the board, (2) the presence or absence of a piece advantage, (3) the side possessing this advantage, (4) the presence or absence of kings on the board, (5) the side having the so-called "move," or opposition advantage, and finally (6) the first moments of the pieces about normal and diagonal axes through the board. During play, newly acquired board positions are saved in the memory until a reasonable number have been accumulated, and they are then merged with those on the "memory tape" and a new memory tape is produced. Board positions within a record are listed in a serial fashion, being sorted with respect to the words which define them. The records are arranged on the tape in the order that they are most likely to be needed during the course of a game; board positions with 12 pieces to a side coming first, et cetera. This method of cataloging is very important because it cuts tape searching time to a minimum.

Reference must be made, of course, to the board positions already saved, and this is done by reading the correct record into the memory and searching through it by a dichotomous search procedure. Usually five or more records are held in memory at one time, the exact number at any time depending upon the lengths of the particular records in question. Normally, the program calls three or four new records into memory during each new move, making room for them as needed, by discarding the records which have been held the longest.

Two different procedures have been found to be of value in limiting the number of board positions that are saved; one based on the frequency of use, and the second on the ply. To keep track of the frequency of use, an age term is carried along with the score. Each new board position to be saved is arbitrarily assigned an age. When reference is made to a stored board position, either to update its score or to utilize it in the look-ahead procedure, the age recorded for this board position is divided by two. This is called *refreshing*. Offsetting this, each board position is automatically aged by one unit at the memory merge times (normally occurring about once every 20 moves). When the age of any one board position reaches an arbitrary maximum value this board position is expunged from the record. This is a form of *forgetting*. New board positions which remain unused are soon forgotten, while board positions which are used several times in succession will be refreshed to such an extent that they will be remembered even if not used thereafter for a fairly long period of time. This form of refreshing and forgetting was adopted on the basis of reflections as to the frailty of human memories. It has proven to be very effective.

In addition to the limitations imposed by forgetting, it seemed desirable to place a restriction on the maximum size of any one record. Whenever an arbitrary limit is reached, enough of the lowest-ply board positions are automatically culled from the record to bring the size well below the maximum.

Before embarking on a study of the learning capabilities of the system as just described, it was, of course, first necessary to fix the terms and coefficients in the evaluation polynomial. To do this, a number of different sets of values were tested by playing through a series of book games and computing the move correlation coefficients. These values varied from 0.2 for the poorest polynomial tested, to approximately 0.6 for the one finally adopted. The selected polynomial contained four terms (as contrasted with the use of 16 terms in later experiments). In decreasing order of importance these were:

1. piece advantage,

2. denial of occupancy,

3. mobility, and

4. a hybrid term which combined control of the center and piece advancement.

3.2 Rote-Learning Tests

After a scoring polynomial was arbitrarily picked, a series of games was played, both self-play and play against many different individuals (several of these being checker masters). Many book games were also followed, some of these being end games. The program learned to play a very good opening game and to recognize most winning and losing end positions many moves in advance, although its midgame play was not greatly improved. This program now qualifies as a rather better-than-average novice, but definitely not as an expert.

At the present time the memory tape contains something over 53,000 board positions (averaging 3.8 words each) which have been selected from a much larger number of positions by means of the culling techniques described. While this is still far from the number which would tax the listing and searching procedures used in the program, rough estimates, based on the frequency with which the saved boards are utilized during normal play (these figures being tabulated automatically), indicate that a library tape containing at least 20 times the present number of board positions would be needed to improve the midgame play significantly. At the present rate of acquisition of new positions this would require an inordinate amount of play and, consequently, of machine time.[10]

The general conclusions which can be drawn from these tests are that:

1. An effective rote-learning technique must include a procedure to give the program a sense of direction, and it must contain a refined system for cataloging and storing information.

2. Rote-learning procedures can be used effectively on machines with the data-handling capacity of the IBM 704 if the information which must be saved and searched does not occupy more than, roughly, one million words, and if not more than one hundred or so references need to be made to this information per minute. These figures are, of course, highly dependent upon the exact efficiency of cataloging which can be achieved.

3. The game of checkers, when played with a simple scoring scheme and with rote learning only, requires more than this number of words for master caliber of play and, as a consequence, is not completely amenable to this treatment on the IBM 704.

4. A game, such as checkers, is a suitable vehicle for use during the development of learning techniques, and it is a very satisfactory device for demonstrating machine learning procedures to the unbelieving.

4. Learning Procedure Involving Generalizations

An obvious way to decrease the amount of storage needed to utilize past experience is to generalize on the basis of experience and to save only the generalizations. This should, of course, be a continuous process if it is to be truly effective, and it should involve several levels of abstraction. A start has been made in this direction by having the program select a subset of possible terms for use in the evaluation polynomial and by having the program determine the sign and magnitude of the coefficients which multiply these parameters. At the present time this subset consists of 16 terms chosen from a list of 38 parameters. The piece-advantage term needed to define the task is computed separately and, of course, is not altered by the program.

After a number of relatively unsuccessful attempts to have the program generalize while playing both sides of the game, the program was arranged to act as two different players, for convenience called *Alpha* and *Beta*. Alpha generalizes on its experience after each move by adjusting the coefficients in its evaluation polynomial and by replacing terms which appear to be unimportant by new parameters drawn from a reserve list. Beta, on the contrary, uses the same evaluation polynomial for the duration of any one game. Program Alpha is used to play against human opponents, and during self-play Alpha and Beta play each other.

At the end of each self-play game a determination is made of the relative playing ability of Alpha, as compared with Beta, by a neutral portion of the program. If Alpha wins—or is adjudged to be ahead when a game is otherwise terminated—the then current scoring system used by Alpha is given to Beta. If, on the other hand, Beta wins or is ahead, this fact is recorded as a black mark for Alpha. Whenever Alpha receives an arbitrary number of black marks (usually set at three) it is assumed to be on the wrong track, and a fairly drastic and arbitrary change is made in its scoring polynomial (by reducing the coefficient of the leading term to zero). This action is necessary on occasion, since the entire learning process is an attempt to find the highest point in multidimensional scoring space in the presence of many secondary maxima on which the program can become trapped. By manual intervention it is possible to return to some previous condition or make some other change if it becomes apparent that the learning process is not functioning properly. In general, however, the program seeks to extricate itself from traps and to improve more or less continuously.

The capability of the program can be tested at any time by having Alpha play one or more book games (with the learning procedure temporarily immobilized) and by correlating its play with the recommendations of the masters or, more interestingly, by pitting it against a human player.

4.1 Polynomial Modification Procedure

If Alpha is to make changes in its scoring polynomial, it must be given some trustworthy criteria for measuring performance. A logical difficulty presents itself, since the only measuring parameter available is this same scoring polynomial that the process is designed to improve. Recourse is had to the peculiar property of the look-ahead procedure, which makes it less important for the scoring polynomial to be particularly good the further ahead the process is continued. This means that one can evaluate the relative change in the positions of two players, when this evaluation is made over a fairly large number of moves, by using a scoring system which is much too gross to be significant on a move by move basis.

Perhaps an even better way of looking at the matter is that we are attempting to make the score, calculated for the current board position, look like that calculated for the terminal board position of the chain of moves which most probably will occur during actual play. Of course, if one could develop a perfect system of this sort it would be the equivalent of always looking ahead to the end of the game. The nearer this ideal is approached, the better would be the play.[11]

In order to obtain a sufficiently large span to make use of this characteristic, Alpha keeps a record of the apparent goodness of its board positions as the game progresses. This record is kept by computing the scoring polynomial for each board position encountered in actual play and by saving this polynomial in its entirety. At the same time, Alpha also computes the backed-up score for all board positions, using the look-ahead procedure described earlier. At each play by Alpha the initial board score, as saved from the previous Alpha move, is compared with the backed-up score for the current position. The difference between these scores, defined as delta, is used to check the scoring polynomial. If delta is positive it is reasonable to assume that the initial board evaluation was in error and terms which contributed positively should have been given more weight, while those that contributed negatively should have been given less weight. A converse statement can be made for the case where delta is negative. Presumably, in this case, either the initial board evaluation was incorrect, or a wrong choice of moves was made, and greater weight should have been given to terms making negative contributions, with less weight to positive terms. These changes are not made directly but are brought about in an involved way which will now be described.

A record is kept of the correlation existing between the signs of the individual term contributions in the initial scoring polynomial and the sign of delta. After each play an adjustment is made in the values of the correlation coefficients, due account being taken of the number of times that each particular term has been used and has had a nonzero value. The coefficient for the polynomial term (other than the piece-advantage term) with the then largest correlation coefficient is set at a prescribed maximum value with proportionate values determined for all of the remaining coefficients. Actually, the term coefficients are fixed at integral powers of 2, this power being defined by the ratio of the correlation coefficients. More precisely, if the ratio of two correlation coefficients is equal to or larger than n but less than $n + 1$, where n is an integer, then the ratio of the two term coefficients is set equal to 2^n. This procedure was adopted in order to increase the range in values of the term coefficients. Whenever a correlation-coefficient calculation leads to a negative sign, a corresponding reversal is made in the sign associated with the term itself.

4.2 Instabilities

It should be noted that the span of moves over which delta is computed consists of a remembered part and an anticipated portion. During the remembered play, use had been made of Alpha's current scoring polynomial to determine Alpha's moves but not to determine the opponent's moves, while during the anticipation play the moves for both sides are made using Alpha's scoring polynomial. One is tempted to increase the sensitivity of delta as an indicator of change by increasing the span of the remembered portion. This has been found to be dangerous since the coefficients in the evaluation polynomial and, indeed, the terms themselves, may change between the time of the remembered evaluation and the time at which the anticipation evaluation is made. As a matter of fact, this difficulty is present even for a span of one move pair. It is necessary to recompute the scoring polynomial for a given initial board position after a move has been determined and after the indicated corrections in the scoring polynomial have been made, and to save this score for future comparisons, rather than to save the score used to determine the move. This may seem a trivial point but its neglect in the initial stages of these experiments led to oscillations quite analogous to the instability induced in electrical circuits by long delays in a feedback loop.

As a means of stabilizing against minor variations in the delta values, an arbitrary minimum value was set, and when delta fell below this minimum for any particular move no change was made in the polynomial. This same minimum value is used to set limits for the initial board evaluation score to decide whether or not it will be assumed to be zero. This minimum is recomputed each time and, normally, has been fixed at the average value of the coefficients for the terms in the currently existing evaluation polynomial.

Still another type of instability can occur whenever a new term is introduced into the scoring polynomial. Obviously, after only a single move the correlation coefficient of this new term will have a magnitude of 1, even though it might go to 0 after the very next move. To prevent violent fluctuations due to this cause, the correlation coefficients for newly introduced terms are computed as if these terms had already been used several times and had been found to have a zero correlation coefficient. This is done by replacing the times-used number in the calculation by an arbitrary number (usually set at 16) until the usage does, in fact, equal this number.

After a term has been in use for some time, quite the opposite action is desired so that the more recent experience can outweigh earlier results. This is achieved, together with a substantial reduction in calculation time, by using powers of 2 in place of the actual times used and by limiting the maximum power that is used. To be specific, at any stage of play defined as the Nth move, corrections to the values of the correlation coefficients C_N are made using 16 for N until N equals 32, whereupon 32 is used until N equals 64, et cetera, using the formula: $C_N = C_{N-1} - (C_{N-1} \pm 1)/N$ and a value for N larger than 256 is never used.

After a minimum was set for delta it seemed reasonable to attach greater weight to situations leading to large values of delta. Accordingly, two additional categories are defined. If a contribution to delta is made by the first term, meaning that a change has occurred in the piece ratio, the indicated changes in the correlation coefficients are doubled, while if the value of delta is so large as to indicate that an almost sure win or lose will result, the effect on the correlation coefficients is quadrupled.

4.3 Term Replacement

Mention has been made several times of the procedure for replacing terms in the scoring polynomial. The program, as it is currently running, contains 38 different terms (in addition to the piece advantage term), 16 of these being included in the scoring polynomial at any one time and the remaining 22 being kept in reserve. After each move a low-term tally is recorded against that active term which has the lowest correlation coefficient and, at the same time, a test is made to see if this brings its tally count up to some arbitrary limit, usually set at 8. When this limit is reached for any specific term, this term is transferred to the bottom of the reserve list, and it is replaced by a term from the head of the reserve list. This new term enters the polynomial with zero values for its correlation coefficient, times used, and low-tally count. On the average, then, an active term is replaced once each eight moves and the replaced terms are given another chance after 176 moves. As a check on the effectiveness of this procedure, the program reports on the usage which has accrued against each discarded term. Terms which are repeatedly rejected after a minimum amount of usage can be removed and replaced with completely new terms.

It might be argued that this procedure of having the program select terms for the evaluation polynomial from a supplied list is much too simple and that the program should generate the terms for itself. Unfortunately, no satisfactory scheme for doing this has yet been devised. With a man-generated list one might at least ask that the terms be members of an orthogonal set, assuming that this has some meaning as applied to the evaluation of a checker position. Apparently, no one knows enough about checkers to define such a set. The only practical solution seems to be that of including a relatively large number of possible terms in the hope that all of the contributing parameters get covered somehow, even though in an involved and redundant way. This is not an undesirable state of affairs, however, since it simulates the situation which is likely to exist when an attempt is made to apply similar learning techniques to real-life situations.

Many of the terms in the existing list are related in some vague way to the parameters used by checker experts. Some of the concepts which checker experts appear to use have eluded the writer's attempts at definition, and he has been unable to program them. Some of the terms are quite unrelated to the usual checker lore and have been discovered more or less by accident. The second moment about the diagonal axis through the double corners is an example. Twenty-seven different simple terms are now in use, the rest being combinational terms, as will be described later.

A word might be said about these terms with respect to the exact way in which they are defined and the general procedures used for their evaluation. Each term relates to the relative standings of the two sides, with respect to the parameter in question, and it is numerically equal to the difference between the ratings for the individual sides. A reversal of the sign obviously corresponds to a change of sides. As a further means of insuring symmetry the individual ratings of the respective sides are determined at corresponding times in the play as viewed by the side in question. For example, consider a parameter which relates to the board conditions as left after one side has moved. The rating of Black for such a parameter would be made after Black had moved, and the rating of White would not be made until after White had moved. During anticipation play, these individual ratings are made after each move and saved for future reference. When an evaluation is desired the program takes the differences between the most recent ratings and those made a move earlier. In general, an attempt has been made to define all parameters so that the individual-side ratings are expressible as small positive integers.

4.4 Binary Connective Terms

In addition to the simple terms of the type just described, a number of combinational terms have been introduced. Without these terms the scoring polynomial would, of course, be linear. A number of different ways of introducing nonlinear terms have been devised but only one of these has been tested in any detail. This scheme provides terms which have some of the properties of binary logical connectives. Four such terms are formed for each pair of simple terms which are to be related. This is done by making an arbitrary division of the range in values for each of the simple terms and assigning the binary values of 0 and 1 to these ranges. Since most of the simple terms are symmetrical about 0, this is easily done on a sign basis. The new terms are then of the form $A \cdot B$, $A \cdot {\sim}B$, ${\sim}A \cdot B$, and ${\sim}A \cdot {\sim}B$, yielding values either of 0 or 1. These terms are introduced into the scoring polynomial with adjustable coefficients and signs, and are thereafter indistinguishable from the other terms.

As it would require some 1404 such combinational terms to interrelate the

27 simple terms originally used, it was found desirable to limit the actual number of combinational terms used at any one time to a small fraction of these and to introduce new terms only as it became possible to retire older ineffectual terms. The terms actually used are given in the appendix to Samuel (1959)

4.5 Preliminary Learning-by-Generalization Tests

An idea of the learning ability of this procedure can be gained by analyzing an initial test series of 28 games[12] played with the program just described. At the start an arbitrary selection of 16 terms was chosen and all terms were assigned equal weights. During the first 14 games Alpha was assigned the White side, with Beta constrained as to its first move (two cycles of the seven different initial moves). Thereafter, Alpha was assigned Black and White alternately. During this time a total of 29 different terms was discarded and replaced, the majority of these on two different occasions.

Certain other figures obtained during these 28 games are of interest. At frequent intervals the program lists the 12 leading terms in Alpha's scoring polynomial with their correlation coefficients and a running count of the number of times these coefficients have been altered. Based on these samplings, one observes that at least 20 different terms were assigned the largest coefficient at some time or other, some of these alternating with other terms a number of times, and two even reappearing at the top of the list with their signs reversed. While these variations were more violent at the start of the series of games and decreased as time went on, their presence indicated that the learning procedure was still not completely stable. During the first seven games there were at least 14 changes in occupancy at the top of the list involving 10 different terms. Alpha won three of these games and lost four. The quality of the play was extremely poor. During the next seven games there were at least eight changes made in the top listing involving five different terms. Alpha lost the first of these games and won the next six. Quality of play improved steadily but the machine still played rather badly. During Games 15 through 21 there were eight changes in the top listing involving five terms; Alpha winning five games and losing two. Some fairly good amateur players who played the machine during this period agreed that it was "tricky but beatable." During Games 22 through 28 there were at least four changes involving three terms. Alpha won two games and lost five. The program appeared to be approaching a quality of play which caused it to be described as "a better than average player." A detailed analysis of these results indicated that the learning procedure did work and that the rate of learning was surprisingly high, but that the learning was quite erratic and none too stable.

4.6 Second Series of Tests

Some of the more obvious reasons for this erratic behavior in the first series of tests have been identified. The program was modified in several respects to improve the situation, and additional tests were made. Four of these modifications are important enough to justify a detailed explanation.

In the first place, the program was frequently fooled by bad play on the part of its opponent. A simple solution was to change the correlation coefficients less drastically when delta was positive than when delta was negative. The procedure finally adopted for the positive delta case was to make corrections to selected terms in the polynomial only. When the scoring polynomial was positive, changes were made to coefficients associated with the negatively contributing terms, and when the polynomial was negative, changes were made to the coefficients associated with positively contributing terms. No changes were made to coefficients associated with terms which happened to be zero. For the negative delta case, changes were made to the coefficients of all contributing terms, just as before.

A second defect seemed to be connected with the too frequent introduction of new terms into the scoring polynomial and the tendency for these new terms to assume dominant positions on the basis of insufficient evidence. This was remedied by the simple expedient of decreasing the rate of introduction of new terms from one every eight moves to one every 32 moves.

The third defect had to do with the complete exclusion from consideration of many of the board positions encountered during play by reason of the minimum limit on delta. This resulted in the misassignment of credit to those board positions which permitted spectacular moves when the credit rightfully belonged to earlier board positions which had permitted the necessary ground-laying moves. Although no precise way has yet been devised to ensure the correct assignment of credit, a very simple expedient was found to be most effective in minimizing the adverse effects of earlier assignments. This expedient was to allow the span of remembered moves, over which delta is computed, to increase until delta exceeded the arbitrary minimum value, and then to apply the corrections to the coefficients as dictated by the terms in the retained polynomial for this earlier board position. In this case, the difficulty which was mentioned in Section 4.2 in connection with an arbitrary increase in span, does not occur after each correction, since no changes are made in the coefficients of the scoring polynomial as long as delta is below the minimum value. Of course, whenever delta does exceed the minimum value the program must then recompute the initial scoring polynomial for the then current board position and so restart the procedure with a span of a single remembered move pair. This over all procedure rectifies the defect of assigning credit to a board position that lies too far along the move chain, but it introduces the possibility of assigning credit to a board position that is not far enough along.

As a partial expedient to compensate for this newly introduced danger, a change was made in the initial board evaluation. Instead of evaluating the ini-

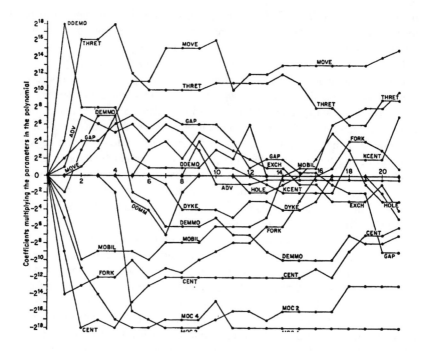

Figure 4. Second series of learning-by-generalization tests. Coefficients assigned by the program to the more significant parameters of the evaluation polynomial plotted as a function of the number of games played. Two regions of special interest might be noted: (1) the situation after 13 or 14 games, when the program found that the initial signs of many of the terms had been set incorrectly, and (2) the conditions of relative stability which are beginning to show up after 31 or 32 games.

tial board positions directly, as was done before, a standard but rudimentary tree search (terminated after the first nonjump move) was used. Errors due to impending jump situations were eliminated by this procedure, and because of the greater accuracy of the evaluation it was possible to reduce the minimum delta limit by a small amount.

Finally, to avoid the danger of having Beta adopt Alpha's polynomial as a result of a chance win on Alpha's part (or perhaps a situation in which Alpha had allowed its polynomial to degenerate after an early or midgame advantage had been gained), it was decided to require a majority of wins on Alpha's part before Beta would adopt Alpha's scoring polynomial.

With these modifications, a new series of tests was made. In order to reduce the learning time, the initial selection of terms was made on the basis of the results obtained during the earlier tests, but no attention was paid to their previously assigned weights. In contrast with the earlier erratic behavior, the revised program appeared to be extremely stable, perhaps at the expense of a

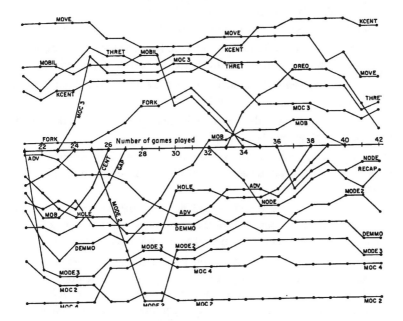

somewhat lower initial learning rate. The way in which the character of the evaluation polynomial altered as learning progressed is shown in Figure 4.

The most obvious change in behavior was in regard to the relative number of games won by Alpha and the prevalence of draws. During the first 28 games of the earlier series Alpha won 16 and lost 12. The corresponding figures for the first 28 games of the new series were 18 won by Alpha, and four lost, with six draws. In all cases the games were terminated, if not finished, in 70 moves and a judgment made in terms of the final positions. Unfortunately, these figures are not strictly comparable because of the decreased frequency with which Beta adopted Alpha's polynomial during the second series, both by design and because a programming error immobilized the adoption procedure during part of the tests. Nevertheless, the great decrease in the number of losses and the prevalence of draws seemed to indicate that the learning process was much more stable. Some typical games from this second series are given in Samuel (1959).

As learning proceeds, it should become harder and harder for Alpha to improve its game, and one would expect the number of wins by Alpha to decrease with time. If secondary maxima in scoring space are encountered, one might even find situations in which Alpha wins less than half of the games. With Beta at such a maximum any minor change in Alpha's polynomial would result in a degradation of its play, and several oscillations about the maximum might occur before Alpha landed at a point which would enable it to beat Beta. Some evidence of this trend is discernible in the play, although many more games will have to be played before it can be observed with certainty.

The tentative conclusions which can be drawn from these tests are:

1. A simple generalization scheme of the type here used can be an effective learning device for problems amenable to tree-searching procedures.

2. The memory requirements of such schemes are quite modest and remain fixed with time.

3. The operating times are also reasonable and remain fixed, independent of the amount of accumulated learning.

4. Incipient forms of instability in the solution can be expected but, at least for the checker program, these can be dealt with by quite straightforward procedures.

5. Even with the incomplete and redundant set of parameters which have been used to date, it is possible for the computer to learn to play a better-than-average game of checkers in a relatively short period of time.

As a final precautionary note, it should be stated that these experiments have not encompassed a sufficiently large series of games to demonstrate unambiguously that the learning procedure is completely stable or that it will necessarily lead to the best possible choice of parameters and coefficients.

5. Rote Learning Versus Generalization

Some interesting comparisons can be made between the playing style developed by the learning-by-generalization program and that developed by the earlier rote-learning procedure. The program with rote learning soon learned to imitate master play during the opening moves. It was always quite poor during the middle game, but it easily learned how to avoid most of the obvious traps during end-game play and could usually drive on toward a win when left with a piece advantage. The program with the generalization procedure has never learned to play in a conventional manner and its openings are apt to be weak. On the other hand, it soon learned to play a good middle game, and with a piece advantage it usually polishes off its opponent in short order. Interestingly enough, after 28 games it had still not learned how to win an end game with two kings against one in a double corner.

Apparently, rote learning is of the greatest help either under conditions when the results of any specific action are long delayed or in those situations where highly specialized techniques are required. Contrasting with this, the generalization procedure is most helpful in situations in which the available permutations of conditions are large in number and when the consequences of any specific action are not long delayed.

5.1 Procedures Involving Both Forms of Learning

The next obvious step is to combine the better features of the rote learning procedure with a generalization scheme. This must be done with some care, since it is not practical to update the previously saved information after every change in the evaluation polynomial. A compromise solution might be to save only a very limited amount of information during the early stages of learning and to increase the amount as warranted by the increasing stability of the evaluation coefficient with learning. For example, the program could be arranged to save only the piece-advantage term at the start. At some stage in the learning process the next term could be added, perhaps when no change had been made in the parameter used for this term during some fairly long period, say for three complete games. If and when the program is able to play an additional period without changes in the next parameter, this could also be added, et cetera. Whenever a change does occur in a parameter previously assumed to be stable, the entire memory tape could be reviewed, all terms involving the changed parameter and those lower on the list could be expunged, and the program could drop back to the earlier condition with respect to its term saving schedule.

Another solution would be to utilize the generalization scheme alone until it had become fairly stable and to introduce rote learning at this time. It is, of course, perfectly feasible to salvage much of the learning which has been accumulated by both of the programs studied to date. This could be done by appending an abridged form of the present memory tape to the generalization scheme in its present stage of learning and by proceeding from there in accordance with the first solution proposed above.

5.2 Future Development

While it is believed that these tests have reached the stage of diminishing returns, some effort might well be expended in an attempt to get the program to generate its own parameters for the evaluation polynomial. Lacking a perfectly general procedure, it might still be possible to generate terms based on theories as proposed by students of the game. This procedure would be at variance with the writer's previous philosophy, but it is highly likely that similar compromises will have to be made when one attempts to apply learning procedures to problems of economic importance.

6. Conclusions

As a result of these experiments (see further detailed analysis of program and games in the appendix to Samuel 1959) one can say with some certainty that it is now possible to devise learning schemes which will greatly outperform

an average person and that such learning schemes may eventually be economically feasible as applied to real life problems.

Notes

1. Some of these are quite profound and have a bearing on the questions raised by Nelson Goodman in *Fact, Fiction and Forecast,* Cambridge, Mass.: Harvard, 1954.

2. Warren S. McCulloch (1949) has compared the digital computer to the nervous system of a
flatworm. To extend this comparison to the situation under discussion would be unfair to the
worm, since its nervous system is actually quite highly organized as compared with the random-
net studies by Farley and Clark (1954), Rochester, Holland, Haibt, and Duda (1956), and by
Rosenblatt (1958).

3. The first operating checker program for the IBM 701 was written in 1952. This was recoded
for the IBM 704 in 1954. The first program with learning was completed in 1955 and demonstrated on television on February 24, 1956.

4. One of the more interesting of these was to express a board position in terms of the first and
higher moments of the white and black pieces separately about two orthogonal axes on the
board. Two such sets of axes were tried, one set being parallel to the sides of the board and the
second set being those through the diagonals.

5. This apt phraseology was suggested by John McCarthy.

6. Not the capture of all the opponent's pieces, as popularly assumed, although all games end in
this fashion.

7. The use of a weight ratio rather than this, conforming more closely to the values assumed by
many players, can lead into certain logical complications, as found by Strachey (1952).

8. The only departure from complete generality of the game as programmed is that the program
requires the opponent to make a permissible move, including the taking of a capture if one is offered. "Huffing" is not permitted.

9. This coefficient is defined as $C = (L - H)/(L + H)$, where L is the total number of different
legal moves which the machine judged to be poorer than the indicated book moves, and H is the
total number which it judged to be better than the book moves.

10. This playing-time requirement, while large in terms of cost, would be less than the time
which the checker master probably spends to acquire his proficiency.

11. There is a logical fallacy in this argument. The program might save only invariant terms
which have nothing to do with goodness of play; for example, it might count the squares on the
checkerboard. The forced inclusion of the piece-advantage term prevents this.

12. The games averaged 68 moves (34 to a side) of which approximately 20 caused changes to
be made in the scoring polynomial.

16

GPS, A Program that Simulates Human Thought

Allen Newell and Herbert A. Simon

1. Introduction

This chapter is concerned with the psychology of human thinking. It sets forth a theory to explain how some humans try to solve some simple formal problems. The research from which the theory emerged is intimately related to the field of information processing and the construction of intelligent automata, and the theory is expressed in the form of a computer program. The rapid technical advances in the art of programming digital computers to do sophisticated tasks have made such a theory feasible.

It is often argued that a careful line must be drawn between the attempt to *accomplish* with machines the same tasks that humans perform, and the attempt to *simulate* the processes humans actually use to accomplish these tasks. The program discussed in the report, GPS (general problem solver), maximally confuses the two approaches—with mutual benefit. GPS has previously been described as an attempt to build a problem-solving program (Newell, Shaw, and Simon 1959a, 1960a), and in our own research it remains a major vehicle for exploring the area of artificial intelligence. Simultaneously, variants of GPS provide simulations of human behavior (Newell and Simon 1961a). It is this latter aspect—the use of GPS as a theory of human problem-solving—that we want to focus on exclusively here, with special attention to the relation between the theory and the data.

As a context for the discussion that is to follow, let us make some brief comments on some history of psychology. At the beginning of this century the prevailing thesis in psychology was *associationism*. It was an atomistic doctrine, which postulated a theory of hard little elements, either sensations or ideas, that became hooked or associated together without modification. It was a mechanistic doctrine, with simple fixed laws of contiguity in time and space to account for the formation of new associations. Those were its assumptions. Behavior proceeded by the stream of associations: Each association produced its successors, and acquired new attachments with the sensations arriving from the environment.

In the first decade of the century a reaction developed to this doctrine through the work of the Wurzburg school. Rejecting the notion of a completely self-determining stream of associations, it introduced the task *(aufgabe)* as a necessary factor in describing the process of thinking. The task gave direction to thought. A noteworthy innovation of the Wurzburg school was the use of systematic introspection to shed light on the thinking process and the contents of consciousness. The result was a blend of mechanics and phenomenalism, which gave rise in turn to two divergent antitheses, Behaviorism and the Gestalt movement.

The behavioristic reaction insisted that introspection was a highly unstable, subjective procedure, whose futility was amply demonstrated in the controversy on imageless thought. Behaviorism reformulated the task of psychology as one of explaining the response of organisms as a function of the stimuli impinging upon them and measuring both objectively. However, Behaviorism accepted, and indeed reinforced, the mechanistic assumption that the connections between stimulus and response were formed and maintained as simple, determinate functions of the environment.

The Gestalt reaction took an opposite turn. It rejected the mechanistic nature of the associationist doctrine but maintained the value of phenomenal observation. In many ways it continued the Wurzburg school's insistence that thinking was more than association—thinking has direction given to it by the task or by the set of the subject. Gestalt psychology elaborated this doctrine in genuinely new ways in terms of holistic principles of organization.

Today psychology lives in a state of relatively stable tension between the poles of Behaviorism and Gestalt psychology. All of us have internalized the major lessons of both: We treat skeptically the subjective elements in our experiments and agree that all notions must eventually be made operational by means of behavioral measures. We also recognize that a human being is a tremendously complex, organized system, and that the simple schemes of modern behavioristic psychology seem hardly to reflect this at all.

2. An Experimental Situation

In this context, then, consider the following situation. A human subject, a student in engineering in an American college, sits in front of a blackboard on which are written the following expressions:

$$(R \supset \sim P) \cdot (\sim R \supset Q) \mid \sim (\sim Q \cdot P)$$

This is a problem in elementary symbolic logic, but the student does not know it. He does know that he has twelve rules for manipulating expressions containing letters connected by "dots" ($\cdot$), "wedges" (V), "horseshoes" ($\supset$), and "tildes" ($\sim$), which stand respectively for "and," "or," "implies," and "not." These rules, given in Figure 1, show that expressions of certain forms (at the tails of the arrows) can be transformed into expressions of somewhat different form (at the heads of the arrows). (Double arrows indicate transformations can take place in either direction.) The subject has practiced applying the rules, but he has previously done only one other problem like this. The experimenter has instructed him that his problem is to obtain the expression in the upper right corner from the expression in the upper left corner using the twelve rules. At any time the subject can request the experimenter to apply one of the rules to an expression that is already on the blackboard. If the transformation is legal, the experimenter writes down the new expression in the left-hand column, with the name of the rule in the right-hand column beside it. The subject's actual course of solution is shown beneath the rules in Figure 1.

The subject was also asked to talk aloud as he worked; his comments were recorded and then transcribed into a "protocol,"—i.e., a verbatim record of all that he or the experimenter said during the experiment. The initial section of this subject's protocol is reproduced in Figure 2.

3. The Problem of Explanation

It is now proposed that the protocol of Figure 2 constitutes data about human behavior that are to be explained by a psychological theory. But what are we to make of this? Are we back to the introspections of the Wurzburgers? And how are we to extract information from the behavior of a single subject when we have not defined the operational measures we wish to consider?

There is little difficulty in viewing this situation through behavioristic eyes.

Objects are formed by building up expressions from letters (P, Q, R, . . .) and connectives · (dot), V (wedge), ⊃ (horseshoe), and ~ (tilde). Examples are P, ~Q, P V Q, ~ (R ⊃ S) · ~P; ~~P is equivalent to P throughout. Twelve rules exist for transforming expressions (where A, B, and C may be any expressions or subexpressions):

R 1. A · B → B · A
      A V B → B V A

R 2. A ⊃ B → ~ B ⊃ ~ A

R 3. A · A ⟷ A
      A V A ⟷ A

R 4. A · (B · C) ⟷ (A · B) · C
      A V (B V C) ⟷ (A V B) V C

R 5. A V B ⟷ ~(~A · ~B)

R 6. A ⊃ B ⟷ ~ A V B

R 7. A · (B V C) ⟷ (A · B) V (A · C)
      A V (B · C) ⟷ (A V B) · (A V C)

R 8. A · B → A   Applies to main
      A · B → B   expression only.

R 9. A → A V X   Applies to main
                       expression only.

R 10. A⎫
       B⎭ → A · B   A and B are two main expressions.

R 11. A   ⎫
       A ⊃ B ⎭ → B   A and A ⊃ B are two main expressions.

R 12. A ⊃ B⎫   A ⊃ B and B ⊃ C
       B ⊃ C⎭ → A ⊃ C are two main expressions.

Example, showing subject's entire course of solution on problem:

1. (R ⊃ ~P) · (~ R ⊃ Q)	~ (~ Q · P)
2. (~R V ~P) · (R V Q)	Rule 6 applied to left and right of 1.
3. (~R V ~P) · (~ R ⊃ Q)	Rule 6 applied to left of 1.
4. R ⊃ ~P	Rule 8 applied to 1.
5. ~R V ~P	Rule 6 applied to 4.
6. ~R ⊃ Q	Rule 8 applied to 1.
7. R V Q	Rule 6 applied to 6.
8. (~R V ~P) · (R V Q)	Rule 10 applied to 5. and 7.
9. P ⊃ ~R	Rule 2 applied to 4.
10. ~Q ⊃ R	Rule 2 applied to 6.
11. P ⊃ Q	Rule 12 applied to 6. and 9.
12. ~P V Q	Rule 6 applied to 11.
13. ~(P · ~Q)	Rule 5 applied to 12.
14. ~(~Q · P)	Rule 1 applied to 13. QED.

Figure 1. The task of symbolic logic.

The verbal utterances of the subject are as much behavior as would be his arm movements or galvanic skin responses. The subject was not introspecting; he was simply emitting a continuous stream of verbal behavior while solving the problem. Our task is to find a model of the human problem solver that explains the salient features of this stream of behavior. This stream contains not only the subject's extemporaneous comments, but also his commands to the experimenter, which determine whether he solves the problem or not.

Although this way of viewing the behavior answers the questions stated above, it raises some of its own. How is one to deal with such variable behavior? Isn't language behavior considered among the most complex human behavior? How does one make reliable inferences from a single sample of data on a single subject?

The answers to these questions rest upon the recent, striking advances that have been made in computers, computer programming and artificial intelligence. We have learned that a computer is a general manipulator of sym-

Well, looking at the left hand side of the equation, first we want to eliminate one of the sides by using rule 8. It appears too complicated to work with first. Now—no, —no, I can't do that because I will be eliminating either the Q or the P in that total expression. I won't do that at first. Now I'm looking for a way to get rid of the horseshoe inside the two brackets that appear on the left and right sides of the equation. And I don't see it. Yeh, if you apply rule 6 to both sides of the equation, From there I'm going to see if I can apply rule 7.

Experimenter writes: 2. $(\sim R \ V \sim P) \bullet (R \ V \ Q)$

I can almost apply rule 7, but one R needs a tilde. So I'll have to look for another rule. I'm going to see if I can change that R to a tilde R. As a matter of fact, I should have used rule 6 on only the left hand side of the equation. So use rule 6, but only on the left hand side.

Experimenter writes: 3. $(\sim R \ V \sim P) \bullet (\sim R \supset Q)$

Now I'll apply rule 7 as it is expressed. Both - excuse me, excuse me, it can't be done because of the horseshoe. So - now I'm looking-scanning the rules here for a second, and seeing if I can change the R to an ~R in the second equation, but I don't see any way of doing it. (Sigh.) I'm just sort of lost for a second.

Figure 2. Subject's protocol on first part of problem.

bols—not just a manipulator of numbers. Basically, a computer is a transformer of patterns. By suitable devices, most notably its addressing logic, these patterns can be given all the essential characteristics of linguistic symbols. They can be copied and formed into expressions. We have known this abstractly since Turing's work in the mid-1930s, but it is only recently that computers have become powerful enough to let us actually explore the capabilities of complex symbol manipulating systems.

For our purpose here, the most important branch of these explorations is the attempt to construct programs that solve tasks requiring intelligence. Considerable success has already been attained (Gelernter 1959b, Kilburn et al. 1959, Minsky 1961a, Newell, Shaw, and Simon 1957a, 1958b, Samuel 1959a, Tonge 1960). These accomplishments form a body of ideas and techniques that allow a new approach to the building of psychological theories. (Much of the work on artificial intelligence, especially our own, has been partly motivated by concern for psychology; hence, the resulting rapprochement is not entirely coincidental.)

We may then conceive of an intelligent program that manipulates symbols in the same way that our subject does—by taking as inputs the symbolic logic expressions, and producing as ouputs a sequence of rule applications that coincides with the subject's. If we observed this program in operation, it would be considering various rules and evaluating various expressions, the same sorts of things we see expressed in the protocol of the subject. If the fit of such a program were close enough to the overt behavior of our human subject—i.e., to the protocol—then it would constitute a good theory of the subject's problem solving.

Conceptually the matter is perfectly straightforward. A program prescribes in abstract terms (expressed in some programming language) how a set of symbols in a memory is to be transformed through time. It is completely analogous to a set of difference equations that prescribes the transformation of a set of numbers through time. Given enough information about an individual, a program could be written that would describe the symbolic behavior of that individual. Each individual would be described by a different program, and those aspects of human problem-solving that are not idiosyncratic would emerge as the common structure and content of the programs of many individuals.

But is it possible to write programs that do the kinds of manipulation that humans do? Given a specific protocol, such as the one of Figure 2, is it possible to induct the program of the subject? How well does a program fit the data? The remainder of the report will be devoted to answering some of these questions by means of the single example already presented. We will consider only how GPS behaves on the first part of the problem, and we will compare it in detail with the subject's behavior as revealed in the protocol. This will shed considerable light on how far we can consider programs as theories of human problem solving.

4. The GPS Program

We will only briefly recapitulate the GPS program, since our description will add little to what has already been published (Newell, Shaw, and Simon 1959a, 1960a). GPS deals with a task environment consisting of *objects* which can be transformed by various *operators;* it detects *differences* between objects; and it organizes the information about the task environment into *goals*. Each goal is a collection of information that defines what constitutes goal attainment, makes available the various kinds of information relevant to attaining the goal, and relates the information to other goals. There are three types of goals:

> Transform object A into object B.
> Reduce difference D between object A and object B.
> Apply operator Q to object A.

For the task of symbolic logic, the objects are logic expressions; the operators are the twelve rules (actually the specific variants of them); and the differences are expressions like "change connective" or "add a term." Thus the objects and operators are given by the task; whereas the differences are something GPS brings to the problem. They represent the ways of relating operators to their respective effects upon objects.

Basically, the GPS program is a way of achieving a goal by setting up sub-

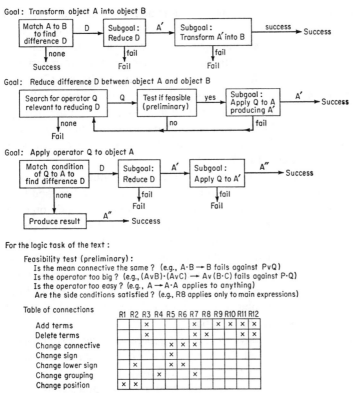

Goal: Transform object A into object B

Goal: Reduce difference D between object A and object B

Goal: Apply operator Q to object A

For the logic task of the text :

Feasibility test (preliminary) :
Is the mean connective the same ? (e.g., A·B → B fails against PvQ)
Is the operator too big ? (e.g., (AvB)·(AvC) → Av(B·C) fails against P·Q)
Is the operator too easy ? (e.g., A → A·A applies to anything)
Are the side conditions satisfied ? (e.g., R8 applies only to main expressions)

Table of connections

	R1	R2	R3	R4	R5	R6	R7	R8	R9	R10	R11	R12
Add terms			x				x		x	x	x	x
Delete terms			x			x	x			x	x	
Change connective					x	x	x					
Change sign					x							
Change lower sign		x			x	x						
Change grouping				x			x					
Change position	x	x										

x means some variant of the rule is relevant. GPS will pick the appropriate variant.

Figure 3. Methods for GPS.

goals whose attainment leads to the attainment of the initial goal. GPS has various schemes, called methods, for doing this. Three crucial methods are presented in Figure 3. one method associated with each goal type.

Thus, to transform an object A into an object B, the objects are first matched—put into correspondence and compared element by element. If the match reveals a difference, D, between the two objects, then a subgoal is set up to reduce this difference. If this subgoal is attained, a new object, A', is produced which (hopefully) no longer has the difference D when compared with object B. Then a new subgoal is created to transform A' into B. If the transformation succeeds, the entire goal has been attained in two steps: from A to A' and from A' to B.

If the goal is to reduce the difference between two objects, the first step is to find an operator that is relevant to this difference. Relevance here means that the operator affects objects with respect to the difference. Operationally, relevance can be determined by applying the matching process already used to the input and output forms of the operators, due account being taken of variables. The results can be summarized in a table of connections, as shown in Figure 3, which lists for each difference the operators that are relevant to it. This table also lists the differences that GPS recognizes. (This set is somewhat different from the one given in Newell, Shaw, and Simon [1959a]; it corresponds to the program we will deal with in this report.) If a relevant operator, Q, is found, it is subjected to a preliminary test of feasibility, one version of which is given in Figure 3. If the operator passes this test, a subgoal is set up to apply the operator to the object. If the operator is successfully applied, a new object, A', is produced which is a modification of the original one in the direction of reducing the difference. (Of course, other modifications may also have occurred which nullify the usefulness of the new object.)

If the goal is to apply an operator, the first step is to see if the conditions of the operator are satisfied. The preliminary test above by no means guarantees this. If the conditions are satisfied, then the output, A, can be generated. If the conditions are not satisfied, then some difference, D, has been detected and a subgoal is created to reduce this difference, just as with the transform goal. Similarly, if a modified object, A', is obtained, a new subgoal is formed to try to apply the operator to this new object.

These methods form a recursive system that generates a tree of subgoals in attempting to attain a given goal. For every new difficulty that is encountered a new subgoal is created to overcome this difficulty. GPS has a number of tests it applies to keep the expansion of this goal tree from proceeding in unprofitable directions. The most important of these is a test which is applied to new subgoals for reducing differences. GPS contains an ordering of the differences, so that some differences are considered easier than others. This ordering is given by the table of connections in Figure 3, which lists the most difficult differences first. GPS will not try a subgoal if it is harder than one of its super goals. It will also not try a goal if it follows an easier goal. That is, GPS insists on working on the hard differences first and expects to find easier ones as it goes along. The other tests that GPS applies involve external limits (e.g., a limit on the total depth of a goal tree it will tolerate) and whether new objects or goals are identical to ones already generated.

5. GPS on the Problem

The description we have just given is adequate to verify the reasonableness, although not the detail, of a trace of GPS's behavior on a specific problem. (In particular we have not described how the two-line rules, R10 through R12, are handled, since they do not enter into the protocol we are examin-

```
L0   ~(~Q·P)
L1   (R⊃~P)·(~R⊃Q)

GOAL 1  TRANSFORM L1 INTO L0
     GOAL 2  DELETE R FROM L1
          GOAL 3  APPLY R8 TO L1
               PRODUCES L2 R⊃~P

     GOAL 4  TRANSFORM L2 INTO L0
          GOAL 5  ADD Q TO L2
               REJECT

     GOAL 2
          GOAL 6  APPLY R8 TO L1
               PRODUCES L3  ~R⊃Q

     GOAL 7  TRANSFORM L3 INTO L0
          GOAL 8  ADD P TO L3
               REJECT

     GOAL 2
          GOAL 9  APPLY R7 TO L1
               GOAL 10  CHANGE CONNECTIVE TO V IN LEFT L1
                    GOAL 11  APPLY R6 TO LEFT L1
                         PRODUCES L4  (~R V ~P)·(~R⊃Q)

          GOAL 12  APPLY R7 TO L4
               GOAL 13  CHANGE CONNECTIVE TO V IN RIGHT L4
                    GOAL 14  APPLY R6 TO RIGHT L4
                         PRODUCES L5  (~R V ~P)·(R V Q)

          GOAL 15  APPLY R7 TO L5
               GOAL 16  CHANGE SIGN OF LEFT RIGHT L5
                    GOAL 17  APPLY R6 TO RIGHT L5
                         PRODUCES L6  (~R V ~P)·(~R⊃Q)

          GOAL 18  APPLY R7 TO L6
               GOAL 19  CHANGE CONNECTIVE TO V
                        IN RIGHT L6
                    REJECT

          GOAL 16
               NOTHING MORE

          GOAL 13
               NOTHING MORE

     GOAL 10
          NOTHING MORE
```

Figure 4. Trace of GPS on first part of the problem.

ing.) In Figure 4, we give the trace on the initial part of the problem. Indentation is used to indicate the relation of a subgoal to a goal. Although the methods are not shown, they can clearly be inferred from the goals that occur.

The initial problem is to transform L1 into L0. Matching L1 to L0 reveals that there are R's in L1 and no R's in L0. This difference leads to the formulation of a reduce goal, which for readability has been given its functional name, *Delete*. The attempt to reach this goal leads to a search for rules which finds rule 8. Since there are two forms of rule 8, both of which are admissible, GPS chooses the first. (Variants of rules are not indicated, but can be inferred easily from the trace.) Since rule 8 is applicable, a new object, L2, is produced. Following the method for transform goals, at the next step a new goal has been generated: to transform L2 into L0. This in turn leads to another reduce goal: to restore a Q to L2. But this goal is rejected by the evaluation, since adding a term is more difficult than deleting a term. GPS then returns to goal 2 and seeks another rule which will delete terms. This time it finds the other form of rule 8 and goes through a similar excursion, ending with the rejection of goal 8.

Returning again to goal 2 to find another rule for deleting terms, GPS obtains rule 7. It selects the variant (A V B) • (A V C) → A V (B • C), since only this one both decreases terms and has a dot as its main connective. Rule 7 is not immediately applicable; GPS first discovers that there is a difference of connective in the left subexpression, and then that there is one in the right subexpression. In both cases it finds and applies rule 6 to change the connective from horseshoe to wedge, obtaining successively L4 and L5. But the new expression reveals a difference in sign which leads again to rule 6—that is, to the same rule as before, but perceived as accomplishing a different function. Rule 6 produces L6, which happens to be identical with L4 although GPS does not notice the identity here. This leads, in goal 19, to the difference in connective being redetected; whereupon the goal is finally rejected as representing no progress over goal 13. Further attempts to find alternative ways to change signs or connectives fail to yield anything. This ends the episode.

6. Comparison of the GPS Trace with the Protocol

We now have a highly detailed trace of what GPS did. What can we find in the subject's protocol that either confirms or refutes the assertion that this program is a detailed model of the symbol manipulations the subject is carrying out? What sort of correspondence can we expect? The program does not provide us with an English language output that can be put into one-one correspondence with the words of the subject. We have not even given GPS a goal to "do the task and talk at the same time," which would be a necessary reformulation if we were to attempt a correspondence in such detail. On the other hand, the trace, backed up by our knowledge of how it was generated, does provide a complete record of all the task content that was considered by GPS, and the order in which it was taken up. Hence, we should expect to find every feature of the protocol that concerns the task mirrored in an essential way in the program trace. The converse is not true, since many things concerning the task surely occurred without the subject's commenting on them (or even being aware of them). Thus, our test of correspondence is one-sided but exacting.

Let us start with the first sentence of the subject's protocol (Figure 2):

Well, looking at the left-hand side of the equation, first we want to eliminate one of the sides by using rule 8.

We see here a desire to decrease L1 or eliminate something from it, and the selection of rule 8 as the means to do this. This stands in direct correspondence with goals 1, 2, and 3 of the trace.

Let us skip to the third and fourth sentences:

Now—no,—no, I can't do that because I will be eliminating either the Q or the P in that total expression. I won't do that at first.

We see here a direct expression of the covert application of rule 8, the subsequent comparison of the resulting expression with L0, and the rejection of this course of action because it deletes a letter that is required in the final expression. It would be hard to find a set of words that expressed these ideas more clearly. Conversely, if the mechanism of the program (or something essentially similar to it) were not operating, it would be hard to explain why the subject uttered the remarks that he did.

One discrepancy is quite clear. The subject handled both forms of rule 8 together, at least as far as his comment is concerned. GPS, on the other hand, took a separate cycle of consideration for each form. Possibly the subject followed the program covertly and simply reported the two results together. However, we would feel that the fit was better if GPS had proceeded something as follows:

GOAL 2 DELETE R FROM L1
    GOAL 3 APPLY R8 TO L1
        PRODUCES L2 R ⊃ ~P OR ~R⊃Q
    GOAL 4 TRANSFORM L2 INTO L0
        GOAL 5 ADD Q TO R⊃~P OR ADD P TO ~R⊃Q
        REJECT

We will consider further evidence on this point later.

Let us return to the second sentence, which we skipped over:

It appears too complicated to work with first.

Nothing in the program is in simple correspondence with this statement, though it is easy to imagine some possible explanations. For example, this could merely be an expression of the matching—of the fact that L1 is such a big expression that the subject cannot absorb all its detail. There is not enough data locally to determine what part of the trace should correspond to this statement, so the sentence must stand as an unexplained element of the subject's behavior.

Now let us consider the next few sentences of the protocol:

Now I'm looking for a way to get rid of the horseshoe inside the two brackets that appear on the left and right side of the equation. And I don't see it. Yeh, if you apply rule 6 to both sides of the equation, from there I'm going to see if I can apply rule 7.

This is in direct correspondence with goals 9 through 14 of the trace. The comment at the end makes it clear that applying rule 7 is the main concern and that changing connectives is required in order to accomplish this. Further, the protocol shows clearly that rule 6 was selected as the means. All three rule selections provide some confirmation that a preliminary test for feasibility was made by the subject—as by GPS—in the reduce goal method. If there was not selection on the main connective, why wasn't rule 5 selected instead of rule 6? Or why wasn't the $(A \cdot B) V (A \cdot C) \rightarrow A \cdot (B V C)$ form of rule 7 selected?

However, there is a discrepancy between trace and protocol, for the subject handles both applications of rule 6 simultaneously, (and apparently was also handling the two differences simultaneously), whereas GPS handles them sequentially. This is similar to the discrepancy noted earlier in handling rule 8. Since we now have two examples of parallel processing, it is likely that there is a real difference on this score. Again, we would feel better if GPS proceeded somewhat as follows:

GOAL 9 APPLY R7 TO L1
    GOAL 10 CHANGE CONNECTIVE TO V IN LEFT L1 AND RIGHT L1
        GOAL 11 APPLY R6 TO LEFT L1 AND RIGHT L1
            PRODUCES L5 (~R V~P) • (RVQ)

A common feature of both these discrepancies is that forming the compound expressions does not complicate the methods in any essential way. Thus, in the case involving rule 8, the two results stem from the same input form, and require only the single match. In the case involving rule 7, a single search was made for a rule and the rule applied to both parts simultaneously, just as if only a single unit was involved.

There are two aspects in which the protocol provides information that the program is not equipped to explain. First, the subject handled the application of rule 8 covertly but commanded the experimenter to make the applications of rule 6 on the board. The version of GPS used here did not make any distinction between internal and external actions. To this extent it fails to be an adequate model. The overt-covert distinction has consequences that run throughout a problem, since expressions on the blackboard have very different memory characteristics from expressions generated only in the head. Second, this version of GPS does not simulate the search process sufficiently well to provide a correspondent to "And I don't see it. Yeh, ..." This requires providing a facsimile of the rule sheet, and distinguishing search on the sheet from searches in the memory.

The next few sentences read:

> I can almost apply rule 7, but one R needs a tilde. So I'll have to look for another rule. I'm going to see if I can change that R to a tilde R.

Again the trace and the protocol agree on the difference that is seen. They also agree that this difference was not attended to earlier, even though it was present. Some fine structure of the data also agrees with the trace. The right-hand R is taken as having the difference (R to ~ R) rather than the left-hand one, although either is possible. This preference arises in the program (and presumably in the subject) from the language habit of working from left to right. It is not without consequences, however, since it determines whether the subject goes to work on the left side or the right side of the expression; hence, it can affect the entire course of events for quite a while. Similarly, in the rule 8 episode the subject apparently worked from left to right and from top to bottom in order to arrive at "Q or P" rather than "P or Q." This may seem like concern with excessively detailed features of the protocol, yet those details support the contention that what is going on inside the human system is quite akin to the symbol manipulations going on inside GPS.

The next portion of the protocol is:

> As a matter of fact, I should have used rule 6 on only the left-hand side of the equation. So use 6, but only on the left-hand side.

Here we have a strong departure from the GPS trace, although, curiously enough, the trace and the protocol end up at the same spot, $(\sim R \vee \sim P) \cdot (\sim R \supset Q)$. Both the subject and GPS found rule 6 as the appropriate one to change signs. At this point GPS simply applied the rule to the current expression; whereas the subject went back and corrected the previous application. Nothing exists in the program that corresponds to this. The most direct explanation is that the application of rule 6 in the inverse direction is perceived by the subject as undoing the previous application of rule 6. After following out this line of reasoning, he then takes the simpler (and less foolish-appearing) alternative, which is to correct the original action.

The final segment of the protocol reads:

> Now I'll apply rule 7 as it is expressed. Both—excuse me, excuse me, it can't be done because of the horseshoe. So—now I'm looking— scanning the rules here for a second, and seeing if I can change the R to ~ R in the second equation, but I don't see any way of doing it. (Sigh). I'm just sort of lost for a second.

The trace and the protocol are again in good agreement. This is one of the few self-correcting errors we have encountered. The protocol records the futile search for additional operators to affect the differences of sign and connective, always with negative results. The final comment of mild despair can be interpreted as reflecting the impact of several successive failures.

7. Summary of the Fit of the Trace to the Protocol

Let us take stock of the agreements and disagreements between the trace and the protocol. The program provides a complete explanation of the subject's task behavior with five exceptions of varying degrees of seriousness.

There are two aspects in which GPS is unprepared to simulate the subject's behavior: in distinguishing between the internal and external worlds, and in an adequate representation of the spaces in which the search for rules takes place. Both of these are generalized deficiencies that can be remedied. It will remain to be seen how well GPS can then explain data about these aspects of behavior.

The subject handles certain sets of items in parallel by using compound expressions; whereas GPS handles all items one at a time. In the example examined here, no striking differences in problem solving occur as a result, but larger discrepancies could arise under other conditions. It is fairly clear how

GPS could be extended to incorporate this feature.

There are two cases in which nothing corresponds in the program to some clear task-oriented behavior in the protocol. One of these, the early comment about "complication," seems to be mostly a case of insufficient information. The program is making numerous comparisons and evaluations which could give rise to comments of the type in question. Thus this error does not seem too serious. The other case, involving the "should have ..." passage, does seem serious. It clearly implies a mechanism (maybe a whole set of them) that is not in GPS. Adding the mechanism required to handle this one passage could significantly increase the total capabilities of the program. For example, there might be no reasonable way to accomplish this except to provide GPS with a little continuous hindsight about its past actions.

An additional general caution must be suggested. The quantity of data is not large considering the size and complexity of the program. This implies that there are many degrees of freedom available to fit the program to the data. More important, we have no good way to assess how many relevant degrees of freedom a program possesses, and thus to know how easy it is to fit alternative programs. All we do know is that numerous minor modifications could certainly be made, but that no one has proposed any major alternative theories that provide anything like a comparably detailed explanation of human problem-solving data.

It would help if we knew something of how idiosyncratic the program was. We have discussed it here only in relation to one sample of data for one subject. We know enough about subjects on logic problems to assert that the same mechanisms show up repeatedly, but we cannot discuss these data here in detail. In addition, several recent investigations more generally support the concept of information processing theories of human thinking (Bruner et al. 1956; Feigenbaum 1961a; Feldman 1961a; Hovland and Hunt 1960; Miller et al. 1960).

8. Conclusion

We have been concerned in this report with showing that the techniques that have emerged for constructing sophisticated problem-solving programs also provide us with new, strong tools for constructing theories of human thinking. They allow us to merge the rigor and objectivity associated with Behaviorism with the wealth of data and complex behavior associated with the Gestalt movement. To this end their key feature is not that they provide a general framework for understanding problem-solving behavior (although they do that, too), but that they finally reveal with great clarity that the free behavior of a reasonably intelligent human can be understood as the product of a complex but finite and determinate set of laws. Although we know this only for small fragments of behavior, the depth of the explanation is striking.

17

STRIPS:

A New Approach to the Application of Theorem Proving to Problem Solving

Richard E. Fikes and Nils J. Nilsson

1. Introduction

This chapter describes a new problem-solving program called STRIPS (Stanford Research Institute Problem Solver). An initial version of the program has been implemented in Lisp on a PDP-10 and is being used in conjunction with robot research at SRI. STRIPS is a member of the class of problem solvers that search a space of "world models" to find one in which a given goal is achieved. For any world model, we assume that there exists a set of applicable operators, each of which transforms the world model to some other world model. The task of the problem solver is to find some composition of operators that transforms a given initial world model into one that satisfies some stated goal condition.

This framework for problem solving has been central to much of the research in artificial intelligence (Nilsson 1971). Our primary interest here is in the class of problems faced by a robot in re-arranging objects and in navigating, i.e., problems that require quite complex and general world models compared to those needed in the solution of puzzles and games. In puzzles and games, a simple matrix or list structure is usually adequate to represent a state of the problem. The world model for a robot problem solver, however, must include a large number of facts and relations dealing with the position of the robot and the positions and attributes of various objects, open spaces, and boundaries. In STRIPS, a world model is represented by a set of well-formed formulas (wffs) of the first-order predicate calculus.

Operators are the basic elements from which a solution is built. For robot problems, each operator corresponds to an *action routine*[1] whose execution causes a robot to take certain actions. For example, we might have a routine that causes it to go through a doorway, a routine that causes it to push a box, and perhaps dozens of others.

Green (1969) implemented a problem-solving system that depended exclusively on formal theorem-proving methods to search for the appropriate sequence of operators. While Green's formulation represented a significant step in the development of problem-solvers, it suffered some serious disadvantages connected with the "frame problem"[2] that prevented it from solving nontrivial problems.

In STRIPS, we surmount these difficulties by separating entirely the processes of theorem proving from those of searching through a space of world models. This separation allows us to employ separate strategies for these two activities and thereby improve the overall performance of the system. Theorem-proving methods are used only *within* a given world model to answer questions about it concerning which operators are applicable and whether or not goals have been satisfied. For searching through the space of world models, STRIPS uses a GPS-like means-end analysis strategy (Ernst and Newell 1969). This combination of means-ends analysis and formal theorem-proving methods allows objects (world models) much more complex and general than any of those used in GPS and provides more powerful search heuristics than those found in theorem-proving programs.

We proceed by describing the operation of STRIPS in terms of the conventions used to represent the search space for a problem and the search methods used to find a solution. We then discuss the details of implementation and present some examples.

2. The Operation of STRIPS

2.1. The Problem Space

The problem space for STRIPS is defined by the initial world model, the set of available operators and their effects on world models, and the goal statement.

As already mentioned, STRIPS represents a world model by a set of well-formed formulas (wffs). For example, to describe a world model in which the robot is at location a and boxes B and C are at locations b and c we would include the following wffs:

ATR(a)
AT(B, b)
AT(C, c).

We might also include the wff

$(\forall u \, \forall x \, \forall y)\{[\mathrm{AT}(u, x) \wedge (x \neq y)] \Rightarrow \sim \mathrm{AT}(u, y)\}$

to state the general rule that an object in one place is not in a different place. Using first-order predicate calculus wffs, we can represent quite complex world models and can use existing theorem-proving programs to answer questions about a model.

The available operators are grouped into families called schemata. Consider for example the operator *goto* for moving the robot from one point on the floor to another. Here there is really a distinct operator for each different pair of points, but it is convenient to group all of these into a family goto (m, n) parameterized by the initial position[3] m and the final position n. We say that goto (m, n) is an operator schema whose members are obtained by substituting specific constants for the *parameters m and n*. In STRIPS, when an operator is applied to a world model, specific constants will already have been chosen for the operator parameters.

Each operator is defined by an operator description consisting of two main parts: a description of the effects of the operator, and the conditions under which the operator is applicable. The effects of an operator are simply defined by a list of wffs that must be added to the model and a list of wffs that are no longer true and therefore must be deleted. We shall discuss the process of calculating these effects in more detail later. It is convenient to state the applicability condition, or *precondition,* for an operator schema as a *wff schema.* To determine whether or not there is an instance of an operator schema applicable to a world model, we must be able to prove that there is an instance of the corresponding wff schema that logically follows from the model.

For example, consider the question of applying instances of the operator subschema goto (m, b) to a world model containing the wff ATR(a), where a and b are constants. If the precondition wff schema of goto (m, n) is ATR(m), then we find that the instance ATR(a) can be proved from the world model. Thus, an applicable instance of goto(m, b) is goto(a, b).

It is important to distinguish between the parameters appearing in wff schemata and ordinary existentially and universally quantified variables that may also appear. Certain modifications must be made to theorem-proving programs to enable them to handle wff schemata, these are discussed later.

Goal statements are also represented by wffs. For example, the task "Get

Boxes B and C to Location a" might be stated as the wff:

AT$(B, a) \land$ AT(C, a).

To summarize, the problem space for STRIPS is defined by three entities:

1. An initial world model, which is a set of wffs describing the present state of the world.

2. A set of operators, including a description of their effects and their precondition wff schemata.

3. A goal condition stated as a wff.

The problem is solved when STRIPS produces a world model that satisfies the goal wff.

2.2. The Search Strategy

In a very simple problem-solving system, we might first apply all of the applicable operators to the initial world model to create a set of successor models. We would continue to apply all applicable operators to these successors and to their descendants (say in breadth-first fashion) until a model was produced in which the goal formula was a theorem. However, since we envision uses in which the number of operators applicable to any given world model might be quite large, such a simple system would generate an undesirably large tree of world models and would thus be impractical.

Instead, we have adopted the GPS strategy of extracting "differences" between the present world model and the goal and of identifying operators that are "relevant" to reducing these differences (Ernst and Newell 1969). Once a relevant operator has been determined, we attempt to solve the subproblem of producing a world model to which it is applicable. If such a model is found, then we apply the relevant operator and reconsider the original goal in the resulting model. In this section, we review this basic GPS search strategy as employed by STRIPS.

STRIPS begins by employing a theorem prover to attempt to prove that the goal wff G_0 follows from the set M_0 of wffs describing the initial world model. If G_0 does follow from M_0, the task is trivially solved in the initial model. Otherwise, the theorem prover will fail to find a proof. In this case, the uncompleted proof is taken to be the "difference" between M_0 and G_0. Next, operators that might be relevant to "reducing" this difference are sought. These are the operators whose effects on world models would enable the proof to be continued. In determining relevance, the parameters of the operators may be partially or fully instantiated. The corresponding instantiated precondition wff schemata (of the relevant operators) are then taken to be new subgoals.

Consider the trivially simple example in which the task is for the robot to go to location b. The goal wff is thus ATR(b), and unless the robot is already at location b, the initial proof attempt will be unsuccessful. Now, certainly the instance goto(m, b) of the operator goto(m, n) is relevant to reducing the difference because its effect would allow the proof to be continued (in this case, completed). Accordingly, the corresponding precondition wff schema, say ATR(m), is used as a subgoal.

STRIPS works on a subgoal using the same technique. Suppose the precondition wff schema G is selected as the first subgoal to be worked on. STRIPS again uses a theorem prover in an attempt to find instances of G that follow from the initial world model M_0. Here again, there are two possibilities. If no proof can be found, STRIPS uses the incomplete proof as a difference, and sets up (sub) subgoals corresponding to their precondition wffs. If STRIPS does find an instance of G that follows from M_0, then the corresponding operator instance is used to transform M_0 into a new world model M_1. In our previous simple example, the subgoal wff schema G was ATR(m). If the initial model contains the wff ATR(a), then an instance of G—namely ATR(a)—can be proved from M_0. In this case, the corresponding operator instance goto(a, b) is applied to M_0 to produce the new model, M_1. STRIPS then continues by attempting to prove G_0 from M_1. In our example, G_0 trivially follows from M_1 and we are through. However, if no proof could be found, subgoals for this problem would be set up and the process would continue.

The hierarchy of goal, subgoals, and models generated by the search process is represented by a *search tree*. Each node of the search tree has the form (<world model>, <goal list>), and represents the problem of trying to achieve the sub-goals on the goal list (in order) from the indicated world model.

An example of such a search tree is shown in Figure 1. The top node (M_0, (G_0)) represents the main task of achieving goal G_0 from world model M_0. In this case, two alternative subgoals G_a and G_b are set up. These are added to the front of the goal lists in the two successor nodes. Pursuing one of these subgoals, suppose that in the node (M_0, (G_a, G_0)), goal G_a is satisfied in M_0; the corresponding operator, say OP_a, is then applied to M_0 to yield M_1. Thus, along this branch, the problem is now to satisfy goal G_0 from M_1, and this problem is represented by the node (M_1, (G_0)). Along the other path, suppose G_c is set up as a subgoal for achieving G_b and thus the node (M_0, (G_c, G_b, G_0)) is created. Suppose G_c is satisfied in M_0 and thus OP_c is applied to M_0 yielding M_2. Now STRIPS must still solve the subproblem G_b before attempting the main goal G_0. Thus, the result of applying OP_c is to replace M_0 by M_2 and to remove G_c from the goal list to produce the node (M_2, (G_b, G_0)).

This process continues until STRIPS produces the node (M_4, (G_0)). Here suppose G_0 can be proved directly from M_4 so that this node is terminal. The solution sequence of operators is thus (OP_c, OP_b, OP_e).

This example search tree indicates clearly that when an operator is found to be relevant, it is not known where it will occur in the completed plan; that is, it may be applicable to the initial model and therefore be the first operator applied, its effects may imply the goal so that it is the last operator applied,

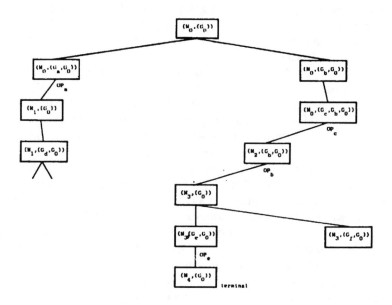

Figure 1. A typical STRIPS search tree.

or it may be some intermediate step toward the goal. This flexible search strategy embodied in STRIPS combines many of the advantages of both forward search (from the initial model toward the goal) and backward search (from the goal toward the initial model).

Whenever STRIPS generates a successor node, it immediately tests to see if the first goal on the goal list is satisfied in the new node's model. If so, the corresponding operator is applied, generating a new successor node; if not, the difference (i.e., the uncompleted proof) is stored with the node. Except for those successor nodes generated as a result of applying operators, the process of successor generation is as follows: STRIPS selects a node and uses the difference stored with the node to select a relevant operator. It uses the precondition of this operator to generate a new successor. (If all of the node's successors have already been generated, STRIPS selects some other node still having uncompleted successors.) A flowchart summarizing the STRIPS search process is shown in Figure 2.

STRIPS has a heuristic mechanism to select nodes with uncompleted successors to work on next. For this purpose we use an evaluation function that takes into account such factors as the number of remaining goals on the goal list, the number and types of predicates in the remaining goal formulas, and the complexity of the difference attached to the node.

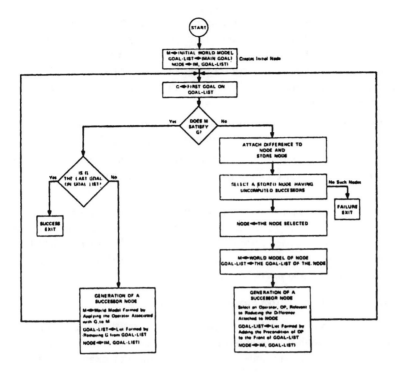

Figure 2. Flow chart for STRIPS.

3. Implementation

3.1 Theorem-Proving with Parameters

In this section, we discuss the more important details of our implementation of STRIPS; we begin by describing the automatic theorem-proving component.

STRIPS uses the resolution theorem-prover QA3.5 (Garvey and Kling 1969) when attempting to prove goal and sub-goal wffs. We assume that the reader is familiar with resolution proof techniques for the predicate calculus (Nilsson 1971). These techniques must be extended to handle the parameters occurring in wff schemas; we discuss these extensions next.

The general situation is that we have some goal wff schema $G(\bar{p})$, that is to be proved from a set M of clauses where $\bar{p}$ is a set of schema parameters. Following the general strategy of resolution theorem provers, we attempt to prove the inconsistency of the set $\{M \cup \sim G(\bar{p})\}$. That is, we attempt to find an instance $\bar{p}'$ of $\bar{p}$ for which $\{M \cup \sim G(\bar{p}')\}$ is inconsistent.

We have been able to use the standard unification algorithm of the resolution method to compute the appropriate instances of schema variables during the search for a proof. This algorithm has the advantage that it finds the most general instances of parameters needed to effect unification. To use the unification algorithm we must specify how it is to treat parameters. The following substitution types are allowable components of the output of the modified unification algorithm:

- Terms that can be substituted for a variable: variables, constants, parameters, and functional terms not containing the variable.

- Terms that can be substituted for a parameter: constants, parameters, and functional terms not containing Skolem functions, variables, or the parameter.

The fact that the same parameter may have multiple occurrences in a set of clauses demands another modification to the theorem prover. Suppose two clauses C_1 and C_2 resolve to form clause C and that in the process some term t is substituted for parameter p. Then we must make sure that p is replaced by t in all of the clauses that are descendants of C.

3.2. Operator Descriptions and Applications

We have already mentioned that to define an operator, we must state the preconditions under which it is applicable and its effects on a world model schema. Preconditions are stated as wff schemata. For example, suppose $G(\bar{p})$ is the operator precondition schema of an operator $O(\bar{p})$, $\bar{p}$ is a set of parameters, and M is a world model. Then if $\bar{p}'$ is a constant instance of $\bar{p}$ for which $\{M \cup \sim G(\bar{p}')\}$ is contradictory, then STRIPS can apply operator $O(\bar{p}')$ to world model M.

We next need a way to state the effects of operator application on world models. These effects are simply described by two lists. On the *delete list* we specify those clauses in the original model that might no longer be true in the new model. On the *add list* are those clauses that might not have been true in the original model but are true in the new model.

For example, consider an operator push(k, m, n) for pushing object k from m to n. Such an operator might be described as follows:

push(k, m, n)
   Precondition: ATR(m)
                  $\wedge$ AT(k, m)
   delete list
                ATR(m);
                AT(k, m)
   add list
                ATR(n); AT(k, n).

The parameters of an operator schema are instantiated by constants at the time of operator application. Some instantiations are made while deciding what instances of an operator schema are relevant to reducing a difference, and the rest are made while deciding what instances of an operator are applicable in a given world model. Thus, when the add and delete lists are used to create new world models, all parameters occurring in them will have been replaced by constants.

(We can make certain modifications to STRIPS to allow it to apply operators with uninstantiated parameters. These applications will produce world model schemata. This generalization complicates somewhat the simple add and delete-list rules for computing new world models and needs further study.)

For certain operators it is convenient to be able merely to specify the *form* of clauses to be deleted. For example, one of the effects of a robot *goto* operator must be to delete information about the direction that the robot was originally facing even though such information might not have been represented by one of the parameters of the operator. In this case we would include the atom FACING($) on the delete list of *goto* with the convention that any atom of the form FACING($), regardless of the value of $, would be deleted.

When an operator description is written, it may not be possible to name explicitly all the atoms that should appear on the delete list. For example, it may be the case that a world model contains clauses that are derived from other clauses in the model. Thus, from AT(B1, a) and from AT(B2, $a+\Delta$), we might derive NEXTTO(B1, B2) and insert it into the model. Now, if one of the clauses on which the derived clause depends is deleted, then the derived clause must also be deleted.

We deal with this problem by defining a set of primitive predicates (e.g., AT, ATR) and relating all other predicates to this primitive set. In particular, we require the delete list of an operator description to indicate all the atoms containing primitive predicates that should be deleted when the operator is applied. Also, we require that any nonprimitive clause in the world model have associated with it those primitive clauses on which its validity depends. (A primitive clause is one which contains only primitive predicates.) For example, the clause NEXTTO(B1, B2) would have associated with it the clauses AT(B1, a) and AT(B2, $a+\Delta$).

By using these conventions, we can be assured that primitive clauses will be correctly deleted during operator applications, and that the validity of nonprimitive clauses can be determined whenever they are used in a deduction by checking to see if all of the primitive clauses on which the nonprimitive clause depends are still in the world model.

3.3. Computing Differences and Relevant Operators

STRIPS uses the GPS strategy of attempting to apply those operators that are relevant to reducing a difference between a world model and a goal or subgoal. We use the theorem prover as a key part of this mechanism.

Suppose we have just created a new node in the search tree represented by $(M, (G_i, G_{i-1}, \ldots, G_0))$. The *theorem prover* is called to attempt to find a contradiction for the set $\{M \cup \sim G_i\}$. If one can be found, the operator whose precondition was G_i is applied to M and the process continues.

Here, though, we are interested in the case in which no contradiction is obtained after investing some prespecified amount of theorem-proving effort. The uncompleted proof P is represented by the set of clauses that form the negation of the goal wff, plus all of their descendants (if any), less any clauses eliminated by editing strategies (such as subsumption and predicate evaluation). We take P to be the difference between M and G_i and attach P to the node.[4]

Later, in attempting to compute a successor to this node with incomplete proof P attached, we first must select a relevant operator. The quest for relevant operators proceeds in two steps. In the first step an ordered list of candidate operators is created. The selection of candidate operators is based on a simple comparison of the predicates in the difference clauses with those on the add lists of the operator descriptions. For example, if the difference contained a clause having in it the negation of a position predicate AT, then the operator *push* would be considered as a candidate for this difference.

The second step in finding an operator relevant to a given difference involves employing the theorem prover to determine if clauses on the add list of a candidate operator can be used to "resolve away" clauses in the difference (i.e., to see if the proof can be continued based on the effects of the operator). If the theorem prover can in fact produce new resolvents that are descendants of the add list clauses, then the candidate operator (properly instantiated) is considered to be a relevant operator for the difference set.

Note that the consideration of one candidate operator schema may produce several relevant operator instances. For example, if the difference set contains the unit clauses $\sim \text{ATR}(a)$ and $\sim \text{ATR}(b)$, then there are two relevant instances of $\text{goto}(m, n)$, namely $\text{goto}(m, a)$ and $\text{goto}(m, b)$. Each new resolvent that is a descendant of the operator's add list clauses is used to form a relevant instance of the operator by applying to the operator's parameters the same substitutions that were made during the production of the resolvent.

3.4. Efficient Representation of World Models

A primary design issue in the implementation of a system such as STRIPS is how to satisfy the storage requirements of a search tree in which each node may contain a different world model. We would like to use STRIPS in a robot or question-answering environment where the initial world model may consist of hundreds of wffs. For such applications it is infeasible to recopy completely a world model each time a new model is produced by application of an operator.

We have dealt with this problem in STRIPS by first assuming that most of the wffs in a problem's initial world model will not be changed by the application of operators. This is certainly true for the class of robot problems with which we are currently concerned. For these problems most of the wffs in a model describe rooms, walls, doors, and objects, or specify general properties of the world, which are true in all models. The only wffs that might be changed in this robot environment are the ones that describe the status of the robot and any objects which it manipulates.

Given this assumption, we have implemented the following scheme for handling multiple world models. All the wffs for all world models are stored in a common memory structure. Associated with each wff (i.e., clause) is a visibility flag, and QA3.5 has been modified to consider only clauses from the memory structure that are marked as visible. Hence, we can "define" a particular world model for QA3.5 by marking that model's clauses visible and all other clauses invisible. When clauses are entered into the initial world model, they are all marked as visible. Clauses that are not changed remain visible throughout STRIPS' search for a solution.

Each world model produced by STRIPS is defined by two clause lists. The first list, DELETIONS, names all those clauses in the initial world model that are no longer present in the model being defined. The second list, ADDITIONS, names all those clauses in the model being defined that are not also in the initial model. These lists represent the changes in the initial model needed to form the model being defined, and our assumption implies they will contain only a small number of clauses.

To specify a given world model to QA3.5, STRIPS marks visible the clauses on the model's ADDITIONS list and marks invisible the clauses on the model's DELETIONS list. When the call to QA3.5 is completed, the visibility markings of these clauses are returned to their previous settings.

When an operator is applied to a world model, the DELETIONS list of the new world model is a copy of the DELETIONS list of the old model plus any clauses from the initial model that are deleted by the operator. The ADDITIONS list of the new model consists of the clauses from the old model's ADDITIONS list, as transformed by the operator, plus the clauses from the operator's add list.

3.5. An Example

Tracing through the main points of a simple example helps to illustrate the various mechanisms in STRIPS. Suppose we want a robot to gather together three objects and that the initial world model is given by:

$$M_0 : \begin{cases} \text{ATR}(a) \\ \text{AT(BOX1},b) \\ \text{AT(BOX2},c) \\ \text{AT(BOX3},d) \end{cases}.$$

The goal wff describing this task is

G_0:$(\exists x)$ [AT(BOX1, x) $\wedge$ AT(BOX2, x) $\wedge$ AT(BOX3, x)].

Its negated form is

$\sim G_0$: $\sim$ AT(BOX1, x) $\vee$ $\sim$ AT(BOX2, x) $\vee$ $\sim$ AT(BOX3, x).

(In $\sim G_0$ the term x is a universally quantified variable.)

We admit the following operators:

1. push (k, m, n): Robot pushes object k from place m to place n.
   Precondition: AT(k, m) $\wedge$ ATR(m)
   Negated precondition: $\sim$ AT(k, m) $\vee$ $\sim$ ATR(m)
   Delete list: ATR(m)
                  AT(k, m)
   Add list: AT(k, n)
                  ATR(n)

2. goto(m, n): Robot goes from place m to place n.
   Precondition:ATR(m)
   Negated precondition: $\sim$ ATR(m)
   Delete list: ATR(m)
   Add list: ATR(n)

Following the flow chart of Figure 2, STRIPS first creates the initial node $(M_0, (G_0))$ and attempts to find a contradiction to $\{M_0 \cup \sim G_0\}$. This attempt is unsuccessful; suppose the incomplete proof is that shown in Figure 3. We attach this incomplete proof to the node and then select the node to have a successor computed.

The only candidate operator is push(k, m, n). Using the add list clause AT(k, n), we can continue the uncompleted proof in one of several ways depending on the substitutions made for k and n. Each of these substitutions produces a relevant instance of push. One of these is: OP_1: push(BOX2, m, b) given by the substitutions BOX2 for k and b for n. Its associated precondition (in negated form) is: $\sim G_1$: $\sim$ AT(BOX2, m) $\vee$ $\sim$ ATR(m). Suppose OP_1 is selected and used to create a successor node. (Later in the search process another successor using one of the other relevant instances of push might be computed if our original selection did not lead to a solution.) Selecting OP_1 leads to the computation of the successor node $(M_0, (G_1, G_0))$.

STRIPS next attempts to find a contradiction for $\{M_0 \cup \sim G_1\}$. The uncompleted proof (difference) attached to the node contains Figure 4. When this node is later selected to have a successor computed, one of the candidate operators is goto(m, n). The relevant instance is determined to be OP_2: goto(m, c) with (negated) precondition $\sim G_2$: ATR(m). This relevant operator results in the successor node $(M_0, (G_2, G_1, G_0))$.

Next STRIPS determines that $(M_0 \cup \sim G_2)$ is contradictory with $m = a$. Thus, STRIPS applies the operator goto(a, c) to M_0 to yield

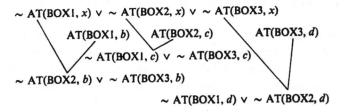

Figure 3. Part of the resolution proof for $M_0 \cup \sim G_0$.

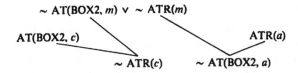

Figure 4. Part of the resolution proof for $M_0 \cup \sim G_1$.

$$M_1 : \begin{cases} \text{ATR}(c) \\ \text{AT}(\text{BOX1}, b) \\ \text{AT}(\text{BOX2}, c) \\ \text{AT}(\text{BOX3}, d) \end{cases}.$$

The successor node is $(M_1, (G1, G_0))$. Immediately, STRIPS determines that $(M_1 \cup \sim G_0)$ is contradictory with $m = a$. Thus, STRIPS applies the operator push(BOX2, c, b) to yield

$$M_2 : \begin{cases} \text{ATR}(b) \\ \text{AT}(\text{BOX1}, b) \\ \text{AT}(\text{BOX2}, b) \\ \text{AT}(\text{BOX3}, d) \end{cases}.$$

The resulting successor node is $(M_2, (G_0))$, and thus STRIPS reconsiders the original problem but now beginning with world model M_2. The rest of the solution proceeds in similar fashion.

Our implementation of STRIPS easily produces the solution {goto(a, c), push(BOX2, c, b), goto(b, d), push(BOX3, d, b)}. (Incidentally, Green's theorem-proving problem-solver (Green 1969) has not been able to obtain a solution to this version of the 3-Boxes problem. It did solve a simpler version of the problem designed to require only two operator applications.)

4. Example Problems Solved by STRIPS

STRIPS has been designed to be a general-purpose problem solver for robot tasks, and thus must be able to work with a variety of operators and with a world model containing a large number of facts and relations. This section describes its performance on three different tasks. The initial world model for all three tasks consists of a corridor with four rooms and doorways (see Figure 3) and is described by the list of axioms in Table 1. Initially, the robot is in ROOM1 at location *e*. Also in ROOM1 are three boxes and a lightswitch: BOX1 at location *a*, BOX2 at location *b*, and BOX3 at location c; and a lightswitch, LIGHTSWITCH1 at location *d*. The lightswitch is high on a wall out of normal reach of the robot.

The first task is to turn on the lightswitch. The robot can solve this problem by going to one of the three boxes, pushing it to the lightswitch, climbing on the box[5] and turning on the lightswitch. The second task is to push the three boxes in ROOM1 together. (This task is a more realistic elaboration of the three-box problem used as an example in the last section.) The third task is for the robot to go to a designated location, *f*, in ROOM4.

The operators that are given to STRIPS to solve these problems are described in Table 1. For convenience we define two "goto" operators, goto1 and goto2. The operator goto1(m) takes the robot to any *coordinate* location *m* in the same room as the robot. The operator goto2(m) takes the robot next to any *item m* (e.g., lightswitch, door, or box) in the same room as the robot. The operator pushto(m, n) pushes any pushable object *m* next to any item *n* (e.g., lightswitch, door or box) in the same room as the robot. Additionally, we have operators for turning on lightswitches, going through doorways, and climbing on and off boxes. The precise formulation of the preconditions and the effects of these operators is contained in Table 1.

We also list in Table 1 the goal wffs for the three tasks and the solutions obtained by STRIPS. Some performance figures for these solutions are shown in Table 2. In Table 2, the figures in the "Time taken" column represent the CPU time (excluding garbage collection) used by STRIPS in finding a solution. Although some parts of our program are compiled, most of the time is spent running interpretive code; hence, we do not attach much importance to these times. We note that in all cases most of the time is spent doing theorem proving (in QA3.5).

The next columns of Table 2 indicate the number of nodes generated and the number of operator applications both in the search tree and along the solution path. (Recall from Figure 2 that some successor nodes do not correspond to operator applications.) We see from these figures that the general search heuristics built into STRIPS provide a highly directed search toward the goal. These heuristics presently give the search a large "depth-first" com-

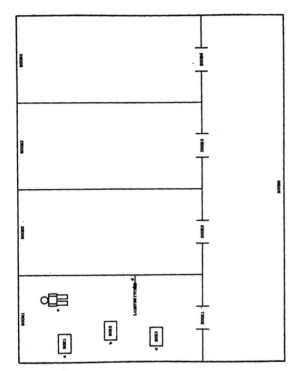

Figure 5. Room plan for the robot tasks.

ponent, and for this reason STRIPS obtains an interesting but nonoptimal solution to the "turn on the light-switch" problem.

5. Future Plans and Problems

The current implementation of STRIPS can be extended in several directions. These extensions will be the subject of much of our problem-solving research activities in the immediate future. We mention some of these briefly.

We have seen that STRIPS constructs a problem-solving tree whose nodes represent subproblems. In a problem-solving process of this sort, there must be a mechanism to decide which node to work on next. Currently, we use an evaluation function that incorporates such factors as the number and the estimated difficulty of the remaining subgoals, the cost of the operators applied so far, and the complexity of the current difference. We expect to devote a good deal of effort to devising and experimenting with various evaluation functions and other ordering techniques.

$(\forall x \forall y \forall z)$CONNECTS$(x,y,z) \Rightarrow$ CONNECTS$(x,z,y)]$
CONNECTS(DOOR1,ROOM1,ROOM5)
CONNECTS(DOOR2,ROOM2,ROOM5)
CONNECTS(DOOR3,ROOM3,ROOM5)
CONNECTS(DOOR4,ROOM4,ROOM5)

LOCINROOM(f,ROOM4)	INROOM(BOX1,ROOM1)
AT(BOX1,a)	INROOM(BOX2,ROOM1)
AT(BOX2,b)	INROOM(BOX3,ROOM1)
AT(BOX3,c)	INROOM(ROBOT,ROOM1)
AT(LIGHTSWITCH1 ,d)	INROOM(LIGHTSWITCH1 ,ROOM1)
ATROBOT(e)	PUSHABLE(BOX1)
TYPE(BOX1,BOX)	PUSHABLE(BOX2)
TYPE(BOX2,BOX)	PUSHABLE(BOX3)
TYPE(BOX3,BOX)	ONFLOOR
TYPE(D4,DOOR)	STATUS(LIGHTSWITCH1,OFF)
TYPE(D3,DOOR)	TYPE(LIGHTSWITCH1,LIGHTSWITCH)
TYPE(D2,DOOR)	
TYPE(D1,DOOR)	

Table 1. Formulation for STRIPS Tasks: Initial World Model.

Another area for future research concerns the synthesis of more complex procedures than those consisting of simple linear sequences of operators. Specifically, we want to be able to generate procedures involving iteration (or recursion) and conditional branching. In short, we would like STRIPS to be able to generate computer programs. Several researchers (Green 1969, Waldinger and Lee 1969, and Manna and Waldinger 1971) have already considered the problem of automatic program synthesis and we expect to be able to use some of their ideas in STRIPS.

We are also interested in getting STRIPS to "learn" by having it define new operators for itself on the basis of previous problem solutions. These new operators could then be used to solve even more difficult problems. It would be important to be able to generalize to parameters any constants appearing in a new operator; otherwise, the new operator would not be general enough to warrant saving. One approach (Hart and Nilsson 1971) that appears promising is to modify STRIPS so that it solves every problem presented to it in terms of generalized parameters rather than in terms of constants appearing in the specific problem statements. Hewitt (1970) discusses a related process that he calls "procedural abstraction." He suggests that, from a few instances of a procedure, a general version can sometimes be synthesized.

This type of learning provides part of our rationale for working on automatic problem solvers such as STRIPS. Some researchers have questioned the value of systems for automatically chaining together operators into higher-level proce-

Operators

    gotol(m): Robot goes to coordinate location *m*.
        Preconditions:
            (ONFLOOR) $\land$ ($\exists x$)[INROOM(ROBOT,x) $\land$ LOCINROOM(m,x)]
        Delete list: ATROBOT($\$$),NEXTTO(ROBOT,$\$$)
        Add list: ATROBOT(m)
    goto2(m): Robot goes next to item *m*.
        Preconditions:
            (ONFLOOR) $\land$ { ($\exists x$)[INROOM(ROBOT,x) $\land$ INROOM(m,x)] $\lor$
                ($\exists x$)($\exists y$) [INROOM(ROBOT,x) $\land$ CONNECTS(m,x,y)]}
        Delete list: ATROBOT($\$$),NEXTTO(ROBOT,$\$$)
        Add list: NEXTTO(ROBOT,m)
    pushto(m,n): robot pushes object *m* next to item *n*
        Precondition:
            PUSHABLE(m) $\land$ ONFLOOR $\land$ NEXTTO(ROBOT,m) $\land$ {($\exists x$)[INROOM(m,x)
                $\land$ INROOM(n,x)] $\lor$ ($\exists x,\exists y$)[INROOM(m,x) $\land$ CONNECTS(n,x,y)]}
        Delete list: AT ROBOT ($\$$), NEXTTO (ROBOT,$\$$), NEXTTO ($\$,m$),
              AT ($m,\$$), NEXTTO ($m,\$$)
        Add list: NEXTTO(m,n)
               NEXTTO(n,m)
               NEXTTO(ROBOT,m)
    turnonlight(m): robot turns on lightswitch *m*.
        Precondition: {($\exists n$)[TYPE(n,BOX) $\land$ ON(ROBOT,n) $\land$ NEXTO(n,m)]}
               $\land$ TYPE(m,LIGHTSWITCH)
        Delete list: STATUS(m,OFF)
        Add list: STATUS(m,ON)
    climbonbox(m). Robot climbs up on box *m*.
        Preconditions:
            ONFLOOR A TYPE(m,BOX) $\land$ NEXTTO(ROBOT,m)
        Delete list: ATROBOT($\$$),0NFLOOR
        Add list: ON(ROBOT,m)
    climboffbox(m) Robot climbs off box *m*.
        Preconditions:
            TYPE(m,BOX) $\land$ ON(ROBOT,m)
        Delete list: ON(ROBOT,m)
        Add list: ONFLOOR
    gothrudoor (k,l,m): Robot goes through door *k* from room *l* into room *m*.
        Preconditions:
             NEXTTO(ROBOT,k) $\land$ CONNECTS(k,l,m) $\land$ INROOM(ROBOT,l) $\land$ ONFLOOR
        Delete list: ATROBOT($\$$),NEXTTO(ROBOT,$\$$),INROOM(ROBOT,$\$$)
        Add list: INROOM(ROBOT,m)

Tasks

1. *Turn on the lightswitch*
    Goal wff: STATUS(LIGHTSWITCHl,ON)
    STRIPS solution: {goto2(BOXl),climbonbox(BOXl),climboffbox(BOXl),
        pushto(BOX1,LIGHTSWITCH1),climbonbox(BOX1),
        turnonlight(LIGHTSWITCH1)}
2. *Push three boxes together*
    Goal wff: NEXTTO(BOX1,BOX2) $\land$ NEXTTO(BOX2,BOX3)
    STRIPS solution: {goto2(BOX2),pushto(BOX2,BOXl),goto2(BOX3),
        pushto(BOX3,BOX2)}
3. *Go to a location in another room*
    Goal wff: ATROBOT(f)
    STRIPS solution: {goto2(DOOR1), gothrudoor(DOOR1,ROOM1,ROOM5),
        goto2(DOOR4),gothrudoor(DOOR4,ROOM5,ROOM4),
        gotol(f)}

Table 1 (continued). Formulation for STRIPS tasks: operators and tasks.

	Time taken (in seconds)		Number of nodes		Number of applications	
	Total	Theorem-proving	On solution path	In search tree	On solution path	In search tree
Turn on the lightswitch	113.1	83.0	13	21	6	6
Push three boxes together	66.0	49.6	9	9	4	4
Go to a location in another room	123.0	104.9	11	12	5	5

Table 2. Performance of STRIPS on three tasks.

dures that themselves could have been "hand coded" quite easily in the first place. Their viewpoint seems to be that a robot system should be provided a priori with a repertoire of all of the operators and procedures that it will ever need.

We agree that it is desirable to provide a priori a large number of specialized operators, but such a repertoire will nevertheless be finite. To accomplish tasks just outside the boundary of a priori abilities requires a process for chaining together existing operators into more complex ones. We are interested in a system whose operator repertoire can "grow" in this fashion. Clearly one must not give such a system a problem too far away from the boundary of known abilities, because the combinatorics of search will then make a solution unlikely. However, a truly "intelligent" system ought always to be able to solve slightly more difficult problems than any it has solved before.

Acknowledgements

The development of the ideas embodied in STRIPS has been the result of the combined efforts of the present authors, Bertram Raphael, Thomas Garvey, John Munson, and Richard Waldinger, all members of the Artificial Intelligence Group at SRI.

The research reported here was sponsored by the Advanced Research Projects Agency and the National Aeronautics and Space Administration under Contract NAS12-2221.

Notes

1. The reader should keep in mind the distinction between an operator and its associated action routine. Execution of action routines actually causes the robot to take actions. Application of operators to world models occurs during the planning (i.e., problem solving) phase when an attempt is being made to find a sequence of operators whose associated action routines will produce a desired state of the world. (See the papers by Munson (1971) and Fikes (1971) for discussions of the relationships between STRIPS and the robot executive and monitoring functions.)

2. Space does not allow a full discussion of the frame problem; for a thorough treatment see Raphael (1970).

3. The parameters m and n are each really vector-valued, but we avoid vector notation here for simplicity. In general, we denote constants by letters near the beginning of the alphabet (a, b, c, ...), parameters by letters in the middle of the alphabet (m, n, ...), and quantified variables by letters near the end of the alphabet (x, y, z).

4. If P is very large we can heuristically select some part of P as the difference.

5. This task is a robot version of the so-called "Monkey and Bananas" problem. STRIPS can solve the problem even though the current SRI robot is incapable of climbing boxes and turning on lightswitches.

18

Blackboard Systems: The Blackboard Model of Problem Solving and the Evolution of Blackboard Architectures

H. Penny Nii

1. The Blackboard Model of Problem Solving

Historically the blackboard model arose from abstracting features of the HEARSAY-II speech-understanding system developed between 1971 and 1976.[1] HEARSAY-II understood a spoken speech query about computer science abstracts stored in a data base. It "understood" in the sense that it was able to respond to spoken commands and queries about the database. From an informal summary description of the HEARSAY-II program, the HASP system was designed and implemented between 1973 and 1975. The domain[2] of HASP was ocean surveillance, and its task[3] was the interpretation of continuous passive sonar data. HASP, as the second example of a blackboard system, not only added credibility to the claim that a blackboard approach to problem solving was general, but it also demonstrated that it could be abstracted into a robust model of problem solving. Subsequently, many application programs have been implemented whose solutions were formulated using the blackboard model. Because of the different characteristics of the application problems and because the interpretation of the blackboard model varied, the design of these programs differed considerably. However, the blackboard model of problem solving has not undergone any substantial changes in the last ten years.

A *problem-solving model* is a scheme for organizing reasoning steps and domain knowledge to construct a solution to a problem. For example, in a *backward-reasoning model,* problem solving begins by reasoning backward from a goal to be achieved toward an initial state (data). More specifically, in a *rule-based backward reasoning model* knowledge is organized as "if-then" rules, and modus ponens inference steps are applied to the rules from a goal rule back to an initial-state rule (a rule that looks at the input data). An excellent example of this approach to problem solving is the MYCIN program (Shortliffe 1976). In a *forward-reasoning model,* however, the inference steps are applied from an initial state toward a goal. The OPS system exemplifies such a model (Forgy and McDermott 1977). In an *opportunistic reasoning model,* pieces of knowledge are applied either backward or forward at the most "opportune" time. Put another way, the central issue of problem solving deals with the question, "What pieces of knowledge should be applied when and how?" A problem solving model provides a conceptual framework for organizing knowledge and a strategy for applying that knowledge.

The blackboard model of problem solving is a highly structured special case of opportunistic problem solving. In addition to opportunistic reasoning as a knowledge application strategy, the blackboard model prescribes the organization of the domain knowledge and all the input and intermediate and partial solutions needed to solve the problem. We refer to all possible partial and full solutions to a problem as its *solution space.*

In the blackboard model, the solution space is organized into one or more application-dependent hierarchies.[4] Information at each level in the hierarchy represents partial solutions and is associated with a unique vocabulary that describes the information. The domain knowledge is partitioned into independent modules of knowledge that transform information on one level, possibly using information at other levels, of the hierarchy into information on the same or other levels. The knowledge modules perform the transformation using algorithmic procedures or heuristic rules that generate actual or hypothetical transformations. Opportunistic reasoning is applied within this overall organization of the solution space and task specific knowledge; that is, which module of knowledge to apply is determined dynamically, one step at a time, resulting in the incremental generation of partial solutions. The choice of a knowledge module is based on the solution state (particularly, the

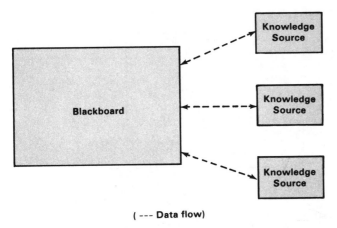

(--- Data flow)

Figure 1. The blackboard model. There is a global database called the blackboard, and there are logically independent sources of knowledge called the knowledge sources. The knowledge sources respond to changes on the blackboard. Note that there is no control flow; the knowledge sources are self-activating.

latest additions and modifications to the data structure containing pieces of the solution) and on the existence of knowledge modules capable of improving the current state of the solution. At each step of knowledge application, either forward- or backward-reasoning methods can be applied.[5]

The blackboard model is a relatively complex problem-solving model prescribing the organization of knowledge and data and the problem solving behavior within the overall organization. This section contains a description of the basic blackboard model. Variations and extensions are discussed in subsequent sections.

1.1 The Blackboard Model

The blackboard model is usually described as consisting of three major components (see Figure 1):

1.1.1 The Knowledge Sources

The knowledge needed to solve the problem is partitioned into knowledge sources, which are kept separate and independent.

1.1.2 The Blackboard Data Structure

The problem solving state data are kept in a global database, the blackboard. Knowledge sources produce changes to the blackboard that lead incrementally to a solution to the problem. Communication and interaction among the knowledge sources take place solely through the blackboard.

1.1.3 Control

The knowledge sources respond opportunistically to changes in the blackboard.[6]

Figure 2. Solving jigsaw puzzles.

The difficulty with this description of the blackboard model is that it only outlines the organizational principles. For those who want to build a blackboard system, the model does not specify how it is to be realized as a computational entity; that is, the blackboard model is a conceptual entity, not a computational specification. Given a problem to be solved, the blackboard model provides enough guidelines for sketching a solution, but a sketch is a long way from a working system. To design and build a system, a detailed model is needed. Before moving on to adding details to the blackboard model, we explore the implied behavior of this abstract model.

Let us consider a hypothetical problem of a group of people trying to put together a jigsaw puzzle. Imagine a room with a large blackboard and around it a group of people each holding over-size jigsaw pieces. We start with volunteers who put their most "promising" pieces on the blackboard (assume it's sticky). Each member of the group looks at his pieces and sees if any of them fit into the pieces already on the blackboard. Those with the appropriate pieces go up to the blackboard and update the evolving solution. The new updates cause other pieces to fall into place, and other people go to the blackboard to add their pieces. It does not matter whether one person holds more pieces than another. The whole puzzle can be solved in complete silence; that is, there need be no direct communication among the group. Each person is self-activating, knowing when his pieces will contribute to the solution. No a priori established order exists for people to go up to the blackboard. The apparent cooperative behavior is mediated by the state of the solution on the blackboard. If one watches the task being performed, the solution is built incrementally (one piece at a time) and opportunistically (as an opportunity for adding a piece arises), as opposed to starting, say, systematically from the left top corner and trying each piece.

This analogy illustrates quite well the blackboard problem-solving behavior implied in the model and is fine for a starter. Now, let's change the layout of the room in such a way that there is only one center aisle wide enough for one person to get through to the blackboard. Now, no more than one person can go up to the blackboard at one time, and a monitor is needed, someone who can see the group and can choose the order in which a person is to go up to the blackboard. The monitor can ask all people who have pieces to add to raise their hands. The monitor can then choose one person from those with their hands raised. To select one person, some criteria for making the choice is needed, for example, a person who raises a hand first, a person with a piece that bridges two solution islands (that is, two clusters of completed pieces), and so forth. The monitor needs a strategy or a set of strategies for solving the puzzle. The monitor can choose a strategy before the puzzle solving begins or can develop strategies as the solution begins to unfold. In any case, it should be noted that the monitor has broad executive power. The monitor could, for example, force the puzzle to be solved systematically from left to right; that is, the monitor has the power to violate one essential characteristic of the original blackboard model, that of opportunistic problem solving.

The last analogy, though slightly removed from the original model, is a useful one for computer programmers interested in building blackboard systems. Given the serial nature of most current computers, the conceptual distance between the model and a running blackboard system is a bit far, and the mapping from the model to a system is prone to misinterpretation. By adding the constraint that solution building physically occur one step at a time in some order determined by the monitor (when multiple steps are possible and desirable), the blackboard model is brought closer to the realities inherent in serial-computing environments.[7]

Although the elaborate analogy to jigsaw puzzle solving gives us additional clues to the nature of the behavior of blackboard systems, it is not a very good example for illustrating the organization of the blackboard or for the partitioning of appropriate knowledge into knowledge sources. To illustrate these aspects of the model, we need another example. This time let us consider another hypothetical problem, that of finding koalas in a eucalyptus forest (see Figure 3).

Imagine yourself in Australia. One of the musts if you are a tourist is to go and look for koalas in their natural habitat. So, you go to a koala preserve

Courtesy, San Diego Zoo.   Courtesy, San Diego Zoo.

Figure 3. Finding koalas.

and start looking for them among the branches of the eucalyptus trees. You find none. You know that they are rather small, grayish creatures which look like bears.[8] The forest is dense, however, and the combination of rustling leaves and the sunlight reflecting on the leaves adds to the difficulty of finding these creatures, whose coloring is similar to their environment.[9] You finally give up and ask a ranger how you can find them. He gives you the following story about koalas: "Koalas usually live in groups and seasonally migrate to different parts of the forest, but they should be around the northwest area of the preserve now. They usually sit on the crook of branches and move up and down the tree during the day to get just the right amount of sun.[10] If you are not sure whether you have spotted one or not, watch it for a while; it will move around, though slowly."[11] Armed with the new knowledge, you go back to the forest with a visual image of exactly where and what to look for. You focus your eyes at about 30 feet with no luck, but you try again, and this time focus your eyes at 50 feet, and suddenly you do find one. Not only one, but a whole colony of them.[12]

Let's consider one way of formulating this problem along the lines of the blackboard model. Many kinds of knowledge can be brought to bear on the problem: the color and shape of koalas, the general color and texture of the environment (the noise characteristics), the behavior of the koalas, effects of season and time of the day, and so on. Some of the knowledge can be found in books, such as *Handbook of Koala Sizes and Color* or *Geography of the Forest.* Some knowledge is informal—the most likely places to find koalas at any given time or the koalas' favorite resting places. How can these diverse sources of knowledge be used effectively? First, we need to decide what constitutes a solution to the problem. Then, we can consider what kinds of information are in the data, what can be inferred from them, and what knowledge might be brought to bear to achieve the goal of finding the koalas.

Think of the solution to this problem as a set of markings on a series of snapshots of the forest. The markings might say, "This is certainly a koala because it has a head, body, and limbs and because it has changed its position since the last snapshot;" "This might be a koala, because it has a blob that looks like a head;" "These might be koalas because they are close to the one we know is a koala and the blobs could be heads, legs, or torsos." The important characteristics of the solution are that the solution consists of bits and pieces of information, and it is a reasoned solution with supporting evidence and supporting lines of reasoning.

Having decided that the solution would consist of partial and hypothetical identifications, as well as complete identifications constructed from partial ones, we need a solution-space organization that can hold descriptions of bits and pieces of the koalas. One such descriptive framework is a part-of hierarchy. For each koala, the highest level of description is the koala itself, which is described on the next level by head and body; the head is described on the next level by ears, nose, and eyes; the body is described by torso, legs, and arms; and so on. At each level, there are descriptors appropriate for that level: size, gender, and height on the koala level, for example. Each primitive body part is described on the lower levels in terms of geometric features, such as shapes and line segments. Each shape has color and texture associated with it as well as its geometric descriptions (see Figure 4). In order to identify a part of the snapshot as a koala, we need to mark the picture with line segments and regions. The regions and pieces of lines must eventually be combined, or synthesized, in such a way that the description of the constructed object can be construed as some of the parts of a koala or a koala itself. For example, a small, black circular blob could be an eye, but it must be surrounded by a bigger, lighter blob that might be a head. The more pieces of information one can find that fit the koala description, the more confident we can be. In addition to the body parts that support the existence of a koala, if the hypothesized koala is at about 30 to 50 feet above ground, we would be more confident than if we found the same object at 5 feet.

The knowledge needed to fill in the koala descriptions falls into place with the decision to organize the solution space as a part-of abstraction hierarchy. We would need a color specialist, a shape specialist, a body-part specialist, a habitat specialist, and so forth. No one source of knowledge can solve the problem; the solution to the problem depends on the combined contributions of many specialists. The knowledge held by these specialists is logically independent. Thus, a color specialist can determine the color of a region without knowing how the shape specialist determined the shape of the region. However, the solution of the problem is dependent on both of them. The

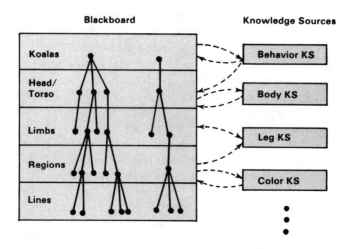

Figure 4. Koalas: Blackboard structure and knowledge sources. The koalas in the scene are described as a part-of hierarchy. Specialist knowledge modules contribute information about what they "see" to help in the search for koalas.

torso specialist does not have to know whether the arm specialist checked if an arm had paws or not (the torso specialist probably doesn't even know about paws), but each specialist must rely on the other specialists to supply the information each one needs. Cooperation is achieved by assuming that whatever information is needed is supplied by someone else.

The jigsaw puzzle and the koala problems illustrate the organization of information on the blackboard database, the partitioning of domain knowledge into specialized sources of knowledge, and some of the characteristic problem-solving behavior associated with the blackboard model.[13] Neither of these, however, answers the questions of how the knowledge is to be represented, or of what the mechanisms are for determining and activating appropriate knowledge. As mentioned earlier, problem solving models are conceptual frameworks for formulating solutions to problems. The models do not address the details of designing and building operational systems. How a piece of knowledge is represented, as rules, objects, or procedures, is an engineering decision. It involves such pragmatic considerations as "naturalness," availability of a knowledge representation language, and the skill of the implementers, to name but a few.[14] What control mechanisms are needed depends on the complexity and the nature of the application task. We can, however, attempt to narrow the gap between the model and operational systems. Now, the blackboard model is extended by adding more details to the three primary components in terms of their structures, functions, and behaviors.

1.2 The Blackboard Framework

Applications are implemented with different combinations of knowledge representations, reasoning schemes, and control mechanisms. The variability in the design of blackboard systems is due to many factors, the most influential one being the nature of the application problem itself. It can be seen, however, that blackboard architectures which underlay application programs have many similar features and constructs. The blackboard framework is created by abstracting these constructs.[15] The blackboard framework, therefore, contains descriptions of the blackboard system components that are grounded in actual computational constructs. The purpose of the framework is to provide design guidelines appropriate for blackboard systems in a serial-computing environment.[16] Figure 5 shows some modifications to Figure 1 to reflect the addition of system-oriented details.

1.2.1 The Knowledge Sources

The domain knowledge needed to solve a problem is partitioned into knowledge sources that are kept separate and independent.

The objective of each knowledge source is to contribute information that will lead to a solution to the problem. A knowledge source takes a set of current information on the blackboard and updates it as encoded in its specialized knowledge.

The knowledge sources are represented as procedures, sets of rules, or logic assertions. To date most of the knowledge sources have been represented as either procedures or as sets of rules. However, systems that deal with signal processing either make liberal use of procedures in their rules or use both rule sets and procedurally encoded knowledge sources.

The knowledge sources modify only the blackboard or control data structures (that also might be on the blackboard), and only the knowledge sources modify the blackboard. All modifications to the solution state are explicit and visible.

Each knowledge source is responsible for knowing the conditions under which it can contribute to a solution. Each knowledge source has preconditions that indicate the condition on the blackboard which must exist before the body of the knowledge source is *activated.*[17]

1.2.2 The Blackboard Data Structure

The problem solving state data are kept in a global database, the *blackboard.* Knowledge sources produce changes to the blackboard that lead incrementally to a solution, or a set of acceptable solutions, to the problem. Interaction among the knowledge sources takes place solely through changes on the blackboard.

The purpose of the blackboard is to hold computational and solution state data needed by and produced by the knowledge sources. The knowledge

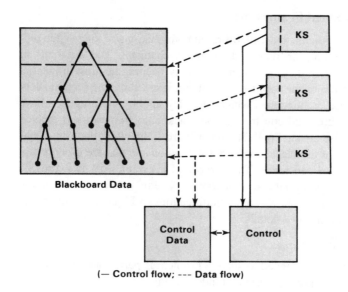

Blackboard Data

(— Control flow; --- Data flow)

Figure 5. The blackboard framework.

sources use the blackboard data to interact with each other indirectly.

The blackboard consists of objects from the solution space. These objects can be input data, partial solutions, alternatives, and final solutions (and, possibly, control data).

The objects on the blackboard are hierarchically organized into levels of analysis. Information associated with objects (that is, their properties) on one level serves as input to a set of knowledge sources, which, in turn, place new information on the same or other levels.

The objects and their properties define the vocabulary of the solution space. The properties are represented as attribute-value pairs. Each level uses a distinct subset of the vocabulary.[18]

The relationships between the objects are denoted by named links.[19] The relationship can be between objects on different levels, such as "part-of" or "in-support-of," or between objects on the same level, such as "next-to" or "follows."

The blackboard can have multiple blackboard panels. That is, a solution space can be partitioned into multiple hierarchies.[20]

The data on the blackboard are hierarchically organized. The knowledge sources are logically independent, self-selecting modules. Only the knowledge sources are allowed to make changes to the blackboard. Based on the latest changes to the information on the blackboard, a control module selects and executes the next knowledge source.

1.2.3 Control

The knowledge sources *respond opportunistically* to changes in the black-board.

There is a set of control modules that monitor the changes on the black-board and decide what actions to take next.

Various kinds of information are made globally available to the control modules. The information can be on the blackboard or kept separately. The control information is used by the control modules to determine the focus of attention.

The focus of attention indicates the next thing to be processed. The focus of attention can be either the knowledge sources (that is, which knowledge sources to activate next) or the blackboard objects (that is, which solution islands to pursue next) or a combination of both (that is, which knowledge sources to apply to which objects).[21]

The solution is built one step at a time. Any type of reasoning step (data driven, goal driven, model driven, and so on) can be applied at each stage of solution formation. As a result, the sequence of knowledge source invocation is dynamic and opportunistic rather than fixed and preprogrammed.

Pieces of problem-solving activities occur in the following iterative sequence:

1. A knowledge source makes change(s) to blackboard object(s). As these changes are made, a record is kept in a global data structure that holds the control information.

2. Each knowledge source indicates the contribution it can make to the new solution state. (This can be defined a priori for an application or dynamically determined.)

3. Using the information from points 1 and 2, a control module selects a focus of attention.

4. Depending on the information contained in the focus of attention, an appropriate control module prepares it for execution as follows:

   a. If the focus of attention is a knowledge source, then a blackboard object (or sometimes, a set of blackboard objects) is chosen to serve as the context of its invocation (knowledge-scheduling approach).

   b. If the focus of attention is a blackboard object, then a knowledge source is chosen which will process that object (event-scheduling approach).

   c. If the focus of attention is a knowledge source and an object, then that knowledge source is ready for execution. The knowledge source is executed together with the context, thus described.

Criteria are provided to determine when to terminate the process. Usually, one of the knowledge sources indicates when the problem solving process is terminated, either because an acceptable solution has been found or because the system cannot continue further for lack of knowledge or data.

1.2.4 Problem-Solving Behavior and Knowledge Application

The problem solving behavior of a system is determined by the knowledge application strategy encoded in the control modules. The choice of the most appropriate knowledge-application strategy is dependent on the characteristics of the application task and on the quality and quantity of domain knowledge relevant to the task.[22] Basically, the acts of choosing a particular blackboard region and choosing a particular knowledge source to operate on that region determine the problem-solving behavior. Generally, a knowledge source uses information on one level as its input and produces output information on another level. Thus, if the input level of a particular knowledge source is on the level lower (closer to data) than its output level, then the application of this knowledge source is at application of bottom-up, forward reasoning.

Conversely, a commitment to a particular type of reasoning step is a commitment to a particular knowledge application method. For example, if we are interested in applying a data-directed, forward reasoning step, then we would select a knowledge source whose input level is lower than its output level. If we are interested in goal-directed reasoning, we would select a knowledge source that puts information needed to satisfy a goal on a lower level. Using the constructs in the control component, one can make any type of reasoning step happen at each step of knowledge application.[23]

How a piece of knowledge is stated often presupposes how it is to be used. Given a piece of knowledge about a relationship between information on two levels, that knowledge can be expressed in top down or bottom-up application forms. These can further be refined. The top-down form can be written as a goal, an expectation, or as an abstract model of the lower-level information. For example, a piece of knowledge can be expressed as a conjunction of information on a lower level needed to generate a hypothesis at a higher level (a goal), or it can be expressed as information on a lower level needed to confirm a hypothesis at a higher level (an expectation), and so on. The framework does not presuppose nor does it prescribe the knowledge-application, or reasoning, methods. It merely provides constructs within which any reasoning methods can be used. Many interesting problem-solving behaviors have been implemented using these constructs.

1.3 Perspectives

The organizational underpinnings of blackboard systems have been the primary focus. The blackboard framework is a system-oriented interpretation of the blackboard model. It is a mechanistic formulation intended to serve as a foundation for system specifications. In problem-solving programs, we are usually interested in their performance and problem-solving behavior, not their organization. We have found, however, that some classes of complex problems become manageable when they are formulated along the lines of the blackboard model. Also, interesting problem solving behavior can be programmed using the blackboard framework as a foundation. Even though the blackboard framework still falls short of being a computational specification, given an application task and the necessary knowledge, it provides enough information so that a suitable blackboard system can be designed, specified, and built.[24]

There are other perspectives on the blackboard model. The blackboard model is sometimes viewed as a model of general problem solving (Hayes-Roth 1983). It has been used to structure cognitive models (McClelland and Rumelhart 1981; Rumelhart and McClelland 1982; and Hayes-Roth et al. 1979); the OPM system, simulates the human planning process. Sometimes the blackboard model is used as an organizing principle for large, complex systems built by many programmers. The ALVan project (Stentz and Shafer 1985) takes this approach.

1.4 Summary

The basic approach to problem solving in the blackboard framework is to divide the problem into loosely coupled subtasks. These subtasks roughly correspond to areas of specialization within the task (for example, there are human specialists for the subtasks). For a particular application, the designer defines a solution space and knowledge needed to find the solution. The solution space is divided into analysis levels of partial or intermediate solutions, and the knowledge is divided into specialized knowledge sources that perform the subtasks. The information on the analysis levels is globally accessible on the blackboard, making it a medium of interaction between the knowledge sources. Generally, a knowledge source uses information on one level of analysis as its input and produces output information on another level. The decision to employ a particular knowledge source is made dynamically using the latest information contained in the blackboard data structure (the current solution state). This particular approach to problem decomposition and knowledge application is very flexible and works well in diverse application domains. One caveat, however: How the problem is partitioned into subproblems makes a great deal of difference to the clarity of the approach, the speed with which solutions are found, the resources required, and even the ability to solve the problem at all.

In order to discuss the details of various blackboard systems, it is helpful to trace the intellectual history of the blackboard concepts. Aside from being interesting in itself, it explains the origins of ideas and reasons for some of the differences between blackboard system designs. The reasons often have no rational basis but have roots in the "cultural" differences between the research laboratories that were involved in the early history of blackboard systems.

2. Evolution of Blackboard Architectures

Metaphorically we can think of a set of workers, all looking at the same blackboard: each is able to read everything that is on it, and to judge when he has something worthwhile to add to it. This conception is just that of Selfridge's Pandemonium: a set of demons, each independently looking at the total situation and shrieking in proportion to what they see that fits their natures... (Newell 1962.)

2.1 Prehistory

The above quotation is the first reference to the term blackboard in the AI literature. Newell was concerned with the organizational problems of programs that existed at the time (for example, checker-playing programs, chess-playing programs, theorem-proving programs), most of which were organized along a generate-and-test search model[25] (Newell 1969). The major difficulty in these programs was rigidity. He notes:

A program can operate only in terms of what it knows. This knowledge can come from only two sources. It can come from assumptions [or] it can come from executing processes... either by direct modification of the data structure or by testing ... but executing processes take time and space [whereas] assumed information does not have to be stored or generated. Therefore the temptation in creating efficient programs is always to minimize the amount of generated information, and hence to maximize the amount of stipulated information. It is the latter that underlies most of the rigidities.

In one example, Newell discusses an organization to synthesize complex processes by means of sequential flow of control and hierarchically organized, closed subroutines. Even though this organization had many advantages (isolation of tasks, space saving by coding nearly identical tasks once, and so on), it also had difficulties. First, conventions required for communication among the subroutines often forced the subroutines to work with impoverished information. Second, the ordered subroutine calls fostered the need for doing things sequentially. Third, and most importantly, it encouraged programmers to think of the total program in terms of only one thing going on at a time. However, in problem solving there are often many possible things to be processed at any given time (for example, exploring various branches of a search tree), and relatively weak and scattered information is necessary to guide the exploration for a solution (for example, observations noticed while going down one branch of a search tree could be used when going down another branch). The primary difficulties with this organization, then, were inflexible control and restricted data accessibility. It is within this context that Newell notes the difficulties "might be alleviated by maintaining the isolation of routines, but allowing all the subroutines to make use of a common data structure." He uses the blackboard metaphor to describe such a system.

The blackboard solution proposed by Newell eventually became the production system (Newell and Simon 1972), which in turn led to the development of the OPS system (Forgy and McDermott 1977). In OPS the subroutines are represented as condition-action rules[26], and the data are globally available in the working memory. One of the many "shrieking demons" (those rules whose "condition sides" are satisfied) is selected through a conflict resolution process. The conflict-resolution process emulates the selection of one of the loudest demons, for example, one that addresses the most specific situation. OPS does reflect the blackboard concept as stated by Newell and provides for flexibility of control and global accessibility to data. However, the blackboard systems as we know them today took a slightly more circuitous route before coming into being.

In a paper first published in 1966 (later published in Simon 1977), Simon mentions the term blackboard in a slightly different context from Newell. The discussion is within the framework of an information-processing theory about discovery and incubation of ideas:

> In the typical organization of a problem-solving program, the solution efforts are guided and controlled by a hierarchy or "tree" of goals and subgoals. Thus, the subject starts out with the goal of solving the original problem. In trying to reach this goal, he generates a subgoal ... If the subgoal is achieved, he may then turn to the now-modified original goal. If difficulties arise in achieving the subgoal, sub-subgoals may be created to deal with them ... we would specify that the goal tree be held in some kind of temporary memory, since it is a dynamic structure, whose function is to guide search, and it is not needed when the problem solution has been found ... In addition, the problem solver is noticing various features of the problem environment and is storing some of these in memory ... What use is made of [a feature] at the time it is noted depends on what subgoal is directing attention at that moment ... over the longer run, this information influences the growth of the subgoal tree ... I will call the information about the task environment that is noticed in the course of problem solution and fixated in permanent (or relatively long-term) memory the "blackboard."

Although Newell's and Simon's concerns appear within different contexts, the problem-solving method they were using was the goal directed, generate-and-test search method. They encountered two common difficulties: the need for previously generated information during problem solving and flexible control. It was Simon who proposed the blackboard ideas to Raj Reddy and Lee Erman for the HEARSAY project.[27]

Although the blackboard metaphor was suggested by Simon to the

HEARSAY designers, the final design of the system, as might be expected, evolved out of the needs of the speech understanding task. Such system characteristics as hierarchically organized analysis levels on the blackboard and opportunistic reasoning, which we now accept as integral parts of blackboard systems, were derived from needs and constraints that were different from Newell's and Simon's. One of the key notions attributable to the speech understanding problem was the notion of the blackboard partitioned into analysis levels. This is a method of using and integrating different "vocabularies," as mentioned earlier, in problem solving. In most problem-solving programs of the time, such as game-playing and theorem proving programs, the problem space had a homogeneous vocabulary. In the speech-understanding problem, there was a need to integrate concepts and vocabularies used in describing grammars, words, phones, and so on.

There are two interesting observations to be made from early history. First, the early allusions to a blackboard are closely tied to search methodologies, and, not surprisingly, the use of generate and test search is evident in HEARSAY-II. Second, although the HEARSAY-II blackboard system was designed independently from the OPS system, there are, as we might expect, some conceptual similarities. For example, the scheduler in HEARSAY-II is philosophically and functionally very similar to the conflict resolution module in OPS, which, in turn, is a way of selecting one of the shrieking demons.

The HASP system, which has its own intellectual history, does not focus so much on search techniques as on knowledge-application techniques. Put another way, HASP was built in a culture that had a tradition of using problem-solving approaches that focused on applying large amounts of situation-specific knowledge rather than on applying a weak method (generate-and-test) using general knowledge about the task.[28] The methodology used to select and apply knowledge in HASP is, therefore, quite different philosophically from the one reflected in the HEARSAY-II scheduler. These and other differences are elaborated on in the next section.[29] Next is examined another branch of a history that influenced the design of HEARSAY-II, the speech-understanding task.

2.2 The HEARSAY Project

Although a blackboard concept was documented in AI literature as early as 1962 by Newell, it was implemented as a system a decade later by people working on a speech understanding project. The first article on the HEARSAY system appeared in *IEEE Transactions on Audio and Electroacoustics* in 1973 (Reddy et al. 1973).[30] There, the authors described the limitations of extant speech recognition systems and proposed a model that would overcome the limitations. To summarize, the article stated that although the importance of context, syntax, semantics, and phonological rules in the recognition of speech was accepted, no system had been built that incorporated these ill-

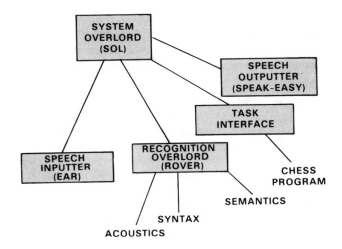

Figure 6. Overview of the HEARSAY-I systems (from Reddy et al. 1973a).

defined sources of knowledge. At the same time, the authors' previous work
indicated (1) that the limitation of syntax directed methods of parsing from
left to right had to be overcome; (2) that parsing should proceed both forward
and backward from anchor points; and (3) that because of the lack of feedback in a simple part-of hierarchical structure, the magnitude of errors on the
lower level propagated multiplicatively up the hierarchy; that is, minor errors
in the signal level, for example, became major errors on a sentence level.

The system architecture described in the Reddy article, later to be known as
the HEARSAY-I architecture, was based on a model that addressed the following requirements: (1) the contribution of each source of knowledge (syntax, semantics, context, and so on) to the recognition of speech had to be measurable;
(2) the absence of one or more knowledge sources should not have a crippling
effect on the overall performance; (3) more knowledge sources should improve
the performance; (4) the system must permit graceful error recovery; (5)
changes in performance requirements, such as increased vocabulary size or
modifications to the syntax or semantics, should not require major
modifications to the model. The functional diagram of the HEARSAY-I architecture is shown in Figure 6, and its behavior is summarized as follows:

> The EAR module accepts speech input, extracts parameters, and performs some
> preliminary segmentation, feature extraction, and labeling, generating a "partial
> symbolic utterance description." The recognition overlord (ROVER) controls the
> recognition process and coordinates the hypothesis generation and verification
> phases of various cooperating parallel processes. The TASK provides the inter-
> face between the task being performed and the speech recognition and genera-
> tion (SPEAK-EASY) parts of the system. The system overlord (SOL) provides
> the overall control for the system.

From Figure 7, which illustrates the recognition process, one can glean the beginnings of an organization of a blackboard system. Note how the overlord (ROVER) controlled the invocation of activities. The beginnings of the scheduler, as well as the knowledge sources, are apparent, as they became incorporated in HEARSAY-II.

Since the different recognizers are independent, the recognition overlord needs to synchronize the hypothesis generation and verification phases of various processes.... Several strategies are available for deciding which subset of the processes generates the hypotheses and which verify. At present this is done by polling the processes to decide which process is most confident about generating the correct hypothesis. In voice chess, [The task domain for HEARSAY-I was chess moves] where the semantic source of knowledge is dominant, that module usually generates the hypotheses. These are then verified by the syntactic and acoustic recognizers. However, when robust acoustic cues are present in the incoming utterance, the roles are reversed with the acoustic recognizer generating the hypotheses.

"Knowledge sources are activated in a lock-step sequence consisting of three phases: poll, hypothesize, and test" (Hayes-Roth et al. 1979). During the polling phase, the overlord queries the knowledge sources to determine which ones have something to contribute to that region of the sentence hypothesis which is "in focus" and with what level of "confidence."[31] In the hypothesizing phase, the most promising knowledge source is activated to make its contribution. Finally, in the testing phase, knowledge sources evaluate the new hypotheses.

Some of the difficulties encountered in HEARSAY-I can be attributed to the way in which the solution to the application task was formulated, and other difficulties arose from the design of the system. The problem was formulated to use the hypothesize and test paradigm only on the word level, that is, the blackboard only contained a description at the word level. This meant that all communication among the knowledge sources was limited to sharing information at the word level. This formulation caused two major difficulties. First, it becomes difficult to add nonword knowledge sources and to evaluate their contributions. Second, the inability to share information contributed by nonword knowledge sources caused the information to be recomputed by each knowledge source that needed it. In other words, the difficulty lay in trying to force the use of a single vocabulary when multiple vocabularies were needed.

The architectural weaknesses of HEARSAY-I, as stated by its designers, lay in (1) the lock-step control sequence that limited "parallelism,"[32] (2) the lack of provision to express relationships among alternative sentence hypotheses, and (3) the built-in problem-solving strategy that made modifications awkward and comparisons of different strategies impossible (Lesser et al. 1974). To overcome these difficulties, information (in the multiple vocabularies needed to understand utterances) used by all the knowledge sources was uniformly represented and made globally accessible on the blackboard in

HEARSAY-II. In addition, a scheduler dynamically selected and activated the appropriate knowledge sources.

During the time that HEARSAY-II was being developed, the staff of the HASP project was looking for an approach to solve its application problem. The search for a new methodology came about because the plan generate and test problem-solving method that was successful for interpreting mass-spectrometry data in the DENDRAL program (Lindsay et al. 1980) was found to be inappropriate for the problem of interpreting passive sonar signals. In the history of blackboard systems, HASP represents a branching point in the philosophy underlying the design of blackboard systems. Generally, later systems can be thought of as modifications of, or extensions to, either the HEARSAYlike or HASPlike designs.

2.3 The HASP Project

The task of HASP was to interpret continuous sonar signals passively collected by hydrophone arrays monitoring an area of the ocean. Signals are received from multiple arrays, with each array consisting of multiple hydrophones. Each array has some directional resolution. Imagine a large room full of plotters, each recording digitized signals from the hydrophones. Now, imagine an analyst going from one plotter to the next trying to discern what each one is hearing, and then integrating the information from all the plots in order to discern the current activity in the region under surveillance. This interpretation and analysis activity goes on continuously day in and day out. The primary objective of this activity is to detect enemy submarines. The objective of the HASP project was to write a program that "emulated" the human analysts, that is to incorporate, in a computer program, the expertise of the analysts, especially their ability to detect submarines.[33] The HASP problem was chosen to work on because it appeared to be similar to the DENDRAL problem, a signal interpretation problem for which there were experts who could do the job. The system designers were confident that the problem-solving approach taken in DENDRAL would work for HASP. What was DENDRAL's task, and what was its approach? To quote from Feigenbaum (1977), the task was

> to enumerate plausible structures (atom-bond graphs) for organic molecules, given two kinds of information: analytic instrument data from a mass spectrometer and a nuclear magnetic resonance spectrometer; and user-supplied constraints on the answers, derived from any other source of knowledge (instrumental or contextual) available to the user.

DENDRAL's inference procedure is a heuristic search that takes place in three stages, without feedback: *plan-generate-and-test.*

Generate is a generation process for plausible structures. Its foundation is a combinatorial algorithm that can produce all the topologically legal candidate structures. Constraints supplied by the user or by the *Plan* process prune and steer the

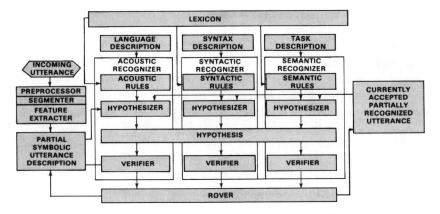

Figure 7. Details of the recognition process (From Reddy et al. 1973b).

generation to produce the plausible set and not the enormous legal set.

Test refines the evaluation of plausibility, discarding less worthy candidates and rank-ordering the remainder for examination by the user. . . It evaluates the worth of each candidate by comparing its predicted data with the actual input data…Thus, test selects the 'best' explanation of the data.

Plan produces direct (that is, not chained) inference about likely substructures in the molecule from patterns in the data that are indicative of the presence of the substructure. In other words, Plan worked with combinatorially reduced abstracted sets to guide the search in a generally fruitful direction.

If some of the words in this description were replaced, the plan-generate-and test approach seemed appropriate for the HASP tasks:

Generate plausible ship candidates and their signal characteristics. *Test* by comparing the predicted signals with the real signals. *Plan* by selecting types of ships that could be in the region of interest. The Plan phase would use intelligence reports, shipping logs, and so on.

The system designers had already talked with the analysts and had read their training manuals. They knew the necessary knowledge could be represented as rules, a form of domain knowledge representation that had proven its utility and power in DENDRAL. Difficulties were encountered immediately; some of these were:

1. The input data arrived in a continuous stream, as opposed to being batched like in DENDRAL. The problem of a continuous data stream was solved by processing data in time-framed batches.

2. The analysis of the activities in the ocean had to be tracked, and updated over time. Most importantly, past activities played an important role in the analysis of current activities.

3. There were numerous types of information that seemed relevant but remote from the interpretation process, for example, the average speeds of ships.

To address the second problem, it was immediately clear that a data structure was needed which was equivalent to a "situation board" used by the analysts; the data structure was called the Current Best Hypothesis (CBH). CBH reflected the most recent hypothesis about the situation at any given point in time. This could serve as the basis for generating a "plan;" that is, the CBH could be used as a basis for predicting the situation to be encountered in the next time frame. The prediction process could also utilize and integrate the variety of information mentioned in item 3. The predicted CBH would then be used (1) to verify that the interpretation from the previous time frame was correct (2) to reduce the number of alternatives generated during past time frames,[34] and (3) to reduce the number of new signals not accounted for in the predicted CBH that needed to be analyzed in full. CBH was thought of as a cognitive "flywheel" that maintained the continuous activities in a region of ocean between time frames. The initial design, a modified version of DENDRAL, was sketched out in December of 1973 (see Figure 8).

Then there came the bad news. There was no plausible generator of the solution space, and there was no simulator to generate the signals of hypothesized platforms. The bad news had a common root; given a platform, there was a continuum of possible headings, speeds, and aspects relative to an array. Each parameter, in addition to variations in the water temperature, depth, and so on, uniquely affected the signals "heard" at an array. Consequently, there was a continuum of possibilities in the solution space as well as for the simulator to simulate. The designers tried to limit the number of possibilities, for example, by measuring the headings by unit degrees, but this left an enormous search space. Moreover, there was not enough knowledge to prune the space to make the generate and test method practical. The DENDRAL approach was abandoned. Then the HEARSAY-II approach was learned of. The description of the approach produced enough of a mental shift in the way the HASP problem was viewed that a new solution could be designed. It should be noted in passing that HEARSAY-II in fact had generators and used them. It was the idea of fusing uncertain and partial solutions to construct solutions, combined with "island driving,"[35] that intrigued the designers.

The sonar analysts solved the problem piecemeal. They first identified a harmonic set in the signals. The "accounted-for" signals were then "subtracted" from the data set. Then another harmonic set would be formed with the remaining data, and so on until all the signals were accounted for.[36] Each harmonic set implied a set of possible sources of sound (for example, a propeller shaft), which in turn implied a set of possible ship types from which the sounds could be emanating. Certain signal characteristics directly implied platform types, but this type of diversion from the incremental analysis was very rare. What the human analysts were doing was what might be called logical induction and synthesis.[37] Hypotheses were synthesized from pieces of data using a large amount of domain-specific knowledge that translated information in one form to information in another form, that is, transformed a description in one vocabulary to one in another vocabulary. For example, a set of frequencies was transformed into a set of possible ship parts (for example, a shaft or a propeller) by using knowledge of the form, "If the harmonic set consists of ..., then it is likely due to ..." The partial solutions thus formed were then combined using other knowledge to construct acceptable solutions.

The analysts were also strongly model driven. There were common shipping lanes used by merchant ships traveling from one port to another. These platforms usually maintained a steady speed and heading. This and similar knowledge served to constrain the number of possible partial solutions. For example, if a hypothetical surface platform traveled across a shipping lane, then the possibility that it might be a merchant ship could be eliminated. In this example, a model of ship movements was able to aid in the platform classification process. Moreover, knowledge about the characteristics of platforms was used to combine lower-level, partial solutions. Suppose a platform type was hypothesized from an acoustic source, for example, a propeller shaft. Knowledge about the platform type (a model) was then used to look for other acoustic sources (for example, engine) belonging to that platform. This type of top-down, model-driven analysis was used as often as the bottom-up signal analysis.

Once it was clear that interpretation in HASP, as in HEARSAY, was a process of piecemeal generation of partial solutions that were combined to form complete solutions, the HEARSAY-II system organization could be exploited. The CBH was partitioned into levels of analysis corresponding to the way analysts were used to thinking (that is, signals, harmonic sets, sources, and ship types). The rule-based knowledge gathered for the purposes of pruning and guiding the search process was organized into sets of rules (knowledge sources) that transformed information on one level to information on another level.[38]

Nothing is as easy as it appears. There were many differences between the speech and the sonar signal understanding tasks that drove the HASP system architecture in a different direction from HEARSAY-II. The use of the blackboard as a situation board that evolves over time has already been mentioned. This is somewhat equivalent to asking a speaker to repeat his utterance over and over again while moving around, and having the interpretation improve with each repeated utterance as well as being able to locate the speaker after each utterance. After each utterance, the CBH would reflect the best that the system could do up to that point. It was also mentioned that sets of rules, as opposed to procedures in HEARSAY-II, were used to represent knowledge sources. Rules were chosen because they were used in DENDRAL and in MYCIN.[39]

There was one global data structure that contained a hypothesis about the

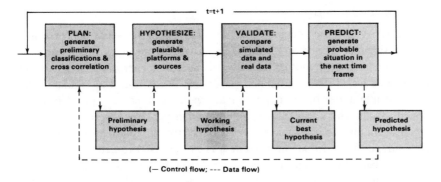

Figure 8. HASP design based on DENDRAL.

situation. After each of the plan, hypothesize, validate, and predict phases, the hypothesis changed states. These states were called the preliminary hypothesis, the working hypothesis, the current best hypothesis, and the predicted hypothesis.

This choice of knowledge representation had a great influence in simplifying the HASP scheduler. The following characteristics influenced the final design of HASP.

2.3.1 Events

The concept of events is inherent in the HASP problem. For example, a certain type of frequency shift in the signal would be an event that implied the ship was changing its speed. An appearance or disappearance of a signal would be an event that implied a new ship was on the scene or a known ship was getting out of the range of the sensors, or it implied an expected behavior of certain types of ships. This inherent task characteristic made it natural for the HASP system to be an event based system; that is, an occurrence of a particular event implied that new information was available for some a priori determined knowledge source to pursue. The goals of the task dictated what events were significant and what were not. This, in turn, meant that the programmer (the knowledge engineer of today) could a priori decide what changes in the blackboard, that is, events, were significant for solving the problem (as opposed to the system noticing every change). Furthermore, the only time a knowledge source needed to be activated was when some events occurred that it knew about. These task characteristics, together with the use of a rule-based knowledge representation, helped redefine and simplify the task of the scheduler in the sense that each piece of knowledge was more or less self-selecting for any given event.[40]

2.32 Temporal Events

In HEARSAY-II "time" meant the sequence in which the words appeared in a spoken sentence. Based on the sequence of words, one could predict or verify the appearance of another set of words later or earlier in the sequence. In HASP time had different connotations. In one sense, time was similar to the separate utterances in the hypothetical repetitive utterances problem mentioned earlier. There was information redundancy, as well as new and different information (no two utterances sound exactly the same), as time went on. Redundancy meant that the system was not pressed to account for every piece of data at each time frame. It could wait to see if a clearer signal appeared later, for example. Also, time meant that the situation at any time frame was a "natural" consequence of earlier situations, and such information as trends and temporal patterns (both signal and symbolic) that occur over time could be used. One of the most powerful uses of time in this sense was the generation and use of expectations of future events.

2.33 Multiple Input Streams

Aside from the digitized data from many hydrophones, HASP had another kind of input—reports. Reports contained information gathered from intelligence or normal shipping sources. These reports tended to use descriptions similar to those used on the ship level on the blackboard (CBH). Whereas the ordinary data came in at the bottom level for both HEARSAY and HASP, HASP had another input "port" at the highest level. Given the input at this level, the system generated the kinds of acoustic sources and acoustic signatures it expected in the future based on information in its taxonomic knowledge base. This type of model-based expectation was one of the methods used to "fuse" report data with signal data.

2.34 Explanation

The purpose of explanation is to understand what is going on in the system from the perspective of the user and the programmer. Because the needs of the users are different from those of the programmers, explanation can take on many forms. Explanation for the user was especially important in HASP, because there was no way to test the correctness of the answer. The only way to test the performance of the system was to get human analysts to agree that the system's situation hypotheses and reasoning were plausible. CBH, with its network of evidential supports served to justify the elements of the hypothesis and their hypothetical properties. It served to "explain" the relationships between the signal data and its various levels of interpretation. The explanation of the reasoning, that is, "explaining" which pieces of knowledge had been applied under what circumstances, was made possible by "playing back" the executed rules.[41]

There were many other differences, but these characteristics had the most impact on the design of the eventual system. The list serves to illustrate how strongly the task characteristics influence blackboard architectures.

Since HEARSAY-II and HASP, there have been a variety of other programs whose system designs are rooted in the blackboard model. These programs include applications in the area of interpretation of electron density maps of protein crystals (Terry 1983), planning (Hayes-Roth et al. 1979), scene analysis (Nagao and Matsuyama 1980), and signal understanding and situation assessment (Spain 1983, and Williams 1985). There are other applications currently being built in the areas of process control, very large-scale integration (VLSI) design, crisis management, image understanding, and signal interpretation. Many applications in the Defense Advanced Research Project Agency's (DARPA) Strategic Computing Program in the areas of military battle management, a pilot's associate and autonomous vehicles utilize the blackboard model. To date, there is no commonly agreed upon architecture for blackboard systems. Rather, there are more or less strict interpretations of the model. The blackboard framework that distills the common constructs and features of many blackboard systems has been introduced.

Acknowledgements

This work was supported by the Defense Advanced Research Projects Agency (N0039-83-C-0136), the National Institutes of Health (5P41 PR-00785), and Boeing Computer Services (W266875).

Notes

1. This document is a part of a retrospective monograph on the AGE project currently in preparation.

2. Domain refers to a particular area of discourse, for example, chemistry.

3. Task refers to a goal-oriented activity within the domain, for example, to analyze the molecular composition of a compound.

4. The hierarchy can be an abstraction hierarchy, a part-of hierarchy, or any other type of hierarchy appropriate for solving the problem.

5. There are various other ways of categorizing reasoning methods, for example, event driven, goal driven, model driven, expectation driven, and so forth. Without getting into the subtle differences between these methods, it is safe to say that any one of these methods can be applied at each step in the reasoning process.

6. There is no control component specified in the blackboard model. The model merely specifies a general problem-solving behavior. The actual locus of control can be in the knowledge sources, on the blackboard, in a separate module, or in some combination of the three. (The need for a control component in blackboard systems is discussed later.)

7. The serialization of the blackboard model is useful only because we tend to work on uniprocessor computers. We are currently conducting research on concurrent problem-solving methods. A starting point for the work is the pure blackboard model. One can see, at least conceptually, much parallelism inherent in the model. The problem is how to convert the model into an

operational system that can take advantage of many (100s to 1000s) processor-memory pairs.

8. More details at this descriptive level would be considered factual knowledge and can be used as a part of a prototypical model of koalas.

9. The signal-to-noise ratio is low.

10. This is knowledge about the prototypical behavior pattern of koalas. The ranger suggests a highly model-driven approach to finding them.

11. This is a method of detection as well as confirmation.

12. This koala problem has a long history. It was invented by Ed Feigenbaum (after his trip to Australia) and myself in 1974, during the time when we were not allowed to write about the HASP project. The primary objective of this example was to illustrate the power of model-directed reasoning in interpreting noisy data. A paper was written about it but has been collecting dust, a victim of our distaste for writing about hypothetical problems. I resurrect it here because it's hard to come up with a good example that does not require specialized domain knowledge.

13. As in the jigsaw problem, the problem-solving behavior in the koala problem would be opportunistic. As new pieces of evidence are found and new hypotheses generated, appropriate knowledge sources analyze them and create new hypotheses.

14. The blackboard model does not preclude the use of human knowledge sources. Interesting interactive and symbiotic expert systems can be built by integrating human expertise during run time.

15. There is an implicit assumption that systems can be described at various levels of abstraction. Thus, the description of the framework is more detailed than the model and less detailed than a specification (a description from which a system can be built). Here, they are called the model, framework, and specification levels.

16. One can view the blackboard framework as a prescriptive model; that is, it prescribes what must be in a blackboard system. However, it must be kept in mind that application problems often demand extensions to the framework, as can be seen in the examples in Part 2.

17. One can view a knowledge source as a large rule. The major difference between a rule and a knowledge source is the grain size of the knowledge each holds. The condition part of this large rule is called the knowledge source precondition, and the action part is called the knowledge source body.

18. Many times, the names of the attributes on different levels are the same, for example, "type." Often these are shorthand notations for "type-of-x-object" or "type-of-y-object." Sometimes they are duplications of the same attribute used for convenience sake.

19. A relationship is a special kind of property.

20. This feature was first used in the CRYSALIS system. The rationale for introducing multiple panels is discussed in Nii (1986).

21. Any given system usually employs one of the three approaches, not all.

22. It might be said that this is a hedge, that there should be a knowledge-application strategy or a set of strategies built into the framework to reflect different problem-solving behaviors. It is precisely this lack of doctrine, however, that makes the blackboard framework powerful and useful. If an application task calls for two forward-reasoning steps followed by three backward-reasoning steps at some particular point, the framework allows for this. This is not to say that a system with built-in strategies cannot be designed and built. If there is a knowledge-application strategy "generic" to a class of applications, then it might be worthwhile to build a skeletal system with that particular strategy.

23. The control component of the framework is extensible in many directions. In the BB-1 system (Hayes-Roth 1983), the control problem is viewed as a planning problem. Knowledge

sources are applied according to a problem-solving plan in effect. The creation of a problem-solving plan is treated as another problem to be solved using the blackboard approach.

24. What about statements such as "Fortran Common is a blackboard" or "Object-oriented systems are blackboard systems?" All I can say is the potential for a thing is not that thing itself. With some effort, one can design and build a blackboard system in Fortran, and the common area is a good candidate for storing blackboard data. However, one also needs to design knowledge sources that are self-selecting and self-contained and control modules that determine the focus of attention and manage knowledge source application. The blackboard framework is a problem-solving framework. It is not a programming language, although an instance of the framework can have a blackboard language associated with it. It is also not a knowledge representation language, although one can use any knowledge representation language for the knowledge sources and the blackboard. Why can't I get away with placing a hunk of ground beef, a can of tomato sauce, a box of spaghetti, and bottles of seasoning in a pile, and call the pile a spaghetti dinner or, better yet, linguine a la pesta rosa? It would certainly simplify my life.

25. "Generate" is a process that produces each element of the solution space one at a time. The "test" process determines if the generated element satisfied some conditions of predicates in the task domain.

26. See Davis and King 1977, for an overview of production systems.

27. These historical notes are communications from Herbert Simon.

28. Most OPS expert systems use strong knowledge, but this came about later (ca. 1979).

29. There is no denying that there are cultural differences in the AI laboratories; they foster different styles, methods, and lines of research. Whatever the research topic, the intellectual effort tends to follow the line of least resistance, and adopts the styles and methods at the researcher's own laboratory. For example, the work of Newell and Simon on general problem solving has a great deal of influence on much of the work at Carnegie-Mellon University. On the other hand, the work of Feigenbaum and Buchanan on applications of domain-specific knowledge influences the work at their Stanford University laboratory.

30. The manuscript was delivered to IEEE on April 30, 1972.

31. The poll portion of the poll, hypothesize, and test is also very characteristic of OPS and HEARSAY-II. This construct takes on a totally different form in HASP and other subsequent systems.

32. The term parallelism was used quite early in the project even though at that time the system ran on uniprocessors. Later (ca. 1976), experiments with parallel executions were conducted on the C.mmp system (Fennell and Lesser 1977).

33. This was in 1973 before the term expert system was coined. The only expert system in existence at the time was DENDRAL, and MYCIN was on its way.

34. There was only one solution hypothesis. However, some attributes, for example, platform type, could have alternative values.

35. Island driving is a problem solving strategy. A relatively reliable partial hypothesis is designated as an "island of certainty," and the hypothesis building pushes out from this solution island in many directions. This is sometimes called a "middle-out" strategy. There can be many islands of certainty driving the problem-solving process.

36. As easy as it sounds, the task of harmonic set formation was a very difficult one, given noisy and missing data, and could produce large combinatorial possibilities. Addressing this problem became one of the major concerns in HASP.

37. An interesting article on this point is "A More Rational View of Logic." by Alex P. Pentland and Martin A. Fischler; it appeared in the Winter 1983 issue of the *AI Magazine*.

38. It is interesting to note that many of the pieces of knowledge intended for pruning purposes could be converted into inductive knowledge. For example, a pruning rule that read "If a signal is coming from outside the normal traffic lane, then its source could not be cargo or cruise ships" could be used directly for reducing alternatives or could be converted to read "..., then its source is either military ships or fishing boats." One can hold the view that this is not surprising, because knowledge is knowledge, and what counts is how and when it's used.

39. This is a good example of the cultural influence. No other representation was even considered.

40. The relationship between events within the task and events in the system are discussed in Nii (1986).

41. In MYCIN and other similar rule-based programs, explanation consists of a playback of rule firings. In HASP the ordinary methos of playback turned out to be useful only to programmers for debugging purposes. For the user, the rules were either too detailed or were applied in a sequence (breadth first) that was hard for them to understand. In HASP the explanation was generated from an execution history with the help of "explanation templates" that selected the appropriate rule activities in some easy-to-understand order.

Reasoning in Complex
and Dynamic Environments

Part IV presents papers marking the emergence of what came to be called *strong method* or *knowledge intensive* problem solvers. Many factors helped shift the AI research emphasis away from *weak method* approaches, where solution strategies were based on the systematic reduction of syntactic differences between state descriptions in the problem space. Weak methods had difficulty addressing, for example, when a difference might have to be radically increased, or the entire representation shifted, before a solution was afforded. Part IV also introduces several of the multitude of approaches that make up modern AI, including model and case based reasoners and solution strategies based on the interactions of autonomous agents.

By the mid-seventies Edward Feigenbaum and his research group at Stanford had demonstrated positive results with knowledge intensive approaches to problem solving. Success in these early programs was often credited to the vast amounts of "knowledge" represented explicitly in the program. Rather than stand-alone solvers, these programs were intended to assist the human expert in his or her tasks. The earliest program, *Dendral* infers the structure of organic molecules from their chemical formulae and mass spectrographic data. The *Meta-Dendral* program infers rules for use of the Dendral program. Meta-Dendral is given the structure for known compounds along with their mass and the relative abundance of the fragments produced by mass spectrography. It interprets this information and induces for use by Dendral, general rules of the relationship between molecular structure and cleavage (Chapter 20).

In another project from Stanford, MYCIN (Chapter 21), the expert reasoner assisted doctors in the analysis of meningitis and bactertemia, or infections of the blood. An important challenge to MYCIN was the need to obtain immediate analysis from data that was often imprecise or not available. The certainty factor algebra developed for MYCIN has been extended and adopted for many subsequent expert systems. These first expert reasoning programs also addressed the demands of humans for relevance and coherence within the context generated by solution methods. Furthermore, it was expected that expert programs should have the ability to explain their search steps as well as results.

There was a great diversity of new problems addressed by the AI research community during the period of the seventies and eighties, including attempts to model commonsense reasoning as well as to create examples of dynamic and default reasoning processes. These approaches pushed both weak method search as well as logic, still a representational commitment of many, in entirely new directions.

In the logic community, for example, McCarthy (Chapter 19) begins a codification of commonsense reasoning. McCarthy wants to make explicit for the problem solver all the assumptions that go into simple problem scenarios, such as stacking blocks on a table or moving a box and then climbing on it to achieve a goal. Hayes, picks up this theme (Chapter 24) with a proposal, the *Naive Physics Manifesto*, to describe with logic many intuitive world situations, for example, human interaction with the world of physical phenomena such as flowing water and the effects of gravity. The combinatorial questions involved in searching through these axiom systems, as well as the global nature of the problem specification and search will be later challenged by researchers including Brooks (Chapter 12) and Agre and Chapman (Chapter 28).

Doyle (Chapter 22) notes that intelligence in the world is marked by the need to constantly refine and amend understanding. Not only are humans revising their models in a changing world, but as a consequence, previous assumptions and conclusions must often be adjusted. Doyle describes such reasoning as *non-monotonic*, and calls a program for the ongoing support of belief revision based on current models a *truth maintenance system*. Doyle's work has important influences on subsequent reasoning systems, with many of them containing truth maintenance subsystems.

One challenge to logic-based representation is termed the *frame problem* (Minsky, Chapter 6, Hayes, Chapter 24). In logic based reasoning schemes, sound inference rules may be applied to axioms describing the world. In STRIPS problem solving (Chapter 17), for example, these inferences create new descriptions of a world changed by a given action or event. But one can ask what happens to the world descriptions to which inference rules *do not* apply, for example, the blocks not picked up by the robot arm. Are they retained as they were in the new world description? What if they are jostled by the movement of the other blocks, or if the table is touched by the action of the arm? Are these invariant or do they change too? Can we state general axioms specifying what can be assumed to be invariant with respect to certain types of actions or events in the world? The answer is, it depends.... McCarthy's *circumscription logic*, (Chapter 23) addresses these issues.

Several different approaches to expert reasoning systems followed the successes of the rule-based system. Two of the most important are *Case-Based* and *Model-Based* reasoning. Janet Kolodner (Chapter 26) describes reasoning based on the collection and reuse of past experiences. Kolodner offers programs for diagnosis as well as for arguing legal precedent. She also notes the important and difficult task of organizing cases for retrieval from memory based on generality, specificity, as well as utility measures. A most difficult aspect of this research is determining how the problem solving experience from one situation might be needed in the future. Chapter 27, presents model-based reasoning. This approach, rather than taking the more traditional analysis based on empirical associations, such as a symptom with its cause, is based on explicit representation of the structure and functionality, as well as the expected interactions, of the constituent components of the application domain. In Chapter 27 this is the diagnosis of electronic circuits.

The 1980s period in AI research also marked a renewed interest in machine learning. This had long been a traditional concern of AI, beginning with the work of Samuel (Chapter 15) and research efforts described in Part II (Holland, Chapter 11 and McClelland, Rumelhart, and Hinton, Chapter 12). Learning is seen again in Part IV, where Meta-Dendral (Chapter 20) induces new rules or chemical relationships for the Dendral program to use in determining the molecular structure of compounds. Carbonell (Chapter 25) surveys a number of important paradigms for machine learning. In fact, machine learning is one area of AI where a collection such as this is simply unable to cover the territory. We recommend sources including the special issue of the AI Journal (40, 1989) and collections of readings (Michalski et al 1986, 1989; Shavlik and Dietterich 1990; Weiss and Kulikowski 1991; Luger and Stubblefield 1993, ch. 12).

Another research direction, beginning in the robotics and planning community (Fikes and Nilsson Chapter 17, Brooks Chapter 13) is problem solving accomplished by distributed agents. In this paradigm, intelligence emerges as an artifact of individual agent's collaboration and interaction. Chapter 28, a description by Agre and Chapman of an interactive, multi-agent board game, creates models and reference that are local to individual agents. This research offers a direct challenge to the traditional approaches taken by the robotics and logic communities. The authors state:

> Before and beneath any activity of plan following, life is a continual improvisation, a matter of deciding what to do now based on how the world is now. Our

empirical and theoretical studies of activity have led us to question the supposition that action derives from the Execution of Plans and the corresponding framework of problem solving and reasoning with representations. We observe that real situations are characteristically complex, uncertain, and *immediate...* (Traditional) planning is inherently combinatorially explosive and so is unlikely to scale up to realistic situations which take thousands of propositions to represent. Most real situations cannot be completely represented; there isn't time to collect all the necessary information. Real situations are rife with uncertainty; the actions of other agents and processes cannot be predicted... Rather than relying on reasoning to intervene between perception and action, we believe activity mostly derives from very simple sorts of machinery interacting with the immediate situation... without requiring explicit models of the world.

This approach, see also Brooks Chapter 13, reflects the modern AI interest in problem solving based on the interactions of autonomous agents. A volume of the AI Journal (72, 1995) presents a survey of this research.

Finally, there are a number of other modern dimensions to AI research, including the study of emergent phenomena and development of connectionist networks, that we lack the space to address. We end by mentioning the beginning of the *Cognitive Science* research community. This group saw its promise in the words of Turing (Chapter 2) and Newell and Simon (Chapters 4, 14, and 16). In fact, Chapter 16, with its analysis of human problem solving subjects using an explicit comparison of their performance with the running *general problem solver* program, is arguably the first empirical research in cognitive science.

In cognitive science the primary task of the researcher is to understand intelligence in humans. Computational mechanisms can add important insight to this analysis. Through the seventies and eighties, Cognitive Science found its independence from AI and came to flourish as an active research community on its own (Norman 1981, Luger 1994). Cognitive Science, often using the tools and techniques created by AI research, has arisen from the assumption that the laws governing cognitive processes and mechanisms are invariant across subjects and modes of embodiment. These issues point forward to the final Chapter of this collection, Simon's *Machine as Mind.*

19

Programs with Common Sense

John McCarthy

1. The Advice Taker

T he "Advice Taker" is a proposed program for solving problems by manipulating sentences in formal languages.[1] The main difference between it and other programs or proposed programs for manipulating formal languages, such as the Logic Theory Machine (Newell 1957) and the Geometry Program of Gelernter (1963), is that in the previous programs the formal system was the subject matter but the heuristics were all embodied in the program. In this program the procedures will be described as much as possible in the language itself and, in particular, the heuristics are all so described.

The main advantages we expect the advice taker to have is that its behavior will be improvable merely by making statements to it, telling it about its symbolic environment and what is wanted from it. To make these statements will require little if any knowledge of the program or the previous knowledge of the advice taker. One will be able to assume that the advice taker will have available to it a fairly wide class of immediate logical consequences of anything it is told and its previous knowledge. This property is expected to have much in common with what makes us describe certain humans as having common sense. We shall therefore say that a program has common sense if it automatically deduces for itself a sufficiently wide class of immediate consequences of anything it is told and what it already knows.

Before describing the advice taker in any detail, I would like to describe more fully our motivation for proceeding in this direction. Our ultimate objective is to make programs that learn from their experience as effectively as humans do. It may not be realized how far we are presently from this objective. It is not hard to make machines learn from experience how to make simple changes in their behavior of a kind which has been anticipated by the programmer. For example, Samuel has included in his checker program (Samuel 1959) facilities for improving the weights the machine assigns to various factors in evaluating positions. He has also included a scheme whereby the machine remembers games it has played previously and deviates from its previous play when it finds a position which it previously lost. Suppose, however, that we wanted an improvement in behavior corresponding, say, to the discovery by the machine of the principle of the opposition in checkers. No present or presently proposed schemes are capable of discovering phenomena as abstract as this.

If one wants a machine to be able to discover an abstraction, it seems most likely that the machine must be able to represent this abstraction in some relatively simple way. There is one known way of making a machine capable of learning arbitrary behavior, and thus to anticipate every kind of behavior: This is to make it possible for the machine to simulate arbitrary behaviors and try them out. These behaviors may be represented either by nerve nets (Minsky 1962), by Turing machines (McCarthy 1956), or by calculator programs (Friedberg 1958). The difficulty is twofold. First, in any of these representations the density of interesting behaviors is incredibly low. Second, and even more important, small interesting changes in behavior expressed at a high level of abstraction do not have simple representations. It is as though the human genetic structure were represented by a set of blueprints: then a mutation would usually result in a wart, a failure of parts to meet, or even an ungrammatical blueprint which could not be translated into an animal at all. It is very difficult to see how the genetic representation scheme manages to be general enough to represent the great variety of animals observed and yet be such that so many interesting changes in the organism are represented by small genetic changes. The problem of how such a representation controls the development of a fertilized egg into a mature animal is even more difficult.

In my opinion, a system which is to evolve intelligence of human order should have at least the following features:

1. All behaviors must be representable in the system. Therefore, the system should either be able to construct arbitrary automata or to program in

some general-purpose programming language.

2. Interesting changes in behavior must be expressible in a simple way.

3. All aspects of behavior except the most routine must be improvable. In particular, the improving mechanism should be improvable.

4. The machine must have or evolve concepts of partial success because on difficult problems decisive successes or failures come too infrequently.

5. The system must be able to create subroutines which can be included in procedures as units. The learning of subroutines is complicated by the fact that the effect of a subroutine is not usually good or bad in itself. Therefore, the mechanism that selects subroutines should have concepts of an interesting or powerful subroutine whose application may be good under suitable conditions.

Of the five points mentioned, our work concentrates mainly on the second. We base ourselves on the idea that in order for a program to be capable of learning something it must first be capable of being told it. In fact, in the early versions we shall concentrate entirely on this point and attempt to achieve a system which can be told to make a specific improvement in its behavior with no more knowledge of its internal structure or previous knowledge than is required in order to instruct a human. Once this is achieved, we may be able to tell the advice taker how to learn from experience.

The main distinction between the way one programs a computer and modifies the program and the way one instructs a human or will instruct the advice taker is this: A machine is instructed mainly in the form of a sequence of imperative sentences, while a human is instructed mainly in declarative sentences describing the situation in which action is required together with a few imperatives that say what is wanted. The advantages of imperative sentences are as follows:

1. A procedure described in imperatives is already laid out and is carried out faster.

2. One starts with a machine in a basic state and does not assume previous knowledge on the part of the machine.

The advantages of declarative sentences are as follows:

1. Advantage can be taken of previous knowledge.

2. Declarative sentences have logical consequences and it can be arranged that the machine will have available sufficiently simple logical consequences of what it is told and what it previously knew.

3. The meaning of declaratives is much less dependent on their order than is the case with imperatives. This makes it easier to have afterthoughts.

4. The effect of a declarative is less dependent on the previous state of the system so that less knowledge of this state is required on the part of the

instructor. The only way we know of expressing abstractions (such as the previous example of the opposition in checkers) is in language. That is why we have decided to program a system which reasons verbally.

1.1 The Construction of the Advice Taker

The advice taker system has the following main features:

1. There is a method of representing expressions in the computer. These expressions are defined recursively as follows: A class of entities called terms is defined and a term is an expression. A sequence of expressions is an expression. These expressions are represented in the machine by list structures (Minsky 1962).

2. Certain of these expressions may be regarded as declarative sentences in a certain logical system which will be analogous to a universal Post canonical system. The particular system chosen will depend on programming considerations but will probably have a single rule of inference which will combine substitution for variables with *modus ponens*. The purpose of the combination is to avoid choking the machine with special cases of general propositions already deduced.

3. There is an immediate deduction routine which when given a set of premises will deduce a set of immediate conclusions. Initially, the immediate deduction routine will simply write down all onestep consequences of the premises. Later this may be elaborated so that the routine will produce some other conclusions which may be of interest. However, this routine will not use semantic heuristics; i.e., heuristics which depend on the subject matter under discussion. The intelligence, if any, of the advice taker will not be embodied in the immediate deduction routine. This intelligence will be embodied in the procedures which choose the lists of premises to which the immediate deduction routine is to be applied. Of course, the program should never attempt to apply the immediate deduction routine simultaneously to the list of everything it knows. This would make the deduction routine take too long.

4. Not all expressions are interpreted by the system as declarative sentences. Some are the names of entities of various kinds. Certain formulas represent objects. For our purposes, an entity is an object if we have something to say about it other than the things which may be deduced from the form of its name. For example, to most people, the number 3812 is not an object: they have nothing to say about it except what can be deduced from its structure. On the other hand, to most Americans the number 1776 is an object because they have filed somewhere the fact that it represents the year when the American Revolution started. In the advice taker each object has a property list in which are listed the specific things we have to

say about it. Some things which can be deduced from the name of the object may be included in the property list anyhow if the deduction was actually carried out and was difficult enough so that the system does not want to carry it out again.

5. Entities other than declarative sentences which can be represented by formulas in the system are individuals, functions, and programs.

6. The program is intended to operate cyclically as follows: The immediate deduction routine is applied to a list of premises and a list of individuals. Some of the conclusions have the form of imperative sentences. These are obeyed. Included in the set of imperatives which may be obeyed is the routine which deduces and obeys.

We shall illustrate the way the advice taker is supposed to act by means of an example. Assume that I am seated at my desk at home and I wish to go to the airport. My car is at my home also. The solution of the problem is to walk to the car and drive the car to the airport. First, we shall give a formal statement of the premises the advice taker uses to draw the conclusions. Then we shall discuss the heuristics which cause the advice taker to assemble these as premises from the totality of facts it has available. The premises come in groups, and we shall explain the interpretation of each group.

1. First, we have a predicate "at." "at(x,y)" is a formalization of "x is at y." Under this heading we have the premises

   1. at (I, desk)
   2. at (desk, home)
   3. at (car, home)
   4. at (home, county)
   5. at (airport, county)

We shall need the fact that the relation "at" is transitive, which might be written directly as

   6. at (x,y), at $(y,z) \to$ at (x,z)

or alternatively we might instead use the more abstract premises

   6'. transitive (at) and

   7'. transitive $(u) \to (u\ (x,y), u\ (y,z) \to (u\ (x,z))$ from which 6. can be deduced.

2. There are two rules concerning the feasibility of walking and driving.

   8. walkable (x), at (y,x), at(z,x), at$(I,y) \to$ can(go$(y,z$, walking))

   9. drivable (x), at (y,x), at (z,x), at (car,y), at (I,car) $\to$ can (go $(y,z,$driving))

There are also two specific facts.

   10. walkable (home)
   11. drivable (county)

3. Next we have a rule concerned with the properties of going.

12. did (go (x,y,z)) → at (I,y)

4. The problem itself is posed by the premise:

13. want (at (I,airport))

5. The above are all the premises concerned with the particular problem. The last group of premises are common to almost all problems of this sort. They are:

14. (x→can(y)), (did(y)→z)→canachult(x,y,z)

The predicate "canachult(x,y,z)" i.e., "can achieve ultimately," means that in a situation to which x applies, the action y can be performed and brings about a situation to which z applies. A sort of transitivity is described by

15. canachult (x,y,z), canachult (z,u,v) → canachult (x,prog (y,u), v).

Here prog(u,v) is the program of first carrying out u and then v. (Some kind of identification of a single action u with the one step program prog(u) is obviously required, but the details of how this will fit into the formalism have not yet been worked out).

The final premise is the one which causes action to be taken.

16. x, canachult (x,prog (y,z), w), want (w) → do (y)

The argument the advice taker must produce in order to solve the problem deduces the following propositions in more or less the following order:

1. at (I,desk) → can (go (desk,car,walking))

2. at (I,car) → can (go (home,airport,driving))

3. did (go (desk,car,walking)) → at (I,car)

4. did (go (home,airport,driving)) → at (I,airport)

5. canachult (at (I,desk), go (desk,car,walking), at (I,car))

6. canachult (at (I,car), go (home,airport,driving), at (I,airport))

7. canachult (at (I,desk), program (go(desk,car,walking),
   go (home,airport, driving)), → at (I,airport))

8. do (go (desk,car,walking))

The deduction of the last proposition initiates action.

This reasoning raises two major questions of heuristics: The first is that of how the 16 premises are collected, and the second is that of how the deduction proceeds once they are found. We cannot give complete answers to either question in the present chapter; they are obviously not completely separate since some of the deductions might be made before some of the premises are collected. Let us first consider the question of where the 16 premises come from.

First of all, we assert that except for the 13th premise (want (at (I,airport)) which sets the goal) and the 1st premise (at(I,desk) which we shall get from a routine which answers the question "where am I"), all the premises can reasonably be expected to be specifically present in the memory of a machine which has competence of human order in finding its way around. That is, none of them is so specific to the problem at hand that assuming its presence in memory constitutes an anticipation of this particular problem or of a class of problems narrower than those which any human can expect to have previously solved. We must impose this requirement if we are to be able to say that the advice taker exhibits common sense.

On the other hand, while we may reasonably assume that the premises are in memory, we still have to describe how they are assembled into a list by themselves to which the deduction routine may be applied. Tentatively, we expect the advice taker to proceed as follows: initially, the sentence "want(at(I,airport))" is on a certain list L, called the main list, all by itself. The program begins with an observation routine which looks at the main list and puts certain statements about the contents of this list on a list called "observations of the main list." We shall not specify at present what all the possible outputs of this observation routine are but merely say that in this case it will observe that "the only statement on L has the form 'want(u(x))'." (We write this out in English because we have not yet settled on a formalism for representing statements of this kind.) The "deduce and obey" routine is then applied to the combination of the "observations of the main list" list, and a list called the "standing orders list." This list is rather small and is never changed, or at least is only changed in major changes of the advice taker. The contents of the "standing orders" list has not been worked out, but what must be deduced is the extraction of certain statements from property lists. Namely, the program first looks at "want(at(I,airport))" and attempts to copy the statements on its property list. Let us assume that it fails in this attempt because "want(at(I,airport))" does not have the status of an object and hence has no property list. (One might expect that if the problem of going to the airport had arisen before, "want(at(I,airport))" would be an object, but this might depend on whether there were routines for generalizing previous experience that would allow something of general use to be filed under that heading.) Next in order of increasing generality the machine would see if anything were filed under "want (at (I,x)" which would deal with the general problem of getting somewhere. One would expect that premises 6 (or 6' and 7'), 8, 9, 12 would be so filed. There would also be the formula

want (at (I,x)) → do (observe (where am I))

which would give us premise 1. There would also be a reference to the next higher level of abstraction in the goal statement which would cause a look at the property list of "want (x)." This would give us 14, 15, and 16.

We shall not try to follow the solution further except to remark that for "want(at(I,x))" there would be a rule that starts with the premises "at(I, y)" and "want(I,x)" and has as conclusion a search for the property list of "go (y,x,z)." This would presumably fail, and then there would have to be heuristics that would initiate a search for a y such that "at(I,y)" and "at (airport,y)." This would be done by looking on the property lists of the origin and the destination and working up. Then premise 9 would be found which has as one of its premises "at(I,car)." A repetition of the above would find premise 8, which would complete the set of premises since the other "at" premises would have been found as by-products of previous searches.

We hope that the presence of the heuristic rules mentioned on the property lists where we have put them will seem plausible to the reader. It should be noticed that on the higher level of abstraction many of the statements are of the stimulus-response form. One might conjecture that division in man between conscious and unconscious thought occurs at the boundary between stimulus-response heuristics which do not have to be reasoned about but only obeyed, and the others which have to serve as premises in deductions.

2. Situations, Actions, and Causal Laws[2]

Although formalized theories have been devised to express the most important fields of mathematics and some progress has been made in formalizing certain empirical sciences, there is at present no formal theory in which one can express the kind of means-ends analysis used in ordinary life. The closest approach to such a theory of which I am aware is made by Freudenthal (1960).

Our approach to the artificial intelligence problem requires a formal theory. We believe that human intelligence depends essentially on the fact that we can represent in language facts about our situation, our goals, and the effects of the various actions we can perform. Moreover, we can draw conclusions from the facts to the effect that certain sequences of actions are likely to achieve our goals.

In Section 1, I discussed the advantages of having a computer program, the Advice Taker, that will reason from collections of facts about its problem and derive statements about what it can do. The name "advice taker" came from the hope that its behavior could be improved by giving it advice in the form of new facts rather than by rewriting the program. The reader is referred to Minsky (1961) for a general introduction to the subject of artificial intelligence.

The first requirement for the advice taker is a formal system in which facts about situations, goals, and actions can be expressed and which contains general facts about means and ends as axioms. A start is made here on providing a system meeting the following specifications:

1. General properties of causality, and certain obvious but until now unformalized facts about the possibility and results of actions, are given as axioms.

2. It is a logical consequence of the facts of a situation and the general axioms that certain persons can achieve certain goals by taking certain actions.

3. The formal descriptions of situations should correspond as closely as possible to what people may reasonably be presumed to know about them when deciding what to do.

2.1 Situations and Fluents

One of the basic entities in our theory is the *situation*. Intuitively, a situation is the complete state of affairs at some instant of time. The laws of motion of a system determine all future situations from a given situation. Thus a situation corresponds to the notion of a point in phase space. In physics, laws are expressed in the form of differential equations which give the complete motion of the points of that space.

Our system is not intended to supply a complete description of situations nor the description of complete laws of motion. Instead, we deal with partial descriptions of situations and partial laws of motion. Moreover, the emphasis is on the simple qualitative laws of everyday life rather than on the quantitative laws of physics. As an example, take the fact that if it is raining and I go outside I will get wet.

Since a situation is defined as a complete state of affairs, we can never describe a situation fully; and we therefore provide no notation for doing so in our theory. Instead, we state facts about situations in the language of an extended predicate calculus. Examples of such facts are:

1. raining(s)

meaning that it is raining in situation s.

2. time $(s) = 1963.7205$

giving the value of the time in situation s. It will usually prove convenient to regard the time as a function of the situation rather than vice versa, because the numerical value of the time is known and important only where the laws of physics are involved.

3. at(I,home,s) or at(I,home)(s)

meaning that I am at home in situation s. We shall use the second of the given notations that isolates the situation variable since in most, if not all, cases we will be able to suppress it completely.

We shall not describe here the logical system we intend to use. Basically, it is a predicate calculus, but we shall use the λ-notation and if necessary conditional expressions, as in Lisp or Algol. We shall extend the meaning of the Boolean operators to operate on predicates. Thus by at(I,home) $\wedge$ raining we mean the same as λs. at(I,home)(s) $\wedge$ raining(s)

A predicate or function whose argument is a situation will be called a *fluent*, the predicate being called a *propositional fluent*. Thus, *raining, time,* and *at(I,home)* are all fluents, the first and last being propositional fluents. The term was used by Newton for a physical quantity that depends on time, and we therefore feel that the present use of the term is justified.

In our formulas we can usually use the fluents without explicitly writing variables that represent situations. This corresponds to the use of random variables in probability theory without using variables representing points in the sample space, even though random variables are supposed to be regarded as functions defined on a sample space. In fact, we shall go further and give an interpretation of our theory as a type of modal logic in which the fluents are not regarded as functions at all.

2.2 Causality

In order to express causal laws, we introduce the second-order predicate cause. The statement cause (π) (s), where π is a propositional fluent, is intended to mean that the situation s will lead in the future to a situation that satisfies the fluent π. Thus, cause (π) is itself a propositional fluent. As an example of its use we write

$$\forall s. \, \forall p. \, [\text{person} \, (p) \wedge \text{raining} \wedge \text{outside} \, (p) \supset \text{cause} \, (\text{wet} \, (p))] \, (s),$$

which asserts that a person who is outside when it is raining will get wet. We shall make the convention that, if π is a fluent, then $\forall \pi$ means the same as

$$\forall s . \, \pi \, (s).$$

With this convention we can write the previous statement as

$$\forall \, \forall p. \, \text{person} \, (p) \wedge \text{raining} \wedge \text{outside} \, (p) \supset \text{cause} \, (\text{wet} \, (p)),$$

thereby suppressing explicit mention of situations.

As a second example we discuss a special case of the law of falling bodies in the form:

$$\forall \, \forall t. \, \forall b. \, \forall t^1 . \, \forall h \, \text{real}(t) \wedge \text{real}(t^1) \wedge \text{real}(h) \wedge \text{body} \, (b)$$
$$\wedge \, \text{unsupported} \, (b) \wedge [\text{height} \, (b) = h] \wedge [\tfrac{1}{2}gt^2 < h] \wedge$$
$$[\text{time} = t'] \supset \text{cause} \, (\text{height} \, (b) = h - \tfrac{1}{2}gt^2 \wedge \text{time} = t' = t).$$

The concept of causality is intended to satisfy the three following general laws, which may be considered as axioms:

C1. $\forall$. cause $(\pi) \wedge [\forall . \pi \supset p] \supset$ cause (p)
C2. $\forall$. cause (cause $(\pi)) \supset$ cause (π)
C3. $\vee$. cause $(\pi_1) \vee$ cause $(\pi_2) \supset$ cause $(\pi_1 \vee \pi_2)$

The fact that we can suppress explicit mention of situations has the following interesting consequence: Instead of regarding the π's as predicates we may regard them as propositions and regard cause as a new modal operator. The operator $\forall$ seems then to be equivalent to the N (necessary) operator of ordinary modal logic. Conversely, it would appear that modal logic of necessity might be regarded as a monadic predicate calculus where all quantifiers are over situations.

In the present case of causality, we have a choice of how to proceed. Regarding the system as a modal logic seems to have the following two advantages:

1. If we use the predicate calculus interpretation, we require second-order predicate calculus in order to handle cause (π) (s), whereas if we take the modal interpretation we can get by with first-order predicate calculus.
2. We shall want decision procedures or at least proof procedures for as much of our system as possible. If we use the modal approach, many problems will involve only substitution of constants for variables in universal statements and will therefore fall into a fairly readily decidable domain.

Another example of causality is given by a 2-bit binary counter that counts every second. In our formalism its behavior may be described by the statement:

$\forall \forall t \, \forall x_0 \, \forall x_1.\text{time} = t \wedge \text{bit0} = x_1 \supset \text{cause }($
$\text{time} = t+1 \wedge (\text{bit0} = x_0 \oplus 1) \wedge (\text{bit1} = x_1 \oplus (x_0 \wedge 1)))$

In this example time, bit0, and bit1 are fluents, while t, x_0, and x_1 are numerical variables. The distinction is made clearer if we use the more long-winded statement

$\forall s \forall t \forall x_0 \forall x_1.\text{time }(s) = t \wedge \text{bit0 }(s) = x_0 \wedge \text{bit1}(s) = x_1 \supset$
$\text{cause } \lambda s'.\text{time }(s'') = t+1 \wedge (\text{bit0}(s') = x_0 \oplus 1) \wedge \text{bit1 }(s') = x_1 \oplus (x_0 \wedge 1)))(s)$

In this case, however, we can rewrite the statement in the form

$\forall s.\text{cause } (\lambda s'.[\text{time }(s') = \text{time }(s) + 1] \wedge [\text{bit0 }(s') = \text{bit0}(s) \oplus 1] \wedge$
$[\text{bit1 }(s') = \text{bit1 }(s) \oplus (\text{bit0 }(s) \wedge 1)])(s)$

Thus we see that the suppression of explicit mention of the situations forced us to introduce the auxiliary quantities t, x_0, and x_1 which are required because we can no longer use functions of two different situations in the same formula. Nevertheless, the s-suppressed form may still be worthwhile because it admits the modal interpretation.

The time as a fluent satisfies certain axioms. The fact that there is only one situation corresponding to a given value of the time may be expressed by the axiom

T1. $\forall \forall \pi \forall \rho \forall t.$ cause $(\text{time} = t \wedge \pi) \wedge$ cause $(\text{time} = t \wedge \rho) \supset$ cause
$(\text{time} = t \wedge \pi \wedge \rho)$

Another axiom is

T2. $\forall \forall t.\text{real }(t) \wedge t > \text{time} \supset$ cause $(\text{time} = t)$

2.3 Actions and the Operator *Can*

We shall regard the fact that a person performs a certain action in a situation as a propositional fluent. Thus moves(person, object, location)(s) is regarded as asserting that person moves object to location in the situation s. The effect of moving something is described by

$\forall \forall \rho \forall o \forall l.\text{moves }(\rho,o,l) \supset$ cause $(\text{at } o,l))$

or in the long form

$\forall s \forall p \forall o \forall l.\text{moves }(p,o,l)(s) \supset$ cause $(\lambda s'.\text{at }(o,l)(s'))(s)$

In order to discuss the ability of persons to achieve goals and to perform actions we introduce the operator *can*. can $(p, \pi)(s)$ asserts that the person p can make the situation s satisfy π. We see that can(p,π) is a propositional fluent and that like *cause, can* may be regarded either as a second-order predicate or a modal operator. Our most common use of *can* will be to assert that a person can perform a certain action. Thus we write can $(p,\text{moves } (p,o,l))$ (s) to assert that in situation s, the person p can move the object o to location l.

The operator *can* satisfies the axioms

K1. $\forall \forall \pi \forall \rho \forall p. [\text{can } (p,\pi) \wedge (\pi \rho) \supset (\text{can } (p,\rho)]$

K2. $\forall \forall \pi \forall p_1 \forall p_2. [\sim \text{can } (p_1, \pi) \wedge \text{can } (p_1, \sim \pi)]$

K3. $\forall \forall p \forall \pi \forall \rho. [\text{can } (p,\pi) \wedge \text{can } (p,\rho) \text{ can } (p, \pi \wedge \rho)]$

Using K1 and can$(p, \text{moves}(p,o,l))$ and $\forall \forall p \forall o \forall l.$ moves $(p,o,l) \supset$ cause (at $(o,l))$, we can deduce can$(p, \text{cause (at } (o,l)))$, which shows that the operators *can* and *cause* often show up in the same formula.

The ability of people to perform joint actions can be expressed by formulas like can$(p_1, \text{can}(p_2, \text{marry}(p_1,p_2)))$, which suggests the commutative axiom

K4. $\forall \forall p_1 \forall p_2 \forall \pi.\text{can } (p_1,\text{can } (p_2 \ \pi)) \supset \text{can } (p_2 ,\text{can } (p_1,\pi))$

A kind of transitivity is empressed by the following

Theorem: From

1. can$(p, \text{cause}(\pi))$; and
2. $\forall .\pi \supset$ can $(p, \text{cause } (p))$; it follows that
3. can$(p, \text{cause}(\text{can}(p, \text{cause}(\rho p))))$.

Proof: Substitute can$(p, \text{cause}(\rho))$ for ρ in axiom Cl and substitute cause (π) for π and cause$(\text{can}(p, \text{cause}(\rho)))$ for ρ in axiom K1. The conclusion then follows by propositional calculus.

In order to discuss the achievement of goals requiring several consecutive actions, we introduce *canult*(p,π) which is intended to mean that the person p can ultimately bring about a situation satisfying π. We connect it with *can* and *cause* by means of the axiom

KC1. $\forall .\forall p \forall \pi.\pi \vee$ can $(p,\text{cause (canult } (p,\pi))) \supset \text{canult } (p,\pi)$

This axiom partially corresponds to the Lisp-type recursive definition:

canult $(p,\pi) = \pi \vee$ can $(p, \text{cause (canult } (p,\pi)))$

We also want the axiom

KC2. $\forall \forall p \forall \pi. \text{ cause (canult } (p,\pi)) \supset \text{canult } (p,\pi)$

2.4 Examples

The first example we shall consider is a situation in which a monkey is in a room where a bunch of bananas is hanging from a ceiling too high to reach. In the corner of the room there is a box, and the solution to the monkey's problem is to move the box under the bananas and climb onto the box from which the bananas can be reached.

We shall describe the situation in such a way that it will follow from our axioms and the description that the monkey can get the bananas. We shall not discuss the heuristic problem of how monkeys might or even do solve the problem. Specifically, we shall prove that canult(monkey, has(monkey, bananas)). The situation is described in a very simplified way by the following statements:

H1. $\forall \forall u$. place $(u) \supset$ can (monkey, move (monkey, box, u))

H2 $\forall \forall u \forall v \forall p$. move $(p,v,u) \supset$ cause at (v,u)

H3. $\forall$ can (monkey,climbs (monkey,box))

H4. $\forall \forall u \forall v \forall p$. at $(v,u) \wedge$ climbs $(p,v) \supset$ cause (at $(v,u) \wedge$ on (p,v))

H5. $\forall$ place (under (bananas))

H6. $\forall$ at (box, under (bananas)) $\wedge$ on (monkey,box) $\supset$ can (monkey,reach (monkey,bananas))

H7. $\forall \forall p \forall x$. reach $(p,x) \supset$ cause (has (p,x))

The reasoning proceeds as follows: From H1 and H5 by substitution of under (bananas) for u and by propositional calculus we get

1. can(monkey, move(box, under(bananas)))

Using 1, H_2, and axiom C1, we get

2. can (monkey,cause(at(box, under (bananas))))

Similarly, H3, H4, and C1 give

3. at (box, under (bananas)) $\supset$ can (monkey,cause (at (box, under (bananas)) $\wedge$ on (monkey,box)))

Then H6 and H7 give

4. at (box, under (bananas)) $\wedge$ on (monkey,box) $\supset$ can (monkey,cause (has(monkey, bananas)))

Now, Theorem 1 is used to combine 2, 3, and 4, to result in

5. can (monkey,cause (can (monkey,cause (can (monkey, cause (has (monkey , bananas))))))

Using KC1, we reduce this to

canult(monkey, has(monkey, bananas)))

Another example concerns a two-person game where player p_1 has two moves, but whichever one he chooses, player p_2 has a move that will beat him. This situation may be described as follows:

1 can $(p_1,m_1) \wedge$ can $(p_1,m_2) \wedge (m_1 \vee m_2)$

2. $[m_1 \supset$ cause $(\pi_1)] \wedge [m_2 \supset$ cause $(\pi_2)]$

3. $\forall .\pi_1 \vee \pi_2 \supset$ [can $(p_2, n_1) \wedge$ can $(p_2 ,n_2) \wedge (n_1 \vee n_2)]$

4. $\forall .(\pi_1 \wedge n_1) \vee (\pi_2 \wedge n_2) \supset$ cause(win(p_2))

We would like to be able to draw the conclusion

3. canult$(p_2 ,$win$(p_2))$ We proceed as follows: From 1 and 2 we get

4. cause (π_1) v cause (π_2) and we use Axiom C3 to get

5. cause $(\pi_1 \vee \pi_2$) Next we weaken 3 to get

6. $\forall . \pi_1 \supset$ can (p_2, n_1) and

7. $\forall . \pi_2 \supset$ can (p_2, n_2) and then we use Kl to get

8. $\forall . \pi_1 \supset$ can $(p_2, \pi_1 \wedge n_1$) and

9. $\forall . \pi_2 \supset$ can$(p_2, \pi_2 \wedge n_2)$ The propositional calculus gives

10. $\forall . \pi_1 \vee \pi_2 \supset$ can $(p_2, \pi_1 \wedge n_1$) can$(p_2, \pi_1 \wedge n_2$) and using K3 we get

11. $\forall . \pi_1 \vee \pi_2 \supset$ can $(p_2, (\pi_1 \wedge n_1$) $(\pi_2 \wedge n_2$)) which together with 4 and K1 gives

12. $\forall . \pi_1 \vee \pi_2 \supset$ can $(p_2, \text{cause} (\text{win} (p_2)))$ which together with 5 and C1 gives

13. cause$(\text{can}(p_2, \text{cause}(\text{win}(p_2)))$ Using the axioms for *canult* we now get

14. canult $(p_2, \text{win} (p_2))$

2.5 Note

After finishing the bulk of this investigation, I came across the work of Prior (1958). He defines modal operators P and F, where P (π) means 'it has been the case that π' and F(π) means 'it will be the case that π.' He subjects these operators to a number of axioms and rules of inference in close analogy to the well-known modal logic of possibility, and also interprets this logic in a restricted predicate calculus where the variables range over times. This logic is then extended to include a somewhat undetermined future and he claims (unconvincingly) that it cannot be interpreted in predicate calculus. I have not yet made a detailed comparison of our logic with Prior's, but here are some tentative conclusions:

1. The causality logic should be extended to allow inference about the past.

2. Causality logic should be extended to allow inference that certain propositional fluents will always hold.

3. Cause(πr) satisfies the axioms for his F(π), which means that his futurity theory possesses, from his point of view, nonstandard models. Specifically, a collection of functions p_1 (t), p_2 (t) may satisfy his futurity axioms and assign truth to p (1) $\wedge \sim$ (Fp) (0). In our system this is acceptable because something can happen without being caused to happen.

4. If we combine his past and futurity axioms, our system will no longer fit his axioms and
   PF1. $p \sim F(\sim P(p))$
   PF2. $p \sim P(\sim F(p))$
   since we do not wish to say that whatever is was always inevitable.

Notes

1. Section 1 is a reprint of a paper taken from "Mechanisation of Thought Processes," Vol. 1, pp. 77-84, Proc. Symposium, National Physical Laboratory, London, November 24-27, 1958.

2. Section 2 copies a memorandum originally distributed in 1963.

20

Dendral and Meta-Dendral: Their Applications Dimension

Bruce G. Buchanan and Edward A. Feigenbaum

1. Introduction

The DENDRAL and Meta-DENDRAL programs are products of a large, interdisciplinary group of Stanford University scientists concerned with many and highly varied aspects of the mechanization of scientific reasoning and the formalization of scientific knowledge for this purpose. An early motivation for our work was to explore the power of existing AI methods, such as heuristic search, for reasoning in difficult scientific problems (Lederberg and Feigenbaum 1968). Another concern has been to exploit the AI methodology to understand better some fundamental questions in the philosophy of science, for example the processes by which explanatory hypotheses are discovered or judged adequate (Churchman and Buchanan 1969). From the start, the project has had an applications dimension (Feigenbaum and Buchanan 1968; Buchanan, Sutherland, and Feigenbaum 1969; Buchanan, Duffield, and

Robertson 1971). It has sought to develop "expert level" agents to assist in the solution of problems in their discipline that require complex symbolic reasoning. The applications dimension is the focus of this chapter.

In order to achieve high performance, the DENDRAL programs incorporate large amounts of knowledge about the area of science to which they are applied, structure elucidation in organic chemistry. A "smart assistant" for a chemist needs to be able to perform many tasks as well as an expert, but need not necessarily understand the domain at the same theoretical level as the expert. The over-all structure elucidation task is described below (Section 2) followed by a description of the role of the DENDRAL programs within that framework (Section 3). The Meta-DENDRAL programs (Section 4) use a weaker body of knowledge about the domain of mass spectrometry because their task is to formulate rules of mass spectrometry by induction from empirical data. A strong model of the domain would bias the rules unnecessarily.

1.1. Historical Perspective

The DENDRAL project began in 1965. Then, as now, we were concerned with the conceptual problems of designing and writing symbol manipulation programs that used substantial bodies of domain-specific scientific knowledge. In contrast, this was a time in the history of AI in which most laboratories were working on general problem solving methods, e.g., in 1965 work on resolution theorem proving was in its prime.

The programs have followed an evolutionary progression. Initial concepts were translated into a working program: the program was tested and improved by confronting simple test cases; and finally a production version of the program including user interaction facilities was released for real applications. This intertwining of short-term pragmatic goals and long-term development of new AI science is an important theme throughout our research. The results presented here have been produced by DENDRAL programs at various stages of development.

2. The General Nature of the Applications Tasks

2.1. Structure Eucidation

The application of chemical knowledge to elucidation of molecular structures is fundamental to understanding important problems of biology and medicine. Areas in which we and our collaborators maintain active interest include: (a) identification of natural products isolated from terrestrial or marine sources, particularly those products which demonstrate biological activity or which are key intermediates in biosynthetic pathways; (b) verification of the identity of new synthetic materials; (c) identification of drugs and their metabolites in clinical studies; and (d) detection of metabolic disorders of genetic, developmental, toxic or infectious origins by identification of organic constituents excreted in abnormal quantities in human body fluids.

In most circumstances, especially in the areas of interest summarized above, chemists are faced with structural problems where direct examination of the structure by X-ray crystallography is not possible. In these circumstances they must resort to structure elucidation based on data obtained from a variety of physical, chemical and spectroscopic methods.

This kind of structure elucidation involves a sequence of steps that is roughly approximated by the following scenario. An unknown structure is isolated from some source. The source of the sample and the isolation procedures employed already provide some clues as to the chemical constitution of the compound. A variety of chemical, physical and spectroscopic data are collected on the sample. Interpretation of these data yields structural hypotheses in the form of functional groups or more complex molecular fragments. Assembling these fragments into complete structures provides a set of candidate structures for the unknown. These candidates are examined and experiments are designed to differentiate among them. The experiments, usually collecting additional spectroscopic data and executing sequences of chemical reactions, result in new structural information which serves to reduce the set of candidate structures. Eventually enough information is inferred from experimental data to constrain the candidates to the correct structure.

As long as time permits and the number of unknown structures is small, a manual approach will usually be successful, as it has been in the past. However, the manual approach is amenable to a high degree of computer assistance, which is increasingly necessary for both practical and scientific reasons. One needs only examine current regulatory activities in fields related to chemistry, or the rate at which new compounds are discovered or synthesized to gain a feeling for the practical need for rapid identification of new structures. More important, however, is the contribution such computer assistance can make to scientific creativity in structure elucidation in particular, and chemistry in general, by providing new tools to aid scientists in hypothesis formation. The automated approaches discussed in this paper provide a systematic procedure for verifying hypotheses about chemical structure and ensuring that no plausible alternatives have been overlooked.

2.2. Structure Elucidation with Constraints from Mass Spectrometry

The Heuristic DENDRAL Program is designed to help organic chemists determine the molecular structure of unknown compounds. Parts of the program have been highly tuned to work with experimental data from an analytical instrument known as a mass spectrometer. *Mass spectrometry* is a new and still developing analytic technique. It is not ordinarily the only analytic technique used by chemists, but is one of a broad array, including nuclear magnetic resonance (NMR), infrared (IR), ultraviolet (UV), and "wet chemistry" analyses. Mass spectrometry is particularly useful when the quantity of the sample to be identified is very small, for it requires only micrograms of sample.

A mass spectrometer bombards the chemical sample with electrons, causing fragmentations and rearrangements of the molecules. Charged fragments are collected by mass. The data from the instrument, recorded in a histogram known as a mass spectrum, show the masses of charged fragments plotted against the relative abundance of the fragments at a mass. Although the mass spectrum for each molecule may be nearly unique, it is still a difficult task to infer the molecular structure form the 100-300 data points in the mass spectrum. The data are highly redundant because molecules fragment along different pathways. Thus two different masses may or may not include atoms from the same part of the molecules. In short, the theory of mass spectrometry is too incomplete to allow unambiguous reconstruction of the structure from overlapping fragments.

Throughout this chapter we will use the following terms to describe the actions of molecules in the mass spectrometer:

1. *Fragmentation*—the breaking of a connected graph (molecule) into fragments by breaking one or more edges (bonds) within the graph.

2. *Atom migration*—the detachment of nodes (atoms) from one fragment and their reattachment to a second fragment. This process alters the masses of both fragments.

3. *Mass spectral process* (or processes)—a fragmentation followed by zero or more atom migrations.

2.3. Structure Elucidation with Constraints from Other Data

Other analytic techniques are commonly used in conjunction with, or instead of, mass spectrometry. Some rudimentary capabilities exist in the DENDRAL programs to interpret proton NMR and Carbon 13 (^{13}C) NMR spectra. For the most part, however, interpretation of other spectroscopic and chemical data has been left to the chemist. The programs still need to be able to integrate the chemist's partial knowledge into the generation of structural alternatives.

3. Heuristic DENDRAL as an Intelligent Assistant

3.1. Method

Heuristic DENDRAL is organized as a plan—generate—test sequence. This is not necessarily the same method used by chemists, but it is easily understood by them. It complements their methods by providing such a meticulous search through the space of molecular structures that the chemist is virtually guaranteed that any candidate structure which fails to appear on the final list of plausible structures has been rejected for explicitly stated chemical reasons.

The three main parts of the program are discussed below, starting with the generator because of its fundamental importance.

3.1.1. The Generator

The heart of a heuristic search program is a generator of the search space. In a chess playing program, for example, the legal move generator completely defines the space of moves and move sequences. In Heuristic DENDRAL the legal move generator is based on the DENDRAL algorithm developed by J. Lederberg (1964, 1965, 1969). This algorithm specifies a systematic enumeration of molecular structures. It treats molecules as planar graphs and generates successively larger graph structures until all chemical atoms are included in graphs in all possible arrangements. Because graphs with cycles presented special problems,[1] initial work was limited to chemical structures without rings (with the exception of Sheikh et al. [1970]).

The number of chemical graphs for molecular formulas of interest to chemists can be extremely large. Thus it is essential to constrain structure generation to only *plausible* molecular structures. The CONGEN program (Carhart, Smith, Brown, and Djerassi 1975),[2] is the DENDRAL hypothesis generator now in use. It accepts problem statements of (a) the number of atoms of each type in the molecule and (b) constraints on the correct hypothesis, in order to generate all chemical graphs that fit the stated constraints. These problem statements may come from a chemist interpreting his own experimental data or from a spectrometric data analysis program.

The purpose of CONGEN is to assist the chemist in determining the chemical structure of an unknown compound by (1) allowing him to specify certain types of structural information about the compound which he has determined from any source (e.g., spectroscopy, chemical degradation, method of isolation, etc.) and (2) generating an exhaustive and non-redundant list of structures that are consistent with the information. The generation is a stepwise process, and the program allows interaction at every stage: based upon partial results the chemist may be reminded of additional information which he can specify, thus limiting further the number of structural possibilities.

CONGEN breaks the problem down into several types of subproblems, for example: (i) hydrogen atoms are omitted; (ii) parts of the graph containing no cycles are generated separately from cyclic parts (and combined at the end); (iii) cycles containing only unnamed nodes are generated before labeling the nodes with names of chemical atoms (e.g., carbon or nitrogen); (iv) cycles containing only three-connected (or higher) nodes (e.g., nitrogen or tertiary carbon) are generated before mapping two-connected nodes (e.g., oxygen or secondary carbon) onto the edges. At each step several constraints may be applied to limit the number of emerging chemical graphs (Carhart and Smith 1976).

At the heart of CONGEN are two algorithms whose validity has been mathematically proven and whose computer implementation has been well tested. The structure generation algorithm (Brown, Masinter, and Hjelmeland 1974; Brown and Masinter 1974; Masinter, Sridharan, Carhart, and Smith 1974; and Masinter, Sridharan, Carhart, and Smith 1974) is designed to determine all topologically unique ways of assembling a given set of atoms, each with an associated valence, into molecular structures. The atoms may be chemical atoms with standard chemical valences, or they may be names representing molecular fragments ("superatoms") of any desired complexity, where the valence corresponds to the total number of bonding sites available within the superatom. Because the structure generation algorithm can produce only structures in which the superatoms appear as single nodes (we refer to these as intermediate structures), a second procedure, the imbedding algorithm (Brown and Masinter 1974, and Carhart, Smith, Brown, and Djerassi 1975) is needed to expand the superatoms to their full chemical identities.

A substantial amount of effort has been devoted to modifying these two basic procedures, particularly the structure generation algorithm, to accept a variety of other structural information (constraints), using it to prune the list of structural possibilities. Current capabilities include specification of good and bad substructural features, good and bad ring sizes, proton distributions and connectivities of isoprene units (Carhart and Smith 1976). Usually, the chemist has additional information (if only some general rules about chemical stability) of which the program has little knowledge but which can be used to limit the number of structural possibilities. For example, he may know that the chemical procedures used to isolate the compound would change organic acids to esters and thus the program need not consider structures with unchanged acid groups. Also, he is given the facility to impart this knowledge interactively to the program.

To make CONGEN easy to use by research chemists, the program has been provided with an interactive "front end." This interface contains EDITSTRUC, an interactive structure editor, DRAW, a teletype-oriented structure display program (Carhart 1976) and the CONGEN "executive" program which ties together the individual subprograms, such as subprograms for defining superatoms and substructures, creating and editing lists of constraints or superatoms, and saving and restoring superatoms, constraints and structures from secondary storage (disc). The resulting system, for which comprehensive user-level documentation has been prepared, is running on the SUMEX computing facility at Stanford and is available nationwide over the TYMNET network (Carhart et al. 1975). The use of CONGEN by chemists doing structure elucidation is discussed in Section 3.4.

3.1.2. The Planning Programs

Although CONGEN is designed to be useful as a stand-alone package some assistance can also be given with the task of inferring constraints for the generator. This is done by *planning* programs that analyze instrument data and infer constraints (see Buchanan, Sutherland, and Feigenbaum 1969; Buchs et al. 1970; and Smith et al. 1972).

The DENDRAL Planner uses a large amount of knowledge of mass spectrometry to infer constraints. For example, it may infer that the unknown molecule is probably a ketone but definitely not a methylketone. Planning information like this is put on the generator's lists of good and bad structural features. Planning has been limited almost entirely to mass spectrometry, but the same techniques can be used with other data sources as well.

The DENDRAL Planner (Smith et al. 1972) allows for cooperative (man-machine) problem solving in the interpretation of mass spectra. It uses the chemist's relevant knowledge of mass spectrometry and applies it systematically to the spectrum of an unknown. That is, using the chemist's definitions of the structural skeleton of the molecule and the relevant fragmentation rules, the program does the bookkeeping of associating peaks with fragments and the combinatorics of finding consistent ways of placing substituents around the skeleton.

The output from the DENDRAL Planner is a list of structure descriptions with as much detail filled in as the data and defined fragmentations will allow. Because there are limits to the degree of refinement allowed by mass spectrometry alone, sets of atoms are assigned to sets of skeletal nodes. Thus the task of fleshing out the plan—specifying possible structures assigned to specific skeletal nodes—is left to CONGEN.

3.1.3. The Testing and Ranking Programs

The programs MSPRUNE (Smith and Carhart 1978) and MSRANK (Varkony, Carhart, and Smith 1977) use a large amount of knowledge of mass spectrometry to make testable predictions from each plausible candidate molecule. Predicted data are compared to the data from the unknown compound to throw out some candidates and rank the others (Buchanan, Sutherland, and Feigenbaum 1969; Varkony, Carhart, and Smith 1977; Smith and Carhart 1978).

MSPRUNE works with (a) a list of candidate structures from CONGEN, and (b) the mass spectrum of the unknown molecule. It uses a fairly simple theory of mass spectrometry to predict commonly expected fragmentations for each candidate structure. Predictions which deviate greatly from the observed spectrum are considered prima facie evidence of incorrectness; the corresponding structures are pruned from the list. MSRANK then uses more subtle rules of mass spectrometry to rank the remaining structures according to the number of predicted peaks found (and not found) in the observed data, weighted by measures of importance of the processes producing those peaks.

3.2. Research Results

The Heuristic DENDRAL effort has shown that it is possible to write a computer program that equals the performance of experts in some limited areas of science. Published papers on the program's analysis of aliphatic ketones, amines, ethers, alcohols, thiols and thioethers (Duffield et al. 1969; Schroll et al. 1969; Buchs et al. 1970a; Buchs et al. 1970b) make the point that although the program does not know more than an expert (and in fact knows far less), it performs well because of its systematic search through the space of possibilities and its systematic use of what it does know. A paper on the program's analysis of estrogenic steroids makes the point that the program can solve structure elucidation problems for complex organic molecules (Smith et al 1972) of current biological interest. Another paper on the analysis of mass spectra of mixtures of estrogenic steroids (without prior separation) establishes the program's ability to do better than experts on some problems (Smith et al 1973). With mixtures, the program succeeds, and people fail, because of the magnitude of the task of correlating data points with each possible fragmentation of each possible component of the mixture. Several articles based on results from CONGEN demonstrate its power and utility for solving current research problems of medical and biochemical importance (Smith 1975; Smith, Konopelski, and Djerassi 1976; Cheer et al. 1976; Smith and Carhart 1976; Smith and Carhart 1978; Carhart 1976).

3.3. Human Engineering

A successful applications program must demonstrate competence, as the previous section emphasized. However, it is also necessary to design the programs to achieve *acceptability,* by the scientists for whom the AI system is written. That is, without proper attention to human engineering, and similar issues, a complex applications program will not be widely used. Besides making the I/O language easy for the user to understand, it is also important to make the scope and limitations of the problem solving methods known to the user as much as possible (Buchanan and Smith 1977). The features designed into DENDRAL programs to make them easier and more pleasant to use include graphical drawings of chemical structures (Carhart 1976), a stylized, but easily understood language of expressing and editing chemical constraints (Carhart, Smith, Brown, and Djerassi 1975), on-line help facilities (Buchanan and Smith 1977), depth-first problem solving to produce some solutions quickly, estimators of problem size and (at any time) amount of work remaining. Documentation and user manuals are written at many levels of detail. And one of our staff is almost always available for consultation by phone or message (Carhart et al. 1975).

3.4. Applications of CONGEN to Chemical Problems

Many persons have used DENDRAL programs (mostly CONGEN) in an experimental mode. Some chemists have used programs on the SUMEX machine, others have requested help by mail, and a few have imported programs to their own computers.

Copies of programs have been distributed to chemists requesting them. However, we have strongly suggested that persons access the local versions by TYMNET to minimize the number of different versions we maintain and to avoid the need for rewriting the InterLisp code for another machine.

Users do not always tell us about the problems they solve using the DENDRAL programs. To some extent this is one sign of a successful application. The list below thus represents only a sampling of the chemical problems to which the programs have been applied. CONGEN is most used, although other DENDRAL subprograms have been used occasionally.

Since the SUMEX computer is available over the TYMNET network, it is possible for scientists in many parts of the world to access the DENDRAL programs on SUMEX directly. Many scientists interested in using DENDRAL programs in their own work are not located near a network access point, however. These chemists use the mail to send details of their structure elucidation problem to a DENDRAL project collaborator at Stanford.

DENDRAL programs have been used to aid in structure determination problems of the following kinds:

- terpenoid natural products from plant and marine animal sources
- marine sterols
- organic acids in human urine and other body fluids
- photochemical rearrangement products
- impurities in manufactured chemicals
- conjugates of pesticides with sugars and amino acids
- antibiotics
- metabolites of microorganisms
- insect hormones and pheremones

CONGEN was also applied to published structure elucidation problems by students in Professor Djerassi's class on spectroscopic techniques to check the accuracy and completeness of the published solutions. For several cases, the program found structures which were plausible alternatives to the published structures (based on problem constraints that appeared in the article). This kind of information thus serves as a valuable check on conclusions drawn from experimental data.

4. Meta-DENDRAL

Because of the difficulty of extracting domain-specific rules from experts for use by DENDRAL, a more efficient means of transferring knowledge into the program was sought. Two alternatives to "handcrafting" each new knowledge base have been explored: interactive knowledge transfer programs and automatic theory formation programs. In this enterprise the separation of domain-specific knowledge from the computer programs themselves has been critical.

One of the stumbling blocks with programs for the interactive transfer of knowledge is that for some areas of chemistry there are no experts with enough specific knowledge to make a high performance problem solving program (see Buchanan, Sutherland, and Feigenbaum 1970). It is desirable to avoid forcing an expert to focus on original data in order to codify the rules explaining those data because that is such a time-consuming process. For these reasons an effort to build an automatic rule formation program (called Meta-DENDRAL) was initiated.

The DENDRAL programs are structured to read their task-specific knowledge from tables of production rules and execute the rules in new situations, under rather elaborate control structures. The Meta-DENDRAL programs have been constructed to aid in building the knowledge base, i.e., the tables of rules.

4.1. The Task

The present Meta-DENDRAL program (Buchanan et al. 1976; Buchanan and Mitchell 1978) interactively helps chemists determine the dependence of mass spectrometric fragmentation on substructural features, under the hypothesis that molecular fragmentations are related to topological graph structural features of molecules. Our goal is to have the program suggest qualitative explanations of the characteristic fragmentations and rearrangements among a set of molecules. We do not now attempt to rationalize all peaks nor find quantitative assessments of the extent to which various processes contribute to peak intensities.

The program emulates many of the reasoning processes of manual approaches to rule discovery. It reasons symbolically, using a modest amount of chemical knowledge. It decides which data points are important and looks for fragmentation processes that will explain them. It attempts to form general rules by correlating plausible fragmentation processes with substructural features of the molecules. Then, as a chemist does, the program tests and modifies the rules.

Each I/O pair for Meta-DENDRAL is: (INPUT) a chemical sample with uniform molecular structure (abbreviated to "a structure"): (OUTPUT) one X-Y point from the histogram of fragment masses and relative abundances of fragments (often referred to as one peak in the mass spectrum).

Since the spectrum of each structure contains 100 to 300 different data points, each structure appears in many I/O pairs. Thus, the program must look for several generating principles, or processes, that operate on a structure to produce many data points. In addition, the data are not guaranteed correct because these are empirical data which may contain noise or contributions from impurities in the original sample. As a result, the program does not attempt to explain every I/O pair. It does, however, choose which data points to explain on the basis of criteria given by the chemist as part of the imposed model of mass-spectrometry.

Rules of mass spectrometry actually used by chemists are often expressed as what AI scientists would call production rules. These rules (when executed by a program) constitute a simulation of the fragmentation and atom migration processes that occur inside the instrument. The left-hand side is a description of the graph structure of some relevant piece of the molecule. The right-hand side is a list of processes which occur: specifically, bond cleavages and atom migrations. For example, one simple rule is

(R1) N—C—C—C → N—C*C—C

where the asterisk indicates breaking the bond at that position and recording the mass of the fragment to the left of the asterisk. (No migration of atoms between fragments is predicted by this rule.)

Although the vocabulary for describing individual atoms in subgraphs is small and the grammar of subgraphs is simple, the size of the subgraph search space is large. In addition to the connectivity of the subgraph, each atom in the subgraph may have up to four (dependent) attributes specified: (a) atom type (e.g., carbon), (b) number of connected neighbors (other than hydrogen), (c) number of hydrogen neighbors, and (d) number of doubly-bonded neighbors. The size of the space to consider, for example, for subgraphs containing 6 atoms, each with any of (say) 20 attribute-value specifications, is 20^6 possible subgraphs.

The language of processes (right-hand sides of rules) is also simple but can describe many combinations of actions: one or more bonds from the left-hand side may break and zero or more atoms may migrate between fragments.

4.2. Method

The rule formation process for Meta-DENDRAL is a three-stage sequence similar to the plan-generate-test sequence used in Heuristic DENDRAL. In Meta-DENDRAL, the generator (RULEGEN), described in section 4.2.2 below, generates plausible rules within syntactic and semantic constraints and within desired limits of evidential support. The model used to guide the generation of rules is particularly important since the space of rules is very large. The model of mass spectrometry in the program is highly flexible and can be modified by the user to suit his own biases and assumptions about the kinds of rules that are appropriate for the compounds under consideration. The model determines (i) the vocabulary to be used in constructing rules, (ii) the syntax of the rules (as before, the lefthand side of a rule describes a chemical graph, the right-hand side describes a fragmentation and/or rearrangement process to be expected in the mass spectrometer), (iii) some semantic constraints governing the plausibility of rules. For example, the chemist can use a subset of the terms available for describing chemical graphs and can restrict the number of chemical atoms described in the lefthand sides of rules and can restrict the complexity of processes considered in the right-hand sides (Buchanan and Mitchell 1978).

The planning part of the program (INTSUM), described in 4.2.1, collects and summarizes the evidential support. The testing part (RULEMOD), described in 4.2.3, looks for counterexamples to rules and makes modifications to the rules in order to increase their generality and simplicity and to decrease the total number of rules. These three major components are discussed briefly in the following subsections.

4.2.1. Interpret Data as Evidence for Processes

The INTSUM program (Smith et al. 1973) (named for data interpretation and summary) interprets spectral data of known compounds in terms of possible fragmentations and atom migrations. For each molecule in a given set, INTSUM first produces the plausible processes which might occur, i.e., breaks and combinations of breaks, with and without atom migrations. These processes are associated with specific bonds in a portion of molecular structure, or skeleton, that is chosen because it is common to the molecules in the given set. Then INTSUM examines the spectra of the molecules looking for evidence (spectral peaks) for each process.

Notice that the association of processes with data points may be ambiguous. For instance, in the molecule CH_3—CH_2—CH_2—NH—CH_2—CH_3 a spectral peak at mass 29 may be attributed to a process which breaks either the second bond from the left or one which breaks the second bond from the right, both producing CH_3—CH_2 fragments.

4.2.2. Generate Candidate Rules

After the data have been interpreted by INTSUM, control passes to a heuristic search program known as RULEGEN (Cheer et al. 1976) for rule generation. RULEGEN creates general rules by selecting "important" features of the molecular structure around the site of the fragmentations proposed by INTSUM. These important features are combined to form a subgraph description of the local environment surrounding the broken bonds. Each subgraph considered becomes the left hand side of a candidate rule whose right hand side is INTSUM's proposed process. Essentially RULEGEN searches (within the constraints) through a space of these subgraph descriptions looking for successively more specific subgraphs that are supported by successively "better" sets of evidence.

Conceptually, the program begins with the most general candidate rule, X*X (where X is any unspecified atom and where the asterisk is used to indicate the broken bond, with the detected fragment written to the left of the asterisk). Since the most useful rules lie somewhere between the overly-general candidate, X*X, and the overly-specific complete molecular structure descriptions (with specified bonds breaking), the program generates refined descriptions by successively specifying additional features. This is a coarse search; for efficiency reasons RULEGEN sometimes adds features to several nodes at a time, without considering the intermediate subgraphs.

The program systematically adds features (attribute-value pairs) to subgraphs, starting with the subgraph X*X, and always making each successor more specific than its parent. (Recall that each node can be described with any or all of the following attributes: atom type, number of non-hydrogen neighbors, number of hydrogen neighbors, and number of doubly bonded neighbors.) Working outward, the program assigns one attribute at a time to all atoms that are the same number of atoms away from the breaking bond. Each of the four attributes is considered in turn, and each attribute *value* for which there is supporting evidence generates a new successor. Although different values for the same attribute may be assigned to each atom at a given distance from the breaking bond, the coarseness of the search prevents examination of subgraphs in which this attribute is totally unimportant on *some* of these atoms.

4.2.3. Refine and Test the Rules

The last phase of Meta-DENDRAL (called RULEMOD) (Buchanan et al. 1976) evaluates the plausible rules generated by RULEGEN and modifies them by making them more general or more specific. In contrast to RULE-GEN, RULEMOD considers negative evidence (incorrect predictions) of rules in order to increase the accuracy of the rule's applications within the training set. While RULEGEN performs a coarse search of the rule space for reasons of efficiency, RULEMOD performs a localized, fine search to refine the rules.

RULEMOD will typically output a set of 5 to 10 rules covering substantially the same training data points as the input RULEGEN set of approximately 25 to 100 rules, but with fewer incorrect predictions. This program is written as a set of five tasks, corresponding to the five points below.

- *Selecting a Subset of Important Rules.* The local evaluation in RULEGEN has ignored negative evidence and has not discovered that different RULEGEN pathways may yield rules which are different but explain many of the same data points. Thus there is often a high degree of overlap in those rules and they may make many incorrect predictions. The initial selection removes most of the redundancy in the rule set.

- *Merging Rules.* For any subset of rules which explain many of the same data points, the program attempts to find a slightly more general rule that (a) includes all the evidence covered by the overlapping rules and (b) does not bring in extra negative evidence. If it can find such a rule, the overlapping rules are replaced by the single compact rule.

- *Deleting Negative Evidence by Making Rules More Specific.* RULEMOD tries to add attribute-value specifications to atoms in each rule in order to delete some negative evidence while keeping all of the positive evidence. This involves local search of the possible additions to the subgraph descriptions that were not considered by RULEGEN. Because of the coarseness of RULEGEN's search, some ways of refining rules are not tried, except by RULEMOD.

- *Making Rules More General.* RULEGEN often forms rules that are more specific than they need to be. Thus RULEMOD seeks a more general form that covers the same (and perhaps new) data points without introducing new negative evidence.

- *Selecting the Final Rule Set.* The selection procedure applied at the beginning of RULEMOD is applied again at the very end of RULEMOD in order to remove redundancies that might have been introduced during generalization and specialization.

4.3. Meta-DENDRAL Results

One measure of the proficiency of Meta-DENDRAL is the ability of the corresponding performance program to predict correct spectra of new molecules using the learned rules. One of the DENDRAL performance programs ranks a list of plausible hypotheses (candidate molecules) according to the similarity of their predictions (predicted spectra) to observed data. The rank of the correct hypothesis (i.e., the molecule actually associated with the observed spectrum) provides a quantitative measure of the "discriminatory power" of the rule set.

The Meta-DENDRAL program has successfully rediscovered known, published rules of mass spectrometry for two classes of molecules. More importantly, it has discovered new rules for three closely related families of structures for which rules had not previously been reported. Meta-DENDRAL's rules for these classes have been published in the chemistry literature (Buchanan et al. 1976). Evaluations of all five sets of rules are discussed in that publication.

Recently Meta-DENDRAL has been adapted to a second spectroscopic technique, 13C-nuclear magnetic resonance (13C-NMR) spectroscopy (Mitchell and Schwenzer 1977; Buchanan and Mitchell 1977). This new version provides the opportunity to direct the induction machinery of Meta-DENDRAL under a model of 13C-NMR spectroscopy. It generates rules which associate the resonance frequency of a carbon atom in a magnetic field with the local structural environment of the atom. 13C-NMR rules have been generated and used in a candidate molecule ranking program similar to the one described above. 13C-NMR rules formulated by the program for two classes of structures have been successfully used to identify the spectra of additional molecules (of the same classes, but outside the set of training data used in generating the rules).

The quality of rules produced by Meta-DENDRAL has been assessed by

a) obtaining agreement from mass spectroscopists that they are reasonable explanations of the training data and provide acceptable predictions of new data, and

b) testing them as discriminators of structures outside the training set.

The question of agreement on previously characterized sets of molecules is relatively easy, since the chemist only needs to compare the program's rules and predictions against published rules and spectra. Agreement has been high on test sets of amines, estrogenic steroids, and aromatic acids. On new data, however, the chemist is forced into spot checks. For example, analyses of some individual androstane spectra from the literature were used as spot checks on the program's analysis of the collections of androstane spectra.

The discrimination test is to determine how well a set of rules allows discrimination of known structures from alternatives on the basis of comparing predicted and actual spectra. For example, given a list of structures (Sl, ..., Sn) and the mass spectrum for structure Sl, can the rules *predict* a spectrum for Sl which matches the *given* spectrum (for Sl) better than spectra *predicted* for S2-Sn match the given spectrum? When this test is repeated for each available spectrum for structures Sl-Sn, the discriminatory power of the rules is determined. The program has found rules with high discriminatory power (Buchanan et al. 1976), but much work remains before we standardize on what we consider an optimum mix of generality and discriminatory power in rules.

4.3.1. Transfer to Applications Problems

The INTSUM program has begun to receive attention from chemists outside the Stanford community, but so far there have been only inquiries about outside use of the rest of Meta-DENDRAL. INTSUM provides careful assistance in associating plausible explanations with data points, within the chemist's own definition of "plausible." This can save a person many hours, even weeks, of looking at the data under various assumptions about fragmentation patterns.

The uses of INTSUM have been to investigate the mass spectral fragmentations of progesterones (Hammerun and Djerassi 1975a; Hammerun and Djerassi 1975b), marine sterols and antibiotics (in progress).

5. Problems

The science of AI suffers from the absence of satellite engineering firms that can map research programs into marketable products. We have sought alternatives to developing CONGEN ourselves into a program that is widely available and have concluded that the time is not yet ripe for a transfer of responsibility. In the future we hope for two major developments to facilitate dissemination of large AI programs: (a) off-the-shelf, small (and preferably cheap) computers that run advanced symbol manipulating languages, especially InterLisp, and (b) software firms that specialize in rewriting AI applications programs to industrial specifications.

While the software is almost too complex to export, our research-oriented computer facility has too little capacity for import. Support of an extensive body of outside users means that resources (people as well as computers) must be diverted from the research goals of the project.

At considerable cost in money and talent, it has been possible to export the programs to Edinburgh.[3] But such extensive and expensive collaborations for technology transfer are almost never done in AI. Even when the software is rewritten for export, there are too few "computational chemists" trained to manage and maintain the programs at local sites.

6. Computers and Languages

The DENDRAL programs are coded largely in InterLisp and run on the DEC KI-10 system under the TENEX operating system at the SUMEX computer resource at Stanford. Parts of CONGEN are written in FORTRAN and SAIL including some I/O packages and graph manipulation packages. We are currently studying the question of rewriting CONGEN in a less flexible language in order to run the program on a variety of machines with less power and memory. Peripheral programs for data acquisition, data filtering, library search and plotting exist for chemists to use on a DEC PDP 11/45 system, but are coupled to the AI programs only by file transfer.

7. Conclusion

CONGEN has attracted a moderately large following of chemists who consult it for help with structure elucidation problems. INTSUM, too, is used occasionally by persons collecting and codifying a large number of mass spectra.

With the exceptions just noted, the DENDRAL and Meta-DENDRAL programs are not used outside the Stanford University community and thus they represent only a successful demonstration of scientific capability. These programs are among the first AI programs to do even this. The achievement is significant in that the task domain was not "smoothed" or "tailored" to fit existing AI techniques. On the contrary, the intrinsic complexity of structure elucidation problems guided the AI research to problems of knowledge acquisition and management that might otherwise have been ignored.

The DENDRAL publications in major chemical journals have introduced to chemists the term "artificial intelligence" along with AI concepts and methods. The large number of publications in the chemistry literature also indicates substantial and continued interest in DENDRAL programs and applications.

Acknowledgments

The individuals who, in addition to the authors, are collectively responsible for most of the AI concepts and code are: Raymond Carhart, Carl Djerassi, Joshua Lederberg and Dennis Smith, Harold Brown, Allan Delfino, Geoff Dromey, Alan Duffield, Larry Masinter, Tom Mitchell, James Nourse, N. S. Sridharan, Georgia Sutherland, Tomas Varkony, and William White.

Other contributors to the DENDRAL project have been: M. Achenbach, C. Van Antwerp, A. Buchs, L. Creary, L. Dunham, H. Eggert, R. Engelmore, F. Fisher, N. Gray, R. Gritter, S. Hammerum, L. Hjelmeland, S. Johnson, J. Konopelski, K. Morrill, T. Rindfleisch, A. Robertson, G. Schroll, G. Schwenzer, Y. Sheikh, M. Stefik, A. Wegmann, W. Yeager, and A. Yeo.

A large number of individuals have worked on programs for data collection and filtering from the mass spectrometer, as well as on operation and maintenance of the instruments themselves. We are particularly indebted to Tom Rindfleisch for overseeing this necessary part of the DENDRAL project.

In its early years DENDRAL research was sponsored by NASA and ARPA. More recently DENDRAL has been sponsored by the NIH (Grant RR-00612). The project depends upon the SUMEX computing facility located at Stanford University for computing support. SUMEX is sponsored by the NIH (Grant RR-00785) as a national resource for applications of artificial intelligence to medicine and biology.

Notes

1. The symmetries of cyclic graphs prevented prospective avoidance of duplicates during generation. Brown, Hjelmeland and Masinter solved these problems in both theory and practice (Smith et al 1973; Brown and Masinter 1974).

2. Named for constrained generator.

3. R. Carhart is working with Professor Donald Michie's group to bring up a version of CONGEN there.

Consultation Systems for Physicians:

The Role of Artificial Intelligence Techniques

Edward H. Shortliffe

1. Introduction

Although computers have had an increasing impact on the practice of medicine, the successful applications have tended to be in domains where physicians have not been asked to interact at the terminal. Few potential user populations are as demanding of computer-based decision aids. This is due to a variety of factors which include their traditional independence as lone decision makers, the seriousness with which they view actions that may have life and death significance, and the overwhelming time demands that tend to make them impatient with any innovation that breaks up the flow of their daily routine.

This chapter examines some of the issues that have limited the acceptance of programs for use by physicians, particularly programs intended to give advice in clinical settings. My goal is to present design criteria which may encourage the use of computer programs by physicians, and to show that AI offers some particularly pertinent methods for responding to the design criteria outlined. Although the emphasis is medical throughout, many of the issues occur in other user communities where the introduction of computer methods must confront similar barriers. After presenting the design considerations and their relationship to AI research, I will use our work with MYCIN to illustrate some of the ways in which we have attempted to respond to the acceptability criteria I have outlined.

1.1 The Nature of Medical Reasoning

It is frequently observed that clinical medicine is more an "art" than a "science." This statement reflects the varied factors that are typically considered in medical decision making; any practitioner knows that well-trained experts with considerable specialized experience may still reach very different conclusions about how to treat a patient or proceed with a diagnostic workup.

One factor which may contribute to observed discrepancies, even among experts, is the tendency of medical education to emphasize the teaching of *facts,* with little formal advice regarding the *reasoning processes* that are most appropriate for decision making. There has been a traditional assumption that future physicians should learn to make decisions by observing other doctors in action and by acquiring as much basic knowledge as possible. More recently, however, there has been interest in studying the ways in which expert physicians reach decisions in hopes that a more structured approach to the teaching of medical decision making can be developed (Kassirer 1978, Elstein 1978).

Computer programs for assisting with medical decision making have tended not to emphasize models of clinical reasoning. Instead they have commonly assigned structure to a domain using statistical techniques such as Bayes' Theorem (deDombal 1972) or formal decision analysis (Gorry 1973). More recently a number of programs have attempted to draw lessons from analyses of actual human reasoning in clinical settings (Wortman 1972, Pauker 1976). Although the other methodologies may lead to excellent decisions in the clinical areas to which they have been applied, many believe that programs with greater dependence on models of expert clinical reasoning will have heightened acceptance by the physicians for whom they are designed.

1.2. The Consultation Process

Accelerated growth in medical knowledge has necessitated greater subspecialization and more dependence upon assistance from others when a patient presents with a complex problem outside one's own area of expertise. Such consultations are acceptable to doctors in part because they maintain the primary physician's role as ultimate decision maker. The consultation generally involves a dialog between the two physicians, with the expert explaining the basis for advice that is given and the nonexpert seeking justification of points found puzzling or questionable. Consultants who offered dogmatic advice they were unwilling to discuss or defend would find that their opinions were seldom sought. After a recommendation is given, the primary physician generally makes the decision whether to follow the consultant's advice, seek a second opinion, or proceed in some other fashion. When the consultant's advice is followed, it is frequently because the patient's doctor has been genuinely educated about the particular complex problem for which assistance was sought.

Since such consultations are accepted largely because they allow the primary physician to make the final management decision, it can be argued that medical consultation programs must mimic this human process. Computer-based decision aids have typically emphasized only the accumulation of patient data and the generation of advice (Shortliffe 1979). On the other hand, an ability to explain decisions may be incorporated into computer-based decision aids if the system is given an adequate internal model of the logic that it uses and can convey this intelligibly to the physician-user. The addition of explanation capabilities may be an important step towards effectively encouraging a system's use.

2. Acceptability Issues

Studies have shown that many physicians are inherently reluctant to use computers in their practice (Startsman 1972). Some researchers fear that the psychological barriers are insurmountable, but we are beginning to see systems that have had considerable success in encouraging terminal use by physicians (Watson 1974). The key seems to be to provide adequate benefits while creating an environment in which the physician can feel comfortable and efficient.

Physicians tend to ask at least seven questions when a new system is presented to them:

1. Is its performance reliable?

2. Do I need this system?

3. Is it fast and easy to use?

4. Does it help me without being dogmatic?

5. Does it justify its recommendations so that I can decide for myself what to do?

6. Does use of the system fit naturally into my daily routine?

7. Is it designed to make me feel comfortable when I use it?

Experience has shown that reliability alone may not be enough to insure system acceptance (Shortliffe 1979); the additional issues cited here are also central to the question of how to design consultation systems that doctors will be willing to use.

3. Design Criteria

The design considerations for systems to be used by physicians can be divided into three main categories: mechanical, epistemological, and psychological.

3.1. Mechanical Issues

It is clear that the best of systems will eventually fail if the process for getting information in or out of the machine is too arduous, frustrating, or complicated. Someday physician-computer interaction may involve voice communication by telephone or microphone, but technology is likely to require manual interaction for years to come. Thus, careful attention to the mechanics of the interaction, the simplicity of the displays, response time, accessibility of terminals, and self-documentation, are all essential for the successful implementation of clinical computing systems.

3.2. Epistemological Issues

As has been discussed, the quality of a program's performance at its decision making task is a basic acceptability criterion. A variety of approaches to automated advice systems have been developed, and many perform admirably (Shortliffe 1979). Thus the capturing or knowledge and data, plus a system for using them in a coherent and consistent manner, are the design considerations that have traditionally received the most attention.

Other potential uses of system knowledge must also be recognized, however. As has been noted, physicians often expect to be educated when they request a human consultation, and a computer-based consultant should also be an effective teaching tool. On the other hand. physicians would quickly reject a pedantic program that attempted to convey every pertinent fact in its knowledge base. Thus it is appropriate to design programs that convey knowledge as well as advice, but which serve this educational function only when asked to do so by the physician-user.

As has been mentioned, physicians also prefer to understand the basis for a consultant's advice so that they can decide for themselves whether to follow the recommendation. Hence the educational role of the consultation program can also be seen as providing an explanation or justification capability. When asked to do so, the system should be able to retrieve and display any relevant fact or reasoning step that was brought to bear in considering a given case. It is also important that such explanations be expressed in terms that are easily comprehensible to the physician.

Since it would be unacceptable for a consultation program to explain *every* relevant reasoning step or fact. it is important that the user be able to request justification for points found to be puzzling. Yet an ability to ask for explanations generally requires that the program be able to understand free-form queries entered by the user. A reasonable design consideration, then, is to attempt to develop an interface whereby simple questions expressed in English can be understood by the system and appropriately answered.

It is perhaps inevitable that consultation programs dealing with complex clinical problems will occasionally reveal errors or knowledge gaps, even after they have been implemented for ongoing use. A common source of frustration is the inability to correct such errors quickly so that they will not recur in subsequent consultation sessions. There is often a lapse of several months between "releases" of a system, with an annoying error recurring persistently in the meantime. It is therefore ideal to design systems in which knowledge is easily modified and integrated; then errors can be rapidly rectified once the missing or erroneous knowledge is identified. This requires a flexible knowledge representation and powerful methods for assessing the interactions of new knowledge with other facts already in the system.

Finally, the acquisition of knowledge can be an arduous task for system developers. In some applications the knowledge may be based largely on statistical data, but in others it may be necessary to extract judgmental information from the minds of experts. Thus another design consideration is the development of interactive techniques to permit acquisition of knowledge from primary data or directly from an expert without requiring that a computer programmer function as an intermediary.

3.3. Psychological Issues

The most difficult problems in designing consultation programs may be the frequently encountered psychological barriers to the use of computers among physicians (Startsman 1972, Croft 1972). Many of these barriers are reflected in the mechanical and epistemological design criteria mentioned above. However, there are several other pertinent observations:

1. It is probably a mistake to expect the physician to adapt to changes imposed by a consultation system.

2. A system's acceptance may be greatly heightened if ways are identified to permit physicians to perform tasks that they have wanted to do but had previously been unable to do (Mesel 1976, Watson 1974).

3. It is important to avoid premature introduction of a system while it is still "experimental."

4. System acceptance may be heightened if physicians know that a human expert is available to back up the program when problems arise.

5. Physicians are used to assessing research and new techniques on the basis of rigorous evaluations; hence novel approaches to assessing both the performance and the clinical impact of medical systems are required.

4. Knowledge Engineering

In recent years the terms "expert systems" and "knowledge-based systems" have been coined to describe AI programs that contain large amounts of specialized expertise that they convey to system users in the form of consultative advice. The phrase "knowledge engineering" has been devised (Michie 1973) to describe the basic AI problem areas that support the development of expert systems. There are several associated research themes:

Representation of Knowledge. A variety of methods for computer-based representation of human knowledge have been devised, each of which is directed at facilitating the associated symbolic reasoning and at permitting the codification and application of "common sense" as well as expert knowledge of the domain.

Acquisition of Knowledge. Obtaining the knowledge needed by an expert program is often a complex task. In certain domains programs may be able to "learn" through experience or from examples, but typically the system designers and the experts being modeled must work closely together to identify and verify the knowledge of the domain. Recently there has been some early experience devising programs that actually bring the expert to the computer terminal where a "teaching session" can result in direct transfer of knowledge from the expert to the system itself (Davis 1979).

Methods of Inference. Closely linked to the issue of knowledge representation is the mechanism for devising a line of reasoning for a given consultation. Techniques for hypothesis generation and testing are required, as are focusing techniques. A particularly challenging associated problem is the development of techniques for quantitating and manipulating uncertainty. Although inferences can sometimes be based on established techniques such as Bayes' theorem or decision analysis, utilization of expert judgmental knowledge typically leads to the development of alternate methods for symbolically manipulating inexact knowledge (Shortliffe 1975).

Explanation Capabilities. For reasons I have explained in the medical context above, knowledge engineering has come to include the development of techniques for making explicit the basis for recommendations or decisions. This requirement tends to constrain the methods of inference and the knowledge representation that is used by a complex reasoning program.

The Knowledge Interface. There are a variety of issues that fall in this general category. One is the mechanical interface between the expert program and the individual who is using it; this problem has been mentioned for the medical user, and many of the observations there can be applied directly to the users in other knowledge engineering application domains. Researchers on these systems also are looking for ways to combine AI techniques with more traditional numerical approaches to produce enhanced system performance. There is growing recognition that the greatest power in knowledge-based expert systems may lie in the melding of AI techniques and other computer science methodologies (Shortliffe 1979).

Thus it should be clear that artificial intelligence, and specifically knowledge engineering, are inherently involved with several of the design considerations that have been suggested for medical consultation systems. In the next section I will discuss how our medical AI program has attempted to respond to the design criteria that have been cited.

5. An Example: The MYCIN System

Since 1972 our research group at Stanford University[1] has been involved with the development of computer-based consultation systems. The first was designed to assist physicians with the selection of antibiotics for patients with serious infections. That program has been termed MYCIN after the suffix utilized in the names of many common antimicrobial agents. MYCIN is still a research tool, but it has been designed largely in response to issues such as those I have described. The details of the system have been discussed in several publications (Shortliffe 1976, Davis 1977, Scott 1977) and may already be well known to many readers. Technical details will therefore be omitted here, but I will briefly describe the program to illustrate the ways in which its structure reflects the design considerations outlined above.

5.1. Knowledge Representation and Acquisition

All infectious disease knowledge in MYCIN is contained in packets of inferential knowledge represented as production rules (Davis 1976). These rules were acquired from collaborating clinical experts during detailed discussions of specific complex cases on the wards at Stanford Hospital. More recently the system has been given the capability to acquire such rules directly through interaction with the clinical expert.[2]

MYCIN currently contains some 600 rules that deal with the diagnosis and treatment of bacteremia (bacteria in the blood) and meningitis (bacteria in the cerebrospinal fluid). These rules are coded in InterLisp (Teitelman 1978), but routines have been written to translate them into simple English so that they can be displayed and understood by the user. For example, one simple rule which relates a patient's clinical situation with the likely bacteria causing the illness is shown in Figure 1. The strengths with which the specified inferences can be drawn are indicated by numerical weights, or certainty factors, that are described further below.

5.2. Inference Methods

5.2.1. Reasoning Model

Production rules provide powerful mechanisms for selecting those that apply to a given consultation. In MYCIN's case the rules are only loosely related to

RULE 300

[This rule applies to all cultures and suspected infections, and is tried in order to find out about the organisms (other than those seen on cultures or smears) which might be causing the infection.]

If: 1) The infection which requires therapy is meningitis, and
     2) The patient does have evidence of serious skin or soft tissue infection, and
     3) Organisms were not seen on the stain of the culture, and
     4) The type of the infection is bacterial

Then: There is evidence that the organism (other than those seen on cultures or smears) which might be causing the infection is staphylococcus-coag-pos (.75) streptococcus-group-a (.5)

Figure 1. A sample MYCIN rule.

one another before a consultation begins; the program selects the relevant rules and chains them together as it considers a particular patient. Two rules chain together if the action portion of one helps determine the truth value of a condition in the premise of the other. The resulting reasoning network, then, is created dynamically and can be seen as a model of one approach to the patient's problem.

MYCIN's strategy in rule selection is goal-oriented. The program "reasons backwards" from its recognized goal of determining therapy for a patient. It therefore starts by considering rules for therapy selection, but the premise portion of each of those rules in turn sets up new questions or subgoals. These new goals then cause new rules to be invoked and a reasoning network is thereby developed. When the truth of a premise condition is best determined by asking the physician rather than by applying rules (e.g., to determine the value of a laboratory test), a question is displayed. The physician enters the appropriate response and the program continues to select additional rules. Once information on the patient is obtained, some rules will fail to be applicable; in this way the invoked applicable rules will provide a customized patient-specific reasoning network for the case under consideration.

Portions of a sample consultation session are shown in Figure 2. The physician's responses are in capital letters and follow a double asterisk. Note that the physician can indicate that he does not know the answer to a question (Question 13) and MYCIN will proceed to do the best it can on the basis of the data available. Typographical or spelling errors are automatically corrected (Question 12) with the presumed meaning printed at the left margin so that the physician knows what assumption has been made. Note also that the physician's responses are generally single words.

In Figure 3, the form of MYCIN's final conclusions and therapy recommendations are demonstrated. Note that the program specifies what organisms are likely to be causing the patient's infection and then suggests a therapeutic regimen appropriate for them. There are also specialized routines to calculate recommended drug doses depending upon the patient's size and kidney function.

5.2.2. Management of Uncertainty

The knowledge expressed in a MYCIN rule is seldom definite but tends to include "suggestive" or "strongly suggestive" evidence in favor of a given conclusion. In order to combine evidence regarding a single hypothesis but derived from a number of different rules, it has been necessary to devise a numeric system for capturing and representing an expert's measure of belief regarding the inference stated in a rule. Although this problem may at first seem amenable to the use of conditional probabilities and Bayes' Theorem, a probabilistic model fails to be adequate for a number of reasons we have detailed elsewhere (Shortliffe 1975). Instead we use a model that has been influenced by the theory of confirmation, and have devised a system of belief measures known as certainty factors. These numbers lie on a -1 to +1 scale with -1 indicating absolute disproof of an hypothesis, +1 indicating its proof, and 0 indicating the absence of evidence for or against the hypothesis (or equally weighted evidence in both directions). The relationship of the model to formal probability theory and the methods for combining evidence from diverse sources (rules and user estimates) have been described (Shortliffe 1975). Although the system has served us well to date, it does have several recognized inadequacies (Adams 1976) and can only be seen as a first step towards the development of a coherent theory for the management of uncertainty in complex reasoning domains.

5.3. Explanation

Perhaps the greatest advantage of the rules used in MYCIN is the way in which they facilitate the development of mechanisms for explaining and justifying system performance. These capabilities also contribute greatly to MYCIN's educational role (Clancey 1979). The explanation program has two options, one of which is limited in scope but fast and easy to use. This option is used during a consultation session and allows examination of the reasoning steps that have generated a specific question. The second option is more powerful but it involves language processing and is therefore less reliable and more time consuming. This question-answering capability is designed to allow full access to all system knowledge, both static (i.e., facts and rules obtained from experts) and dynamic (i.e., conclusions reached by the program for the specific consultation session). Each system is briefly described below.

5.3.1. Answers To Questions About The Reasoning Status

```
-----PATIENT-538----
1) Patient's name:
** PT538
2) Age:
** 45
3) Sex:
** MALE
4) Race:
** CAUC
```
=CAUCASIAN

5) Are there any cultures for Pt538 which may be related to the present illness, and from which organisms have been grown successfully in the microbiology laboratory?
```
** NO
```
6) Are there any pending cultures?
```
** YES
    -----CULTURE-1-----
```
7) From what site was the specimen for CULTURE-1 taken?
```
**  CSF
```
8) Please give the date and time when the pending csf culture (CULTURE-1) was obtained.
```
** 1 1/28/78
```
9) Was a smear examined at the time that the specimen for the pending csf culture (CULTURE-1) was obtained?
```
*   YES
```
10) Were any organisms seen on the smear of the specimen submitted as the pending csf culture (CULTURE-1)?
```
** YES
    -----ORGANISM-1-----
```
11) The stain (Gram. India ink, or Ziehl-Neelsen acid-fast) of ORGANISM-1:
```
**  GRAMNEG
```
12) Is ORGANISM-1 a rod or coccus (etc.):
```
**  ROOD
```
=ROD

13) What is the form of the individual organisms (e.g. Lancet-shaped for cocci. fusiform for rods, etc.)?
```
** ??
```
Expected responses are: FUSIFORM, PLUMP or DUMBBELL-SHAPED
Enter HELP for list of options.
```
**  UNKNOWN
```
14) Any other organisms noted on the smear?
```
** NO
```

Figure 2. The beginnings of a sample consultation.

My therapy recommendations will be designed to treat for organisms that either are very likely or, although less likely, would have a significant effect on therapy selection if they were present. It is important to cover for the following probable infection(s) and associated organism(s):

INFECTION-1 is MENINGITIS
+ <ITEM-1> E.COLI
+ <ITEM-2> PSEUDOMONAS-AERUGINOSA
+ <ITEM-3> KLEBSIELLA-PNEUMONIAE
+ <ITEM-4> DIPLOCOCCUS-PNEUMONIAE
41) Does Pt538 have a clinically significant allergic reaction to any antimicrobial agent?
** NO
42) Do you have reason to suspect that Pt538 may have impaired renal function?
** NO
43) Pt538's weight in kilograms:
** 70
[REC-1] My preferred therapy recommendation is:
In order to cover for Items <1 2 3 4>:
Give the following in combination:
1) AMPICILLIN
Dose: 3.5g (28.0 ml) q4h IV
          [calculated on basis of 50 mg/kg]
2) GENTAMICIN
Dose: 119 mg (3.0 ml, 80mg/2ml ampule) q8h IV [calculated on basis of 1.7 mg/kg]
          plus consider giving 5 mg q24h intrathecally
Since high concentrations of penicillins can inactivate aminoglycosides, do not mix these two antibiotics in the same bottle.

Figure 3. Example of MYCIN's recommendations.

During the consultation, MYCIN may ask questions which the physician finds puzzling, either because they appear irrelevant or because the details of their applicability are unclear. When this occurs, the physician can digress momentarily and seek an explanation of the question. Instead of answering the question MYCIN has asked, the user enters the word "WHY" and the program responds with a translation of the rule which generated the question. An example of this feature is shown in Figure 4. Note that MYCIN begins its response by phrasing in English its understanding of the "WHY question" asked by the physician. It then displays the relevant rule, specifying which conditions in the premise are already known to be true and which conditions remain to be investigated. In many cases this single rule displayed is an adequate explanation of the current line of reasoning and the physician can then proceed with the consultation by answering the question.

35)Is this a hospital-acquired infection?
** Why

[i.e. WHY is it important to determine whether the infection was acquired while the patient was hospitalized?]

[2.0] This will aid in determining the organisms (other than those seen on cultures or smears) which might be causing the infection.
    It has already been established that
        [2.1] the infection which requires therapy is meningitis, and
        [2.2] organisms were not seen on the stain of this pending csf culture, and
        [2.3] the type of the infection is bacterial, and
        [2.4] neurosurgery is not one of the relevant items from the history of pt538, and
        [2.5] the age of pt538 is greater than 10 days
    Therefore, if
        [2.6] the infection was acquired while the patient was hospitalized
then:
        there is evidence that the organism (other than those seen on cultures or smears) which might be causing the infection is e.coli (.75)
        staphylococcus-coag-pos (.3) pseudomonas-aeruginosa (.3)
        klebsiella-pneumoniae (.5)
[back to question 35...]
**

Figure 4. Example of the WHY command.

The user can alternatively continue to investigate the current reasoning by repeating the "WHY" command several times. Each additional "WHY" is interpreted by MYCIN as a request for display of the next rule in the current reasoning chain. For example, in Figure 4 another "WHY" would be equivalent to asking, "Well then, why are you trying to determine the organisms which might be causing the infection?" After responding to each "WHY," MYCIN returns to the current question and awaits the physician's response.

The "HOW" command is used in conjunction with the "WHY" command. Note that MYCIN places a unique number before each condition in the premise of a displayed rule (Figure 4). If the user does not understand how a specified condition was met (or will be met), the "HOW" command, followed by the identifying number of the premise clause in question, can be used. Hence "HOW" requires an argument as shown in Figure 5. This example follows immediately on the "WHY" example in Figure 4; thus the argument "2.3" refers to the third condition in the premise of RULE545 in Figure 4 and "2.5" refers to the fifth. MYCIN's responses to "HOW" commands are self-explanatory. Note also that components of all explanations are given identifiers so that, in Figure 5, the command "HOW 3.1" would have resulted in a display of RULE526.

Other features of the capability to assess the reasoning status during a consultation are described elsewhere (Davis 1977, Scott 1977, Davis 1979). Two points require emphasis here, however. First, these features require no English language processing since the user gives simple single-word commands; hence the capability is fast, efficient, and reliable. On the other hand, questions are limited to the immediate reasoning environment surrounding the question asked by MYCIN. Hence general access to other system knowledge or other conclusions previously made by the program is not possible. To provide a more general explanation capability, MYCIN must be able to respond to questions expressed in simple English as described below.

5.3.2. Answers To Questions about the Consultation and Knowledge Base

MYCIN's general question-answering feature is automatically made available to the user at the end of each consultation session. After a therapy recommendation has been given, the physician may still have several questions regarding details of the consultation and the basis for diagnostic and therapeutic advice. Figure 6 shows an example of a simple English question which MYCIN understands and attempts to answer. Our approach to natural language understanding is very simplistic (Scott 1977) but often adequate if questions are kept short without subordinate clauses. In many cases questions are best answered simply by retrieving relevant rules and displaying them in a format suitable for the question being asked. In Figure 6 MYCIN offers a detailed explanation of how it had decided that the patient might be infected with an E. coli. All rules are specified by number so that the physician can have them displayed if full details are desired.

Figure 7 demonstrates the way in which a physician can ask general questions of the knowledge base (static knowledge); neither the questions nor MYCIN's responses refer to any specific consultation session. Note that MYCIN has a sense of its limitations and makes it clear that it has no knowledge specific to pneumonia. Also, a large dictionary includes synonyms and hence permits MYCIN to recognize that "pneumococcal" refers to "pneumococcus" which in turn is the same as "diplococcus-pneumoniae."

Despite their utility, the language understanding features demonstrated in Figs. 6 and 7 have significant limitations. The associated computer code is large, complex, and very slow. Furthermore, we have found that it takes novice users several sessions before they learn the best ways to phrase questions so that MYCIN will interpret them properly.

5.4. Evaluating MYCIN

As work on MYCIN has progressed, we have begun to devise techniques for analyzing formally the system's performance. It must be emphasized, however, that the decision making performance is only one aspect of overall system acceptability; as I have discussed, many of the most significant prob-

[back to question 35...]
** HOW 2.3
[i.e. HOW was it established that, the type of the infection is bacterial?]

The following rules concluded about the likelihood that the type of the infection is bacterial:

	Rule	Certainty
[2.7]	RULE148	(.19)
[2.8]	RULE500	(.51)
[2.9]	RULE501	(.95)
[3.0]	RULE502	(.97)
[3.1]	RULE526	(.98)
[3.2]	RULE504	(.97)
[3.3]	RULE524	(.98)

Thus, it has been established that the type of the infection is bacterial.

[back to question 35...]
* * HOW 2.5
[i.e. HOW was it established that the age of pt538 is greater than 10 days?]

In answer to question 2 you said that the age of pt538 is 34 years. Thus, it has been established that the age of pt538 is greater than 10 days.

[back to question 35...]

Figure 5. Examples of the HOW command.

lems occur when attempts are made to encourage physicians to use a program, even after it has been shown to reach good decisions.

The details of the evaluation studies will not be presented here,[4] but a number of specific points are of interest. First, any evaluation is difficult because there is so much difference of opinion in this domain, *even among experts*. Hence, it is unclear how to select a "gold standard" by which to measure the system's performance.

Actual clinical outcome cannot be used because each patient of course is treated in only one way and because a poor outcome in a gravely ill patient cannot necessarily be blamed on the therapy that had been selected.

Second, although MYCIN performed at or near expert level in almost all cases, the evaluating experts in one study (Yu 1979a) had serious reservations about the clinical utility of the program. It is difficult to assess how much of this opinion is due to actual inadequacies in system knowledge or design and how much is related to inherent bias against any computer-based consultation aid. In a subsequent study we attempted to eliminate this bias from the study by having the evaluators unaware of which recommendations

** WHY DID YOU TREAT E.COLI?

ITEM-1 is E.coli associated with meningitis. I decided to treat ITEM1 on the basis of clinical evidence only.

The following rules concluded about: the likelihood that e.coli is one of the organisms (other than those seen on cultures or smears) which might be causing the infection

RULE545 was used to conclude that e.coli is one of the organisms
> (other than those seen on cultures or smears) which might be causing the infection (.74).

RULE557 was used to conclude that e.coli is one of the organisms
> (other than those seen on cultures or smears) which might be causing the infection (.93).

The parameters most frequently used in these rules:
   the infection which requires therapy
   whether a smear of the culture was examined
   whether organisms were seen
   the type of the infection

Figure 6. Response to a free text question.

** HOW DO YOU DECIDE THAT AN ORGANISM IS AN E.COLI?

The following rules conclude about: the likelihood that the identity of the organism is E.coli.
555, 304, 243, 3
Which of the rules do you wish to see?
   **   NONE

** WHAT IS THE TREATMENT FOR PNEUMOCOCCAL PNEUMONIA?

The MYCIN system currently can treat the following infections: BACTERIA MENINGI-TIS CYSTITIS. Because the knowledge base is incomplete, all other infections will be treated like bacteremia.

For treatment of DIPLOCOCCUS-PNEUMONIAE in BACTEREMIA, the drugs of choice (ranked by relative efficacy, assuming sensitivity) are:
   1st choice:
         PENICILLIN or AMPICILLIN
   Second Choice:
         NAFCILLIN, CEPHALOTHIN, ERYTHROMYCIN, or CLINDAMYCIN
   3rd choice:
         TETRACYCLINE, CHLORAMPHENICOL, or VANCOMYCIN

** WHAT DOSE OF ERYTHROMYCIN DO YOU RECOMMEND?

When ERYTHROMYCIN is given for BACTEREMIA, the recommended dosage is:
if age is > 12 yrs then 12 mg/kg q6h IV
else if age > .08 yrs then 5 mg/kg q6h IV
else if age > .02 yrs then 5 mg/kg q12h IV

Figure 7. Requests for MYCIN's general knowledge.

were MYCIN's and which came from actual physicians (Yu 1979b). In that setting MYCIN's recommendations were uniformly judged preferable to, or equivalent to, those of five infectious disease experts who recommended therapy for the same patients.

Finally, those cases in which MYCIN has tended to do least well are those in which serious infections have been simultaneously present at sites in the body about which the program has been given no rules. It is reasonable, of course, that the program should fail in areas where it has no knowledge. However, a useful antimicrobial consultation system must know about a broad range of infectious diseases, just as its human counterpart does. Even with excellent performance managing isolated bacteremias and meningitis, the program is therefore not ready for clinical implementation.

There will eventually be several important questions regarding the clinical impact of MYCIN and systems like it. Are they used? If so, do the physicians follow the program's advice? If so, does patient welfare improve? Is the system cost effective when no longer in an experimental form? What are the legal implications in the use of, or failure to use, such systems? The answers to all these questions are years away for most consultation systems, but it must be recognized that all these issues are ultimately just as important as whether the decision making methodology manages to lead the computer to accurate and reliable advice.

6. Conclusion

Although I have asserted that AI research potentially offers solutions to many of the important problems confronting researchers in computer-based clinical decision making, the field is not without its serious limitations. However, AI has reached a level of development where it is both appropriate and productive to begin applying the techniques to important real world problems rather than purely theoretical issues. The difficulty lies in the fact that such efforts must still dwell largely in research environments where short term development of systems for service use is not likely to occur.

It is also important to recognize that other computational techniques may meld very naturally with AI approaches as the fields mature. Thus we may see, for example, direct links between AI methods and statistical procedures, decision analysis, pattern recognition techniques, and large databanks. As researchers in other areas become more familiar with AI, it may gradually be brought into fruitful combination with these alternate methodologies. The need for physician acceptance of medical consultation programs is likely to make AI approaches particularly attractive, at least in those settings where hands-on computer use by physicians is desired or necessary. This paper has attempted to explain why the wedding of AI and medical consultation systems is a natural one and to show, in the setting of the MYCIN system, how one early application has responded to design criteria identified for a user community of physicians.

Notes

1. Several computer scientists, physicians, and a pharmacist have been involved in the development of the MYCIN System. These include J. Aikins, S. Axline, J. Bennett, A. Bonnet, B. Buchanan, W. Clancey, S. Cohen, R. Davis, L. Fagan, F. Rhame, C. Scott, W. vanMelle, S. Wraith, and V. Yu.

2. This capability was implemented in rudimentary form in early versions of the system (Shortliffe 1976) but was substantially broadened and strengthened by Davis in his Teiresias program (Davis 1979).

3. The mechanisms for examining the reasoning status using "WHY" and "HOW" commands were largely the work of Davis in his Teiresias program (Davis 1979). The techniques he developed are general in their applicability and have been implemented in nonmedical domains as well.

4. See (Yu 1979a) for the details of the bacteremia evaluation, and (Yu 1979b) for the data on MYCIN's performance selecting therapy for patients with meningitis.

22

A Truth Maintenance System

Jon Doyle

1. Introduction

Computer reasoning programs usually construct computational models of situations. To keep these models consistent with new information and changes in the situations being modeled, the reasoning programs frequently need to remove or change portions of their models. These changes sometimes lead to further changes, for the reasoner often constructs some parts of the model by making inferences from other parts of the model. We study both the problem of how to make changes in computational models, and the underlying problem of how the models should be constructed in order to make making changes convenient. The approach is to record the reasons for believing or using each program belief, inference rule, or procedure. To allow new information to displace previous conclusions, we employ "non-monotonic" reasons for beliefs, in which one belief depends on a lack of belief in some other statement. We use a program called the *Truth Maintenance System*[1] (TMS) to determine the current set of beliefs from the current set of reasons, and to update the current set of beliefs in accord with new reasons in a (usually) incremental fashion. To perform these revisions, the TMS traces the reasons for beliefs to find the consequences of changes in the set of assumptions.

This chapter describes the representations and mechanisms used to structure and revise the current set of beliefs and assumptions. We stress the need of problem solvers to choose between alternative systems of beliefs, illustrate methods for embedding control structures in patterns of assumptions, describe how to organize problem solvers into "dialectically arguing" modules, and outline a mechanism by which a problem solver can employ rules guiding choices of what to believe, what to want, and what to do.

1.1. The Essence of the Theory

Many treatments of formal and informal reasoning in mathematical logic and artificial intelligence have been shaped in large part by a seldom acknowledged view: the view that the process of reasoning is the process of deriving new knowledge from old, the process of discovering new truths contained in known truths. This view, as it is simply understood, has several severe difficulties as a theory of reasoning. In this section, I propose another, quite different view about the nature of reasoning. I incorporate some new concepts into this view, and the combination overcomes the problems exhibited by the conventional view.

Briefly put, the problems with the conventional view of reasoning stem from the *monotonicity* of the sequence of states of the reasoner's beliefs: his beliefs are true, and truths never change, so the only action of reasoning is to augment the current set of beliefs with more beliefs. This monotonicity leads to three closely related problems involving commonsense reasoning, the frame problem, and control. To some extent, my criticisms here of the conventional view of reasoning will be amplifications of Minsky's (1974) criticisms of the logistic approach to problem solving.

One readily recalls examples of the ease with which we resolve apparent contradictions involving our commonsense beliefs about the world. For example, we routinely make assumptions about the permanence of objects and the typical features or properties of objects, yet we smoothly accommodate corrections to the assumptions and can quickly explain our errors away. In such cases, we discard old conclusions in favor of new evidence. Thus, the set of our commonsense beliefs changes non-monotonically.

Our beliefs of what is current also change non-monotonically. If we divide the trajectory of the temporally evolving set of beliefs into discrete temporal situations, then at each instant the most recent situation is the set of current beliefs, and the preceding situations are past sets of beliefs. Adjacent sets of beliefs in this trajectory are usually closely related, as most of our actions have only a relatively small set of effects. The important point is that the trajectory does not form a sequence of monotonically increasing sets of beliefs, since many actions change what we expect is true in the world. Since we base our actions on what we currently believe, we must continually update our current set of beliefs. The problem of describing and performing this updating efficiently is sometimes called the *frame problem*. In connection with the frame problem, the conventional view suffers not only from monotonicity, but also from *atomicity*, as it encourages viewing each belief as an isolated statement, related to other beliefs only through its semantics. Since the semantics of beliefs are usually not explicitly represented in the system, if they occur there at all, atomicity means that these incremental changes in the set of current beliefs are difficult to compute.

The third problem with the conventional view actually subsumes the problem of commonsense reasoning and the frame problem. The problem of control is the problem of deciding what to do next. Rather than make this choice blindly, many have suggested that we might apply the reasoner to this task as well, to make inferences about which inferences to make. This approach to the problem of control has not been explored much, in part because such control inferences are useless in monotonic systems. In these systems, adding more inference rules or axioms just increases the number of inferences possible, rather than preventing some inferences from being made. One gets the unwanted inferences together with new conclusions confirming their undesirability.

Rather than give it up, we pursue this otherwise attractive approach, and make the deliberation required to choose actions a form of reasoning as well. For our purposes, we take the desires and intentions of the reasoner to be represented in his set of current beliefs as beliefs about his own desires and intention. We also take the set of inference rules by which the reasoning process occurs to be represented as beliefs about the reasoner's own computational structure. By using this self-referential, reflexive representation of the reasoner, the inference rules become rules for self-modification of the reasoner's set of beliefs (and hence his desires and intentions as well). The control problem of choosing which inference rule to follow takes the form "Look at yourself as an object (as a set of beliefs), and choose what (new set of beliefs) you would like to become."

The language of such inference rules, and the language for evaluating which self-change to make, are for the most part outside the language of inference rules encouraged by the conventional view of reasoning. For example, when the current set of beliefs is inconsistent, one uses rules like "Reject the smallest set of beliefs possible to restore consistency" and "Reject those beliefs which represent the simplest explanation of the inconsistency." These sorts of rules are all we have, since we cannot infallibly analyze errors or predict the future, yet these rules are non-monotonic, since they lead to removing beliefs from the set of current beliefs.

To repeat, one source of each of these problems is the monotonicity inherent in the conventional view of reasoning. I now propose a different view, and some new concepts which have far reaching consequences for these issues.

Rational thought is the process of finding reasons for attitudes.

To say that some attitude (such as belief, desire, intent, or action) is rational is to say that there is some acceptable reason for holding that attitude. Rational thought is the process of finding such acceptable reasons. Whatever purposes the reasoner may have, such as solving problems, finding answers, or taking action, it operates by constructing reasons for believing things, desiring things, intending things, or doing or willing things. The actual attitude in the reasoner occurs only as a by-product of constructing reasons. The current set of beliefs and desires arises from the current set of reasons for beliefs and desires, reasons phrased in terms of other beliefs and desires. When action is taken, it is because some reason for the action can be found in terms of the beliefs and desires of the actor. I stress again, the only *real* component of thought is the current set of reasons—the attitudes such as beliefs and desires arise from the set of reasons, and have no independent existence.

One consequence of this view is that to study rational thought, we should study justified belief or reasoned argument, and ignore questions of truth. Truth enters into the study of extra-psychological rationality and into what common-sense truisms we decide to supply to our programs, but truth does not enter into the narrowly psychological rationality by which our programs operate.

Of course, this sort of basic rationality is simpler to realize than human belief. Humans exhibit "burn-in" phenomena in which longstanding beliefs come to be believed independently of their reasons, and humans sometimes undertake "leaps of faith" which vault them into self-justifying sets of beliefs, but we will not study these issues here. Instead, we restrict ourselves to the more modest goal of making rational programs in this simpler sense.

The view stated above entails that for each statement or proposition P just one of two states obtains: Either

a) P has at least one currently acceptable *(valid)* reason, and is thus a member of the current set of beliefs, or

b) P has no currently acceptable reasons (either no reasons at all, or only unacceptable ones), and is thus not a member of the current set of beliefs.

If P falls in state (a), we say that P is *in* (the current set of beliefs), and otherwise, that P is *out* (of the current set of beliefs). These states are not symmetric, for while reasons can be constructed to make P *in,* no reason can make P *out.* (At most, it can make ¬P *in* as well.)

This shows that the proposed view also succumbs to monotonicity problems, for the set of reasons grows monotonically, which (with the normal sense of "reason") leads to only monotonic increases in the set of current beliefs. To solve the problem of monotonicity, we introduce novel meanings for the terms "a reason" and "an assumption."

Traditionally, a reason for a belief consists of a set of other beliefs, such that if each of these basis beliefs is held, so also is the reasoned belief. To get off the ground, this analysis of reasons requires either circular arguments between beliefs (and the appropriate initial state of belief) or some fundamental type of belief which grounds all other arguments. The traditional view takes these fundamental beliefs, often called assumptions (or premises), as believed without reason. On this view, the reasoner makes changes in the current set of beliefs by removing some of the current assumptions and adding some new ones.

To conform with the proposed view, we introduce meanings for "reason" and "assumption" such that assumptions also have reasons. A *reason* (or justification) for a belief consists of an ordered pair of sets of other beliefs, such that the reasoned belief is *in* by virtue of this reason only if each belief in the first set is *in,* and each belief in the second set is *out.* An *assumption* is a current belief one of whose valid reasons depends on a non-current belief, that is, has a non-empty second set of antecedent beliefs. With these notions we can create "ungrounded" yet reasoned beliefs by making assumptions. (E.g., give P the reason ({ }, {¬P}).) We can also effect non-monotonic changes in the set of current beliefs by giving reasons for some of the *out* statements used in the reasons for current assumptions. (E.g., to get rid of P, justify ¬P.) We somewhat loosely say that when we justify some *out* belief supporting an assumption (e.g., ¬P), we are *denying* or *retracting* the assumption (P).

These new notions solve the monotonicity problem. Following from this solution we find ways of treating the commonsense reasoning, frame, and control problems plaguing the conventional view of reasoning. Commonsense default expectations we represent as new style assumptions. Part of the frame problem, namely how to non-monotonically change the set of current beliefs, follows from this non-monotonic notion of reason. However, much of the frame problem (e.g., how to give the "laws of motion" and how to retrieve them efficiently) lies outside the scope of this discussion. The control problem can be dealt with partially by embedding the sequence of procedural states of the reasoner in patterns of assumptions.

Other advantages over the conventional view also follow. One of these advantages involves how the reasoner retracts assumptions. With the traditional notion of assumption, retracting assumptions was unreasoned. If the reasoner removed an assumption from the current set of beliefs, the assumption remained out until the reasoner specifically put it back into the set of current beliefs, even if changing circumstances obviated the value of removing this belief. The new notions introduce instead the *reasoned retraction of assumptions.* This means that the reasoner retracts an assumption only by giving a reason for why it should be retracted. If later this reason becomes invalid, then the retraction is no longer effective and the assumption is restored to the current set of beliefs.

The reasoned retraction of assumptions helps in formulating a class of backtracking procedures which revise the set of current assumptions when inconsistencies are discovered. The paradigm procedure of this sort we call dependency-directed backtracking after Stallman and Sussman (1977). It is the least specialized procedure for revising the current set of assumptions in the sense that it only operates on the reasons for beliefs, not on the form or content of the beliefs. In short, it traces backwards through the reasons for the conflicting beliefs, finds the set of assumptions reached in this way, and then retracts one of the assumptions with a reason involving the other assumptions. Dependency-directed backtracking serves as a template for more specialized revision procedures. These specialized procedures are necessary in almost all practical applications, and go beyond the general procedure by taking the form of the beliefs they examine into account when choosing which assumption to reject.

1.2. Basic Terminology

The TMS records and maintains arguments for potential program beliefs, so as to distinguish, at all times, the current set of program beliefs. It manipulates two data structures: *nodes,* which represent beliefs, and *justifications,* which represent reasons for beliefs. We write St(N) to denote the statement of the potential belief represented by the node N. We say the TMS believes in (the potential belief represented by) a node if it has an argument for the node and believes in the nodes involved in the argument. This may seem circular, but some nodes will have arguments which involve no other believed nodes, and so form the base step for the definition.

As its fundamental actions,

1. The TMS can create a new node, to which the problem solving program using the TMS can attach the statement of a belief (or inference rule, or procedure, or data structure). The TMS leaves all manipulation of the statements of nodes (for inference, representation, etc.) to the program using the TMS.

2. It can add (or retract) a new justification for a node, to represent a step of an argument for the belief represented by the node. This argument step usually represents the application of some rule or procedure in the problem solving program. Usually, the rules or procedures also have TMS nodes, which they include in the justifications they create.

3. Finally, the TMS can mark a node as a *contradiction,* to represent the inconsistency of any set of beliefs which enter into an argument for the node.

A new justification for a node may lead the TMS to believe in the node. If the TMS did not believe in the node previously this may in turn allow other nodes to be believed by previously existing but incomplete arguments. In this case, the TMS invokes the *truth maintenance* procedure to make any necessary revisions in the set of beliefs. The TMS revises the current set of beliefs by using the recorded justifications to compute non-circular arguments for nodes from premises and other special nodes, as described later. These non-circular arguments distinguish one justification as the *well-founded supporting justification* of each node representing a current belief. The TMS locates the set of nodes to update by finding those nodes whose well-founded arguments depend on changed nodes.

The program using the TMS can indicate the inconsistency of the beliefs represented by certain currently believed nodes by using these nodes in an argument for a new node, and by then marking the new node as a contradiction. When this happens, another process of the TMS, *dependency-directed backtracking,* analyzes the well-founded argument of the contradiction node to locate the *assumptions* (special types of nodes defined later) occurring in the argument. It then makes a record of the inconsistency of this set of assumptions, and uses this record to change one of the assumptions. After this change, the contradiction node is no longer believed.

The TMS employs a special type of justification, called a *non-monotonic justification,* to make tentative guesses. A non-monotonic justification bases an argument for a node not only on current belief in other nodes, as occurs in the most familiar forms of deduction and reasoning, but also on lack of current belief in other nodes. For example, one might justify a node N-1 representing a statement P on the basis of lack of belief in node N-2 representing the statement ¬P. In this case, the TMS would hold N-1 as a current belief as long as N-2 was not among the current beliefs, and we would say that it had assumed belief in N-1. More generally, by an *assumption* we mean any node whose well-founded support is a non-monotonic justification.

As a small example of the use of the TMS, suppose that a hypothetical office scheduling program considers holding a meeting on Wednesday. To do this, the program assumes that the meeting is on Wednesday. The inference system of the program includes a rule which draws the conclusion that due to regular commitments, any meeting on Wednesday must occur at 1:00 PM. However, the fragment of the schedule for the week constructed so far has some activity scheduled for that time already, and so another rule concludes the meeting cannot be on Wednesday. We write these nodes and rule-constructed justifications as follows:

Node	Statement	Justification	Comment
N-1	DAY(M) = WEDNESDAY	(SL ( ) (N-2))	*an assumption*
N-2	DAY(M) ≠ WEDNESDAY		*no justification yet*
N-3	TIME(M) = 13:00	(SL (R-37 N-1) ( ))	

The above notation for the justifications indicates that they belong to the class of *support-list* (SL) justifications. Each of these justifications consists of two lists of nodes. A SL-justification is a *valid* reason for belief if and only if each of the nodes in the first list is believed and each of the nodes in the second list is not believed. In the example, if the two justifications listed above are the only existing justifications, then N-2 is not a current belief since it has no justifications at all. N-1 is believed since the justification for N-1 specifies that this node depends on the lack of belief in N-2. The justification for N-3 shows that N-3 depends on a (presumably believed) node R-37. In this case, R-37 represents a rule acting on (the statement represented by) N-1.

Subsequently another rule (represented by a node R-9) acts on beliefs about the day and time of some other engagement (represented by the nodes N-7 and N-8) to reject the assumption N-1.

N-2   DAY(M) ≠ WEDNESDAY   (SL (R-9 N-7 N-8) ( ))

To accommodate this new justification, the TMS will revise the current set of beliefs so that N-2 is believed, and N-1 and N-3 are not believed. It does this by tracing "upwards" from the node to be changed, N-2, to see that N-1 and N-3 ultimately depend on N-2. It then carefully examines the justifications of each of these nodes to see that N-2's justification is valid (so that N-2 is *in*). From this it follows that N-1's justification is invalid (so N-1 is *out*), and hence that N-3's justification is invalid (so N-3 is *out*).

2. Representation of Reasons for Beliefs

2.1. States of Belief

A node may have several justifications, each justification representing a different reason for believing the node. These several justifications comprise the node's *justification-set*. The node is believed if and only if at least one of its justifications is *valid*. We described the conditions for validity of SL-justifications above, and shortly will introduce the other type of justification used in the TMS. We say that a node which has at least one valid justification is *in* (the current set of beliefs), and that a node with no valid justifications is *out* (of the current set of beliefs). We will alternatively say that each node has a *support-status* of either *in* or *out*. The distinction between *in* and *out* is not that between *true* and *false*. The former classification refers to current possession of valid reasons for belief. *True* and *false*, on the other hand, classify statements according to truth value independent of any reasons for belief.

In the TMS, each potential belief to be used as a hypothesis or conclusion of an argument must be given its own distinct node. When uncertainty about some statement (e.g., P) exists, one must (eventually) provide nodes for both the statement and its negation. Either of these nodes can have or lack well-founded arguments, leading to a four-element belief set (similar to the belief set urged by Belnap (1976)) of neither P nor ¬P believed, exactly one believed, or both believed.

The literature contains many proposals for using three-element belief sets of *true, false,* and *unknown.* With no notion of justified belief, these proposals have some attraction. I urge, however, that systems based on a notion of justified belief should forego three-valued logics in favor of the four-valued system presented here, or risk a confusion of truth with justified belief. Users of justification-based three-valued systems can avoid problems if they take care to interpret their systems in terms of justifications rather than truth-values, but the danger of confusion seems greater when the belief set hides this distinction. One might argue that holding contradictory beliefs is just a transient situation, and that any stable situation uses only three belief states: *true*—only P believed, *false*—only ¬P believed, and *unknown*—neither believed. But the need for the four-element system cannot be dismissed so easily. Since we make the process of revising beliefs our main interest, we concern ourselves with those processes which operate during the transient situation. For hard problems and tough decisions, these "transient" states can be quite long-lived.

2.2. Justifications

Justifications, as recorded in the TMS, have two parts; the external form of the justification with significance to the problem solver, and the internal form of significance to the TMS. For example, a justification might have the external form "Modus Ponens *A* *A*⊃*B*" and have the internal form (SL (N-1 N-2 N-3) ()), supposing that N-1 represents the rule Modus Ponens, N-2 represents A, and N-3 represents *A* ⊃ *B*. The TMS never uses or examines the external forms of justifications, but merely records them for use by the problem solver in constructing externally meaningful explanations. Henceforth, we will ignore these external forms of justifications.

Although natural arguments may use a wealth of types of argument steps or justifications, the TMS forces one to fit all these into a common mold. The TMS employs only two (internal) forms for justifications, called *support-list* (SL) and *conditional-proof* (CP) justifications. These are inspired by the typical forms of arguments in natural deduction inference systems, which either add or subtract dependencies from the support of a proof line. A proof in such a system might run as follows:

Line	Statement	Justification	Dependencies
1.	A ⊃ B	Premise	{1}
2.	B ⊃ C	Premise	{2}
3.	A	Hypothesis	{3}
4.	B	MP 1, 3	{1, 3}
5.	C	MP 2, 4	{1, 2, 3}
6.	A ⊃ C	Discharge 3, 5	{1, 2}

Each step of the proof has a line number, a statement, a justification, and a set of line numbers on which the statement depends. Premises and hypotheses depend on themselves, and other lines depend on the set of premises and hypotheses derived from their justifications. The above proof proves $A \supset C$ from the premises $A \supset B$ and $B \supset C$ by hypothesizing A and concluding C via two applications of Modus Ponens. The proof of $A \supset C$ ends by discharging the assumption A, which frees the conclusion of dependence on the hypothesis but leaves its dependence on the premises.

This example displays justifications which sum the dependencies of some of the referenced lines (as in line 4) and subtract the dependencies of some lines from those of other lines (as in line 6). The two types of justifications used in the TMS account for these effects on dependencies. A support-list justification says that the justified node depends on each node in a set of other nodes, and in effect sums the dependencies of the referenced nodes. A conditional-proof justification says that the node it justifies depends on the validity of a certain hypothetical argument. As in the example above, it subtracts the dependencies of some nodes (the hypotheses of the hypothetical argument) from the dependencies of others (the conclusion of the hypothetical argument). Thus we might rewrite the example in terms of TMS justifications as follows (here ignoring the difference between premises and hypotheses, and ignoring the inference rule MP):

N-1	$A \supset B$	(SL ( ) ( ))	*Premise*
N-2	$B \supset C$	(SL ( ) ( ))	*Premise*
N-3	A	(SL ( ) ( ))	*Premise*
N-4	B	(SL (N-1 N-3) ( ))	*MP*
N-5	C	(SL (N-2 N-4) ( ))	*MP*
N-6	$A \supset C$	(CP N-5 (N-3) ( ))	*Discharge*

CP-justifications, which are explained in greater detail in Doyle (1979), differ from ordinary hypothetical arguments in that they use two lists of nodes as hypotheses, the *in*hypotheses and the *out*hypotheses. In the above justification for N-6, the list of *in*hypotheses contains just N-3, and the list of *out*hypotheses is empty. This difference results from our use of non-monotonic justifications, in which arguments for nodes can be based both on *in* and *out* nodes.

To repeat the definition scattered throughout the previous discussion, the support-list justification has the form

(SL <*in*list> <*out*list>),

and is valid if and only if each node in its *in*list is *in,* and each node in its *out*list is *out.* The SL-justification form can represent several types of deductions. With empty *in*list and empty *out*list, we say the justification forms a *premise* justification. A premise justification is always valid, and so the node it justifies will always be *in.* SL-justifications with nonempty *in*lists and empty *out*lists represent normal deductions. Each such justification represents a monotonic argument for the node it justifies from the nodes of its *in*-

list. We define *assumptions* to be nodes whose supporting-justification has a nonempty *out*list. These assumption justifications can be interpreted by viewing the nodes of the *in*list as comprising the reasons for wanting to assume the justified node; the nodes of the *out*list represent the specific criteria authorizing this assumption. For example, the reason for wanting to assume "The weather will be nice" might be "Be optimistic about the weather"; and the assumption might be authorized by having no reason to believe "The weather will be bad." We occasionally interpret the nodes of the *out*list as "denials" of the justified node, beliefs which imply the negation of the belief represented by the justified node.

CP-justifications take the form

(CP <consequent> <*in*hypotheses> <*out*hypotheses>).

A CP-justification is valid if the consequent node is *in* whenever

(a) each node of the *in*hypotheses is *in* and

(b) each node of the *out*hypotheses is *out*.

The TMS can easily determine the validity of a CP-justification only when the justification's consequent and *in*hypotheses are *in* and the *out*hypotheses are *out*, since determining the justification's validity with other support-statuses for these nodes may require switching the support-statuses of the hypothesis nodes and their repercussions to set up the hypothetical situation in which the validity of the conditional-proof can be evaluated. This may require truth maintenance processing, which in turn may require validity checking of further CP-justifications, and so the whole process becomes extremely complex. Instead of attempting such a detailed analysis (for which I know no algorithms), the TMS uses the opportunistic and approximate strategy of computing new SL-justifications which, at the time of their creation, are equivalent to the CP-justifications in terms of the dependencies they specify, and are easily checked for validity. Whenever the TMS finds a CP-justification valid, it computes an equivalent SL-justification by analyzing the well-founded argument for the consequent node of the CP-justification to find those nodes which are not themselves supported by any of the *in*hypotheses or *out*hypotheses but which directly enter into the argument for the consequent node along with the hypotheses (see Doyle (1979) for a precise characterization). The TMS checks the derived SL-justifications first in determining the support-status of a node, and uses them in explanations. It uses only SL-justifications (derived or otherwise) as supporting-justifications of nodes.

2.3. Terminology of Dependency Relationships

The set of *supporting-nodes* of a node is the set of nodes which the TMS used to determine the support-status of the node. For *in* nodes, the supporting-nodes are just the nodes listed in the *in*list and *out*list of its supporting-justification, and in this case we also call the supporting-nodes the *antecedents* of the node. For the supporting-nodes of *out* nodes, the TMS picks one node from each justification in the justification-set. From SL-justifications, it picks either an *out* node from the *in*list or an *in* node from the *out*list. From CP-justifications, it picks either an *out* node from the *in*hypotheses or consequent or an *in* from the *out*hypotheses. We define the supporting-nodes of *out* nodes in this way so that the support-status of the node in question cannot change without either a change in the support-status of one of the supporting-nodes, or without the addition of a new valid justification. We say that an *out* node has no antecedents. The set of *foundations* of a node is the transitive closure of the antecedents of the node, that is, the antecedents of the node, their antecedents, and so on. This set is the set of nodes involved in the well-founded argument for belief in the node. In the other direction, the set of *consequences* of a node is the set of all nodes which mention the node in one of the justifications in their justification-set. The *affected-consequences* of a node are just those consequences of the node which contain the node in their set of supporting-nodes. The set of *repercussions* of a node is the transitive closure of the affected-consequences of the node, that is, the affected-consequences of the node, their affected-consequences, and so on. The TMS keeps the supporting-nodes and the consequences of each node as part of the node data-structure, and computes the antecedents, foundations, affected-consequences, and repercussions of the node from these lists.

3. Truth Maintenance Mechanisms

3.1. Circular Arguments

Suppose a program manipulates three nodes as follows:

F $(= (+ X Y) 4)$ ...   *omitted*
G $(= X 1)$ $(SL (J) ( ))$
H $(= Y 3)$ $(SL (K) ( ))$.

(We sometimes leave statements and justifications of nodes unspecified when they are not directly relevant to the presentation. We assume that all such omitted justifications are valid.) If J is *in* and K is *out,* then the TMS will make F and G *in,* and H *out.* If the program then justifies H with

$(SL (F G) ( ))$,

the TMS will bring H *in.* Suppose now that the TMS makes J *out* and K *in,* leading to G becoming *out* and H remaining *in.* The program might then justify G with

$(SL (F H) ( ))$.

If the TMS now takes K *out,* the original justification supporting belief in H

becomes invalid, leading the TMS to reassess the grounds for belief in *H*. If it makes its decision to believe a node on the basis of a simple evaluation of each of the justifications of the node, then it will leave both *G* and *H in,* since the two most recently added justifications form circular arguments for *G* and *H* in terms of each other.

These circular arguments supporting belief in nodes motivate the use of well-founded supporting justifications, since nodes imprudently believed on tenuous circular bases can lead to ill-considered actions, wasted data base searches, and illusory inconsistencies which might never have occurred without the misleading, circularly supported beliefs. In view of this problem, the algorithms of the TMS must ensure that it believes no node for circular reasons.

Purported arguments for nodes can contain essentially three different kinds of circularities. The first and most common type of circularity involves only nodes which can be taken to be *out* consistently with their justifications. Such circularities arise routinely through equivalent or conditionally equivalent beliefs and mutually constraining beliefs. The above algebra example falls into this class of circularity.

The second type of circularity includes at least one node which must be *in*. Consider, for example

F   TO-BE   (SL ( ) (*G*))
G   ¬TO-BE   (SL ( ) (*F*)).

In the absence of other justifications, these justifications force the TMS either to make *F in* and *G out,* or *G in* and *F out.* This type of circularity can arise in certain types of sets of alternatives.

In unsatisfiable circularities, the third type, no assignment of *in* or *out* to nodes is consistent with their justifications. Consider

F   ...   (SL ( ) (*F*)).

With no other justifications for *F*, the TMS must make *F in* if and only if it makes *F out,* an impossible task. Unsatisfiable circularities sometimes indicate real inconsistencies in the beliefs of the program using the truth maintenance system, and can be manifest, for example, when prolonged backtracking rules out all possibilities. The current version of the TMS does not handle unsatisfiable circularities (it goes into a loop), as I removed the occasionally costly check for the presence of such circularities to increase the normal-case efficiency of the program. A robust implementation would reinstate this check.

3.2. The Truth Maintenance Process

The truth maintenance process makes any necessary revisions in the current set of beliefs when the user adds to or subtracts from the justification-set of a node. Retracting justifications presents no important problems beyond those of adding justifications, so we ignore retractions to simplify the discussion.

In outline, the truth maintenance process starts when a new justification is added to a node. Only minor bookkeeping is required if the new justification is invalid, or if it is valid but the node is already *in*. If the justification is valid and the node is *out*, then the node and its repercussions must be updated. The TMS makes a list containing the node and its repercussions, and marks each of these nodes to indicate that they have not been given well-founded support. The TMS then examines the justifications of these nodes to see if any are valid purely on the basis of unmarked nodes, that is, purely on the basis of nodes which do have well-founded support. If it finds any, these nodes are brought *in* (or *out* if all their justifications are invalid purely on the basis of well-founded nodes). Then the marked consequences of the nodes are examined to see if they too can now be given well-founded support. Sometimes, after all of the marked nodes have been examined in this way, well-founded support-statuses will have been found for all nodes. Sometimes, however, some nodes will remain marked due to circularities. The TMS then initiates a constraint-relaxation process which assigns support-statuses to the remaining nodes. Finally, after all this, the TMS checks for contradictions and CP-justifications, performs dependency-directed backtracking and CP-justification processing if necessary, and then signals the user program of the changes in support-statuses of the nodes involved in truth maintenance.

For more detail, see Doyle (1979), or better still, the chapter on data dependencies in Charniak, Riesbeck, and McDermott (1979), which presents a simplified Lisp implementation of a TMS-like program along with a proof of its correctness. McAllester (1978) presents an alternative implementation of a truth maintenance system, and Doyle (1978a) presents a program listing of one version of the TMS in an appendix.

4. Dependency-Directed Backtracking

When the TMS makes a contradiction node *in,* it invokes dependency-directed backtracking to find and remove at least one of the current assumptions in order to make the contradiction node *out.* The steps of this process follow. We enclose commentary in bracket-asterisk pairs ([*, *]).

Step 1 (Find the maximal assumptions). Trace through the foundations of the contradiction node C to find the set $S = \{A_1,..., A_n\}$, which contains an assumption A if and only if A is in C's foundations and there is no other assumption B in the foundations of C such that A is in the foundations of B. [* We call S the set of the *maximal* assumptions underlying C. *]

[* Just as the TMS relies on the problem solving program to point out inconsistencies by marking certain nodes as contradictions, it also relies on the problem solver to use non-monotonic assumptions for any beliefs to which backtracking might apply. Because the TMS does not inspect the statements represented by its nodes, it forgoes the ability, for example, to retract premise justifications of nodes. *]

Step 2 (Summarize the cause of the inconsistency). If no previous backtracking attempt on C discovered S to be the set of maximal assumptions, create a new node NG, called a *nogood*, to represent the inconsistency of S. [* We call S the *nogood-set.* *] If S was encountered earlier as a nogood-set of a contradiction, use the previously created nogood node. [* Since C represents a false statement, NG represents

$$St(A_1) \wedge \cdots \wedge St(A_n) \supset \text{\textit{false}},$$

or

$$\neg(St(A_1) \wedge \cdots \wedge St(A_n)) \tag{1}$$

by a simple rewriting. *]

Justify NG with

$$(CP \ C \ S \ (\ )). \tag{2}$$

[* With this justification, NG will remain *in* even after Step 3 makes one of the assumptions *out*, since the CP-justification means that NG does not depend on any of the assumptions. *]

Step 3 (Select and reject a culprit). Select some A_i, the *culprit*, from S. Let $D_1 \ldots, D_k$ be the *out* nodes in the *out*list of A_i's supporting-justification. Select D_j from this set and justify it with

$$(SL \ (NG \ A_1 \cdots A_{i-1} \ A_{i+1} \ \cdots \ A_n) \ (D_1 \cdots D_{j-1} \ D_{j+1} \cdots D_k)). \tag{3}$$

[* If one takes these underlying D nodes as "denials" of the selected assumption, this step recalls *reductio ad absurdum.* The backtracker attempts to force the culprit *out* by invalidating its supporting-justification with the new justification, which is valid whenever the nogood and the other assumptions are *in* and the other denials of the culprit are *out*. If the backtracker erred in choosing the culprit or denial, presumably a future contradiction will involve D_j and the remaining assumptions in its foundations. However, if the *out*list of the justification (3) is nonempty, D_j will be an assumption, of higher level than the remaining assumptions, and so will be the first to be denied.

The current implementation picks the culprit and denial randomly from the alternatives, and so relies on blind search. Blind search is inadequate for all but the simplest sorts of problems, for typically one needs to make a guided choice among the alternative revisions of beliefs. I will return to this problem in Section 6. *]

Step 4 (Repeat if necessary). If the TMS finds other arguments so that the contradiction node C remains in after the addition of the new justification for D_j, repeat this backtracking procedure. [* Presumably the previous culprit A_i will no longer be an assumption. *] Finally, if the contradiction becomes *out*, then halt; or if no assumptions can be found in C's foundations, notify the problem solving program of an unanalyzable contradiction, then halt.

End of the dependency-directed backtracking procedure.

As an example, consider a program scheduling a meeting, to be held preferably at 10 A.M. in either room 813 or 801.

N-1	TIME(M) = 1000	(SL ( ) (N–2))
N-2	TIME(M) ≠ 1000	
N-3	ROOM(M) = 813	(SL ( ) (N–4)
N-4	ROOM(M) = 801	

With only these justifications, the TMS makes N–l and N–3 *in* and the other two nodes *out.* Now suppose a previously scheduled meeting rules out this combination of time and room for the meeting by supporting a new node with N–1 and N–3 and then declaring this new node to be a contradiction.

N-5   CONTRADICTION   (SL (N-1 N-3) ( ))

The dependency-directed backtracking system traces the foundations of N-5 to find two assumptions, N–l and N–3, both maximal.

N-6	NOGOOD N-1 N-3	(CP N-5 (N-1 N-3) ( ))	*here* ≡ (SL ( ) ( ))
N-4	ROOM(M) = 801	(SL (N-6 N-1) ( ))	

The backtracker creates N-6 which means, in accordance with form (1) of Step 2,

$$\neg(\text{TIME}(M) = 1000 \wedge \text{ROOM}(M) = 813)$$

and justifies N-6 according to form (2) above. It arbitrarily selects N-3 as the culprit, and justifies N-3's only *out* antecedent, N-4, according to form (3) above. Following this, the TMS makes N-1, N-4 and N-6 *in,* and N-2, N-3 and N-5 *out.* N-6 has a CP-justification equivalent to a premise SL-justification, since N-5 depends directly on the two assumptions N-1 and N-3 without any additional intervening nodes.

A further rule now determines that room 801 cannot be used after all, and creates another contradiction node to force a different choice of room.

N-7	CONTRADICTION	(SL (N-4) ( ))	
N-8	NOGOOD N-1	(CP N-7 (N-1) ( ))	*here* ≡ (SL (N-6) ( ))
N-2	TIME(M) ≠ 1000	(SL (N-8) ( ))	

Tracing backwards from N-7 through N-4, N-6 and N-1, the backtracker finds that the contradiction depends on only one assumption, N-1. It creates the no-good node N-8, justifies it with a CP-justification, in this case equivalent to the SL-justification (SL (N-6) ( )), since N-7's foundations contain N-6 and N-1's repercussions do not. The loss of belief in N-1 carried N-5 away as well, for the TMS makes N-2, N-3, N-6 and N-8 *in,* and N-1, N-4, N-5 and N-7 *out.*

5. Dialectical Arguments

Quine (1953) has stressed that we can reject any of our beliefs at the expense of making suitable changes in our other beliefs. For example, we either can change our beliefs to accommodate new observations, or can reject the new observations as hallucinations or mistakes. Notoriously, philosophical arguments have argued almost every philosophical conclusion at the expense of other propositions. Philosophers conduct these arguments in a discipline called dialectical argumentation, in which one argues for a conclusion in two steps; first producing an argument for the conclusion, then producing arguments against the arguments for the opposing conclusion. In this discipline, each debater continually challenges those proposed arguments which he does not like by producing new arguments which either challenge one or more of the premises of the challenged arguments, or which challenge one or more steps of the challenged argument. We can view each debater as following this simplified procedure:

Step 1 (Make an argument). Put forward an argument A for a conclusion based on premises thought to be shared between debaters.

Step 2 (Reply to challenges). When some debater challenges either a premise or a step of A with an argument B, either (1) make a new argument for the conclusion of A, or (2) make an argument for the challenged premise or step of A challenging one of the premises or steps of B.

Step 3 (Repeat). Continue to reply to challenges, or make new arguments.

In this section we show how to organize a problem solving program's use of the TMS into the form of dialectical argumentation. Several important advantages and consequences motivate this. As the first consequence, we can reject any belief in a uniform fashion, simply by producing a new, as yet unchallenged, argument against some step or premise of the argument for the belief. We were powerless to do this with the basic TMS mechanisms in any way other than physically removing justifications from the belief system. This ability entails the second consequence, that we must explicitly provide ways to choose what to believe, to select which of the many possible revisions of our beliefs we will take when confronting new information. Quine has urged the fundamentally pragmatic nature of this question, and we must find mechanisms for stating and using pragmatic belief revision rules. As the third consequence of adopting this dialectical program organization, the belief system becomes additive. The system never discards arguments, but accumulates them and uses them whenever possible. This guides future debates by keeping them from repeating past debates. But the arguments alone comprise the belief system, since we derive the current set of beliefs from these arguments. Hence all changes to beliefs occur by adding new arguments to a monotonically growing store of arguments. Finally, as the fourth consequence, the inference system employed by the program becomes modular. We charge each component of the inference system with arguing for its conclusion and against opposing conclusions. On this view, we make each module be a debater rather than an inference rule.

We implement dialectical argumentation in the TMS by representing steps of arguments both by justifications and by beliefs. To allow us to argue against argument steps, we make these beliefs assumptions.

Suppose some module wants to justify node N with the justification (SL I O). Instead of doing this directly, the module creates a new node, J, representing the statement that I and O SL-justify N; in other words, that belief in each node of I and lack of belief in each node of O constitute a reason for believing in N. The module justifies N with the justification (SL $J+I$ O), where $J+I$ represents the list I augmented by J. The TMS will make N in by reason of this justification only if J is *in*. The module then creates another new node, $\neg J$, representing the statement that J represents a challenged justification. Finally, the module justifies J with the justification (SL ( ) ($\neg J$)). In this way, the module makes a new node to represent the justification as an explicit belief, and then assumes that the justification has not been challenged.

For example, suppose a module wishes to conclude that $X = 3$ from $X + Y = 4$ and $Y = 1$. In the dialectical use of the TMS, it proceeds as follows:

N-1	$X + Y = 4$	...
N-2	$Y = 1$	...
N-3	$X = 3$	(SL (N-4 N-1 N-2) ( ))
N-4	(N-1) AND (N-2) SL-JUSTIFY N-3	(SL ( ) (N-5))
N-5	N-4 IS CHALLENGED	*no justifications yet*

Since N-5 has no justifications, it is *out,* so N-4, and hence N-3, are *in.*

In this discipline, conflicts can be resolved either by challenging premises of arguments, or by challenging those justifications which represent arguments steps. Actually, premise justifications for nodes now become assumptions, for the explicit form of the premise justification is itself assumed. In either case, replies to arguments invalidate certain justifications by justifying the nodes representing the challenges. The proponent of the challenged argument can reply by challenging some justification in the challenging argument.

This way of using the TMS clearly makes blind dependency-directed backtracking useless, since the number of assumptions supporting a node becomes very large. Instead, we must use more refined procedures for identifying certain nodes as the causes of inconsistencies.

6. Assumptions and the Problem of Control

How a problem solver revises its beliefs influences how it acts. Problem solvers typically revise their beliefs when new information (such as the expected effect of an action just taken or an observation just made) contradicts previous beliefs. These inconsistencies may be met by rejecting the belief that the action occurred or that the observation occurred. This might be thought of as the program deciding it was hallucinating. Sometimes, however, we choose to reject the previous belief and say that the action made a change in the world, or that we had made some inappropriate assumption which was corrected by observation. Either of these ways of revising beliefs may be warranted in different circumstances. For example, if during planning we encounter a contradiction by thinking through a proposed sequence of actions, we might decide to reject one of the proposed actions and try another action. On the other hand, if while carrying out a sequence of actions we encounter a contradiction in our beliefs, we might decide that some assumption we had about the world was wrong, rather than believe that we never took the last action. As this example suggests, we might choose to revise our beliefs in several different ways. Since we decide what to do based on what we believe and what we want, our choice of what to believe affects what we choose to do.

How can we guide the problem solver in its choice of what to believe? It must make its choice by approximating the set of possible revisions by the set of assumptions it can change directly, for it cannot see beforehand all the consequences of a change without actually making that change and seeing what happens. We have studied two means by which the problem solver can decide what to believe, the technique of encoding control information into the set of justifications for beliefs, and the technique of using explicit choice rules. Both of these approaches amount to having the reasoner deliberate about what to do. In the first case, the reasoning is "canned." In the second, the reasoning is performed on demand.

We encode some control information into the set of justifications for beliefs by using patterns of non-monotonic justifications. We can think of a non-monotonic justification (SL ( ) (N-2 N-3)) for N-1 as suggesting the order in which these nodes should be believed, N-1 first, then N-2 or N-3 second. On this view, each non-monotonic justification contributes a fragment of control information which guides how the problem solver revises its beliefs. In Sections 6.1 and 6.2, we illustrate how to encode two standard control structures in patterns of justifications, namely default assumptions and sequences of alternatives. These examples should suggest how other control structures such as decision trees or graphs might be encoded.

Even with these fragments of control information, many alternative revisions may appear possible to the problem solver. In such cases, we may wish to provide the problem solver with rules or advice about how to choose which revision to make. If we are clever (or lazy), we might structure the problem solver so that it uses the same language and mechanisms for these revision rules as for rules for making other choices, such as what action to perform next, how to carry out an action, or which goal to pursue next. In de Kleer, Doyle, Steele, and Sussman (1977) my colleagues and I incorporated this suggestion into a general methodology which we call *explicit control of reasoning,* and implemented AMORD, a language of pattern-invoked procedures controlled by the TMS. I am currently studying a problem solver architecture, called a *reflexive interpreter,* in which the problem solver's structure and behavior are themselves domains for reasoning and action by the problem solver (Doyle 1978b). This sort of interpreter represents its own control state to itself explicitly among its beliefs as a *task network* similar to that used in McDermott's (1978) NASL, in which problems or intentions are represented as *tasks*. The interpreter also represents to itself its own structure as a program by means of a set of *plans,* abstract fragments of task network. It represents the important control state of having to make a choice by creating a *choice task,* whose carrying out involves making a choice. The interpreter can then treat this choice task as a problem for solution like any other task. In this framework, we formulate rules for guiding belief revision as plans for carrying out choice tasks. We index these revision plans by aspects of the problem solver state, for example, by the historical state, by the control state, by the state of the problem solution, by the domain, by the action just executed, and by other circumstances. Each revision plan might be viewed as a specialization of the general dependency-directed backtracking procedure. Such refinements of the general backtracking procedure take the form of the beliefs (and thus the problem solver state) into account when deciding which assumptions should be rejected.

6.1. Default Assumptions

Problem solving programs frequently make specifications of default values for the quantities they manipulate, with the intention either of allowing specific reasons for using other values to override the current values, or of rejecting the default if it leads to an inconsistency. (See Reiter (1978) for a lucid exposition of some applications.) The example in Section 1.2 includes such a default assumption for the day of the week of a meeting.

To pick the default value from only two alternatives, we justify the default node non-monotonically on the grounds that the alternative node is *out.* We generalize this binary case to choose a default from a larger set of alternatives. Take $S = \{A_1, ..., A_n\}$ to be the set of alternative nodes, and if desired, let G be a node which represents the reason for making an assumption to choose the default. To make A_i the default, justify it with

(SL (G) $(A_1 \cdots A_{i-1} A_{i+1} \cdots A_n)$)

If no additional information about the value exists, none of the alternative nodes except A_i will have a valid justification, so A_i will be *in* and each of the other alternative nodes will be *out.* Adding a valid justification to some other alternative node causes that alternative to become *in,* and invalidates the support of A_i, so A_i goes *out.* When analyzing a contradiction derived from A_i, the dependency-directed backtracking mechanism recognizes A_i as an assumption because it depends on the other alternative nodes being *out.* The backtracker may then justify one of the other alternative nodes, say A_j, causing A_i to go *out.* This backtracker-produced justification for A_j will have the form

(SL <various nodes> <remainder nodes>)

where <remainder nodes> is the set of A_k's remaining in S after A_i and A_j are taken away. In effect, the backtracker removes the default node from the set of alternatives, and makes a new default assumption from the remaining alternatives. As a concrete example, our scheduling program might default a meeting day as follows:

N-1	PREFER W. TO M. OR F.	...
N-2	DAY(M) = MONDAY	
N-3	DAY(M) = WEDNESDAY	(SL (N-1) (N-2 N-4))
N-4	DAY(M) = FRIDAY	

The program assumes Wednesday to be the day of the meeting M, with Monday and Friday as alternatives. The TMS will make Wednesday the chosen day until the program gives a valid reason for taking Monday or Friday instead.

We use a slightly different set of justifications if the complete set of alternatives cannot be known in advance but must be discovered piecemeal. This ability to extend the set of alternatives is necessary, for example, when the default is a number, due to the large set of possible alternatives. Retaining the above notation, we represent the negation of St(A_i) with a new node, $\neg A_i$. We arrange for A_i to be believed if $\neg A_i$ is *out*, and set up justifications so that if A_j is distinct from A_i, A_j supports $\neg A_i$. We justify A_i with

(SL (G) ($\neg A_i$)),

and justify $\neg A_i$ with a justification of the form

(SL (A_j) ( ))

for each alternative A_j distinct from A_i. As before, A_i will be assumed if no reasons for using any other alternative exist. Furthermore, new alternatives can be added to the set S simply by giving $\neg A_i$ a new justification corresponding to the new alternative. As before, if the problem solving program justifies an unselected alternative, the TMS will make the default node *out*. Backtracking, however, has a new effect. If A_i supports a contradiction, the backtracker may justify $\neg A_i$ so as to make A_i become *out*. When this happens, the TMS has no way to select an alternative to take the place of the default assumption. The extensible structure requires an external mechanism to construct a new default assumption whenever the current default is ruled out. For example, a family planning program might make assumptions about the number of children in a family as follows:

N-1	PREFER 2 CHILDREN	...
N-2	#-CHILDREN(F) = 2	(SL (N-1) (N-3))
N-3	#-CHILDREN(F) ≠ 2	(SL (N-4) ( ))
		(SL (N-5) ( ))
		(SL (N-6) ( ))
		(SL (N-7) ( ))
N-4	#-CHILDREN(F) = 0	

N-5   #-CHILDREN(F) = 1
N-6   #-CHILDREN(F) = 3
N-7   #-CHILDREN(F) = 4

With this system of justifications, the TMS would make N-2 *in*. If the planning program finds some compelling reason for having 5 children, it would have to create a new node to represent this fact, along with a new justification for N-3 in terms of this new node.

6.2. Sequences of Alternatives

Linearly ordered sets of alternatives add still more control information to a default assumption structure, namely the order in which the alternatives should be tried. This extra heuristic information might be used, for example, to order selections of the day of the week for a meeting, of a planning strategy, or of the state of a transistor in a proposed circuit analysis.

We represent a sequence of alternatives by a controlled progression of default assumptions. Take $\{A_1, ..., A_n\}$ to be the heuristically ordered sequence of alternative nodes, and let G be a node which represents the reason for this heuristic ordering. We justify each A_i with

(SL (G ¬A_{i-1}) (¬A_i))

A_1 will be selected initially, and as the problem solver rejects successive alternatives by justifying their negations, the TMS will believe the successive alternatives in turn. For example, our scheduling program might have:

N-1	SEQUENCE N-2 N-4 N-6	...
N-2	DAY(M) = WEDNESDAY	(SL (N-1) (N-3))
N-3	DAY(M) ≠ WEDNESDAY	
N-4	DAY(M) = THURSDAY	(SL (N-1 N-3) (N-5))
N-5	DAY(M) ≠ THURSDAY	
N-6	DAY(M) = TUESDAY	(SL (N-1 N-5) ( ))

This would guide the choice of day for the meeting M to Wednesday, Thursday and Tuesday, in that order.

Note that this way of sequencing through alternatives allows no direct way for the problem solving program to reconsider previously rejected alternatives. If, say, we wish to use special case rules to correct imprudent choices of culprits made by the backtracking system, we need a more complicated structure to represent linearly ordered alternatives. We create three new nodes for each alternative A_i: PA_i, which means that A_i is a possible alternative; NSA_i, which means that A_i is not the currently selected alternative; and ROA_i, which means that A_i is a ruled-out alternative. We suggest members for the set of alternatives by justifying each PA_i with the reason for including A_i in the set of alternatives. We leave ROA_i unjustified, and justify each A_i and NSA_i with

$$A_i: \quad (SL \ (PA_i \ NSA_1 \bullet \bullet \bullet NSA_{i-1}) \ (ROA_i))$$

$$NSA_i: \quad (SL \ (\ ) \ (PA_i))$$

$$(SL \ (ROA_i) \ (\ ))$$

Here the justification for A_i is valid if and only if A_i is an alternative, no better alternative is currently selected, and A_i is not ruled out. The two justifications for NSA_i mean that either A_i is not a valid alternative, or that A_i is ruled out. With this structure, different parts of the problem solver can independently rule in or rule out an alternative by justifying the appropriate A or ROA node. In addition, we can add new alternatives to the end of such a linear order by constructing justifications as specified above for the new nodes representing the new alternative.

7. Discussion

The TMS solves part of the belief revision problem, and provides a mechanism for making non-monotonic assumptions. Artificial intelligence researchers recognized early on that AI systems must make assumptions, and many of their systems employed some mechanism for this purpose. Unfortunately, the related problem of belief revision received somewhat less study. Hayes (1973) emphasized the importance of the belief revision problem, but most work on revising beliefs appears to have been restricted to the study of backtracking algorithms operating on rather simple systems of states and actions. Minsky (1980) presents a theory of memory which includes a more general view of reasoning exhibiting similarities to the view presented here. McDermott and I (1980) attempt to formalize the logic underlying the TMS with what we call *non-monotonic logic*.

Many philosophers study evaluative criteria for judging which belief revisions are best, based on the connections between beliefs. Quine and Ullian (1978) survey this area, Rescher (1964) presents a framework for belief revision motivated by Quine's (1953, 1970) "minimum mutilation" principle, and Lewis (1973) proposes means for filling in this framework. Scriven (1959) relates these questions to the problem of historical explanation in a way quite reminiscent of our non-monotonic arguments for beliefs.

I have used the term "belief" freely in the preceding sections, so much so that one might think the title "Belief Revision System" more appropriate, if no less ambitious, than "Truth Maintenance System." Belief, however, for many people carries with it a concept of grading, yet the TMS has no nontrivial grading of beliefs. Perhaps a more accurate label would be "opinion revision system," where I follow Dennett (1978) in distinguishing between binary judgmental assertions (opinions) and graded underlying feelings (beliefs). As Dennett explains, this distinction permits description of those circumstances in which reasoned arguments force one to assert a conclusion, even though one does not believe the conclusion. Hesitation, self-deception, and other complex states of belief and opinion can be described in this way. I feel it particularly apt to characterize the TMS as revising opinions rather than beliefs. Choosing what to "believe" in the TMS involves making judgments, rather than continuously accreting strengths or confidences. A single new piece of information may lead to sizable changes in the set of opinions, where new beliefs typically change old ones only slightly. I also find this distinction between binary judgments and graded approximations useful in distinguishing non-monotonic reasoning from imprecise reasoning, such as that modeled by Zadeh's (1975) fuzzy logic.

Shrobe (1979, and in personal communications) has suggested modifying the TMS to use multiple supporting-justifications whenever several well-founded arguments can be found for a node, to signal the problem solver whenever the argument for some node changes, and to develop a language for describing and efficiently recognizing patterns in arguments for nodes, well-founded or otherwise. Other worthy problems include how to incorporate truth maintenance techniques into "virtual-copy" representational systems (Fahlman 1979) and making the TMS more incremental. The TMS normally avoids examining the entire data base when revising beliefs, and instead examines only the repercussions of the changed nodes, but can leave most of them in their original state after finding alternate non-circular arguments for the supposedly changed nodes. Moreover, apparently unsatisfiable circularities can occur which require examining nodes not included in these repercussions in order to construct the set of beliefs. One might hope to find clues about how to organize the TMS's analysis of potential arguments for beliefs by studying what types of arguments humans find easy or difficult to understand. Statman (1974) indicates that humans have difficulty following arguments which have many back-references to distant statements, and attempts to formalize some notions of the complexity of proofs using measures based on the topology of the proof graph.

One final note: the overhead required to record justifications for every program belief might seem excessive. Some of this burden might be eliminated. However, the pressing issue is not the expense of keeping records of the sources of beliefs. Rather, we must consider the expense of *not* keeping these records. If we throw away information about derivations, we may be condemning ourselves to continually rederiving information in large searches caused by changing irrelevant assumptions. This original criticism of MICROPLANNER (in Sussman and McDermott 1972) applies to the context mechanisms of CONNIVER and QA4 as well. If we discard the sources of beliefs, we may make impossible the correction of errors in large, evolving data bases. We will find such techniques not just desirable, but necessary, when we attempt to build truly complex programs and systems. Lest we follow the tradition of huge, incomprehensible systems which spawned software engineering, we must, in Gerald Sussman's term, make "responsible" programs which can explain their actions and conclusions to a user. (Cf. Rich, Shrobe, and Waters 1979.)

Acknowledgements

This chapter abbreviates Doyle (1979), and is based on a master's thesis submitted to the department of Electrical Engineering and Computer Science of the Massachusetts Institute of Technology on May 12, 1977.[2] I implemented the first of many versions of the TMS (see Doyle 1976) as an extension (in several ways) of the "fact garbage collector" of Stallman and Sussman's (1977) ARS electronic circuit analysis program. I thank Gerald Jay Sussman (thesis advisor), Johan de Kleer, Scott Fahlman, Philip London, David McAllester, Drew McDermott, Marvin Minsky, Howard Shrobe, Richard M. Stallman, James Stansfield, Guy L. Steele, Jr., and Alan Thompson for ideas and comments. de Kleer, Steele, Marilyn Matz, Richard Fikes, Randall Davis, Shrobe, and the referees of the journal *Artificial Intelligence* gave me valuable editorial advice. I thank the Fannie and John Hertz Foundation for supporting my research with a graduate fellowship.

Notes

1. The term "truth maintenance system" not only sounds like Orwellian Newspeak, but also is a misnomer. I retained it at the time partly for consistency with my previous publications, and partly for lack of a better term. Names involving belief or opinion seemed inapt in light of the use of nodes to represent desires, intentions, and procedures as well as beliefs, and I finally found the more accurate term "reason maintenance system" or RMS shortly after publication of this paper. While the new name enjoys wide usage, the original predominates through subsequent reinforcements, e.g., de Kleer (1986).

2. Large subsequent literatures on both reason maintenance and nonmonotonic logics contribute improved algorithms, systems, formalizations, and understanding of the issues. My own subsequent work has returned to these issues again and again. McDermott and I (1980) constructed our initial nonmonotonic logic in 1978. My doctoral thesis (Doyle 1980) used dialectical deliberation in addressing issues of reasoned control of reasoning and action, and also moved closer to the memory model of Minsky (1980) by abandoning, at least to some extent, the—call it hope, call it fiction—coercion of all types of mental attitudes and substructures into things called "beliefs" that sometimes tortures my English in the preceding sections. My mathematical theory of reasoned assumptions (Doyle 1983, 1994a) completed this move, providing, among other things, variable degrees of well-foundedness, a formally justified critique of the TMS, and close formal connections between the structures of reasons and reasoned states on the one hand and economic preferences and equilibria on the other, connections that in some ways vindicate the association of nonmonotonic reasons and control so prominent in the preceding. I later elaborated on these economic connections in (Doyle 1988, 1992b), and in collaboration with Michael Wellman (Doyle and Wellman 1991), the latter work explicating the ordinary ambiguity of reasoned states as a reflection of the general impossibility of ideally rational social choice procedures. These economic considerations also help relate reasons and reason maintenance with recent theories of belief revision in philosophical logic (Doyle 1991, Doyle 1992a). My most recent return (Doyle and Wellman 1990, Doyle 1994b) seeks to carry out the promise of (Doyle 1983) by constructing reason maintenance *services* that provide rational, distributed, piecemeal

revisions of information, with effort guided by balancing supply of resources and demand for revisions. (Many of these references may be obtained electronically through my home page http://www.medg.lcs.mit.edu/people/doyle/doyle.html.)

Doyle (1979) bore a dedication to the memory of John Sheridan Mac Nerney. For this reprinting, I extend the dedication to include the memories of David G. Bourgin and Jürgen Schmidt as well.

23

Circumscription
A Form of Non-Monotonic Reasoning

John McCarthy

1. Introduction—The Qualification Problem

McCarthy (1960) proposed a program with 'common sense' that would represent what it knows (mainly) by sentences in a suitable logical language. It would decide what to do by deducing a conclusion that it should perform a certain act. Performing the act would create a new situation, and it would again decide what to do. This requires representing both knowledge about the particular situation and general common sense knowledge as sentences of logic.

The 'qualification problem,' immediately arose in representing general common sense knowledge. It seemed that in order to fully represent the conditions for the successful performance of an action, an impractical and implausible number of qualifications would have to be included in the sentences expressing them. For example, the successful use of a boat to cross a river requires, if the boat is a rowboat, that the oars and rowlocks be present and unbroken, and that they fit each other. Many other qualifications can be added, making the rules for using a rowboat almost impossible to apply, and yet anyone will still be able to think of additional requirement not yet stated.

Circumscription is a rule of conjecture that can be used by a person or program for 'jumping to certain conclusions.' Namely, *the objects that can be shown to have a certain property P by reasoning from certain facts A are all the objects that satisfy P*. More generally, circumscription can be used to conjecture that the tuples <*x, y,* …, *z*> that can be shown to satisfy a relation *P*(*x, y,* …, *z*) are all the tuples satisfying this relation. Thus we *circumscribe* the set of relevant tuples.

We can postulate that a boat can be used to cross a river unless 'something' prevents it. Then circumscription may be used to conjecture that the only entities that can prevent the use of the boat are those whose existence follows from the facts at hand. If no lack of oars or other circumstance preventing boat use is deducible, then the boat is concluded to be usable. The correctness of this conclusion depends on our having 'taken into account' all relevant facts when we made the circumscription.

Circumscription formalizes several processes of human informal reasoning. For example, common sense reasoning is ordinarily ready to jump to the conclusion that a tool can be used for its intended purpose unless something prevents its use. Considered purely extensionally, such a statement conveys no information; it seems merely to assert that a tool can be used for its intended purpose unless it can't. Heuristically, the statement is not just a tautologous disjunction; it suggests forming a plan to use the tool.

Even when a program does not reach its conclusions by manipulating sentences in a formal language, we can often profitably analyze its behavior by considering it to *believe* certain sentences when it is in certain states, and we can study how these *ascribed beliefs* change with time (see McCarthy 1979). When we do such analyses, we again discover that successful people and programs must jump to such conclusions.

2. The Need for Non-Monotonic Reasoning

We cannot get circumscriptive reasoning capability by adding sentences to an axiomatization or by adding an ordinary rule of inference to mathematical logic. This is because the well known systems of mathematical logic have the following *monotonicity property*. If a sentence q follows from a collection A of sentences and $A \subseteq B$, then q follows from B. In the notation of proof theory: if $A \vdash q$ and $A \subseteq B$, then $B \vdash q$. Indeed a proof from the premisses A is a sequence of sentences each of which is either a premiss, an axiom or follows from a subset of the sentences occurring earlier in the proof by one of the rules of inference. Therefore, a proof from A can also serve as a proof from B. The semantic notion of entailment is also monotonic; we say that A entails q (written $A \models q$) if q is true in all models of A. But if $A \models q$ and $A \subset B$, then every model of B is also a model of A, which shows that $B \models q$.

Circumspection is a formalized *rule of conjecture* that can be used along with the *rules of inference* of first order logic. *Predicate circumscription* assumes that entities satisfy a given predicate only if they have to on the basis of a collection of facts. *Domain circumscription* conjectures that the 'known' entities are all there are. It turns out that domain circumscription, previously called *minimal inference,* can be subsumed under predicate circumscription.

We will argue using examples that humans use such 'non-monotonic' reasoning and that it is required for intelligent behavior. The default case reasoning of many computer programs (Reiter 1980) and the use of THNOT in MICROPLANNER (Sussman 1971) programs are also examples of non-monotonic reasoning, but possibly of a different kind from those discussed in this paper. Hewitt (1972) gives the basic ideas of the PLANNER approach.

The result of applying circumscription to a collection A of facts is a sentence schema that asserts that the only tuples satisfying a predicate $P(x, ..., z)$ are those whose doing so follows from the sentences of A. Since adding more sentences to A might make P applicable to more tuples, circumscription is not monotonic. Conclusions derived from circumscription are conjectures that A includes all the relevant facts and that the objects whose existence follows from A are all the relevant objects.

A heuristic program might use circumscription in various ways. Suppose it circumscribes some facts and makes a plan on the basis of the conclusions reached. It might immediately carry out the plan, or be more cautious and look for additional facts that might require modifying it.

Before introducing the formalism, we informally discuss a well known problem whose solution seems to involve such non-monotonic reasoning.

3. Missionaries and Cannibals

The *Missionaries and Cannibals* puzzle, much used in AI, contains more than enough detail to illustrate many of the issues.

> Three missionaries and three cannibals come to a river. A rowboat that seats two is available. If the cannibals ever outnumber the missionaries on either bank of the river, the missionaries will be eaten. How shall they cross the river?

Obviously the puzzler is expected to devise a strategy of rowing the boat back and forth that gets them all across and avoids the disaster.

Amarel (1971) considered several representations of the problem and discussed criteria whereby the following representation is preferred for purposes of AI, because it leads to the smallest state space that must be explored to find the solution. A state is a triple comprising the numbers of missionaries, cannibals and boats on the starting bank of the river. The initial state is 331, the desired final state is 000, and one solution is given by the sequence (331, 220, 321, 300, 311, 110, 221, 020, 031, 010, 021, 000).

We are not presently concerned with the heuristics of the problem but rather with the correctness of the reasoning that goes from the English statement of the problem to Amarel's state space representation. A generally intelligent computer program should be able to carry out this reasoning. Of course, there are the well known difficulties in making computers understand English, but suppose the English sentences describing the problem have already been rather directly translated into first order logic. The correctness of Amarel's representation is not an ordinary logical consequence of these sentences for two further reasons.

First, nothing has been stated about the properties of boats or even the fact that rowing across the river doesn't change the numbers of missionaries or cannibals or the capacity of the boat. Indeed it hasn't been stated that situations change as a result of action. These facts follow from common sense knowledge, so let us imagine that common sense knowledge, or at least the relevant part of it, is also expressed in first order logic.

The second reason we can't *deduce* the propriety of Amarel's representation is deeper. Imagine giving someone the problem, and after he puzzles for a while, he suggests going upstream half a mile and crossing on a bridge. "What bridge," you say. "No bridge is mentioned in the statement of the problem." And this dunce replies, "Well, they don't say there isn't a bridge." You look at the English and even at the translation of the English into first order logic, and you must admit that "they don't say" there is no bridge. So you modify the problem to exclude bridges and pose it again, and the dunce proposes a helicopter, and after you exclude that, he proposes a winged horse or that the others hang onto the outside of the boat while two row.

You now see that while a dunce, he is an inventive dunce. Despairing of getting him to accept the problem in the proper puzzler's spirit, you tell him the solution. To your further annoyance, he attacks your solution on the grounds that the boat might have a leak or lack oars. After you rectify that omission from the statement of the problem, he suggests that a sea monster may swim up the river and may swallow the boat. Again you are frustrated, and you look for a mode of reasoning that will settle his hash once and for all.

In spite of our irritation with the dunce, it would be cheating to put into the statement of the problem that there is no other way to cross the river than using the boat and that nothing can go wrong with the boat. A human doesn't need such an ad hoc narrowing of the problem, and indeed the only watertight way to do it might amount to specifying the Amarel representation in English. Rather we want to avoid the excessive qualification and get the

Amarel representation by common sense reasoning as humans ordinarily do.

Circumscription is one candidate for accomplishing this. It will allow us to conjecture that no relevant objects exist in certain categories except those whose existence follows from the statement of the problem and common sense knowledge. When we *circumscribe* the first order logic statement of the problem together with the common sense facts about boats etc., we will be able to conclude that there is no bridge or helicopter. "Aha," you say, "but there won't be any oars either." No, we get out of that as follows: It is a part of common knowledge that a boat can be used to cross a river *unless there is something wrong with it or something else prevents using it,* and if our facts do not require that there be something that prevents crossing the river, circumscription will generate the conjecture that there isn't. The price is introducing as entities in our language the 'somethings' that may prevent the use of the boat.

If the statement of the problem were extended to mention a bridge, then the circumscription of the problem statement would no longer permit showing the non-existence of a bridge, i.e., a conclusion that can be drawn from a smaller collection of facts can no longer be drawn from a larger. This non-monotonic character of circumscription is just what we want for this kind of problem. The statement, "There is a bridge a mile upstream, and the boat has a leak." doesn't contradict the text of the problem, but its addition invalidates the Amarel representation.

In the usual sort of puzzle, there is a convention that there are no additional objects beyond those mentioned in the puzzle or whose existence is deducible from the puzzle and common sense knowledge. The convention can be explicated as applying circumscription to the puzzle statement and a certain part of common sense knowledge. However, if one really were sitting by a river bank and these six people came by and posed their problem, one wouldn't take the circumscription for granted, but one *would* consider the result of circumscription as a hypothesis. In puzzles, circumscription seems to be a rule of inference, while in life it is a rule of conjecture.

Some have suggested that the difficulties might be avoided by introducing probabilities. They suggest that the existence of a bridge is improbable. The whole situation involving cannibals with the postulated properties cannot be regarded as having a probability, so it is hard to take seriously the conditional probability of a bridge given the hypotheses. More to the point, we mentally propose to ourselves the normal non-bridge, non-sea-monster interpretation *before* considering these extraneous possibilities, let alone their probabilities, i.e., we usually don't even introduce the sample space in which these possibilities are assigned whatever probabilities one might consider them to have. Therefore, regardless of our knowledge of probabilities, we need a way of formulating the normal situation from the statement of the facts, and non-monotonic reasoning seems to be required. The same considerations seem to apply to fuzzy logic.

Using circumscription requires that common sense knowledge be expressed in a form that says a boat can be used to cross rivers unless there is something that prevents its use. In particular, it looks like we must introduce into our ontology (the things that exist) a category that includes something wrong with a boat or a category that includes something that may prevent its use. Incidentally, once we have decided to admit *something wrong with the boat,* we are inclined to admit a *lack of oars* as such a something and to ask questions like, "Is a lack of oars all that is wrong with the boat?"

Some philosophers and scientists may be reluctant to introduce such *things,* but since ordinary language allows "something wrong with the boat" we shouldn't be hasty in excluding it. Making a suitable formalism is likely to be technically difficult as well as philosophically problematical, but we must try.

We challenge anyone who thinks he can avoid such entities to express in his favorite formalism, "Besides leakiness, there is something else wrong with the boat." A good solution would avoid counter-factuals as this one does.

Circumscription may help understand natural language, because if the use of natural language involves something like circumscription, it is understandable that the expression of general common sense facts in natural language will be difficult without some form of non-monotonic reasoning.

4. The Formalism of Circumscription

Let A be a sentence of first order logic containing a predicate symbol $P(x_1, \ldots, x_n)$ which we will write $P(\bar{x})$. We write $A(\Phi)$ for the result of replacing all occurrences of P in A by the predicate expression O. (As well as predicate symbols, suitable A-expressions are allowed as predicate expressions).

Definition. The *circumscription* of P in $A(P)$ is the sentence schema

$$A(\Phi) \wedge \forall \bar{x}.(\Phi(\bar{x}) \supset P(\bar{x})) \supset \forall \bar{x}. (P(\bar{x}) \supset \Phi(\bar{x})). \tag{1}$$

(1) can be regarded as asserting that the only tuples $(\bar{x})$ that satisfy P are those that have to—assuming the sentence A. Namely, (1) contains a predicate parameter Φ for which we may substitute an arbitrary predicate expression. (If we were using second order logic, there would be a quantifier $\forall \Phi$ in front of (1).) Since (1) is an implication, we can assume both conjuncts on the left, and (1) lets us conclude the sentence on the right. The first conjunct $A(\Phi)$ expresses the assumption that Φ satisfies the conditions satisfied by P. and the second $\forall \bar{x} . (\Phi(\bar{x}) \supset P(\bar{x}))$ expresses the assumption that the entities satisfying Φ are a subset of those that satisfy P. The conclusion asserts the converse of the second conjunct which tells us that in this case, Φ and P must coincide.

We write $A \vdash_\rho q$ if the sentence q can be obtained by deduction from the result of circumscribing P in A. As we shall see $\vdash$ is a nonmonotonic form of inference, which we shall call *circumscriptive inference.*

A slight generalization allows circumscribing several predicates jointly; thus jointly circumscribing P and Q in $A(P, Q)$ leads to

$$A(\Phi, \Psi) \wedge \forall \bar{x}.(\Phi(\bar{x}) \supset P(\bar{x})) \wedge \forall \bar{y}\ (\Psi(\bar{y}) \supset Q(\bar{y}))$$
$$\supset \forall \bar{x}.\ (P(\bar{x}) \supset \Phi(\bar{x})) \wedge \forall \bar{y}.(Q(\bar{y}) \supset \Psi(\bar{y})) \tag{2}$$

in which we can simultaneously substitute for Φ and Ψ. The relation $A \vdash_{P,Q} q$ is defined in a corresponding way. Although we do not give examples of joint circumscription in this chapter, we believe it will be important in some AI applications.

Consider the following examples:

Example 1. In the blocks world, the sentence A may be

$$isblock\ A \wedge isblock\ B \wedge isblock\ C \tag{3}$$

asserting that A, B and C are blocks. Circumscribing $isblock$ in (3) gives the schema

$$\Phi(A) \wedge \Phi(B) \wedge \Phi(C) \wedge \forall x\ (\Phi(x) \supset isblock\ x) \supset \forall x.(isblock\ x \supset \Phi(x)). \tag{4}$$

If we now substitute

$$\Phi(x) \equiv (x = A \vee x = B \vee x = C) \tag{5}$$

into (4) and use (3), the left side of the implication is seen to be true, and this gives

$$\forall x.(isblock\ x \supset (x = A \vee x = B \vee x = C)), \tag{6}$$

which asserts that the only blocks are A, B and C, i.e., just those objects that (3) requires to be blocks. This example is rather trivial, because (3) provides no way of generating new blocks from old ones. However, it shows that circumscriptive inference is non-monotonic since if we adjoin $isblock\ D$ to (3), we will no longer be able to infer (6).

Example 2. Circumscribing the disjunction

$$isblock\ A \vee isblock\ B \tag{7}$$

leads to

$$(\Phi(A) \vee \Phi(B)) \wedge \forall x.\ (\Phi(x) \supset isblock\ x) \supset \forall x.(isblock\ x \vee \Phi(x)). \tag{8}$$

We may then substitute successively $\Phi(x) \equiv (x = A)$ and $\Phi(x) \equiv (x = B)$, and these give respectively

$$(A = A \vee A = B) \wedge \forall x.\ (x = A \supset isblock\ x) \supset \forall x\ .\ (isblock\ x \supset x = A), \tag{9}$$

which simplifies to

$$isblock\ A \supset \forall x.(isblock\ x \supset x = A) \tag{10}$$

and

$$(B = A \vee B = B) \wedge \forall x.(x = B \supset isblock\ x) \supset \forall x.(isblock\ x \supset x = B), \tag{11}$$

which simplifies to

$$isblock\ B \supset \forall x.(isblock\ x \supset x = B). \tag{12}$$

(10), (12) and (7) yield

$$\forall x.(isblock\ x \supset x = A) \vee \forall x.(isblock\ x \supset x = B), \tag{13}$$

which asserts that either A is the only block or B is the only block.

Example 3. Consider the following algebraic axioms for natural numbers, i.e., non-negative integers, appropriate when we aren't supposing that natural numbers are the only objects.

$$isnatnum\ 0 \land \forall x.\ (isnatnum\ x \supset isnatnum\ succ\ x). \tag{14}$$

Circumscribing *isnatnum* in (14) yields

$$\Phi(0) \land \forall x.(\Phi(x) \supset \Phi(succ\ x)) \land \forall x.(\Phi(x) \supset isnatnum\ x)$$
$$\supset \forall x.(isnatnum\ x \supset \Phi(x)). \tag{15}$$

(15) asserts that the only natural numbers are those objects that (14) forces to be natural numbers, and this is essentially the usual axiom schema of induction. We can get closer to the usual schema by substituting $\Phi(x) \equiv \Psi(x) \land isnatnum\ x$. This and (14) make the second conjunct drop out giving

$$\Psi(0) \land \forall x.(\Psi(x) \supset \Psi(succ\ x)) \supset \forall x.(isnatnum\ x \supset \Psi(x)). \tag{16}$$

Example 4. Returning to the blocks world, suppose we have a predicate *on*(*x, y, s*) asserting that block *x* is on block *y* in situation *s*. Suppose we have another predicate *above*(*x, y, s*) which asserts that block *x* is above block *y* in situation *s*. We may write

$$\forall x\ y\ s.(on(x, y, s) \supset above(x, y, s)) \tag{17}$$

and

$$\forall x\ y\ z\ s.(above(x, y, s) \land above(y, z, s) \supset above(x, z, s)), \tag{18}$$

i.e. *above* is a transitive relation. Circumscribing *above* in (17) and (18) gives

$$\forall x\ y\ s.\ (on(x, y, s) \supset \Phi(x, y, s))$$
$$\land \forall x\ y\ z\ s.\ (\Phi(x, y, s) \land \Phi(y, z, s) \supset \Phi(x, z, s))$$
$$\land \forall x\ y\ s.\ (\Phi(x, y, s) \supset above(x, y, s))$$
$$\supset \forall x\ y\ s.\ (above(x, y, s) \supset \Phi(x, y, s)) \tag{19}$$

which tells us that *above* is the transitive closure of *on*.

In the preceding two examples, the schemas produced by circumscription play the role of axiom schemas rather than being just conjectures.

5. Domain Circumscription

The form of circumscription described in this chapter generalizes an earlier version called *minimal inference*. Minimal inference has a semantic counterpart called *minimal entailment,* and both are discussed in McCarthy (1977) and more extensively in Davis (1980). The general idea of minimal entailment is that a sentence *q* is minimally entailed by an axiom *A*, written $A \models_m q$, if *q* is true in all *minimal models* of *A*, where one model is considered less than another if they agree on common elements, but the domain of the larger may contain elements not in the domain of the smaller. We shall call the earlier form *domain circumscription* to contrast it with the *predicate circumscription* discussed in this chapter.

The domain circumscription of the sentence A is the sentence

$$Axiom(\Phi) \wedge A^{\Phi} \supset \forall x.\Phi(x). \tag{20}$$

where A^{Φ} is the relativization of A with respect to Φ and is formed by replacing each universal quantifier $\forall x$. in A by $\forall x$. $\Phi(x) \supset$ and each existential quantifier $\exists x$. by $\exists x.\Phi(x) \wedge$. $Axiom(\Phi)$ is the conjunction of sentences $\Phi(a)$ for each constant a and sentences $\forall x$. $(\Phi(x) \supset \Phi(f(x)))$ for each function symbol f and the corresponding sentences for functions of higher arities.

Domain circumscription can be reduced to predicate circumscription by relativizing A with respect to a new one place predicate called (say) *all*, then circumscribing *all* in $A^{all} \wedge Axiom(all)$, thus getting

$$Axiom(\Phi) \wedge A^{\Phi} \wedge \forall x.(\Phi(x) \supset all(x)) \supset \forall x.(all(x) \supset \Phi(x)). \tag{21}$$

Now we justify our using the name *all* by adding the axiom $\forall x.all(x)$ so that (21) then simplifies precisely to (20).

In the case of the natural numbers, the domain circumscription of true, the identically true sentence, again leads to the axiom schema of induction. Here *Axiom* does all the work, because it asserts that 0 is in the domain and that the domain is closed under the successor operation.

6. The Model Theory of Predicate Circumscription

This treatment is similar to Davis's (1980) treatment of domain circumscription. Pat Hayes (1979) pointed out that the same ideas would work.

The intuitive idea of circumscription is saying that a tuple $\bar{x}$ satisfies the predicate P only if it has to. It has to satisfy P if this follows from the sentence A. The model theoretic counterpart of circumscription is *minimal entailment*. A sentence q is minimally entailed by A, iff q is true in all minimal models of A, where a model is minimal if as few as possible tuples $\bar{x}$ satisfy the predicate P. More formally, this works out as follows.

Definition. Let $M(A)$ and $N(A)$ be models of the sentence A. We say that *M is a submodel of N in P,* writing $M \leqslant_p N$, if M and N have the same domain, all other predicate symbols in A besides P have the same extensions in M and N, but the extension of P in M is included in its extension in N.

Definition. A model M of A is called *minimal* in P iff $M' \leqslant_p M$ only if $M' = M$. As discussed by Davis (1980), minimal models do not always exist.

Definition. We say that A *minimally entails q with respect to P,* written $A \models_p q$ provided q is true in all models of A that are minimal in P.

Theorem. *Any instance of the circumscription of P in A is true in all models of A minimal in P, i.e., is minimally entailed by A in P.*

Proof. Let M be a model of A minimal in P. Let P' be a predicate satisfying the left side of (1) when substituted for Φ. By the second conjunct of the left side, P is an extension of P'. If the right side of (1) were not satisfied, P

would be a proper extension of P'. In that case, we could get a proper sub-model M' of M by letting M' agree with M on all predicates except P and agree with P' on P. This would contradict the assumed minimality of M.

Corollary. If $A \vdash_p q$, then $A \models_p q$.

While we have discussed minimal entailment in a single predicate P, the relation $<_{P,Q}$, models minimal in P and Q. and $\models_{P,Q}$ have corresponding properties and a corresponding relation to the syntactic notion $\vdash_{P,Q}$ mentioned earlier.

7. More on Blocks

The axiom

$$\forall x\, y\, s.\ (\forall z.\ \neg\, prevents(z, move(x, y), s) \supset on(x, y, result(move(x, y), s))) \qquad (22)$$

states that unless something prevents it, x is on y in the situation that results from the action $move(x, y)$.

We now list various 'things' that may prevent this action.

$$\forall x\, y\, s\,.\ (\neg\, isblock\ x \vee \neg\, isblock\ y$$
$$\supset prevents(NONBLOCK, move(x, y), s)) \qquad (23)$$

$$\forall x\, y\, s.\ (\neg\, clear(x, s) \vee \neg clear(y, s)$$
$$\supset prevents(COVERED, move(x, y), s)) \qquad (24)$$

$$\forall x\, y\, s.\ (tooheavy\ x \supset prevents(weight\ x, move(x, y),s)). \qquad (25)$$

Let us now suppose that a heuristic program would like to move block A onto block C in a situation s0. The program should conjecture from (22) that the action $move(A, C)$ would have the desired effect, so it must try to establish $\forall z.\ \neg\, prevents(z, move(A, C), s0)$. The predicate $\lambda z.prevents(z, move(A, C), s0)$ can be circumscribed in the conjunction of the sentences resulting from specializing (23), (24) and (25), and this gives

$$(\neg isblock\ A \vee \neg\, isblock\ C \supset \Phi(NONBLOCK))$$
$$\wedge\ (\neg clear(A, s0) \vee \neg clear(C, s0) \supset \Phi(COVERED))$$
$$\wedge\ (tooheavy\ A \supset \Phi(weight\ A))$$
$$\wedge\ \forall z.(\Phi(z), \supset\ prevents(z, move(A, C), s0))$$
$$\supset \forall z\,.\ (prevents(z, move\ (A, C), s0) \supset \Phi(z)) \qquad (26)$$

which says that the only things that can prevent the move are the phenomena described in (23)–(25). Whether (26) is true depends on how good the program was in finding all the relevant statements. Since the program wants to show that nothing prevents the move, it must set $\forall z.\ (\Phi(z) \equiv false)$, after which (26) simplifies to

$$(isblock\ A \wedge isblock\ B \wedge clear(A,s0) \wedge clear(B,s0) \wedge \neg tooheavy\ A$$
$$\supset \forall z\,.\ \neg\, prevents(z, move(A, C), s0). \qquad (27)$$

We suppose that the premises of this implication are to be obtained as follows:

1) *isblock A* and *isblock B* are explicitly asserted.

2) Suppose that the only *on*ness assertion explicitly given for situation $s0$ is $on(A, B. s0)$. Circumscription of $\lambda x\, y\,.\, on(x, y, s0)$ in this assertion gives

$$\Phi(A,B) \wedge \forall x\, y.(\Phi(x,y) \supset on(x,y, s0)) \supset \forall x\, y.(on(x,y,s0) \supset \Phi(x,y)) \tag{28}$$

and taking $\Phi(x, y) \equiv x = A \wedge y = B$ yields

$$\forall x\, y.(on(x, y, s0) \supset x = A \wedge y = B). \tag{29}$$

Using

$$\forall x\, s\,.\, (clear(x, s) \equiv \forall y\,.\, \neg\, on(y, x, s)) \tag{30}$$

as the definition of *clear* yields the second two desired premisses.

3) $\neg\, tooheavy(x)$ might be explicitly present or it might also be conjectured by a circumscription assuming that if x were too heavy, the facts would establish it.

Circumscription may also be convenient for asserting that when a block is moved, everything that cannot be proved to move stays where it was. In the simple blocks world, the effect of this can easily be achieved by an axiom that states that all blocks except the one that is moved stay put. However, if there are various sentences that say (for example) that one block is attached to another, circumscription may express the heuristic situation better than an axiom.

8. Remarks

(1) Circumscription is not a 'non-monotonic logic.' It is a form of non-monotonic reasoning augmenting ordinary first order logic. Of course, sentence schemata are not properly handled by most present general purpose resolution theorem provers. Even fixed schemata of mathematical induction when used for proving programs correct usually require human intervention or special heuristics, while here the program would have to use new schemata produced by circumscription. In McCarthy (1979), we treat some modalities in first order logic instead of in modal logic. In our opinion, it is better to avoid modifying the logic if at all possible, because there are many temptations to modify the logic, and it would be very difficult to keep them compatible.

(2) The default case reasoning provided in many systems is less general than circumscription. Suppose, for example, that a block x is considered to be on a block y only if this is explicitly stated, i.e., the default is that x is not on y. Then for each individual block x, we may be able to conclude that it isn't on block A, but we will not be able to conclude, as circumscription would allow, that there are no blocks on A. That would require a separate default statement that a block is clear unless something is stated to be on it.

(3) The conjunct $\forall \overline{x}.\ (\Phi(\overline{x}) \supset P(\overline{x}))$ in the premiss of (1) is the result of

suggestions by Ashok Chandra (1979) and Patrick Hayes (1979) whom I thank for their help. Without it, circumscribing a disjunction, as in the second example in Section 4, would lead to a contradiction.

(4) The most direct way of using circumscription in AI is in a heuristic reasoning program that represents much of what it believes by sentences of logic. The program would sometimes apply circumscription to certain predicates in sentences. In particular, when it wants to perform an action that might be prevented by something it circumscribes the prevention predicate in a sentence A representing the information being taken into account.

Clearly the program will have to include domain dependent heuristics for deciding what circumscriptions to make and when to take them back.

(5) In circumscription it does no harm to take irrelevant facts into account. If these facts do not contain the predicate symbol being circumscribed, they will appear as conjuncts on the left side of the implication unchanged. Therefore, the original versions of these facts can be used in proving the left side.

(6) Circumscription can be used in other formalisms than first order logic. Suppose for example that a set a satisfies a formula $A(a)$ of set theory. The circumscription of this formula can be taken to be

$$\forall x.(A(x) \wedge (x \subset a) \supset (a \subset x)). \tag{31}$$

If a occurs in $A(a)$ only in expressions of the form $z \in a$, then its mathematical properties should be analogous to those of predicate circumscription. We have not explored what happens if formulas like $a \in z$ occur.

(7) The results of circumscription depend on the set of predicates used to express the facts. For example, the same facts about the blocks world can be axiomatized using the relation *on* or the relation *above* considered in Section 4 or also in terms of the heights and horizontal positions of the blocks. Since the results of circumscription will differ according to which representation is chosen, we see that the choice of representation has epistemologieal consequences if circumscription is admitted as a rule of conjecture. Choosing the set of predicates in terms of which to axiomatize as set of facts, such as those about blocks, is like choosing a coordinate system in physics or geography. As discussed in McCarthy (1979), certain concepts are definable only relative to a theory. What theory admits the most useful kinds of circumscription may be an important criterion in the choice of predicates. It may also be possible to make some statements about a domain like the blocks world in a form that does not depend on the language used.

Acknowledgments

This investigation was supported in part by ARPA Contract MDA-903-76-CO206, ARPA Order No. 2494, in part by NSF Grant MCS 78-00524, in part by the IBM 1979 Distinguished Faculty Program at the T. J. Watson Research Center, and in part by the Center for Advanced Study in the Behavioral Sciences.

The Second Naive Physics Manifesto

Patrick J. Hayes

1. Preface

Five years ago I wrote a paper, "The Naive Physics Manifesto," complaining about AI's emphasis on toy worlds and urging the field to put away childish things by building large-scale formalizations, suggesting in particular that a suitable initial project would be a formalization of our knowledge of the everyday physical world: of naive physics (NP). At that time, l felt rather alone in making such a suggestion (which is why the paper had such a proselytizing tone) and quite optimistic that success in even this ambitious a project could be achieved in a reasonable time scale. As the chapters in Hobbs and Moore (1985) testify, both feelings are no longer appropriate. There is a lot of work going on, and there is more to be done than I had foreseen. A whole layer of professionalism has emerged, for example, in the business of finding out just what people's intuitive ideas are about such matters as falling rocks or evaporating liquids, a matter I had relegated to disciplined introspection. In 1978, I predicted that the overall task was an order of magnitude (but not ten orders of magnitude) more difficult than any that had been undertaken so far. I now think that two or three orders of magnitude is a better estimate. It's still not impossible, though.

My old paper now seems dated and, in places, inappropriately naive on some deep issues. The following is a revised version which attempts to correct some of these shortcomings, and repeats the points which need repeating because nobody seems to have taken any notice of them.

This is a revised version of the original, not a sequel to it. Since several years have passed, some of the passion may have gone, being replaced with (I hope) more careful discussion.

2. Introduction

Artificial intelligence is full of 'toy problems': small, artificial axiomatizations or puzzles designed to exercise the talents of various problem-solving programs or representational languages or systems. The subject badly needs some non-toy worlds to experiment with. In other areas of cognitive science, also, there is a need to consider the organization of knowledge on a larger scale than is currently done, if only because quantitatively different mental models may well be qualitatively different.

In this chapter I propose the construction of a formalization of a sizable portion of common-sense knowledge about the everyday physical world: about objects, shape, space, movement, substances (solids and liquids), time, etc. Such a formalization could, for example, be a collection of assertions in a first-order logical formalism, or a collection of KRL units, or a microplanner program, or one of a number of other things, or even a mixture of several. It should have the following characteristics.

2.1 Breadth

It should cover the whole range of everyday physical phenomena: not just the blocks world, for example. Since in some important sense the world (even the everyday world) is infinitely rich in possible phenomena, this will never be perfect. Nevertheless, we should *try* to fill in all the major holes, or at least identify them.

It should be reasonably detailed. For example, such aspects of a block in a block world as shape, material, weight, rigidity and surface texture should be available as concepts in a blocks-world description, as well as support relationships.

2.2 Density

The ratio of facts to concepts needs to be fairly high. Put another way: the units have to have *lots* of slots. Low-density formalizations are in some sense trivial: they fail to say enough about the concepts they mention to pin down the meaning of their symbols at all precisely. Sometimes, for special purposes, as for example in foundational studies, this can be an advantage: but not for us.

2.3 Uniformity

There should be a common formal framework (language, system, etc.) for the whole formalization, so that the inferential connections between the different parts (axioms, frames, ...) can be clearly seen, and divisions into subformalizations are not prejudged by deciding to use one formalism for one area and a different one for a different area.

I (still) believe that a formalization of naive physics with these properties can be constructed within a reasonable time-scale. The reasons for such optimism are explained later. It is important however to clearly distinguish this proposal from some others with which it may be confused, because some of these seem to be far less tractable.

3. What the Proposal Isn't

It is *not* proposed to make a computer program which can 'use' the formalism in some sense. For example, a problem-solving program, or a natural language comprehension system with the representation as target. It is tempting to make such demonstrations from time to time. (They impress people; and it is satisfying to have actually *made* something which works, like building model railways; and one's students can get Ph.D.'s that way.) But they divert attention from the main goal. In fact, I believe they have several more dangerous effects. It is perilously easy to conclude that, because one has a program which *works* (in some sense), its representation of its knowledge must be more or less *correct* (in some sense). Now this is true, in some sense. But a representation may be adequate to support a limited kind of inference, and completely unable to be extended to support a slightly more general kind of behavior. It may be wholly limited by scale factors, and therefore tell us nothing about thinking about realistically complicated worlds. Images as internal pictures and the STRIPS representation of actions by add and delete lists are two good examples. I suspect that the use of state variables to represent time is another. Such representational devices are traps, tempting the unwary into dead ends where they struggle to overcome insurmountable difficulties, difficulties generated by the representation itself. I now believe, although I know this view is very controversial, that the famous frame problem is such a difficulty: an apparently deep problem which is largely artifact.

I emphasize this point because there is still a prevailing attitude in AI that research which does not result fairly quickly in a working program of some kind is somehow useless or, at least, highly suspicious. Of course implementability is the ultimate test of the validity of ideas in AI, and I do not mean to argue against this. But we must not be too hasty.

This is no more than a reiteration of John McCarthy's emphasis, since the inception of AI as a subject, on the importance of representational issues (McCarthy 1957, McCarthy and Hayes 1969). In 1969, McCarthy proposed the "Missouri Program," which would make no inferences of its own but would be willing to check proposed arguments submitted to it: a proof checker for common sense. Those who find it repugnant to be told to ignore programming considerations may find it more congenial to be urged to imagine the project of building a proof *checker* for naive physics.

It is *not* proposed to develop a new formalism or language to write down all this knowledge in. In fact, 1 propose (as my friends will have already guessed) that first-order logic is a suitable basic vehicle for representation. However, let me at once qualify this.

I have no particular brief for the usual syntax of first-order logic. Personally I find it agreeable: but if someone likes to write it all out in KRL, or semantic networks of one sort or another, or OMEGA, or KRYPTON, or what have you; well, that's fine. The important point is that one *knows what it means:* that the formalism has a clear *interpretation* (I avoid the word 's*m*nt*cs' deliberately). At the level of interpretation, there is little to choose between any of these, and most are strictly weaker than predicate calculus, which also has the advantage of a clear, explicit model theory, and a well understood proof theory.

I have pointed out elsewhere (Hayes 1977, 1978) that virtually all known representational schemes are equivalent to first-order logic (with one or two notable exceptions, primarily to do with nonmonotonic reasoning). This is still true in 1983, but I should perhaps emphasize that care is needed in making comparisons. First, in claiming equivalence, one is speaking of representational (expressive) power, not computational efficiency. Given a simple "dumb" interpreter (i.e., a "uniform" theorem-prover), these may be at odds with one another. The moral is that simple, dumb interpreters are a bad idea, and interpreters should be sensitive to 'control' information, meta-information about the inferential process itself. This idea brings its own representational problems. I am not arguing that these should be ignored. On the contrary, they raise some of the most important questions in AI. But until we have some idea of the sorts of inferences we might want to control, speculation on the matter is premature. Second, in making comparisons between systems one must exercise care. Many "computational" systems have invisible, buried, assumptions about their domain, not explicitly documented in publications, which must be rendered explicit in a logical axiomatization.[1] Third, the use of logic imposes almost no restrictions on the kinds of thing about which we wish to speak: sequences of actions or views of a room or plans or goals, etc., are all perfectly fine candidates. One must not let lack of imagination in axiomatizing lead one to conclude that logical formalisms are weaker than some of the more superficially baroque systems which AI has devised. (In particular, first-order logic can be taken to quantify over some properties, functions and relations and still be essentially first-order. What makes it higher-order is when its quantifiers have to range over all^2 properties, functions and relations, a condition which cannot be enforced without something like a rule of λ-abstraction or a comprehension schema.)

Finally, let me emphasize that idiosyncratic notations may sometimes be useful for idiosyncratic subtheories. For example, in sketching an axiomatic theory of fluids (Hayes 1985) I found it useful to think of the possible physical states of fluids as being essentially states of a finite-state machine. This summarizes a whole lot of lengthy, and rather clumsy, first-order axioms into one neat diagram. Still, it *means* the same as the axioms: first-order logic is still, as it were, the reference language. It is essential that there be some standard reference language in this way, so that the different parts of the formalism can be related to one another.

It is *not* proposed to find a philosophically exciting reduction of all ordinary concepts to some special collection of concepts (such as sets, or Goodmanesque "individuals," or space-time points, or qualia.) Maybe some such reduction will eventually turn out to be possible. I think it extremely unlikely and not especially desirable, but whether or not it is, is not the present issue. First we need to formalize the naive world view, using whatever concepts seem best suited to that purpose—thousands or tens of thousands of them if necessary. Afterwards we can try to impose some a priori ontological scheme upon it. But until we have the basic theory articulated, we don't know what our subject matter is.

Now, this is not to say that we should not exercise some care in avoiding unnecessary proliferation of axioms, or some aesthetic sensibility in designing axioms to give clean proofs and to interact as elegantly as possible. But these are matters of general scientific style, not ends in themselves.

4. Theories, Tokens and Closure

Let us imagine that a NP formalization exists. It consists of a large number of assertions *(or:* frames, scripts, networks, etc.) involving a large number of relation, function and constant symbols *(or:* frame headers, slot names, node and arc labels, etc. From now on I will not bother to reemphasize these obvious parallels). For neutral words, let us call these formal symbols *tokens,* and the collection of axioms the *theory* (in the sense of 'formal theory' in logic, not 'scientific theory' in history of science).

The success of a NP theory is measured by the extent to which it provides a vocabulary of tokens which allows a wide range of intuitive concepts to be expressed, and to which it then supports conclusions mirroring those which we find correct or reasonable. People know, for example, that if a stone is released, it falls with increasing speed until it hits something, and there is then an impact, which can cause damage if the velocity is high. The theory should provide tokens allowing one to express the concept of releasing a stone in space. And it should then be possible to infer from the theory that it will fall, etc.: so there must be tokens enabling one to express ideas of velocity, direction, impact, and so on. And then these same tokens must be usable in describing other kinds of circumstance, and the theory support the appropriate conclusions there, and so on. We want the overall pattern of consequences produced by the theory to correspond reasonably faithfully to our own intuition in both breadth and detail. Given the hypothesis that our own intuition is itself realized as a theory of this kind inside our heads, the NP theory we construct will then be equipotent with this inner theory.

More subtle tests than mere matching against intuition might be applied to an NP theory. Consequences which are *very* obvious should have shorter derivations then those which require some thought, perhaps. If, in proving p from q, the theory must make use of some concept token, perhaps psychologists can devise an experiment in which the "activation" of that concept can be tested for, while people are deciding whether or not q, given p. Pylyshyn (1979) discusses ways in which intermediate psychological states might be investigated: I will not discuss them further here, but focus instead on questions connected with getting a theory constructed in the first place.

The practical task of building such a theory begins with some 'target' concepts and desired inferences. Take the familiar example of formalizing a world of cubical wooden blocks on a flat table, with the goal of being able to reason about processes of piling these into vertical stacks and rearranging such piles by moving blocks from place to place: the familiar blocks world. Notice that we have put quite a constraint on what inferences we are interested in. An actual tabletop of blocks admits of many more interesting and complicated activities: building walls and pyramids, pushing blocks around horizontally, juggling, etc.; but we deliberately exclude such matters from consideration for now.

I will go through this toy world in detail, in order to illustrate some general points. It is not intended as a serious exercise in naive physics. First, we obviously need the concept of block (a predicate $Block(b)$), and there will be several states of the little universe as things are moved, so we also need that concept ($State(s)$). A block will be on some other block or on the table in every state ($On(b,c,s)$, and the name $table$): four tokens so far, and now we can write some axioms, such as:

$$\forall s,b.\ State(s) \wedge Block(b) \supset$$
$$(\exists c.\ Block(c) \wedge On(b,\ c,\ s)) \vee On(b,\ table,\ s) \tag{1}$$

(We could have done it differently: for example, a function *below(b,s)* instead of the relation *On*, so that *On(b,c,s)* translates into *below(b,s)* = *c*. Or a function *above(b,s)*, with the obvious meaning, and a constant, *air*, so that *above(b,s)* = *air* corresponds to: ∀*c*. ~*On(c,b,s)*, and being careful never to apply *above* to the table. We could have decided not to use states at all, but to have thought of each block as having a temporal history. No doubt other variations are possible. (In the future, I will—to save paper and to improve readability—omit such antecedents as *Block(b)* and *State(s)* from formulae. It is straightforward to enrich the logic to a many-sorted logic in which this omission is syntactically normal. The concepts are there, though, and need inferential machinery of one kind or another, so they should be shown in the "reference language.")

Now, to describe change we need the idea of a state-transition. There are several ways to do this. We could have a relation *Next(s,t)* between states, for example, or a function *next(s)*, corresponding to the intuitive feeling that one moment follows another, and there is always a unique next thing that will in fact happen (que sera, sera). Or we might say that, since we are talking about actions, and there are usually several things one *might* do in a given situation, so there are several different next-states. This leads to McCarthy's idea—now standard—of actions as state to state functions. We might have actions *pickup(b,s)* and *putdown(b,s)*, for example. The result of picking up *b* is a state in which *b* is no longer on anything but rather is held in the hand:

$$Held(b, pickup(b)) \qquad (2)$$

$$Held(b,s) \supset \forall x.\ \sim On(b,x,s) \qquad (3)$$

We must now modify (1) by adding *Held(b,s)* as a third possibility. The result of put downing on *b* is that whatever is held gets to rest on *b*; provided of course there is nothing there already. To make this neater, let's define *Clear*:

$$Clear(x,s) \equiv \forall c.\ On(c,x,s) \lor x{=}table \qquad (4)$$

Then we can say:

$$Held(b,s) \land Clear(c,s) \supset On(b,c,putdown(c,s)) \qquad (5)$$

(This still doesn't explain what *putdown(c,s)* is like if nothing is *Held* in *s*. We might decide there are two sorts of states, those in which the hand is holding something and those in which it is empty, and insist that *putdown* applies only to the former. Or we might just say that:

$$\forall x.\ \sim Held(x,s) \supset putdown(c,s) = s \qquad (6)$$

We can now begin to see how the desired kinds of conclusion might follow. If we know that *A* is on *C* on the table and *B* is on the table and *A* and *C* are clear, then we can infer from (2) that after a suitable pickup, *A* is held. Unfortunately, we can't conclude that *B* is still clear: *C* may have jumped onto it, as far as our axioms are concerned. (Consider a world of jumping blocks, or stackable frogs, in which every time one is lifted, the one beneath hops onto a different block. This is a possible world, and all five of the axioms are true in it. So, nothing that they say rules this possibility out.) This is a tiny illustration of the notorious frame problem (McCarthy and Hayes 1969). We need to say that during a pickup of a block, no other *On* relations change.

Now, for the first time, we don't need to introduce any new tokens. We have a rich enough vocabulary at hand to state our axiom:

$$On(b,c,s) \supset \forall d.\sim On(b,c,pickup(d,s)) \veebar b = d \tag{7}$$

Here, $\veebar$ is exclusive-or, so that if b is not d, then $On(b,c)$ must still be true in $pickup(d,s)$; and we are sure that $\sim On(b,c,pickup(b,s))$ under any circumstances. Notice that the block picked up might itself carry others, and they go right along with it.

Given (7), we can quickly conclude that B is still clear and still on the table, so we can now putdown onto it and have a state in which A is on B—no longer clear, by (4)—and C is clear ... well, not quite, since putting down might yet disturb things. But we can fix this with an even simpler frame axiom:

$$On(b,c,s) \supset On(b,c,putdown(d,s)) \tag{8}$$

and we can now discuss states reached by picking up and putting down things all over the place, as we desired. Given a sufficiently complete description of a layout of blocks, and a goal of some other configuration, then if there is a sequence of block movements which get us from the former to the latter, then this theory will show that there is.

For some time now we have not needed to introduce any other tokens. We can do the changes by adding or modifying axioms, working entirely in the given vocabulary. This collection of tokens (*block, table, state, on, held, pickup, putdown*) is enough to work with.[3] Alternative worlds can be constructed within it. It is a large enough collection to support axioms describing general properties of the universe we have in mind, and descriptions of particular worlds in enough detail to allow the sorts of conclusion we wanted to be inferred. No subset will do the job, as we have seen: but this is just enough to let us say what needs saying. We have reached what might be called a *conceptual closure*. This phenomenon is familiar to anyone who has tried to axiomatize or formalize some area. Having chosen one's concepts to start on, one quickly needs to introduce tokens for others one had not contemplated, and the axioms which pin down their meanings introduce others, and so on: until one finds suddenly there are enough tokens around that it is easy to say enough "about" them all: enough, that is, to enable the inferences one had had in mind all along to be made.

This sort of closure is by no means trivial. Suppose we had tried to use $next(s)$, following the idea that world-states are, after all, linearly ordered; then it becomes quite hard to achieve. We can say that a block may stay where it is, or become picked up:

$On(b,c,s) \wedge \forall x. \sim Held(x,s) \supset On(b,c,next(s)) \vee Held(b,next(s)))$ \hfill (9)

and we can insist that only one is held at once:

$Held(b,s) \wedge Held(c,s) \supset b = c$ \hfill (10)

But putting down is more difficult. If we say

$Held(b,s) \wedge Clear(c,s) \supset On(b,c,next(s))$ \hfill (11)

then the held block has been put down into every clear space. We certainly want to say that the held block is put down in one of the potential putdown sites:

$Held(b,s) \supset \exists c. Clear(c,s) \wedge On(b,c,next(s))$ \hfill (12)

But we now have no way of inferring that the held block can actually be placed in any particular clear place. This axiom is consistent with a world in which blocks can be placed only on the table, for example, or in which blocks are always released from on high and falleth gently upon some random stack or other. There is no way within this vocabulary to describe one possible future state's properties as distinct from those of a different possible future state. We have no way of stating the properties we need: closure eludes us. It can be achieved, but only by bringing possible futures in by the back door.

Our theory, though closed, is by no means perfect. As stated, it can support all the inferences we had in mind. Unfortunately, it can also support some others which we didn't have in mind. For example, nothing in the axioms so far prevents two successive pickups, giving a handful of blocks (or, somewhat less plausibly, a handful of towers of blocks). This would be fine, except that (5) has it that anything held is deposited by a putdown, thus leaving several blocks on one; but they were supposed to be all the same size. The neatest way to fix this is to modify (2), say as follows:

$\forall x. \sim Held(x,s) \supset Held(b, pickup(b,s))$ \hfill (13)

We can also insist that only single blocks are picked up by adding $Clear(b,s)$ as another antecedent condition. Again: if a block is *Clear*, then we can pick it up—its still *Clear*—and put it down on *itself:* there's nothing in (5) to prevent this. (Consider a zero-gravity world in which blocks can be released in space, and they then just hang there: and say that in this case the block is *On* itself. Clearly all the axioms are satisfied in this world too.) So to rule this out we need another axiom, and to modify (5) slightly. Finding other such bugs is left as an exercise for the reader.

It is important to bear such negative properties of a formalization in mind even though they make the formalizer's life more complex. It is easy to overlook them.

5. Meanings, Theories and Model Theory

In developing this toy theory, I have several times used an example world to show that something we wanted to follow didn't, or that something we didn't want to be true might be. This ability to interpret our axioms in a possible world, see what they say and whether it is true or not, is so useful that I cannot imagine proceeding without it. But it is only possible if there is an idea of a *model* of the formal language in which the theory is written: a systematic notion of what a possible world is and how the tokens of the theory can be mapped into entities (or structures or values or whatever) in such worlds. We have to be able to *imagine* what our tokens *might* mean.

Now this semantic metatheory may be relatively informal, but the more exactly it is defined, the more useful it will be as a tool for the theory-builder. The main attraction of formal logics as representational languages is that they have very precise model theories, and the main attraction of first-order logic is that its model theory is so simple, so widely applicable, and yet so powerful.

A first-order model is a set of entities and suitable mappings from tokens to functions and relations, of appropriate arity, over it.[4] Any collection of things will do: for example, for our blocks world, I could take the collection of papers on my desk, and interpret *On* to be the relation which holds between two pieces of paper when one partially or wholly overlaps the other, and *pickup* to be the action of picking up, and so on. (In fact, this isn't a model, because my desk is too crowded: axiom (5) is false. But it would be if I tidied my desk up.)

This is very satisfying, since we have found a model which is very close to the original intuition. But there are other models. Consider a table and a single block and the two states, one—call it *A*—with the block on the table, and the other—call it *B*—with the block held above the table. Let *pickup* and *putdown* denote the functions $(A \rightarrow B, B \rightarrow B)$ and $(B \rightarrow A, A \rightarrow A)$ respectively, let *Held* be true just of the block in state *B*, and let *On* be true just of the block and the table in state *A*. All the axioms are true, so this is a possible world. This one is much simpler than my desk, and its existence shows that the axioms really say rather less than one might have thought they did: specifically, they say nothing about *how many* blocks or states there are, or about the direction of time's arrow.

One can find other very simple models, for example models made of dots being moved on a screen—so the theory says nothing about the three-dimensionality of the world.

This illustrates how the existence of a model theory for our formal language is not just a methodological convenience. It tells us what our formalizations could mean and hence, what they couldn't mean. We may think that we have captured some concept in a theory, but unless the theory is sufficiently rich to guarantee that *all* its models reveal the kind of structure we had in mind, then we are deluded: *a token of a theory means no more than it means in the simplest model of the theory.*

Returning to methodology for a moment, a crucial property of this way of characterizing meaning is that it transcends syntactic and operational variations. A given theory might be realized operationally in innumerable ways. Even ignoring heuristic 'control' issues, we have such variations as natural deduction rules, or semantic tableaux or Hilbert-style axiomatizations. We can make the theory look like a semantic network or a collection of frames or MOPS or any one of innumerable other variations. None of these variations will give the theory an ounce more expressive power. None of them could ever make good a representational inadequacy of the theory. It is easy to lose sight of this basic and uncomfortable truth. Thinking model-theoretically helps us to keep it in mind.

It also gives us a powerful theoretical tool. For example, I mentioned earlier that defined concept tokens, such as *Clear,* added no real expressiveness to a theory. This seems kind of intuitive once it is pointed out, but it has a quite conclusive model-theoretic statement (Beth's definability theorem) which completely settles the matter, and frees up time for more productive discussions.

An objection to the idea of models goes as follows. Any particular formalization or implementation consists entirely of the expressions and the inference rules or procedures which manipulate them. The idea of a model, and the mappings which relate expressions to denotations, etc., are just metatheorists' ideas, imposed from without. But we could have a different model theory for the same formal language, and declare that *this* semantic theory assigned meanings to the formal symbols. (e.g., see D. Israel [... 1985]) And who is to say which of the many possible semantic theories is the right one?

But the relationship between a model theory and the (purely formal) inference rules or procedures attached to the formal language is not arbitrary in this way. Each model theory sanctions certain inferences (the ones that preserve truth in those models) and not others. And, sometimes, we also get the converse, viz., if some assertion is true in all those models, then the rules will indeed eventually declare it so. This is the content of the completeness theorem for a formal language. We should treasure completeness theorems: they are rare and beautiful things. Without them, we have no good justification for our claims that we know how our theories say what we claim they say about the worlds we want them to describe. To emphasize this, consider enriching the formal language by introducing a new kind of symbol, say a quantifier M which I claim means 'most' so that $MxP(x)$ means P is true of *most* things. I can easily give a model theory: $MxP(x)$ is true in a model just when P is true of more than half the universe (with a little more subtlety for infinite domains, but let that pass). I can *claim* this, but the claim is premature until I can describe some mechanism of inference which captures that interpretation, generating all the inferences which it justifies and none which it refutes. And this might be difficult. For some model theories we know it is impossible.

A model theory can determine the actual meaning of the logical symbols of the formal language, but it does not determine the actual meaning of the tokens. The only way to do that is by restricting the set of possible models of the theory, for example by adding axioms. All we can say of a token is that in this model it means this, in that one it means that. There is no single 'meaning' of a formal token (unless there is only a single model): we cannot point to something and say, *that* is the meaning.

We might restate the goal of building a formal theory as being that of ensuring that all the models of the theory are recognizable as the kind of possible world we were trying to describe, so that in each one, each token denotes what it should. But this notion of meaning raises a well-known philosophical specter, a second objection to a model-theoretic view of meaning. For no model theory can specify what kinds of entity constitute the universes of its models. It refers only to the presence of functions and relations defined over a set, not to what the set is a set *of.* And we could always make our universes out of entirely unsuitable things, in particular the tokens themselves.

Suppose we have a 'suitable' model of a theory. Make a ghost model as follows. Let each name denote itself. Every token which should denote an operation on things, interpret it rather as an operation on the *names* of things, whose result is the expression which would have referred to the thing got by performing the operation on the things named, so that for example a unary function symbol f denotes the function on expressions which takes the expression 'e' to the expression '$f(e)$,' '$g(h(a))$' to '$f(g(h(a)))$,' and so on. And interpret each relation symbol as that relation on expressions which is true when the relation is true of the thing named by the expressions in the 'suitable' model: so that 'P' denotes the predicate which is true of the symbol 'a' just if '$P(a)$' is true in the first model. In general, whenever you need to decide a question of fact, go and check in the "suitable" model to see what its facts are, and use those.

There is one of these ghostly (Herbrand) models for every model, and it makes exactly the same axioms true. So there could be no way of adding axioms (or frames or scripts or demons or MOPS or anything else, just to re-emphasize the point) which could ensure that all a theory is talking about might not be its own symbols.

This is an important point, considered as a criticism of a theory of meaning. Indeed, no formal operations, no matter how complex, can ever ensure that tokens denote any particular kinds of entity. There are, I think, three ways in which tokens can be attached to their denotations more rigidly (so to speak). One: if the token is itself in a metatheory of some internal part of the theory, then the connection can simply be directly made by internal, formal, manipulations. Formally, these are "reflection principles," or rules of translation between a language and its metalanguage.

Two: if the theory is in a creature with a body—a robot, like us—then some of the tokens can be attached to sensory and motor systems so that the truth of some propositions containing them is kept in correspondence to the way the real world actually is. These tokens—they might include the concept *vertical* connected to the inner ear, and those of a whole intricate theory of lighting and surfaces and geometry and texture and movement connected with visual perception, and a whole other collection associated with proprioceptive awareness of the body's position in space—have a special status. We might say that the body's sensorimotor apparatus *was* the model theory of this part of the internal formalization.

Three: tokens could be attached to the world through language. Again, let the theory be built into a physical computer, one without senses, but with a natural language comprehension and production system. The tokens of the internal theory are now related to English words in the way we expect, so that the deep semantic meaning of a sentence is a collection of axiomatic statements in the formalism. Such a system could talk about things to other language users and could come to learn facts about an external world by communicating with them. Assuming that *their* beliefs and conversations really were about things—that they managed to actually refer to external entities—then I think we would have no reason to refuse the same honor to the conversing system.

These matters require and deserve fuller discussion elsewhere. But I suggest that for the purposes of developing a naive physics, this whole issue can be safely ignored. We can take out a promissory loan on *real* meanings. One way or another, parts of our growing formalization will have eventually to be attached to external worlds through senses or language or maybe some other way, and ghost models will be excluded. We must go ahead trying to formalize our intuitive world; paying attention indeed to the complexity and structural suitability of our models, but not worrying about what sort of stuff they are made from.

We have then to be ready to repay the loan, by looking out for areas of axiomatization where the tokens might be attachable to perceptual or motor or linguistic systems. For example, ideas connected with time must make some contact with our internal "clocks" of various sorts. Much of our intuitive knowledge of force and movement comes from *what it feels like* when we push, pull, lift and move. Much of our knowledge of three-dimensional space is connected with how things *look;* and so on.

6. Discovering Intuitions and Building Theories

We have been assuming all along that we are able to interpret tokens of the theory in intuitive terms. But this assumes that we can identify our own intuitive concepts sufficiently clearly to assign them to tokens. In practice, building axiomatic theories is in large part an exploration and clarification of our own intuitions. Just as professional grammarians tend to acquire an astonishingly acute sense of exactly which syntactic constructions are acceptable to a native speaker, so naive physicists will need to develop an acute sense of intuitive reasonableness of descriptions of the everyday physical world. It is not at all an easy thing to do.

Consider the earlier toy blocks-world example. It might be argued that here is a small theory with complete conceptual closure. But it is closed only with respect to the very limited range of inferences we required initially; this is exactly what makes it a toy theory. Try to expand it to deal with our own ideas of putting things on things. We have the token *On*: what exactly did that mean? It had a component of pure geometry, referring to the spatial arrangement of the blocks. It also seemed to have some idea of support contained within it: if *A* is on *B*, then *B* is holding *A* up; *B* is the reason why *A* isn't falling, it is bearing *A*'s weight. Now these are very different ideas. For example, the geometric *On* is asymmetrical (nothing is on anything which is on it—although it doesn't seem that this should be an axiom so much as a consequence of some more basic spatial theory), but the support *On* can be, e.g., two long blocks leaning on one another. They come together here in that the geometric *On* implies the support *On*, because blocks are rigid and strong, so they will bear weight without deforming or breaking. And this is because the stuff they are made of has these properties. To emphasize the separateness of these two ideas, imagine the alternative possible world with no gravity. The geometry is unchanged, but the 'support' idea is absent. So they must have distinct subtheories.

Both concepts are linked to clusters of others which we have not yet begun to formalize. The experience of doing so may well sharpen our sense of what the concept is, perhaps separating it out further into several slightly (or very) different ideas, each requiring its own axiomatic connections to the rest of the theory.

We have taken a proposed concept and seen it as a blend of two distinct components. As well as this analytic "division" of concepts there is what we might call a process of "broadening"; extending the range of a concept, trying it out in other areas where it seems natural. For example, imagine four blocks arranged in a compact square on the table, with adjacent faces in contact (the very fact that you can do that says a lot about the richness of the spatial geometry part of our internal theories) and place a fifth block neatly on top, in the center. What is this block on? We might say it is on *each* of the other blocks, but this is a very different notion (e.g. pick up one of the lower blocks). Perhaps it is on the set of the four blocks ... but a set hardly seems the kind of thing that can bear weight, and anyway only some sets will work. Perhaps we should abandon the notion of *On* altogether in this case in favor of some other, more subtle, relationship between the blocks. But it seems intuitively clear that the top block *is* on *something,* in much the same way that it could be on one block. The only reasonable conclusion, I believe, is that the fifth block is indeed on a (single) thing, which is made up of the four other blocks. By arranging them thus in a compact square, one has created a new object; we might call it a platform. (If someone points to it and asks;

what is *that?*, the question is quite intelligible: there is some *thing* there. One might of course answer: nothing, its just four blocks.) So blocks can be on other things than blocks and tables. Its the same concept, but using it in a different situation forces a reevaluation of what can be said about it. We need to be able to state some criterion of put-on-ability, which seems to be having a firm horizontal surface. But now we have a new concept, that of a surface. This requires more axioms to relate it to existing concepts, and these in turn introduce other concepts (edge, side of a surface, direction, adjacency, contact, the object-surface relation, etc.: see Hobbs and Moore 1985, Chapter 3 for a first attempt at such a list) and these require more axioms, each typically introducing other concepts, and so on. Conceptual closure becomes much harder to achieve: perhaps impossible to achieve completely.

This is what typically happens when one extends the scope of a concept. Closure is fragile, sensitive to the demands placed on the theory. Toy theories achieve it only by having very restricted demands placed on them. In developing naive physics we expect far more of the theory, forcing it to be larger and making closure more remote. There is a constant tension between wanting a closed theory and wanting to pin down the meanings of tokens as precisely as we can: between closure and breadth.

This example illustrates an important and basic fact about the enterprise of knowledge representation. We want breadth and density: but you can't have the density without the breadth. If we want the theory to say a *lot* about a concept, the only way to do so is to relate that concept to many others. If there are many axioms in the theory which contain a certain token, there must ipso facto be many other tokens to which it is axiomatically related. It is exactly this, being tightly caught in a dense web of inferential connections to other parts of the theory, which gives a token meaning, by cutting out unwanted implausible models. And this is what we want, since the goal of the axiomatizing enterprise is to produce a theory from which we can rapidly draw the many conclusions corresponding to our intuitions, and this inferential richness goes along with model theoretic constraint.

7. [9] Why It Needs To Be Done*

In the earlier version of this chapter I argued at length that tackling a large-scale project such as this is essential for long-term progress in artificial intelligence. I will briefly review those arguments here, before turning to other reasons why large-scale formalization of "mental models" (Gentner and

*Editor's Note: Sections 7 and 8 from the original paper have been removed from this reprint with the permission of the author. We have renumbered the sections from this point forward, but included the original section numbers in brackets to avoid confusion with any extant references.

Stevens 1983) is of basic importance to other parts of cognitive science.

For AI there are three arguments: the importance of scale effects, the need to develop techniques of inference control, and the motivation of adequate representational languages.

AI has the aim of constructing working systems. This might be taken as the defining methodology of the field, in fact, in contrast to cognitive psychology. But there is a real danger in applying this criterion too early and too rigorously, so that a doctoral thesis must demonstrate a working program in order to be acceptable. Several areas of AI have outgrown this state, but work on knowledge representation is only just beginning to. As I have argued earlier, scale limitations mean that no matter how many short forays into small areas we make, we will never get an adequate formalization of common sense knowledge. We have to take density seriously, and density requires breadth.

That weak, general techniques of controlling inference are inadequate to cope with the combinatorially explosive search spaces defined by large-scale assertional databases is now a matter for the textbooks. The moral is that the inference-makers need to be informed about what they are doing; they need a theory of control. I will not emphasize this point here, but note that the really large spaces which broad, dense formalizations yield may need qualitatively different meta-theories of control, or other search processes entirely. I believe that the study of inferential control (which subsumes many questions of system architecture generally) is one of the most important facing AI at present. *But until we have some dense theories to experiment on, we won't know what the real problems are. Many* of the current ideas on controlling deductive search may be useful only on relatively sparse spaces; contrariwise, richly connected spaces may present new opportunities for effective strategies (the widespread use of relaxation, for example, may become newly effective). It would be interesting to find out, but something like naive physics has to be done first, otherwise our control theories will be little more than formalizations of the weak, general heuristics we already have.[7]

I will bet that there are more representational languages, systems and formalisms developed by AI workers in the last ten years than there are theories to express in them. This is partly because of the pressure to implement already mentioned, but is also due to a widespread feeling that the *real* scientific problems are concerned with how to represent knowledge rather than with what the knowledge is. When inadequacies arise in formalizations, the usual response is to attribute the cause less to the formalization than to a limitation of the language which was used to express it.[8] Many major recent efforts in the development of special knowledge representation languages are concerned with issues which have to do with the structure of the theories which are to be expressed in them. KLONE, for example appears to be a complex notation for describing interrelationships between concepts in a theory, including those between a concept and its constituent parts. The scientific questions of interest are to do with these relationships, not the idiosyncrasies of any particular notation for recording them. But all of this could be carried out in first order logic. The KLONE authors attribute considerable importance to the distinction between the structure of individual concepts on the one hand and the relationships between concepts on the other. In our terms this amounts to an extra layer of structural distinctions added on top of the simple axiomatic theory. Whether or not the distinction is worthwhile, it should not obscure the need to construct the underlying theory itself first.[9]

Progress in building nontrivially large axiomatizations of common sense knowledge is also of importance to other fields than AI. Any theorizing about cognition has to take into account the structure of the internal theories which—if the whole computational view of mind is anything like correct—support it. If this is taken seriously, then large parts of cognitive and developmental psychology and psycholinguistics must refer to internal conceptual structures. This is a truism of cognitive science by now, but what is less widely appreciated is the need to be sensitive to the *details* of these inner theories. Much work concerns itself with broad hypotheses about the functional architecture of cognitive structure, without paying attention to the detailed inferences which constitute the internal activities of the system. Some work assumes very simple internal theories, expressed in terms of "schemata," for example, or as an associative network of concept-nodes. But we know that internal theories, if they exist at all, must be extremely large and complex; and we know that we do not yet have any very reliable ideas about their structure, still less about their dynamics. Under these circumstances it seems risky at best to attempt to relate observable behavior to general hypotheses about cognitive structure. Word meanings in psycholinguistic theorizing, for example, often seem to be regarded as atomic entities related by some kind of association. But, as much AI work on language understanding even in restricted domains has shown, words must map into internal concepts in very complex and idiosyncratic ways, and the concepts themselves must be embedded in a network of internal theory, even to make possible such elementary operations as pronoun disambiguation or the interpretation of indirect speech acts.

The medieval alchemists had much empirical knowledge, and very grandiose but simple theories, and some success in relating the two together. Their view of the world attempted to make direct connections between philosophical and religious ideas and the colors and textures of the substances in their retorts. Modern chemistry began when the search for the Philosophers Stone was abandoned for the more modest goal of understanding the details of what was happening in the retorts. Cognitive Science is sometimes reminiscent of alchemy. We should, perhaps, give up the attempt to make grand, simple theories of the mind, and concentrate instead on the details of what must be in the heads of thinkers. Discovering them will be a long haul, no doubt, but when we know what it is that people know, we can begin to make realistic theories about how they work. Because they work largely by using this knowledge.

8. [10] Is This Science?

The earlier manifesto ended on a note of exquisite methodological nicety: whether this activity could really be considered *scientific*. This second manifesto will end on a different note. Doing this job is necessary, important, difficult and fun. Is it really scientific? Who cares?

Acknowledgments

It is impossible to name all the people who have contributed to these ideas. I would, however, like to especially thank Maghi King, who let me get started; and Jerry Hobbs, who made me finish.

Notes

1. This touches on a basic terminological ambiguity. Shall we regard an axiom as a statement *in* a logic; or as a new *rule* to be *added* to the logic, so that the logic is somehow made stronger but the axiomatization is not enlarged? One always has the option: the second route tends to lead to less expressive but operationally more efficient systems, since a rule can often be neatly characterized as an axiom with a restriction imposed on its use, so that less can be inferred from it. I think we should take our axioms unrestricted for a while, until we can see more realistically what sorts of restriction we shall have to impose on their inferential behavior to achieve practical systems.

2. There are two versions, in fact: "all nameable," which you get with the rule or schema, and "all," which can't be enforced by any schema or rule or computational device of *any* kind, since the set of theorems is then not recursively enumerable. If anyone claims to have implemented a reasoning system which can handle full higher order reasoning, he is wrong.

3. I omitted *clear* deliberately. It has an explicit definition and could be eliminated entirely at no real cost of expressive power. Having that token makes axioms more compact and deductions shorter, but it does not enable us to say anything new, since we could have replaced it everywhere else by its definition and gotten an equivalent set of axioms. Definitions don't add to the expressive power of a theory.

4. This is usually presented, in textbooks of elementary logic, in a rather formal, mathematical way: and this fact may have given rise to the curious but widespread delusion that a first-order model is merely another formal description of the world, just like the axiomatization of which it is a model; and that the Tarskian truth recursion is a kind of translation from one formal system to another (e.g., Wilks 1977). This is quite wrong. For a start, the relationship between an axiomatization and its models (or, dually, between a model and the set of axiomatizations which are true of it) is quite different from a translation. It is many-many rather than one-one, for example. Moreover, it has the algebraic character called a Galois connection, which is to say, roughly, that as the axiomatization is increased in size (as axioms are added), the collection of models—possible states of affairs—decreases in size. It is quite possible for large, complex axiomizations to have small, simple models, and vice versa. In particular, a model can always be gratuitously complex (e.g., contain entities which aren't mentioned at all in the axiomization). But the deeper mistake in this way of thinking is to confuse a formal description of a model—found in the textbooks which are developing a mathematical approach to the metatheo-

ry of logic—with the actual model. This is like confusing a mathematical description of Sydney Harbour Bridge in a textbook of structural engineering with the actual bridge. A Tarskian model can be a piece of reality. If I have a blocks-world axiomatization which has three block-tokens, '*A*,' '*B*,' and '*C*' and if I have a (real, physical) table in front of me, with three (real, physical) wooden blocks on it, then the set of those three blocks can be the set of entities of a model of the axiomatization (provided, that is, that I can go on to interpret the relations and functions of the axiomatization as physical operations on the wooden blocks, or whatever, in such a way that the assertions made about the wooden blocks, when so interpreted, are in fact true). There is nothing in the model theory of first-order logic which a priori prevents the real world being a model of an axiom system.

5. The felt need for a nontrivially complex axiomatization to try out search heuristics on was my original motivation for embarking on this whole enterprise.

6. This may be connected with the fact that in computer science generally, development of programming languages is a respectable academic concern, while the development of particular programs isn't. After all, who knows what a language might be used for, especially a *general-purpose* language? And knowledge representation systems are almost invariably proud of their generality. This attitude is especially easy to comprehend when the Krep language is considered a species of programming language itself, which was a widespread confusion for several years.

7. The deliberate eschewal of control (= computational) issues in the naive physics proposal represents a very *conservative* approach to questions of such structuring. First order logic makes very weak assumptions about the structure of theories couched in it, almost the weakest possible. They can be summarized as: the universe consists of individual entities, with relations between them. Nothing is said about the nature of the entities. (An attempt to find an area where this "discreteness" assumption breaks down was what led me to the liquids formalization, and an individualization assumption was, unexpectedly, crucial to its success.) It makes no assumptions whatever about control. Any insight into theory structure which is obtainable within naive physics must be readily transferable to more elaborate notations or systems of representation, therefore. It seems wisest, at this early stage in the development of large "knowledge bases," to be as conservative as possible. One might think that attempting to use first-order logic as a representational vehicle would be doomed to failure by its expressive inadequacy. In fact, however, the limitations seem to be on our ability to think of things to say in it.

Paradigms for Machine Learning

Jaime G. Carbonell

1. Historical Perspectives

Machine learning (ML) played a central role in artificial intelligence at its very beginning. Although the AI limelight has wandered away from machine learning in the advent of other significant developments, such as problem solving, theorem proving, planning, natural language processing, robotics, and expert systems, ML has returned cast in multiple guises, playing increasingly more significant roles. For instance, early work in linear perceptrons faded away in light of theoretical limitations, but resurged this decade with much fanfare as connectionist networks with hidden units able to compute and learn nonlinear functions. In the interim, many symbolic machine learning paradigms flourished, and several have evolved into powerful computational methods, including inductive concept acquisition, classifier systems, and explanation based learning. Today, there are many active research projects spanning the gamut of machine learning methods, several focusing on the theory of learning and others on improving problem solving performance in complex domains. In the 1980s, the field of machine learning has reemerged as one of the major areas of artificial intelligence, with an annual ML conference, an established 1,000 subscriber journal, dozens of books, and ample representation in all major AI conferences.

Perhaps the tenacity of ML researchers in light of the undisputed difficulty of their ultimate objectives, and in light of early disappointments, is best explained by the very nature of the learning process. The ability to learn, to adapt, to modify behavior is an inalienable component of human intelligence. How can we build truly artificially intelligent machines that are not capable of self-improvement? Can an expert system be labeled "intelligent," any more than the *Encyclopedia Britannica* be labeled intelligent, merely because it contains useful knowledge in quantity? An underlying conviction of many ML researchers is that learning is a prerequisite to any form of true intelligence—therefore it must be investigated in depth, no matter how formidable the challenge. Philosophical considerations aside, machine learning, like knowledge representation and reasoning, cuts across all problem areas of AI: problem solving, theorem proving, analogical and nonmonotonic reasoning, natural language processing, speech recognition, vision, robotics, planning, game playing, pattern recognition, expert systems, and so on. In principle, progress in ML can be leveraged in all these areas; it is truly at the core of artificial intelligence.

Recently, machine learning research has begun to pay off in various ways: solid theoretical foundations are being established; machine learning methods are being successfully integrated with powerful performance systems; and practical applications based on the more established techniques have already made their presence felt. Recent successes in machine learning include decision tree induction applied to industrial process control (based on Quinlan's ID3 [Quinlan 1983] and its successors), the integration of explanation-based learning into general knowledge-intensive reasoning systems (such as SOAR [Laird et al. 1986], PRODIGY [Minton et al. 1987] and THEO), and extended forms of neural network learning to produce phonemic level speech recognition at an accuracy surpassing conventional methods (such as hidden Markoff models) in modular time delay neural networks.

To date one can identify four major ML paradigms and multiple subparadigms under active investigation: inductive learning, e.g., acquiring concepts from sets of positive and negative examples; analytic learning, e.g., explanation-based learning and certain forms of analogical and case-based learning methods; genetic algorithms, e.g., classifier systems (Holland 1975); and connectionist learning methods, e.g., nonrecurrent "backprop" hidden layer neural networks. These machine learning paradigms emerged from quite different scientific roots, employ different computational methods, and often rely on subtly different ways of evaluating success, although all share the common goal of building machines that can learn in significant ways for a wide variety of task domains. In all cases, learning can be defined operationally to mean the ability to perform new tasks that could not be performed before or perform old tasks better (faster, more accurately, etc.) as a result of changes produced by the learning process. Except for this basic consensus on what it means to learn, there are precious few assumptions shared by all four paradigms.

2. The Inductive Paradigm

The most widely studied method for symbolic learning is one of inducing a general concept description from a sequence of instances of the concept and (usually) known counter examples of the concept. The task is to build a concept description from which all the previous positive instances can be rederived by universal instantiation but none of the previous negative instances (the counter examples) can be rederived by the same process. At this level of abstraction, the problem may sound simple, but it is not even well posed. The design space of potential inductive systems is determined by many important dimensions, such as the following.

1. *Description Language:* The language in which input instances and output concepts are expressed can vary in representational power (e.g., propositional calculus, first-order logic, or beyond), in whether the domain of variables in the description language is discrete, continuous or mixed, and in whether individual values are points in the domain or probability distributions among the possible domain values. Most early concept acquisition systems handled only certain classes of propositional representations (attribute-value lists) with single-valued variables drawn from a finite nominal domain. Continuous variables were arbitrarily partitioned into discrete intervals. Present systems explore the full range of possibilities. However, most systems make a fixed vocabulary assumption in that all the relevant descriptors must be present at the outset. Lately, some researchers are starting to consider the implications of description languages that grow during the learning cycle, labeling the process *representational shift.*

2. *Noise and Instance Classification:* Most early learning-from-examples systems assumed that every instance was correctly classified as positive or negative with respect to the desired concept; that is, they assumed a benign and accurate teacher providing a stream of well-formed data (Winston 1975). Since such an assumption is much too restrictive for real-world applications, new systems explore the possibility of inaccurately labeled and unlabeled instances, of partially specified instances (where some attributes may be unknown), of measurement errors in the values of the attributes, and of differential relevance among the attributes. So long as the signal-to-noise ratio is acceptable, and the number of instances is sufficiently high, statistical techniques integrated into

the learning method come to the rescue.

3. *Concept Type:* Some learning systems strive for *discriminant concepts,* where the concept description is a set of tests which strive to separate all instances of the concept apart from all instances of every other concept known to the system. Often discriminant concept descriptions are encoded as paths from the root to the leaves of incrementally acquired decision trees. Other learning systems acquire *characteristic concepts,* which strive for compactness and elegance in the concept descriptions. Such concepts are far easier to communicate to human users and often prove more usable when they must be interpreted by some other part of the performance system. However, the tradeoff for simplicity of description is often loss of complete accuracy; characteristic concepts do not necessarily comply with the strict discrimination criterion. Characteristic concept descriptions are often encoded as frames or logical formulae. The *inductive bias* of a learning system is often expressed as preferences in the type of concept to be acquired, and simplicity of the concept description is the most prevalent form of domain-independent inductive bias.

4. *Source of Instances:* The initial learning-from-examples model called for an external teacher to supply a stream of classified examples for a single concept to be acquired at one time. In addition to considering the possibility of noise in the data (discussed above), one can remove the teacher entirely and use the external world as a source of data. In such cases, the learner must be proactive in seeking examples, must cope with multiple concepts at one time, and must seek its own classification of instances by appealing to an external oracle (if available), by performing experiments (if possible), or by conceptual clustering techniques (Michalski and Stepp 1983). Current work also addresses the judicious selection of instances to reduce maximally the uncertainty in partially formed concepts (a complex form of multi-dimensional binary search).

5. *Incremental Versus One-Shot Induction:* One-shot inductive learning systems consider all the positive and negative instances that will ever be seen as training data at one time and produce a concept description not open to further modification (Dietterich and Michalski 1983). Incremental techniques produce the best-guess concept (Winston 1975) or the range of concepts consistent with the data so far, as in version spaces (Mitchell 1978), and can interleave learning and performance. As the latter reflect more accurately real-world situations in which learning is an ongoing process, they are currently the ones more heavily investigated.

3. The Analytic Paradigm

A more recent but very widely studied paradigm for learning is based on analytical learning from few exemplars (often a single one) plus a rich underlying domain theory. The methods involved are deductive rather than inductive, utilizing past problem solving experience (the exemplars) to guide which deductive chains to perform when solving new problems, or to formulate search control rules that enable more efficient application of domain knowledge. Thus, analytic methods focus on improving the efficiency of a system without sacrificing accuracy or generality, rather than extending its library of concept descriptions. The precursors of modern analytic learning methods are macro-operators (Fikes and Nilsson 1971—Chapter 17 of this volume), and formal methods such as weakest precondition analysis. Presently, analytic learning methods focus on explanation-based learning (DeJong and Mooney 1986, Mitchell, Keller, and Kedar-Cabelli 1986), multi-level chunking (Laird, Rosenbloom, and Newell 1986), iterative macro-operators (Cheng and Carbonnel 1986), and derivational analogy (Carbonell 1986). Some fundamental issues cut across all analytic methods:

1. *Representation of Instances:* In analytic methods an instance corresponds to a portion of a problem solving trace, and learning uses that single instance plus background knowledge (often called a *domain theory*). In the simplest case an instance is just a sequence of operators, which can be grouped into macro-operators, modified in analogical transfer, or viewed as steps in a "proof" of the problem solution for explanation-based learning. More recently, problem solving traces carry with them the justification structure (i.e., the goal-subgoal tree, annotations on why each operator was selected, and a trace of failed solution attempts, all interconnected with dependency links). These traces permit richer learning processes such as generalized chunking, derivational analogy, and explanation-based specialization (Minton et al. 1987).

2. *Learning from Success or Failure:* The earliest analytic techniques acquired only the ability to replicate success more efficiently (e.g., macro-operators, early EBL, and early chunking). However, much can be learned from failure in order to avoid similar pitfalls in future situations sharing the same underlying failure causes. Recent EBL techniques, analogical methods, and to some extent chunking in systems like SOAR (Laird, Rosenbloom, and Newell 1986) learn both from success and from failure.

3. *Degree of Generalization:* The control knowledge acquired in analytical learning can be specific to the situation in the exemplar or generalized as permitted by the domain theory. Generalization strategies range from

the elimination of irrelevant information (in virtually all analytical methods) to the application of general meta-reasoning strategies to elevate control knowledge to the provably most general form in the presence of a strong domain and architectural theory (Minton et al. 1987).

4. *Closed Versus Open Loop Learning:* Open loop learning implies one-pass acquisition of new knowledge, regardless of later evidence questioning its correctness or utility. In contrast, closed loop learning permits future evaluation of the new knowledge for modification or even elimination should it not improve system performance as desired. Performance measures of newly acquired knowledge are often empirical in nature; only the acquisition of the control knowledge is purely analytical.

4. The Genetic Paradigm

Genetic algorithms (also called "classifier systems") represent the extreme empirical position among the machine learning paradigms. They have been inspired by a direct analogy to mutations in biological reproduction (crossovers, point mutations, etc.) and Darwinian natural selection (survival of the fittest in each ecological niche). Variants of a concept description correspond to individuals of a species, and induced changes and recombinations of these concepts are tested against an objective function (the natural selection criterion) to see which to preserve in the gene pool. In principle, genetic algorithms encode a parallel search through concept space, with each process attempting coarse-grain hill climbing.

Stemming from the work of Holland (1975) the genetic algorithm community has grown largely independent of other machine learning approaches, and has developed its own analysis tools, applications, and workshops. However, many of the underlying problems and techniques are shared with the mainline inductive methods and with the connectionist paradigm. For instance, as in all empirical learning, assigning credit (or blame) for changes in performance as measured by the objective function is difficult and indirect. There are a multiplicity of methods to address this problem in the inductive approaches, dating back to Samuel (1963 and Chapter 15 of this volume). For genetic algorithms, Holland developed the *bucket brigade* algorithm (Holland 1986, and Chapter 11 of this volume). And, credit/blame assignment is positively central to all connectionist learning methods, as exemplified by the back propagation technique.

5. The Connectionist Paradigm

Connectionist learning systems, also called "neural networks" (NNets) or "parallel distributed processing systems" (PDPs), have received much attention of late. They have overcome the theoretical limitations of perceptrons and early linear networks by the introduction of "hidden layers" to represent intermediate processing and compute nonlinear recognition functions. There are two basic types of connectionist systems: those that use distributed representations—where a concept corresponds to an activation pattern spanning, potentially, the entire network—and those that use localized representations where physical portions of the network correspond to individual concepts. The former is the more prevalent, although hierarchical modularization for complex systems limits the physical extent of concept representations.

Connectionist systems learn to discriminate among equivalence classes of patterns from an input domain in a holistic manner. They are presented with training sets of representative instances of each class, correctly labeled (with some noise tolerance), and they learn to recognize these and other instances of each representative class. Learning consists of readjusting weights in a fixed topology network via different learning algorithms such as *Boltzmann* (Hinton, Sejnowski, and Ackley 1984) or *back propagation*. These algorithms, in essence, calculate credit assignment from the final discrimination back to the individual weights on all the active links in the network. There are, of course, many more complex issues and many subtle variations involved.

Amidst structural diversity, one can find strong functional similarities between connectionist learning systems and their symbolic counterparts, namely discriminant learning in inductive systems and genetic algorithms. Induced symbolic decision trees and NNets both are trained on a number of preclassified instance patterns, both are noise-tolerant, and after training both are given the task of classifying new instances correctly. In order to evaluate the appropriateness of each technique to the task at hand, one must ask some detailed quantitative questions, such as comparing the ease of casting training data into acceptable representations, the amount of training data required for sufficiently accurate performance, the relative computational burden of each technique in both training and performance phases, and other such metrics.

6. Cross-Paradigmatic Observations

Consider the larger picture, contrasting the three symbolic paradigms and connectionist systems in general. But, rather than engaging in the perennial sectarian debate of supporting one paradigm at the expense of the other, let us summarize the properties of a domain problem that favor the selection of each basic approach:

1. *Signal-Symbol Mapping:* From continuous signals such as wave forms into meaningful discrete symbols such as phonemes in speech recognition. Best approach: Connectionism (or traditional statistical learning methods such as dynamic programming or hidden Markoff models).

2. *Continuous Pattern Recognition:* From analog signals to a small discrete set of equivalence classes. Best approach: Connectionism. Inductive or genetic approaches require that the signal-symbol map be solved first, or that a predefined feature set with numerical ranges be given a priori.

3. *Discrete Pattern Recognition:* From collections of features to membership in a predefined equivalence class (e.g., noninteractive medical diagnosis). Best approach: Inductive learning of decision trees. Other inductive approaches, genetic algorithms, and even connectionist methods can apply.

4. *Acquiring New Concept Descriptions:* From examples to general descriptions. Best approach: Induction with characteristic concept descriptions, permitting explanation to human users or manipulation by other system modules. Genetic algorithms and connectionist approaches do not produce characteristic concept descriptions.

5. *Acquiring Rules for Expert Systems:* From behavioral traces to general rules. If a strong domain theory is present, analogical or EBL approaches are best. If not, inductive or genetic approaches prevail. Connectionist systems do not preserve memory of earlier states and therefore cannot emulate well multi-step inferences or deductive chains.

6. *Enhancing the Efficiency of Rule-Based Systems:* From search guided only by weak methods to domain-dependent focused behavior. Best approach: Analytic techniques ranging from macro-operators and chunking to EBL and analogy. Here is where background knowledge can be used most effectively to reformulate control decisions for efficient behavior by analytic means.

7. *Instruction and Symbiotic Reasoning:* From stand-alone system to collaborative problem solving. When user and system must pool resources and reason jointly, or when either attempts to instruct the other, knowledge must be encoded in an explicit manner comprehensible to both. Best approaches: Inductive (with characteristic concept descriptions) or analytic (often case-based analogical) reasoning. Neither genetic systems nor (especially) connectionist ones represent the knowledge gained in a manner directly communicable to the user or other system modules.

Imagine attempting to understand the external significance of a huge matrix of numerical connection strengths.

8. *Integrated Reasoning Architectures:* From general reasoning principles to focused behavior in selected domains. In principle all methods of learning should apply, although the analytic ones have been most successful thus far.

At the risk of oversimplification, one may make a general observation: Connectionist approaches are superior for single-step gestalt recognition in unstructured continuous domains, if very many training examples are present. At the opposite end of the spectrum, analytic methods are best for well-structured knowledge-rich domains that require deep reasoning and multi-step inference, even if few training examples are available. Inductive and genetic techniques are best in the center of the wide gulf between these two extreme points. Clearly there are many tasks that can be approached by more than one method, and evaluating which might be the best approach requires detailed quantitative analysis. Perhaps more significantly, there are complex tasks where multiple forms of learning should co-exist, with connectionist approaches at the sensor interface, inductive ones for formulating empirical rules of behavior, and analytic ones to improve performance when the domain model is well enough understood.

26

Improving Human Decision Making through Case-Based Decision Aiding

Janet L. Kolodner

1. Introduction

Much of AI is sold to the world as fully automated expert systems, that is, systems based on rules that, given a problem statement, will produce a solution. Such systems have been highly successful in solving problems in many well-circumscribed domains. They have not been successful, however, in solving problems requiring creativity, broad commonsense knowledge, or esthetic judgment.

There are three ways we might deal with this problem: First, we might throw our hands up in despair, claiming that after 30 years, if AI can't solve these problems, it isn't worth continuing the endeavor. The opponents of AI have been vocal about this approach. However, this approach is the wrong way to deal with the failings of expert systems. After all, the technology is young and has been useful to many industries in solving important but narrow problems.

A second approach is to continue trying to give the computer the full capabilities people have. The majority of AI researchers are involved in this effort. Doug Lenat, for example, is attempting to put all human consensus knowledge into the machine in CYC (Guha and Lenat 1990; Lenat and Guha 1990). Others are working on a variety of necessary reasoning methods and knowledge representations. Indeed, much of the research in the AI lab at the Georgia Institute of Technology is aimed in this direction. This approach is the one that will lead us into the AI future. It will allow us to better understand what cognition is about and will allow us to eventually develop systems with improved cognitive capabilities.

The third approach is aimed toward the present. Researchers ask, "Is there a way to take what we know now about AI and create systems that can do better than current ones?" The answer to this question is, "Yes, if we can develop an appropriate symbiotic relationship between people and machines." We are then left with a set of other more substantial questions: How can we make sure that computers and people have the right interactions? What responsibilities should the computer take on? What should people be responsible for? What methodologies are available for building these symbiotic systems?

One way to approach these problems is to examine the natural reasoning people do, develop a cognitive model of this reasoning, and explore which parts of the process are easy for people and which parts are hard. At the same time, it is appropriate to ask whether the machine can provide help in those areas where people have trouble. One hopes a complement can be found. Such an approach has the advantage of producing a system that can be useful now and that can be made even better as we begin to better understand what else people need and how to make the computer perform these services.

My approach to these questions comes from experience with a reasoning methodology called case-based reasoning (Kolodner 1988; Kolodner, Simpson, and Sycara 1985; Hammond 1986, 1989). *Case-based reasoning* is an analogical reasoning method. It means reasoning from old cases or experiences in an effort to solve problems, critique solutions, explain anomalous situations, or interpret situations. Many computer programs have been written that use case-based reasoning for problem solving or interpretation. MEDIATOR (Simpson 1985; Kolodner and Simpson 1989) and PERSUADER (Sycara 1987), for example, use cases to resolve disputes. JULIA (Kolodner 1987a, 1987b; Hinrichs 1988, 1989), CLAVIER (Barletta and Hennessy 1989), and KRITIK (Goel 1989; Goel and Chandrasekaran 1989) use case-based reasoning for design. CHEF (Hammond 1986, 1989) and PLEXUS (Alterman 1988) are case-based planners. HYPO (Ashley 1988; Ashley and Rissland 1987) is a case-based legal reasoner. CASEY (Koton 1988), PROTOS (Bareiss 1989), CELIA (Redmond 1989), and MEDIC (Turner 1989) use case-based reasoning for diagnosis.

Case-based reasoning provides both a methodology for building systems and a cognitive model of people. It is consistent with much that psychologists have observed in the natural problem solving that people do (for example, Read and Cesa 1990; Klein and Calderwood 1988; and Ross 1986). People tend to be comfortable using case-based reasoning for decision making.[1] In dynamically changing situations and other situations where much is unknown and when solutions are not clear cut, it seems to be the preferred method of reasoning (Klein and Calderwood 1988).

Psychologists have observed, however, that people have several problems in doing analogical or case-based reasoning. Although they are good at using analogs to solve new problems, they are not always good at remembering the right ones (Read and Cesa 1990; Holyoak 1985; Gentner 1987, 1989). However, computers are good at remembering. The idea in case-based decision aiding is that the computer augments the person's memory by providing cases (analogs) for a person to use in solving a problem. The person does the actual decision making using these cases as guidelines. In essence, computer augmentation of a person's memory allows this person to make better case-based decisions because it makes more cases (and perhaps better ones) available to the person than would be available without the machine. At the same time, the person is free to use a reasoning method that comes naturally to make these decisions.

In this chapter, I first present a short overview of case-based reasoning, then discuss the analogical problem solving people do and the help they need and what the computer can provide. I continue with a technical description of the *indexing problem,* the problem of making sure cases are available at appropriate times, and then discuss how cases might be chosen to put into such a system. I close with the implications of such a system for human decision making, for both novices and experts.[2]

2. Case-Based Reasoning: An Overview

A host is planning a meal for a set of people who include, among others, several people who eat no meat or poultry, one of whom is also allergic to milk products, several meat-and-potatoes men, and her friend Anne. Because it is tomato season, she wants to use tomatoes as a major ingredient in the meal. As she plans the meal, she remembers the following:

> I once served tomato tart (made from mozzarella cheese, tomatoes, dijon mustard, basil, and pepper, all in a pie crust) as the main dish during the summer when I had vegetarians come for dinner. It was delicious and easy to make. But I can't serve that to Elana (the one allergic to milk).

She considers whether she can adapt this solution to suit Elana. Another case suggests an adaptation.

> I have adapted recipes for Elana before by substituting tofu products for cheese. I could do that, but I don't know how good the tomato tart will taste that way.

She decides not to serve tomato tart and continues planning. Because it is summer, she decides that grilled fish would be a good main course. However, she now remembers something else:

> Last time I tried to serve Anne grilled fish, she wouldn't eat it. I had to put hot dogs on the grill at the last minute.

This memory suggests to her that she shouldn't serve fish, but she wants to anyway. She considers whether there is a way to serve fish so that Anne will eat it.

> I remember seeing Anne eat mahi-mahi in a restaurant. I wonder what kind of fish she will eat. The fish I served her was whole fish with the head on. The fish in the restaurant was a fillet and more like steak than fish. I guess I need to serve a fish that is more like meat than fish. Perhaps swordfish will work. I wonder if Anne will eat swordfish. Swordfish is like chicken, and I know she eats chicken.

Here, she is using examples and counterexamples of a premise (Anne doesn't eat fish) to try to derive an interpretation of the premise that stands up to scrutiny.

The hypothetical host is utilizing case-based reasoning to plan a meal. In *case-based reasoning,* a reasoner remembers previous situations similar to the current one and uses them to help solve the new problem. In the previous example, remembered cases are used to suggest a means of solving the new problem (for example, to suggest a main dish), suggest a means of adapting a solution that doesn't fit (for example, substitute a tofu product for cheese), warn of possible failures (for example, Anne won't eat fish), and interpret a situation (for example, why didn't Anne eat the fish; will she eat swordfish?).

Case-based reasoning can mean adapting old solutions to meet new demands, using old cases to explain new situations, using old cases to critique new solutions, or reasoning from precedents to interpret a new situation (much like lawyers do) or create an equitable solution to a new problem (much like labor mediators do).

If we watch the way people around us solve problems, we are likely to observe case-based reasoning in constant use. Attorneys are taught to use cases as precedents for constructing and justifying arguments in new cases. Mediators and arbitrators are taught to do the same. Other professionals are not taught to use case-based reasoning but often find that it provides a way to efficiently solve problems. Consider, for example, a doctor faced with a patient who has an unusual combination of symptoms. If s/he's previously seen a patient with similar symptoms, s/he is likely to remember the old case and propose the old diagnosis as a solution to the new problem. If proposing these disorders was previously time consuming, this approach is a big time savings. Of course, the doctor can't assume the old answer is correct. S/he must still validate it for the new case in a way that doesn't prohibit considering other likely diagnoses. Nevertheless, remembering the old case allows him(her) to easily generate a plausible answer.

Similarly, a car mechanic faced with an unusual mechanical problem is likely to remember other similar problems and consider whether these solutions explain the new problem. Doctors evaluating the appropriateness of a therapeutic procedure or judging which of several are appropriate are also likely to remember instances using each procedure and make their judgments based on previous experiences. Problem instances of using a procedure are particularly helpful here; they tell the doctor what could go wrong, and when an explanation is available that explains why the old problem occurred, they focus the doctor in finding the information s/he needs to make sure the problem won't show up again. We hear cases being cited time and again by our political leaders in explaining why some action was taken or should be taken. Many management decisions are also made based on previous experience.

Case-based reasoning is also used extensively in day-to-day commonsense reasoning. The meal-planning example presented previously is typical of the reasoning we all do from day to day. When we order a meal in a restaurant, we often base decisions about what might be good on our other experiences in this restaurant and those like it. As we plan our household activities, we remember what previously worked and didn't work and use this information to create our new plans. A childcare provider mediating an argument between two children remembers what previously worked and didn't work in calming such situations and bases his(her) suggestion on this information.

In general, the second time solving some problem or doing some task is easier than the first because we remember and repeat the previous solution. We are more competent the second time because we remember our mistakes and go out of our way to avoid them.

There are two styles of case-based reasoning: problem solving and interpretive. In the *problem-solving style* of case-based reasoning, solutions to new problems are derived using old solutions as a guide. Old solutions can provide almost-right solutions to new problems, and they can provide warnings of potential mistakes or failures. In the previous example, past cases suggest tomato tart as a main dish, a method of adapting tomato tart for those who don't eat cheese, and a type of fish that Anne will eat. A case also warns of the potential for a failure—Anne won't eat certain kinds of fish. Case-based reasoning of this variety can support a variety of problem-solving tasks, including planning, diagnosis, and design.

In the *interpretive style,* new situations are evaluated in the context of old situations. A lawyer, for example, uses interpretive case-based reasoning when s/he uses a series of old cases to justify an argument in a new case. A child who says "But you let sister do it" is using a case to justify his(her) argument. Managers making strategic decisions use the interpretive style. We often use interpretive case-based reasoning to evaluate the pros and cons of a problem solution. In general, the interpretive style of case-based reasoning is useful for situation classification; the evaluation of a solution; argumentation; the justification of a solution, interpretation, or plan; and the projection of effects of a decision or plan. Interpretive case-based reasoning can also be used during problem solving, as we saw the host in our initial example do when trying to justify serving swordfish to a guest who is known to not like some kinds of fish.

Interpretive case-based reasoning is most useful when there are no computational methods available to evaluate a solution or position. Often, in these situations, there are so many unknowns that even if computational methods were available, the knowledge necessary to run them would usually be absent. A reasoner who uses cases to help evaluate and justify decisions or interpretations is making up for his(her) lack of knowledge by assuming that the world is consistent.

Both styles of case-based reasoning depend heavily on a case-retrieval mechanism that can recall useful cases at appropriate times, and also in both styles, storage of new situations in memory allows learning from experience. The problem-solving style is characterized by the substantial use of adaptation processes to generate solutions and interpretive processes to judge derived solutions. The interpretive style uses cases to provide justifications for solutions, allowing the evaluation of solutions when no clear-cut methods are available and the interpretation of situations when definitions of the situation's boundaries are open ended or fuzzy.

The major processes shared by reasoners that do case-based reasoning are case retrieval and case storage (also called memory update). To make sure that poor solutions are not repeated along with the good ones, case-based reasoners must also evaluate their solutions.

The two styles of case use, however, require that different reasoning be done once cases are retrieved. In problem-solving case-based reasoning, a ballpark solution to the new problem is *proposed* by extracting the solution from some retrieved case. This step is followed by *adaptation,* the process of fixing an old solution to fit a new situation, and *criticism,* the process of evaluating the new solution before trying it out. In interpretive case-based reasoning, a ballpark interpretation or desired result is proposed, sometimes based on retrieved cases, sometimes imposed from the outside (for example, when a lawyer's client requires a certain result). This step is followed by *justification,* the process of creating an argument for the proposed solution, which is done by comparing and contrasting the new situation to prior cases, and *criticism,* the process of debugging the argument, which is done by generating hypothetical situations and trying the argument out on them.

These steps are, in some sense, recursive. The criticize and adapt steps, for example, often require new cases to be retrieved. There are also several loops in the process. Criticism can lead to additional adaptation, so might evaluation. In addition, when reasoning is not progressing well using one case, the whole process might need to be restarted from the top, with a new case chosen.

3. Human Use of Case-Based and Analogical Reasoning

In the context of case-based and analogical reasoning, let us examine what people do well, what people do badly, and the reasons behind using case-based reasoning.

3.1 What People Do Well

Psychologists observing the problem-solving and decision-making procedures of people see them using case-based reasoning under a variety of circumstances. Ross (1986, 1989), for example, shows that people learning a new skill often refer to previous problems to refresh their memories on how to do the task. Research conducted in the lab at Georgia Tech shows that both novice and experienced car mechanics use their own experiences and those of others to help them generate hypotheses about what is wrong with a car, recognize problems (for example, a testing instrument is not working), and remember how to test for different diagnoses (Lancaster and Kolodner 1988, Redmond 1989). Other research in the lab shows that physicians extensively use previous cases to generate hypotheses about what is wrong with a patient; help them interpret test results; and select therapies when several are available, and none are well understood. Researchers also observed architects and caterers recalling, merging, and adapting old design plans to create new ones.

Klein and Calderwood (1988) observed expert decision makers in complex, dynamically changing situations. These experts use analogs to understand situational dynamics, generate options, and predict the effects of implementing an option in several different naturalistic decision-making situations. They observed experts using cases to both suggest solutions that were then adapted and evaluate solutions and situations. In the naturalistic situations they observed, the use of analogs was far more important than the application of abstract principles, rules, or conscious deliberation about alternatives. Analogs or cases provided concrete manifestations of the rules or principles that allow them to easily be applied. Cases also allowed decision makers to be alert to causal factors operating during an incident, anticipate what might happen if a course of action was implemented, suggest options, and be reassured that an option worked and could be relied on. Their primary power, claims Klein (Klein, Whitaker, and King 1988), is that they allow the decision maker to deal with unknown and uncertain information. An analog reflects the ways variables affected solutions in the past. In the same study, Klein and Whitaker found that the case-based method is much more reliable than unstructured prediction when there are many unknowns.

Read (Read and Cesa 1990) observed people using old cases to explain anomalous occurrences and found them particularly adept at using this approach when the anomalous event reminded them of a personal experience.

The conclusion I draw from these studies is that reasoning using analogs is a natural process for people, especially when there is much uncertainty or many unknowns and during early learning. People know well how to use analogs to reason, and the use of analogs in reasoning (at least for experts) results in reliable solutions.

3.2 What People Do Badly

Despite the fact that people use cases well to reason, there are a number of pitfalls for people when using cases. Some people blindly use case-based reasoning, relying on previous experience without validating it in the new situation. A case-based reasoner might allow cases to bias him(her) too much in solving a new problem (Gilovich 1981), and often, people are not reminded of the most appropriate sets of cases when they are reasoning (Holyoak 1985, Gentner 1989). In addition, when there is much to remember, people cannot always access the right information when they need it.

Novices have a variety of other problems. They cannot do analogical reasoning well for two of reasons. First, they are missing the experiences they need to make good analogical decisions. Second, they are missing the experiences that tell them which parts of a situation are the important ones to focus on; that is, their criteria for judging the similarity of cases is deficient.

3.3 Why Case-Based Reasoning?

People use case-based or analogical reasoning in the whole variety of situations previously illustrated and discussed. One question we might want to consider is "why"? We start by considering why a doctor or anyone else trained in the practice of making logical decisions would make case-based inferences. After all, the doctor is trained to use facts and knowledge, and case-based reasoning looks like it is based on hearsay. The answer is simple. The doctor is trained to recognize disorders in isolation and to recognize common combinations of disorders. S/he also knows the etiology of disorders, that is, how they progress. However, s/he cannot be trained to recognize every combination of disorders, and the knowledge s/he has of disease processes is time consuming to use to generate plausible diagnoses. If s/he once used his(her) knowledge of the disease process to solve a hard problem, it makes sense to cache the solution in such a way that it can be reused. That is, once s/he has learned to recognize a novel combination of disorders, if s/he remembers this experience, s/he will be able to recognize it again, just as s/he recognizes more common combinations, without the difficult reasoning that was necessary the first time. The logical medical judgment comes later in deciding whether the patient does indeed have the proposed set of diseases.

Thus, case-based reasoning is useful to people who know a lot about a task and domain because it gives them a way to reuse hard reasoning that they've done in the past. It is equally useful, however, to those who know little about a task or domain. Consider, for example, a person who has never done any entertaining yet has to plan the meal specified in the introduction. His(her) own entertaining experience won't help. However, if s/he has been to dinner parties, s/he has a place to start. If s/he remembered meals s/he'd been served under circumstances similar to those s/he has to deal with, s/he could use one of these meals to get started. For example, if s/he could generate a list of large dinner parties s/he has attended, then for each one, s/he could figure out whether it was easy to make and inexpensive, and when s/he remembered one, adapt it to fit.

Case-based reasoning is also useful when knowledge is incomplete, or evidence is sparse. Logical systems have trouble dealing with either of these situations because they want to base their answers on what is well known and sound. More traditional AI systems use certainty factors and other methods of inexact reasoning to counter these problems, all of which require considerable effort on the part of the computer, and none of which seem intuitively plausible. Case-based reasoning provides another method for dealing with incomplete knowledge. A case-based reasoner makes assumptions to fill in incomplete or missing knowledge based on what his(her) experience tells him(her) and goes on from there. Solutions generated in this way won't always be optimal or even right, but if the reasoner is careful about evaluating proposed answers, the case-based methodology provides a way to easily generate answers.

4. Using Case-Based Reasoning to Aid Human Decision Making

We now have several facts at our disposal to use in exploring how decision making in people can be improved. First, people find it easy to use analogs in reasoning, but they often find it hard to remember the right ones. Second, the use of analogs in solving problems and making decisions has many advantages if analogs are used well: They help in dealing with uncertainty, assessing situations, deriving solutions, and so on. Third, the methodology called case-based reasoning, which has been implemented in several computer programs, provides us with computational methods for case retrieval, adaptation, and evaluation.

My proposal is to use the computational methods we have available to implement systems that help people, both novices and experts, to better do analogical reasoning. Because people have trouble remembering appropriate cases, the system will augment their memories by providing, at appropriate times, the relevant experiences of others. However, because people are better at dealing with esthetics, ethics, creative adaptation, and judgment, we leave the real decision making to people. That is, the computer will provide cases to human problem solvers at appropriate times to help them with such tasks as coming up with solutions, adapting old solutions, critiquing and evaluating solutions, and warning of potential problems.

Two hypothetical systems illustrate the division of labor. The first system is a design assistant. The second is a mediator's assistant. In both systems, the language of discourse is English, which is the easiest way to explain the interactions between a system and a person. A better interface than the one presented here, however, would probably be more graphic and allow communication through menus and mice.

4.1 An Architect's Assistant

The hypothetical system I show here helps an architect in doing design. An architect has to deal with a number of issues: The function must be appropriate, the design must fit the site, costs must be within limits, and so on. In the example I show, the architect's problem is to design a geriatric hospital. Let us assume that the computer screen is configured with a space for notes, a space for graphic manipulations, a space for the problem specification, and a space where cases are presented. Let us further assume that each case has both a picture part and a textual part.

On the screen, we see the new problem in the problem specification space and a representation of the site, showing its contour, size, and shape, in the graphic space.[3]

> *Problem:* Design a geriatric hospital: The site is a 4-acre wooded sloping square; the hospital will serve 150 inpatients and 50 outpatients daily; offices for 40 doctors are needed. Both long-term and short-term facilities are needed. It should be more like a home than an institution, and it should allow easy visitation by family members.

> *Screen:* The site, its contour and shape, is shown.

The person now uses the mouse to highlight those parts of the problem specification that s/he feels need to be addressed at this point early in the design.

> *Person:* Hospital, homeyness, provision of visitation, long-term and short-term care, and geriatric are the elements highlighted.

The computer uses these highlighted parts of the problem as preferences in finding useful cases in memory. The most useful cases will match all these features; less useful ones (that perhaps can address only some part of the problem) will match some subset of these features. The computer finds many cases and partitions them according to how well they match the highlighted criteria. It presents its ordered partitions and asks the person which s/he would like to see more detail on. At the same time, the computer does some bookkeeping (invisible right now). It tracks which cases in its lists achieve which of the requested features.

Computer: I know of many long-term facilities for the elderly, many acute-care hospitals, and one geriatric hospital: Wesley Woods in Atlanta. Of the acute-care hospitals, Piedmont Hospital in Atlanta is the most homey. Of the long-term facilities, the Jewish Home in Fairfield County, Connecticut, is closest in the type of care it provides and the ability to provide opportunities for family visitation. What would you like to see?

The person chooses to see Wesley Woods, the only geriatric hospital with both long-term and short-term facilities. The computer shows a picture of the layout of Wesley Woods and provides a commentary.

Person: Show Wesley Woods.

Screen: Picture and layout of Wesley Woods are shown.

Computer: The goal in designing Wesley Woods was to create a homey atmosphere. To achieve this goal, they used residential, rather than institutional, furnishings, forms, and materials and made sure it was cheery and colorful. They made all the corridors short, so people would feel like they were in a home-sized place. The functional units of the hospital were hidden from normal sight, so the patients didn't feel like they were in a hospital. The design did a very good job of providing homeyness. However, there was one big problem. It is hard for patients and staff to find their way around because the views give no distinguishing landmarks or orienting features, and it is not possible to see one's destination until nearly there. It looks so much like a home that patients and visitors are not sure what to do once they arrive there.

The person makes some notes based on the Wesley Woods successes and failures (make sure corridors have views; make sure corridors have distinguishing features), decides that there are large portions of this design s/he can borrow, and begins to manipulate this design (using icons) to make it fit the new site. It won't fit on the site because of the slope. S/he adapts its design by adding a lower floor, subtracting part of the lower floor of Wesley Woods, and putting the two main entries on different levels.

The computer, which is responsible for bookkeeping, now notices that the building has entries on two levels. It knows this configuration to be a difficult design problem and, therefore, attempts to retrieve cases that can help the designer. It retrieves several cases that show how to use two entrances. It interrupts the designer and makes a suggestion. The architect uses this information.

Computer: I have several examples of hospital buildings with entrances on two levels. Georgia Baptist Hospital has lobbies on two levels, one for inpatients, one for outpatients. Brighams and Womens in Boston has entries on two levels with a two-floor lobby that combines inpatient and outpatient functions. The lobbies are connected by a ceremonial escalator.

Person: I'll put the outpatient lobby on the bottom level and the inpatient lobby on the second level.

The computer has tracked the goals of the designer and how they were achieved in other cases that the designer might not have seen yet. It has a mechanism for noticing when design goals are violated by design decisions. In this case, because the inpatient entrance is above usable ground, and the Jewish Home in Fairfield had provided for easy visitation by providing easy access to the usable outdoors, the program notices a violation of design goals. It is also able to retrieve another case, where even though the ground sloped, access to the outside was easily provided. It interrupts the architect to warn of the potential problem and suggest a solution.

Computer: One of the nice features of the Jewish Home in Fairfield is the access to the outside that patients have. That's a potential problem if the inpatient lobby is on the upper floor.

I know of another institution where access was important and was provided by putting patient rooms and gathering places against the same slope, so people could walk right outside. In another, the two functions were divided between two different buildings, each on a different part of the slope, so everyone had access to the outside.

I do not continue with the example here but stop to point out the responsibilities of the machine and the person. The computer has two responsibilities: bookkeeping and retrieval. The bookkeeping it does is of two varieties. First, it tracks the good points of designs it remembers. The Jewish Home, for example, had the advantage of providing patients with easy access to the outside. This configuration made visitation by family members pleasant. In addition, the computer makes easy inferences to make sure, to the best of its knowledge, that good points of designs it knows of are not violated and that bad points are not repeated.

The case retrieval done by the system has three purposes: First, cases suggest solutions to problems or methods for computing solutions. Second, cases provide warnings of potential problems. Third, cases help in critiquing.

Everything the computer does is in service of the responsibilities of the person using the system. Thus, the human user is responsible for hard adaptation, the choice of features to consider, the choice of cases to consider, the evaluation of suggestions, the evaluation of warnings, and all decision making.

4.2 A Mediator's Assistant

In the architect's assistant, the computer looked over the person's shoulder and provided warnings and suggestions as necessary. In this example, also hypothetical, we see the user requesting cases from the system to help him(her) in answering several necessary questions to assess the situation and come up with a solution. This example is based on the reasoning done by an automated case-based mediation system called PERSUADER (Sycara 1987). PERSUADER's task was to mediate labor-management disputes.

In this example, we see the mediator presented with a problem. The union wants a large salary increase, but the company cannot afford it. To figure out what to do, the mediator must collect some information. S/he wants to know why the company is losing money. The system helps him(her) by providing several cases of companies losing money, each of which suggests a different explanation. Note again that I use English interaction because it is easy to show. The person might actually interact with the system in some other way.

Problem: Southern Airlines presents its employees with the ultimatum that if they don't take wage cuts of 8 percent, the company, which has become noncompetitive, will go bankrupt.

Mediator: Get me cases to suggest why the company is losing money although the industry is prosperous.

Computer:

Great Railroad Company: When it was losing money in prosperous times, it was because the union was insisting on featherbedding, an expensive and unnecessary practice.

Northern Airlines Shuttle: When it was losing money in prosperous times, it was because the management was not treating the employees well. The employees, in turn, were not as productive as they should have been.

Western Trucking: When it was losing money in prosperous times, it was because of mismanagement by the executive board. Board members were using the resources of Northern Airlines for purposes unrelated to the company.

The mediator considers each alternative, collecting the information s/he needs and decides that this situation is a case of mismanagement. S/he now needs to find a solution. S/he adds to the representation of the problem that there is mismanagement in the company and asks the computer to suggest solutions. The computer responds with several cases.

Computer:

Western Trucking: Management was forced to resign, and the employees took a pay cut until things were back to normal. It took time to get back on the road, but the consensus is that the new management did better than the old management could have.

Foobaz Airlines: Employees took a pay cut to avoid bankruptcy, but management was forced to put employees on the board and give them a share in the company. The president took things under control, firing those managers who had been involved in mismanagement. S/he made it clear that employees on the board were to be taken seriously. Because employees felt responsible for their share of the company and also that they were listened to, productivity went up immediately, and the company began making more money. Two years later, the employees not only regained their old salaries but began making more than their counterparts in other airlines. This approach could not have been taken without the willingness of both parties to cooperate in the agreement.

In this hypothetical example, the aiding system is much more passive than in the previous example. Even so, cases that are recalled by the system provide the user with much important data. We can think of this system as a smart interface for a database system. It is able to recall partially matching cases that a decision maker can base analysis and decisions on. It is more than a database because it does its retrieval based on the specifics of a situation and finds partially matching cases that can be used to answer the specific questions of the user. It does not require the full matching of features, nor does it require a database administrator to formulate queries. Rather, it allows the decision maker to ask the questions and be close to the data decisions are based on.

5. Implementing Case-Based Decision-Aiding Systems

The examples show us that case-based decision-aiding systems can be passive or active. They can be used to aid novices or experts, and they can be used to help a wide variety of decision-making activities. Some function of such a system depends on the use it will be put to, but much of the function of any such system depends on the cases that are in the system and the means of retrieving them. Several issues come up in discussing implementation. We could consider how to build the systems, what retrieval algorithms to use, what memory update algorithms to use, and so on, or we can consider some conceptual issues that are independent of any particular implementation. We choose to do the latter, making the assumption that a smart programmer can program a retrieval algorithm or that case-based reasoning shells will be available and used. In this section, therefore, I first consider the representation of cases; then the issue of assigning indexes to cases such that they can be retrieved at appropriate times; and, finally, the choice of cases to seed a case-based decision aider.

5.1 Representing Cases

Representations of cases can be in any of several forms, including predicate representations, frame representations, or representations resembling database entries. What is important to this discussion is the content that must be represented.

There are three major parts to any case, although for any particular case, they might not all be filled in: First is the *problem-situation description,* the state of the world at the time the case was happening and, if appropriate, what problem needed solving at this time. Second is the *solution,* the stated or derived solution to the problem specified in the problem description. Some case-based reasoners also store traces of how the problem was solved. Third is the *outcome,* the resulting state of the world when the solution was carried out.

Depending on what is included in a case, the case can be used for a variety of purposes. For example, cases that include a problem and solution can be used in deriving solutions to new problems. Those cases with a situation description and outcome can be used in evaluating new situations. If the case also has a specified solution, it can be used in evaluating proposed solutions and anticipating potential problems before they occur.

In addition, a case is as useful in later reasoning as the information it holds. Several items might be represented in an outcome, for example. The baseline is *execution feedback,* that is, what the state of the world was after (and while) the solution was carried out. With this information, a case-based reasoner can anticipate potential problems and project the outcome of new solutions to aid in evaluation. If the case also includes an explanation of why an outcome came about (that is, the causal connections between the initial situation, the solution, and the outcome) and the way in which it was repaired, the case can also be used for guidance in repairing a similar failure in the future.

Similarly, if the solution part of a case designates only a solution, it can be used to help in proposing a solution to a new case. If the solution also includes a store of how it was derived, then the old solution method can be attempted in cases where the old solution is inapplicable. If it includes connections between the problem description, the situation, and the solution, they can be used to help in guiding adaptation.

5.2 The Indexing Problem

Perhaps the biggest issue in case-based reasoning and the design of case-based decision-making aids is the retrieval of appropriate cases. How can we make the computer find the right ones at the right times? As I stated earlier, I call this problem the indexing problem. Essentially, the problem is assigning appropriate labels to cases at the time they are entered into the case memory to ensure that they can be retrieved at appropriate times. In general, these labels designate under what circumstances the case might appropriately be retrieved. They are used at retrieval time to judge the appropriateness of an old case to a new situation.

The analysis of some remindings (something that serves as a reminder of something else) collected from people, coupled with experience in building case-based reasoning systems, has led the case-based reasoning community to propose several guidelines for index (label) selection: (1) indexes should be predictive, (2) indexes should be abstract enough to make a case useful in a variety of future situations, (3) indexes should be concrete enough to be recognizable in future cases, and (4) predictions that can be made should be useful.

5.2.1 Predictive Features

I begin by explaining what predictive means. As previously stated, at the most basic level, a case is a description of a problem, its solution, and the outcome of carrying out the solution. Different combinations of problem descriptors are taken into account in coming up with the solution and are responsible for choices made about the solution. Other combinations of problem and solution descriptors, coupled with descriptors of the world, are responsible for parts of the outcome. Any descriptor combination that is responsible for some piece of the solution or its outcome is said to be *predictive* of the part of the solution or outcome that it influenced.

Some examples illustrate. First, consider a meal that was a failure because some guest, a vegetarian, could not eat the main dish, which was meat. The combination of descriptors, "guest was a vegetarian" and "meat was an ingredient in the main dish," was responsible for the failure. If we see this combination again in a meal we plan, we can predict the same failure (the vegetarian won't be able to eat the main dish). These descriptors are predictive of a particular outcome.

Predictive descriptors can also predict better-than-expected outcomes. Consider a cook who decided to try a new recipe that included a combination of novel ingredients, for example, peanut butter, ginger, and eggplant. She might have been leery of the result but willing to take a chance. The dish turned out to be good; eggplant, peanut butter, and ginger complemented each other well. This combination of descriptors—"peanut butter is an ingredient," "ginger is an ingredient," and "eggplant is an ingredient"—was responsible for a successful outcome, the tasty dish. If a dish with this combination of descriptors is considered again, this case can be used to predict that it will be tasty. Alternatively, if these ingredients are available again, this case can be used to suggest a dish that combines them.

Two more examples complete the illustration. Consider now a doctor whose patient had a novel set of symptoms. She considered many different diagnoses and tried many different treatments before finally figuring out what the combination of disorders was and what treatment was effective. The combination of symptoms, which is responsible for the difficulty in reasoning and predicts a diagnosis and treatment, is a good index. Finally, consider a legal decision that was determined by a loophole. Those features of the case that enabled the loophole are the predictive ones. They allowed the loophole to be used in this case and, if seen again, predict that the loophole can be used again.

5.2.2 Abstractness of Indexes

Although cases are specific, indexes to cases need to be chosen so that the case can be used in as broad a selection of situations as appropriate. Often, this approach means indexes should be more abstract than the details of a particular case. Consider, for example, a case from CHEF (Hammond 1986, 1989). CHEF just created a recipe for beef and broccoli, a stir-fried dish. When it first created the recipe and tried it out, it found that the broccoli got soggy. It fixed the order of the steps in the recipe so that the broccoli remained crisp. This case could be indexed in several ways: (1) dish is prepared by stir frying, dish includes beef, and dish includes broccoli and (2) dish is prepared by stir frying, dish includes meat, and dish includes a crisp vegetable.

The first set allows this case to be recalled whenever beef and broccoli are to be stir fried together. This index, however, would not allow recall of this case, for example, when chicken and snow peas are to be stir fried. However, the order of the steps probably has to be the same as for beef and broccoli—snow peas are also a crisp vegetable that should remain crisp. Indexing by the second set of descriptors makes this case more generally applicable.

5.2.3 Concreteness of Indexes

The danger of abstract indexes is that they can be so abstract that the reasoner would never realize that a new situation had these descriptors except through extensive inference. Thus, although indexes need to be generally applicable, they need to be concrete enough so that they can be recognized with little inference. Consider another example from CHEF to illustrate this point. CHEF just created a new recipe for a strawberry souffle. It created this dish by adapting a recipe for vanilla souffle. When it first made the souffle, it fell. CHEF figured out that the problem was that the liquids and leavening were not balanced: There was too much liquid for the amount of leavening in the recipe. It also figured out that the extra liquid was because of the juice in the strawberries. It solved the problem by increasing the leavening to counter the effect of the liquid in the strawberries. This case could be indexed in several ways: (1) dish is of type souffle, and liquids and leavening are not balanced; (2) dish is of type souffle, and dish includes strawberries; (3) dish is of type souffle, and dish includes fruit; and (4) dish is of type souffle, and dish has a lot of liquid.

The last three indexes are clearly better than the first because their features are directly recognizable without inference. The fourth is okay but probably not as good as 2 and 3 because it is hard to tell the difference between too much liquid and the right amount. Indexes 2 and 3 are the most concrete and recognizable, and of them, the third, which mentions fruit rather than strawberries, is more generally applicable.

5.2.4 Usefulness

A final consideration in choosing indexes is the criterion of usefulness. Indexes should be chosen to make the kinds of predictions that will be useful in later reasoning. In general, any issue that came up in solving one problem could come up again in another one. All combinations of descriptors that predict how to deal with reasoning issues or predict the outcome are, thus, useful. In practice, however, a particular case-based decision aider will be responsible for aiding some subset of decisions that must be made. Guidelines for the kinds of indexes that are useful for retrieving cases to aid with different reasoning tasks are as follows:

> To use cases to help generate solutions to problems, index on combinations of descriptors responsible for the choice of a particular solution, solution component, or solution method.

For example, if a reasoner must choose a means of achieving goals, it should index cases by goal, constraint, or feature combinations that were responsible for solving a problem in a particular way.

> Cases recalled based on combinations of descriptors that were responsible for failures are useful for a number of reasoning tasks: anticipating potential problems, explaining reasoning errors and failures, and recovering from reasoning errors and failures.
>
> To use cases for evaluating proposed solutions, index on combinations of case descriptors that were responsible for each case's outcome and on combinations of descriptors that describe outcomes.

Note that any case can have several indexes associated with it. Consider again the strawberry souffle example. Analyzing it again based on the criterion of usefulness, the first descriptor feature set (including "liquids and leavening are not balanced") would be a good index in a system that helps a person to determine how to recover from its failures and knows how to assign blame for failures when they occur. If the same system helps with the creation of solutions, the third descriptor set (including "dish includes fruit") is also a good index.

5.2.5 A Method for Selecting Indexes for Cases

The method for identifying appropriate indexes for chosen cases has the following steps: First, determine what the case could be useful for. Second, determine under what circumstances the case would be useful for each of these tasks. Third, massage the circumstances to make them as recognizable and generally applicable as possible.

To illustrate, consider the following case:

Problem: Twenty people were coming to dinner; it was summer, and tomatoes were in season; we wanted a vegetarian meal; and one person was allergic to milk products.

Solution: We served tomato tart (a cheese-and-tomato pie). To accommodate the person allergic to milk, we used tofu cheese substitute instead of cheese in one of the tarts.

The first step is to determine what the case could be useful for. There are two possible uses for this case: (1) it provides guidelines for choosing a vegetarian main dish with tomatoes and (2) it provides guidelines for accommodating a person allergic to milk when a main dish with cheese is being served.

The next step is to determine under what circumstances this case would be useful for each of these purposes. For the first purpose, it would be useful in two circumstances; for the second, it would be useful in one:

First Purpose: (1) Goal is to choose a main dish, dish is to be vegetarian, and dish is to include tomatoes. (2) Goal is to chose a main dish, dish is vegetarian, and time is summer.

Second Purpose: Main dish has cheese as an ingredient, one or a few guests are allergic to milk products, and goal is to accommodate these guests.

These three circumstances provide the general framework for the indexes to this case. The next step is to massage them to make them as recognizable and generally applicable as possible. There is no massaging necessary for the first two sets of features. For the last index set, we need to change "goal is to accommodate these guests" to something more informative for a case-based reasoner. We change the descriptor to "goal is to adapt the main dish."

5.3 Choosing Cases and Choosing Indexes

The cardinal rule in choosing cases for a case-based aiding system is that cases must be chosen according to the needs of the users. That is, an analysis of the reasoning goals of system users must be done before choosing cases. This analysis is similar to a task analysis. A user might have several kinds of reasoning goals. Some systems will help with the derivation of a solution, some with critiquing, and some with both.

When a system is to help with the derivation of solutions, those reasoning subgoals that people have in deriving solutions must be discovered. Car mechanics, for example, need to come up with hypotheses about what's wrong with the car, test their hypotheses, select repairs for a car's "disorder," and carry out the repairs. Mechanics have particular hypotheses about what's wrong with cars, particular tests that are done for each, and particular repairs. A system to help a car mechanic needs cases that suggest hypotheses about what's wrong with a car under particular conditions, ways of testing hypotheses, and repairs for particular problems.

In addition, if a system is to help with the anticipation of problems before they arise, it must have cases that point out potential problems, and each case must be indexed by those features that were responsible for its failure.

Systems that help in evaluating or critiquing solutions must store solutions with both good and poor outcomes. These cases must be indexed by those features of the problem and solution that predict outcome. A system whose job is to help explain the reasons for poor solutions also needs to index these cases by descriptions of their outcomes.

In general then, cases must cover the range of problems that will come up in the course of reasoning. They should also cover the range of mistakes that are already well known. At the same time, however, system builders must remember that collecting cases is incremental. A system can start incomplete and be augmented with use. In fact, system builders should think of a training phase for case-based systems. The system is first seeded with a variety of problems, then trained with another set of problems to make sure the range of subgoals is covered. This approach results in additional cases being added to the case library. In addition, in domains where there are many unknowns, one should count on adding new cases as they are encountered in the normal course of using the case-based decision aider.

6. Implementations to Date

Several case-based decision-aiding systems have been built to date. All resemble the hypothetical mediation system that was previously shown. That is, the computer acts to augment human memory by retrieving cases but takes a fairly passive role in doing this retrieval: It retrieves what it is asked to retrieve. Some systems also have analysis capabilities built in that draw generalizations based on the retrieved cases. In these systems, both the cases and the generalizations drawn from them are available to the user.

Cognitive System's Battle Planner (Goodman 1989) was the first major case-based decision-aiding system to be built. It is being used in some classes at West Point to help teach battle planning. It holds approximately 600 cases, all of them battles, primarily from World War II. The system helps users to analyze and repair their doctrine-based solutions. The user inputs a description of the battle situation and his(her) solution. Because the armed services provide doctrine about how to deal with different kinds of battle situations, a user who knows the doctrine finds it fairly easy to create these doctrine-based solutions. The problem, of course, is that the doctrine does not account for the subtle factors of a situation.

It is these subtle factors that Battle Planner helps with. The system recalls cases with similar situations and similar solutions and presents their outcomes to the user. It also attempts to analyze outcomes to provide an accounting of why, in general, the proposed type of solution succeeded or failed in these kinds of situations. The user uses the analysis, plus the individual cases, to modify the original solution and begins the process again, this time attempting to debug the new solution. The process continues until the user is satisfied with his(her) solution.

Figure 1 illustrates: The person enters the description of a battle situation

Scenario Situation: Soviet invasion of Europe, a U.S. Division at Fulda Gap, facing a salient (bulge) in the Soviet line, with a hill behind U.S. troops.

	Attacker	Defender
Nationality	Soviets	U.S
Troop Strength	3700	1100
Heavy Tanks	54	34
Light Tanks	30	30
Morale	tired	fresh
Initiative	-	+
Terrain	Rugged, mixed	
Mission	Seize hill	Hold territory
Method	Frontal Assault	Static defensive line

Retrieved Cases: 9 cases from WWII, all attacker wins
  • In one battle, rapid assault ————▶ major victory
  • In two other battles, delaying actions ————▶ successful second defense

Comparative Analysis: Significant factors generated by retriever from its clustering:

These factors favor Attacker Win:
    Defender lacks reserves
    Defender lacks depth

New Mission and Method:

	Attacker	Defender
Nationality	Soviets	U.S.
Mission	Seize hill	Delay
Method	Frontal Assault	Defend in depth

Retrieved Cases: 18 cases, all defender wins

Figure 1. A sample session with Battle Planner.

and his(her) solution. Here, the mission and method fields describe the solution; the other fields describe the battle situation. The user is planning for the American (defender) side. Battle Planner retrieves nine World War II cases, all in which the attacker wins. It provides commentary about what options and variations were tried in prior cases (and their outcomes) and then supplies a comparative analysis. Armed with this information, the user reformulates his (her) solution. This time, the cases retrieved tell him(her) that the solution is satisfactory.

Another case-based decision-aiding system, LADIES (Duncan 1989), is being used by Bell Canada to aid the development of *depreciation* studies (predictions of how long an item will last). The system helps users specify factors that are important in predicting depreciation and then helps the user predict depreciation.

Many other such systems are currently under development. At Georgia

Tech, one system, called ARCHIE, will help architects design a building. Another version of it will help facility managers lay out the office space and furniture for an organization. Another system under development at Georgia Tech, ED, will help elementary school science teachers plan hands-on science lessons. In addition to lesson planning, it will help teachers anticipate the questions students will ask and will help them understand the circumstances in which they should be interacting with the students during hands-on exploratory activities.

Such systems can also be used (with some additions) for training. Several systems of this sort are under development in industry and universities. Trouble shooting seems to be an area where there is particular interest in developing this kind of system.

7. Implications for Human Decision Making

Case-based reasoning seems to be a natural reasoning methodology in people. The thesis of the researchers at Georgia Tech is that if we view case-based reasoning as a cognitive model, it can inform the design of decision-aiding systems. In particular, because people are good at using cases but not as good at recalling the right ones, useful systems could be built that augment human memory by providing people with cases that might help them to reason but allowing all the complex reasoning and decision making to be done by the person.

There are a variety of decision-making situations in which case-based decision aids could usefully be deployed. Case-based decision aids could help with such problem-solving tasks as diagnosis, design, planning, scheduling, and explanation. Evaluation tasks that cases can help with include criticism (evaluating the goodness of a solution or interpretation), justification, interpretation (classification), and projection (given a solution, project outcome or effect when carried out).

There are, of course, advantages and disadvantages in all decision-making methods. The major disadvantage of the case-based method is that the solution space is not fully explored, and as a result, there is no guarantee of an optimal solution. In addition, it requires the collection of hundreds or thousands of concrete cases. However, there seems to be a pretty good match between what people naturally do and what case-based systems can do. The hope is that the pitfalls of the analogical reasoning that people do can be ameliorated by using these kinds of tools.

It is important to note here that the case-based reasoning approach to analogical reasoning provides some new pragmatic ways of dealing with problems that the analogical reasoning community has been grappling with for many years. One issue that has been a focus of research in analogical reasoning is judging similarity. Case-based reasoning focuses instead on usefulness. A case is useful if it can help achieve the goals of the reasoner. Similarity becomes an issue only at the point where two cases look equally useful—when this situation arises, a more similar case might win out. Rather than attempting to come up with algorithms and heuristics for judging similarity, the goal at Georgia Tech has been to come up with a way of marking cases for their usefulness. Indexes are this means. They designate which of several case descriptors are the more important ones to consider in judging how useful a case might be.

Of course, one cannot predict all the situations in which a case can be useful. When information about usefulness is unavailable, a retriever must be able to retrieve and match cases based only on similarity. The preferred and more usual mode, however, is to select cases based on usefulness, falling back on strict similarity judgments only when absolutely necessary. Methods for dynamically judging usefulness that can fall back on similarity judgments are being developed (for example, Kolodner 1989).

Related to the issue of judging similarity is the issue of what features to use for analog retrieval. Although the analogical community has been debating whether people use surface or abstract features, individual features or combinations, or descriptors or relationships, the case-based reasoning community concentrates on the content of useful indexes. Sometimes surface features are the right ones to index on, sometimes abstract features, sometimes individual features, sometimes combinations of features, sometimes relationships between features, and sometimes relationships between relationships. It depends what reasoning tasks the reasoner is responsible for and what descriptors of an old case were responsible for its solution or outcome.

This concentration on pragmatics allows us to propose systems that can help people to do a better job of analogical reasoning. Although people tend to use surface features for retrieval when they are unfamiliar with a task or domain, a case-based system that is retrieving based on pragmatics can provide the person with cases that s/he would have been unable to retrieve from his(her) own memory. This ability could be a great boon to novices. Although people tend to discount solutions that are inconsistent with what they want a solution to be, a case-based system can present cases with failed solutions, along with explanations of why they better watch out, giving them less reason to discount negative results and helping them to make use of these negative results to create informed solutions.

More concretely, there are a variety of potential benefits to using case-based aiding systems for novices, experts, and corporations. For novices, such a system can provide a range of experience they haven't had. Rather than solving problems from scratch, the wisdom of many experts is available. There are several areas where novices should be able to perform better using such a system. First, with more cases available, they will be able to recognize more situations and the solutions or evaluations that go with these cases. Second, if cases that are available include failure cases, novices will be able to benefit from the failures of others. With failed cases available and presented to the novice by the system, the novice will be able to recognize potential problems and work to avoid them. This skill is one that novices rarely have. Third, novices will have available to them the unanticipated successes—and, therefore, the tricks—of experts that they wouldn't otherwise have. Fourth, retrieved cases will allow novices to better recognize what is important in a new situation. Cases indexed by experts and retrieved on the basis of a description of a new situation will be those that experts would recall and will show the novice ways of looking at a problem that s/he might not have the expertise for without the system. Fifth, the ability to recognize what is important will allow for better critiquing of solutions and situations. Additionally, novices will have access to obscure cases that they otherwise would not be able to make use of. These obscure cases can help with any of the tasks previously listed.

Using these systems during a training period also provides students with a model of the way decision making ought to be done, for example, what things ought to be considered, and provides them with concrete examples on which to hang their more abstract knowledge. Much of the expert decision-making skill people have comes from observing experts and discussing with experts why they solved problems in certain ways. A case-based aiding system can provide at least some of this experience.

The benefits of these systems are not just for novices. In some domains, there is much to remember. For tasks where there is much to remember, case-based aiding systems can augment the memories of even expert decision makers. In addition, as previously discussed, both experts and novices tend to focus on too few possibilities when reasoning analogically or to focus on the wrong cases. Case-based aiding systems can help to alleviate these problems.

Finally, consider the potential benefits of such systems for corporations. An extension to the notion of a case-based aiding system is the notion of *corporate memory*, a means of maintaining the knowledge and wisdom of corporate employees in a corporate database. Such systems would allow corporations to have the knowledge of its employees even after they leave the corporation, would alleviate the bottleneck that arises when one person owns the expertise that many need, and could facilitate communication between different branches of the corporation. It is this last function that I concentrate on here.

A case-based system provides the potential for feedback from one part of an organization to be considered by other parts of the organization. Such a system would work as follows: All employees of the organization working on some project would record their feedback and decisions in the system. All work on one project would be gathered into one case. The case would be indexed in the case library in ways that would aid the decision making of all employees. Each employee using the system would have available the feedback, solutions, and rationale of all the other employees working on the project. Those working on design, for example, would have available the feedback from those in manufacturing who assembled the design, those in testing who verified the artifact, those in marketing who had to sell it, and those users who used it. As the case library was expanded, feedback from different divisions of the corporation could be used to inform decision makers in another division. Designers, for example, could take manufacturability, testability, and usability into account as they created the design, resulting in better design decisions. Of course, there are many new problems that need to be addressed before such systems can be built, not the least of which is organizing and accessing the huge amounts of data within one case representation. Case-based technology provides a platform to begin thinking about such future projects.

Acknowledgments

This research was supported in part by the National Science Foundation under grant IST-8608362 and in part by the Defense Advanced Research Projects Agency under contract F49620-88-C-0058, which is monitored by the Air Force Office of Scientific Research. Thanks to Elaine Rich for helpful comments on the first draft.

Notes

1. Some psychologists call it analogical reasoning (for example, Gentner 1987; Holyoak 1985; Ross 1986), and others call it comparison-based prediction (Klein 1982; Klein, Whitaker, and King 1988).

2. Readers wanting additional information about case-based reasoning should read the article by Steven Slade (1991) in the spring 1991 issue of *AI Magazine*. For more technical detail, see Riesbeck and Schank (1989) and Kolodner (1988).

3. I thank Craig Zimring for this example.

27

Diagnosis Based on Description of Structure and Function

Randall Davis, Howard Shrobe, Walter Hamscher,
Kären Wieckert, Mark Shirley, & Steve Polit

1. Introduction

While expert systems have traditionally been built using large collections of rules based on empirical associations (e.g., Shortliffe 1976) interest has grown recently in the use of systems that reason from representations of structure and function (e.g., Patil, Szolovits, and Schwartz 1981; Genesereth 1981; and Davis 1982). Our work explores the use of such models in troubleshooting digital electronics.

We view the task as a process of reasoning from behavior to structure, or more precisely, from misbehavior to structural defect. We are typically presented with a machine exhibiting some form of incorrect behavior and must infer the structural abberation that is producing it. The task is interesting and difficult because the devices we want to examine are complex and because there is no well developed theory of diagnosis for them.

Our ultimate goal is to provide a level of performance comparable to that of an experienced engineer, including reading and reasoning from schematics; selecting, running, and interpreting the results of diagnostics; selecting and interpreting the results of input test patterns, etc. The initial focus of our work has been to develop three elements that appear to be fundamental to all of these capabilities. We require (i) a language for describing structure, (ii) a language for describing function, and (iii) a set of principles for troubleshooting that uses the two descriptions to guide its investigation. This chapter describes our progress to date on each of those elements.

In discussing troubleshooting, we show why the traditional approach to reasoning about digital electronics—test generation—solves a different problem and we discuss a number of its practical shortcomings. We consider next the style of debugging known as violated expectations and demonstrate why it is a fundamental advance over traditional test generation. Further exploration of the violated expectation approach, however, demonstrates that it is incapable of dealing with commonly known classes of faults. We explain the shortcoming as arising from the use of a fault model that is both implicit and inseparable from the basic troubleshooting methodology. We argue for the importance of fault models that are explicit, separated from the troubleshooting mechanism, and retractable in much the same sense that inferences are retracted in current systems.

2. Structure Description

By structure description we mean topology—the connectivity of components. A number of structure description languages have been developed but most, having originated in work on machine design, deal exclusively with *functional* components, rarely making any provision for describing *physical* organization.[1] In doing machine diagnosis, however, we are dealing with a collection of hardware whose functional and physical organizations are both important. The same gate may be both (i) functionally a part of a muitipiexor, which is functionally a part of a datapath, etc., and (ii) physically a part of chip E67, which is physically part of board 5, etc. Both of these hierarchies are relevant at different times in the diagnosis and both are included in our language.

We use the functional hierarchy as the primary organizing principle because, as noted, our basic task involves reasoning from function to structure rather than the other way around.[2] The functional organization is also typically richer than the structural (more levels to the hierarchy, more terms in the vocabulary), and hence provides a useful organizing principle for the

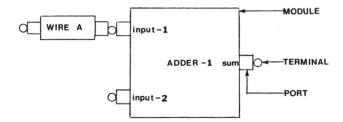

Figure 1. The basic terms used in structure description.

large number of individual physical components. Compare, for example, the functional organization of a board (e.g., a memory controller with cache, address translation hardware, etc.) with the physical organization (1 pc board, 137 chips).

The most basic level of our description vocabulary is built on three concepts: *modules, ports, and terminals* (Figure 1). A module can be thought of as a standard black box. A module has at least two ports; ports are the place where information flows into or out of a module. Every port has at least two terminals, one terminal on the outside of the port and one or more inside. Terminals are primitive elements; they store logic levels representing the information flowing into or out of a device through their port, but are otherwise devoid of substructure.

Two modules are attached to one another by superimposing their terminals. In Figure 1, for example, wire A is a module that has been attached to input-1 of the adder module in this fashion.

The language is hierarchical in the usual sense; modules at any level may have substructure. In practice, our descriptions terminate at the gate level in the functional hierarchy and the chip level in the physical hierarchy, since for our purposes, these are black boxes—only their behavior (or misbehavior) matters. Figure 2 shows the next level of structure of the adder and illustrates why ports may have multiple terminals on their inside: ports provide the important function of shifting level of abstraction. It may be useful to think of the information flowing along wire A as an integer between 0 and 15, yet we need to be able to map those four bits into the four single-bit lines inside the adder. Ports are the place where such information is kept. They have machinery (described below) that allows them to map information arriving at their outer terminal onto their inner terminals. The default provided in the system accomplishes the simple map required in Figure 2.

Since our ultimate intent is to deal with hardware on the scale of a mainframe computer, we need terms in the vocabulary capable of describing levels

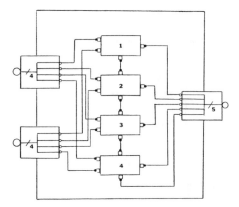

Figure 2. Next level of structure of the adder.

of organization more substantial than the terms used at the circuit level. We can, for example, refer to *horizontal, vertical,* and *bitslice* organizations, describing a memory, for instance, as "two rows of five 1K RAM's." We use these specifications in two ways: as a description of the organization of the device and a specification for the pattern of interconnections among the components.

Our eventual aim is to provide an integrated set of descriptions that span the levels of hardware organization ranging from interconnection of individual modules, through higher levels of organization of modules, and eventually on up through the register transfer and PMS level (Bell and Newell 1971). Some of this requires inventing vocabulary like that above, in other places (e.g., PMS) we may be able to make use of existing terminology and concepts.

The structural description of a module is expressed as a set of commands for building the module. Hence, the adder of Figure 2 is described by indicating how to "build" it (Figure 3). These commands are then executed by the system, causing it to build data structures that model all the components and connections shown. The resulting data structures are organized around the individual components. Executing the first expression of Figure 3, for example, produces 4 data structures that model the individual slices of the adder.

This approach to structure description offers two interesting properties: (a) a natural merging of procedural and object-oriented descriptions, and (b) the use of analogic representations.

To see the merging of descriptions, note that we have two different ways of thinking about structure. We describe a device by indicating how to build it (the procedural view), but then want to think about it as a collection of individual objects (the object-oriented view). The first view is convenient for *describing* structure, the second makes it easy to answer questions about it, questions like connectivity, location, etc., that are important in signal tracing

```
(definemodule adder
   (repeat 4 i
        (part slice-1 adder-slice)
        (run-wire (input-1 adder) (input-1 slice-i))
        (run-wire (input-2 adder) (input-2 slice-i))
        (run-wire (output slice-i) (sum adder))

   (repeat 3 i
        (run-wire (carry-out slice-i)
                  (carry-in slice-[i+1])) ))
```

Figure 3. Parts are described by a pathname through the part hierarchy, e.g., (input-1 adder). (This description can be abbreviated as a bitslice organization, but is expanded here for illustration.)

and other troubleshooting techniques. The two descriptions are unified because the system simply "runs" the procedural description to produce the data structures modeling the device. This gives us the benefit of both approaches with no additional effort and no chance that the two will get out of sync.

The representation is analogic because the data structures that are built are isomorphic to the structure being described. "Superimposing" two terminals, for instance, is implemented as a merging of the structure representing the terminals. The resulting data structures are thus connected in the Lisp sense in the same ways that the objects are connected in Figure 2. The benefit here is primarily conceptual, it simply makes the resulting structures somewhat easier to understand.

Our description language has been built on a foundation provided by a subset of DPL (Batali and Hartheimer 1980). While DPL as originally implemented was specific to VLSI design, it proved relatively easy to "peel off" the top level of language (which dealt with chip layout) and rebuild on that base the new layers of language described above.

Since pictures are a fast, easy and natural way to describe structure, we have developed a simple circuit drawing system that permits interactive entry of pictures like those in Figures 2 and 4. Circuits are entered with a combination of mouse movements and key strokes; the resulting structures are then "parsed" into the language shown in Figure 3.

3. Behavior Description

A variety of techniques have been explored in describing behavior, including simple rules for mapping inputs to outputs, petri nets, and unrestricted

chunks of code. Simple rules are useful where device behavior is uncompli-
cated, petri nets are useful where the focus is on modeling parallel events,
and unrestricted code is often the last resort when more structured arms of
expression prove too limited or awkward. Various combinations of these
three have also been explored.

Our initial implementation uses constraints (Sussman and Steele 1980) to
represent behavior. Conceptually a constraint is simply a relationship. The
behavior of the adder of Figure 1, for example, can be expressed by saying
that the logic levels of the terminals on ports *input-1, input-2* and *sum* are related in the obvious fashion. This is an expression of a relationship, not a
commitment to a particular computation—the logic level at any one of the
terminals can be computed given the other two.

In practice, this is accomplished by defining a set of rules covering all
different computations (the three for the adder are shown below) and setting
them up as demons that watch the appropriate terminals. A complete description of a module, then, is composed of its structural description as outlined
earlier and a behavior description in the form of rules that interrelate the
logic events at its terminals.

```
to get sum from ( input-1 input-2) do (+ input-1 input-2)
to get input-1 from (sum input-2) do (- sum input-2)
to  get input-2 from (sum input-1) do (- sum input-1)
```

A set of rules like these is in keeping with the original conception of constraints, which emphasized the non-directional, relationship character of the
information. When we attempt to use it to model causality and function,
however, we have to be careful. This approach is well suited to modeling
causality and behavior in the world of analog circuits, where devices are
largely one directional. But we can hardly say that the last two rules above
are a good description of the *behavior* of an adder chip—the device doesn't
do subtraction; putting logic levels at its output and one input does not cause
a logic level to appear on its other input.

The last two rules really model the *inferences we make* about the device.
Hence we find it useful to distinguish between rules representing *flow of
electricity* (digital behavior, the first rule above) and rules representing *flow
of inference* (conclusions we can make about the device, the next two rules).
This not only keeps the representation "clean," but as we will see, it provides
part of the foundation for the troubleshooting mechanism.

A set of constraints is a relatively simple mechanism for specifying behavior, in that it offers no obvious support for expressing behavior that falls outside the "relation between terminals" view. The approach also has known
limits. For example, constraints work well when dealing with simple quantities like numbers or logic levels, but run into difficulties if it becomes necessary to work with symbolic expressions.[3]

The approach has, nevertheless, provided a good starting point for our work and offers two important advantages. First, the DPL and constraint machinery includes mechanisms for keeping track of dependency information —an indication of how the system determined the value at a terminal—expressed in terms of what rule computed the value and what other values the rule used in performing its computation. This is very useful in tracing backward to the source of the misbehavior.

Second, the system provides machinery for detecting and unwinding contradictions. A contradiction arises if two rules try to set different values for the same terminal. As we illustrate below, the combination of dependency information and the detection of contradictions provides a useful starting place for troubleshooting.

Our system design offers a number of features which, while not necessarily novel, do provide useful performance. For example, our approach offers a unity of device description and simulation, since the descriptions themselves are "runnable." That is, the behavior descriptions associated with a given module allow us to simulate the behavior of that module; the interconnection of modules specified in the structure description then causes results computed by one module to propagate to another. Thus we don't need a separate description or body of code as the basis for the simulation, we can simply "run" the description itself. This ensures that our description of a device and the machinery that simulates it can never disagree about what to do, as can be the case if the simulation is produced by a separately maintained body of code.

Our use of a hierarchic approach and the terminal, port, module vocabulary makes multi-level simulation very easy. In simulating any module we can either run the constraint associated with the terminals of that module (simulating the module in a single step), or "run the substructure" of that module, simulating the device according to its next level of structure. Since the abstraction shifting behavior of ports is also implemented with the constraint mechanism, we have a convenient uniformity and economy of machinery: we can enable either the constraint that spans the entire module or the constraint that spans the port.

Varying the level of simulation is useful for speed (no need to simulate verified substructure), and provides as well a simple check on structure and behavior specification: we can compare the results generated by the module's behavior specification with those generated by the next lower level of simulation. Mismatches typically mean a mistake in structure specification at the lower level.

We believe it is important in this undertaking to include descriptions of both design and implementation, and to distinguish carefully between them. A wire, for example, is a device whose behavior is specified simply as the guarantee that a logic level imposed on one of its terminals will be propagated to the other terminal. Our structure description allows us to indicate the intended direction of information flow along a wire, but our simulation is not misled by this. This is, of course, important in troubleshooting, since some of the more difficult faults to locate are those that cause devices to behave not as we know they "should," but as they are in fact electrically capable of doing. Our representation machinery allows us to include both design specifications (the functional hierarchy) and implementation (the physical hierarchy) and keep them distinct.

Finally, the behavior description is also a convenient mechanism for fault insertion. A wire stuck at zero, for example, is modeled by giving the wire a behavior specification that maintains its terminals at logic level 0 despite any attempt to change them. Bridges, opens, etc., are similarly easily modeled.

5. Troubleshooting

The traditional approach to troubleshooting digital circuitry (e.g., Breuer and Friedman 1976) has, for our purposes, a number of significant drawbacks. Perhaps most important, it is a theory of *test generation,* not a theory of diagnosis. Given a specified fault, it is capable of determining a set of input values that will detect the fault (i.e., a set of values for which the output of the faulted circuit differs from the output of a good circuit). The theory tells us how to move from faults to sets of inputs; it provides little help in determining what fault to consider, or which component to suspect.

These questions are a central issue in our work for several reasons. First, the level of complexity we want to deal with precludes the use of diagnosis trees, which can require exhaustive consideration of possible faults. Second, our basic task is repair, rather than initial testing. Hence the problem confronting us is "Given the following piece of misbehavior, determine the fault." We are not asking whether a machine is free of faults, we know that it fails and know how it fails. Given the complexity of the device, it is important to be able to use this information as a focus for further exploration.

A second drawback of the existing theory is its use of a set of explicitly enumerated faults. Since the theory is based on Boolean Logic, it is strongly oriented toward faults whose behavior can be modeled as some form of permanent binary value, typically the result of stuck-ats and opens. One consequence of this is the paucity of useful results concerning bridging faults.

A response to these problems has been the use of what we may call the "violated expectation" approach (deKleer 1976; Brown, Burton, and deKleer 1981; Genesereth 1981). The basic insight of this technique is the substitution of violated expectations for specific fault models. That is, instead of postulating a possible fault and exploring its consequences, the technique simply looks for mismatches between the values it expected from correct operation and those actually obtained. This allows detection of a wide range of faults because misbehavior is now simply defined as anything that isn't correct, rather than only those things produced by a struck-at on a line.

This approach has a number of advantages. It is, first of all, fundamentally a diagnostic technique, since it allows systematic isolation of the possibly faulty devices, and does so without having to precompute fault dictionaries, diagnosis trees, or the like. Second, it appears to make it unnecessary to specify a set of expected faults (we comment further on this below). As a result, it can detect a much wider range of faults, including any systematic misbehavior exhibited by a single component. The approach also allows natural use of hierarchical descriptions, a marked advantage for dealing with complex structures.

This approach is a good starting point, but has a number of important limitations built into it. We work through a simple example to show the basic idea and use the same example to comment on its shortcomings.

Consider the circuit in Figure 4.[4] If we set the inputs as shown, the behavior descriptions will indicate that we should expect 12 at F. If, upon measuring, we find the value at F to be 10, we have a conflict between observed results and our model of correct behavior. We check the dependency record at F to find that the value expected there was determined using the behavior rule for the adder and the values emerging from the first and second multiplier. One of those three must be the source of the conflict, so we have three hypotheses: either the adder behavior rule is inappropriate (i.e., the first adder is broken), or one of the two inputs did not have the expected values (and the problem lies further back).

If the second input to adder-1 was good, then the first input must have been a 4 (reasoning from the result at F, valid behavior of the adder, and one of the inputs). But that conflicts with our expectation that it should be a 6. That expectation was based on the behavior rule for the multiplier and the expected value of its inputs. Since the inputs to the multiplier are primitive (supplied by the user), the only alternative along this line of reasoning is that the multiplier is broken. Hence hypothesis # 2 is that adder-1 is good and multiplier-1 is faulty.

If the first input to adder-1 is good, then the second input must have been a 4 (suggesting that the second multiplier might be bad). But if that were a 4, then the expected value at G would be 10 (reasoning forward through the second adder). We can check this and discover in this case that the output at G is 12. Hence the value on the output of the second multiplier can't be 4, it must be 6, hence the second multiplier can't be causing the current problem.

So we are left with the hypotheses that the malfunction lies in either the first multiplier or the first adder. The diagnosis proceeds in this style, dropping down levels of structural detail as we begin to isolate the source of the error.

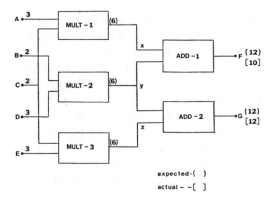

Figure 4. Troubleshooting example using violated expectations.

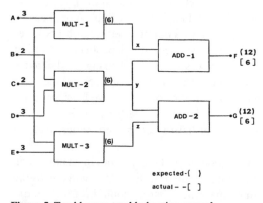

Figure 5. Troublesome troubleshooting example.

This approach is a useful beginning, but has some clear shortcomings that result from hidden assumptions about faults. Consider the slightly revised example shown in Figure 5. Reasoning just as before,[5] the fault at F leads us to suspect adder-1. But if adder-1 is faulty, then everything else is good. This implies a 6 on lines y and z, and (reasoning forward) a 12 at G. But G has been measured to be 6, hence adder-1 can't be responsible for the current set of symptoms. If adder-1 is good, then the fault at F might result from bad inputs (lines x and y). If the fault is on x, then y has a 6. But (reasoning forward) this means a 12 at G. Once again we encounter a contradiction and eliminate line x as a candidate. We turn to line y, postulate that it is 0. This is consistent with the faults at both F and G, and is in fact the only hypothesis we can generate.

The key phrase here is "the only hypothesis we can generate." In fact, there is another quite reasonable hypothesis: the third multiplier might be bad.[6] But how could this produce errors at both F and G? The key lies in being wary of our models. The thought that digital devices have input and output ports is a convenient abstraction, not an electrical reality. If, as sometimes happens (due to a bent pin, bad socket, etc.), a chip fails to get power, its inputs are no longer guaranteed to act unidirectionally as inputs. If the third multiplier were a chip that failed to get power, it might not only send out a 0 along wire z, but it might also pull down wire C to 0. Hence the symptoms result from a single point of failure (multiplier-3), but the error propagates along an "input" line common to two devices.

The problem with the traditional violated expectation approach lies in its implicit acceptance of unidirectional ports and the reflection of that acceptance in the basic dependency-unwinding machinery. That machinery implicitly believes that inputs only get information from outputs—when checking the inputs to multiplier-1, we said they were "primitive." We looked only at the input terminals A and C, never at the other end of the wire at multiplier-3.

Bridges are a second common fault that illustrates an interesting shortcoming in the contradiction detection approach. The reasoning style used above can never hypothesize a bridging fault, again because of implicit assumptions about the model and their subtle reflection in the method. Bridges can be viewed as wires that don't show up in the design. But the traditional approach makes an implicit "closed world" assumption—the structure description is assumed to be complete and anything not shown there "doesn't exist." Clearly this is not always true. Bridges are only one manifestation; wiring errors during assembly are another possibility.

Let's review for a moment. One problem with the traditional test generation technology was its use of a very limited fault model. The contradiction detection approach improves on this substantially by defining a fault as anything that produces behavior different from that expected. This seems to be perfectly general, but, as we illustrated, it is in fact limited in some important ways.

So what do we do? If we toss out the assumption that input and output ports are unidirectional, we take care of that class of errors; the cost is generating more hypotheses. Perhaps we can deal with the increase. If we toss out the closed-word assumption and admit bridges, we're in big trouble. Even if we switch to our physical representation; to keep the hypotheses constrained to those that are physically plausible, the number is vast. It we toss out the assumption that the device was wired as the description indicates, we're in big trouble even if we invoke the single point of failure constraint and assume only one such error. But some failures are due to multiple errors... and transients are an important class of errors ... and .... Wait, down this road appears to lie madness, or at the very least, chaos.

What can we do? We believe that the important thing to do is what human experts seem to do:

- Make all the simplifying assumptions we have to to keep the problem tractable.
- Be explicitly aware of what those assumptions are.
- Be aware of the effect the assumptions have on candidate generation and testing.
- Be able to discard each assumption in turn if it proves to be misleading.

The key, it seems, lies in determining what are the appropriate layers of assumptions for a given domain and in determining their effects on the diagnostic process. In our domain, for example, a sample list of the assumptions underlying correct function of a circuit might be:

- no wires are stuck
- no wires present other than those shown
- ports functioning in specified direction
- actual assembly matches design specifications
- original design is correct

Surrendering these one by one leads us to consider stuck-ats, then bridges. then power loss, etc. We have significant work yet to do in determining a more complete and correct list, and in determining the consequences of each assumption on the diagnostic process. But we feel this is a key to creating more interesting and powerful diagnostic reasoners.

Acknowledgments

This report describes research done at the Artificial Intelligence Laboratory of the Massachusetts Institute of Technology. Support for the laboratory's artificial intelligence research on electronic trouble-shooting is provided in part by the Digital Equipment Corporation.

Notes

1. This is curiously true even for languages billing themselves as *computer hardware description languages*. They rarely mention a piece of physical hardware.

2. We are typically confronted with a machine that misbehaves, not one that has visible structural damage.

3. What, for example, do we do if we know that the output of an or-gate is 1 but we don't know the value at either input? We can refrain from making any conclusion about the inputs, which makes the rules easy to write but misses some information. Or we can write a rule which express the value on one input in terms of the value on the other input. This captures the information but produces problems when trying to use the resulting symbolic expression elsewhere.

4. As is common in the field, we make the usual assumptions that there is only a single source of error and the error is not transient. Both of these are important in the reasoning that follows.

5. The eager reader has no doubt already chosen a likely hypothesis. We go through the reasoning in any case, to show that the method outlined generates the same hypothesis and is in fact simply a more formal way of doing what we often do intuitively.

6. Or the first.

7. Remember, we said it was important to have one.

28

Pengi: An Implementation of a Theory of Activity

Philip E. Agre and David Chapman

1. Pengo

Let us distinguish two different uses of the word "planning."[1] AI has traditionally interpreted the organized nature of everyday activity in terms of capital-P Planning, according to which a smart Planning phase constructs a Plan which is carried out in a mechanical fashion by a dumb Executive phase. People often engage in lowercase-p planning. Though a plan might in some sense be mental, better prototypes are provided by recipes, directions, and instruction manuals. Use of plans regularly involves rearrangement, interpolation, disambiguation, and substitution. Before and beneath any activity of plan following, life is a continual improvisation, a matter of deciding what to do *now* based on how the world is *now*. Our empirical and theoretical studies of activity have led us to question the supposition that action derives from the execution of plans and the corresponding framework of problem solving and reasoning with representations. We observe that real situations are characteristically *complex, uncertain,* and *immediate.* We have shown in Chapman, (1985) that Planning is inherently combinatorially explosive, and so is unlikely to scale up to realistic situations which take thousands of propositions to represent. Most real situations cannot be completely represented; there isn't time to collect all the necessary information. Real situations are rife with uncertainty; the actions of other agents and processes cannot be predicted. At best, this exponentially increases the size of a Planner's search space; often, it may lose the Planner completely. Life is fired at you point blank: when the rock you step on pivots unexpectedly, you have only milliseconds to react. Proving theorems is out of the question.

Rather than relying on reasoning to intervene between perception and action, we believe activity mostly derives from very simple sorts of machinery interacting with the immediate situation. This machinery exploits regularities in its interaction with the world to engage in complex, apparently planful activity without requiring explicit models of the world.

This chapter reports on an implementation in progress of parts of our more general theory of activity (Agre 1985a, Agre 1985b, Agre 1988, Chapman and Agre 1987, Chapman 1985). We are writing a program, Pengi, that plays a commercial arcade video game called Pengo. Pengo is played on a 2-d maze made of unit-sized ice blocks. The player navigates a penguin around in this field with a joystick. Bees chase the penguin and kill him if they get close enough. The penguin and bees can modify the maze by kicking ice blocks to make them slide. If a block slides into a bee or penguin, it dies. A snapshot of a Pengo game appears in Figure 1. In the lower left-hand corner, the penguin faces a bee across a block. Whoever kicks the block first will kill the other.

Although Pengo is much simpler than the real world, it is nonetheless not amenable to current or projected Planning techniques because it exhibits the three properties of complexity, uncertainty, and real-time involvement. With several hundred objects of various sorts on the screen, some moving, representing any situation would require well over a thousand propositions, too many for any current planner. The behavior of the bees has a random component and so is not fully predictable. Real-time response is required to avoid being killed by bees. Still, Pengo is only a toy. There are no real vision or manipulation problems; it's a simulation inside the computer. Nothing drastically novel ever happens. This makes it a tractable first domain for demonstrating our ideas.

In a typical Pengo game, the penguin will run to escape bees, hunt down bees when it has the advantage, build traps and escape routes, maneuver bees into corners, and collect "magic blocks" (shown as concentric squares in Figure 1) for completing the "magic square" structure that wins the game. Naturally we ascribe the player's seeming purposefulness to its models of its envi-

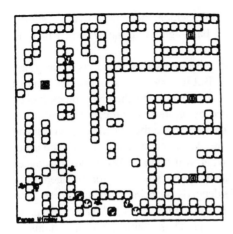

Figure 1. A Pengo game in progress.

ronment, its reasoning about the world, and its planful efforts to carry out its tasks. But as with Simon's ant the complexity of the player's activity may be the result of the interaction of simple opportunistic strategies with a complex world. Instead of sticking to a rigid plan, Pengi lives in the present, continually acting on its immediate circumstances. It happens upon each situation with only a set of goals and a stock of skills. It can take advantage of unexpected opportunities and deal with unexpected contingencies, not because they've been written into a script, but because they are apparent in the situation.

2. Interactive Routines

Routines are patterns of interaction between an agent and its world. A routine is not a plan or procedure; typically it is not represented by the agent. An agent can reliably enter into a particular routine without representing it because of regularities in the world. For example, imagine the penguin running from a bee. The penguin will run as far as it can, until it runs into a wall made of blocks. Then it will have to kick its way through the wall. Then it will run some more. Then it will hit another wall. This process could be described by a procedure with two nested loops: running until it hits something, kicking the obstacle, and repeating.

But this same pattern of activity could equally well arise from a pair of rules: (R1) when you are being chased, run away; (R2) if you run into a wall, kick through it. These rules don't represent the iteration; the loop emerges as a result of the interaction of the rules with the situation. Causality flows into the system from the world, drives the rules which chose what to do, resulting in action which changes the world, and back again into the system, which responds to the changes.

An agent executing a plan is inflexible: it has a series of actions to carry out, and it performs them one after another. But it sometimes happens that while a bee is pursuing the penguin, the bee is accidentally crushed by a block kicked by a different bee. A penguin controlled by an iterative procedure would then either continue running needlessly or have to notice that it had gone wrong and switch to executing a different procedure. An agent engaging in a routine is not driven by a preconceived notion of what will happen. When circumstances change, other responses become applicable; there's no need for the agent even to register the unexpected event. (R1) depends on being chased; if there is no bee chasing, it is no longer applicable, and other rules, relevant perhaps to collecting magic blocks, will apply instead. Thus, routines are opportunistic, and therefore robust under uncertainty. Responses can be individually very simple, requiring almost no computation; this allows real-time activity.

3. Indexical-Functional Aspects

Pengi's activity is guided by relevant properties of the immediate situation we call *indexical—functional aspects,* or "aspects" for short. Registering and acting on aspects is an alternative to representing and reasoning about complex domains, and avoids combinatorial explosions.

A traditional problem solver for the Pengo domain would represent each situation with hundreds or thousands of such representations as (AT BLOCK-213 427 991), (ISA BLOCK-213 BLOCK), and (NEXT-TO BLOCK-213 BEE-23). These representations do not make reference to the penguin's situation or goals. Instead of naming each individual with its own gensym, Pengi employs *indexical-functional entities,* such as the following, which are useful to find at times when playing Pengo:

- the-block-I'm-pushing
- the-corridor-I'm-running-along
- the-bee-on-the-other-side-of-this-block-next-to-me
- the-block-that-the-block-I-just-kicked-will-collide-with
- the-bee-that-is-heading-along-the-wall-that-I'm-on the-other-side-of

As we will see later, the machinery itself does not directly manipulate names for these entities. They are only invoked in particular aspects. If an entity looks like a hyphenated noun phrase, an aspect looks like a hyphenated sentence. For example:

- the-block-I'm-going-to-kick-at-the-bee-is-behind-me
  (so I have to backtrack)

- there-is-no-block-suited-for-kicking-at-the-bee
  (so just hang out until the situation improves)
- I've-run-into-the-edge-of-the-screen (better turn and run along it)
- the-bee-I-intend-to-clobber-is-closer-to-the-projectile-than-I-am
  (dangerous!)
- ...-but-it's-heading-away-from-it (which is OK)
- I'm-adjacent-to-my-chosen-projectile (so kick it)

These aspects depend on the Pengo player's circumstances; this is the *indexicality* of aspects. At any given time, Pengi can ignore most of the screen because effects propagate relatively slowly. It's important to keep track of what's happening around the penguin and sometimes in one or two other localized regions. When Pengi needs to know where something is, it doesn't look in a database, it looks at the screen. This eliminates most of the overhead of reasoning and representation. (The next section will describe how Pengi can *find* an entity in, or *register* some aspect of, a situation.)

Entities and aspects are relative to the player's purposes; they are *functional.* Each aspect is used for a specific purpose: it's important to register various aspects of the-bee-on-the-other-side-of-this-block-next-to-me, because it is both vulnerable (if the penguin kicks the block) and dangerous (because it can kick the block at the penguin). Which aspects even make sense depends on the sort of activity Pengi is engaged in. For example, when running away, it's important to find the-bee-that-is-chasing-me and the-obstacle-to-my-flight and the-edge-I'll-run-into-if-I-keep-going-this-way; when pursuing, you should find the-bee-that-I'm-chasing and the block-I-will-kick-at-the-bee and the-bee's-escape-route. Aspects are not defined in terms of specific individuals such as BEE-69. The-bee-that-is-chasing-me at one minute may be the same bee or a different one from the-bee-that-is-chasing-me a minute later. Pengi cannot tell the difference, but it doesn't matter because the same action is right in either case: run away or hit it with a block. Moreover, the same object might be two entities at different times, or even at the same time. Depending on whether you are attacking or running away, the same block might be a projectile to kick at the bee or an obstacle to your flight.

Avoiding the representation of individuals bypasses the overhead of instantiation: binding constants to variables. In all existing knowledge representation systems, from logic to frames, to decide to kick a block at a bee requires reasoning from some general statement that in every situation satisfying certain requirements there will be some bee (say SOME-BEE) and some block (SOME-BLOCK) that should be kicked at it. To make this statement concretely useful, you must instantiate it: consider various candidate bees and blocks and bind a representation of one of these bees (perhaps BEE-29) to SOME-BEE and a representation of one of the blocks (BLOCK-237) to SOME-BLOCK. With n candidate bees and m blocks, this may involve $n \times m$ work. Clever indexing schemes and control heuristics can help, but the scheme for registering aspects we present in the next section will always be faster.

Entities are not logical categories because they are indexical: their extension depends on the circumstances. In this way, indexical-functional entities are intermediate between logical individuals and categories. Aspects make many cases of generalization free. If the player discovers in a particular situation that the-bee-on-the-other-side-of-this-block-next-to-me-is-dangerous because it can easily kick the block into the penguin, this discovery will apply automatically to other specific bees later on that can be described as the-bee-on-the-other-side-of-this-block-next-to-me.

4. Simple Machinery

We believe that a simple architecture interacting with the world can participate in most forms of activity. This architecture is made up of a *central system* and *peripheral systems*. The central system is responsible, loosely, for cognition: registering and acting on relevant aspects of the situation. The peripheral systems are responsible for perception and for effecter control. Because routines and aspects avoid representation and reasoning, the central system can be made from very simple machinery.

We believe that *combinational networks* can form an adequate central system for most activity. The inputs to the combinational network come from perceptual systems; the outputs go to motor control systems. The network decides on actions that are appropriate given the situation it is presented with. Many nodes of the network register particular aspects. As the world changes, the outputs of the perceptual system change; these changes are propagated through the network to result in different actions. This interaction can result without Pengi maintaining any state in the central system.

5. Visual Routines

Aspects, like routines, are not datastructures. They do not involve variables bound to symbols that represent objects. Aspects are registered by routines in which the network interacts with the perceptual systems and with the world. The actions in these routines get the world and the peripheral systems into states in which the aspects will become manifest.

Shimon Ullman (1983) has developed a theory of vision based on *visual routines* which are patterns of interaction between the central system and a *visual routines processor* (VRP). The VRP maintains several modified internal copies of the two-D sketch produced by early vision. It can perform oper-

Figure 2. Finding the-block-that-the-block-I-just-kicked-will-collide-with using ray tracing and dropping a marker. The two circle-crosses are distinct visual markers, the one on the left marking the-block-that-I-just-kicked and the one on the right marking the-block-that-the-block-just-kicked-will-collide-with.

ations on these images such as coloring in regions, tracing curves, keeping track of locations using visual markers (pointers into the image), indexing interesting features, and detecting and tracking moving objects. The VRP is guided in what operations it applies to what images by outputs of the central network, and outputs of the VRP are inputs to the network. A visual routine, then, is a process whereby the VRP, guided by the network, finds entities and registers aspects of the situation, and finally injects them into the inputs of the network.

The first phase of the network registers aspects using boolean combinations of inputs from the VRP. Some visual routines are run constantly to keep certain vital aspects up to date; it is always important to know if there is a bee-that-is-chasing-me. Other routines are entered into only in certain circumstances. For example, when you kick the-block-that-is-in-my-way-as-I'm running-away-from-some-bee, it is useful to find the-block-that-the-block-I just-kicked-will-collide-with. This can be done by directing the VRP to trace a ray forward from the kicked block over free space until it runs into something solid, dropping a visual marker there, and checking that the thing under the marker is in fact a block. This is illustrated in Figure 2.

As another example, if the penguin is lurking behind a continuous wall of blocks (a good strategy) and a bee appears in front of the wall heading toward it, the-block-to-kick-at-the-bee can be found by extending a ray along the path of the bee indefinitely, drawing a line along the wall, and dropping a marker at their intersection. This is shown in Figure 3.

6. Action Arbitration

Actions are suggested only on the basis of local plausibility. Two actions may conflict. For example, if a bee is closing in on the penguin, the penguin

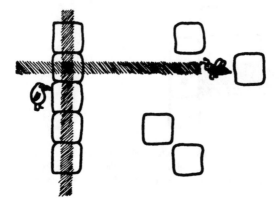

Figure 3. Finding the-block-to-kick-at-the-bee when lurking behind a wall.

should run away. On the other hand, if there is a block close to the penguin and a bee is on the other side, the penguin should run over to the block and kick it at the bee. These two aspects may be present simultaneously, in which case both running away and kicking the block at the bee will be suggested. In such cases one of the conflicting actions must be selected. In some cases, one of the actions should always take precedence over the other. More common-ly, which action to take will depend on other aspects of the situation. In this case, the deciding factor is whether the penguin or the bee is closer to the block between them: whichever gets to it first will get to kick it at the other. Therefore, if the penguin is further from the block it should run away, other-wise it should run toward the block. This is not always true, though: for ex-ample, if the penguin is trapped in a narrow passage, running is a bad strate-gy; the ice block cannot be evaded. In this case, it is better to run toward the block in the hope that the bee will be distracted (as often happens); a severe risk, but better than facing certain death. On the other hand, if the block is far enough away, there may be time to kick a hole in the side of the passage to escape into. We see here *levels* of arbitration: an action is suggested; it may be overruled; the overruling can be overruled, or a counter-proposal be put forth; and so forth.

Action arbitration has many of the benefits of Planning, but is much more efficient, because it does not require representation and search of future worlds. In particular, a designer who understands the game's common pat-terns of interaction (its "dynamics") can use action arbitration to produce ac-tion sequencing, nonlinear look ahead to resolve goal interactions, and hier-archical action selection. Unfortunately, space does not permit us to describe the boundaries of the large but restricted set of dynamics in which this sort of machinery can participate. We should comment, though, on Pengi's central system's lack of state. We do not believe that the human central system has no state. Our point is simply that state is less necessary and less important than is often assumed.

7. Status & Other Work

Currently, Pengi has a network of several hundred gates and a VRP with about thirty operators. It plays Pengo badly, in near real time. It can maneuver behind blocks to use as projectiles and kick them at bees and can run from bees which are chasing it. We expect to expand the network sufficiently that the program will play a competent if not expert game.

Pengi is an implementation of parts of a theory of cognitive architecture which will be described in greater detail in Agre (1988). In constructing the theory we learned from the cognitive-architectural theories of Batali, Drescher, Minsky, Rosenschein, and the SOAR group, among other sources. Rosenschein's is the most similar project. His situated automata use compiled logic gates to drive a robot based on a theory of the robot's interactions with its world. But these use the ontology of first-order logic, not that of aspects. The robot does not use visual routines and its networks contain latches.

We chose Pengo as a domain because it is utterly unlike those AI has historically taken as typical. It is one in which events move so quickly that little or no planning is possible, and yet in which human experts can do very well. Many everyday domains are like this: driving to work, talking to a friend, or dancing. Yet undeniably other situations do require planning. In Agre, (1988) we will outline a theory of planning that builds on the theory of activity that Pengi partly implements. Planning, on this view, is the internalization of social communication about activity.

We are wiring Pengi's central system by hand. Evolution, similarly, wired the central system of insects. But humans and intelligent programs must be able to extend their own networks based on experience with new sorts of situations. This will be a focus of our next phase of research.

Acknowledgments

This work couldn't have been done without the support and supervision of Mike Brady, Rod Brooks, Pat Hayes, Chuck Rich, Stan Rosenschein, and Marty Tenenbaum. We thank Gary Drescher, Leslie Kaelbling, and Beth Preston for helpful comments, David Kirsh for reading about seventeen drafts, and all our friends for helping us develop the theory. Agre has been supported by a fellowship from the Fanny and John Herts Foundation.

This report describes research done at the Artificial Intelligence Laboratory of the Massachusetts Institute of Technology. Support for the laboratory's artificial intelligence research has been provided in part by the Advanced Research Projects Agency of the Department of Defense under Office of Naval Research contract N00014-80-C-05, in part by National Science

Foundation grant MCS-8117633, and in part by the IBM Corporation.

The views and conclusions contained in this document are those of the authors, and should not be interpreted as representing the policies, neither expressed nor implied, of the Department of Defense of the National Science Foundation, nor of the IBM Corporation.

PART FIVE

Foundations Revisited

E ach generation brings the tools of their times to address the questions of the ages. Each scientific community employs the artifacts and metaphors of their day to help understand otherwise mysterious phenomena. We have seen this throughout Western thought with the use of calculation, hydraulics, and galvanism to describe human intelligence and performance (Chapter 1). For the late twentieth century, this has meant the use of computation along with an understanding of the power and limits of formalism and mechanism to address the issues of intelligence. This is the challenge Turing proposed in Chapter 2, and that was extended and amplified through the other chapters of this collection.

It is appropriate that we end our presentation of papers supporting the role of computation in our understanding of intelligence with the 1990s analyses of two of the designers of the original AI experiment, two of the authors of the foundation papers of Part I.

Marvin Minsky's paper, Chapter 29, is a call for synthesis. To face the myriad exciting issues still before us requires the integration of present architectures, blending the connectionist approaches with the best of the symbolic. These hybrid architectures must be able to manage and exploit the advantages of several types of representations. Minsky writes:

> AI research must now move from its traditional focus on particular schemes. There is no best way to represent knowledge or to solve problems and the limitations of current machine intelligence largely stem from seeking unified theories or trying to repair the deficiencies of theoretically neat but conceptually impoverished ideological positions. Our purely connectionist networks are inherently deficient in abilities to reason well; our purely symbolic logical systems are inherently deficient in the abilities to represent the all-important heuristic connections between things-the uncertain, approxi-

mate, and analogical links that we need for making new hypotheses.

Herb Simon, the author of Machine asd Mind (Chapter 30), summarizes the forty years of progress in understanding intelligence made since Turing's challenge. Simon reminds the reader of the utility of the programmed computer for describing cognitive processes. To demonstrate that computer problem solving is not just a *simulation* of thinking but *actual* thought, Simon states:

> It has been argued that a computer simulation of thinking is no more thinking than a simulation of digestion is digestion. The analogy is false. A computer simulation of digestion is not capable of taking starch as an input and producing fructose or glucose as outputs. It deals only with symbolic or numerical quantities representing these substances.

> In contrast a computer simulation of thinking thinks. It takes problems as its inputs and (sometimes) produces solutions as its outputs. It represents these problems and solutions as symbolic structures, as the human mind does, and performs transformations on them, as the human mind does. The materials of digestion are chemical substances, which are not replicated in a computer simulation. The materials of thought are symbols—patterns which can be replicated in a great variety of materials (including neurons and chips), thereby enabling physical symbol systems fashioned of these materials to think.

There are a large number of other important developments in modern artificial intelligence besides those presented in our chapters. These include the attempts to address the philosophical and psychological issues introduced with the emergence of Cognitive Science. There is also the creation of more sophisticated connectionist networks for modeling perception, learning, and other diverse aspects of intelligence. There is the study of the phenomena of emergent intelligence using genetic and agent-based architectures. Throughout its brief history, it seems that a major strength of AI is that it is marked by its individual insights and its heterogeneity of opinion. Rather than creating synthesis, the AI community seems to gather strength through its diversity.

Besides considering the cumulative issues of Part V, the reader should revisit Part I: Turing's seminal conjectures of Chapter 2, Minsky's introduction of programming and design tools for AI in Chapter 3, and Newell and Simon's claims for scientific veridicality in Chapter 4. So many of their insights and conjectures have been realized in the first four decades of research in artificial intelligence and yet, as Alan Turing said almost fifty years ago, so much work remains to be done.

29

Logical Versus Analogical
or Symbolic Versus Connectionist
or Neat Versus Scruffy

Marvin Minsky

1. Introduction

Why is there so much excitement about neural networks today, and how is this related to research in AI? Much has been said, in the popular press, as though these were conflicting activities. This seems exceedingly strange to me because both are parts of the same enterprise. What caused this misconception?

The symbol-oriented community in AI has brought this rift upon itself by supporting models in research that are far too rigid and specialized. This focus on well-defined problems produced many successful applications, no matter that the underlying systems were too inflexible to function well outside the domains for which they were designed. (It seems to me that this oc-

Figure 1. Conflict between theoretical extremes.

curred because of the researchers' excessive concern with logical consistency
and provability. Ultimately, this concern would be a proper one but not in the
subject's current state of immaturity.) Thus, contemporary symbolic AI systems are now too constrained to be able to deal with exceptions to rules or to
exploit fuzzy, approximate, or heuristic fragments of knowledge. Partly in reaction to this constraint, the connectionist movement initially tried to develop
more flexible systems but soon came to be imprisoned in its own peculiar
ideology—trying to build learning systems endowed with as little architectural structure as possible, hoping to create machines that could serve all
masters equally well. The trouble with this attempt is that even a seemingly
neutral architecture still embodies an implicit assumption about which things
are presumed to be similar.

The field called AI includes many different aspirations. Some researchers
simply want machines to do the various sorts of things that people call intelligent. Others hope to understand what enables people to do such things. Still
other researchers want to simplify programming. Why can't we build, once
and for all, machines that grow and improve themselves by learning from experience? Why can't we simply explain what we want, and then let our machines do experiments or read some books or go to school—the sorts of
things that people do. Our machines today do no such things: Connectionist
networks learn a bit but show few signs of becoming smart; symbolic systems are shrewd from the start but don't yet show any common sense. How
strange that our most advanced systems can compete with human specialists
yet are unable to do many things that seem easy to children. I suggest that
this stems from the nature of what we call *specialties*—because the very act
of naming a specialty amounts to celebrating the discovery of some model of
some aspect of reality, which is useful despite being isolated from most of
our other concerns. These models have rules that reliably work—as long as
we stay in their special domains. But when we return to the commonsense
world, we rarely find rules that precisely apply. Instead, we must know how
to adapt each fragment of knowledge to particular contexts and circumstances, and we must expect to need more and different kinds of knowledge
as our concerns broaden. Inside such simple "toy" domains, a rule might

seem to be general, but whenever we broaden these domains, we find more and more exceptions, and the early advantage of context-free rules then mutates into strong limitations.

AI research must now move from its traditional focus on particular schemes. There is no one best way to represent knowledge or to solve problems, and the limitations of current machine intelligence largely stem from seeking unified theories or trying to repair the deficiencies of theoretically neat but conceptually impoverished ideological positions. Our purely numeric connectionist networks are inherently deficient in abilities to reason well; our purely symbolic logical systems are inherently deficient in abilities to represent the all-important *heuristic connections* between things—the uncertain, approximate, and analogical links that we need for making new hypotheses. The versatility that we need can be found only in larger-scale architectures that can exploit and manage the advantages of several types of representations at the same time. Then, each can be used to overcome the deficiencies of the others. To accomplish this task, each formally neat type of knowledge representation or inference must be complemented with some scruffier kind of machinery that can embody the heuristic connections between the knowledge itself and what we hope to do with it.

2. Top Down Versus Bottom Up

Although different workers have diverse goals, all AI researchers seek to make machines that solve problems. One popular way to pursue this quest is to start with a top-down strategy: Begin at the level of commonsense psychology, and try to imagine processes that could play a certain game, solve a certain kind of puzzle, or recognize a certain kind of object. If this task can't be done in a single step, then break things down into simpler parts until you can actually embody them in hardware or software.

This basically reductionist technique is typical of the approach to AI called *heuristic programming.* These techniques have developed productively for several decades, and today, heuristic programs based on top-down analysis have found many successful applications in technical, specialized areas. This progress is largely the result of the maturation of many techniques for representing knowledge. However, the same techniques have seen less success when applied to commonsense problem solving. Why can we build robots that compete with highly trained workers to assemble intricate machinery in factories but not robots that can help with ordinary housework? It is because the conditions in factories are constrained, and the objects and activities of everyday life are too endlessly varied to be described by precise, logical definitions and deductions. Commonsense reality is too disorderly to represent in terms of universally valid axioms. To deal with such variety and novelty, we need more flexible styles of thought, such as those we see in human commonsense reasoning, which is based more on analogies and approximations than on precise formal procedures. Nonetheless, top-down procedures have important advantages in being able to perform efficient, systematic search procedures, manipulate and rearrange the elements of complex situations, and supervise the management of intricately interacting subgoals—all functions that seem beyond the capabilities of connectionist systems with weak architectures.

Shortsighted critics have *always* complained that progress in top-down symbolic AI research is slowing. In one way, this slowing is natural: In the early phases of any field, it becomes ever harder to make important new advances as we put the easier problems behind us; in addition, new workers must face a squared challenge because there is so much more to learn. However, the slowdown of progress in symbolic AI is not just a matter of laziness. Those top-down systems are inherently poor at solving problems that involve large numbers of weaker kinds of interactions such as occur in many areas of pattern recognition and knowledge retrieval. Hence, there has been a mounting clamor for finding another, new, more flexible approach, which is one reason for the recent popular turn toward connectionist models.

The bottom-up approach goes the opposite way. We begin with simpler elements—they might be small computer programs, elementary logical principles, or simplified models of what brain cells do—and then move upward in complexity by finding ways to interconnect these units to produce larger-scale phenomena. The currently popular form of this, the connectionist neural network approach, developed more sporadically than heuristic programming. This development was sporadic in part because heuristic programming developed so rapidly in the 1960s that connectionist networks were swiftly outclassed. Also, the networks needed computation and memory resources that were too prodigious for that period. Now that faster computers are available, bottom-up connectionist research has shown considerable promise in mimicking some of what we admire in the behavior of lower animals, particularly in the areas of pattern recognition, automatic optimization, clustering, and knowledge retrieval. However, their performances have been far weaker in precisely the areas in which symbolic systems have successfully mimicked much of what we admire in high-level human thinking, for example, in goal-based reasoning, parsing, and causal analysis. These weakly structured connectionist networks cannot deal with the sorts of tree search explorations and complex, composite knowledge structures required for parsing, recursion, complex scene analysis, or other sorts of problems that involve functional parallelism. It is an amusing paradox that connectionists frequently boast about the massive parallelism of their computations, yet the homogeneity and interconnectedness of these structures make them virtually unable to do more than one thing at a time—at least, at levels above that of their basic associative function. This is essentially because they lack the architecture needed to maintain adequate short-term memories.

Thus, the current systems of both types show serious limitations. The top-down systems are handicapped by inflexible mechanisms for dealing with very numerous, albeit very weak, interactions, while the bottom-up systems are crippled by inflexible architectures and organizational limitations. Neither type of system has been developed to be able to exploit multiple, diverse varieties of knowledge.

Which approach is best to pursue? This question itself is simply wrong. Each has virtues and deficiencies, and we need integrated systems that can exploit the advantages of both. In favor of the top-down side, AI research has told us a little—but only a little— about how to solve problems by using methods that resemble reasoning. If we understood more about such processes, perhaps we could more easily work down toward finding out how brain cells do such things. In favor of the bottom-up approach, the brain sciences have told us something—but again only a little—about the workings of brain cells and their connections. More research in this area might help us discover how the activities of brain cell networks support our higher-level processes. However, right now we're caught in the middle; neither purely connectionist nor purely symbolic systems seem able to support the sorts of intellectual performances we take for granted even in young children. This article aims at understanding why both types of AI systems have developed to become so inflexible. I'll argue that the solution lies somewhere between these two extremes, and our problem will be to find out how to build a suitable bridge. We already have plenty of ideas at either extreme. On the connectionist side, we can extend our efforts to design neural networks that can learn various ways to represent knowledge. On the symbolic side, we can extend our research on knowledge representations to the designing of systems that can more effectively exploit the knowledge thus represented. However, above all, we currently need more research on how to combine both types of ideas.

3. Representation and Retrieval: Structure and Function

In order that a machine may learn, it must represent what it will learn. The knowledge must be embodied in some form of mechanism, data structure, or representation. AI researchers have devised many ways to embody this knowledge, for example, in the forms of rule-based systems, frames with default assignments, predicate calculus, procedural representations, associative databases, semantic networks, object-oriented data-structures, conceptual dependency, action scripts, neural networks, and natural language.

In the 1960s and 1970s, students frequently asked, "Which kind of representation is best," and I usually replied that we'd need more research before answering. But now I would give a different reply: "To solve really hard problems, we'll have to use several different representations." This is because each particular kind of data structure has its own virtues and deficiencies, and none by itself seems adequate for all the different functions involved with what we call common sense. Each has domains of competence and efficiency, so that one might work where another fails. Furthermore, if we only rely on any single, unified scheme, then we'll have no way to recover from failure. As suggested in section 6.9 of *The Society of Mind* (Minsky 1987), "The secret of what something means lies in how it connects to other things we know. That's why it's almost always wrong to seek the real meaning of anything. A thing with just one meaning has scarcely any meaning at all."

To get around these limitations, we must develop systems that combine the expressiveness and procedural versatility of symbolic systems with the fuzziness and adaptiveness of connectionist representations. Why has there been so little work on synthesizing these techniques? I suspect that it is because both of these AI communities suffer from a common cultural-philosophical disposition: They would like to explain intelligence in the image of what was successful in physics—by minimizing the amount and variety of its assumptions. But this seems to be a wrong ideal. We should take our cue from biology rather than physics because what we call thinking does not directly emerge from a few fundamental principles of wave-function symmetry and exclusion rules. Mental activities are not the sort of unitary or elementary phenomenon that can be described by a few mathematical operations on logical axioms. Instead, the functions performed by the brain are the products of the work of thousands of different, specialized subsystems, the intricate product of hundreds of millions of years of biological evolution. We cannot hope to understand such an organization by emulating the techniques of those particle physicists who search for the simplest possible unifying conceptions. Constructing a mind is simply a different kind of problem—how to synthesize organizational systems that can support a large enough diversity of different schemes yet enable them to work together to exploit one another's abilities.

To solve typical real-world commonsense problems, a mind must have at least several different kinds of knowledge. First, we need to represent goals: What is the problem to be solved. Then, the system must also possess adequate knowledge about the domain or context in which this problem occurs. Finally, the system must know what kinds of reasoning are applicable in this area. Superimposed on all this knowledge, our systems must have management schemes that can operate different representations and procedures in parallel, so that when any particular method breaks down or gets stuck, the system can quickly shift to analogous operations in other realms that might be able to continue the work. For example, when you hear a natural language ex-

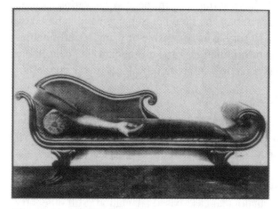

Figures 2A and 2B. Armchair.

pression such as "Mary gave Jack the book," you will produce, albeit unconsciously, many different kinds of thoughts (Minsky 1987, section 29.2), that is, mental activities in such different realms as a visual representation of the scene; postural and tactile representations of the experience; a script sequence for a typical act of giving; representations of the participants' roles; representations of their social motivations; default assumptions about Jack, Mary, and the book; and other assumptions about past and future expectations.

How could a brain possibly coordinate the use of such different kinds of processes and representations? The conjecture is that our brains construct and maintain them in different brain agencies. (The corresponding neural structures need not, of course, be entirely separate in their spatial extents inside the brain.) However, it is not enough to maintain separate processes inside separate agencies; we also need additional mechanisms to enable each of them to support the activities of the others or, at least, to provide alternative operations in case of failures. Chapters 19 through 23 of *The Society of Mind* (Minsky 1987) sketch some ideas about how the representations in different agencies could be coordinated. These sections introduce the concepts of the *polyneme*, a hypothetical neuronal mechanism for activating corresponding slots in different representations; the *microneme,* a context-representing mechanism that similarly biases all the agencies to activate knowledge related to the current situation and goal; and the *paranome,* yet another mechanism that can simultaneously apply corresponding processes or operations to the short-term memory agents—called *pronomes*—of these various agencies.

It is impossible to briefly summarize how all these mechanisms are imagined to work, but section 29.3 of *The Society of Mind* (Minsky 1987) gives some of the flavor of the theory. What controls those paranomes? I suspect that in human minds, this control comes from the mutual exploitation of a long-range planning agency (whose scripts are influenced by various strong goals and ideals; this agency resembles the Freudian superego and is based on early imprinting), another supervisory agency capable of using semiformal inferences and natural language reformulations, and a Freudian-like censorship agency that incorporates massive records of previous failures of various sorts.

3.1 Relevance and Similarity

Problem solvers must find relevant data. How does the human mind retrieve what it needs from among so many millions of knowledge items? Different AI systems have attempted to use a variety of different methods for this. Some assign keywords, attributes, or descriptors to each item and then locate data by feature-matching or using more sophisticated associative database methods. Others use graph matching or analogical case-based adaptation. Still others try to find relevant information by threading their way through systematic, usually hierarchical classifications of knowledge—sometimes called *ontologies.* To me, all such ideas seem deficient because it is not enough to classify items of information simply in terms of the features or structures of the items themselves: We rarely use a representation in an intentional vacuum, but we always have goals—and two objects might seem similar for one purpose but different for another purpose. Consequently, we must also account for the functional aspects of what we know, and therefore, we must classify things (and ideas) according to what they can be used for or which goals they can help us achieve. Two armchairs of identical shape might seem equally comfortable as objects for sitting in, but these same chairs might seem very different for other purposes, for example, if they differ much in weight, fragility, cost, or appearance. The further a feature or difference lies from the surface of the chosen representation, the harder it will be to respond to, exploit, or adapt to, which is why the choice of representation is so important. In each functional context, we need to represent particularly well the heuristic connections between each object's internal features and relationships and the possible functions of that object. That is, we must be able to easily relate the structural features of each object's repre-

Figure 3. Functional similiarity.

sentation to how this object might behave in regard to achieving our current goals (see sections 12.4, 12.5, 12.12, and 12.13, Minsky 1987).

New problems, by definition, are different from those we have already encountered; so, we cannot always depend on using records of past experience. However, to do better than random search, we have to exploit what was learned from the past, no matter that it might not perfectly match. Which records should we retrieve as likely to be the most relevant?

Explanations of relevance in traditional theories abound with synonyms for nearness and similarity. If a certain item gives bad results, it makes sense to try something different. However, when something we try turns out to be good, then a similar one might be better. We see this idea in myriad forms, and whenever we solve problems, we find ourselves using metrical metaphors: We're "getting close" or "on the right track," using words that express proximity. But what do we mean by "close" or "near?" Decades of research on different forms of this question have produced theories and procedures for use in signal processing, pattern recognition, induction, classification, clustering, generalization, and so on, and each of these methods has been found useful for certain applications but ineffective for others. Recent connectionist research has considerably enlarged our resources in these areas. Each method has its advocates, but I contend that it is now time to move to another stage of research: Although each such concept or method might have merit in certain domains, none of them seem powerful enough alone to make our machines more intelligent. It is time to stop arguing over which type of pattern-classification technique is best because that depends on

Figure 4. "Heureka!"

our context and goal. Instead, we should work at a higher level of organization and discover how to build managerial systems to exploit the different virtues and evade the different limitations of each of these ways of comparing things. Different types of problems and representations may require different concepts of similarity. Within each realm of discourse, some representation will make certain problems and concepts appear more closely related than others. To make matters worse, even within the same problem domain, we might need different notions of similarity for descriptions of problems and goals, descriptions of knowledge about the subject domain, and descriptions of procedures to be used.

For small domains, we can try to apply all our reasoning methods to all our knowledge and test for satisfactory solutions. However, this approach becomes impractical when the search becomes too huge—in both symbolic and connectionist systems. To constrain the extent of mindless search, we must incorporate additional kinds of knowledge, embodying expertise about problem solving itself and, particularly, about managing the resources that might be available. The spatial metaphor helps us think about such issues by providing us with a superficial unification: If we envision problem solving as searching for solutions in a spacelike realm, then it is tempting to analogize between the ideas of similarity and nearness, to think about similar things as being in some sense near or close to one another.

But near in what sense? To a mathematician, the most obvious idea would be to imagine the objects under comparison to be like points in some abstract space; then each representation of this space would induce (or reflect) some sort of topologylike structure or relationship among the possible objects being represented. Thus, the languages of many sciences, not merely those of AI and psychology, are replete with attempts to portray families of concepts in terms of various sorts of spaces equipped with various measures of similarity. If, for example, you represent things in terms of (allegedly independent) properties, then it seems natural to try to assign magnitudes to each and then to sum the squares of their differences—in effect, representing these objects as vectors in Euclidean space. This approach further encourages us to formulate the function of knowledge in terms of helping us to decide "which way to go." This method is often usefully translated into the popular metaphor of hill climbing because if we can impose a suitable metric structure on this space, we might be able to devise iterative ways to find solutions by analogy with the method of hill climbing or gradient ascent; that is, when any experiment seems more or less successful than another, then we exploit this metrical structure to help us make the next move in the proper direction. (Later, I emphasize that having a sense of direction entails a little more than a sense of proximity: It is not enough just to know metrical distances; we must also respond to other kinds of heuristic differences, and these differences might be difficult to detect.)

Whenever we design or select a particular representation, this particular choice will bias our dispositions about which objects to consider more or less similar to us (or to the programs we apply to them) and, thus, will affect how we apply our knowledge to achieve goals and solve problems. Once we understand the effects of such commitments, we will be better prepared to select and modify these representations to produce more heuristically useful distinctions and confusions. Thus, let us now examine, from this point of view, some of the representations that have become popular in the AI field.

4. Heuristic Connections of Pure Logic

Why have logic-based formalisms been so widely used in AI research? I see two motives for selecting this type of representation. One virtue of logic is clarity, its lack of ambiguity. Another advantage is the preexistence of many technical mathematical theories about logic. But logic also has its disadvantages. Logical generalizations only apply to their literal lexical instances, and logical implications only apply to expressions that precisely instantiate their

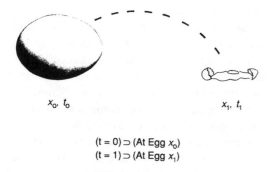

$$(t = 0) \supset (\text{At Egg } x_0)$$
$$(t = 1) \supset (\text{At Egg } x_1)$$

Figure 5. Default assumption.

antecedent conditions. No exceptions are allowed, no matter how closely they match. This approach permits you to use no near misses, no suggestive clues, no compromises, no analogies, and no metaphors. To shackle yourself so inflexibly is to shoot your own mind in the foot—if you know what I mean.

These limitations of logic begin at the foundation with the basic connectives and quantifiers. The trouble is that worldly statements of the form "For all x, $P(x)$" are never beyond suspicion. To be sure, such a statement can indeed be universally valid inside a mathematical realm; however, this validity is because such realms are themselves based on expressions of this kind. The use of such formalisms in AI has led most researchers to seek universal validity, to the virtual exclusion of practicality or interest, as though nothing would do except certainty. Now, this approach is acceptable in mathematics (wherein we ourselves define the worlds in which we solve problems), but when it comes to reality, there is little advantage in demanding inferential perfection when there is no guarantee that even our assumptions will always be correct. Logic theorists seem to have forgotten that any expression in actual life—that is, in a world that we find but don't make—such as $(x)(Px)$ must be seen as only a convenient abbreviation for something more like the following: "For any thing x being considered in the current context, the assertion $P\{x\}$ is likely to be useful for achieving goals like G, provided that we apply it in conjunction with other heuristically appropriate inference methods." In other words, we cannot ask our problem-solving systems to be absolutely perfect or even consistent; we can only hope that they will grow increasingly better than blind search at generating, justifying, supporting, rejecting, modifying, and developing evidence for new hypotheses.

It has become particularly popular in AI logic programming to restrict the representation to expressions written in first-order predicate calculus. This practice, which is so pervasive that most students engaged in it don't even know what "first order" means here, facilitates the use of certain types of inference but at a high price: The predicates of such expressions are prohibited from referring in certain ways to one another. This restriction prevents the representation of metaknowledge, rendering these systems incapable, for example, of describing what the knowledge that they contain can be used for. In effect, it precludes the use of functional descriptions. We need to develop systems for logic that can reason about their own knowledge and make heuristic adaptations and interpretations of it by using knowledge about this knowledge; however, the aforementioned limitations of expressiveness make logic unsuitable for such purposes.

Furthermore, it must be obvious that to apply our knowledge to commonsense problems, we need to be able to recognize which pairs of expressions are similar in whatever heuristic sense may be appropriate. But this seems too technically hard to do—at least for the most commonly used logical formalisms—namely, expressions in which absolute quantifiers range over stringlike normal forms. For example, to use the popular method of resolution theorem proving, one usually ends up using expressions that consist of logical disjunctions of separate, almost meaningless conjunctions. Consequently, the natural topology of any such representation will almost surely be heuristically irrelevant to any real-life problem space. Consider how dissimilar these three expressions seem when written in conjunctive form:

$A \lor B \lor C \lor$,
$AB \lor AC \lor AD \lor BC \lor BD \lor CD$,

and

$ABC \lor ABD \lor ACD \lor BCD$.

The simplest way to assess the distances or differences between expressions is to compare such superficial factors as the numbers of terms or subexpressions they have in common. Any such assessment would seem meaningless for expressions such as these. In most situations, however, it would almost surely be useful to recognize that these expressions are symmetric in their arguments and, hence, will clearly seem more similar if we rerepresent them—for example, by using S_n to mean n of S's arguments have truth value T—so that they can then be written in the form S_1, S_2, and S_3. Even in mathematics itself, we consider it a great discovery to find a new representation for which the most natural-seeming heuristic connection can be recognized as close to the representation's surface structure. However, such a discovery is too much to expect in general, so it is usually necessary to gauge the similarity of two expressions by using more complex assessments based, for example, on the number of set-inclusion levels between them, or on the number of available operations required to transform one into the other, or on the basis of the partial ordering suggested by their lattice of common generalizations and

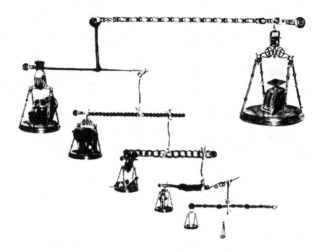

Figure 6. Weighty decisions.

instances. This means that making good similarity judgments might itself require the use of other heuristic kinds of knowledge, until eventually—that is, when our problems grow hard enough—we are forced to resort to techniques that exploit knowledge that is not so transparently expressed in any such "mathematically elegant" formulation.

Indeed, we can think about much of AI research in terms of a tension between solving problems by searching for solutions inside a compact and well-defined problem space (which is feasible only for prototypes) versus using external systems (that exploit larger amounts of heuristic knowledge) to reduce the complexity of that inner search. Compound systems of this sort need retrieval machinery that can select and extract knowledge that is relevant to the problem at hand. Although it is not especially hard to write such programs, it cannot be done in first-order systems. In my view, this can best be achieved in systems that allow us to simultaneously use object-oriented structure-based descriptions and goal-oriented functional descriptions.

How can we make logic more expressive given that each fundamental quantifier and connective is defined so narrowly from the start? This deficiency could well be beyond repair, and the most satisfactory replacement might be some sort of object-oriented frame-based language. After all, once we leave the domain of abstract mathematics and free ourselves from these rigid notations, we can see that some virtues of logiclike reasoning might remain, for example, in the sorts of deductive chaining we used and the kinds of substitution procedures we applied to these expressions. The spirit of some of these formal techniques can then be approximated by other, less formal techniques of making chains (see chapter 18, Minsky 1987). For example, the mechanisms of defaults and frame arrays could be used to approximate the formal effects of instantiating generalizations. When we use heuristic chaining, of course, we cannot assume absolute validity of the result; so, after each reasoning step, we might have to look for more evidence. If we notice exceptions and disparities, then later we must return to each or else remember them as assumptions or problems to be justified or settled at some later time, all things that humans so often do.

5. Heuristic Connections of Rule-Based Systems

Although logical representations have been used in research, rule-based representations have been more successful in applications. In these systems, each fragment of knowledge is represented by an *if-then* rule, so that whenever a description of the current problem situation precisely matches the rule's antecedent *if* condition, the system performs the action described by this rule's *then* consequent. What if no antecedent condition applies? The answer is simple: The programmer adds another rule. It is this seeming modularity that made rule-based systems so attractive. You don't have to write complicated programs. Instead, whenever the system fails to perform or does something wrong, you simply add another rule. This approach usually works well at first, but whenever we try to move beyond the realm of toy problems and start to accumulate more and more rules, we usually get into trouble because each added rule is increasingly likely to interact in unexpected ways with the others. Then, what should we ask the program to do when no antecedent fits perfectly? We can equip the program to select the rule whose antecedent most closely describes the situation; again, we're back to "similar." To make any real-world application program resourceful, we must supplement its formal reasoning facilities with matching facilities that are heuristically appropriate for the problem domain it is working in.

What if several rules match equally well? Of course, we could choose the first on the list, choose one at random, or use some other superficial scheme—but why be so unimaginative? In *The Society of Mind,* I try to regard conflicts as opportunities rather than obstacles, as openings that we can use to exploit other kinds of knowledge. For example, section 3.2 of *The Society of Mind* (Minsky 1987) suggests invoking a principle of *noncompromise* to discard sets of rules with conflicting antecedents or consequents. The general idea is that whenever two fragments of knowledge disagree, it may be better to ignore them both and refer to some other, independent agency. In effect, this approach is managerial: One agency can engage some other body of expertise to

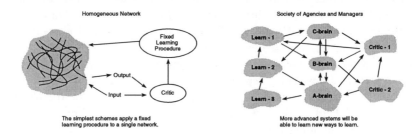

Figure 7. Homostructural vs. heterostructural.

help decide which rules to apply. For example, one might turn to case-based reasoning to ask which method worked best in similar previous situations.

Yet another approach would be to engage a mechanism for inventing a new rule by trying to combine elements of those rules that almost fit already. Section 8.2 of *The Society of Mind* (Minsky 1987) suggests using K-line representations for this purpose. To do so, we must be immersed in a society-of-agents framework in which each response to a situation involves activating not one but a variety of interacting processes. In such a system, all the agents activated by several rules can then be left to interact, if only momentarily (both with one another and with the input signals) to make a useful self-selection about which of the agents should remain active. This could be done by combining certain current connectionist concepts with other ideas about K-line mechanisms. But that can't be done until we learn how to design network architectures that can support new forms of management and supervision of developmental staging.

In any case, current rule-based systems are still too limited in ability to express "typical" knowledge. They need better default machinery. They deal with exceptions too passively; they need censors. They need better "ring-closing" mechanisms for retrieving knowledge (see Minsky 1987, section 19.10). Above all, we need better ways to connect them with other kinds of representations so that we can use them in problem-solving organizations that can exploit other kinds of models and search procedures.

6. Connectionist Networks

Up to this point, we have considered ways to overcome the deficiencies of symbolic systems by augmenting them with connectionist machinery. However, this kind of research should go both ways. Connectionist systems have equally crippling limitations, which might be ameliorated by augmentation with the sorts of architectures developed for symbolic applications. Perhaps such extensions and synthesis will recapitulate some aspects of how the primate brain grew over millions of years by evolving symbolic systems to supervise its primitive connectionist learning mechanisms.

What do we mean by *connectionist?* The use of this term is still rapidly evolving, but here it refers to attempts to embody knowledge by assigning numeric conductivities or weights to the connections inside a network of nodes. The most common form of such a node is made by combining an analog, nearly linear part that "adds up evidence" with a nonlinear, nearly digital part that makes a decision based on a threshold. The most popular such networks today take the form of *multilayer perceptrons,* that is, sequences of layers of such nodes, each layer sending signals to the next. More complex arrangements are also under study that can support cyclic internal activities; hence, they are potentially more versatile but harder to understand. What makes such architectures attractive? Mainly, they appear to be so simple and homogeneous. At least on the surface, they can be seen as ways to represent knowledge without any complex syntax. The entire configuration state of such a net can be described as nothing more than a simple vector—and the network's input-output characteristics as nothing more than a map from one vector space into another. This arrangement makes it easy to reformulate pattern recognition and learning problems in simple terms, for example, of finding the best such mapping. Seen in this way, the subject presents a pleasing mathematical simplicity. It is often not mentioned that we still possess little theoretical understanding of the computational complexity of finding such mappings, that is, of how to discover good values for the connection weights. Most current publications still merely exhibit successful small-scale examples without probing into either assessing the computational difficulty of these problems themselves or of scaling these results to similar problems of larger size.

However, we now know of many situations in which even such simple systems have been made to compute (and, more important, to learn to compute) interesting functions, particularly in such domains as clustering, classification, and pattern recognition. In some instances, this has occurred without any external supervision; furthermore, some of these systems have also performed acceptably in the presence of incomplete or noisy input and, thus, correctly recognized patterns that were novel or incomplete. This achievement means that the architectures of those systems must indeed have embodied heuristic connectivities that were appropriate for those particular problem domains. In such situations, these networks can be useful for the kind of reconstruction-retrieval operations we call *ring closing*.

However, connectionist networks have limitations as well. The next few sections discuss some of these limitations along with suggestions on how to overcome them by embedding such networks in more advanced architectural schemes.

7. Limitation of Fragmentation: The Parallel Paradox

In the Epilogue to *Perceptrons,* Papert and I argued as follows:

> It is often argued that the use of distributed representations enables a system to exploit the advantages of parallel processing. But what are the advantages of parallel processing? Suppose that a certain task involves two unrelated parts. To deal with both concurrently, we would have to maintain their representations in two decoupled agencies, both active at the same time. Then, should either of those agencies become involved with two or more sub-tasks, we'd have to deal with each of them with no more than a quarter of the available resources! If that proceeded on and on, the system would become so fragmented that each job would end up with virtually no resources assigned to it. In this regard, distribution may oppose parallelism: the more distributed a system is—that is, the more intimately its parts interact—the fewer different things it can do at the same time. On the other side, the more we do separately in parallel, the less machinery can be assigned to each element of what we do, and that ultimately leads to increasing fragmentation and incompetence. This is not to say that distributed representations and parallel processing are always incompatible. When we simultaneously activate two distributed representations in the same network, they will be forced to interact. In favorable circumstances, those interactions can lead to useful parallel computations, such as the satisfaction of simultaneous constraints. But that will not happen in general; it will occur only when the representations happen to mesh in suitably fortunate ways. Such problems will be especially serious when we try to train distributed systems to deal with problems that require any sort of structural analysis in which the system must represent relationships between substructures of related types—that is, problems that are likely to demand the same structural resources. (Minsky and Papert 1988, p. 277) (See also Minsky 1987, section 15.11.)

For these reasons, it will always be hard for a homogeneous network to perform parallel *high-level* computations, unless we can arrange for it to become divided into effectively disconnected parts. There is no general remedy for this problem, and it is no special peculiarity of connectionist hardware; computers have similar limitations, and the only answer is providing more hardware. More generally, it seems obvious that without adequate memory buffering, homogeneous networks must remain incapable of recursion, as long as successive function calls have to use the same hardware. This inability is because without such facilities, either the different calls will cause side effects for one another, or some of them must be erased, leaving the system unable to execute proper returns or continuations. Again, this might easily be fixed by providing enough short-term memory, for example, in the form of a stack of temporary K-lines.

8. Limitations of Specialization and Efficiency

Each connectionist net, once trained, can only do what it has learned to do. To make it do something else—for example, to compute a different measure of similarity or to recognize a different class of patterns—would, in general, require a complete change in the matrix of connection coefficients. Usually, we can change the function of a computer much more easily (at least, when the desired functions can each be computed by compact algorithms) because a computer's memory cells are so much more interchangeable. It is curious how even technically well-informed people tend to forget how computationally massive a fully connected neural network is. It is instructive to compare its size with the few hundred rules that drive a typically successful commercial rule-based expert system.

How connected do networks need to be? Several points in *The Society of Mind* suggest that commonsense reasoning systems might not need to increase the density of physical connectivity as fast as they increase the complexity and scope of their performances. Chapter 6 (Minsky 1987) argues that knowledge systems must evolve into clumps of specialized agencies, rather than homogeneous networks, because they develop different types of internal representations. As this evolution proceeds, it will become decreasingly feasible for any of these agencies directly to communicate with the interior of others. Furthermore, there will be a tendency for most newly acquired skills to develop from the relatively few that are already well developed, which again will bias the largest-scale connections toward evolving into recursively clumped, rather than uniformly connected, arrangements. A different tendency to limit connectivities is discussed in section 20.8, which proposes a sparse connection scheme that can simulate in real time the behavior of fully connected nets—in which only a small proportion of agents are simultaneously active. This method, based on a half-century–old idea of Calvin Mooers, allows many intermittently active agents to share the same relatively narrow, common connection bus. This might seem, at first, a mere economy, but section 20.9 suggests that this technique could also induce a more heuristically useful tendency if the separate signals on that bus were to represent meaningful symbols. Finally, chapter 17 suggests other developmental reasons why minds might virtually be forced to grow in relatively discrete stages rather than as homogeneous networks. Our progress in making theories about this area might parallel our progress in understanding the stages we see in the growth of every child's thought.

If our minds are assembled of agencies with so little intercommunication, how can those parts cooperate? What keeps them working on related aspects of the same problem? The first answer I propose in *The Society of Mind* is that it is less important for agencies to cooperate than to exploit one another

Figure 8. Recognition in context.

because those agencies tend to become specialized, developing their own internal languages and representations. Consequently, they cannot understand each other's internal operations well—and each must learn to exploit some of the others for the effects that those others produce—without knowing in any detail how these other effects are produced. Similarly, there must be other agencies to manage all these specialists, to keep the system from too much fruitless conflict for access to limited resources. These management agencies cannot directly deal with all the small interior details of what happens inside their subordinates. Instead, they must work with summaries of what those subordinates seem to do. This also suggests that there must be constraints on internal connectivity: Too much detailed information would overwhelm those managers. Such constraints also apply recursively to the insides of every large agency. Thus, in chapter 8 of *The Society of Mind* (Minsky 1987), I argue that relatively few direct connections are needed except between adjacent level bands.

All this suggests (but does not prove) that large commonsense reasoning systems will not need to be fully connected. Instead, the system could consist of localized clumps of expertise. At the lowest levels, these clumps would have to be densely connected to support the sort of associativity required to learn low-level pattern-detecting agents. However, as we ascend to higher levels, the individual signals must become increasingly abstract and significant, and accordingly, the density of connection paths between agencies can become increasingly (but only relatively) smaller. Eventually, we should be able to build a sound technical theory about the connection densities required for commonsense thinking, but I don't think that we have the right foundations yet. The problem is that contemporary theories of computational complexity are still based too much on worst-case analyses or coarse statistical assumptions, neither of which suitably represents realistic heuristic conditions. The worst-case theories unduly emphasize the intractable versions of problems that, in their usual forms, present less practical difficulty. The statistical theories tend to uniformly weight all instances for lack of systematic ways to emphasize the types of situations of most practical interest. However, the AI systems of the future, like their human counterparts, will normally prefer to satisfice rather than optimize—and we don't yet have theories that can realistically portray these mundane sorts of requirements.

9. Limitations of Context, Segmentation, and Parsing

When we see seemingly successful demonstrations of machine learning in carefully prepared test situations, we must be careful about how we draw more general conclusions. This is because there is a large step between the abilities to recognize objects or patterns when they are isolated and when they appear as components of more complex scenes. In section 6.6 of *Perceptrons* (Minsky and Papert 1988), we see that we must be prepared to find that even after training a certain network to recognize a certain type of pattern, we might find it unable to recognize this same pattern when embedded in a more complicated context or environment. (Some reviewers have objected that our proofs of this fact applied only to simple three-layer networks; however, most of these theorems are much more general, as these critics might see if they'd take the time to extend those proofs.) The problem is that it is usually easy to make isolated recognitions by detecting the presence of various features and then computing weighted conjunctions of them. This is easy to do in three-layer acyclic nets. But in compound scenes, this method won't work unless the separate features of all the distinct objects are somehow properly assigned to the correct objects. Similarly, we cannot expect neural networks generally to be able to parse the treelike or embedded structures found in the phrase structure of natural language.

How could we augment connectionist networks to make them able to do such things as analyze complex visual scenes or extract and assign the referents of linguistic expressions to the appropriate contents of short-term memories? It will surely need additional architecture to represent the structural analysis of a visual scene into objects and their relationships, for example, by protecting each midlevel recognizer from seeing input derived from other objects, perhaps by arranging for the object-recognizing agents to compete in assigning each feature to itself, but denying it to competitors. This method has been successfully used in symbolic systems, and parts have been done in connectionist systems (for example, by Waltz and Pollack), but many conceptual missing links remain in this area, particularly in regard to how a second connectionist system could use the output of one that managed to parse the scene. In any case, we should not expect to see simple solutions to these problems. It might be an accident that so much of the brain is occupied with such functions.

10. Limitations of Opacity

Most serious of all is what we might call the problem of *opacity,* that the knowledge embodied inside a network's numeric coefficients is not accessible outside that net. This challenge is not one we should expect our connectionists to easily solve. I suspect it is so intractable that even our own brains have evolved little such capacity over the billions of years it took to evolve from anemonelike reticulae. Instead, I suspect that our societies and hierarchies of subsystems have evolved ways to evade the problem by arranging for some of our systems to learn to model what some of our other systems do (see Minsky 1987, section 6.12). They might do this modeling in part by using information obtained from direct channels into the interiors of these other networks, but mostly, I suspect, they do it less directly—so to speak, behavioristically—by making generalizations based on external observations, as though they were like miniature scientists. In effect, some of our agents invent models of others. Regardless of whether these models might be defective or even entirely wrong (and here I refrain from directing my aim at peculiarly faulty philosophers), it suffices for these models to be useful in enough situations. To be sure, it might be feasible, in principle, for an external system to accurately model a connectionist network from outside by formulating and testing hypotheses about its internal structure. However, of what use would such a model be if it merely repeated redundantly? It would not only be simpler but also more useful for that higher-level agency to assemble only a pragmatic, heuristic model of this other network's activity based on concepts already available to that observer. (This is evidently the situation in human psychology. The apparent insights we gain from meditation and other forms of self-examination are only infrequently genuine.)

The problem of opacity grows more acute as representations become more distributed—that is, as we move from symbolic to connectionist poles—and it becomes increasingly more difficult for external systems to analyze and reason about the delocalized ingredients of the knowledge inside distributed representations. It also makes it harder to learn, past a certain degree of complexity, because it is hard to assign credit for success, or formulate new hypotheses (because the old hypotheses themselves are not "formulated").

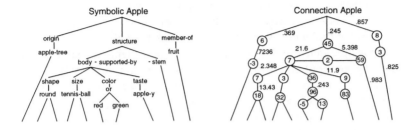

Figure 9. Numerical opacity.

Thus, distributed learning ultimately limits growth, no matter how convenient it might be in the short term, because "the idea of a thing with no parts provides nothing that we can use as pieces of explanation" (Minsky 1987).

For such reasons, although homogeneous, distributed learning systems may work well to a certain point, they eventually may tend to fail when confronted with problems of larger scale—unless we find ways to compensate the accumulation of many weak connections with some opposing mechanism that favors internal simplification and localization. Many connectionist writers positively seem to rejoice in the holistic opacity of representations within which even they are unable to discern the significant parts and relationships. However, unless a distributed system has enough ability to crystallize its knowledge into lucid representations of its new subconcepts and substructures, its ability to learn will eventually slow, and it will be unable to solve problems beyond a certain degree of complexity. In addition, although this situation suggests that homogeneous network architectures might not work well past a certain size, this restriction should be bad news only for those ideologically committed to minimal architectures. For all we currently know, the scales at which such systems crash are large enough for our purposes. Indeed, the society of mind thesis holds that most of the agents that grow in our brains only need to operate on scales so small that each by itself seems no more than a toy. But when we combine enough of them—in ways that are not too delocalized—we can make them do almost anything.

In any case, we should not assume that we always can—or always should—avoid the use of opaque schemes. The circumstances of daily life compel us to make decisions based on "adding up the evidence." We frequently find (when we value our time) that even if we had the means, it wouldn't pay to analyze. The society of mind theory of human thinking doesn't suggest otherwise; on the contrary, it leads us to expect to encounter incomprehensible representations at every level of the mind. A typical agent does little more than exploit other agents' abilities; hence, most of our agents accomplish their job knowing virtually nothing of how it is done.

Analogous issues of opacity arise in the symbolic domain. Just as networks sometimes solve problems by using massive combinations of elements, each of which has little individual significance, symbolic systems sometimes solve problems by manipulating large expressions with similarly insignificant terms, such as when we replace the explicit structure of a composite Boolean function with a locally senseless canonical form. Although this technique simplifies some computations by making them more homogeneous, it disperses knowledge about the structure and composition of the data and, thus, disables our ability to solve harder problems. At both extremes—in representations that are either too distributed or too discrete—we lose the structural knowledge embodied in the form of intermediate-level concepts. This loss might not be evident as long as our problems are easy to solve, but those intermediate concepts might be indispensable for solving more advanced problems. Comprehending complex situations usually hinges on discovering a good analogy or variation on a theme. However, it is virtually impossible to do this with a representation, such as a logical form, a linear sum, or a holographic transformation—each of whose elements seem meaningless because they are either too large or too small—thus leaving no way to represent significant parts and relationships.

Many other problems invite the synthesis of symbolic and connectionist architectures. How can we find ways for nodes to refer to other nodes or to represent knowledge about the roles of particular coefficients? To see the difficulty, imagine trying to represent the structure of the arch in Patrick Winston's thesis—without simply reproducing its topology. Another critical issue is how to enable nets to make comparisons. This problem is more serious than it might seem. Section 23.1 of *The Society of Mind* discusses the importance of differences and goals, and section 23.2 points out that connectionist networks deficient in short term memory will find it peculiarly difficult to detect differences between patterns (Minsky 1987). Networks with weak architectures will also find it difficult to detect or represent (invariant) abstractions; this problem was discussed as early as the Pitts-McCulloch paper of 1947. Still another important problem for memory-weak, bottom-up mechanisms is controlling search: To solve hard problems, one might have to consider different alternatives, explore their subalternatives, and then make comparisons among them—yet still be able to return to the initial situation without forgetting what was accomplished. This kind of activity, which we call thinking, requires facilities for temporarily storing partial states of the system without confusing these memories. One answer is to provide, along with the required memory, some systems for learning and executing control scripts, as suggested in section 13.5 of *The Society of Mind* (Minsky 1987). To do this effectively, we must have some insulationism to counterbalance our connectionism. Smart systems need both of these components, so the symbolic-connectionist antagonism is not a valid technical issue but only a transient concern in contemporary scientific politics.

11. Mind Sculpture

The future work of mind design will not be much like what we do today. Some programmers will continue to use traditional languages and processes. Other programmers will turn toward new kinds of knowledge-based expert systems. However, eventually all this work will be incorporated into systems that exploit two new kinds of resources. On one side, we will use huge pre-programmed reservoirs of commonsense knowledge. On the other side, we will have powerful, modular learning machines equipped with no knowledge at all. Then, what we know as programming will change its character entirely—to an activity that I envision to be more like sculpturing. To program today, we must describe things very carefully because nowhere is there any margin for error. But once we have modules that know how to learn, we won't have to specify nearly so much—and we'll program on a grander scale, relying on learning to fill in details.

This doesn't mean, I hasten to add, that things will be simpler than they are now. Instead, we'll make our projects more ambitious. Designing an artificial mind will be much like evolving an animal. Imagine yourself at a terminal, assembling various parts of a brain. You'll be specifying the sorts of things that were only heretofore described in texts about neuroanatomy. "Here," you'll find yourself thinking, "we'll need two similar networks that can learn to shift time signals into spatial patterns so that they can be compared by a feature extractor sensitive to a context about this wide." Then, you'll have to sketch the architectures of organs that can learn to supply appropriate input to those agencies and draft the outlines of intermediate organs for learning to suitably encode the output to suit the needs of other agencies. Section 31.3 of *The Society of Mind* (Minsky 1987) suggests how a genetic system might mold the form of an agency that is predestined to learn to recognize the presence of particular human individuals. A functional sketch of such a design might turn out to involve dozens of different sorts of organs, centers, layers, and pathways. The human brain might have many thousands of such components.

A functional sketch is only the start. Whenever you use a learning machine, you must specify more than just the sources of input and the destinations of output. It must also somehow be impelled toward the sorts of things you want it to learn—what sorts of hypotheses it should make, how it should compare alternatives, how many examples should be required, how to decide when enough has been done, when to decide that things have gone wrong, and how to deal with bugs and exceptions. It is all very well for theorists to speak about "spontaneous learning and generalization," but there are too many contingencies in real life for such words to mean anything by themselves. Should this agency be an adventurous risk taker or a careful, conservative reductionist? One person's intelligence is another's stupidity. And how should that learning machine divide and budget its resources of hardware, time, and memory?

How will we build such grand machines when so many design constraints are involved? No one will be able to track all the details because just as a human brain is constituted by interconnecting hundreds of different kinds of highly evolved subarchitectures, so will these new kinds of thinking machines. Each new design will have to be assembled by using libraries of already developed, off-the-shelf subsystems already known to be able to handle particular kinds of representations and processes. Also, the designer will be less concerned with what happens inside these units and more concerned with their interconnections and interrelationships. Because most components will be learning machines, the designer will have to specify not only what each one will learn but also which agencies should provide what incentives and rewards for which others. Every such decision about one agency imposes additional constraints and requirements on several others and, in turn, on how to train those others. In addition, as in any society, there must be watchers to watch each watcher, lest any one or a few of them get too much control of the rest.

Each agency will need nerve bundle–like connections to certain other ones for sending and receiving signals about representations, goals, and constraints, and we'll have to make decisions about the relative size and influence of every such parameter. Consequently, I expect that the future art of brain design will have to be more like sculpturing than like our current craft of programming. It will be much less concerned with the algorithmic details of the submachines than with the balancing of their relationships; perhaps this situation better resembles politics, sociology, or management than present-day engineering.

Some neural network advocates might hope that all this will be superfluous. Why not seek to find, instead, how to build one single, huge net that can learn to do all these things by itself. Did not our own human brains come about as the outcome of one great learning search? We could only regard this as feasible by ignoring the facts—the unthinkable scale of that billion-year venture and the octillions of lives of our ancestors. Remember, too, that even so, in all that evolutionary search, not all the problems have yet been solved. What will we do when our sculptures don't work? Consider a few of the wonderful bugs that still afflict even our own grand human brains: obsessive preoccupation with inappropriate goals; inattention and inability to concentrate; bad representations; excessively broad or narrow generalizations; excessive accumulation of useless information; superstition: defective credit-assignment schema; unrealistic cost-benefit analyses; unbalanced, fanatical search strategies; formation of defective categorizations; inability to deal with exceptions to rules; improper staging of development, or living in the past; unwillingness to acknowledge loss; depression or maniacal optimism; and excessive confusion from cross-coupling.

Seeing this list, one has to wonder, "Can people think?" I suspect there is no simple and magical way to avoid such problems in our new machines; it will require a great deal of research and engineering. I suspect that it is no accident that human brains contain so many different and specialized brain centers. To suppress the emergence of serious bugs, both those natural systems and the artificial ones we shall construct will probably need intricate arrangements of interlocking checks and balances, in which each agency is supervised by several others. Furthermore, each of these other agencies must themselves learn when and how to use the resources available to them. How, for example, should each learning system balance the advantages of immediate gain over those of conservative, long-term growth? When should it favor the accumulation of competence over comprehension? In the large-scale design of our human brains, we still don't know much of what all the different organs do, but I'm willing to bet that many of them are largely involved in regulating others, to keep the system as a whole from falling prey to the sorts of bugs that were mentioned above. Until we start building brains ourselves to learn what bugs are most probable, it will remain hard for us to guess the actual functions of much of that hardware.

There are countless wonders yet to be discovered in these exciting new fields of research. We can still learn a great many things from experiments on even the simplest nets. We'll learn even more from trying to make theories about what we observe. And surely, soon we'll start to prepare for that future art-of-mind design by experimenting with societies of nets that embody more structured strategies—and, consequently, make more progress on the networks that make up our own human minds. And in doing all these experiments, we'll discover how to make symbolic representations that are more adaptable and connectionist representations that are more expressive.

It is amusing how persistently people express the view that machines based on symbolic representations (as opposed, presumably, to connectionist representations) could never achieve much or ever be conscious and self-aware. I maintain it is precisely because our brains are still mostly connectionist, that we humans have so little consciousness! It's also why we're capable of so little parallelism of thought—and why we have such limited insight into the nature of our own machinery.

Acknowledgment

This research was funded over a period of years by the Computer Science Division of the Office of Naval Research. Illustrations by Juliana Minsky.

Notes

1. Adapted from Logical versus Analogical or Symbolic versus Connectionist or Neat versus Scruffy. In *AI at MIT: Expanding Frontiers,* eds. Patrick H. Winston, with S. A. Shellard, 219–243. Cambridge, Mass.: MIT Press.

30

Machine as Mind

Herbert A. Simon

1. Introduction

In this chapter I will start with the human mind and what psychological research has learned about it, I will proceed to draw lessons from cognitive psychology about the characteristics we must bestow upon computer programs when we wish those programs to think. I speak of "mind" and not "brain." By "mind" I mean a system that produces thought, viewed at a relatively high level of aggregation: say, at or above the level of elementary processes that require 100 milliseconds or more for their execution. At that level, little or nothing need be said about the structure or behavior of individual neurons, or even small assemblages of them. Our units will be larger and more abstract.

It is well known that the language and representation best adapted to describing phenomena depends on the level of aggregation at which we model them. Physicists concerned with quarks and similar particles on minute temporal and spatial scales do not use the same vocabulary of entities and processes as geneticists describing how DNA informs protein synthesis.

Whatever our philosophical position with respect to reduction, it is practically necessary to build science in levels. The phenomena at each level are described in terms of the primitives at that level, and these primitives become, in turn, the phenomena to be described and explained at the next level below.

The primitives of mind, at the level I wish to consider, are symbols, complex structures of symbols, and processes that operate on symbols (Newell and Simon 1976). The simplest among these processes require tens to hundreds of milliseconds for their execution. Simple recognition of a familiar object takes at least 500 milliseconds. At this level, the same software can be implemented with radically different kinds of hardware—protoplasm and silicon among them.

My central thesis is that, at this level of aggregation, conventional computers can be, and have been, programmed to represent symbol structures and carry out processes on those structures in a manner that parallels, step by step, the way the human brain does it. The principal evidence for my thesis are programs that do just that. These programs demonstrably think.

It has been argued that a computer simulation of thinking is no more thinking than a simulation of digestion is digestion. The analogy is false. A computer simulation of digestion is not capable of taking starch as an input and producing fructose or glucose as outputs. It deals only with symbolic or numerical quantities representing these substances.

In contrast, a computer simulation of thinking thinks. It takes problems as its inputs and (sometimes) produces solutions as its outputs. It represents these problems and solutions as symbolic structures, as the human mind does, and performs transformations on them, as the human mind does. The materials of digestion are chemical substances, which are not replicated in a computer simulation. The materials of thought are symbols—patterns, which can be replicated in a great variety of materials (including neurons and chips), thereby enabling physical symbol systems fashioned of these materials to think. Turing (1950) was perhaps the first to have this insight in clear form, forty years ago.

2. Nearly Decomposable Systems

The successive levels in the architecture of nature are not arbitrary (Simon 1981). Most complex systems are hierarchical and *nearly decomposable*. Consider a building divided into rooms, which are, in turn, divided into cubicles. Starting from a state of radical temperature disequilibrium—every cubic foot of space being momentarily at quite a different temperature from the adjoining spaces—within a matter of minutes the temperature within each cubicle will approach some constant value, a different value for each cubicle.

After a somewhat longer time, all the cubicles in a given room will reach a common temperature. After a still longer interval, all the rooms in the building will reach a common temperature.

In a hierarchical system of this kind, we do not have to consider the behavior at all levels simultaneously. We can model the cubicles, the rooms, and the building semi-independently. In the short run, we can analyze the changes in individual cubicles while disregarding their interaction with the other cubicles. In the middle run, we can analyze the individual rooms, replacing the detail of each cubicle by its average temperature. For the longer run, we can consider the building as a whole, replacing the detail of each room by its average temperature.

In layered hierarchical systems of this kind, each subcomponent has a much higher rate of interaction with the other subcomponents in the same component than it does with subcomponents outside that component. Elsewhere (Simon 1981) I have shown how the behavior of nearly decomposable systems can be analyzed mathematically and why, from an evolutionary standpoint, we should expect most of the complex systems that we find in nature to be nearly decomposable.

For present purposes, what is important about nearly-decomposable systems is that we can analyze them at a particular level of aggregation without detailed knowledge of the structures at the levels below. These details do not "show through" at the next level above; only aggregate properties of the more microscopic systems affect behavior at the higher level. In our temperature example, only the average temperatures of the cubicles affect the changes in temperature in the rooms, and only the average temperatures of the rooms are relevant to the course of equilibration of the building as a whole.

Because mind has shown itself to behave as a nearly-decomposable system, we can model thinking at the symbolic level, with events in the range of hundreds of milliseconds or longer, without concern for details of implementation at the "hardware" level, whether the hardware be brain or computer.

3. The Two Faces of AI

AI can be approached in two ways. First, we can write smart programs for computers without any commitment to imitating the processes of human intelligence. We can then use all of the speed and power of the computer and all of its memory capacity, unconcerned with whether people have the same computational speed and power or the same memory capacity.

Alternatively, we can write smart programs for computers that do imitate closely the human processes, forgoing the computer's capacities for rapid processing of symbols and its almost instantaneous memory storage. We can slow the computer down to human speeds, so to speak, and test whether it can absorb the cunning that will permit it to behave intelligently within these limitations.

Chess-playing programs illustrate the two approaches. DEEPTHOUGHT is a powerful program that now plays chess at grandmaster level and can defeat all but a few hundred human players. It demonstrably does not play in a humanoid way, typically exploring tens of millions of branches of the game tree before it makes its choice of move. There is good empirical evidence (de Groot 1965) that human grandmasters seldom look at more than 100 branches on the tree. By generally searching the *relevant* branches, they make up with chess knowledge for their inability to carry out massive searches.

However, DEEPTHOUGHT by no means "explores all possibilities." "All possibilities" would mean at least 10^{50} branches, 10^{40} times more than the program can manage, and obviously more than any computer, present or prospective can explore. DEEPTHOUGHT exercises a certain degree of selectivity in the branches it explores, but more important, it halts its explorations about a dozen ply deep—far short of the end of the game—and applies an evaluation function to measure the relative goodness of all the positions it reaches. A great deal of chess knowledge, supplied by the human programmers, is incorporated in the evaluation function. Hence DEEPTHOUGHT's chess prowess rests on a combination of brute force, unattainable by human players, and extensive, if "mediocre," chess knowledge.

Consider now a much earlier program, MATER (Baylor and Simon 1966) which is not nearly as good a chess player as DEEPTHOUGHT. In fact, MATER is a specialist designed only to exploit those game positions where an immediate mating combination (possibly a quite deep one) might be hidden. MATER has shown substantial ability to discover such mating combinations—rediscovering many of the most celebrated ones in chess history. What is more interesting, MATER ordinarily looks at fewer than 100 branches of the tree in order to accomplish this feat. It is as selective in its search as human players are in these kinds of situations, and in fact, it looks at nearly the same parts of the game tree as they do.

We can go even farther in comparing MATER with human players. For these kinds of positions (where a possible checkmate lurks), MATER uses the same rules of thumb to guide its search and select promising lines that human masters use. It examines forceful moves first, and it examines first those branches along which the opponent is most constrained. These heuristics, while powerful, do not always lead to the shortest mate. We have found at least one historical instance (a game between Edward Lasker and Thomas) in which both human player and computer required an extra move because the shortest path to a checkmate did not satisfy these heuristics—did not correspond with the most plausible search path.

The remainder of my remarks are concerned with programs that are intelligent in more or less humanoid ways—that carry out only modest computations to perform their tasks. These programs resemble MATER rather than DEEPTHOUGHT. This does not mean that programs for AI should always be built in this way, but my aim here is to consider machine as mind rather than to celebrate the achievements of rapid computation.

4. The View from Psychology

4.1 Selective Heuristic Search

How does intelligence look to contemporary cognitive psychology? I have already mentioned one fact that has been verified repeatedly in the laboratory—human problem solvers do not carry out extensive searches. Even examining 100 possibilities in a game tree stretches human memory and patience. Since many of the spaces in which people solve problems are enormous (I have mentioned the figure of 10^{50} for chess), "trying everything" is not a viable search strategy. People use knowledge about the structure of the problem space to form heuristics that allow them to search extremely selectively.

4.2 Recognition: The Indexed Memory

A second important fact is also well illustrated by the game of chess. A chess grandmaster can play fifty or more opponents "simultaneously," moving from board to board and seldom taking more than a few seconds for each move. If the opponents are not stronger than experts, say, the grandmaster will win almost every game, although his play will perhaps be only at master level. This fact demonstrates that much of grandmasters' knowledge (not all of it) is accessed by recognition of cues on the board, for in simultaneous play they have no time for deep analysis by search (Chase and Simon 1973).

Grandmasters, questioned on how they play simultaneous games, report that they make "standard" developing moves until they notice a feature of the board that indicates a weakness in the opponent's position (doubled pawns, say). Noticing this feature gives access to information about strategies for exploiting it. The grandmaster's memory is like a large indexed encyclopedia (with at least 50,000 index entries). The perceptually noticeable features of the chessboard (the cues) trigger the appropriate index entries and give access to the corresponding information. This information often includes relevant strategies.

Solving problems by responding to cues that are visible only to experts is sometimes called solving them by "intuition." A better label would be "solving by recognition." Intuition consists simply of noting features in a situation that index useful information. There is no mystery in intuition, or at least no more mystery than there is in recognizing a friend on the street and recalling what one knows about the friend.

In computers, recognition processes are generally implemented by productions: the condition sides of the productions serving as tests for the presence of cues, the action sides holding the information that is accessed when the cues are noticed. Hence, it is easy to build computer systems that solve problems by recognition, and indeed recognition capability is the core of most AI expert systems.

The number, 50,000, suggested above as the number of features a grandmaster can recognize on a chessboard, has been estimated empirically, but only by indirect means (Simon and Gilmartin 1973). Confidence rises that the figure is approximately correct when one notes that it is roughly comparable to the native language vocabularies of college graduates (usually estimated at 50,000 to 100,000 words).

Items that, by their recognizability, serve to index semantic memory are usually called "chunks" in the psychological literature. Generalizing, we hypothesize that an expert in any domain must acquire some 50,000 familiar chunks (give or take a factor of four). Although existing expert systems for computers are not this large, the figure is not a daunting one.

By way of footnote, extensive data show that it takes at least 10 years of intensive training for a person to acquire the information (presumably including the 50,000 chunks) required for world-class performance in any domain of expertise. This has been shown for chess playing, musical composition, painting, piano playing, swimming, tennis, neuropsychological research, research in topology, and other fields (Bloom 1985, Hayes 1989). Mozart, who began composing at four, produced no world-class music before at least the age of 17, 13 years later. Child prodigies are not exempt from the rule.

4.3 Seriality: The Limits of Attention

Problems that cannot be solved by recognition generally require the application of more or less sustained attention. Attention is closely associated with human short-term memory. Symbols that are attended to—the inputs, say, to an arithmetic calculation—must be retained during use in short-term memory, which has a capacity of only about seven chunks, a limit that is based on extensive experimental data (Simon 1976). The need for all inputs and outputs of attention-demanding tasks to pass through short-term memory essentially serializes the thinking process. Generally, we can only think of one thing at a time. (Sometimes, by time sharing, we can think of two, if they are not too complex. Light conversation and driving are compatible activities for most people when the traffic is not too heavy!)

Hence, whatever parallel processes may be going on at lower (neural) levels, at the symbolic level the human mind is fundamentally a serial machine, accomplishing its work through temporal sequences of processes, each typically requiring hundreds of milliseconds for execution.

In contrast, the evidence is equally strong that the sensory organs, especially the eyes and ears, are highly parallel systems. We are confronted with a hybrid system, the sensory (and possibly perceptual) processes operating in parallel, and the subsequent symbolic processes (after patterns of stimuli have been recognized and chunked) serially.

Within the limits of present knowledge, there is a no-man's-land between the parallel and serial components of the processor, whose exact boundaries are not known. For example, there are implementable schemes that execute all processing down to the point of recognition in parallel (for example, so-called demon schemes), but there are also workable serial recognition systems (e.g., EPAM: Feigenbaum and Simon 1984, Richman and Simon 1989). The available evidence does not make a clear choice between these alternatives.

4.4 The Architecture of Expert Systems

Psychology, then, gives us a picture of the expert as having a sensory system that is basically parallel in structure, interfaced with a cognitive system that is basically serial. Somewhere in the imprecise boundary between the two is a mechanism (serial or parallel or both) capable of recognizing large numbers (hundreds of thousands) of patterns in the domain of expertise and of obtaining access through this recognition to information stored in short-term memory. The information accessed can be processed further (using heuristic search) by a serial symbol-processing system.

Recognition takes approximately a half second or second (Newell and Simon 1972). The individual steps in search also require hundreds of milliseconds, and search is highly selective, the selectivity based on heuristics stored in memory. People can report orally the results of recognition (but not the cues used in the process) and are aware of many of the inputs and outputs of the steps they take in search. It appears that they can report most of the symbols that reside temporarily in short-term memory (i.e., the symbols in the focus of attention).

One reason for thinking that this structure is sufficient to produce expert behavior is that AI has now built many expert systems, capable of performing at professional levels in restricted domains, using essentially the architecture we have just described. In general, the AI expert systems (for example, systems for medical diagnosis) have fewer "chunks" than the human experts and make up for the deficiency by doing more computing than people do. The differences appear to be quantitative, not qualitative: human and computer experts alike depend heavily upon recognition, supplemented by a little capacity for reasoning (i.e., search).

5. The Matter of Semantics

It is sometimes claimed that the thinking of computers, symbolic systems that they are, is purely syntactical. Unlike people, it is argued, computers do not have intentions, and their symbols do not have semantic referents. The argument is easily refuted by concrete examples of computer programs that demonstrably understand the meanings (at least some of the meanings) of their symbols and that have goals, thus exhibiting at least two aspects of intention.

Consider, first, a computer-driven van, of which we have an example on our university campus, equipped with television cameras and capable of steering its way (slowly) along a winding road in a nearby park. Patterns of light transmitted through the cameras are encoded by the computer program as landscape features (e.g., the verge of the road). The program, having the intention of proceeding along the road and remaining on it, creates internal symbols that denote these features, interprets them, and uses the symbols to guide its steering and speed-control mechanisms.

Consider, second, one of the commercially available chess-playing programs that use an actual chess board on which the opponent moves the men physically and that senses these moves and forms an internal (symbolic) representation of the chess position. The symbols in this internal representation denote the external physical pieces and their arrangement, and the program demonstrates quite clearly, by the moves it chooses, that it intends to beat its opponent.

There is no mystery about what "semantics" means as applied to the human mind. It means that there is a correspondence, a relation of denotation, between symbols inside the head and objects (or relations among objects) outside. In particular, the brain is (sometimes) able to test whether sensory signals received from particular objects identify those objects as the meanings of particular symbols (names). And the human brain is sometimes able to construct and emit words, phrases, and sentences whose denotation corresponds to the sensed scene.

There is also no mystery about human intentions. Under certain circumstances, for example, a human being senses internal stirrings (usually called hunger) that lead him or her to seek food. Under other circumstances, other stirrings create the goal of defeating an opponent in chess. Now the two computer programs I described above also have goals: in the one case to drive along a road, in the other case to win a chess game. It would not be hard to store both programs in the same computer, along with input channels that would, from time to time, switch its attention from the one goal to the other. Such a system would then have not a single intention, but a capacity for several, even as you and I.

It may be objected (and has been) that the computer does not "understand" the meanings of its symbols or the semantic operations on them, or the goals it adopts. This peculiar use of the word "understand" has something to do with the fact that we are (sometimes) *conscious* of meanings and intentions. But then, my evidence that you are conscious is no better than my evidence that the road-driving or chess-playing computers are conscious.

Moreover, in formal treatments of semantics, consciousness has never been one of the defining characteristics; denotation has. What is important about semantic meaning is that there be a correspondence (conscious or not) between the symbol and the thing it denotes. What is important about intention is that there be a correspondence (conscious or not) between the goal symbol and behavior appropriate to achieving the goal in the context of some belief system.

Finally, Searle's Chinese Room parable proves not that computer programs cannot understand Chinese, but only that the particular program Searle described does not understand Chinese. Had he described a program that could receive inputs from a sensory system and emit the symbol "cha" in the presence of tea and "bai cha" in the presence of hot water, we would have to admit that it understood at least a *little* Chinese. And the vocabulary and grammar could be extended indefinitely. Later, I will describe a computer program, devised by Siklóssy (1972), that learns language in exactly this way (although the connection with external senses was not implemented).

6. "Ill-Structured" Phenomena

Research on human thinking has progressed from relatively simple and well-structured phenomena (for example, rote verbal learning, solving puzzles, simple concept attainment) to more complex and rather ill-structured tasks (e.g., use of natural language, learning, scientific discovery, visual art). "Ill-structured" means that the task has ill-defined or multi-dimensional goals, that its frame of reference or representation is not clear or obvious, that there are no clear-cut procedures for generating search paths or evaluating them—or some combination of these characteristics.

When a problem is ill-structured in one or more of these senses, a first step in solving it is to impose some kind of structure that allows it to be represented—that is, symbolized—at least approximately, and attacked in this symbolized form. What does psychology tell us about problem representations, their nature and how they are constructed for particular problems?

6.1 Forms of Representation

We do not have an exhaustive taxonomy of possible representations, but a few basic forms show up prominently in psychological research. First, situations may be represented in words or in logical or mathematical notations. All of these representations are basically propositional and are more or less equivalent to a set of propositions in some formal logic. Propositional representation immediately suggests that the processing will resemble logical reasoning or proof.

When problems are presented verbally, the propositional translation of these words may be quite literal or may comprise only the semantic content of the input without preserving syntactic details. In both cases, we will speak of propositional representation. There is a great deal of psychological evidence that input sentences are seldom retained intact but that, instead, their semantic content is usually extracted and stored in some form.

Second, situations may be represented in diagrams or pictures ("mental pictures"). Internally, a picture or diagram can be represented by the equivalent of a raster of pixels (for example, the cerebral image associated with the direct signals from the retina) or by a network of nodes and links that capture the components of the diagram and their relations. Possibly there are other ways (for example, as the equations of analytic geometry), but these two have been given most consideration by psychologists. A picture or diagram amounts to a *model* of the system, with processes that operate on it to move it through time or to search through a succession of its states.

Most psychological research on representations assumes, explicitly or implicitly, one of the representations mentioned in the preceding paragraphs: propositional, raster-like "picture," or node-link diagram, or some combination of them. All of these representations are easily implemented by computer programs.

6.2 Equivalence of Representations

What consequences does the form of representation have for cognition? To answer that question, we must define the notion of *equivalence of representations*. Actually, we must define two notions: informational equivalence and computational equivalence (Larkin and Simon 1987). Two representations are *informationally* equivalent if either one is logically derivable from the other—if all the information available in the one is available in the other. Two representations are *computationally* equivalent if all the information easily available in the one is easily available in the other, and vice versa.

"Easily" is a vague term, but it is adequate for our purpose. Information is easily available if it can be obtained from the explicit information with a small amount of computation—small relative to the capacities of the processor. Thus, defining a representation includes specifying the primitive processes, those that are not further analyzed and that can be carried out rapidly.

Representations of numerical information in Arabic and Roman numerals are informationally equivalent, but not computationally equivalent. It may be much easier or harder to find the product of two numbers in the one notation than in the other. Similarly, representations of the same problem, on the one hand as a set of declarative propositions in PROLOG, and on the other hand as a node-link diagram in LISP, are unlikely to be computationally equivalent (Larkin and Simon 1987). It may be far easier to solve the problem in the one form than in the other—say, easier by heuristic search than by resolution theorem proving.

6.3 Representations Used by People

There is much evidence that people sometimes use "mental pictures" to represent problems, representations that have the properties of rasters or of node-link networks (Kosslyn 1980). There is little evidence that they use propositions in the predicate calculus to represent them, or operate on their representations by theorem-proving methods. Of course, engineers, scientists, and others do represent many problems with mathematical formalisms, but the processes that operate upon these formalisms resemble heuristic search much more than they do logical reasoning (Larkin and Simon 1987, Paige and Simon 1966).

Research on problem solving in algebra and physics has shown that subjects typically convert a problem from natural language into diagrams and then convert the latter into equations. A direct translation from language to equations seems to take place, if at all, only in the case of very simple familiar problems. AI models of the diagrammatic representations that problem solvers use in these domains can be found in Larkin and Simon (1987) and Novak (1977).

Evidence is lacking as to whether there exists a "neutral" semantic representation for information that is neither propositional nor pictorial. At least in simple situations, much information is readily transformed from one representation to the other. For example, in one common experimental paradigm, subjects are presented with an asterisk above or below a plus sign and, simultaneously, with a sentence of the form, "The star is above/below the plus" (Clark and Chase 1972). The subject must respond "true" or "false." Before responding, the subject must, somehow, find a common representation for the visual display and the sentence—converting one into the other, or both into a common semantic representation. But the experiments carried out in this paradigm do not show which way the conversion goes. From the physics and algebra experiments, we might conjecture that, for most subjects, the internal (or semantic) representation is the diagrammatic one, but we must be careful in generalizing across tasks.

I have barely touched on the evidence from psychology about the representations people use in their problem-solving activities. The evidence we have throws strong doubt on any claim of hegemony for either propositional or pictorial representations. If either tends to be dominant, it is probably the pictorial (or diagrammatic) rather than the propositional. The evidence suggests strongly that, whatever the form of representation, the processing of information almost always resembles heuristic search rather than theorem proving.

We can only conjecture that these preferences have something to do with computational efficiency. I have elsewhere spelled out some of the implications of the computational inequivalence of representations for such issues as logic programming versus rule-based computation.

6.4 Insight Problems

Problems that tend to be solved suddenly, with an "aha!" experience, often after a long period of apparently fruitless struggle, have attracted much attention. Can we say anything about the mystery of such insightful processes? Indeed, we can. We can say enough to dissipate most or all of the magic.

One problem of this kind is the "Mutilated Checkerboard." We are given an ordinary checkerboard of 64 squares and 32 dominoes, each domino exactly covering two adjoining squares of the board. Obviously we can cover the entire board with the 32 dominoes. Now we cut off the northwest square and the southeast square of the board, and ask whether the remaining 62 squares can be covered exactly by 31 dominoes (Kaplan and Simon 1990).

Subjects generally attack this problem by attempting coverings, and persist for an hour or more, becoming increasingly frustrated as they fail to achieve a solution. At some point, they decide that a covering is impossible and switch their effort to proving the impossibility. They recognize that to do so they need a new problem representation, but unfortunately, people do not appear to possess a general-purpose generator of problem representations. It is not enough to say, "I need a new representation." How does one go about constructing it?

Some subjects do, after a shorter or longer time, succeed in constructing a new representation and then solve the problem in a few minutes. The new representation records the *number* of squares of each color and the number of each color that is covered by a single domino. The geometric arrangement of the squares, a central feature of the original representation, is simply ignored. But since the mutilated checkerboard has two more squares of one color than of the other, and since dominoes, no matter how many, can cover only the same number of squares of each color, the impossibility of a covering is immediately evident.

The power of the abstraction is obvious, but how do subjects achieve it? Experiments show that they achieve it when their attention focuses on the fact that the remaining uncovered squares, after unsuccessful attempts at covering, are always the same color. How the attention focus comes about is a longer story, which I won't try to tell here, but which is quite understandable in terms of ordinary mechanisms of attention.

Much remains to be done before we understand how people construct their problem representations and the role those representations play in problem solving. But we know enough already to suggest that the representations people use—both propositional and pictorial—can be simulated by computers. Diagrammatic representations of the node-link type are naturally represented in list-processing languages like Lisp. Rasters pose a more difficult problem, for we must define appropriate primitive processes to extract information from them. Finding such processes is more or less synonymous with developing efficient programs for visual pattern recognition.

7. The Processing of Language

Whatever the role it plays in thought, natural language is the principal medium of communication between people. What do we know about how it is processed and how it is learned?

7.1 Some Programs that Understand Language

Enormous amounts of research on language have been done within the disciplines of linguistics and psycholinguistics. Until quite recent times, the greater part of that research was focused on lexical issues, syntax, and phonetics, seldom straying beyond the boundaries of the individual sentence. Without disputing the importance of this activity, it might be argued that far more has been learned about the relation between natural language and thinking from computer programs that use language inputs or outputs to perform concrete tasks. An example is Novak's (1977) ISMC program, which extracts the information from natural-language descriptions of physics problems, and transforms it into an internal "semantic" representation suitable for a problem-solving system. In a somewhat similar manner, Hayes and Simon's (1974) UNDERSTAND program reads natural-language instructions for puzzles and creates internal representations ("pictures") of the problem situations and interpretations of the puzzle rules for operating on them.

Systems like these give us specific models of how people extract meaning from discourse with the help of semantic knowledge they already hold in memory. For example, Novak's system interprets the natural-language input using schemas that encapsulate its knowledge about such things as levers and masses and assembles this knowledge into a composite schema that pictures the problem situation.

At a more abstract level, UNDERSTAND extracts knowledge from prose about the objects under discussion, the relations among them, and the ways of changing these relations. It uses this information to construct a system of internal nodes, links, and processes that represent these objects, relations, and operations. In simple puzzle situations, UNDERSTAND can go quite a long way with a minimum of semantic knowledge, relying heavily on syntactic cues.

7.2 Acquiring Language

Of equal importance is the question of how languages are acquired. Siklóssy (1972) simulated the process of language acquisition, guided by I.A. Richards' plan for learning language by use of pictures. Siklóssy's program, called ZBIE, was given (internal representations of) simple pictures (a dog chasing a cat, a hat on a woman's head). With each picture, it was given a sentence describing the scene. With the aid of a carefully designed sequence of such examples, it gradually learned to associate nouns with the objects in the pictures and other words with their properties and the relations.

Siklóssy tested ZBIE in novel situations whose components were familiar by requiring it to construct sentences describing these new situations. It learned the fundamentals of a number of European languages, including the appropriate conventions for word order.

7.3 Will Our Knowledge of Language Scale?

These are just a few illustrations of current capabilities for simulating human use and acquisition of language. Since all of them involve relatively simple language with a limited vocabulary, it is quite reasonable to ask how they would scale up to encompass the whole vast structure of a natural language as known and used by a native speaker. We do not know the answer to this question—and won't know it until it has been done—but we should not overemphasize the criticality of the scaling-up issue. When we wish to understand basic physical phenomena, we do not look for complex real-world situations in which to test them, but instead design the simplest conceivable laboratory situations in which to demonstrate and manipulate them.

Even in classical mechanics, physicists are far from a full understanding of the three-body problem, much less the behavior of n bodies, where n is a large number. Most scientific effort goes into the study of toy systems rather than the study of a complex "real world." We usually understand the mechanisms that govern the complex world long before we are able to calculate or simulate the behavior of that world in detail.

Similarly, to demonstrate an understanding of human thinking, we do not need to model thinking in the most complex situations we can imagine. It is enough for most purposes that our theory explain the phenomena in a range of situations that would call for genuine thinking in human subjects. Research has already met that criterion for language processing.

7.4 Discovery and Creativity

We should not be intimidated by words like "intuition" that are often used to describe human thinking. We have seen that "intuition" usually simply means problem solving by recognition, easily modeled by production systems. We have also seen that the "insight" that leads to change in representation and solution of the mutilated checkerboard problem can be explained by mechanisms of attention focusing. What about "creative" processes? Can we give an account of them, too?

Making scientific discoveries is generally adjudged to be both ill-structured and creative. As it is also a very diverse activity, with many aspects, a theory that explains one aspect might not explain others. Scientists sometimes examine data to discover regularities—scientific laws and new concepts for expressing the laws parsimoniously. They sometimes discover new scientific problems or invent new ways of representing problems. They sometimes deduce new consequences from theories.

Scientists sometimes conceive of mechanisms to explain the empirical laws that describe phenomena. They sometimes develop and execute experimental strategies to obtain new data for testing theories or evolving new theories. They sometimes invent and construct new instruments for gathering new kinds of data or more precise data. There are other things that scientists do, but this list at least illustrates the variety of activities in which they engage, any of which may produce a creative discovery.

A number of these activities, but not all, have been simulated by computer. In addition, historians of science have recounted the courses of events that led to a substantial number of important discoveries.

A computer program called BACON (Langley, Simon, Bradshaw, and Zytkow 1987), when given the data available to the scientists in historically important situations, has rediscovered Kepler's Third Law, Ohm's Law, Boyle's Law, Black's Law of Temperature Equilibrium, and many others. In the course of finding these laws, BACON has reinvented such fundamental concepts as inertial mass, atomic weight and molecular weight, and specific heat. We do not have to speculate about how discoveries of these kinds are made; we can examine the behavior of programs like BACON and compare them with the historical record (or with the behavior of human subjects presented with the same problems).

The KEKADA program (Kulkarni and Simon 1988) plans experimental strategies, responding to the information gained from each experiment to plan the next one. On the basis of its knowledge and experience, it forms expectations about the outcome of experiments and switches to a strategy for exploiting its surprise when these expectations are not fulfilled. With the aid of these capabilities, the program is able to track closely the strategy that Hans Krebs used to elucidate the synthesis of urea in vivo and Faraday's strategy in investigating the production of electrical currents by the variation of magnetic fields. Here, the accuracy with which the program explained the human processes was tested through a comparison of its behavior with the day-to-day course of the original research as gleaned from laboratory notebooks.

Programs like BACON and KEKADA show that scientists use essentially the same kinds of processes as those identified in more prosaic kinds of problem solving (solving puzzles or playing chess). Very high quality thinking is surely required for scientific work, but thinking of basically the same kind is used to solve more humdrum problems.

These successes in simulating scientific work put high on the agenda the simulation of other facets of science (inventing instruments, discovering appropriate problem representations) that have not yet been tackled. There is no reason to believe that they will disclose thinking processes wholly different from those that have been observed in the research I have just sketched.

8. Affect, Motivation, and Awareness

I have said nothing about the motivation required for successful human thinking. Motivation comes into the picture through the mechanism of attention. Motivation selects particular tasks for attention and diverts attention from others. When the other conditions for success are present, strong motivation sustained over long periods of time may secure the cognitive effort that is required to find a problem solution. In this manner, motivation and the mechanisms that strengthen and weaken it can be brought into models of problem solving in a quite natural manner.

Putting the matter in this over-simple way does not demean the importance of motivation in human thinking but suggests that its impact on thought processes is rather diffuse and aggregative rather than highly specific. Moreover, if affect and cognition interact largely through the mechanisms of attention, then it is reasonable to pursue our research on these two components of mental behavior independently. For example, in laboratory studies of problem solving, as long as we establish conditions that assure the subjects' attention to the task, we can study the cognitive processes without simultaneously investigating just how the motivation is generated and maintained.

The theory of thinking I have been describing says very little about consciousness—except in equating ability to report information with its presence in short-term memory. Many of the symbolic processes that support thought are in conscious awareness, but others are not. The presence or absence of awareness has strong implications for the ease or difficulty of testing the details of the theory, but few other implications. I will not try to pursue this difficult topic further here.

9. Conclusion: Computers Think
—and Often Think like People

The conclusion we can draw from the evidence I have sketched is simple: Computers can be programmed, and have been programmed, to simulate at a symbolic level the processes that are used in human thinking. We need not talk about computers thinking in the future tense; they have been thinking (in smaller or bigger ways) for 35 years. They have been thinking "logically" and they have been thinking "intuitively"—even "creatively."

Why has this conclusion been resisted so fiercely, even in the face of massive evidence? I would argue, first, that the dissenters have not looked very hard at the evidence, especially the evidence from the psychological laboratory. They have grasped and held on to a romantic picture of the human mind that attributes to it capabilities that it simply does not have—not even the minds of Mozart and Einstein, to say nothing of the rest of us poor mortals.

The human mind does not reach its goals mysteriously or miraculously. Even its sudden insights and "ahas" are explainable in terms of recognition processes, well-informed search, knowledge-prepared experiences of surprise, and changes in representation motivated by shifts in attention. When we incorporate these processes into our theory, as empirical evidence says we should, the unexplainable is explained.

Perhaps there are deeper sources of resistance to the evidence. Perhaps we are reluctant to give up our claims for human uniqueness—of being the only species that can think big thoughts. Perhaps we have "known" so long that machines can't think that only overwhelming evidence can change our belief. Whatever the reason, the evidence is now here, and it is time that we attended to it. If we hurry, we can catch up to Turing on the path he pointed out to us so many years ago.

Bibliography

Abelson, R. P. (1973). The structure of belief systems. In R. C. Schank, & K. Colby (Eds.), *Computer models of thoughtand language*. San Francisco: W.H. Freeman.

Ackley, D. H., Hinton, G. E., & Sejnowski, T. J. (1985). A learning algorithm for Boltzmann machines. *Cognitive Science*, 9, 147-169.

Adams, J. B. (1976). A probability model of medical reasoning and the MYCIN model. *Mathmatical Biosciences*, 32, 177-186.

Agre, P. E. (1985a). *Routines* (MIT AI Memo 828). Cambridge: MIT.

Agre, P. E. (1985b).*The structures of everyday life* (MIT Working Paper 267). Cambridge: MIT.

Agre, P. E. (1988).*The dynamic structure of everyday life*. Unpublished Ph.D. Thesis, Cambridge: MIT Department of Electrical Engineering and Computer Science.

Agre, P. E., & Chapman, D. (1986). Unpublished memo, MIT Artificial Intelligence Laboratory. Cambridge. MA .

Alterman, R. (1988). Adaptive planning. *Cognitive Science,* 12, 393–422.

Amarel, S. (1971). On representation of problems of reasoning about actions. In D. Michie (Ed), *Machine Intelligence 3* (pp. 131-171). Edinburgh: Edinburgh University Press.

Amari, S. A. (1977a). A mathematical approach to neural systems. In J. Metzler (Ed.), *Systems neuroscience*(pp. 67-117). New York: Academic Press.

Amari, S. A. (1977b). Neural theory of association and concept formation. *Biological Cybernetics*, 26, 175-185.

Anderson, J. A. (1970). Two models for memory organization using interacting traces. *Mathematical Biosciences*, 8, 137-160.

Anderson, J. A. (1973). A theory for the recognition of items from short memorized lists. *Psychological Review*, 80, 417-438.

Anderson, J. A. (1977). Neural models with cognitive implications. In D. La Berge & S. J. Samuels (Eds.), *Basic processes in reading perception and comprehension* (pp. 27-90). Hillsdale, NJ: Erlbaum.

Anderson, J. A. (1983). Cognitive and psychological computation with neural models. *IEEE Transactions on Systems, Man, and Cybernetics*, 13, 799-815.

Anderson, J. A., & Mozer, M. C. (1981). Categorization and selective neurons. In G. E. Hinton & J. A. Anderson (Eds.), *Parallel models of associative memory* (pp. 213-236). Hillsdale, NJ: Erlbaum.

Anderson, J. A., Silverstein, J. W., Ritz, S. A., & Jones, R. S. (1977). Distinctive features, categorical perception, and probability learning: Some applications of a neural model. *Psychological Review*, 84, 413-451

Anderson, J. R. (1982). Acquisition of cognitive skill. *Psychological Review*, 89, 369-406.

Anderson, J. R. (1983). *The architecture of cognition*. Cambridge, MA: Harvard University Press.

Anderson, J. R., & Bower, G. (1973). *Human associative memory*. Washington, D.C.: Winston-Wiley.

Aragon, C. R., Johnson, D. S., & McGeoch, L. A. (1985). *Optimization by simulated annealing: An experimental evaluation*. Unpublished manuscript.

Ashby, W. R. (1952a). *Design for a brain*. New York: Wiley. (rev. ed. 1960).

Ashby, W. R. (1952b). Can a mechanical chess player outplay its designer? *British Journal of Philosophy of Science*, 3, 44-57.

Ashby, W. R. (1956a). *An introduction to cybernetics*. New York: Wiley.

Ashby, W. R. (1956b). Design for an intelligence amplifier. In C. E. Shannon, & J. McCarthy (Eds.), *Automata studies, Annuals of Mathematics Studies, Vol. 34*(pp. 215-234). Princeton: Princeton.

Ashley, K. D. (1988). *Modelling legal argument: Reasoning with cases and hypotheticals*. Ph.D. diss., Dept. of Computer and Information Science, Univ. of Massachusetts at Amherst.

Ashley, K. D., & Rissland, E. L. (1987). Compare and contrast: A test of expertise. In *Proceedings of the sixth national conference on artificial intelligence*, 273-278. Menlo Park, CA: American Association for Artificial Intelligence.

Aspray, W. (1981). *From mathematical constuctivity to computer science: Turing, Neumann, and the origins of computer science in mathematical logic*. Ann Arbor, Michigan: University Microfilms International.

Augarten, S. (1985). *Bit by Bit*. London: Unwin.

Bacon, F. (1620). *Novum organum*.

Bahl, L. R., Jelinek, F., & Mercer, R. L. (1983). A maximum likelihood approach to continuous speech recognition. *IEEE Transactions on Pattern Analysis and Machine Intelligence*, 5, 179-190.

Ballard, D. H. (1986). Cortical connections and parallel processing: Structure and function. *Behavioral and Brain Sciences*, 9(1).

Ballard, D. H., Hinton, G. E., & Sejnowski, T. J. (1983). Parallel visual computation. *Nature*, 306, 21-26.

Bareiss, E. R. (1989). *Exemplar-based knowledge acquisition: A unified approach to concept representation, classification, and learning*. Boston: Academic.

Barletta, R., & Hennessy, D. (1989). Case adaptation in autoclave layout design. In K. Hammond (Ed), *Proceedings of the DARPA workshop on case-based reasoning*, 2, 203-207. San Mateo, CA: Morgan Kaufmann.

Bartlett, F. C. (1932). *Remembering a study in experimental and social psychology*. Cambridge: The University Press (revised 1961).

Barto, A. G. (1985). *Learning by statistical cooperation of selfinterested neuronlike computing elements* (COINS Tech. Rep. 85-11). Amherst: University of Massachusetts, Department of Computer and Information Science.

Barto, A. G., & Anandan, P. (1985). Pattern recognizing stochastic learning automata. *IEEE Transactions on Systems, Man, and Cybernetics*, I5, 360-375.

Barto, A. G., & Sutton, R. S. (1981). Landmark learning: An illustration of associative search. *Biological Cybernetics*, 42, 1-8.

Barwise, J., & Perry, J. (1983). *Situations and attitudes*. Cambridge: MIT Press/Bradford.

Batali, J., & Hartheimer, A. (1980).*The design procedure language manual* (MIT AI Memo 598). Cambridge: MIT.

Baylor, G. W., & Simon, H. A. (1966). A chess mating combinations program. *AFIPS Conference Proceedings, Spring Joint Computer Conference, 28*, 431-47. Washington, DC: Spartan Books.

Bell, C. G., & Newell A. (1971).*Computer structures: Readings and examples*. New York: Mc-Graw-Hill.

Bell, C. G., Grason, J., & Newell, A. (1972). *Designing computers and digital systems using PDP16 register transfer modules*. Maynard: Digital Press.

Bellman, R. (1957). *Dynamic programming*. Princeton: Princeton University Press.

Belnap, N. D. (1976). How a computer should think. In G. Ryle (Ed), *Contempoorary Aspects Philosophy*. Stocksfield: Oriel.

Berko, J. (1958). The child's learning of English morphology.*Word*, 14, 150-177.

Berliner, H. J. (1975). *Chess as problem solving: The development of a tactics analyzer*. Unpublished doctoral dissertation, Carnegie-Mellon University.

Berliner, H. J. (1980). Backgammon computer program beats world champion. *Artificial Intelligence*, 14, 205-220.

Berliner, H. J., & Ebeling, C. (1986). The SUPREME architecture: A new intelligent paradigm. *Artificial Intelligence*, 28.

Bernstein, A., & Roberts, M. deV. (1958). Computer vs. chess-player. *Scientific American*, 198, 96-105.

Bernstein, A., de V. Roberts M., Arbuckle, T., & Belskdy, M. A. (1958). A chess-playing program for the IBM 704 computer. *Proceedings of the Western Joint Computer Conference*(pp. 157-159).

Bernstein, J. (1981, Dec). Profiles: AI, Marvin Minsky. *The New Yorker*, pp. 50-126.

Bethke, A . D. (1980). *Genetic algorithms as function optimizers*. Unpublished doctoral dissertation, University of Michigan, Michigan.

Bienenstock, E. L., Cooper, L. N., & Munro, P. W. (1982). Theory for the development of neuron activity: Orientation specificity and binocular interaction in visual cortex. *Journal of Neuroscience*, 2, 32-48.

Binder, K. (1979). *Monte Carlo methods in statistical physics*. Berlin: SpringerVerlag.

Blake, A. (1983). The least disturbance principle and weak constraints. *Pattern Recognition Letters*, 1, 393-399.

Blakemore, C. (1977). *Mechanics of the mind*. Cambridge: Cambridge University Press.

Bledsoe, W. W., & Browning, I. (1959). Pattern recognition and reading by machine. In *Proceedings of the Eastern Joint Computer Conferece*(pp. 225-232).

Bloom, B. S. (Ed.). (1985). *Developing Talent in Young People*. New York: Ballantine.

Bobrow, D. G. & Brown, J. S. (1975). Systematic understanding: synthesis, analysis, and contingent knowledge in specialized understanding systems. In D. G. Bobrow, & A. M. Collins (Eds.), *Representation and understanding*(pp. 103-129). New York: Academic Press.

Bobrow, D. G. (1967). Natural language input for a computer problem solving system. In M. Minsky (Ed.), (1968). *Semantic information processing*(pp. 133-215). Cambridge: MIT Press.

Bobrow, D. G. (1977). A panel on knowledge representation. *Proceedings of the Fifth International Joint Conference on Artificial Intelligence*. Palo Alto: Morgan Kaufmann.

Bobrow, D. G. (Ed.). (1980). Special issue on non-monotonic logic. *Artificial Intelligence*, 13, 1-174.

Bobrow, D. G., & Raphael, B. (1974). New programming languages for AI research. *Computer Surveys*, 6, 153-174.

Bobrow, D. G., & Winograd, T. (1976). *An overview of KRL, a knowledge representation language*. Palo Alto: Xerox PARC.

Bobrow, D. G., & Winograd, T. (1977). An overview of KRL, a knowledge representation language. *Cognitive Science*, 1(1), 3-46.

Bobrow, D. G., et al. (1976). *GUS, a frame-driven dialog system*. Palo Alto: Xerox PARC.

Bomba, J. S. (1959). Alpha-numeric character recognition using local operations. In *Proceedings of the Eastern Joint Computer Conferece*(pp. 218-224).

Booker, L. (1982). *Intelligent behavior as an adaptation to the task environment*. Unpublished doctral disseration, University of Michigan, Michigan.

Boole, G. (1854). *An investigation of the laws of thought*. London: Walton & Maberly.

Boole, G. (1951). *The laws of thought*. New York: Dover.

Bowden, B. V. (Ed.). (1953). *Faster than thought*. New York: Pitman.

Brachman, R. J., & Smith, B. C. (1980). Special issue on knowledge representation. *SIGART Newsletter*, 70, 1-138.

Brady, M., & Wielinga, R. (1977). Reading the writing on the wall. *Proceeding of the Workshop on Computer Vision*. Amherst.

Brentano, F. (1973). *Psychology from an empirical standpoint*. New York: Humanities Press. (Original work published in 1874).

Breuer, M., & Friedman, A. (1976). *Diagnosis and reliable design of digital systems*. New York: Computer Science Press.

Broadbent, D. (1985). A question of levels: Comment on McClelland and Rumelhart. *Journal of Experimental Psychology: General*, 114, 189-192.

Brooks, R. A. (1986). A robust layered control system for a mobile robot. *IEEE J. Rob. Autom.*, 2, 14-23.

Brooks, R. A. (1987). A hardware retargetable distributed layered architecture for mobile robot control. *Proceedings IEEE Robotics and Automationtomation*(pp.106-110). Raleigh, NC.

Brooks, R. A., & Connell, J. H. (1986). Asynchronous distributed control system for a mobile robot. *In Proceedingss SPIE*(pp. 77-84). Cambridge, MA.

Brooks, R. A., & Rowbury (1976). *An EVIL primer*. (Memo CSM-14). Essex: Essex University.

Brown, H., & Masinter, L., (1974). An algorithm for the construction of the graphs of organic molecules. *Discrete Mathematics*, 8, 227.

Brown, H., Masinter, L., & Hjelmeland, L. (1974). Constructive graph labeling using double cosets. *Discrete Mathematics*, 7, 1.

Brown, J. S., Burton, R., & deKleer J. (1981). *Pedagogical and knowledge engineering techniques in the SOPHIE systems* (Xerox Report CIS-14). Palo Alto: Xerox PARC.

Bruner, J. S., Goodnow, J. J., & Austin, G. A. (1956). *A study of thinking*. New York: Wiley.

Buchanan, B. G. (1975). Applications of artificial intelligence to scientifie reasoning. In *Proceedings of Second USA-Japan Computer Conference*. American Federation of Information Processing Societies Press.

Buchanan, B. G., & Lederberg, J. (1971). The heuristic DENDRAL program for explaining empirical data. In *Proceedings of the IFIP Congress*, 71. Ljubljana, Yugoslavia.

Buchanan, B. G., & Mitchell, T. M. (1978). Model-directed learning of production rules. In Waterman, D. A., & Hayes-Roth, F. (Eds.), *Pattern-Directed Inference Systems*. New York: Academic Press.

Buchanan, B. G., & Smith, D. H. (1977). Computer assisted chemical reasoning. In Ludena, E. V., Sabelli, N. H., & Wahl A. C. (Eds.), *Computers in Chemical Education and Research*(p. 388). New York: Plenum Publishing.

Buchanan, B. G., & Sridharan, N. S. (1973, Aug). Rule formation on non-homogeneous classes of objects. In *Proceedings of the Third International Joint Conference on Artificial Intelligence*. Palo Alto: Morgan Kaufmann.

Buchanan, B. G., Duffield, A. M., & Robertson, A. V. (1971). An application of artificial intelligence to the interpretation of mass spectra. In G. W. A. Milne (Ed.), *Mass spectrometry techniques and applications*(p. 121). New York: Wiley .

Buchanan, B. G., Feigenbaum, E. A., & Lederberg, J. (1971, Sept). A heuristic programming study of theory formation in science. In *Proceedings of the Second International Joint Conference on Artificial Intelligence*. Palo Alto: Morgan Kaufmann.

Buchanan, B. G., Feigenbaum, E. A., & Sridharan, N. S. (1972). Heuristic theory formation: data interpretation and rule formation. In B. Meltzer, & D. Michie (Eds.), *Machine Intelligence 7*. Edinburgh: Edinburgh University Press.

Buchanan, B. G., Smith, D. H., White, W. C., Gritter, R., Feigenbaum, E. A., Lederberg, J., & Djerassi, C. (1976). Applications of artifieial intelligence for chemical inference. XXII. Automatic rule formation in mass speetrometry by means of the meta-DENDRAL program. *Journal of the American Chemical Society*, 96, 61-68.

Buchanan, B. G., Sutherland, G. L., & Feigenbaum, E. A. (1969). Heuristic DENDRAL: a program for generating explanatory hypotheses in organic chemistry. In B. Meltzer, & D. Michie (Eds.), *Machine Intelligence 4*. Edinburgh: Edinburgh University Press.

Buchanan, B. G., Sutherland, G. L., & Feigenbaum, E. A. (1970). Toward an understanding of information processes of scientific inference in the context of organic chemistry. In B. Meltzer, & D. Michie (Eds.), *Machine Intelligence 5*. Edinburgh: Edinburgh University Press.

Buchs, A., Delfino, A. B., Djerassi, C., Duffield, A. M., Buchanan, B. G., Feigenbaum, E. A., Lederberg, J., Schroll, G., & Sutherland, G. L. (1971). The application of artificial intelligence in the interpretation of low-resolution mass spectra. *Advances in Mass Spectromefry*, 5, 314.

Buchs, A., Delfino, A. B., Duffield, A. M., Djerassi, C., Buchanan, B. G., Feigenbaum, E. A., & Lederberg, J. (1970). Applications of artificial intelligence for chemical inference. VI. Approach to a general method of interpreting low resolution mass spectra with a computer. *Helvetica Chimica Acta*, 53, 1394.

Buchs, A., Duffield, A. M., Schroll, G., Djerassi, C., Delfino, A. B., Buchanan, B. G., Sutherland, G. L., Feigenbaum, E. A., & Lederberg, J. (1970). Applications of artificial intelligence for chemical inference. IV. Saturated amines diagnosed by their low resolution mass spectra and nuclear magnetic resonance spectra. *Journal of the American Chemical Society*, 92, 6831.

Bush, R. R., & Mosteller, F. (1955). *Stochastic Models for Learning*. New York: Wiley.

Carbonell, J. G. (1986). Derivational analogy: A theory of reconstructive problem solving and expertise acquisition. In R. S. Michalski, J. G. Carbonell & T. M. Mitchell (Eds.), *Machine Learning: An Artificial Intelligence Approach 2*. Palo Alto: Morgan Kaufmann.

Carhart, R. E. (1976). A model-based approach to the teletype printing of chemical structures. *Journal of Chemical Information and Computer Sciences*, 16, 82.

Carhart, R. E., & Djerassi, C. (1973). Applications of artificial intelligence for chemical inference. XI. The analysis of C13 NMR data for structure elucidation of acyclic amines. *Journal of the Chemical Society*, (Perkin II), 1753.

Carhart, R. E., & Smith, D. H. (1976). Applications of artificial intelligence for chemical inference. XX. "intelligent" use of constraints in eomputer-assisted structure elucidation. *Computers and Chemistry*, 1, 79.

Carhart, R. E., Johnson, S. M., Smith, D. H., Buchanan, B. G., Dromey, R. G., & Lederberg, J. (1975). Networking and a collaborative research community: a case study using the DENDRAL program In P.Lykos (Ed.), *Computer Networking and Chemistry*(p. 192). Washington, D.C.: American Chemical Society.

Carhart, R. E., Smith, D. H., Brown, H., & Djerassi, C. (1975). Applications of artificial intelligence for chemical inference. XVII. An approach to computer-assisted elucidation of molecular structure. *Journal of the American Chemical Society*, 97, 5755.

Carhart, R. E., Smith, D. H., Brown, H., & Sridharan, N. S. (1975). Applications of artificial intelligence for chemical inference. XVI. Computer generation of vertex graphs and ring systems. *Journal of Chemical Information and Computer Science*, 15, 124.

Carnap, R. (1967). *The logical structure of the world: Pseudoproblems in philosophy*. Berkeley: University of California Press. [Originally published in 1928.]

Chandra, A. (1979). personal conversation.

Chapman, D. (1985). *Planning for conjunctive goals* (MIT AI Technical Report 802). Cambridge: MIT.

Chapman, D., & Agre, P. E. (1987). Abstract reasoning as emergent from concrete activity. In M. P. Georgeff and A. L. Lansky (Eds.), *Reasoning about actions and plans*(pp. 411-424). Los Altos CA: Morgan Kaufmann.

Charniak, E. (1974a). *He will make you take it back: A study in the pragmatics of language.* (Technical Report). Castagnola, Switzerland: Instituto per gli studi Semantici e Cognitivi.

Charniak, E. (1974b). *Toward a model of children's story comprehension.* Unpublished doctoral dissertation, MIT, and AI Lab Tech Report 266.

Charniak, E., Riesbeck, C., & McDermott, D. (1979). *Artificial intelligence programming*. Hillsdale NJ: Erlbaum.

Chase, W. G., & Simon, H. A. (1973). Perception in chess. *Cognitive Psychology*, 4, 55-81.

Cheer, C., Smith, D. H., Djerassi, C., Tursch, B., Braekman, J. C., & Daloze, D. (1976). Applications of artifieial intelligence for chemical inference. XXI. Chemical studies of marine invertebrates. XVII. The eomputer-assisted identifieation of [+]-palustrol in the marine organism eespitularia sp., aff. subvirdis. Tetrahedron, 32, 1807.

Cheng, P. W., & Carbonnel, J. G. (1986). Inducing iterative rules from experience: The FERMI experiment. In *Proceedings AAAI-86*, 490-495. Palo Alto: Morgan Kaufmann .

Chomsky, N. (1957). *Syntactic structures*. The Hague: Mouton.

Chomsky, N. (1965). *Aspects of the theory of syntax*. Cambridge: MIT Press.

Chomsky, N. (1975). Knowledge of language. In K. Gunderson (Ed.), *Language, Mind and Knowledge*. Minneapolis: University of Minnesota Press.

Chomsky, N., & Halle, M. (1968). *The sound pattern of English*. New York: Harper & Row.

Chomsky, N., & Miller, G. A. (1957). *Pattern conception* (AFCRC, Technical Note Report AFCRCRTN-57-57, Astia Document 110076). Bedford, Mass.

Chomsky, N., and Miller, G. A. (1958). Finite state languages. *Information and Control*, 1(3), 91-112.

Christensen, R. (1981). *Entropy minimax sourcebook (Vols. 1-4)*. Lincoln MA: Entropy Limited.

Church, A. (1936). An unsolvable problem of elementary number theory. *American Journal of Mathematics*, 58, 345-363.

Church, A. (1941). The calculi of lambda-conversion. *Annals of Mathematical Studies*, 6. Princeton: Princeton Univ. Press.

Churchman, C. W., & Buchanan, B. G. (1969). On the design of inductive systems: some philosophical problems. *British Journal for the Philosophy of Science*, 20, 311.

Clancey, W.J. (1979, Sept). Transfer of Rule-Based Expertise Through a Tutorial Dialogue. Unpublished doctoral dissertation and Technical memo STAN-CS-79-769. Stanford: Stanford University.

Clark, H. H., & Chase, W. G. (1972). On the process of comparing sentences against pictures.*Cognitive Psychology*, 3, 472-517.

Collins, A. M., & Loftus, E. F. (1975). A spreading-activation theory of semantic processing. *Psychological Review*, 82, 407-425.

Collins, A. M., & Quillian, M. R. (1969). Retrieval time from semantic memory. *Journal of Verbal Learning and Verbal Behavior*, 8.

Coltheart, M., Patterson, K., & Marshall, J. C. (1980). *Deep dyslexia*. London: Routledge & Kegan.

Conrad, C. (1972). Cognitive economy in semantic memory. *Journal of Experimental Psychology*, 92(2).

Craik, K. J. W. (1952). *The nature of explanation*. New York: Cambridge.

Crick, F., & Mitchison, G. (1983). The function of dream sleep. *Nature*, 304, 111-114.

Croft, D. J. (1972). Is computerized diagnosis possible? *Comp. Biomed. Res.*, 5,351-367.

Darlington, C. D. (1958). *The evolution of genetics*. New York: Basic Books.

Davis, M. (1980). Notes on the mathematics of non-monotonic reasoning. *Artificial Intelligence*, 13.

Davis, M., & Putnam, H. (1960). A computing procedure for qualification. *Journal of the Association for Computing Machinery*, 7(2).

Davis, R. (1979). Interactive transfer of expertise: acquisition of new inference rules. *Artificial Intellignce*, 12, 121-157.

Davis, R. (1982). Expert systems: Where are we and where do we go from here? *AAAI Magazine*, summer.

Davis, R., & King, J. (1977). An overview of production systems. In E. W. Elcock, & D. Michie (Eds.), *Machine Intelligence 8*. New York: American Elsevier.

Davis, R., Buchanan, B. G., & Shortliffe, E. H. (1977). Production rules as a representation for a knowled8e-based consultation system. *Artificial Intelligence*, 8,15-45.

De Kleer, J., Doyle, J., Steele, G. L. Jr., & Sussman, G. J. (1977). Explicit control of reasoning, *Proc. ACM Symp. on Artificial Intelligence and ProprammingLanguages* also (MIT At Lab, Memo 427).

de Dombal, F. T., Leaper, D. J., Staniland, J. R., McCann, A. P., & Horrocks, J. C. (1972). Computer-aided diagnosis of acute abdominal pain. *Brit. Med. Journal*, 2, 9-13.

de Groot, A. (1965).*Thought and Choice in Chess*. The Hague: Mouton. (2nd ed., 1978).

DeJong, G. F., & Mooney, R. (1986). Explanation-based learning: An alternative view, *Mach. Learning*, 1, 145-176.

DeJong, K. A. (1980). Adaptive system design a genetic approach. *IEEE Transactions: Systems, Man, and Cybernetics*, 10(9).

deKleer, J. (1976). *Local methods for localizing faults in electronic circuits* (MIT Al Memo 394), Cambridge: MIT.

deKleer, J. (1986). An assumption-based TMS, *Artificial Intelligence*, 28, 127-162.

DeMarzo, P. M. (1984). *Gibbs potentials, Boltzmann machines, and harmony theory*. Unpublished manuscript.

Dempster, A. P., Laird, N. M., & Rubin, D. B. (1976). Maximum likelihood from incomplete data via the EM algorithm. *Proceedings of the Royal Statistical Society*, 1-38.

Dennent, D. C. (1978a). *Brainstorms: Philosophical essays on mind and psychology*. Montgomery: Bradford.

Dennett, D.C. (1978b). How to change your mind. In *Brainstorms*, 300-309, Montgomery VT: Bradford.

Derthick, M. (1984). *Variations on the Boltzmann machine learning algorithm* (Tech. Rep. No. CMU-CS-84-120). Pittsburgh: CarnegieMellon University, Department of Computer Science.

Dietterich, T. G., & Michalski, R. S. (1983). A comparative review of selected methods for learning structural descriptions. In R. S. Michalski, J. G. Carbonell, & T. M. Mitchell (Eds.), *Machine Learning: An Artificial Intelligence Approach* . Palo Alto, CA:Tioga.

Dinneen, G. P. (1955). Programming pattern recognition. In *Proceedings of the 1955 Western Joint Computer conferece, Session on Learning Machines*(pp. 94-100).

Doran, J. E., & Michie, D. (1966). Experiments with the graph traverser program. *Proceedings of the Royal Society (A)*, 294, 235-59.

Doyle, J. (1976). *The use of dependency relationships in the control of reasoning* (MIT AI Lab, Working Paper 133).

Doyle, J. (1978a). *Truth maintenance systems for problem solving* (MIT AI Lab, TR-419).

Doyle, J. (1978b). Reflexive interpreters, MIT Department of Electrical Engineering and Computer Science, Ph.D. proposal.

Doyle, J. (1979). A truth maintenance system. *Artificial Intelligence*, 12, 231-272.

Doyle, J. (1980). *A model for deliberastion, action, and introspection* (MIT-AI Tech. Report 581), Cambridge: MIT.

Doyle, J. (1983). *Some theories of reasoned assumptions: An essay in rational psychology*(Tech. Report CS-83-125). Pittsburgh: Carnegie Mellon University.

Doyle, J. (1988). *Artificial intelligence and rational self-government* (Tech. Report CS-88-124). Pittsburgh: Carnegie Mellon University.

Doyle, J. (1991). Rational belief revision (preliminary report). In R. E. Fikes & E. Sandewall (Eds), *Proceedings of the second conference on principles of knowledge representation and reasoning*, 163-174. San Mateo CA: Morgan Kaufmann.

Doyle, J. (1992a). Reason Maintenance and belief revision: Foundations vs coherence theories. In *Belief revision*. London: Cambridge Univ. Press.

Doyle, J. (1992b). Rationality and its roles in reasoning. *Computational Intelligence*, 8(2), 376-409.

Doyle, J. (1994a). Reasoned assumptions and rational psychology. *Fundamenta Informaticae*, 20, 1-3, 35-73.

Doyle, J. (1994b). A reasoned economy for planning and replanning. In M. H. Burstein (Ed.), *Proceedings of the 1994 ARPA/Rome Laboratory knowledge-based planning and scheduling workshop*. San Fransisco CA: Morgan Kaufmann.

Doyle, J., & Wellman, M. P. (1990). Rational distributed reason maintenance for planning and replanning of large-scale activities. In K. Sycara (Ed.), *Proceedings of the DARPA workshop on planning and scheduling*. San Mateo CA: Morgan Kaufmann.

Doyle, J., & Wellman, M. P. (1991). Impediments to universal preference-based default theories. *Artificial Intelligence*, 49, 1-3, 97-128.

Doyle, W. (1960). Recognition of sloppy hand-printed characters. *Proceedings of the Western Joint computer Conferece*(pp. 133-142).

Dretske, F. (1981). *Knowledge and theflow of information*. Cambridge: MIT Press/Bradford.

Dreyfus, H. L. (1978). *What computers can't do: A critique of artificial reason, 2nd ed.* New York: Harper and Row.

Dromey, R. G., Buchanan, B. G., Lederberg, J., & Djerassi, C. (1975). Applications of artificial intelligence for chemical inference. XIV. A general method for predicting molecular ions in mass spectra. *Journal of Organic Chemistry*, 40, 770.

Dromey, R. G., Stefik, M. J., Rindfleisch, T., & Duffield, A. M. (1976). Extraction of mass spectra free of background and neighboring component contributions from gas chromatography mass speetrometry data. *Analytical Chemistry*, 48, 1368.

Duda, R. O., & Shortliffe, E. H. (1983). Expert systems research. *Science*, 220, 261-68.

Duffield, A. M., Robertson, A. V., Djerassi, C., Buchanan, B. G., Sutherland, G. L., Feigenbaum, E. A., & Lederberg, J. (1969). Application of artificial intelligence for chemical inference. II. Interpretation of low resolution mass spectra of ketones. *Journal of the American Chemical Society*, 91, 11.

Duncan, N. M. (1989). *Case-based reasoning applied to decision support systems*. Master's thesis, Queen's Univ., Kingston, Ontario, Canada.

Dunham, L. L., Henriek, C. A., Smith, D. H., & Djerassi, C. (1976). Mass speetrometry in structural l and stereoehemieal problems. CCXLVI. Electron impact induced fragmentation of juvenile hormone analogs. *Organic Mass Spectrometry*, 11, 1120.

Edwards, A. (1987). *Pascal's arithmetical triangle*. Oxford University Press.

Eisen, M. (1969). *Introduction to mathematical probability theory*. Englewood Cliffs: Prentice Hall.

Elcock, E. W., & Foster, J. M. (1969). ABYSY 1: an incremental compiler for assertions; an introduction. In B. Meltzer, & D. Michie (Eds.), *Machine Intelligence 4*. Edinburgh: Edinburgh University Press.

Elstein, A. S., Shulman, L. S., & Sprafka, S. A. (1978). Medical Problem Solving: An Analysis of Clinical Reasoning. Cambridge: Harvard Univ. Press.

Erman, L. D., Hayes-Roth, F., Lesser V. R., & Reddy, D. R. (1980). The Hearsay-II speach-understanding system: Integrating knowledge to resolve uncertainty. *Computer Surveys*, 12,(2), 213-253.

Ernst, G. & Newell, A. (1969). *GPS: A Case Study in Generality and Problem Solving*. ACM Monograph Series. New York: Academic Press.

Evans, T. G. (1964). A heuristic program to solve geometric analogy problems. In M. Minsky (Ed.), (1968), *Semantic informsation processing*. Cambridge: MIT Press.

Fahlman, S. E. (1974). A planning system for robot construction tasks. *Artifical Intelligence Journal*, 5, 1-49.

Fahlman, S. E. (1979). *NETL: A system for representing and using real-world knowledge*. Cambridge: MIT Press.

Fahlman, S. E. (1980). *The lEashnet interconnection scheme* (Tech. Rep. CMUCS-80-125). Pittsburgh: Carnegie-Mellon University, Department of Computer Science.

Fahlman, S. E., Hinton, G. E., & Sejnowski, T. J. (1983). Massively parallel architectures for AI: NETL, Thistl, and Boltzmann machines. *Proceedings of the National Conference on Artificial Intelligence AAAI-83.*

Farley B. G., & Clark, W. A. (1954). Simulation of self-organizing systems by digital computer. *IRE Transactions of Information Theory, 4,* 76-84.

Feigenbaum, E. A. (1961). The simulation of verbal learning behavior. *Proceedings of the Western Joint Computer Conference,* 19, 121-132.

Feigenbaum, E. A. (1968, Aug). Artificial intelligence: themes in the second decade. In *Final Supplement to Proceedings of the •FIP68 International Congress.* Edinburgh.

Feigenbaum, E. A. (1977). The art of artificial intelligence: Themes and case studies in knowledge engineering. *Proceedings of the 5th International Joint Conference on Artificial Intelligence.* Palo Alto: Morgan Kaufmann.

Feigenbaum, E. A., & Buchanan, B. G. (1968). Heuristic DENDRAL: a program for generating explanatory hypotheses in organic chemistry. In B. J. Kinariwala, & F. Kuo (Eds.), *Proceedings, Hawaii International Conference on System Sciences.* University of Hawaii Press

Feigenbaum, E. A., & Feldman, J. A. (Eds.). (1963). *Computers and thought.* San Francisco: McGraw-Hill.

Feigenbaum, E. A., & Simon, H. A. (1984). EPAM-like models of recognition and learning. *Cognitive Science,* 8, 305-36.

Feigenbaum, E. A., Buchanan, B. G., & Lederberg, J. (1971). On generality and problem solving: A case study using the DENDRAL program. In B. Meltzer, & D. Michie (Eds.), *Machine Intelligence 6.* Edinburgh: Edinburgh University Press.

Feldman, J. (1961). Simulation of behavior in the binary choice experiment. In *Proceedings of the Western Joint Computer Conference*(pp. 133-144).

Feldman, J. A. (1981). A connectionist model of visual memory. In G. E. Hinton & J. A. Anderson (Eds.), *Parallel models of associative memory* (pp. 49-81). Hillsdale: Erlbaum.

Feldman, J. A. (1982). Dynamic connections in neural networks. *Biological Cybernetics,* 46, 27-39.

Feldman, J. A. (1985). Connectionist models and their applications: Introduction. *Cognitive Science,* 9, 1-2.

Feldman, J. A., & Ballard, D. H. (1982). Connectionist models and their properties. *Cognitive Science,* 6, 205-254.

Fennel, R. D., & Lessor, V. R. (1977). Parallelism in AI problem solving: A case study of HEARSAY-II. *IEEE Transactions on Computers,* 98-111.

Fikes, R. E. (1971, Aug). Monitored execution of robot plans produced by STRIPS. In *Proceedings IFIP,* 71. Ljubljana, Yugoslavia.

Fikes, R. E., & Nilsson, N. J. (1971). STRIPS: A new approach to the application of theorem proving to problem solving. *Artificial Intelligence,* 2, 189-208. (Chapter 17 this volume).

Fodor, J. A. (1983). *Modularity of mind: An essay on faculty psychology.* Cambridge: MIT Press.

Forgy, C., & McDermott, J. (1977). OPS, a domain-independent production system language. *IJCAI,* 5, 933-939.

Forrest, S. (1982). *A parallel algorithm for classification of KL-ONE networks* (Consul Note No. 15). USC/ Information Sciences Institute.

Frege, G. (1884). *Die grundlagen der arithmetic*. Breslau: W. Koeber.

Freimer, M. (1960). *Topics in Dynamic Programming, 11* (Lincoln Laboratory Report 52-G-0020). Lexington: MIT.

Freudenthal, H. A. (1960). *Lincos: Design of l language for cosmic intercourse*. Amsterdam: North-Holland.

Friedberg, R. M. (1958). A learning machine, part I. *IBM Journal of Research and Development*, 2, 2-13.

Friedberg, R. M., Dunham, B., & North, J. H. (1959). A learning machine, part II. *IBM Journal of Research and Development*, 3, 282-287.

Fukushima, K. (1975). Cognitron: A self-organizing multilayered neural network. *Biological Cybernetics*, 20, 121-136.

Fukushima, K. (1980). Neocognitron: A self-organizing neural network model for a mechanism of pattern recognition unaffected by shift in position. *Biological Cybernetics*, 36, 193-202.

Gallistel, C. R. (1980). *The organization of action: A new synthesis*. Hillsdale: Erlbaum.

Gardner, M. (1968). *Logic machines, diagrams and Boolean algebra*. New York: Dover.

Garvey, T., & Kling, R. (1969, Dec). User's guide to QA3.5 question-answering system (SRI Artificial Intelligence Group Technical Note 15). Menlo Park, CA.

Gelernter, H. (1959a). A note on syntactic symmetry and the manipulation of formal systems by machine. *Information and Control*, 2, 80-89.

Gelernter, H. (1963). Realization of a geometry-theorem proving machine. In *Proceedings of an international conference on information processing*(pp. 273-282). Paris: UNESCO House.

Gelernter, H. (1959b). Realization of a geometry theorem-proving machine. *Proceedings of the International Conference on Information Processing*(pp. 273-282). Paris: UNESCO House.

Gelernter, H., & Rochester, N. (1958). Intelligent behavior in problem-solving machines. *IBM Journal of Research and Development*, 2(4), 336-345.

Geman, S., & Geman, D. (1984). Stochastic relaxation, Gibbs distributions, and the Bayesian restoration of images. *IEEE Transactions on Pattern Analysis and Machine Intelligence*, 6, 721741.

Genesereth, M. (1981). *The use of hierarchical models in the automated diagnosis of computer systems* (Stanford HPP memo 81-20) Palo Alto: Stanford Univ.

Gentner, D. (1987). The mechanisms of analogical learning. In S. Vosniadou & A. Ortony (Eds.),*Similarity and analogical reasoning*. New York: Cambridge University Press.

Gentner, D. (1989). Finding the needle: Accessing and reasoning from prior cases. In K. Hammond (Ed.), *Proceedings of the DARPA workshop on case-based reasoning*, 2, 137–143. San Mateo, CA: Morgan Kaufmann.

Gentner, D., & Stevens, A. (Eds.). (1983). *Mental models*. Hillsdale NJ: Erlbaum.

Gilovich, T. (1981). Seeing the past in the present: The effect of associations to familiar events on judgments and decisions. *Journal of Personality and Social Psychology*, 40(5), 797–808.

Ginsburg, H. P. (1983). *The development of mathematical thinking*. New York: Academic Press.

Glorioso, R. M., & Colon Osorio, F. C. (1980). *Engineering intelligent systems*. Bedford: Digital Press.

Glushko, R. J. (1979). The organization and activation of orthographic knowledge in reading words aloud. *Journal of Experimental Psychology: Human Perception and Performance*, 5, 674-691.

Glymour, C. (1991). Freud's androids. In J. Neu (Ed.), *The Cambridge companion to Freud.* Cambridge University Press.

Glymour, C. (1992). *Thinking Things Through.* Cambridge, MA: MIT Press.

Gödel, K. (1931). Uber formal unentscheidbare Satze der Principia Mathematica und verwandter Systeme, I. *Monatshefte for Mathematica and Physics*(pp. 173-189).

Goel, A. (1989). *Integration of case-based reasoning and model-based reasoning for adaptive design poblem solving.* Ph.D. diss., Dept. of Computer and Information Science, The Ohio State Univ.

Goel, A., & Chandrasekaran, B. (1989). Use of device models in adaptation of design cases. In K. Hammond (Ed.),*Proceedings of the DARPA workshop on case-based reasoning*, 2, 100–109. San Mateo, CA: Morgan Kaufmann.

Goldberg, D. (1983). Computer aided gas pipeline operation using genetic algorithms and rule learning. Unpublished doctoral dissertation, University of Michigan, Michigan.

Goldman, N., & Riesbeck, C. (1973). *A conceptually based sentence paraphraser* (Stanford AI Memo 196). Stanford: Stanford University.

Goldstein, I. (1974). *Understanding simple picture programs.* Unpublished doctoral dissertation, MIT, and Al Lab Tech Report 294.

Goldstein, I., & Papert, S. (1971). Artificial intelligence, language and the study of knowledge. *Cognitive Science*, 1, 84-194.

Golomb, S. (1960). A mathematical theory of discrete classification. In C. Cherry (Ed.), *Proceedings of the 4th London Sympoium on Information Theory.* New York: Academic Press.

Goodman, M. (1989). CBR in battle planning. In K. Hammond (Ed.),*Proceedings of the DARPA workshop on case-based reasoning*, 2, 246–269. San Mateo, CA: Morgan Kaufmann.

Goodman, N. (1954). *Fact, fiction and forecast.* Cambridge: Harvard.

Goodwin, G. L. (1959). *Machine recognition of hand sent Morse code* (IRE Transactions on Information Theory).

Gorn, S. (1959). On the mechanical simulation of learning and habitforming. *Information and Control*, 2(3), 226-259.

Gorry, G. A., Kassirer, J. P., Essig, A., & Schwartz, W. B. (1973). Decision analysis as the basis for computer-aided management of acute renal failure. *Amer. J. Medicine*, 55, 473-484.

Gould, J. L., & Marier, P. (1986). Learning by instinct. *Scientific American*, 74-85.

Green, C. (1969). Application of theorem proving to problem solving. In *Proceedings of the first international conference on artificial intelligence.* Menlo Park CA: Morgan Kaufmann

Green, D. M., & Swets, J. A. (1966). *Signal detection theory and psychophysics.* New York: Wiley.

Grimsdale, R. L., Sumner, F. H., Tunis, C. J., & Kilburn, T. (1959). A system for the automatic recognition of patterns. *Proceedings of the Institute of Electrical Engineers*, 106(26), 215.

Grossberg, S. (1976). Adaptive pattern classification and universal recoding: Part I. Parallel development and coding of neural feature detectors. *Biological Cybernetics*, 23, 121-134.

Grossberg, S. (1978). A theory of visual coding, memory, and development. In E. L. J. Leeuwenberg & H. F. J. M. Buffart (Eds.), *Formal theories of visual perception.* New York: Wiley.

Grossberg, S. (1980). How does the brain build a cognitive code? *Psychological Review*, 87, 1-51.

Guha, R. V., and Lenat, D. (1990). cyc: A mid-term report. *AI Magazine* , 11(3), 33–59.

Haller, N. (1959). *Line tracing for character recognition*, MSEE thesis, Massachusetts Institute of Technology, MA.

Halliday, M. A. K. (1970). Functional diversity in language as seen from a consideration of modality and mood in English. *Foundations of Language*, 6, 322-361.

Halmos, P. R. (1974). *Finite-dimensional vector spaces*. New York: Springer-Verlag.

Hammerum, S., & Djerassi, C. (1975). Mass spectrometry in structural and stereochemieal problems. CCXLV The electron impact induced fragmentation reactions of 17-oxygenated progesterones. *Steroids*, 25, 817.

Hammerum, S., & Djerassi, C. (1975). Mass spectrometry in structural and stereoehemieal problems. CCXLIV. The influenee of substituents and stereochemistry on the mass spectral fragmentation of progesterone. *Tetrahedron*, 31, 2391.

Hammond, K. J. (1986). chef: A model of case-based planning. In *Proceedings of the fifth national conference on artificial intelligence*, 65–95. Menlo Park, CA: American Association for Artificial Intelligence.

Hammond, K. J. (1989). *Case-based planning: Viewing planning as a memory task*. Boston: Academic.

Hart, P. E., & Nilsson, N. J. (1971, April). *The construction of generalized plans as an approach toward learning*. SRI Artificial Intelligence Group Memo Menlo Park, California

Hartree, D. R. (1949). *Calculating instruments and machines*. Urbana: University of Illinois Press.

Haugeland, J. (1985). *Artificial intelligence: The very idea*. Cambridge, MA: MIT Press.

Hawkins, J. K. (1961). Self-organizing systems•a review and commentary. In *Proceedings of the IRE, special computer issue*(pp. 31-48).

Hayek, F. A. (1952). *The sensory order*. Chicago: University of Chicago Press.

Hayes, J. R. (1989).*The complete problem solver* (2nd ed.). Hillsdale, NJ: Earlbaum.

Hayes, J. R., & Simon, H. A. (1974). Understanding written problem instructions. In L. W. Gregg (Ed.), *Knowledge and Cognition*. Potomac, MD: Erlbaum.

Hayes, P. (1971). A logic of actions. In B.Meltzer, & D. Michie (Eds.), *Machine Intelligence 6*. Edinburgh: Edinburgh University Press.

Hayes, P. (1973). The frame problem and related problems in artificial intelligence. In A. Elithorn and D. Jones (Eds), *Artificial and human thinking*. San Francisco: Josey-Bass.

Hayes, P. (1977). In defence of logic. *Proceeding of the Fifth International Joint Conference on Artificial Intelligence*. Palo Alto: Morgan Kaufmann. (Chapter 10 of this volume).

Hayes, P. (1978). The naive physics manifesto. In D. Michie (Ed), *Expert systems in the microelectronic age*. Edinburgh, UK: The Edinburgh University Press.

Hayes, P. (1979). personal conversation.

Hayes, P. (1985). Naive physics I: Ontology for liquids. In J.R. Hobbs, & R. C.Moore (Eds), *Formal theories of the commonsense world*. Norwood NJ: Ablex.

Hayes-Roth, B. (1983). *The blackboard architecture: A general framework for problem solving?* (Tech. Rep. HPP-83-30) Knowledge Systems Laboratory, Computer Science Department, Stanford University.

Hayes-Roth, B. (1985). Blackboard architecture for control. *Journal of Artificial Intelligence*, 26, 251-321.

Hayes-Roth, B., Hayes-Roth, F., Rosenschein, S., & Cammarata, S. (1979). Modelling planning as an incremental, opportunistic process. *IJCAI*, 6, 375-383.

Hebb, D. O. (1949). *The organization of behavior*. New York: Wiley.

Hewitt, C. (1970, Aug). *PLANNER: A language for Manipulating models and proving theorems in a robot* (Artificial Intelligence Memo No. 168 (Revised)). Cambridge: MIT, Project MAC.

Hewitt, C. (1971). Procedural embedding of knowledge in PLANNER. In *Proceedings of the second international conference on artificial intelligence*, 167-182. Menlo Park CA: Morgan Kaufmann.

Hewitt, C. (1972). *Description and theoretical analysis (using schemata) of PLANNER: a language for proving theorems and manipulating models in a robot* (MIT AI Laboratory TR-258), Cambridge: MIT.

Hewitt, C. (1975). Stereotypes.as an ACTOR approach towards solving the problem of procedural attachment in FRAME theories. *Proceedings of Theoretical Issues in Natural Language Processing: An interdisciplinary workshop*. Cambridge, MA: Bolt, Beranek, & Newman.

Hewitt, C., Bishop, P., & Steiger, R. (1973). A universal modular ACTOR formalism for artificial intelligence. *Proceedings of the 3rd International Joint Conference on Artificial Intelligence*. Palo Alto: Morgan Kaufmann.

Highleyman, W. K., & Kamentsky, L. A. (1960). Comments on a character recognition method of Bledsoe and Browning. *IRE Transactions on Electronic Computers*, BC-9:163.

Hinrichs, T. R. (1988). Toward an architecture for open-world problem solving. In J. Kolodner (Ed.), *Proceedings of the DARPA workshop on case-based reasoning*, 1, 182–189. San Mateo, CA: Morgan Kaufmann.

Hinrichs, T. R. (1989). Strategies for adaptation and recovery in a design problem solver. In K. Hammond (Ed.), *Proceedings of the DARPA workshop on case-based reasoning*, 2, 115–118. San Mateo, CA: Morgan Kaufmann.

Hintikka, J. (1962). *Knowledge and belief*. Ithaca: Cornell University Press.

Hinton, G. E. (1977). *Relaxation and its role in vision*. Unpublished doctoral dissertation, University of Edinburgh.

Hinton, G. E. (1981a). A parallel computation that assigns canonical objectbased frames of reference. *Proceedings of the 7th International Joint Conference on Artificial Intelligence*. Palo Alto: Morgan Kaufmann.

Hinton, G. E. (1981b). Implementing semantic networks in parallel hardware. In G. E. Hinton & J. A. Anderson (Eds.), *Parallel models of associative memory* (pp. 161-188). Hillsdale: Erlbaum.

Hinton, G. E. (1984). Parallel computations for controlling an arm. *Journal of Motor Behavior*, 6, 171-194.

Hinton, G. E., & Anderson, J. A. (Eds.). (1981). *Parallel models of associative memory*. Hillsdale: Erlbaum.

Hinton, G. E., & Lang, K. (1985). Shape recognition and illusory conjunctions. *Proceedings of the Ninth International Joint Conference on Artifeial Intelligence*. Palo Alto: Morgan Kaufmann.

Hinton, G. E., & Sejnowski, T. J. (1983a). Analyzing cooperative computation. *Proceedings of the Fifth Annual Conference of the Cognitive Science Society*.

Hinton, G. E., & Sejnowski, T. J. (1983b). Optimal perceptual inference. *Proceedings of the IEITE Computer Society Conference on Computer Vision and Pattern Recognition*, 448-453.

Hinton, G. E., Plaut, D.C., & Shallice, T. (1993). Simulating brain damage. *Scientific American*, 269, 4, 76-82.

Hinton, G. E., Sejnowski, T. J., & Ackley, D. H. (1984). *Boltzmann machines: Constraint satis-faction networks that learn* (Tech. Rep. No. CMU-CS-84-119) . Pittsburgh, PA: Carnegie-Mellon University, Department of Computer Science.

Hobbes, T. (1962). *Body, man and citizen*. New York: Collier.

Hobbs, J. R., & Moore, R. C. (1985). *Formal theories of the commonsense world*. Norwood NJ: Ablex.

Hofstadter, D. R. (1979). *Godel, Escher, Bach: An eternal golden braid*. New York: Basic Books.

Hofstadter, D. R. (1983a). Artificial intelligence: subcognition as computation. In E. Machlup, & U. Mansfield (Eds.), *The study of information*. New York: Wiley.

Hofstadter, D. R. (1983b). The architecture of Jumbo. *Proceedings of the International Machine Learning Workshop*.

Hofstadter, D. R. (1985). *Metamagical themas*. New York: Basic Books.

Hogg, T., & Huberman, B. A. (1984). Understanding biological computation. *Proceedings of the National Academy of Sciences*, USA, 81, 6871-6874.

Hohn, F. E., Seshu, S., & Aufenkamp, D. D. (1957). The theory of nets. *IRE Transactions on Electronic Computers*, EC-3(3), 154-161.

Holland, J. H. (1960). Iterative circuit computers. *Proceedings of the Western Joint computer Conferece*(pp. 259-266).

Holland, J. H. (1975). *Adaptation in natural and artificial systems*. Ann Arbor: University of Michigan Press.

Holland, J. H. (1986). Escaping brittleness: The possibilities of general purpose learning algo-rithms applied to parallel rule-based systems. In R.S. Michalski, J.G. Carbonell, & T. M. Mitchell (Eds.), *Machine Learning: An Artificial Intelligence Approach 2* ,593-624. Los Altos, CA.: Morgan Kaufmann. (Chapter 11 this volume).

Holland, J. H., & Reitman, J. S. (1978). Cognitive systems based on adaptive algorithms. In D. A. Waterman, & E. Hayes-Roth (Eds.), *Pattern directed inference systems*. New York: Aca-demic Press.

Holyoak, K. J. (1985). The pragmatics of analogical transfer. In G. Bower (Ed.), *The psychology of learning and motivation, 59–88*. New York: Academic.

Hopfield, J. J. (1982). Neural networks and physical systems with emergent collective computa-tional abilities. *Proceedings of the National Academy of Sciences*, USA, 79, 2554-2558.

Hopfield, J. J. (1984). Neurons with graded response have collective computational properties like those of two-state neurons. *Proceedings of the National Academy of Sciences*, USA, 81, 3088-3092.

Hopfield, J. J., Feinstein, D. I., & Palmer, R. G. (1983). l'Unlearning" has a stabilizing effect in collective memories. *Nature*, 304, 158-159.

Hovland, C. I., & Hunt, E. B. (1960). The computer simulation of concept attainment. *Behav-ioral Science*, 5, 265-267.

Huet, G. (1972). *Constrained resolution* (Report 1117). Cleveland: Case Western University.

Hummel, R. A., & Zucker, S. W. (1983). On the foundations of relaxation labeling processes. *IEEE Transactions on Pattern Analysis and Machine Intelligence*, 5, 267-287.

Isenberg, D., Walker, E. C. T., Ryder, J. M., & Schweikert, J. (1980, Nov). *A top-down effect on the identifeation of function words*. Paper presented at the Acoustical Society of America, Los Angeles.

Israel, D. (1985). A short companion to the naive physics manifesto. In J. R. Hobbs & R. C. Moore (Eds.), *Formal theories of the commonsense world*. Norwood NJ: Ablex.

Jackson, J. H. (1958). On localization. In *Selected writings (Vol. 2)*. New York: Basic Books. (Original work published 1869)

Julesz, B. (1971). *Foundations of cyclopean perception*. Chicago: University of Chicago Press.

Kanerva, P. (1984). *Self-propagating search: A unifed theory of memory* (Rep. No. CSLI-84-7). Stanford, CA: Stanford University, Center for the Study of Language and Information.

Kaplan, C., & Simon, H. A. (1990). In search of insight.*Cognitive Psychology*, 22(3), 374-420.

Kaplan, R. (1971). Augmented transition networks as psychological models of sentence comprehension. In *Proceedings of the second international conference on artificial intelligence*. Menlo Park CA: Morgan Kaufmann.

Kassirer, J. P., & Gorry, G. A. (1978). Clinical problem solving: a behavioral analysis. *Anns. Int. Med.*, 89, 245-255.

Kawamoto, A. H., & Anderson, J. A. (1984). Lexical access using a neural network. *Proceedings of the Sixth Annual Conference of the Cognitive Science Society*, 204-213.

Kienker, P. K., Sejnowski, T. J., Hinton, G. E., & Schumacher, L. E. (1985). *Separating fgure from ground with a parallel network*. Unpublished.

Kilburn, T., Grimsdale, R. L., & Summer, F. H. (1959). Experiments in machine learning and thinking *Proceedings of the International Conference on Information Processing*. Paris: UNESCO House.

Kirkpatrick, S., Gelatt, C. D. Jr., & Vecchi, M. P. (1983). Optimization by simulated annealing. *Science*, 22Q, 671-680.

Kirsch, R. A., Cahn, L., Ray, L. C., & Urban, G. H. (1957). Experiments with processing pictorial information with a digital computer. In *Proceedings of the Eastern Joint Computer Conference*(pp. 221-229).

Kister, J., Stein, P., Ulam, S., Walden, W., & Wells, M. (1957). Experiments in chess. *Journal of the Association for Computing Machinery*, 4(2), 174-177.

Kleene, S. C. (1935). General recursive functions of natural numbers. *American Journal of Mathematics*, 57, 153-157 & 219-244.

Klein, G. (1982). The use of comparison cases. In *IEEE Proceedings of the international conference on cybernetics and society*, 88–91. Washington, D.C.: IEEE Computer Society.

Klein, G., & Calderwood, R. (1988). How do people use analogues to make decisions? In J. Kolodner (Ed), *Proceedings of the DARPA workshop on case-based reasoning*, 1, 209–223. San Mateo, CA: Morgan Kaufmann.

Klein, G., Whitaker, L., & King, J. (1988). Using analogues to predict and plan. In J. Kolodner (Ed.), *Proceedings of the DARPA workshop on case-based reasoning*, 1, 224–232. San Mateo, CA: Morgan Kaufmann.

Kohler, W. (1929). *Gestalt psychology*. New York: Liveright.

Kohonen, T. (1974). An adaptive associative memory principle. *ZEEE Transactions*, C-23, 444-445.

Kohonen, T. (1977). *Associative memory: A system theoretical approach*. New York: Springer.

Kohonen, T. (1982). Clustering, taxonomy, and topological maps of patterns. In M. Lang (Ed.), *Proceedings of the Sixth International Conference on Pattern Recognition* (pp. 114-125). Silver Spring, MD: IEEE Computer Society Press.

Kohonen, T. (1984) . *Self-organization and associative memory*. Berlin: Springer-Verlag.

Kolodner, J. L. (1987a). Capitalizing on failure through case-based inference. In *Proceedings of the ninth annual conference of the cognitive science society*, 715–726. Hillsdale, N.J.: Lawrence Erlbaum.

Kolodner, J. L. (1987b). Extending problem-solving capabilities through case-based inference. In *Proceedings of the fourth international machine learning workshop*, 167–178. San Mateo, CA: Morgan Kaufmann.

Kolodner, J. L. (1989). Selecting the best case for a case-based reasoner. In *Proceedings of the eleventh annual conference of the cognitive science society*, 155–162. Hillsdale, N.J.: Lawrence Erlbaum.

Kolodner, J. L. (Ed.). (1988). *Proceedings of the DARPA case-based reasoning workshop*, 1. San Mateo, CA: Morgan Kaufmann.

Kolodner, J. L., & Simpson, R. L. (1989). The mediator: Analysis of an early case-based problem solver. *Cognitive Science*, 13(4), 507–549.

Kolodner, J. L., Simpson, R. L., & Sycara, K. (1985). A process model of case-based reasoning in problem solving. In *Proceedings of the ninth international joint conference on artificial intelligence*(pp. 284–290). Menlo Park, CA: International Joint Conferences on Artificial Intelligence.

Konolige, K. (1980, Dec). *A first-order formalization of knowledge and action for a multiagent planning system.* (SRI International technical Note 232).

Kosslyn, S. M. (1980). *Image and Mind.* Cambridge, MA: Harvard University Press.

Koton, P. (1988). Reasoning about evidence in causal explanation. In *Proceedings of the seventh national conference on artificial intelligence*, 256–261. Menlo Park, CA: American Association for Artificial Intelligence.

Kowalski, R. (1975a). Predicate calculus as a programming language. *Proceedings I.F.I.P.*, 75.

Kowalski, R. (1979b). *Logic for problem solving.* Amsterdam: North Holland.

Kuhn, T. (1970). *The structure of scientific revolutions, 2nd ed.* Chicago: University of Chicago Press.

Kulkarni, D., & Simon, H. A. (1988). The processes of scientific discovery: The strategy of experimentation. *Cognitive Science*, 12, 139-176.

Kullback, S. (1959). *Information theory and statistics.* New York: Wiley.

Kuno, S. (1965). The predictive analyzer and a path elimination technique. *Comm. of the Assoc. for Computing Machinery*, 8, 687-698.

Laird, J. E., Rosenbloom, P. S. & Newell, A. (1986). Chunking in Soar: The anatomy of a general learning mechanism. *Mach. Learning*, 1, 11-46.

Lamperti, J. (1977). *Lecture notes in applied mathematical sciences: Stochastic processes.* Berlin: Springer-Verlag.

Lancaster, J. S., & Kolodner, J. L. (1988). Varieties of learning from problem-solving experience. In *Proceedings of the tenth annual conference of the cognitive science society*. Hillsdale, N.J.: Lawrence Erlbaum.

Langley, P., Simon, H. A., Bradshaw, G. L., & Zytkow, J. M. (1987). *Scientific Discovery.* Cambridge, MA: MIT Press.

Larkin, J. H. (1983). The role of problem representation in physics. In D. Gentner & A. L. Stevens (Eds.), *Mental models* (pp. 75-98). Hillsdale, NJ: Erlbaum.

Larkin, J. H., & Simon, H. A. (1987). Why a diagram is (sometimes) worth 10,000 words. *Cognitive Science*, 11, 65-99.

Lashley, K. S. (1950). In search of the engram. In *Sociery of Experimental Biology Symposium No. 4: Psychological mechanisms in animal behavior* (pp. 478-505). London: Cambridge University Press.

Lavoisier, A. (1949). *Elements of chemistry.* Chicago: Regnery.

Le Cun, Y. (1985, June). Une procedure d'apprentissage pour reseau a seuil assymetrique [A learning procedure for assymetric threshold network]. *Proceedings of Cognitiva*, 85, 599-604. Paris.

Lederberg, J. (1964). *Compuration of Molecular Formulas for Mass Spectrometry.* Holden-Day, Inc.

Lederberg, J. (1964, 1965, & 1969). DENDRAL-64, a system for computer construction, enumeration and notation of organic molecules as tree structures and cyclic graphs (technical reports to NASA, also available from the author and summarized in [12]). (la) Part I. Notational algorithm for tree structures (1964), CR.57029; (lb) Part II. Topology of cyclic graphs (1965), CR.68898; (lc) Part III. Complete chemical graphs; embedding rings in trees (1969).

Lederberg, J. (1965a). *Systematics of organic molecules, graph topology and Hamilton circuits. A general outline of the DENDRAL system* (NASA CR-48899).

Lederberg, J. (1965b). Topological mapping of organic Molecules. *Proc. Nat. Acad. Sci.*, 53, 1.

Lederberg, J. (1967). Hamilton circuits of convex trivalent polyhedra (up to 18 vertices). *Am. Math. Monthly*, 74, 5

Lederberg, J. (1968). *Online computation of molecular formulas from mass number* (NASA CR94977).

Lederberg, J. (1969). *Topology of Molecules, in The Mathematical Sciences—A Collection of Essays, Edited by the National Research Council's Committee on Support of Research in the Mathematical Sciences (COSRIMS).* Cambridge: The M.I.T. Press.

Lederberg, J. (1972). Rapid calculation of molecular formulas from mass values. *Journal of Chemical Education*, 49, 613.

Lederberg, J., & Feigenbaum, E. A. (1968). Mechanization of inductive inference in organic chemistry. In B. Kleinmuntz (Ed.), *Formal Representations for Human Judgment.* New York: Wiley.

Lederberg, J., Sutherland, G. L., Buchanan, B. G., & Feigenbaum, E. A. (1970). A heuristic program for solving a scientific inference problem: summary of motivation and implementation. In R. Banerji, & M. D. Mesarovic (Eds.), *Theoretical Approaches to Non-Numerical Problem Solving.* New York: Springer-Verlag.

Lederberg, J., Sutherland, G. L., Buchanan, B. G., Feigenbaum, E. A., Robertson, A. V., Duffield, A. M., & Djerassi, C. (1969). Applications of artificial intelligence for chemical inference I. The number of possible organic compounds: acyclic structures containing C, H. O and N. *Journal of the American Chemical Society*, 91, 2973.

Leibniz, G. W. (1679). *De progression dyadica—Pars I, in the collection of Niedersächsische Landesbibliothek, Hanover.* [Reprinted in Herrn von Leibniz, Rechnung mit Null und Eins (pp. 42-47). Siemens Aktiengesellschaft: Berlin.]

Lenat, D. B. (1983). The role of heuristics in learning by discovery: Three case studies. In R. S. Michalski, J. G. Carbonell, & T. M. Mitchell (Eds.), *Machine learning: An artificial intelligence approach.* Palo Alto: Tioga.

Lenat, D., & Guha, R. (1990). *Building large knowledge-based systems.* Reading, MA: Addison-Wesley.

Lesser, V. R., Fennell, R. D., Erman, L. D., & Reddy, D. R. (1974). Organization of the

HEARSAY-II speech understanding system. In *IEEE Symposium on Speech Recognition*(pp. ll-M2-21-M2).

Lettvin, J. Y., Maturana, H., McCulloch, W. S., & Pitts, W. (1959). What the frog's eye tells the frog's brain. *Proceedings of the IRE*, 47, 1940-1951.

Levesque, H. J. (1984). Foundations of a functional approach to knowledge representation. *Artifical Intelligence*, 23, 155-212.

Levin, J. A. (1976). *Proteus: An activationframeworkfor cognitive process models* (Tech. Rep. No. ISI/WP-2). Marina del Rey, CA: University of Southern California, Information Sciences Institute.

Levine, R. D., & Tribus, M. (1979). *The maximum entropy formalism.* Cambridge, MA: MIT Press.

Lewis, A. C. (1986). Memory constraints and flower choice in pieris rapae. *Science*, 232, 863-865.

Lewis, C. H. (1978). *Production system models of practice effects.* Unpublished doctoral dissertation, University of Michigan.

Lewis, D. (1973). *Counterfactuals.* London: Basil Blackwell.

Lindsay, P. H., & Norman, D. A. (1972). *Human information processing: An introduction to psychology.* New York: Academic Press.

Lindsay, R., Buchanan, B. G., Feigenbaum, E. A., & Lederberg, J. (1980). *Applications of artificial intelligence for organic chemistry: The Dendral project.* New York, McGraw-Hill.

Lovelace, (Countess) A. A. (1842). Translator's notes to an article on Babbage's Analytical Engine. In R. Taylor (Ed.), *Scientific Memoirs 3*(pp.691-731).

Loveland, D. W. (1978). *Automated theorem proving: A logical basis.* Amsterdam: North-Holland.

Luce, R. D., & Raiffa, H. (1957). Games and decisions. New York: Wiley.

Luger, G. F. (1994). *Cognitive Science.* San Diego: Academic Press.

Luger, G. F., & Stubblefield, W. A. (1993). *Artificial intelligence: Structures and strategies for complex problem solving, 2nd ed.* Palo Alto: Addison Wesley.

Luria, A. R. (1966). *Higher corticalfunctions in man.* New York: Basic Books.

Luria, A. R. (1973). *The working brain.* London: Penguin.

MacKay, D. M. (1956a). Towards an information-flow model of human behavior. *British Journal of Philosophy*, 47(1), 30-43.

MacKay, D. M. (1956b). The epistemological problem for automata. In L. A. Jeffress (Ed.), *Cerebral mechanisms in behavior: The Hixon symposium*(pp. 235-251). New York: Wiley.

MacKay, D. M. (1956c). The place of "meaning" in the theory of information. In C. Cherry (Ed.), *Proceedings of the 4th London Sympoium on Information Theory*(pp. 215-225). New York: Academic Press.

MacKay, D. M. (1959). Operational aspects of intellect. In D. V. Blake, & A. M. Uttley (Eds.), *Proceedings of the Sympoium on Mechanisation of Thought Processes*(pp. 39-54). Paris: UNESCO House.

Manna, Z., & Waldinger, R. (1971). Towards automatic program synthesis. *Communications of the ACM*, 14(3).

Marr, D. (1982). *Vision.* San Francisco: Freeman.

Marr, D., & Poggio, T. (1976). Cooperative computation of stereo disparity. *Science*, 194, 283-287.

Marr, D., & Poggio, T. (1979). A computational theory of human stereo vision. *Proceedings of the Royal Society of London, Series B,* 204, 301-328.

Marslen-Wilson, W. D., & Welsh, A. (1978). Processing interactions and lexical access during word recognition in continuous speech. *Cognitive Psychology,* 10, 29-63.

Martin, W. (1974). *Memos on the OWL system.* Cambridge: Project MAC, MIT.

Masinter, L., Sridharan, N. S., Carhart, R., & Smith, D. H. (1974a). Application of artificial intelligence for chemical inference XII: exhaustive generation of cyclic and acyclic isomers. *Journal of the American Chemical Society,* 96, 7702.

Masinterf, L., Sridharan, N. S., Carhart, R., & Smith, D. H. (1974b). Applications of artificial intelligence for chemical inference. XIII. Labeling of objects having symmetry. *Journal of the American Chemical Society,* 96, 7714.

McAllester, D. A. (1978). *A three-valued truth maintenance system* (MIT AI Lab., Memo 473).

McCarthy, J. (1956). *Inversion of functions defined by turing machines.* Princton: Automatic Studies.

McCarthy, J. (1957). *Situations, actions, and causal laws* (AI Memo 1, Artificial Intelligence Project). Palo Alto: Stanford Univ.

McCarthy, J. (1959a). Comments. In Mechanisation of thought processes: *Proceedings of a symposium held at the National Physical Laboratory,* November 1958. Vol. 1 (p. 464). London: Her Majesty's Stationery Office.

McCarthy, J. (1959b). Programs with common sense. In D. V. Blake, & A. M. Uttley (Eds.), *Proceedings of the Sympoium on Mechanisation of Thought Processes*(pp. 75-84). Paris: UNESCO House.

McCarthy, J. (1960a). Programs with common sense. In *Proceedings of the Teddington conference on the mechanization of thought processes.* London: H.M. Stationery Office.

McCarthy, J. (1960b). Recursive functions of symbolic expressions and their computation by machine. *Communictions of the ACM,* 3(4), 184-195.

McCarthy, J. (1977a). Epistemological problems in artificial intelligence. In *Proceedings of IJCAI-77,* 1038-1044. San Mateo CA: Morgan Kaufmann.

McCarthy, J. (1977b). Predicate calculus. *Proceeding of the Fifth International Joint Conference on Artificial Intelligence.* Palo Alto: Morgan Kaufmann.

McCarthy, J. (1979a). Ascribing mental qualities to machines. In M. Ringle (Ed.), *Philosophical perspecaves in artificial intelligence.* New York: Harvester.

McCarthy, J. (1979b). First order theories of individual concepts and propositions. In D. Michie (Ed.), *Machine Intelligence 9.* Edinburgh: Edinburgh University Press.

McCarthy, J. (1980). Circumscription - A form of non-monotonic reasoning. *Artificial Intelligence,* 13.

McCarthy, J., & Hayes, P. J. (1969). Some philosophical problems from the standpoint of artificial intelligence. In B.Meltzer, & D. Michie (Eds.), *Machine Intelligence 4.* Edinburgh: Edinburgh University Press.

McClelland, J. L. (1979). On the time-relations of mental processes: An examination of systems of processes in cascade. *Psychological Review,* 86, 287-330.

McClelland, J. L. (1981). Retrieving general and specific information from stored knowledge of specifics. *Proceedings of the Third Annual Meeting of the Cognitive Science Society,* 170-172.

McClelland, J. L., & Rumelhart, D. E. (1981). An interactive activation model of context effects in letter perception: Part 1. An account of basic findings. *Psychological Review*, 88, 375-407.

McClelland, J. L., & Rumelhart, D. E. (1985). Distributed memory and the representation of general and specific information. *Journal of Experimental Psychology: General*, 114, 159-188.

McClelland, J. L., Rumelhart, D. E., & The PDP Research Group (1986). *Parallel distributed processing (vols I & II)*. Cambridge: MIT Press.

McCulloch, W. S. (1949). The brain as a computing machine. *Electrical Engineering*, 68 (6), 492.

McCulloch, W. S. (1954). Through the den of the metaphysician. *British Journal of Philosophy of Science*, 5, 18-31.

McCulloch, W. S., & Pitts, W. (1943). A logical calculus of the ideas immanent in nervous activity. *Bulletin of Mathematical Biophysics*, 5, 115-133.

McDermott, D. (1978). Planning and acting. *Cognitive Science*, 2, 71-109.

McDermott, D., & Doyle, J. (1980). Non-monotonic logic I. *Artificial Intelligence*, 13, 41-72.

McDermott, J., & Forgy, C. (1978). Production system conflict resolution strategies In D. A. Waterman, & F. Hayes-Roth (Eds.), Pattern-directed inference systems. New York: Academic Press.

McGinn, C. (1982). *The character of mind*. Oxford: Oxford University Press.

Mead, G. H. (1934). *Mind, self and society from the standpoint of a social behaviorist*. Chicago: University of Chicago Press.

Meditch, J. S. (1969). *Stochastic optimal linear estimation and control*. New York: McGraw-Hill.

Meltzer, B., & Michie, D. (Eds.). (1970). *Machine Intelligence*, 5. Edinburgh: Edinburgh University Press.

Mesel, E., Wirtschafter, D. D., Carpenter, J. T., Durant, J. R., Hende, C., & Gray, E. A. (1976). Clinical algorithms for cancer chemotherapy systems for community-based consultant-extenders and oncology centers. *Meth. Inform. Med.*, 15,168-173.

Metropolis, N., Rosenbluth, A. W., Rosenbluth, M. N., Teller, A. H., & Teller, E. (1953). Equation of state calculations for fast computing machines. *Journal of Chemical Physics*, 6, 1087.

Michalski, R. S., & Stepp R. E. (1983). Learning from observation: Conceptual clustering. In R. S. Michalski, J. G. Carbonell, & T. M. Mitchell (Eds.), *Machine Learning: An Artificial Intelligence Approach* . Palo Alto: Tioga.

Michalski, R. S., Carbonell, J. G., & Mitchell, T. M. (1983, 1986). *Machine learning: An artificial intelligence approach (vols I & II)*. San Mateo: Morgan Kaufmann.

Michie, D. (1973). Knowledge engineering.*Cybernetics*, 2, 197-200.

Michie, D., & Buchanan, B. G. (1973). Current status of the heuristic DENDRAL program for applying artificial intelligence to the interpretation of mass spectra. In R. A. G. Carrington (Ed.), *Computers for Spectroscopy*. London: Adam Hilger.

Miller, G. A., Galanter, E., & Pribram, K. (1960). *Plans and the structure of behavior*. New York: Holt.

Miller, L., Minker, J., Reed., W. G., & Shindle, W. E. (1960). A multilevel file structure for information processing. *Proceedings of the Western Joint Computer Conference*, 17, 53-59.

Milner, P. M. (1960). Learning in neural systems. In Yovitts, M., & Cameron, S. (Eds.), *Self-organizing systems*. New York: Pergamon.

Minot, O. N. (1959). *Automatic devices for recognition of visible two-dimensional patterns: A survey of the field* (Report TM-364, June 25). San Diego: U.S. Navy Electronics Laboratory.

Minsky, M. (1954). *Discrete selection processes* (Report 1954-494-03-21, Navy Contract Nonr-494(03). Medford: Tufts College.

Minsky, M. (1954). *Neural nets and the brain-model problem.* Unpublished doctoral dissertation, Princeton University.

Minsky, M. (1956). *Heuristic aspects of the artificial intelligence problem* (Group Report 34-55, ASTIA Document AD 236885) (MIT Hayden Library No. H-58). Lexington: MIT, Lincoln Laboratories.

Minsky, M. (1956). Some universal elements for finite automata. In C. E. Shannon, & J. McCarthy (Eds.), *Automata studies, Annuals of Mathematics Studies, Vol. 34*. Princeton: Princeton.

Minsky, M. (1956, Aug). *Notes on the geometry problem, I and II.* Artificial Intelligence Project, Dartmouth College, Hanover, Vt., mimeographed.

Minsky, M. (1959). Physicial machines and their abstract counterparts (Group Report 54-4, March). Lexington: MIT, Lincoln Laboratories.

Minsky, M. (1959). Some methods of artificial intelligence and heuristic programming. *In Mechanisation of thought processes: Proceedings of a symposium - held at the National Physical Laboratory*, November 1958. Vol. 1 (pp. 3-28). London: Her Majesty's Stationery Office.

Minsky, M. (1961). Steps toward artificial intelligence. *Proceedings of the IRE*, 49(1).

Minsky, M. (1962). Neural models for memory. *Proc. Internatl. Congr. Physiological Sciences*, Vol. III.

Minsky, M. (1970, Jan). Form and content in computer science. *Journal of the ACM*, 17, 197-215.

Minsky, M. (1972). *Progress report on artificial intelligence.* (MIT AI Lab Memo 252). Cambridge: MIT AI Lab.

Minsky, M. (1974). A framework for representing knowledge (Memo, MIT A I Lab, unexpurgated version). Cambrigde: MIT University.

Minsky, M. (1974). *A framework for representing knowledge* (MIT AI Lab., Memo 306).

Minsky, M. (1974). *A framework for representing knowledge* (Report AIM, 306, Artificial Intelligence Laboratory, MIT). Reprinted in P. H. Winston (Ed.), The psychology of computer vision, 211-277. New York: McGraw-Hill. (Revised, Chapter 6 this volume).

Minsky, M. (1975). A framework for representing knowledge. In P. H. Winston (Ed.), *The psychology of computer vision.*(pp. 211-277) New York: McGraw-Hill.

Minsky, M. (1977). Plain talk about neurodevelopmental epistemology. *Proceedings of the Fifth International Joint Conference on Artificial Intelligence*. Palo Alto: Morgan Kaufmann.

Minsky, M. (1980). K-lines: A theory of memory. *Cognitive Science*, 4, 117-133.

Minsky, M. (1986). *Society of Mind*. New York: Simon and Schuster.

Minsky, M. (1988). Preface. In D. L. Waltz & J. Feldman (Eds.), *Connectionist models and their implications: Readings from cognitive science*(pp. vii-xvi). Norwood, N.J.: Ablex.

Minsky, M. (Ed.). (1968). *Semantic information processing*. Cambridge: MIT Press.

Minsky, M., & Papert, S. (1969). *Perceptrons: An introduction to computational geometry*. Cambridge: MIT Press.

Minsky, M., & Papert, S. (1988). *Perceptrons, 2d ed*. Cambridge, MA: MIT Press.

Minsky, M., & Selfridge, O. G. (1960). Learning in random nets. In C. Cherry (Ed.), *Proceedings of the 4th London Sympoium on Information Theory*. New York: Academic Press, and ASTIA Document AD-238220.

Minton, S., Carbonell, J. G., Etzioni, O., Knoblock, C. A., & Kuokka, D. R. (1987). Acquiring effective search control rules: Explanation-based learning in the PRODIGY system. In *Proceedings Fourth International Workshop on Machine Learning*, 122-133. Irvine, CA.

Mitchell, T. M. (1978).*Version spaces: An approach to concept learning.* Unpublished doctral dissertation. Stanford: Stanford University.

Mitchell, T. M., & Schwenzer, G. M. (1978). Applications of artificial intelligence for chemical inference. XXV. A computer program for automated empirical 13C NMR rule formation. *Organic Magnetic Resonance*, 11, 378-384.

Mitchell, T. M., Keller, R., & Kedar-Cabelli, S. (1986). Explanation-based generalization: A unifying view. *Mach. Learning*, 1, 47-80.

Mooers, C. N. (1956a). ZATOCODING and developments in information retrieval. *Aslib Proceedings*, 8(1), 3-22.

Mooers, C. N. (1956b). Information retrieval on structured content. In C. Cherry (Ed.), *Proceedings of the 3th London Sympoium on Information Theory*(pp. 212-234). New York: Academic Press.

Moore, E. F. (1959). On the shortest path through a maze. Proceedings of an International Symposium on Switching Theory. In *Annals of the Computation Laboratory (Vols. 29 & 30)*. Cambridge: Harvard.

Moore, R. C. (1980, Oct). *Reasoning about knowledge and action.* (SRI International technical Note 191).

Moravec, H. R. (1984). Locomotion, vision and intelligence. In M. Brady & R. Paul (Eds.), *Robotics Research 1*(pp.215-224). Cambridge: MIT Press.

Morton, J. (1969). Interaction of information in word recognition. *Psychological Peview*, 76, 165-178.

Moussouris, J. (1974). Gibbs and Markov random systems with constraints. *Journal of Statistical Physics*, 10, 11-33.

Mozer, M. C. (1984). *The perception of multiple objects: A parallel, distributed processing approach.* Unpublished manuscript, University of California, San Diego, Institute for Cognitive Science.

Munson, J. H. (1971). Robot planning, execution, and monitoring in an uncertain environment. In *Proceedings of the 2nd International Joint Conference on Artificial Intelligence*. Palo Alto: Morgan Kaufmann.

Nagao, Makoto, & Matsuyama, Takashi. (1980). *A structural analysis of eomplez aerial photographs.* New York: Plenum Press.

Neisser, U. (1967). *Cognitive psychology.* New York: Appleton Century-Crofts.

Neisser, U. (1981). John Dean's memory: A case study. *Cognition*, 9, 1-22.

Newell, A. (1955). The chess machine. In *Proceedings of the 1955 Western Joint Computer conferece, Session on Learning Machines*(pp. 101-108).

Newell, A. (1960). On programming a highly parallel machine to be an intelligent technician. *Proceedings of the Western Joint computer Conferece*(pp. 267-282).

Newell, A. (1962). Some problems of basic organization in problem-solving programs. In M. C. Yovits, G. T. Jacobi, & G. D. Goldstein (Eds.), *Conference on Self-Oryanizing Systems*(pp. 393-423). Washington, D. C.: Spartan Books.

Newell, A. (1965). Limitations of the current stock of ideas for problem solving. In A. Kent, & O. Taulbee (Eds.), *Conference on electronic information handling*. Washington, DC: Spartan.

Newell, A. (1969). Heuristic programming: Ill-structured problems. *Progress in operations research*, III, 360-414. New York: John Willey.

Newell, A. (1973). Artificial intelligence and the concept of mind. In R. C. Schank, & K. Colby (Eds.),*Computer models of thoughtand language*. San Francisco: W.H. Freeman.

Newell, A. (1980). AAAI President's message. *AI Magazine*, 1, 14.

Newell, A. (1980). Physical symbol systems. *Cognitive Science*, 4, 135-183.

Newell, A. (1981). Review of Nils Nilsson, Principles of Artificial Intelligence. *Comtemporary Psychology*, 26, 50-51.

Newell, A. (1982). The knowledge level. *Artifical Intelligence*, 18, 87-127.

Newell, A. (1990). *Unified theories of cognition*. Cambridge: Harvard Univ. Press.

Newell, A., & Shaw, J. C. (1957). Empirical explorations of the logic theory machine: A case study in Heurisitcs. *Proceedings of the Western Joint Computer Conference*(pp. 230-240).

Newell, A., & Simon, H. A. (1956a). The logic theory machine. *IRE Transactions on Information Theory*, IT-2(3), 61-79.

Newell, A., & Simon, H. A. (1956b). *Problem-solving in humans and computers* (Paper P-987). Santa Monica: RAND Corporation.

Newell, A., & Simon, H. A. (1961). GPS-a program that simulates human problem-solving. Proceedings of a Conference on Learning Automata. Munich: Oldenbourg.

Newell, A., & Simon, H. A. (1972). *Human Problem Solving*. Englewood Cliffs: Prentice-Hall.

Newell, A., & Simon, H. A. (1976). Computer science as empirical inquiry: Symbols and search. *Communications of the ACM*, 19(3), 113-126. (Chaper 4 of this volume).

Newell, A., & Tonge, F. M. (1960). An introduction to information processing language IPL-V. *Communications of the ACM*, 3, 205-211.

Newell, A., Shaw, J. C., & Simon, H. A. (1958). Chess-playing programs and the problem of complexity. *IBM Journal of Research and Development*, 2(4), 320-335.

Newell, A., Shaw, J. C., & Simon, H. A. (1958). Elements of a theory of human problemsolving. *Psychological Review*, 65, 151-166.

Newell, A., Shaw, J. C., & Simon, H. A. (1958). *The processes of creative thinking* (Paper P-1320) Santa Monica: RAND Corporation.

Newell, A., Shaw, J. C., & Simon, H. A. (1959). Report on a general problem solving program. *Proceedings of the International Conference on Information Processing*(pp. 256 264). Paris: UNESCO House.

Newell, A., Shaw, J. C., & Simon, H. A. (1960). A variety of intelligent learning in a general problem solver. In Yovitts, M., & Cameron, S. (Eds.), *Self-organizing systems*(pp. 153-189). New York: Pergamon.

Nilsson, N. J. (1971). *Problem solving methods in artificial intellligence*. New York: McGraw Hill.

Nilsson, N. J. (1980). *Principles of artificial intelligence*. Palo Alto: Tioga.

Nilsson, N. J. (1984). *Shakey the robot* (Tech. Note 323). SRI Al Center: Menlo Park.

Norman, D. A. (1973). Memory, knowledge and the answering of questions. In R. L. Solso (Ed.), *Contempory issues in cognitive psychology: The Loyloa symposium.*. Washington D.C.: V.H. Winston and Sons.

Norman, D. A. (1981). *Perspectives on cognitive science*. Hillsdale NJ: Erlbaum.

Norman, D. A., & Bobrow, D. G. (1975). On data-limited and resourcelimited processes. *Cognitive Psychology*, 7, 44-64.

Norman, D. A., & Bobrow, D. G. (1976). On the role of active memory processes in perception and cognition. In C. N. Cofer (Ed.), *The structure of human memory* (pp. 114-132). Freeman: San Francisco.

Norman, D. A., & Bobrow, D. G. (1979). Descriptions: An intermediate stage in memory retrieval. *Cognitive Psychology*, 11, 107-123.

Novak, G. S. (1977). Representation of knowledge in a program for solving physics problems. *Proceedings of the Fifth International Joint Conference on Artificial Intelligence*. San Francisco, CA: Morgan Kaufmann.

Orchard-Hays, W. (1961). The evolution of programming systems. In *Proceedings of the IRE, special computer issue*(pp. 283-295).

Paige, J. M., & Simon, H. A. (1966). Cognitive processes in solving algebra word problems. In B. Kleinsuntz (Ed.), *Problem solving*. New York: Wiley.

Palmer, S. E. (1980). What makes triangles point: Local and global effects in configurations of ambiguous triangles. *Cognitive Psychology*, 9, 353-383.

Papert, S. (1961). Some mathematical models of learning. In C. Cherry (Ed.), *Proceedings of the 4th London Sympoium on Information Theory*. New York: Academic Press.

Papert, S. (1972). Teaching children to be mathematicians vs. teaching about mathematics. *International Journal of Mathematical Education for Science and Technology*, 3, 249-262.

Papert, S., & Minsky, M. (1973). *Proposal to ARPA for research on intelligent automata and micro-automation*. (MIT AI Lab Memo 299). Cambridge: MIT AI Lab.

Parker, D. B. (1985). *Learning-logic (TR-47)*. Cambridge, MA: Massachusetts Institute of Technology, Center for Computational Research in Economics and Management Science.

Pascal, B. (1932). *Pensées*. New York: E.P. Dutton. [Originally published in 1670.]

Pask, G. (1958). Organic control and the cybernetic method. *Cybernetica*, 1(3), 155-173.

Pask, G. (1959). Physical analogues to the growth of a concept. In D. B. Blake, & A. M. Uttley (Eds.), *Proceedings of the symposium on mechanistion of thought processes*. Teddington: National Physical Laboratory.

Patil, R., Szolovits, P., & Schwartz, W. (1981). Causal understanding of patient illness in medical diagnosis. In *Proceedings of the international joint conference on artificial intelligence*, Palo Alto: Morgan Kaufmann.

Pauker, S. G., Gorry, G. A., Kassirer, J. P., & Schwartz, W. B. (1976). Towards the simulation of clinical cognition: taking a present illness by computer. *Amer. J. Med.*, 60, 981-996.

Pearl, J. (1984). *Heuristics: Intelligent search strategies for computer problem solving*. Reading: Addison-Wesley.

Phillips, E. W. (1936). Binary calculation. *Journal Inst. Actuaries*, 67, 187-221.

Pietrykowski & Jensen (1973). *Mechanising w-order type theory through unification* (Report CS-73-16). Waterloo: University of Waterloo.

Pillsbury, W. B. (1897). A study in apperception. *American Journal of Psychology*, 8, 315-393.

Pitts, W., & McCulloch, W. S. (1947). How we know universals. *Bulletin of Mathematical Biophysics*, 9, 127-147.

Poggio, T., & Torre, V. (1978). A new approach to synaptic interactions. In R. Heim, & G. Palm (Eds.), *Approaches to complex systems*. Berlin: Springer-Verlag.

Poincare, H. (1913). *Foundations of science* (G. B. Halstead, Trans.). New York: Science Press.

Polya, G. (1954). *How to solve it*. Princeton, N.J.: Princeton (rev. ed., Anchor A-93). ****1945?

Polya, G. (1954). Induction and analogy in mathematics. In *Mathematics and Plausible Reasoning, vol. 1*. Princeton, N.J.: Princeton; also New York: Dover.

Post, E. (1943). Formal reductions of the general combinatorial problem. *American Journal of Mathematics*, 65, 197-268.

Prior, A. N. (1958). *The syntax of time distinctions*. Franciscan Studies.

Pylyshyn, Z. (1979). Computational models and empirical constraints. *The behavioral and brain sciences*, 3, 111-132.

Quillian, M. R. (1967). Word concepts: A theory and simulation of some basic semantic capabilities. *Behavioral Science*, 12, 410-430.

Quillian, M. R. (1968).Semantic memory. In M. Minsky (Ed.), *Semantic information processing*. Cambridge: Massachusetts Institute of Technology Press.

Quillian, M. R. (1969). The teachable language comprehender: A simulation program and theory of language. *Communications Assn. Comp. Mach.*, 12, 459-476.

Quine, W. V. (1953). Two dogmas of empiricism. In *From a Logical Point of View*. Cambridge: Harvard University Press.

Quine, W. V. (1970). *Philosophy of logic*. Englewood Cliffs NJ: Prentice-Hall.

Quine, W. V., & Ullian, J. S. (1918). *The web of belief*. New York: Random House.

Quinlan, J. R. (1983). Learning efficient classification procedures and their application to chess end games. In R. S. Michalski, J. G. Carbonell, & T. M. Mitchell (Eds.), *Machine Learning: An Artificial Intelligence Approach* . Palo Alto: Tioga.

Rao, C. R., & Mitra, S. K. (1971). Generalized inverse of a matrix and applications. *Sixth Berkeley Symposium on 11 Mathematical Statistics and Probability*, 1, 601-620.

Raphael, B. (1970). The frame problem in problem-solving systems. In *Proc. Adv. Study Inst. on Artificial Intelligence and Heuristic Programming*. Menaggio, Italy.

Rashevsky, N. (1960). *Mathematical Biophysics*. Chicago: University of Chicago Press, 1938 (rev. ed., New York: Dover, 2 vols.).

Read, S., & Cesa, I. (1990). This reminds me of the time when . . . : Expectation failures in reminding and explanation. *Journal of Experimental Social Psychology*, 26.

Reddy, D. R. (1976). Speech recognition by machine: A review. *Proceedings of IEEE*, 64.

Reddy, D. R., Erman, L. D., & Neely, R. B. (1973). A model and a system for machine recognition of speech. *IEEE Transaetions on Audio and Electroaeousties AU*, 21, 229-238.

Reddy, D. R., Erman, L. D., & Neely, R. B. (1973). The HEARSAY speech understanding system: An example of the recognition process. *IJCAI*, 3, 185-193.

Redmond, M. (1989). Combining case-based reasoning, explanation-based learning, and learning from instruction. In A. Segre (Ed.), *Proceedings of the sixth international workshop on machine learning*. San Mateo, CA: Morgan Kaufmann.

Reiter, R. (1978). On reasoning by default. In *Proc. Second Symp. on Theoretical Issues in Natural Language Processing*, Urbana, IL.

Reiter, R. (1980). A logic for default reasoning, *Artificial Intelligence*,13.

Rescher, N. (1964). *Hypothetical Reasoning*. Amsterdam: North-Holland.

Rich, C., Shrobe, H. E., & Waters, R. C. (1979). *Computer aided evolutionary design for software engineering* (MIT AI Lab., Memo 506).

Richman, H. B., & Simon, H. A. (1989). Context effects in letter perception: Comparison of two theories. *Psychological Review*, 96, 417-32.

Rieger, C. (1975). Conceptual memory. In R. Schank (Ed.), *Conceptual information processing*. Amsterdam: North-Holland.

Riesbeck, C. (1975). Conceptual analysis. In R. Schank (Ed.), *Conceptual information processing*. Amsterdam: North-Holland.

Riesbeck, C., & Schank, R. (1989). *Inside case-based reasoning*. Hillsdale, N.J.: Lawrence Erlbaum.

Riley, M. S. (1984). *Strucrural understanding in performance and learning*. Unpublished doctoral dissertation, University of Pittsburgh.

Riley, M. S., & Smolensky, P. (1984). A parallel model of (sequential) problem solving. *Proceedings of the Sixth Annual Conference of the Cognitive Science Society*.

Roberts, L. G. (1960). Pattern recognition with an adaptive network. *IRE International Convention Record, pt. 2*(pp. 66-70).

Robinson, J. A. (1965). A machinc-oriented logic based on the resolution principle. *Journal of the ACM*, 12, 23-41.

Robinson, J. A. (1965). A machine-oriented logic based on the resolution principle. *Journal of the Assoc. for Computing Machinery*, 12, 23-41.

Rochester, N., Holland, J. H., Haibt, L. H., & Duda, W. L. (1956). Test on a cell assembly theory of the action of the brain, using a large digital computer. *IRE Transaction on Information Theory*, IT-2(3), 80-93.

Rock, I. (1973). *Orientation and form*. New York: Academic Press.

Rosenblatt, F. (1958). The perceptron: A probabalistic model for information storage and organization in the brain. *Psychological Review*, 65, 386-408.

Rosenblatt, F. (1959). Two theorems of statistical separability in the perceptron. *In Mechanisation of thought processes: Proceedings of a symposium held at the National Physical Laboratory*, November 1958. Vol. I (pp. 421-456). London: HM Stationery Office.

Rosenblatt, F. (1962). *Principles of neurodynamics*. New York: Spartan.

Rosenbloom, P. C. (1950). *The elements of mathematical logic*. New York: Dover.

Rosenfeld, A., Hummel, R. A., & Zucker, S. W. (1976). Scene labeling by relaxation operations. *IEEE Transactions on Systems*, Man, and Cybernetics, 6, 420-433.

Rosenschein, S. J., & Kaelbling, L. P. (1986). The synthesis of digital machines with provable epistemic properties. In J. Y. Halpern, (Ed.), *Theoretieal aspeets of reasoning about knowledge*(pp. 83-98). Los Altos CA: Morgan Kauffman.

Ross, B. H. (1986). Remindings in learning: Objects and tools. In S. Vosniadou and A. Ortony (Eds.), *Similarity and analogical reasoning*, New York: Cambridge University Press.

Ross, B. H. (1989). Some psychological results on case-based reasoning. In K. Hammond (Ed.), *Proceedings of the DARPA workshop on case-based reasoning*, 2, 144–147. San Mateo, CA: Morgan Kaufmann.

Rumelhart, D. E. (1975). Notes on a schema for stories. In D. G. Bobrow, & A. Collins (Eds.), *Representation and understanding* (pp. 211-236). New York: Academic Press.

Rumelhart, D. E. (1977). Toward an interactive model of reading. In S. Dornic (Ed.), *Attention & Performance Vl*. Hillsdale, NJ: Erlbaum.

Rumelhart, D. E. (1979). Some problems with the notion of literal meanings. In A. Ortony (Ed.), *Metaphor and thought*. Cambridge, England: Cambridge University Press.

Rumelhart, D. E. (1980). Schemata: The building blocks of cognition. In R. Spiro, B. Bruce, & W. Brewer (Eds.), *Theoretical issues in reading comprehension* (pp. 33-58). Hillsdale, NJ: Erlbaum.

Rumelhart, D. E., & McClelland, J. L. (1982). An interactive activation model of context effects in letter perception: Part 2. The contextual enhancement effect and some tests and extensions of the model. *Psychological Review*, 89, 60-94.

Rumelhart, D. E., & McClelland, J. L. (1985). Levels indeed! A response to Broadbent. *Journal of Experimental Psychology: General*, 114, 193-197.

Rumelhart, D. E., & Norman, D. A. (1982). Simulating a skilled typist: A study of skilled cognitive-motor performance. *Cognitive Science*, 6, 1-36.

Rumelhart, D. E., & Zipser, D. (1985). Feature discovery by competitive learning. *Cognitive Science*, 9, 75- 112.

Rumelhart, D. E., Lindsay, P. H., & Norman, D. A. (1972). A process model for long-term memory. In E. Tulving & W. Donaldson (Eds.), *Organization of memory*. New York: Academic Press.

Russell, B. (1926). *Our knowledge of the external world as a field for scientific method in philosophy*. London: G. Allen & Unwin.

Russell, B. (1948). *Human knowledge: Its scope and limits*. New York: Simon & Schuster.

Samuel, A. L. (1959a). Some studies in machine learning using the game of checkers. *IBM Journal of Research and Development*, 3(3), 210-229.

Samuel, A. L. (1960). Letter to the editor, Science, 132(6), 3429.

Samuel, A. L. (1963). Some studies in machine learning using the game of checkers. In E. A. Feigenbaum & J. Feldman (Eds.), *Computers and thought*. New York: McGraw-Hill, New York. (Chapter 15 of this volume).

Samuel, A. L. (l959b). Machine learning. *Technology Review*, 62, 42-45.

Sandewall, E. (1970). Representing natural language information in predicate calculus. In B. Meltzer, & D. Michie (Eds.), *Machine Intelligence, Vol. 5*. Edinburgh: Edinburgh University Press.

Schank, R. C. (1971). Finding the conceptual content and intention in an utterance in natural language conversation, In *Proceedings of the second international conference on artificial intelligence*. Menlo Park CA: Morgan Kaufmann.

Schank, R. C. (1973a). *Causality and reasoning* (Technical Report 1). Castagnola, Switzerland: Instituto per gli studi Semantici e Cognitivi.

Schank, R. C. (1973b). Identification of conceptualizations underlying natural language. In R. C. Schank and K. Colby (Eds.), *Computer models of thought and language*. San Francisco: Freeman.

Schank, R. C. (1973c). The fourteen primitive actions and their inferences. (Stanford AI Lab Memo 183). Stanford: Stanford University.

Schank, R. C. (1974). Conceptual dependency: A theory of natural language understanding. *Cognitive Psychology*, 3(4).

Schank, R. C. (1975). *Conceptual information processing*. Amsterdam: North-Holland.

Schank, R. C. (1976). The role of memory in language processing. In C. N. Cofer (Ed.), *The structure of human memory* (pp. 162-189). Freeman: San Francisco.

Schank, R. C. (1980). Language and memory. *Cognitive Science*, 4, 243-284.

Schank, R. C., & Ableson, R. (1977). *Scripts, plans, goals and understanding*. Hillsdale: Erlbaum.

Schank, R. C., & Colby, K. (Eds.). (1973). *Computer models of thoughtand language*. San Francisco: W. H. Freeman.

Schank, R. C., Goldman, N. M., Rieger, C., & Riesbeck, C. (1973). MARGIE: Memory, analysis, response generation, and inference in English. *Proceedings of the Third International Joint Conference on Artificial Intelligence*. Palo Alto: Morgan Kaufmann.

Schroll, G., Duffield, A. M., Djerassi, C., Buchanan, B. G., Sutherland, G. L., Feigenbaum, E. A., & Lederberg, J. (1969). Application of artificial intelligence for chemical inference. III. Aliphatic ethers diagnosed by their low resolution mass spectra and NMR data. *Journal of the American Chemical Society*, 91, 7440.

Schubert, L. K. (1975). Extending the expressive power of semantic networks. *Artificial Intelligence*, 7(2), 163-198.

Schwartz, M. F., Marin, O. S. M., & Saffran, E. M. (1979). Dissociations of language function in dementia: A case study. *Brain and Language*, 7, 277-306.

Schwenzer, G. M. (1977). Computer assisted structure elucidation using automatically acquired 13C NMR rules. In D. Smith (Ed.), *Computer Assisted structure Elucidation*. ACS Symposium, 54, 58.

Scott, A. C., Clancey, W., Dsvis, R., & Shortliffe, E, H. (1977). Explanation capabilities Of knowledge-based production systems. *American Journal of Computational Linguistics*, Microfiche 62.

Scott, P. (1983). Knowledge-oriented learning. *Proceedings of the Eighth International Joint Conference on Artificial Intelligence*, 432-35. Palo Alto: Morgan Kaufmann.

Scriven, M. (1959). Truisms as the grounds for historical explanations. In P. Gardiner (Ed) *Theories of history*. New York: Free Press.

Sejnowski, T. J. (1981). Skeleton filters in the brain. In G. E. Hinton & J. A. Anderson (Eds.), *Parallel models of associative memory* (pp. 4982). Hillsdale, NJ: Erlbaum.

Sejnowski, T. J., & Hinton, G. E. (in press). Separating figure from ground with a Boltzmann machine. In M. A. Arbib & A. R. Hanson (Eds.), *Vision, brain, and cooperative computotion*. Cambridge, MA: MIT Press/Bradford.

Sejnowski, T. J., Hinton, G. E., Kienker, P., & Schumacher, L. E. (1985). *Figure-ground separation by simulated annealing*. Unpublished manuscript.

Selfridge, O. G. (1955). Pattern recognition in modern computers. *Proceedings of the Western Joint Computer Conference*.

Selfridge, O. G. (1956). Pattern recognition and learning. In C. Cherry (Ed.), *Proceedings of the 3rd London Sympoium on Information Theory*(p. 345). New York: Academic Press.

Selfridge, O. G. (1959). Pandemonium: A paradigm for learning. In *Proceedings of the Symposium on the Mechanization of Thought Processes*(pp. 511-529).

Selfridge, O. G., & Neisser, U. (1960). Pattern recognition by machine. *Scientific American*, 203, 60-68.

Shannon, C. E. (1949). Synthesis of two-terminal switching networks. *Bell System Technical Journal*, 28(1), 59-98.

Shannon, C. E. (1950a). Automatic chess player. *Scientific American*, 182, 48.

Shannon, C. E. (1950b). Programming a digital computer for playing chess. *Philosophy Magazine*, 41, 356-375.

Shannon, C. E. (1955). Game-playing machines. *Journal of the Franklin Institute*, 260(6), 447-453.

Shannon, C. E. (1956). A universal Turing machine with two internal states. In C. E. Shannon, & J. McCarthy (Eds.), *Automata studies, Annuals of Mathematics Studies, Vol. 34*(pp. 215-234). Princeton: Princeton.

Shannon, C. E. (1963). The mathematical theory of communication. In C. E. Shannon & W. Weaver (Eds.), *The mathematical theory of communication* (pp 29-125). Urbana: University of Illinois Press. (Reprinted from Bell System Technical Journal, 1948, July and October)

Shavlik, J. & Dietterich, T. (Eds.) (1990). *Readings in machine learning.* San Mateo CA: Morgan Kaufmann.

Sheikh, Y. M., Buchs, A., Delfino, A. B., Schroll, G., Duffield, A. M., Djerassi, C., Buchanan, B. G., Sutherland, G. L., Feigenbaum, E. A., & Lederberg, J. (1970). Applications of artificial intelligence for chemical inference. V. An approach to the computer generation of cyclic structures. Differentiation between all the possible isomeric ketones of composition C6H100. *Organic Mass Spectrometry*, 4, 493.

Shepard, R. N. (1984). Ecological constraints on internal representation: Resonant kinematics of perceiving, imagining, thinking, and dreaming. *Psychological Review*, 91, 417-447.

Sherman, H. (1959). A quasi-topological method for machine recognition of line patterns. In *Proceedings of the international conference on information processing.* Paris: UNESCO House.

Shortliffe, E, H., Buchanan, B. G., & Feigenbaum, E. A. (1979). Knowledge engineering for medical decision making: a review of computerbased clinical decision aids. In *Proceedings Of the IEEE*, 67, 1207-1224.

Shortliffe, E. H. (1976). *Computer-based medical consultations: MYCIN.* New York: American Elsevier.

Shortliffe, E. H. (1980). Medical consultation systems: designing for doctors. In M. Sime and M. Fitter (Eds.), Communication With Computers. New York: Academic Press.

Shortliffe, E. H., & Buchanan, B. G. (1975). A model Of inexact reasoning in medicine. *Math. Biosci.*, 23, 351-379.

Shrobe, H. E. (1979). *Dependency directed reasoning for complex program understanding* (MIT AI Lab., TR-503).

Siklóssy, L. (1972). Natural language learning by computer. In H. A. Simon & L. Siklóssy (Eds.), *Representation and meaning.* Englewood Cliffs, NJ: Prentice-Hall.

Simmons, R. F. (1973). Semantic networks their computation and use for understanding english sentences. In Schank, R. C. & Colby, K.*Computer models of thoughtand language.* San Francisco: W.H. Freeman.

Simon, H. A. (1947). *Administrative Behavior.* New York: MacMillan.

Simon, H. A. (1969). *The sciences of the artificial.* Cambridge: MIT Press.

Simon, H. A. (1976). The information-storage system called 'human memory.' In M. R. Rosenzweig & E. L. Bennett (Eds.), *Neural mechanisms of learning and memory.* Cambridge, MA: MIT Press.

Simon, H. A. (1977). Scientific discovery and the psychology of problem solving. In *Models of discovery.* Boston: D. Reidel Publishing Company.

Simon, H. A. (1980). Cognitive science: The newest of the artificial sciences. *Cognitive Science*, 4, 33-46.

Simon, H. A. (1981). *The Sciences of the Artificial.* Cambridge, Cambridge: MIT Press.

Simon, H. A., & Gilmartin, K. A. (1973). A simulation of memory for chess positions. *Cognitive Psychology*, 5, 29-46.

Simpson, R. L. (1985). *A computer model of case-based reasoning in problem solving: An investigation in the domain of dispute mediation*. Ph.D. diss., School of Information and Computer Science, Georgia Institute of Technology.

Skinner, B. F. (1953). *Science and human behavior*. New York: Macmillan.

Slade, S. (1991). Case-based reasoning: A research paradigm. *AI Magazine* 12(1), 42–55.

Slagle, J. R. (1961). *A Computer program for solving problems in freshman calculus (SAINT)*, doctoral dissertation, Massachusetts Institute of Technology, Cambridge, Mass.

Slagle, J. R. (1963). A heuristic program that solves symbolic integration problems in freshman calculus. *Journal for the Assoc. for Computing Machinery*, 10, 4.

Sloman, A. (1976). (personal communication).

Smith, D. H. (1975a). Applications of artificial intelligence for chemical inference. XV. Constructive graph labeling applied to chemical problems. Chlorinated hydrocarbons. *Analytical Chemistry*, 47, 1176.

Smith, D. H. (1975b). Applications of artificial intelligence for chemical inference. XVII. The scope of structural isomerism. *Journal of Chemical Information and Computer Science*, 15, 203.

Smith, D. H., & Carhart, R. E. (1970). Applications of artificial intelligence for chemical inference. XXIV. Structural isomerism of mono- and sesquiterpenoid skeletons. *Tetrahedron*, 32, 2513.

Smith, D. H., & Carhart, R. E. (1978). Structure elucidation based on computer analysis of high and low resolution mass spectral data. In M. L. Gross (Ed.), *Proceedings of the Symposium on Chemical Applications of High Performance Spectrometry*. Washington, D.C.: American Chemical Society.

Smith, D. H., Buchanan, B. G., Engelmore, R. S., Adlercreutz, H., & Djerassi, C. (1973). Applications of artificial intelligence for chemical inference. IX. Analysis of mixtures without prior separation as illustrated for estrogens. *Journal of the American Chemical Society*, 95, 6078.

Smith, D. H., Buchanan, B. G., Engelmore, R. S., Duffield, A. M., Yeo, A., Feigenbaum, E. A., Lederberg, J., & Djerassi, C. (1972). Applications of artificial intelligence for chemical inference VIII. An approach to the computer interpretation of the high resolution mass spectra of complex molecules. Structure elucidation of estrogenic steroids. *Journal of the American Chemical Society*, 94, 5962.

Smith, D. H., Buchanan, B. G., White, W. C., Feigenbaum, E. A., Djerassi, C., & Lederberg, J. (1973). Applications of artificial intelligence for chemical inference. X.-Intsum: a data interpretation program as applied to the collected mass spectra of estrogenic steroids. *Tetrahedron*, 29, 3117.

Smith, D. H., Konopelski, J. P., & Djerassi, C. (1976). Applications of artifieial intelligence for chemical inference. XIX. Computer generation of ion structures. *Organic Mass Spectrometry*, 11, 86.

Smith, D. H., Masinter, L. M., & Sridharan, N. S. (1974). Heuristic DENDRAL: analysis of molecular structure. In W. T. Wipke, S. Heller, R. Feldmann, & E. Hyde (Eds.), *Computer Representation and Manipulation of Chemical Information*(p. 287). New York: Wiley.

Smith, E. E. (1967). Effects of familiarity on stimulus recognition and categorization. *Journal of Experimental Psychology*, 74, 324-332.

Smith, E. E. (1968). Choice reaction time: An analysis of the major theoretical positions. *Psychological Bulletin, 69*, 77-110.

Smith, P. T., & Baker, R. G. (1976). The influence of English spelling patterns on pronunciation. *Journal of Verbal Learning and Verbal Behavior, 15*, 267-286.

Smith, S. (1980). A learning system based on genetic algorithms. Unpublished doctral dissertation, University of Pittsburgh, Pennsylvania.

Smolensky, P. (1981). *Lattice renormalization of 04 theory*. Unpublished doctoral dissertation, Indiana University.

Smolensky, P. (1983). Schema selection and stochastic inference in modular environments. *Proceedings of the National Conference on Artifcial Intelligence AAAI-83*, 109-113.

Smolensky, P. (1984). The mathematical role of self-consistency in parallel computation. *Proceedings of the Sixth Annual Conference of the Cognitive Science Society*.

Smolensky, P., & Riley, M. S. (1984). *Harmony theory: Problem solving, parallel cognitive models, and thermal physics* (Tech. Rep. No. 8404). La Jolla: University of California, San Diego, Institute for Cognitive Science.

Solomonoff, R. J. (1957). An inductive inference machine. In *IRE National Convention Record, pt. 2*(pp. 56-62).

Solomonoff, R. J. (1958). The mechanization of linguistic learning. In *2nd International Congress on Cybernetics*. Namur: Assoc. de Cybernétique; also in Zator Technical Bulletin ZTB-125 and ASTIA Document AD 212226.

Solomonoff, R. J. (1959). A new method for discovering the grammars of phrase structure languages. In *Proceedings of the international conference on information processing*. Paris: UNESCO House; also ASTIA Document AD 210390.

Solomonoff, R. J. (1960). *A preliminary report on a general theory of inductive inference* (Zator Technical Bulletin ZTB-138, Contract AF 49(638)376). Cambridge: Zator Company.

Solso, R. L. (Ed.). (1973). *Contemporary issues in cognitive psychology: The Loyola symposium*. Washington, D.C.: V. H. Winston and Sons.

Spain, D. S. (1983, Sept). Application of artificial intelligence to tactical situation assessment. In *Proceedings of the 16th EASCON 83*.

Spoehr, K., & Smith, E. (1975). The role of orthographic and phonotactic rules in perceiving letter patterns. *Journal of Experimental Psychology: Human Perception and Performance, 1*, 2134.

Stallman, R. M., & Sussman, G. J. (1977). Forward reasoning and dependency-directed backtracking in a system for computer-aided circuit analysis. *Artificial Intelligence, 9* (2), 135-196.

Startsman, T. S., & Robinson, R. E. (1972). The attitudes Of medical and paramedical personnel towards computers. *Comp. Biomed. Res., 5*, 218-227.

Statman, R. (1974). *Structural complexity of proofs*. Stanford University Department of Mathematics, Ph.D. Thesis.

Stentz, A., & Shafer, S. (1985, Aug). *Module programmer's guide to local map builder for ALVan* (Technical Report, CarnegieMellon University Computer Science Department).

Sternberg, S. (1966). High-speed scanning in human memory. *Science, 153*, 652-654.

Sternberg, S. (1969). Memory scanning: Mental processes revealed by reaction-time experiments. *American Scientist, 57*, 421-457.

Stevens, M. E. (1957). A survey of automatic reading techniques (Report 5643). Washington, D.C.: National Bureau of Standards.

Stockton, F. R. (1895). The lady or the tiger? In: *A chosen few: Short stories*. New York: Charles Scribner's Sons.

Strachey, C. S. (1952). Logical or non-mathematical programmed. In *Proceedings of the Association for Computing Machinery* (ACM).

Strang, G. (1976). *Linear algeora and its applications*. New York: Academic Press.

Sussman, G. J. (1973). *A computational model of skill acquisition*. New York: American Elsevier. (Also AI Lab Technical Report 297).

Sussman, G. J., & McDermott, D. (1972). From PLANNER to CONNIVER—A genetic approach. In *Proc. AFIPS FJCC*, 1171-1179.

Sussman, G. J., & Steele, G. (1980). Constraints - a language for expressing almost-hierarchical descriptions, *Artificial Intelligence Journal*, 14, 1-40.

Sussman, G. J., Winograd, I., & Charniak, E. (1970). *Micro-planner reference manual* (MIT AI Memo 203). Cambridge: MIT University.

Sutherland, G. L. (1967, Feb). DENDRAL—A computer program for generating and filtering chemical structures (Stanford Heuristic Programming Project Memo HPP-67-1).

Sutherland, G. L. (1969, March). Heuristic DENDRAL: a family of LISP programs (Stanford Heuristic Programming Project Memo HPP-69-1).

Sutton, R. S., & Barto, A. G. (1981). Toward a modern theory of adaptive networks: Expectation and prediction. *Psychological Review*, 88, 135-170.

Sycara, E. P. (1987). *Resolving adversarial conflicts: An approach to integrating case-based and analytic methods*. Ph.D. diss., School of Information and Computer Science, Georgia Institute of Technology.

Tarski, A. (1944). The semantic conception of truth and the foundations of semantics. *Philos and Phenom Res,* 4, 341-376.

Teitelbaum, P. (1967). The biology of drive. In G. Quarton, T. Melnechuk, & F. O. Schmitt (Eds.), *The neurosciences: A study program*. New York: Rockefeller Press.

Teitelman, W. (1978, Oct). INTERLISP Reference Manual. Palo Alto: XEROX Corporation, & Cambridge: Bolt , Beranek and Newman.

Terrace, H. S. (1963). Discrimination learning with and without errDrS. Journal of the Experimental Analysis of Behavior, 6, 1-27.

Terry, A. (1983). *The CRYSALIS Project: Hierarchical control of production systems* (Tech. Rep. HPP-83-19). Stanford University, Heuristic Programming Project.

Thomas, G. B. Jr. (1968). *Calculus and analytic geometry (4th ed.)*. Reading, MA: Addison-Wesley.

Thorndike, E. L., & Lorge, I. (1944). *The teacher s word book of 30,000 words*. New York: Columbia University Press.

Tinbergen, N. (1951). *The study of instinct*. New York: Oxford.

Tonge, F. M. (1960). An assembly line balancing procedure. *Management Science*, 7(1), 21-42.

Tulving, E. (1972). Episodic and semantic memory. In E. Tulving & W. Donaldson (Eds.), *Organization of memory*. New York: Academic Press.

Turing, A. M. (1950). Computing machinery and intelligence. *Mind*, 59, 422-460.

Turner, R. M. (1989). *A schema-based model of adaptive problem solving*. Ph.D. diss., School of Information and Computer Science, Georgia Institute of Technology.

Ullman, S. (1983). *Visual routines* (MIT AI Memo 723). Cambridge: MIT.

Unger, S. H. (1959). Pattern detection and recognition. *Proceedings of the IRE*, 47(10), 1737-1752.

Uttley, A. M. (1956a). Temporal and spatial patterns in a conditional probability machine. In C. E. Shannon, & J. McCarthy (Eds.), *Automata studies, Annuals of Mathematics Studies, Vol. 34*(pp. 215-234). Princeton: Princeton.

Uttley, A. M. (1956b). Conditional probability as a principle of learning. In *Proceedings of the 1st International congress on Cybernetics*(pp. 830-856). Namur, Belium.

Uttley, A. M. (1959). The design of conditional probability computers. *Information and Control*, 2, 1-24.

Varkony, T. H., Carhart, R. E., & Smith, D. H. (1977). Computer assisted structure elucidation, ranking of candidate structures, based on comparison between predicted and observed mass spectra. In *Proceedings of the ASMS Meeting*. Washington, D.C.

Varkony, T. H., Smith, D. H., & Djerassi, C. (1978). Computer-assisted structure manipulation-studies in the biosynthesis of natural products. *Tetrahedron*, 34, 841-852.

Venesky, R. L. (1970). *The structure of English orthography*. The Hague: Mouton.

Von Neumann, J. & Morgenstern, O. (1947). *The theory of games and economic behavior*. Princeton: Princeton University Press.

Von Uexküll, J. (1921). *Umwelt und Innenwelt der Tiere*. Berlin.

von der Malsberg, C. (1973). Self-organizing of orientation sensitive cells in the striate cortex. *Kybernetik*, 14, 85-100.

Waldinger, R., & Lee, R. (1969). PROW: A step toward automatic program writing. In *Proceedings of the International Joint Conference on Artificial Intelligence*. Washington, D.C.

Wang, H. (1960a). Toward mechanical mathematics. *IBM Journal of Research and Development*, 4(1), 2-22.

Wang, H. (1960b). Proving theorems by pattern recognition, I. *Communications of the ACM*(p. 220).

Warren, R. M. (1970). Perceptual restoration of missing speech sounds. *Science*, 167, 393-395.

Waterman, D. A., & Hayes-Roth, E. (Eds.). (1978). *Pattern-directed inference systems*. New York: Academic Press.

Watson, R. J. (1974). Hedical staff response to a medical information system with direct physician-computer interface. *HEDINFO*, 74, 299-302.

Weiss, S. M., & Kulikowski, C. A. (1991). *Computer systems that learn*. San Mateo CA: Morgan Kaufmann.

Weizenbaum, J. (1965). ELIZA. *Comm. of the Assoc. of Computing Machinery*, 9(1), 36-45.

Wertheimer, M. (1959). *Productive thinking*. New York: Harper and Row.

Widrow, G., & Hoff, M. E. (1960). Adaptive switching circuits. *Institute of Radio Engineers, Western Electronic Show and Convention, Convention Record*, Part 4, 96-104.

Wiener, N. (1948). *Cybernetics*. New York: Wiley.

Wilks, Y. (1973). An artificial intelligence approach to machine translation. In R. C. Schank, & K. Colby (Eds.), *Computer models of thoughtand language*. San Francisco: W.H. Freeman.

Wilks, Y. (1975). Primitives and words. *Proceedings of the Conference on Theoretical Issues in Natural Language Processing*. Association for Computational Linguistics.

Wilks, Y. (1977). *Good and bad arguments about semantic primitives* (DAI Memo 42).Edinburgh University: Department of Artificial Intelligence.

Williams, M. A. (1985). *Distributed, cooperating expert systems for signal understanding*. Seminar on AI Applications to Battlefield 3.4-1-3.4-6.

Williams, R. J. (1983). *Unit activation rules for cognitive network models* (Tech. Rep. No. ICS 8303). La Jolla: University of California, San Diego, Institute for Cognitive Science.

Willshaw, D. J. (1971). *Models of distributed associative memory*. Unpublished doctoral dissertation, University of Edinburgh.

Willshaw, D. J. (1981). Holography, associative memory, and inductive generalization. In G. E. Hinton & J. A. Anderson (Eds.), *Parallel models of associative memory* (pp. 83-104). Hillsdale, NJ: Erlbaum.

Wilson, S. (1982). *Adaptive 'cortical' pattern recognition* (Internal Report, Research Laboratories, Polaroid Corporation). Rochester: Polaroid Corp.

Winograd, T. (1972). *Understanding natural language*. New York: Academic Press.

Winograd, T. (1974). *Five lectures on artificial intelligence*. (Stanford AI Lab Memo 246). Stanford: Stanford University.

Winograd,T. (1975). Frames and the declarative procedural controversy. In D. G. Bobrow, & A. Collins (Eds.), *Representation and Understanding*. New York: Academic Press.

Winston, P. H. (1975). Learning structural descriptions from examples. In P. H. Winston (Ed.), *The psychology of computer vision*. New York: McGraw-Hill.

Wood, C. C. (1978). Variations on a theme by Lashley: Lesion experiments on the neural model of Anderson, Silverstein, Ritz, & Jones. *Psychological Review*, 85, 582-591.

Woods, W. (1973). An experimental parsing system for transition network grammars. In R. Rustin (Ed.), *Natural language processing*. New York: Algorithmics Press.

Woods, W. (1975). What's in a link. In D. G. Bobrow, & A. Collins, (Eds.), *Representation and Understanding*. New York: Academic Press.

Woods, W. (1985). What's in a link: Foundations for semantic networks. In R. J. Brachman & H. J. Levesque (Eds.), *Readings in knowledge representation*. San Mateo CA: Morgan Kaufmann.

Woods, W., & Kaplan, R. (1971). *The lunar sciences natural language information system* (Rep. No. 2265). Cambridge, MA: Bolt, Beranek, and Newman.

Wortman, P. M. (1972). Medical diagnosis: an information processing approach. *Comput. Biomed. Res.*, 5, 315-328.

Wozencraft, J., & Horstein, M. (1961). Coding for two-way channels. In C. Cherry (Ed.), *Proceedings of the 4th London Sympoium on Information Theory*. New York: Academic Press.

Yu, V. L., Buchanan, B. G. Shortliffe. E. H., Wraith, S.M., Davis, R. Scott, H. C., & Cohen, S. N. (1979). Evaluating the performance of a computer-based consultant. *Comput. Prog. Biomed.*, 9, 95-102.

Yu, V. L., Fagan, L. M. Wraith, S. M., Clancey, W. J., Scott, A. C., Hannigan, J., Blum, R. L., Buchanan, B. G., & Cohen, S N. (1979). Antimicrobial selection by a computer. A blinded evaluation by infectious diseases experts. *J. Amer. Med. Assoc.*, 242(12, 1279-1282.

Zadeh, L. A. (1965). Fuzzy sets. *Information and Control*, 8, 338-353.

Zadeh, L. A. (1975). Fuzzy logic and approximate reasoning, *Synthese,* 30, 407-428.

Index